Special Edition

USING
VISUAL J++

Special Edition

USING
VISUAL J++

Written by Mark Culverhouse with

Clayton Walnum • Nelson Howell • Greg Perry

Special Edition Using Visual J++

Credits

PRESIDENT
Roland Elgey

PUBLISHER
Joseph B. Wikert

PUBLISHING MANAGER
Fred Slone

TITLE MANAGER
Bryan Gambrel

EDITORIAL SERVICES DIRECTOR
Elizabeth Keaffaber

MANAGING EDITOR
Sandy Doell

DIRECTOR OF MARKETING
Lynn E. Zingraf

ACQUISITIONS EDITOR
Al Valvano

PRODUCTION EDITOR
Sarah Rudy

EDITORS
Jim Bowie
Kate Givens
Judith Goode
Brian Sweany
Nick Zafran

ASSISTANT PRODUCT MARKETING MANAGER
Christy M. Miller

STRATEGIC MARKETING MANAGER
Barry Pruett

TECHNICAL EDITORS
Matthew Brown
Nelson Howell
Steve Tallon

TECHNICAL SUPPORT SPECIALIST
Nadeem Muhammed

ACQUISITIONS COORDINATOR
Carmen Krikorian

SOFTWARE RELATIONS COORDINATOR
Patty Brooks

EDITORIAL ASSISTANT
Mark D. Kane

BOOK DESIGNER
Ruth Harvey

COVER DESIGNER
Dan Armstrong

PRODUCTION TEAM
Stephen Adams
Debra Bolhuis
Erin Danielson
Jason Hand
Daniel Harris
Kay Hoskin
Steph Mineart
Casey Price
Laura Robbins
Bobbi Satterfield
Staci Somers
Paul Wilson

INDEXER
Tim Taylor

Composed in *Century Old Style* and *ITC Franklin Gothic* by Que Corporation.

To Linda Roos, Rick Greenwald, and all my friends in River Valley.

About the Authors

Mark Culverhouse received a degree in Computer Science from Northern Illinois University. The past eight years were spent at Gupta Corporation as lead developer of ReportWindows. A Microsoft Windows developer since Windows 1.0, Mark previously did IBM MVS systems software development for Candle Corporation, MASSTOR Systems, and Cambridge Systems Group. He also worked as an IBM MVS systems programmer in the banking industry. Mark can be reached on the Internet at LoneRock@execpc.com or by visiting his Web site at http://www.execpc.com/~lonerock.

Clayton Walnum, who has a degree in Computer Science, has been writing about computers for almost 15 years and has published hundreds of articles in major computer publications. He is also the author of over 25 books that cover such diverse topics as programming, computer gaming, and application programs. His most recent book is *Windows 95 Game SDK Strategy Guide,* also published by Que. His other titles include the award-winning *Building Windows 95 Applications with Visual Basic* (Que), *3-D Graphics Programming with OpenGL* (Que), *Borland C++ 4.x Tips, Tricks, and Traps* (Que), *Turbo C++ for Rookies* (Que), *Dungeons of Discovery* (Que), *PC Picasso: A Child's Computer Drawing Kit* (Sams), *Powermonger: The Official Strategy Guide* (Prima), *DataMania: A Child's Computer Organizer* (Alpha Kids), *Adventures in Artificial Life* (Que), and *C-manship Complete* (Taylor Ridge Books). Mr. Walnum lives in Connecticut with his wife Lynn and their four children, Christopher, Justin, Stephen, and Caitlynn.

Nelson Howell is a veteran of the computer industry. Starting with IBM mainframes in 1967, he has survived the changes from mainframes to minis to microcomputers. He has had the opportunity to meet some of the founders of computers including J. Presper Eckert and Admiral Grace Hooper. In addition to writing, he is now engaged in providing support to users of software for Integra Technology International. Now at home in Tucson, Arizona, he is surrounded by his family of four sons and a very tolerant wife.

We'd Like to Hear from You!

As part of our continuing effort to produce books of the highest possible quality, Que would like to hear your comments. To stay competitive, we *really* want you, as a computer book reader and user, to let us know what you like or dislike most about this book or other Que products.

You can mail comments, ideas, or suggestions for improving future editions to the address below, or send us a fax at (317) 581-4663. For the online inclined, Macmillan Computer Publishing has a forum on CompuServe (type **GO QUEBOOKS** at any prompt) through which our staff and authors are available for questions and comments. The address of our Internet site is **http://www.mcp.com** (World Wide Web).

In addition to exploring our forum, please feel free to contact me personally to discuss your opinions of this book: I'm **74671,3710** on CompuServe, and I'm **avalvano@que.mcp.com** on the Internet.

Thanks in advance—your comments will help us to continue publishing the best books available on computer topics in today's market.

Al Valvano
Acquisitions Editor
Que Corporation
201 W. 103rd Street
Indianapolis, Indiana 46290
USA

Contents at a Glance

V | Appendixes

Table of Contents

V | Appendixes

Introduction

by Clayton Walnum

The Internet is growing by leaps and bounds. It won't be too long before you can contact just about anyone online— not only your friends and acquaintances, but also every major company in the country. This incredible growth is the pathway to opportunity. Everybody who's anybody in the world of telecommunications is looking for ways to enhance online experience on the Internet. One company that has scored a big hit on the Internet is Sun Microsystems, which recently released an unusual programming language called Java. Once people used Java, the Internet was guaranteed to never be the same again.

What's so special about Java? Java enables programmers to create something called *applets*. Applets are special computer programs that can be included as an element of a Web page. When the user views a Web page containing one of these applets, the machine he's connected to automatically sends the applet to the user and the user's own Java-compatible browser runs the applet. Because applets are transferred in a non-machine-specific form, they can run on any machine that has a Java interpreter.

Using Java, you can do everything from adding simple animation to your Web pages, to writing sophisticated computer programs that your Web page visitors can use online. Applets that have already been released include games, spreadsheets, graphing programs, animation controllers, simulators, and much, much more. Java is so intriguing and so successful that even major players in the industry, including Netscape and Microsoft, are providing Java-compatible software for the Internet.

Specifically, Microsoft has not only added full Java compatibility to their excellent Web browser, Microsoft Internet Explorer, but they've also released a new Java development system called Visual J++. Visual J++ includes many of the features that C++ programmers have enjoyed over the last few years, including a source-code generator that can create a complete Java applet. All you have to do is concentrate on adding the details, without worrying about writing a lot of boilerplate code.

In this book, you'll learn not only how Java applets work on the Internet, but also how to include Java applets in your Web pages. More importantly, you'll learn, step-by-step, how to write your own applets using Visual J++. You can write these applets for your own personal use or for general release on the Internet. Imagine the thrill of seeing one of your own Java creations being used on Web pages all over the world! ■

Who This Book Is for

This book is the perfect starting point for anyone who wants to learn about Visual J++ and Java. Although it's helpful to have previous programming experience (especially with C or C++), this book includes a complete tutorial on the Java language and how to build applets with Visual J++. The Visual J++ tools, such as AppletWizard and Java Type Library Wizard, that you can use to create your own applets are described in detail. Moreover, you'll learn the Java language starting with the basics and working your way toward writing full-featured applets and applications.

Although this book is suitable for programming novices, more experienced programmers will find much of interest as well. If you're already familiar with languages such as C and C++, you'll be able to skim over the Java language introduction and dive right into the business of creating applets. Although the Java language is very much like C++, the way it's used is unique. Up until Java, you've never seen anything quite like applets.

To summarize, this book is for both novice and intermediate programmers. Novice programmers will get an introduction to the Java language, whereas more experienced programmers can concentrate on getting the most from the language by quickly learning how to use Visual J++ to build powerful applets for the Internet. Even expert programmers may find this book to be a useful introduction to the world of Java. To understand this book, however, you should at least be familiar with basic programming constructs such as functions and loops.

Hardware and Software Requirements

The minimum system requirements for Windows 95 or NT users are as follows:

- An IBM-compatible 80486 with at least 16M of memory
- Windows 95 or Windows NT
- A hard drive
- A CD-ROM drive
- A Microsoft-compatible mouse
- 256-color graphics
- A Windows-compatible sound card (If you don't care about hearing sound files with Java's applets, you don't need a sound card.)

Compiling the Programs in This Book

As you work through the examples in this book, you'll learn how to install Visual J++ and compile the example programs that are presented in each chapter. In general, though, you can compile the programs in this book by following the procedures given here.

1. Start Visual J++.
2. Select File, Open from Visual C++'s menu bar.
3. Open the Java source code file that you want to compile. (All Java source-code files have the .java file extension.)
4. Select Build, Build from Visual C++'s menu bar.
5. When asked if you want to create a default workspace, click the Yes button. Visual J++ then compiles the applet.
6. To run the newly compiled applet, select Build, Execute from Visual J++'s menu bar.

A Word to the Wise

As every programmer knows, a good program is virtually crash-proof. Error-checking must be done for every action that may fail, and appropriate error messages must be given to the user. Unfortunately, good error-checking requires a lot of extra program code. For the programmer working on his next magnum opus, this is all just part of the game. But for an author writing a programming book, this extra code has different implications.

A programming book should present its topics in as clear a manner as possible. This means featuring programs whose source code is not obscured by a lot of details that don't apply directly to the topic at hand. For this reason, the programs in this book do not always employ proper error-checking. For example, user input often goes unverified and dynamic construction of objects is assumed to be successful.

In short, if you use any of the code in this book in your own programs, it's up to you to add whatever error-checking may have been left out. Never assume anything in your programs. If you aren't 100 percent sure of your program's state, you must add error-checking to ensure that the program doesn't come crashing down on your user. Just because this book's author may have been lax in his error-checking (for good reasons), that doesn't let you off the hook.

Conventions Used in This Book

In order to make the text easier to understand, this book adopts several style conventions. For example, you'll notice that variable names, function names, and other types of program code that are part of a text paragraph are printed in computer type (monospaced) in order to set the code off from the surrounding text.

Another example is menu commands, which are shown like this: File, Open. In this case, you can click the File menu, then click the Open option. Alternatively, you can press Alt+F to access the File menu, then press O; or use the arrow keys to highlight Open, then press Enter. Finally, you can use the mouse to click the Open file button on the toolbar.

When you need to hold down the first key while you press a second key, a plus sign (+) is used for the combination:

Alt+F or Ctrl+M

The Shift, Ctrl, and Alt keys must all be used in this way.

When a letter in a menu or dialog box is underlined, it indicates that you can press the Alt key plus that letter (or that letter alone in submenus and dialog boxes) to choose that command. In File, Open you can access the menu by pressing Alt+F; then with the File menu selected, you can choose Open by pressing the letter O. Often, the underlined letter is the first letter in the word; at other times it is not. For instance, to choose Edit, Properties, you would press the Alt key and hold it down while you press the O key.

Bold text is used to indicate text you are asked to type. *Italic* text is used for new terms.

N O T E Notes provide additional information that might help you avoid problems, or offer advice or general information related to the current topic. ▪

T I P Tips provide extra information that supplements the current topic. Often, tips offer shortcuts or alternative methods for accomplishing a task.

CAUTION

Cautions warn you if a procedure or description in the topic could lead to unexpected results, or even data loss or damage to your system. If you see a caution, proceed carefully.

What About Sidebars?

Sidebars are sprinkled throughout the book to give you the author's insight into a particular topic. The information in a sidebar supplements the material in the chapter.

On into the Wonderful World of Visual J++

If you're still reading this introduction, you're probably convinced that Visual J++ and Java is something you really want to learn about. If you're interested in the Internet, that decision is a wise one. At this point, Java is virtually guaranteed its place in Internet history. Want to know why? Turn the page and keep reading. ●

Introducing Java

Why Java Is Hot

by Clayton Walnum

Anyone who's had anything to do with computers in the '90s knows that the Internet is all the rage. The immense growth of this global computer network has not only created a handy way to download files and information, but has also sparked major controversies over freedom of speech, copyright law, and computer security. Hardly a day goes by without the Internet making the news.

But not all Internet activity is steeped in controversy. One of the more positive Internet newsmakers has been the release of Java, a computer programming language that enables folks like you and me to easily create applications that can be used across the Internet without worrying about platform compatibility or network security. The two types of Java applications—applets for use within World Wide Web pages and stand-alone Java applications—are guaranteed to do more to liven up the World Wide Web than even the most heated controversy. ■

How Java was developed

Java's history is a long and winding road.

The attributes of Java that make it perfect for Web applets

Transferring executable files across the Internet is safer using Java applets.

About local and remote applets

Some applets don't have to be transferred over the Internet, whereas others do.

How the client/server relationship relates to Java applets

When an HTML document must load an applet, it must rely on the applet's server to obtain the file.

How Java maintains network security

Java applets protect you from network hanky-panky.

The Java Story

Java was conceived long before its suitability for the Internet was noted and taken advantage of. You may be surprised to learn that Java was developed for a very different use. In fact, "Java" isn't even the language's original name.

Back in 1990, a gentleman by the name of James Gosling was given the task of creating programs to control consumer electronics. Gosling and his team of people at Sun Microsystems started designing their software using C++, the language that most programmers were praising as the next big thing because of its object-oriented nature. Gosling, however, quickly found that C++ was not suitable for the projects he and his team had in mind. They ran into trouble with complicated aspects of C++ such as multiple inheritance of classes and program bugs such as memory leaks. Gosling soon decided that he was going to have to come up with his own, simplified computer language that would avoid all the problems he had with C++.

Although Gosling didn't care for the complexity of languages such as C++, he did like the basic syntax and object-oriented features of the language. So when he sat down to design his new language, he used C++ as its model, stripping away all the features of C++ that made that language difficult to use with his consumer-electronics projects. When Gosling completed his language-design project, he had a new programming language that he named Oak. (The story goes that the name Oak came to Gosling as he gazed out his office window at an oak tree.)

Oak was first used in something called the Green project, wherein the development team attempted to design a control system for use in the home. This control system would enable the user to manipulate a list of devices, including TVs, VCRs, lights, and telephones, all from a handheld computer called *7 (Star Seven). The *7 system featured a touch-sensitive screen that the owner used to select and control the devices supported by the control.

The next step for Oak was the video-on-demand (VOD) project, in which the language was used as the basis for software that controlled an interactive television system. Although neither *7 nor the VOD project led to actual products, they gave Oak a chance to develop and mature. By the time Sun Microsystems discovered that the name "Oak" was already claimed and they changed the name to Java, they had a powerful, yet simple, language on their hands.

More importantly, Java is a platform-neutral language, which means that programs developed with Java can run on any computer system with no changes. This platform independence is attained by using a special format for compiled Java programs. This file format, called byte-code, can be read and executed by any computer system that has a Java interpreter. The Java interpreter, of course, must be written specially for the system on which it will run.

In 1993, after the World Wide Web had transformed the text-based Internet into a graphics-rich environment, the Java team realized that the language they had developed would be perfect for Web programming. The team came up with the concept of Web applets, small programs that could be included in Web pages, and even went so far as to create a complete Web browser (now called HotJava) that demonstrated the language's power.

In the second quarter of 1995, Sun Microsystems officially announced Java. The "new" language was quickly embraced as a powerful tool for developing Internet applications. Netscape

Communications, the developer of the popular Netscape Navigator Web browser, added support for Java to its new Netscape Navigator 2.0. Other Internet software developers would follow suit, including Microsoft, whose Internet Explorer 3.0 offers Java support. After more than five years of development, Java has found its home.

Introducing Java

By now, you may be curious why Java is considered such a powerful tool for Internet development projects. You already know that Java is a simplified version of C++. Anyone who has struggled with learning C++ knows that the key word in the previous sentence is "simplified." C++ added so much to the C language that even professional programmers often have difficulty making the transition.

According to Sun Microsystems, Java is "simple, object-oriented, statically typed, compiled, architecture neutral, multithreaded, garbage collected, robust, secure, and extensible." That's a mouthful, but this description of Java probably doesn't help you understand the language much. The following list of Java's attributes, however, should clear out some of the cobwebs:

- *Simple.* Java's developers deliberately left out many of the unnecessary features of other high-level programming languages. For example, Java does not support pointer math, implicit typecasting, structures or unions, operator overloading, templates, header files, or multiple inheritance.

- *Object-oriented.* Just like C++, Java uses classes to organize code into logical modules. At runtime, a program creates objects from the classes. Java classes can inherit from other classes, but multiple inheritance, wherein a class inherits methods and fields from more than one class, is not allowed.

- *Statically typed.* All objects used in a program must be declared before they are used. This enables the Java compiler to locate and report type conflicts.

- *Compiled.* Before you can run a program written in the Java language, the program must be compiled by the Java compiler. The compilation results in a "byte-code" file that, while similar to a machine-code file, can be executed under any operating system that has a Java interpreter. This interpreter reads in the byte-code file and translates the byte-code commands into machine-language commands that can be directly executed by the machine that's running the Java program. You could say, then, that Java is both a compiled and interpreted language.

- *Multithreaded.* Java programs can contain multiple threads of execution, which enables programs to handle several tasks concurrently. For example, a multithreaded program can render an image on the screen in one thread, while continuing to accept keyboard input from the user in the main thread. All applications have at least one thread, which represents the program's main path of execution.

- *Garbage collected.* Java programs do their own garbage collection, which means that programs are not required to delete objects that they allocate in memory. This relieves programmers of virtually all memory-management problems.

- *Robust*. Because the Java interpreter checks all system access performed within a program, Java programs cannot crash the system. Instead, when a serious error is discovered, Java programs create an exception. This exception can be captured and managed by the program without any risk of bringing down the system.

- *Secure*. The Java system not only verifies all memory access but also ensures that no viruses are hitching a ride with a running applet. Because pointers are not supported by the Java language, programs cannot gain access to areas of the system for which they have no authorization.

- *Extensible*. Java programs support native methods, which are functions written in another language, usually C++. Support for native methods enables programmers to write functions that may execute faster than the equivalent functions written in Java. Native methods are dynamically linked to the Java program; that is, they are associated with the program at runtime. As the Java language is further refined for speed, native methods will probably be unnecessary.

- *Well-understood*. The Java language is based upon technology that's been developed over many years. For this reason, Java can be quickly and easily understood by anyone with experience with modern programming languages such as C++.

As you can tell from the preceding list of features, a great deal of thought went into creating a language that would be fairly easy to use but still provide the most powerful features of a modern language like C++. Thanks to features such as automatic garbage collection, programmers can spend more time developing their programs rather than wasting valuable man-hours hunting for hard-to-find memory-allocation bugs. However, features such as Java's object-oriented nature, as well as its ability to handle multiple threads of execution, ensure that the language is both up-to-date and powerful.

Java Programs

As mentioned previously, Java can be used to create two types of programs: applets and stand-alone applications. An applet is simply a part of a Web page, just as an image or a line of text can be. Just as a browser takes care of displaying an image referenced in an HTML document, a Java-enabled browser locates and runs an applet. When your Java-capable Web browser loads the HTML document, the Java applet is also loaded and executed.

Using applets, you can do everything from adding animated graphics to your Web pages to creating complete games and utilities that can be executed over the Internet. Some applets that have already been created with Java include Bar Chart, which embeds a configurable bar chart in an HTML document; Crossword Puzzle, which enables users to solve a crossword puzzle on the Web; and LED Sign, which presents a scrolling, computerized message to viewers of the Web page within which the applet is embedded. Figure 1.1 shows a spreadsheet applet running in Netscape Navigator.

FIG. 1.1
Applets are small programs that are run from within an HTML document.

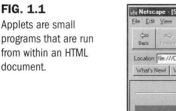

Although most Java programmers are excited by the ability to create applets, Java can also be used to create stand-alone applications—that is, applications that don't need to be embedded in an HTML document. The most well-known application is the HotJava Web browser itself, shown in Figure 1.2. This basic browser is completely written in the Java language, showing how Java handles not only normal programming tasks such as looping and evaluating mathematical expressions, but also how it can handle the complexities of telecommunications programming.

FIG. 1.2
The HotJava Web browser is written completely in the Java programming language.

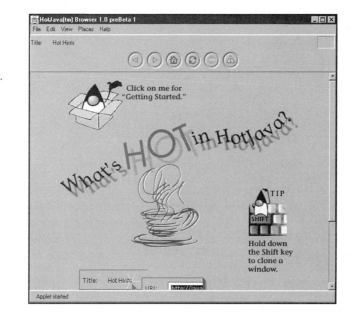

Applets and the Internet

It's an applet's ability to hitch a ride on the Information Superhighway that makes it so unique. In fact, applets are really the first step towards making the Internet a true extension of your computer's local storage system. When you view a Web page containing applets, those applets may be coming to you from just about anywhere on the Web—from the office down the street or from a software distributor in Hong Kong. In this section, you discover just how this interaction works.

Local and Remote Applets

One of Java's major strengths is that you can use the language to create dynamic content for your Web pages. That is, thanks to Java applets, your Web pages are no longer limited to the tricks you can perform with HTML. Now your Web pages can do just about anything you want them to. All you need to do is write the appropriate applets.

But writing Java applets is only half the story. How your Web page's users obtain and run the applets is equally as important. It's up to you to not only write the applet (or use someone else's applet), but also to provide users access to the applet. Basically, your Web pages can contain two types of applets: local and remote. These applet types are named after the location at which they are stored.

A local applet is one that is stored on your own computer system (see Figure 1.3). When your Web page must find a local applet, it doesn't need to retrieve information from the Internet—in fact, your browser doesn't even need to be connected to the Internet at that time.

FIG. 1.3

Local applets are stored on and loaded from your computer system.

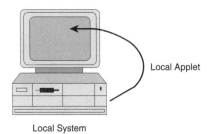

Local Applet

Local System

A remote applet is one that is located on another computer system (see Figure 1.4). This computer system may be located in the building next door, or it may be on the other side of the world—it makes no difference to your Java-compatible browser. No matter where the remote applet is located, it's downloaded onto your computer via the Internet. Your browser must, of course, be connected to the Internet at the time it needs to display the remote applet.

To reference a remote applet in your Web page, you must know the applet's URL (where it's located on the Web) and any attributes and parameters that you need to supply in order to display the applet correctly. If you didn't write the applet, you'll need to find the document that describes the applet's attributes and parameters. This document is usually written by the applet's author.

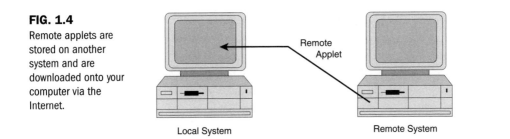

FIG. 1.4
Remote applets are stored on another system and are downloaded onto your computer via the Internet.

Local System

Remote System

Clients and Servers

If a required applet is not located on your system, it can be downloaded automatically to your system and then run. To the user, this exchange of applets over the Internet is mostly transparent. All the user knows is that she's looking at a page that contains a game of tictactoe, an animated image of Duke, or some other Java-based content. In this way, the Internet becomes almost an extension of the user's basic system, sort of a gigantic hard drive that contains a practically infinite number of accessible applets and applications.

Currently, there's a client/server relationship between a browser that wants to display an applet and the system that can supply the applet. The client is a computer that requires services from another system; the server is the computer that provides those services. In the case of a Java applet, the client is the computer that's trying to display an HTML document that contains a reference to an applet. The server is the computer system that uploads the applet to the client, thereby allowing the client to use the applet. In Figure 1.4, you could call the local system the client and the remote system the server.

It won't be long, however, before the difference between a client and a server begins to get muddy. When Java browsers can send as well as receive applets, computers will constantly switch between being a client and a server. For example, suppose a user loads up his favorite Java-compatible browser and connects to a Web site. The home page on the Web site contains an animated title, so your system downloads the applet that displays this title. For the time being, your system is the client and the remote system is the server.

Now, however, you decide that you want to search the remote system's public databases for a particular file. Because you've just written a handy search application that can do the job for you, your system transmits the application to the remote computer, where it sets to work finding the file you specified. Suddenly, your computer is the server and the remote computer is the client.

This sort of switching between client and server tasks is a step toward making the Internet a huge extension of your computer. That is, more and more, the Internet will seem to be a part of your own local system, rather than a collection of computers located all over the world. You'll be able to access the Internet almost as easily as your own hard drive. In fact, you might not even need a hard drive at all! You can just run applications located somewhere else on the Internet and store your data in any number of special storage sites.

Security

You may have heard horror stories about people who have downloaded programs from the Internet only to find, after running the program, that it infected their system with a virus or otherwise wreaked havoc with their computer. Therefore, you may be reluctant to jump on the applet bandwagon. After all, with so many applets flying around the Internet, trouble could rear its ugly head like a demon from a Clive Barker novel.

The truth, however, is that Java applets are a secure way to transmit programs on the Internet. This is because the Java interpreter will not allow an applet to run until the interpreter has confirmed that the applet's byte-code has not been corrupted or changed in some way (see Figure 1.5). Moreover, the interpreter determines whether the byte-code representation of the applet sticks to all of Java's rules. For example, a Java applet can never use a pointer to gain access to portions of computer memory for which it doesn't have access. The bottom line is that, not only are Java applets secure, they are virtually guaranteed not to crash the system.

FIG. 1.5
Applets are verified
before they are run, so
they are virtually
guaranteed to be safe
and secure.

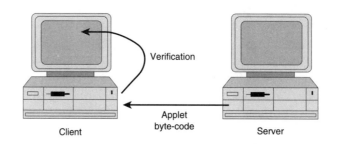

Verification

Applet
byte-code

Client

Server

Java just may be the biggest thing to hit the World Wide Web since, well, the Web itself. As you'll see in the forthcoming chapters, Java not only provides a way to create secure applications that can be used safely on the Internet, but the language also represents a complete shift in the way people may think about their computers in the future. Because a Java applet can be located anywhere on the Web, yet still be executable on your computer, your computer's storage may well expand from its tiny hard drive to include all of the Internet.

Thanks to a Java-compatible browser's ability to download applets, users who log on to Java-powered Web pages can enjoy the Java experience without even realizing what's going on behind the scenes. This is unlike other types of applications on the Internet that the user must explicitly download before they can be run. When more and more applets start running rampant on the Information Superhighway, the Internet just might start living up to its hype.

Microsoft and Java

As anyone who owns a computer knows, Microsoft is not one to sit back and watch another software company grab all the glory associated with a major advancement. Once Java became a success, the folks at Microsoft knew they were going to have to join the party or be left behind.

In response to Java's success, Microsoft added Java support to the snazzy Web browser, Microsoft Internet Explorer. Then, they started work on Visual J++, a programming environment that would take Java programming away from the command line and thrust it back into the world of graphical user interfaces where it belongs.

For programmers familiar with Visual C++, using Visual J++ produces an eerie sense of déjà vu. The two programming environments are so similar, in fact, that they look almost exactly alike on the screen. In any case, Visual J++ greatly simplifies the process of creating Java applets and applications, while at the same time adding the power of Microsoft's wizards to speed Java development.

Finally, Microsoft is hard at work refining a set of programming APIs called ActiveX that enables programmers to use OLE technology to create browsers and ActiveX controls (previously known as OLE controls) for use with Internet applications. Moreover, ActiveX will support Java applets, eventually running those applets as ActiveX controls in HTML documents—an impressive feat, indeed!

From Here...

Where will it all end? Who knows? For now, you can get to work on those Java applets you've been dying to write without having to rely on the clunky command-line tools that were part of the original JDK (Java Developer's Kit). Using Visual J++, you can get started fast and easily on the road to Internet programming wizardry. For more information, please refer to the following chapters:

- Chapter 2, "Java and Visual J++," explains the details of how Java keeps applets safe for transmission over the Internet.
- Chapter 3, "The Java Language," provides an introduction to the Java language.

Java and Visual J++

By Greg Perry

Even Internet old-timers are new to most evolving Internet products. Whether Internet newcomer or pro, Java technology is still a mysterious unknown to most Internet users and programmers. Microsoft decided *not* to be the first on the market with a Java tool. Microsoft's delay let the software giant produce one of the most powerful, integrated, and workable Java tools available: Visual J++.

This chapter explains what the Java hype is all about, discusses how Microsoft's new Visual J++ platform improves upon the Java standard, and explores the Visual J++ technology in a way that prepares you to use it as soon as possible. A Visual J++ user is both the programmer who writes Visual J++ applications and the Internet's end-users who use the technology that Visual J++ provides.

Get ready to learn about Visual J++, one of the most powerful Internet products ever developed. ■

Understand the HTML language

HTML carries the Web page instructions for formatting and placing text, graphics, and applications.

Learn the history of Web browsers

Mosaic-like graphic Web-browsing software quickly replaced the older text-based Web browsers.

Interact with Web pages

Web pages with embedded Java applets can instantly become interactive.

Enhance Java with Visual J++

Visual J++ enhances your Java development by giving you powerful development tools that speed Java's Web page development and appeal.

Watch Java Web page interaction

See a Java-based Internet page to get a glimpse of the interaction Java makes possible.

Master Visual J++'s tool assortment

Visual J++ includes a feature-packed assortment of tools found only on professional development systems such as Visual C++.

Get Ready for Visual J++: What's It All About?

We could jump right into Visual J++ and write an application here in Chapter 2, but doing so would do most readers a disservice. Despite the popularity of the Internet and the huge number of newly-added users each month, the Internet is still in its infancy.

Hardly anyone is a true Internet expert due to new Internet technologies, such as Visual J++, that emerge almost daily. Most Internet consultants specialize in only one or two areas of the Net; it simply has not been around long enough for a complete mastery by most people.

Fortunately, one does not have to be an Internet guru to take advantage of the Internet by exploring its sites. In addition, you don't even have to have a degree in programming to tackle advanced Internet topics, such as creating Web pages and using Visual J++. People will be able to use Visual J++ on many different levels, creating Internet sites and applications from many different points of view and with different goals in mind for the end-user. You might use Visual J++ to add simple interaction to your Internet development or you might use Visual J++ to write complete stand-alone applications that you sell to end-users.

The following sections explore some of the history that is indispensable to mastering Visual J++. Visual J++ is more than just a programming language, and yet many people will be able to create applications with Visual J++ without any previous programming experience. To orient you, read the following sections to solidify your basic understanding of today's Internet Web pages. Once you cover the basics, you'll know exactly where Visual J++ fits into the Internet equation.

The Need for Simple Navigation

If you have used the Internet in the last couple of years, you probably explored *home pages*, those graphical Internet screens with hot spots that you click to move around the intricate Internet. Your Web browsing software takes you on a journey through an intricate graphical maze (a spider web of interrelated connections, hence the term *Web*). An Internet *site* might contain several Web pages; the first screen you visit for any site generally is that site's home page. The home page often contains links to other pages on the site and to other home pages on the Internet.

For example, if you visit Microsoft's site at **www.microsoft.com**, you'll see Microsoft's home page. The mouse cursor changes shape when you move it over a hypertext link to another page or to a definition box, which pops up when you click the mouse. Figure 2.1 shows Microsoft's home page.

N O T E This book does not require that you be an Internet guru to understand and use Visual J++. Nevertheless, be sure that you've used the Internet enough to understand home pages and maneuver around the *WWW* (*World Wide Web*, or just *Web*). If you've programmed in *HTML* (*Hypertext Markup Language*), you'll be even further ahead of the game. If you've never written HTML code, don't fret because this book explains enough to get by for most Visual J++ developers. ▪

FIG. 2.1

Web pages are graphical and often connected to other sites.

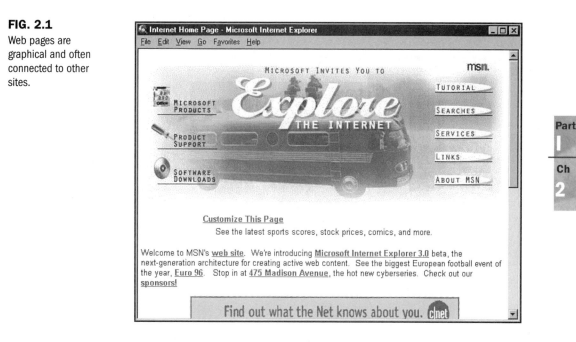

Each page you see on the Web is located *somewhere* on someone's computer. How in the world does your Web-browser find the correct page? Each Web page contains a unique address called the URL (*Uniform Resource Locator*). Instead of requiring that you type each page's URL (which can become quite lengthy), the current page's hypertext links direct your Web browsing software to the next URL that you want to display. Literally, surfing the Web is as easy as flipping through pages in a book.

TIP   The Web works a lot like the Windows hypertext help system. By clicking hypertext links (sometimes called *hot spots*) or by directing users to another page, you can maneuver throughout the World Wide Web just as you do with online help. Instead of viewing another help screen from your application's directory, however, you could be viewing an Italian museum's images of its masterpieces.

The first Web browsers on the market were known as *Mosaic* browsers, named after the first true Internet graphical browsing program called *Mosaic*. Students at the University of Illinois at Urbana-Champaign created Mosaic for the National Center for Supercomputing Applications (NCSA). Mosaic took the Web one giant leap forward, making Web-crawling (Internet style, of course!) accessible to anyone with an Internet connection and the Mosaic software.

A Web page might contain text, graphics, and even icons you can click to view multimedia events. One of the goals of Web designers is to make Web pages appear uniform no matter what kind of computer (or, more accurately, which *platform*) the end-user uses to view the page. The HTML language is a machine-independent language that Web page developers use to design Web pages. One page's HTML listing is actually a set of text commands that, when viewed with a Web browser, produces a Web page that conforms to the look the author intended. Listing 2.1 contains the HTML commands that produced Figure 2.1's Web page.

NOTE Once again, if this is old hat to you, you're well ahead of the game. Nevertheless, this quick Web page introduction will serve us well throughout the rest of the book. This background material, although brief, ensures that all readers will be on the same basic level when the Visual J++ material is introduced below. ■

Listing 2.1 HTML Commands that Produce the Microsoft Home Page

```
<HTML>
<HEAD>
<TITLE>MSN Welcomes You To The Internet!</TITLE>
</HEAD>
<!--MSN Web Team: RC, New Scripting-->
<!-- This is the Header -->
<BODY TopMargin=20 LeftMargin=5 BGCOLOR=#FFFFFF LINK=#336600
 VLINK=#808080 ALINK=#FF0000>
<FONT FACE="Arial, Geneva" SIZE=2>
<CENTER>
<A HREF="/maps/msn-home.map"><IMG SRC="/images/msn-home.jpg"
 ALT="Clickable Map Image" WIDTH=590 HEIGHT=224 BORDER=0  USEMAP="#home"
 ISMAP></A>
</CENTER>
<P>
<MAP NAME="home">
<AREA SHAPE=RECT COORDS="7,36,120,88" HREF=/products/msprod.htm>
<AREA SHAPE=RECT COORDS="7,97,120,141" HREF=http://www.microsoft.com/support/>
<AREA SHAPE=RECT COORDS="7,151,120,198" HREF=/products/intprod.htm>
<AREA SHAPE=RECT COORDS="473,28,576,50" HREF=/tutorial/default.html>
<AREA SHAPE=RECT COORDS="473,64,576,87" HREF=/access/allinone.asp>
<AREA SHAPE=RECT COORDS="473,100,576,124" HREF=/access/ref.asp>
<AREA SHAPE=RECT COORDS="473,138,576,162" HREF=/access/links/other.htm>
<AREA SHAPE=RECT COORDS="473,174,576,199" HREF=/about/msn.htm>
<AREA SHAPE=RECT COORDS="134,4,433,116" HREF=/letter.htm>
</MAP>
     <CENTER> <TABLE Border=0> <TR> <TD>
     <A HREF="/choices.asp"><FONT SIZE=2 FACE="Arial, Helv">
     <B>Customize This Page</B></FONT></A> </TD> </TR> <TR>
     <TD><FONT SIZE=2 FACE="Arial, Helv">
     <MARQUEE BEHAVIOR=SLIDE ALIGN=MIDDLE BGCOLOR=#FFFFFF SCROLLAMOUNT=10>
     See the latest sports scores, stock prices, comics, and more. 
     </MARQUEE> </FONT> </TD> </TR> </TABLE> </CENTER>
<P>Welcome  to MSN's <A HREF="/letter.htm"><B>web site</B></A>. 
 We're introducing <A HREF="http://www.microsoft.com/ie/"><B>Microsoft Internet
 Explorer 3.0</B></A> beta, the next-generation architecture for creating
 active web content.
  See the biggest European football event of the year,
 <A HREF="http://www.euro96.com/"><B>Euro 96</B></A>.   Stop in at
 <A HREF="http://475Madison.msn.com"><b>475 Madison Avenue</B>
 </A>, the hot new cyberseries.  Check out our
 <A HREF="http://www.msn.com/guides/sitesee/"><B>sponsors!</B></A>
 </Html>
```

Take a moment to see how Listing 2.1's HTML commands produced Figure 2.1's Web page. The Microsoft home page is fairly advanced so the HTML listing looks a little forbidding at first. Nevertheless, as you compare the HTML code to the home page, you'll soon see that the HTML language is extremely simple.

The terms within angled brackets (< and >) are called *tag references* (or *tag commands*). Tag controls are central to the HTML program. Many commands contain a beginning and ending tag (a forward slash, /, precedes an ending tag). The non-bracketed text items are literal constants, such as Web page text that is to appear on the resulting Web page. The tags primarily determine the placement of figures, the location of links to other Web sites, and the formatting of text. For example, <TITLE> marks the beginning of a title and </TITLE> marks the end. Many of the tags in Listing 2.1 are formatting tag codes that specify font style and size instructions for the Web browser.

In reality, the tags do not format text; they offer instructions that your Web browser is to follow. Therefore, when your Web browser sees the <CENTER> tag, your Web browser knows to center the text that runs up to the subsequent </CENTER> ending tag.

N O T E   When you navigate to a Web page, the server sends to your browser only the HTML text, not the graphical image of the Web page. Your browser then reads the text and responds to the commands by formatting text appropriately and placing links and graphic images where the HTML dictates they should appear. Your browser first receives the full HTML page and then receives whatever graphic images are required to complete the page. Most browsers offer a Stop button you can press to keep from receiving the graphic images for the times when you don't want to wait on the images but you only want to see the text. In place of those images, your Web browser will display icons that represent the unsent images.

When this book looks at a Web site in detail, simpler Web sites than the Microsoft home page will be offered as examples. You should not get bogged down in advanced HTML commands when learning a new technology such as Visual J++. Even simple HTML commands can produce quite attractive Web pages. For example, consider how simple Listing 2.2's HTML code appears. You should have little trouble following the HTML commands even if HTML is new to you.

Listing 2.2   Simple HTML Commands Can Produce Nice-Looking Web Pages

```
<HTML>
<HEAD>
<TITLE>Your Page Title</TITLE>
</HEAD>
<BODY>
<CENTER>
<H1>Fancy, yet Simple!</H1><P>
</CENTER>
<HR NOSHADE>
```

continues

Part
I

Ch
2

Listing 2.2 Continued

```
HTML is your key to Visual J++ applications. You will eventually load
Visual J++ programs onto other Internet user's computers through an
HTML tag command pair.<center>
<IMG SRC="Apple.gif" ALT="">
</CENTER>
<H1><I><A HREF=www.microsoft.com> Click here to see Microsoft's Web site
</A></I></H1><MARQUEE >This text scrolls across the screen</MARQUEE><P>
</BODY>
</HTML>
```

Figure 2.2 shows the resulting Web page that Listing 2.2's HTML commands produce. As you can see, the Web page is attractive and fairly complex looking despite the simple HTML code that created it.

FIG. 2.2

A nice Web page that requires simple HTML.

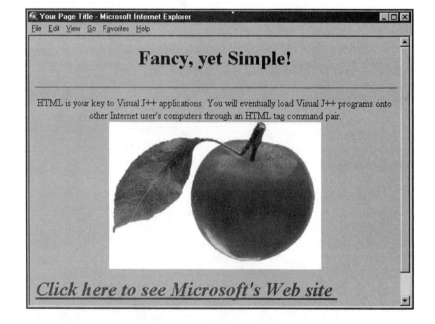

Why all this talk about HTML? HTML is the vehicle with which you'll eventually link Visual J++ applications to Web pages. As you'll see throughout this book, one simple HTML tag command embeds a complete Visual J++ application into any Web site you create.

 The next time you log on to the Internet, locate your menu option that lets you view the HTML source code. If you use Internet Explorer, the source display command is View, Source and if you use Netscape Navigator, the command is View, Document Source.

Transferring the HTML text listing takes much less transfer time than would transferring a graphical representation of the page. Your browser reads the HTML commands and then formats the text or graphic images according to their instructions. Although your browser must be more capable than a simple graphics viewer, your CPU's time is much less precious than modem downloading time.

Although several tools exist to create Web pages using modern graphical cut-and-paste methods, you can create a fancy Web page simply by using a text editor and knowing the HTML language. There are several good books available that dedicate themselves to the HTML language. If you are interested, here are some of the best:

- *Special Edition Using HTML*
- *HTML by Example*
- *HTML Quick Reference*

Part

I

Ch

2

Internet: From Text to Multimedia

The World Wide Web is not the Internet—it is only a tool that dynamically links Web sites to one another and makes for uniform Web retrieval and navigation. The Internet is defined as the collection of interconnected computers all over the globe.

When the Internet first appeared, users had a difficult time locating information on other computers connected to the Internet. One had to be a master of the UNIX operating system to utilize the Internet effectively. Successful Internet usage required a mastery both of your own computer's hardware and operating system, as well as a fairly in-depth knowledge of Internet connections. Internet retrievals required sitting at a text-based terminal and issuing commands to get where you wanted to go.

In the early 1980s, computer users realized that additional tools were needed to make the Internet usable for more people. Not only were early text-based navigation tools cryptic to use, but they were also machine-dependent: An individual user could not often go to another computer and access information using a common interface. Internet developers began linking their information together into a simple hypertext system, which let users jump from topic to topic.

Given the transition of computers in the 1980s from a text interface to graphical user interface (*GUI*), the development of Mosaic in late 1993 finally provided the necessary commonality and graphic access to give Internet users a mouse-driven, graphical Web-browsing vehicle. In addition, the Web solidified the Internet as a tool usable by the masses—both computer literate users and novices.

Going the Next Step

The colorful, Mosaic-like browsers changed the Internet by taking its technological development out of the exclusive hands of scientific, corporate, and educational researchers. The new Web browsers made the Internet accessible to *anybody* and *everybody* with their simple to-and-fro navigational tools and appealing graphical nature. Soon, millions of users all over the world were moving back and forth between Web sites as easily as they moved from page to page in their word processors.

The Mosaic browser filled its job requirements better than anyone could have imagined. Yet, Mosaic is already considered outdated due to the static nature of its screens. In other words, despite the colorful and cross-linked site pages that Mosaic makes available to the world, the pages don't have enough action in them to keep users occupied; more important, the browser technology is too static to make Web sites truly come alive.

Users seem to want more from the Internet than just a distributed set of interconnected graphical screens. Despite the Web's hypertext nature, those hypertext links simply take you from page location to page location without really doing any work for you except finding appropriate data quickly. Users want real computing power coming at them from the Web sites they visit. For example, instead of reading about the rules of chess, you might want to see a chess game in action or get an introductory graphical tutorial on effective opening moves.

Java, developed by Sun Microsystems in the mid-1990s, changes the way that Web sites operate. Java is a programming language with language features similar to C++. Instead of using Web browsers to view data, the browsers seamlessly download programs written in the Java language and *those Java programs execute on the user's computer.* When you view a Java-enabled Web page, you'll not only see the usual graphical page, but you'll also be able to interact with a program that runs on your own computer, brought to your computer via the Web's connection.

CAUTION

Don't make the mistake of thinking that the sounds and animation you've seen on Web pages represent the Java technology. For example, when you listen to a Web page's sound file, your own computer's sound-producing software is probably playing the sound data that comes from the Web site to your browser. Java takes computer interaction a step further than that.

There are two kinds of programs you can write with the Java language. They are:

- *Java applets* Java applets are small programs that travel with HTML code and execute on the Web user's computer.
- *Java Applications* Java applications are complete stand-alone programs that do not require a Web browser or HTML to execute.

Most Java programs to date reside in applets. After all, the primary goal of Java is to place executable code on Web pages so that users gain more interactivity with Web sites. In addition to writing applets that appear in your Web pages, you can also create stand-alone programs that execute without the need for a Web browser. For example, if you wanted to write a rental property management application that ran independently of an Internet connection, you could select Java as the programming language you use to develop the application.

Java Provides Executable Content

When working with Visual J++ and Java, you'll often hear and read about *executable content*. Executable content is what Java is really all about. A Web page contains executable content, via HTML commands, in the form of a Java applet. Any Web page's Java *content* is *executable* on the target user's computer. Figure 2.3 shows an overview of an HTML document with two embedded Java applets.

FIG. 2.3
HTML serves up Java's executable content.

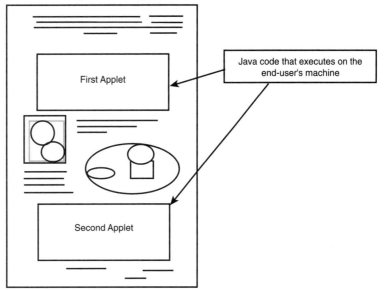

When the end-user enters the URL that displays Figure 2.3's page (or hypertext links to the page), the user's Web-browsing software loads the HTML code, formats the page's text according to the HTML tags, displays any graphic images that appear on the page, and loads the executable content (applets) so the content can execute either immediately or upon a predetermined event, such as a mouse click over a hotspot on the Web page.

N O T E As you'll see in this book's code, the <APPLET> tag indicates that a Java-enabled applet appears inside HTML. The Java code follows the <APPLET> tag until the closing </APPLET> appears. <APPLET> replaces the older <APP> tag used in previous releases of Java. ▩

> **CAUTION**
> You will only be able to run applets if you have a Java-enabled browser, such as Microsoft's Internet Explorer 3.0 or Netscape Navigator 2.0 or later.

The best method of running Java applets is not always obvious to the end-user. The user might think he or she is viewing a busy Web page when, in reality, an applet is providing animation. The look of that animation is smooth because the animation software runs on the user's computer. Because of the applet, the speed of the animation is not dependent on the download time or on Internet traffic.

Before Java-enabled Web pages, the user did have some interaction with the remote site. Nevertheless, that interaction was severely limited. Web page animation was controlled by the user's animation software: If a computer system had no software that could display animation, that feature of the Web page was lost for that system's users. If the user were to interact with the remote site in a question-answer session, such as in order-taking, the user would often have to fill out the form completely before error-checking could be done to any of the user's responses. The user would have to trigger any and all interactions with the remote site; the response would then be limited to the remote site's speed and the current traffic flow on the Internet.

N O T E *CGI* programming (*Common Gateway Interface*) programming provides for the primitive interaction you often see on non-Java Web sites.

Surely, you have traveled into a remote Web site, downloaded software, and then logged off to execute that software. Java makes this process seamless. When you travel to a remote site, the software you want to run can run without your doing anything at all. In addition, the software applet automatically downloads itself to your computer, runs when you trigger its execution, and then goes away when you leave the Web site without taking up permanent disk space! Think of the possibilities for software developers: You'll be able to test-drive software without running an installation program and without having to remove the software when you finish the demonstration.

Multi-Platform Executable Content

Now that you've seen how Java-enabled Web sites appear to the user, think about the requirements of such executable content. When you write a Java-based Web page, you want the code to work on the end-user's remote computer *no matter what kind of computer the remote user uses*. Successfully writing a single program that compiles and operates on multiple platforms is almost impossible and yet, Java easily accomplishes the task.

A Coding Background

Before going further, you may need a review of programming terms if you are new to programming or your skills need refreshing. A program is a set of instructions, written in a programming language such as Java, that tells the computer what to do. Both Java applets and Java applications are programs.

You'll use Visual J++ to write the *code*, or program instructions, that will form your Java programs. Once you write the code, you'll have to *compile* the code. No computer can really understand a programming language such as Java. Programming languages exist for humans. When you compile the program, the *compiler* (Visual J++ includes a compiler) translates your human-readable code into machine-readable code.

Due to the *virtual machine* nature of Java (see the text that follows this sidebar), Java code is not completely compiled, but the Java compiler compiles the code into an in-between stage called *bytecode*. Your Java-enabled Web browsing software then translates this compiled bytecode into instructions that your computer can then execute.

The secret to a Java program's multi-platform operation is *bytecode*. Whereas most programming compilers such as Visual C++ and Visual Basic compile code into a machine-dependent executable program, Java development tools such as Visual J++ do not go quite that far. All Java compilers compile your Java instructions into a special machine-independent module called bytecode.

No computer can really read bytecode but each computer's Java-enabled browser can. In other words, given the same Java applet bytecode, a PC can run the applet using Internet Explorer 3.0 and a UNIX-based minicomputer can run that *very same bytecode* by using its own Java-enabled browser such as *HotJava*. Each Web browser actually interprets the machine-dependent bytecode and then translates that bytecode into machine-specific instructions that particular computer can understand.

N O T E   Figure 2.4 shows the Java compilation/translation scenario. You'll use Visual J++ to write Java code for a virtual machine, you'll then instruct Visual J++ to compile the code into machine-independent bytecode that follows the Web page that is to contain the applet, and when the end-user requests that Web page, the user's Web browser reads the bytecode and automatically interprets the bytecode into code readable by the user's computer. The user is unaware that all this took place; he or she simply displays the Web page and sees the executing applet along with the rest of the Web page's content.

The idea is that you're not writing for one particular *real* computer, but a universal computer that represents *all* computers (at least all those that support a Java-enabled Web browser). This universal computer, called the "virtual machine," only runs the bytecode. Each computer's Java-enabled Web browser software translates the bytecode into machine-readable code.

The Web browser automatically runs the Visual J++ applet. Some applets run automatically, and some run in response to a user event such as a mouse click. It's important that you realize that the user does not necessarily know or care that a small program is running. To the user, the Web page simply does more and responds much more quickly, as fast as the user's computer can translate the bytecode's executable content. All traces of the program then go away when the applet ends, or when the user leaves the Web page.

T I P   When you want the fastest response time possible for a user's interaction with a Web page, you will almost certainly want to use Visual J++ to write a Java applet. Although the user still has to wait for the Web page to download, and although the user still has to wait for the bytecode to get to the computer, the applet (the Web page's executable content) executes as quickly as the user's computer can run the applet. The user is no longer bound to download time once the computer gets the executable content. All other forms of Web page interaction, such as Web page interaction written in CGI, are slaves to download response time and current Internet activity.

FIG. 2.4
Your Visual J++ session produces compiled bytecode that subsequent computers translate.

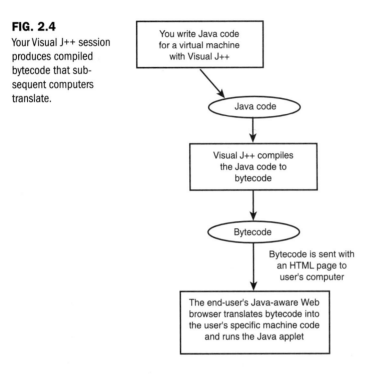

Java is considered *architecture neutral* in that a Java program is not written for a specific machine but rather for the universal virtual machine.

The Java Usage Summary

If you are new to Java technology, as most people still are, you might appreciate a summary of the process one goes through when they are viewing a Java-enabled Web page with a Java-aware Web browser such as Internet Explorer. Here are the steps that occur:

1. You log on to the Internet, using your Web-browsing software.
2. You see your Web browser's default home page.
3. You enter a Java-enabled Web site's URL (location) to view.
4. The serving computer sends the HTML document to your Web browser.
5. The document's <APPLET> tag informs your Web browser of the Web page's Java-based executable content.
6. Your Web browser downloads graphic images from the server, if any graphics appear on the Web page.
7. Depending on how the Java applet is to be triggered (either automatically or by a user's event), the server will also send the bytecode to your computer (the *target*) when the time is right.

8. Your computer's Web browser interprets the bytecode and executes the Java executable content.

9. When you leave the Web page, the executable content goes away. (Some Web browsers will keep the Java code in memory for a while in case you return to the page.)

Perhaps this would also be a good time to explain what you, a Visual J++ developer, will go through when creating Web pages with Java applets. Here are the general steps you'll follow:

1. Start Visual J++ if you have not already done so. (Starting Visual J++ actually means starting the *Developer Studio*, a complete programming language development support system.) You'll learn how to install and start Visual J++ in Chapter 14, "Getting Started with Visual J++."

2. Create your Java applet.

3. Create the HTML Web page that will contain the Java applet. Use appropriate tags to indicate the applet and its parameters.

4. Compile the Java applet. The Developer Studio keeps track of Java applets using the project concept. You'll store each applet in the project and all associated files for that project will also reside in the project, including the HTML Web page.

5. If the compiler finds errors, fix them and recompile the project's files.

6. Test your applet. You can test Visual J++ project applications without logging onto the Internet. If the Java applet does not do what you intended, fix the problem and recompile the applet.

7. Store the applet and HTML on your Web server, where it will await an Internet user's request.

Multithreaded Applications

A *multithreaded application* is a program that might spin off into more than one *thread*, or a single line of execution. Without multithreading, a program can only execute sequentially. Many programs, however, might be able to perform multiple calculations or processing of tasks in parallel. Of course, if one calculation depends on a the result of a second calculation, both cannot execute in parallel because one must complete before the next calculation can begin.

You've already experienced multithreading if you've navigated through the Web. You can be reading and scrolling through text while graphic images are loading elsewhere on the page. In addition, you can download a file or image by clicking on an icon and then, while the downloading takes place, you can start the download of yet another image or file.

As you develop Java programs, Visual J++ lets you specify various threads that can act independently of one another.

> **CAUTION**
>
> Don't be fooled. At its lowest level, a computer can only execute one instruction at a time. Nevertheless, computers run so quickly that they can appear to perform more than one task at the same time. Although there are a handful of computers that contain multiple processors, these multi-processor computers are not yet in the mainstream; most people still use a single processor machine.

No More Missing Viewers!

A Java applet can deliver two separate items that will make Java-based Web pages more successful and popular than those Web pages that are not Java-enabled. Your Java-enabled Web page can transmit a *protocol handler* to the end-user's computer that accepts downloaded data in a format that the user's computer would not otherwise be able to receive. For example, if you decide to transmit data to your Web page, and you transmit that data using a special error-correction protocol that you developed to match your particular data format, you'll be able to send first a protocol handler that explains to the target computer how to receive the incoming data.

Your users will not have to know about the protocol handler either. Think of a protocol handler as an automatic protocol selector. For example, if you've ever downloaded a file from a BBS, you've probably had to choose a download protocol such as XMODEM or ZMODEM. The protocol that the BBS sends to you must match the protocol you select or the two computers will not be able to communicate. By first sending a protocol handler *before* sending the data, the protocol handler teaches the target computer how to receive the data so your users will not have to bother with protocol selection themselves.

In addition to protocol handlers, Java-enabled programs can send *content handlers* to receiving computers. For example, if your Java-enabled page contains a graphic image that resides in your own, new, specially-developed graphics format, you can send a content handler first. For example, if your Web page contains a .JPG graphic image, almost anyone will be able to see the images because the .JPG format is so common. However, if you send a uniquely-formatted graphic image, you can first send a content handler that teaches the target computer how to display the image; then your Java applet can send the image.

> **N O T E** You'll never have to worry about an end-user being able to receive your data or display your graphic images again as long as you provide the appropriate protocol handler or content handler when you send unusual information.

Is Security an Issue?

The answer to this question is that security is *always* an issue. It could be that Java-enabled applets are prone to security problems. After all, when you visit a Java-enabled Web page, you are not always sure if an applet is running or what exactly that applet is trying to do to your computer's disk or memory.

Fortunately, Sun Microsystems developed Java from inception to be a network-based programming language. Therefore, security is inherent in the language, both for the developer and for the Internet user. What follows are some of the security-related protections built into the Java language:

- A Java applet is not allowed to venture into memory areas where it does not belong.
- A Java applet cannot create, read, rename, copy, or write files on the end-user's file system.
- A Java applet cannot connect to additional machines on the end-user's network.
- Applets cannot call system routines on the end-user's system.

Part
I

Ch
2

CAUTION

You can locally load and run a Java applet from your own browser by loading an applet from your own disk drive or network. In the case of a locally-loaded applet, the applet does generally have permission to read and write to the local file system. In addition, some applet viewers do let the end-user specify a list of files that a Web applet can access.

As you can see, Java developers do understand the need for security and the most obvious security footholds are barred from an applet's access. As more people write Java applets, additional security concerns are sure to enter into the picture.

Give Java a Spin

Now that you know more about Java, why not look at a Java-enabled Web page? Use Internet Explorer 3.0 or Netscape's Navigator to locate the following Web site:

> **http://www2.nando.net/nt/nando.cgi**

This Web site displays a colorful newspaper-like Web page that details current news events of the day called the *NandO Times*. From this site's URL address, perhaps you can tell that this Web page is a CGI-based Web page as most non-Java pages are. Although the Web page is fancy, the page is static and does nothing more than display text and graphics. Notice the four still pictures at the top of the page.

Scroll down to the list of choices at the bottom of the Web page and look for the choice labeled JAVA VERSION. Click this choice. Once the Java version appears on your screen, you'll see the same Web page as before; the Java version of the page displays an eye-catching scrolling text display of headline news and the four graphic images change regularly (about once a second—fast for the Internet). Figure 2.5 shows the Web page and calls out where to find the moving text and images when you browse the NandO Times Web site.

TIP

In the future, if you want to go directly to the Java-based NandO Times page, set your browser's URL address to:

> **http://www2.nando.net/nt/?java**

FIG. 2.5
In the NandO Times Web site, the four graphic images change regularly.

The flashing graphic images and the scrolling text do *not* come from a CGI program that is behind the Web page. You are seeing the results of a Java applet that the server sent to your computer along with the HTML page when you requested the Web page. Your computer is running the code that scrolls the text and changes the graphics.

Visual J++ Takes Java Farther

Visual J++ is *not* a Java competitor. Microsoft makes it very clear that the Visual J++ technology supports the entire Sun Microsystems-developed Java language. Visual J++ is a programming platform used to develop Java-enabled applets and applications. Visual J++ includes not only a Java compiler (the tool that translates your Java programs to bytecode), but also an editor, debugger, and online documentation provider. (The end of this section explores Visual J++'s features more fully.)

Therefore, if you already know Java, you'll feel at home with Visual J++ once you learn Visual J++'s interface. Learning Visual J++'s interface may at first seem extremely difficult. Figure 2.6 shows a sample Visual J++ session. The numerous windows and screen elements often frighten the novice programmer, but you'll soon see that the Visual J++ tools are there to make your life easier, not more complicated.

FIG. 2.6
Visual J++ sessions can appear confusing to newcomers.

TIP This book takes its title seriously! Instead of a dry in-depth explanation of every Visual J++ feature, command, and option, this book shows you how to get up and running quickly with Visual J++, so that you'll be using the system as soon as possible. This book will explain the most common components of the Visual J++ system and then dive into Visual J++'s uses and programming fundamentals. You'll find that this book's hands-on approach makes using Visual J++ a pleasure from the very beginning.

The early Java compilers were command-line based. Surprisingly, the graphical nature of computers and the Web did not make it to the Java language development tools until programmers used Java for about a year. In late 1995 and early 1996, graphical Java development tools began to appear on the market.

Microsoft was not the first on the market with a Java development tool. As a matter of fact, Microsoft entered the Java race fairly late in the game. Although late, Microsoft did things right when they introduced Visual J++.

Keep in mind that Visual J++ is not a Java replacement, nor is Visual J++ a competing product to the Java language. In fact, Microsoft makes it clear that Visual J++ implements the very same Java technology developed by Sun Microsystems. Therefore, when you work with Visual J++, you are working with the Java language, just as Visual C++ programmers write code in C++. Visual J++ is a complete development platform, or program development tool, with which you can create Java-enabled applets.

The following are just a few Visual J++ features you'll find and use:

■ The Visual J++ compiler can compile over one million lines of Java code each minute. That's really fast!

■ The Visual J++ editor contains virtually a word processing set of powerful text features including the usual search, cut, and paste, as well as multi-pane viewing, moving, and copying between windows, bookmarks, full-screen viewer, and advanced windowing features.

■ Visual J++ contains a complete online help system that includes all available documentation, including a version of Microsoft's Books Online technology.

■ You'll want to take advantage of Visual J++'s interactive debugger. The debugger lets you specify breakpoints and examine data contents at any point in your program.

■ Microsoft's famous wizard technology builds your initial Java applet or application. You then can fill in the missing pieces to customize your own Java program requirements.

■ You can use the Visual J++ applet viewer, *JView*, to test the applets and applications you write before sending those applets out onto the Web with your Web server.

■ You will create dialog boxes and menus with the Resource Wizard.

■ For speed, use Visual Visual J++'s keyboarding macro technology to create shortcuts.

■ The included Java wizards can also create your initial HTML Web page containing your Java-based executable content.

■ Visual J++ integrates the *COM* (*Common Object Model*) so that you can integrate external applications, such as a working Excel spreadsheet, into your own Java applets and applications.

■ One of the newest technologies that should reinvent the way we develop applications is the *ActiveX* technology, an integrated part of Visual J++. ActiveX is the modern-day next-step evolution for OLE and VBX (Visual Basic) controls that you may already be used to.

N O T E   Visual J++ uses the same development platform, the Developer Studio, that other powerful Microsoft development languages also use, such as Visual C++ and the FORTRAN Powerstation. Although the Developer Studio is Windows-based, that is, you must have Windows to use the Developer Studio. Java applets and applications that you create can run on any Java-enabled platform. ■

CAUTION

If you've studied Java before, you may have heard of *content* and *protocol handlers* that the Java supports. A content handler teaches a Web browser how to display new kinds of data and a protocol handler teaches a Web browser how to send and receive data using various formats. Although the Java language portion of Visual J++ lets you write content and protocol handler development, Visual J++ does not support content or protocol handlers. The only Web browser on the market that does support the two handlers is HotJava, a Sun Microsystems product. Visual J++'s ActiveX and COM technologies replace content and protocol handler requirements.

Get Ready for Visual J++

Now that you have a brief historical background of the Java language, you know how Java applets and applications fit into the world of the Internet. Java applets travel along with an HTML document and execute *on the end-user's computer*. That execution gives you the ability to produce much more real-time Web page action, which could include the following interactive content:

Part

I

Ch

2

- Question and answer sessions with instant feedback and error correction.

- Integrated external object embedding. Include an Excel worksheet directly inside your Web page for users to use for calculating loan rate scenarios or mortgage payment amounts.

- Animation that is limited only by the user's computing speed and that is not dependent on Internet traffic or download speed.

- A protocol-independent data receiver for real-time stock quotes or other fast-paced data display.

- A scientific graphics-drawing program, such as a CAD/CAM package, that uses the end-user's computing power to generate the points drawn.

- Interactive games sent directly to users. You could even charge a small monthly fee to keep your users in video games that come to them directly on the Net. When the game credits are gone, the applet can remove itself from the user's computer.

From Here...

The goal of this chapter was to provide you with an introduction to Java technology and to the Visual J++ development system. You now know that Visual J++ is not a Java replacement, but a Java development system with which you can create robust interactive Internet applications. Now that you've mastered an overview of the features and functions of Java and Visual J++, you're ready to jump right into the Visual J++ Developer Studio in the next chapter and learn how to maneuver through Visual J++ and take advantage of the power you'll find in Visual J++.

The following points were covered in this chapter:

- The Internet became more usable for mass consumption as soon as the World Wide Web came onto the scene with Mosaic-like browsers that displayed graphic pages and allowed for simple navigation between Web sites.

- Java-enabled Web pages provide true interaction and animation.

- A Java program is actually an applet, or a miniature application, that executes on the end-user's computer as soon as the user looks at the Web page and triggers the Java program.

- Java is a robust but fairly secure system that respects many security boundaries and provides safe content for both developers and users.

■ The Java language provides for both protocol handlers and content handlers so you need not worry about your user's successful receipt of the data you send with your Java applet.

■ Visual J++ is one of the most powerful Java development systems available.

■ As you progress with your Visual J++ development, you'll soon learn how to take advantage of the new ActiveX and COM technologies that let you integrate powerful pre-written applications, such as Excel, into your own Java-enabled Web pages.

CHAPTER 3

The Java Language

by Mark Culverhouse

In Chapter 2, "Java and Visual J++," you learned about the Internet and some of the requirements of a dynamic, distributed environment. In this chapter, you will learn about the Java programming language and how its features meet the requirements for secure, distributed computing on the Internet and intranets. You will see how simple, yet powerful, the Java language is. After learning about the elements of the language in this chapter, you will then examine the standard Java API Packages in the following chapters.

Java is a pure, object-oriented language. You should be familiar with C++, another object-oriented language, or at least object-oriented concepts. This chapter should familiarize you with the core Java language. ■

Simple data types

Java has fewer simple data types, but they are familiar.

Reference data type

New with Java is the reference data type that replaces traditional pointers.

Arrays

Java arrays are what you would expect, but they are also objects.

Classes

Classes are the heart of Java's completely object-oriented architecture.

Interfaces

Java interfaces are a simple but powerful mechanism to deal with the object capabilities.

Methods

Methods define the behavior of objects.

Packages

Java packages provide a way to manage source code and name spaces.

Other highly recommended basic sources of information about the Java language are:

- The Java Documentation page. Sun's JavaSoft **http://java.sun.com/doc/index.html**
- "The Java Language Specification" JavaSoft **http://java.sun.com/doc/ language_specification.html**
- "Java API Documentation" JavaSoft **http://java.sun.com/doc/ api_documentation.html**
- "The Java Tutorial" JavaSoft **http://java.sun.com/doc/tutorial.html**
- "The Java Virtual Machine Specification" JavaSoft **http://java.sun.com/doc/ language_vm_specification.html**
- "General Information and White Papers" JavaSoft **http://java.sun.com/doc/ general.html**
- "The Java Language, An Overview" JavaSoft **http://java.sun.com/doc/Overviews/ java/**
- "The Java Language Environment White Paper" JavaSoft **http://java.sun.com/doc/ language_environment/**
- This book's companion CD-ROM contains "The Java QuickReference" HTML document.
- The Java language news group **comp.lang.java**
- Visual J++ Books Online on the Visual J++ CD-ROM.

Examining Java's Goals

Programming languages are created to meet a set of design goals. Java has a very well-defined set of design goals. By examining these goals, you will better understand the features of the language.

Java is designed for distributed computing on the Internet. Some of the requirements for distributed computing include the following:

- Simplicity: Keep it simple. Make it easier to learn and use.
- Familiarity: Use existing standards like C++ syntax to give the language a familiar feel.
- Robustness: Eliminate error-prone features and require programmers to "cast away" correctness.
- Portability: Compile into hardware and OS independent executable code.
- Security: Provide an environment with levels of security for Java programs to run.
- High Performance: Multitasking.

Many code examples are used to illustrate how the language works. Many other examples illustrate common mistakes you might make when starting out with Java. By learning about them now, you can avoid them later.

As you learn more about Java, you will appreciate its consistency with respect to object orientation. Below is the Java HelloWorld program. The familiar `main` still exists, but notice it is inside a class definition. A `static, system` object contains the system output stream, `out`, which contains a method, `println`:

```
class HelloWorld {
        static public void main(String args[]) {
        System.out.println("Hello World!");
        }
}
```

In this chapter, the Java language is presented using many code examples. Each example will consist of one or more complete classes. Many early examples show simple sample statements in a static block. This is the easiest Java class to use to illustrate simple statements. The static block is executed once. The events that can cause a class's static initialization block(s) to be executed include the first time an object of that class is created using the `new operator`, or when the first call to a `static class` method is made.

In many examples, statements that cause compile errors are left in the code, but are commented out. The statement in error is usually followed by a comment beginning with "`//error`." This is done to resolve ambiguities about how Java works. All of these sample classes are available on the accompanying CD-ROM.

Here is a sample of some example code. Notice the use of a class static initialization block instead of introducing methods:

```
class Class3Static{
    static{
        System.out.println("Class3Static loaded");
        //1+2; // error "Invalid expression statement" not allowed in Java
    }
}
```

Facts about the Java language:

- Every class in Java is a subclass of the object class.
- Local variables can be declared and initialized anywhere in a block.

Table 3.1 contains the list of Java reserved keywords. These keywords have special meaning in the Java language and must be used as designed. Not all keywords are implemented, but they still are reserved and should not be used.

Table 3.1   List of Java Reserved Keywords

abstract	do	if	outer	this
boolean	double	implements	package	throw
break	else	import	private	throws
byte	extends	inner	protected	transient
byvalue	false	instanceof	public	true
case	final	int	rest	try
catch	finally	interface	return	var
char	float	long	short	void
class	for	native	static	volatile
const	future	new	super	while
continue	generic	null	switch	
default	goto	operator	synchronized	

The following list enumerates the different statements in the Java language. Anywhere a single statement is allowed, one of the entries in the list below can be substituted.

List of Java Statements

VariableDeclaration

Expression;

{ Statements }

if (Expression)
Statement else Statement

while (Expression) Statement

do Statement while(Expression);

try Statement catch(Parameter)
Statement finally Statement

switch(Expression){ Statements }

synchronized(Expression) Statement

return Expression;

throw Expression;

case Expression:

default:

Identifier: Statement

break Identifier;

continue Identifier;

;

Simple Data Types

Each variable and expression in a program has one, and only one, data type. Data types represent different sets of data values and determine which standard operators can be applied. There are two kinds of data types: simple and composite. *Simple* data types are the built-in Java data types. *Composite* data types are composed by the programmer using simple types, arrays, classes, and interfaces.

Java has a limited set of simple, built-in data types. Each Java data type is defined to have the same respective fixed length on all platforms.

Table 3.2 lists the simple data types and some associated attributes.

Table 3.2 Simple Data Types and Attributes

Type	Bits	Default	Signed	Range
boolean	1	false	N/A	true and false
byte	8	0	yes	-128 to 127
char	16	\u0000	no	\u0000 to \uFFFF
short	16	0	yes	-32768 to 32768
int	32	0	yes	-2,147,483,648 to 2,147,483,647
long	64	0	yes	-2**63 to 2**63-1
float	32	0.0	yes	~ -10**39 to 10**39
double	64	0.0	yes	~ -10**317 to 10**317
reference	n/a	null	n/a	n/a

TIP Simple data types are defined to have default initial values. However, the compiler may still give error messages when a non-initialized variable is referenced. The rule is that local variables *must* be initialized before being used, or a compile-time error results. Static class variables do *not* have to be initialized before being used. Static variables use the default values listed above. The best practice has always been to assign a value to a variable before using it. Java makes this mandatory for local variables. The default values are also used to initialize array elements.

Facts About Simple Data Types:

- Simple data types are passed by value as method parameters or during assignment.
- Because simple data types are built-in, the new operator is never used to create a simple data type instance.

> **TIP** Later, when we discuss Java's API packages, you will find that each of these simple data types also has a corresponding object wrapper class in the java.lang package. These wrapper classes add more functionality to each data type and allow passing of values by reference.

Boolean

Something as basic as a Boolean data type should not be left to each programmer to define. Java defines Boolean as a built-in type. A Boolean is one-bit wide and takes on the values true or false. The initial value of a Boolean variable is false.

A Boolean is not a number and cannot be cast to a number or any other type. Nor can numeric operators be used with Booleans. If necessary, Booleans must be converted to numbers and vice versa. The code sample below in Listing 3.1 illustrates the points made above.

Listing 3.1   Boolean Number Conversion (\msdev\samples\que\QueChap3.java)

```
class Class3Boolean{
    static{
        int n = 0;
        boolean b = true;

        b = ( n != 0 );    // convert 0 to false else true
        b = ( n != 0 ? true : false ); // same as above
        n = ( b ? 1 : 0 ); // convert true to 1 false to 0

        //b = n; // error! can't convert int to boolean
        //b = (boolean)n; // error! can't even cast it!

        //n = b;    // error! can't convert boolean to int
        //n = (int)b; // error! invalid cast

        //if( n )    // error! Incompatible type can't convert int to
boolean
        //      n = 1;
        //b = ( n ? true : false); // error! same thing n is not a boolean
    }
}
```

At first, the stricter type checking may seem annoying, but, in return, many costly programming errors are eliminated from all Java code.

Character

Java defines one character built-in type, char. A char is a two-byte Unicode character. This makes character data and strings use more memory, but internationalization becomes easier.

The initial default value for a char is \u0000. A char can be treated as an unsigned 16-bit number. However, if any data loss occurs, then casting will be required.

Listing 3.2 illustrates some basic uses of the char data type.

Listing 3.2   Character Example (\msdev\samples\que\QueChap3.java)

```
class Class3Character{
    static{
        char c = 'a';
        int n = 0;
        float f = (float)0.0; // cast is needed
        double d = 0.0;
        boolean b = false;
        byte y = 0;
        short s = 0;

        //c = b; // error can't convert boolean to char
        //b = c; // error can't convert char to boolean

        c = (char)n; // ok
        //c = n; // error explicit cast needed
        n = c;      // ok

        c = (char)f; // ok
        //c = f;  // error explicit cast needed
        f = c;   // ok

        c = (char)y; // ok
        //c = y;  // error explicit cast needed
        y = (byte)c;   // ok
        //y = c;  // error! explicit cast needed

        c = (char)s; // ok
        //c = s;  // error explicit cast needed
        s = (short)c;   // ok
        //s = c;  // error! explicit cast needed

        if(c < 0)     // ok
            c = ' ';
        ++c; // ok

        // be careful casting

        c = 0x8000;  // c is now 32,768 this could be Chinese
        s = (short)c; // s is now -32,768
        b = c == s;   // b is false!
    }
}
```

Part

I

Ch

3

Table 3.3 shows some common character literals. Use the values under the Literal column in your source code.

Table 3.3   Character Literals

Character	ASCII	Literal
Continuation		\
Back Space	BS	\b
Form Feed	FF	\f
New Line	LF	\n
Carriage Return	CR	\r
Horizontal Tab	HT	\t
Back Slash	\	\\
Single Quote	'	\'
Double Quote	"	\"
Hex Pattern	0xdd	\xdd
Octal Pattern	0ddd	\ddd
Unicode Pattern	0xdddd	\udddd

Numbers

Java has four integer and two floating-point, built-in data types. All six of these numeric data types are signed. There is no unsigned keyword in Java.

Built-in integer number data types are all signed and take on integral values only. The range of integers spans a negative minimum and a positive maximum value depending on the size of the respective data type.

Built-in floating-point number data types are also signed and take on real values, i.e., an integral and decimal part. Floating-point numbers range from a negatively signed minimum value and a positively signed maximum value. The minimum and maximum are dependent on the size of the floating-point data type.

Integers   The four integer data types are:

- `byte`—8 bits
- `short`—16 bits
- `int`—32 bits
- `long`—64 bits

Conversion is done during assignment. If any data loss would occur, then casting is required.

A `long` literal is specified with a trailing L or l.

Listing 3.3 has some common coding examples using integer data types.

Listing 3.3 Integer Examples (\msdev\samples\que\QueChap3.java)

```
class Class3Integers{
    static{
        byte b = 1;
        short s = 2;
        int i = 3;
        long l = 4L;

        l = i = s = b; // ok no data loss
        //b = s = i = l; // error 3 casts needed
        b = (byte)s;   // ok
        s = (short)i; // ok
        i = (int)l;    // ok
    }
}
```

Floating Point   The two floating-point data types are:

- float—32-bit single precision IEEE 754-1985 floating point number.
- double—64-bit double precision IEEE 754-1985 floating point number.

Facts About Floating Point Numbers:

- A float literal is specified with a trailing F or f.
- A double literal is specified with a trailing D or d.
- Floating point literals can be specified in scientific notation: 2.34E-10d -4e14F -12.876E8D.
- If a literal such as 3.1415 is specified without a D or F, then double is assumed.

Java enforces strict type checking to avoid programming errors. If an assignment results in data loss, then explicit action by the programmer is required to avoid compile-time errors. In Listing 3.4 casting is used to avoid compile errors.

Listing 3.4 Floating Point Examples (\msdev\samples\que\QueChap3.java)

```
class Class3FloatingPoint{
    static{
        float f = 2147483647F;
        double d = 4.5E+4;
        long l = 1011;

        //f = 3.1415; // error need to cast double to float
        //f = 3.1E12; // error need to cast double to float

        f = (float).1e12; // ok
        f = 2F;      // ok
        f = 2.3F;    // ok
```

continues

Listing 3.4   Continued

```
        f = 2.3E5F;  // ok
        f = 2.3e5F;  // ok

        d = f; // ok
        //f = d; // error need to cast double to float

        d = l; // ok
        //l = d; // error need to cast double to long

        f = l; // ok
        //l = f; /// error need to cast float to long
    }
}
```

Reference Data Type

Simple, built-in data types have been discussed above. Composite data types will be discussed later, but first the reference data type will be examined. Composite data types are objects, interfaces, and arrays. In Java you never actually define an object instance; you must explicitly create one using new. The new operator returns a "reference" to the new object. The value of the reference is stored in a reference data type.

The default value of a reference is null. The null value is a Java keyword; it is not a typedef as in C. Java has no typedef.

A reference data type is like a simple, built-in data type, in that it contains a value. The difference is that the value is a reference to an object. The reference data type is simple; the object it references is composite.

TIP

Note that you cannot create a new int using new in Java as you can in C++. The new operator in Java can only create objects. However, Java arrays are actually objects, so you can create a one-element array of ints.

A reference is as close to a pointer as you will get in Java. References are more than pointers; they are smart pointers. They are smart because they collectively manage created objects. There is no delete in Java. As a programmer, you do not have to worry about freeing objects or their memory in Java. An object is deleted when it goes out of "scope," i.e., when it is no longer referenced. When is an object no longer referenced? When no reference contains its reference value.

An important fact about references: The value null is not a number. It is a keyword like true and false.

How Big Is a Reference?

How many bits does it take to store a reference? There is no way to find out. There is no `sizeof` operator in Java.

TIP

If Java has no pointers then how can a method return values through output parameters? For example, suppose a method is to return the current temperature in degrees Centigrade and degrees Fahrenheit using two output parameters. In C++ the parameters would be pointers or references to say, `int`s or `double`s. The pointers would be de-referenced or the equivalent C++ "references" used to save the new values.

The answer is to use arrays. For example, pass one element array as the output parameter. Update the array element with the new value.

Part

I

Ch

3

The code example in Listing 3.5 shows two string objects being created. The references to the new strings are initially stored in reference variables, s1 and s2. Initially s1 and s2 are not equal because new will return unique reference values for each new object. Comparing s1 and s2 compares the reference values, not the values of the objects referenced, i.e., not "S1" and "S2."

When the value of s1 is assigned to s2, they both reference the same object, the string "S1." The string "S2" can no longer be referenced because there is no reference variable still containing a reference to it. The "S2" string gets tossed into the Recycling Bin.

Listing 3.5   References Examples 1 of 2
(\msdev\samples\que\QueChap3.java)

```
class Class3References1{
     static{
          String s1, s2; // no Strings yet, just String references
          boolean b;

          s1 = new String("S1"); // create a new string
          s2 = new String("S2"); // create a new string
          b = s1 == s2;   // b is false

          s2 = s1; // s2 now has same reference as s1
          b = s1 == s2;   // b is true

          // "S2" is no longer referenced! It's gone.
     }
}
```

Comparing reference values and comparing referenced object values can be confusing. To compare the values of two `String` objects you can use the `compareTo` method. The `String` class provides the `compareTo` method to compare a `String`'s value with another `String`'s value. Comparing references is to test for the equivalence of objects, not object values. Listing 3.6 has some examples of comparing `String` objects and values.

Listing 3.6 References Examples 2 of 2
(\msdev\samples\que\QueChap3.java)

```
class Class3References2{
    static{
        String s1;
        String s2a, s2b;
        boolean b;

        s1 = new String("S1");  // create a new string
        s2a = new String("S2"); // create a new string
        s2b = new String("S2"); // create a new string
        b = s1 == s2a;  // b is false
        b = s2a == s2b; // b is false
        b = s2a.equals(s2b);  // now b is true
        b = s2a.compareTo(s2b) == 0; // now b is true
    }
}
```

Arrays

Java arrays are implemented as objects; therefore, arrays are referenced the same as any other object. Java maintains an array class for each simple data type and for each class. Java uses these classes to implement arrays; however, you cannot extend an array class yourself.

In this section you will learn:

- How to create and initialize arrays.
- How multidimensional arrays are supported.

Facts About Java Arrays:

- Arrays are objects.
- The first element in an array has index 0.
- The array class has a public, read-only variable named length that can be used to get the number of elements in the array.
- Arrays are accessed through references, like any other object.
- Arrays are created using new and disposed of by garbage collection.
- Arrays can be created using static initializers.
- Elements of new arrays are initialized to data type defaults.
- Multidimensional arrays are supported as arrays of arrays.
- Array exceptions thrown include: ArrayIndexOutOfBoundsException and ArrayStoreException.

Listing 3.7 shows the notation used to declare array references in Java. The array brackets can come after the name of the variable, or after the name of the array element type. Note that the `instanceof` operator tests the actual object referenced, not just the declared type of the reference. A `null` reference is not an instance of any class.

Listing 3.7 Arrays Examples 1 of 5
(\msdev\samples\que\QueChap3.java)

```
class Class3Arrays0{
    static{
        int i[];          // i is an int array reference
        int[] j;          // j is an int array reference
        int i1[], i2[];   // i1 and i2 are int array references
        int[] j1, j2;     // j1 and j2 are int array references

        // next statement is ok because
        // all variables are instances of int[]
        i = i1 = i2 = j = j1 = j2 = new int[2];

        boolean b;
        // note that
        b = i instanceof int[]; // b is true
        i = null;
        b = i instanceof int[]; // b is false
    }
}
```

Listing 3.8 shows how an array is just a reference to an array object. Notice the use of the `length` variable in the `Array` class.

Listing 3.8 Arrays Examples 2 of 5
(\msdev\samples\que\QueChap3.java)

```
class Class3Arrays1{
    static{
        int i[];  // i is null reference to array of ints

        i = new int[7]; // i is a reference to array of 7 ints

        boolean b;
        b = i.length == 7; // b is true
    }
}
```

The next example, Listing 3.9, shows `String` objects used in an array. Note that the array variable is a reference for the array object. Each `String` object must be created and stored in each array element.

Listing 3.9   Arrays Examples 3 of 5
(\msdev\samples\que\QueChap3.java)

```
class Class3Arrays2{
     static{
          String s[]; // s is a null reference to an array of String references

          s = new String[2]; // s is a reference to an array of 2 null
          ➡references to Strings

          s[0] = new String("Day"); // first element in array s is reference to
          ➡"Day"
          s[1] = new String("Night");
          s[1] = "Night";  // same as above Java shortcut for String constructor

          //s[1] = String("Night");  // error new is needed
     }
}
```

The next example, Listing 3.10, shows how an array can be treated as an object. An int array is cast to an object and then back to an int array. Note the declaration of the static int array.

Listing 3.10   Arrays Examples 4 of 5
(\msdev\samples\que\QueChap3.java)

```
class Class3Arrays3{
     static int i[] = {1,2,3,4,5,6,7}; // create static array

     static{
          Object o;
          o = i;

          int j[];

          j = (int[])o;

          boolean b;

          b = i.length == 7; // b = true
          b = j.length == 7; // b = true
          b = i == j;        // b = true
          b = i[3] == j[3];  // b = true 4==4
     }
}
```

Multidimensional arrays are supported in Java. They are similar to C arrays, i.e., arrays of arrays. Listing 3.11 illustrates a two-dimensional array, s, that is statically initialized, and another two-dimensional array, S, which is created dynamically to contain the same contents as s. Notice that S could have been created as String[3][2], which would have caused the creation of the sub-arrays. Dimensions must be specified continuously from left to right, but can stop at any level after the first.

Listing 3.11   Arrays Examples 5 of 5 (\msdev\samples\que\QueChap3.java)

```java
class Class3Arrays4{
    static String s[][] =
        {    {"CA", "California"},
             {"IL", "Illinois"},
             {"VA", "Virginia"}
        };

    static{
        int i;

        i = s.length;     // i == 3
        i = s[0].length; // i == 2
        i = s[1].length; // i == 2
        i = s[2].length; // i == 2

        // create equivalent of statically initialized s
        String S[][];
        S = new String[3][]; // we could have used String[3][2]
        S[0] = new String[2];
        S[1] = new String[2];
        S[2] = new String[2];
        S[0][0] = new String("CA");
        S[0][1] = new String("California");
        S[1][0] = new String("IL");
        S[1][1] = new String("Illinois");
        S[2][0] = new String("VA");
        S[2][1] = new String("Virginia");

        boolean b;

        b = S instanceof String;      // b == false
        b = S instanceof String[];    // b == false
        b = S instanceof String[][]; // b == true
        b = S instanceof Object;      // b == true
    }
}
```

Part
I

Ch
3

Classes

Java is a pure, object-oriented language. Classes are the kernel of the language. This section will cover:

- The definition of a Java class.
- How to create objects from classes.

- Defining class methods and variables.
- Using `private` and `public` access modifiers to encapsulate data.
- The use of `static` initialization.
- Constructors.
- Extending classes.
- Overriding classes.
- Garbage collection.

A class is a set of data and methods that define the attributes and behavior of an object.

Facts About Java Classes:

- The `this` reference variable is the value of the current object.
- The `super` variable refers to the base class of the current object.
- Classes contain data variables and methods.
- Classes cannot be nested.

Classes are used to model objects in the real world. The following examples, Listings 3.12 through 3.14, illustrate the use of classes by building a thermometer. The first design (see Listing 3.12) has a `Thermometer` class that contains a single data variable to hold the thermometer's current temperature in degrees Fahrenheit. Because `temperature` is `public`, its value can be accessed using the dot notation.

Listing 3.12 Thermometer1 Examples (\msdev\samples\que\QueChap3.java)

```
class Class3Class1a{
    static{
        Thermometer1 t = new Thermometer1();

        t.temperature = 72.0f;  // set temp

        float temp = t.temperature; // get temp
    }
}
class Thermometer1{
    public float temperature = 0;
}
```

The first release of the thermometer worked, but didn't sell in the marketplace. Marketing says we need to meet the features of our competition. Some engineers meet and decide to add the following enhancements:

1. Ability to read temperature in degrees Centigrade.
2. Instructions that prohibit using the thermometer outside its engineered limits.
3. Ability to read the most recent highest and lowest temperatures.

Release 2 of the thermometer (see Listing 3.13) implements the features set out above. The test driver class, Class3Class1b, has been updated to reflect the new thermometer's specifications.

This upgrade will introduce several new Java features, as well as introduce some object-oriented design concepts.

The getMaximum and getMinimum methods are static or class methods. They are associated with the class itself and not any particular instance (so no use of this within a class method). Class methods can be accessed through an instance reference or by using the class name.

Listing 3.13 Thermometer2 Test Example (\msdev\samples\que\QueChap3.java)

```
class Class3Class1b{
    static{
        Thermometer2 t = new Thermometer2();

        t.setTemperature( 72.0f );  // set temp

        float temperature;

        temperature = t.getTemperature(); // get temperature in F
        temperature = t.getCelsius(); // get temperature in C
        temperature = t.getHigh(); // get highest temperature
        temperature = t.getLow(); // get lowest temperature
        temperature = t.getMaximum(); // get maximum temperature
        temperature = Thermometer2.getMinimum(); // get minimum temperature
        t.resetHighLow(); // reset the high and low temperatures to current
temp
    }
}
```

The first thing to notice when looking at the new Thermometer2 class (see Listing 3.14) is its name. A new release was necessary because compatibility with the old release could not be maintained. In Thermometer1 the variable temperature was declared to be public. This means that clients of Thermometer1 directly referenced the temperature variable to get and set its value. The new requirements to validate settings of the thermometer temperature and to support high and low temperature recordings cannot be implemented if clients are allowed to directly set the temperature value.

In Thermometer2, the temperature variable has been made private so that clients cannot access it. Two new methods, getTemperature and setTemperature were added for access to temperature by clients. If temperature had originally been private, it would have been possible to ship a new Thermometer1 class with the new features that would still be compatible with the old version.

One of the concepts of object-oriented design is called *encapsulation*, which states that a client should only see the services that a server offers, and not the data or internal details of how those services are provided. As you can see from the simple thermometer example, following this rule can help to avoid problems down the road.

The next thing to notice are the variables, TEMPERATURE_MAX and TEMPERATURE_MIN. These are the Java equivalents of constants. The static keyword makes the variable a class variable instead of an instance variable. The value is the same for all thermometers, so it should be a class variable. The final keyword says that the value, after initialization, will never change, i.e., it is constant. These constants are still made private and access is provided with methods.

The variable fiveninths is a simple example of how class static initializers can be used. These blocks of code are executed once when the class is first loaded. In this example, the value of 5/9 is computed once and saved in a private class variable for use later in calculations. This is a trivial example with little, if any, actual benefit.

The setTemperature method, besides checking for valid values of a potential new temperature setting, also demonstrates the use of the this reference. Notice that the parameter to setTemperature is the same name as the class instance variable used to store the current temperature setting. The this reference is used to resolve the reference to the instance variable whose name was pushed out of scope by the method parameter name.

The value of this is always a reference to the current object being run. This is true within instance methods, but not within class static methods, where there is no instance. The this keyword could be explicitly used for each reference to an instance variable or method, but it is not required.

Listing 3.14   Thermometer2 Class (\msdev\samples\que\QueChap3.java)

```java
class Thermometer2{
    private static final float TEMPERATURE_MAX = 260.0F;
    private static final float TEMPERATURE_MIN = -80.0F;
    private static float fiveninths;

    private float temperature = 0;
    private float temperatureHigh = 0;
    private float temperatureLow = 0;

    static{
        fiveninths = 5.0F/9.0F; // calculate number one time for use later
    }

    float getTemperature(){
        return temperature;
    }

    boolean setTemperature(float temperature){
        if(temperature > TEMPERATURE_MAX || temperature < TEMPERATURE_MIN)
            return false;

        this.temperature = temperature; // use this reference to unambiguate
        if(temperature > temperatureHigh)
            temperatureHigh = temperature;
        if(temperature < temperatureLow)
            temperatureLow = temperature;
```

```
        return true;
    }

    static float getMaximum(){
        return TEMPERATURE_MAX;
    }

    static float getMinimum(){
        return TEMPERATURE_MIN;
    }

    float getHigh(){
        return temperatureHigh;
    }

    float getLow(){
        return temperatureLow;
    }

    float getCelsius(){
        return (temperature - 32.0F) * fiveninths;
    }

    void resetHighLow(){
        temperatureHigh = temperature;
        temperatureLow = temperature;
    }
}
```

Constructors

You have already seen the use of class static initialization blocks, which are executed once per class. Constructors are special methods that are executed once per object as it is created. The thermometer classes did not have a constructor. Java supplies a default constructor with no parameters if one is not specified. The new operator allocates memory for the object and calls the constructor with the parameters. The this reference is set to refer to the new object. The constructor should initialize the object.

Facts About Constructors:

- Constructors have the same name as their class.
- If no constructor is specified for a class, then a default constructor with no parameters is used.
- If any constructor with parameters is specified, then a default (no parameter) constructor is no longer provided automatically. If one is needed, it must be specified in the class.
- A class can have multiple constructors. Each must have a unique sequence of parameter data types so the compiler can tell them apart.
- A constructor may invoke one, and only one, other constructor in the first statement using this(...).

Constructors are used to initialize objects. A class can have more than one constructor; the difference is the set of parameters passed in to initialize the object. Listing 3.15 shows a class called Person. When a Person object is created, different amounts of information are available. A constructor is defined for each combination of available data.

Listing 3.15   Person Test (\msdev\samples\que\QueChap3.java)

```java
class Class3Class2{
    static{
        Person p;
        p = new Person();
        p = new Person("Frank Lloyd Wright");
        p = new Person("Frank Lloyd Wright ", "Spring Green");
        p = new Person("Frank Lloyd Wright ", "Spring Green", 58893);
    }
}
```

The Person class (see Listing 3.16) contains a default constructor with no parameters, so a Person object can be created with no information known. If this state of Person was not wanted, then the default constructor definition could be removed from the class definition, and those types of objects would not be allowed.

It may be useful to "call" or invoke one constructor from another to share some initialization code. This is possible by using the this reference with parameters. Invoking another constructor can only be done in the first statement of a constructor.

Listing 3.16   Person Class (\msdev\samples\que\QueChap3.java)

```java
class Person{
    String name;
    String city;
    int zipcode;

    Person(){// default constructor
    }

    Person(String name){
        this();
        //this();  // error only one constructor can be invoked
        this.name = name;
    }

    Person(String name, String city){
        this(name);
        this.city = city;
        //this(); // error constructor call must be first
    }

    Person(String name, String city, int zipcode){
        this(name, city);
```

```
            this.zipcode = zipcode;
      }
}
```

The *finalize* Method

You have seen how constructors are invoked when an object is created. What happens when the object is destroyed? Suppose in an object's constructor a network connection is opened for the life of the object. Where should the connection be closed? It should be closed just before the object is destroyed. When Java objects are destroyed, their `finalize` method is called.

Java objects are destroyed after the following sequence of steps:

1. When there are no more references to the object.
2. After the garbage collector runs to queue pending `finalize` methods.
3. And, when the finalize thread runs and processes pending `finalize` methods.

Facts About `finalize` Methods:

- The `finalize` method is called after the object has been garbage collected.
- There is no guarantee that `finalize` will ever be called, but it will never be called more than once.
- The `finalize` method may be called by your code, but it will still be processed the same as if it had not been called by user code.

The example below shows how to "free" a Java object. Simply null the last reference of the object, and that's it. Later, possibly when the system is idle, the garbage collector will identify the object as having no references. It will then be marked as a candidate for destruction. Before actually being destroyed, the `finalize` method is called. You might want to make the `finalize` method private or protected to prevent it from being called explicitly by a client.

The `finalize` method may not always be called implicitly by Java. If resources that are not freed by the operating system are to be freed in `finalize`, then it might be necessary to *force* the processing of `finalize` methods. This is shown in Listing 3.17.

Part I Ch 3

Listing 3.17 NetworkConnection Example (\msdev\samples\que\QueChap3.java)

```
class Class3Class3{
    static{
        NetworkConnection c;
        System.out.println("Class3Class3 static called");
        c = new NetworkConnection("Localhost");
        // ... use connection
        c = null; // eliminate last reference to connection
        // let's nudge Java into "deleting" object
        Runtime runtime = Runtime.getRuntime();
```

continues

Listing 3.17   Continued

```
        runtime.gc(); // run garbage collector
        runtime.runFinalization(); // run pending finalize methods
    }
     static void doNothing(){
    }

}
class NetworkConnection{
    NetworkConnection(String connect){
        // establish network connection ...
    }
    protected void finalize(){
        // close network connection ...
    }
}
```

Extending Classes

Java classes can be extended or subclassed. If class B extends class A, then B is a subclass of A and A is a superclass of B. This is one of the most useful object-oriented concepts, inheritance. Programs can be better organized with the proper use of inheritance. The java.lang.Object class is the default root class of all Java objects.

Java supports only single inheritance, i.e., a subclass can have only a single immediate super-class. Multiple inheritance allows multiple immediate superclasses. However, use of multiple inheritance has been avoided because it has proven to be too complex to apply effectively. Java has a language feature called interfaces, which provides many of the benefits of multiple inheritance. Interfaces are discussed later.

Uses of Inheritance:

- Layering sets of functionality.
- Extending the functionality of existing read-only classes.

Software engineers are always on the lookout for techniques that simplify complex implementations. If it isn't simple, then there is a nagging suspicion that it isn't right.

To illustrate inheritance, a hypothetical case study involving electronic devices is used. The examples are described in Listings 3.18 through 3.24.

An electronics application evolved which controlled electrical appliances like televisions and VCRs. The first release was an X-10 based system that was fairly simple; it only turned appliances on and off. But in the future new Java chips would be used to control these devices, so new functionality was added.

The first release (see Listing 3.18) produced the two classes: TV1 and VCR1. No inheritance was used. Each device was developed independently. Each performed the same function, and each had a different interface to perform the on/off function. There was no special relationship between these classes.

Listing 3.18   TV1 and VCR1 Classes (\msdev\samples\que\QueChap3.java)

```java
class TV1{
    boolean bOn;
    void setOnOff(boolean bOn){ this.bOn = bOn; }
}
class VCR1{
    boolean bPower;
    void turnOn(){ bPower = true; }
    void turnOff(){ bPower = false; }
}
```

The code Listing 3.19 shows how TV1 and VCR1 objects would be manipulated in client code. Each must be created and called through its own class interface. To store TV1 and VCR1 objects in an array, it was necessary to use an Object array because Object is the only superclass that both have in common.

Because the TV1 and VCR1 objects are stored as objects, they must be tested for their class; then casting must be used to access their respective methods.

Listing 3.19   TV1 and VCR1 Test (\msdev\samples\que\QueChap3.java)

```java
class Class3Extends1{
    static{
        TV1 tv = new TV1();
        VCR1 vcr = new VCR1();

        // turn on each device
        tv.setOnOff(true);
        vcr.turnOn();

        // put all devices in array
        Object device[] = new Object[2];
        device[0] = tv;
        device[1] = vcr;

        // turn off all devices
        for(int i = 0; i < 2; ++i){
            if(device[i] instanceof TV1)
                ((TV1)device[i]).setOnOff(false);
            else if(device[i] instanceof VCR1)
                ((VCR1)device[i]).turnOff();
        }
    }
}
```

This next example, Listing 3.20, shows how inheritance can be used to move the on/off functionality to a single class called SwitchedDevice1. TV2 and VCR2 each extend the SwitchedDevice1 class. The similar on/off interfaces were normalized into one interface. The TV2 and VCR2 class definitions only contain data and methods that pertain to their respective use.

If it is discovered that all SwitchedDevice1s should perform some new function, then new methods can be added to the SwitchedDevice1 class and be available by all subclasses.

Listing 3.20   TV2 and VCR2 Class (\msdev\samples\que\QueChap3.java)

```java
class SwitchedDevice1{
    boolean bOn;
    void setOnOff(boolean bOn){ this.bOn = bOn; }
}
class TV2 extends SwitchedDevice1{
}
class VCR2 extends SwitchedDevice1{
}
```

The above class definitions lead to some simplification in the client (see Listing 3.21). The Object array can be replaced by a SwitchedDevice array. The runtime class identification and casting are now eliminated. Being able to call the setOnOff method in the same manner for objects from different classes is an example of *polymorphism*.

Listing 3.21   TV2 and VCR2 Test (\msdev\samples\que\QueChap3.java)

```java
class Class3Extends2{
    static{
        TV2 tv = new TV2();
        VCR2 vcr = new VCR2();

        // turn on each device
        tv.setOnOff(true);
        vcr.setOnOff(true);

        // put all devices in array
        SwitchedDevice1 device[] = new SwitchedDevice1[2];
        device[0] = tv;
        device[1] = vcr;

        // turn off all devices
        for(int i = 0; i < 2; ++i){
            device[i].setOnOff(false);
        }
    }
}
```

Abstract Classes

An abstract class is any class containing an abstract method, or any class extended from an abstract class that does not implement every remaining unimplemented inherited abstract method. An abstract class must have the abstract keyword modifier.

An abstract method is a method with the abstract keyword modifier specified. The abstract method uses a semi-colon in place of the normal bracketed body of statements. Declaring a method abstract is a way to *require* that subclasses implement certain methods.

Facts About Abstract:

- Abstract classes cannot be instantiated (i.e., the new operand cannot be applied to an abstract class).
- Static methods and constructors cannot be abstract.
- Private methods cannot be abstract.

Here are our TV and VCR classes redesigned to use an abstract class in Listing 3.22. The SwitchedDevice2 now has its method declared as abstract with no implementation specified. Each subclass now must implement the method.

Part

I

Ch

3

**Listing 3.22   TV3 and VCR3 Classes
(\msdev\samples\que\QueChap3.java)**

```
abstract class SwitchedDevice2{
    abstract void setOnOff(boolean bOn);
}
class TV3 extends SwitchedDevice2{
    boolean bOn;
    void setOnOff(boolean bOn){ this.bOn = bOn; }
}
class VCR3 extends SwitchedDevice2{
    boolean bPower;
    void setOnOff(boolean bPower){ this.bPower = bPower; }
}
```

Making the method and class abstract does not affect the client interface (see Listing 3.23).

**Listing 3.23   TV3 and VCR3 Client Test
(\msdev\samples\que\QueChap3.java)**

```
class Class3Abstract1{
    static{
        TV3 tv = new TV3();
        VCR3 vcr = new VCR3();

        // turn on each device
        tv.setOnOff(true);
        vcr.setOnOff(true);
```

continues

Listing 3.23   Continued

```
         // put all devices in array
         SwitchedDevice2 device[] = new SwitchedDevice2[2];
         device[0] = tv;
         device[1] = vcr;

         // turn off all devices
         for(int i = 0; i < 2; ++i){
             device[i].setOnOff(false);
         }
     }
}
```

The examples below (see Listings 3.24 and 3.25) show how abstract classes are used. The Abstract1 class (see Listing 3.24) contains an abstract method myMethodA. Notice the ";" instead of "{...}." There is no body. The abstract modifier means that some subclass must implement the myMethodA method, or no objects with the Abstract1 class can be created. As soon as the abstract keyword is added to a method within a class, that class becomes abstract and the abstract keyword must be added to the class declaration or get a compile error.

The Concrete1 class (see Listing 3.24) extends the Abstract1 class and implements myMethodA. Now, new objects of class Concrete1 can be created. The Abstract2 class extends the Abstract1 class. Although Abstract2 contains no abstract methods, it is still an abstract class because it does not implement the inherited myMethodA method. Because Abstract2 is abstract, it must specify the abstract keyword. Concrete2 extends Abstract2 and implements myMethodA, so instances of Concrete2 can be created.

Listing 3.24   Abstract Classes (\msdev\samples\que\QueChap3.java)

```
abstract class Abstract1{
    public abstract void myMethodA();
}

class Concrete1 extends Abstract1{
    public void myMethodA(){  }
}

abstract class Abstract2 extends Abstract1{
}

class Concrete2 extends Abstract2{
    public void myMethodA(){ }
}
```

The next example (see Listing 3.25 and 3.26) shows how the above abstract and "concrete" classes are used. Notice that object references can be implicitly cast to superclass references.

Listing 3.25   Abstract Test (\msdev\samples\que\QueChap3.java)

```
abstract class Class3Abstract2{
    //abstract static void initialize(); // error static methods cannot be
abstract
    //abstract Class3Abstract1();      // error constructors cannot be abstract
    abstract   void defaultMethod();//
    abstract public void publicMethod();// ok
    abstract protected void protectedMethod();//
    abstract private void privateMethod();// error - this should produce a
compile error but does not
...
```

Listing 3.26   Abstract Test Continued
(\msdev\samples\que\QueChap3.java)

```
...
static{
        Abstract1 abstract1; // ok, we haven't tried to create one yet
        Abstract2 abstract2;
        //abstract1 = new Abstract1(); // error abstract class cannot be
instantiated
        Concrete1 concrete1 = new Concrete1();
        abstract1 = concrete1;
        //abstract2 = concrete1; // error can't convert
        Concrete2 concrete2;
        concrete2 = new Concrete2();
        abstract1 = concrete2;
        abstract2 = concrete2;
        //concrete1 = concrete2;// error incompatible types
        //concrete1 = (Concrete1)concrete2;// error invalid cast
        //concrete2 = (Concrete2)concrete1;// error invalid cast
        //concrete2 = abstract1; // error cast needed
        //concrete2 = abstract2; // error cast needed
        concrete2 = (Concrete2)abstract1;
        concrete2 = (Concrete2)abstract2;
        abstract1.myMethodA();
        abstract2.myMethodA();
        concrete1.myMethodA();
        concrete2.myMethodA();
    }
}
```

Part
I

Ch
3

Programmers are always trying to organize their code better. Java inheritance is a great tool to apply whenever possible. In the next section another similar tool, the Java `interface`, is discussed.

Interfaces

A Java `interface` is a named set of "abstract" methods and constants. The methods and constants define a protocol, but not an implementation. This sounds a lot like `abstract` classes, but there is a big difference. Up until now, references have been used to refer to class objects. For an object to be assigned to a class object reference it must be of the same class or a subclass of the class type of the reference.

Interfaces provide a mechanism to use variables and method parameters to store references to objects related not by class inheritance, but by interface implementation. An interface reference variable could store a reference to an interface implemented by an insect, a bird, a plane, and a space ship as long as each class `implements` the Fly interface.

In this section you will learn:

- What an interface is.
- How to define an interface.
- How to define interface methods and variables.
- How to use interfaces as variables and parameters.
- How to combine and extend interfaces.

Facts About Interfaces:

- Interfaces consist of `public` methods and `public static final` variables.
- Interfaces are either `public` or `private` (the default if one is not specified).
- An interface is a data type that can be used to define variables and parameters.
- The `implements` keyword is used to indicate that an interface is implemented by a class.

Here are the TV and VCR classes (see Listing 3.27) implemented using an interface. `Interface` methods are always `public`, so `public` keywords were added to the implemented methods that were `private` by default. Notice the use of `implements` instead of `extends`.

Listing 3.27   TV4 and VCR4 Classes
(\msdev\samples\que\QueChap3.java)

```
interface SwitchedDevice3{
    void setOnOff(boolean bOn);
}
class TV4 implements SwitchedDevice3{
    boolean bOn;
    public void setOnOff(boolean bOn){ this.bOn = bOn; }
}
class VCR4 implements SwitchedDevice3{
    boolean bPower;
    public void setOnOff(boolean bPower){ this.bPower = bPower; }
}
```

The client interface (see Listing 3.28) does not change with the use of interfaces, even though TVs and VCRs no longer share any superclasses (except the root class, Object).

Listing 3.28 TV4 and VCR4 Test (\msdev\samples\que\QueChap3.java)

```
class Class3Interface1{
    static{
        TV4 tv = new TV4();
        VCR4 vcr = new VCR4();

        // turn on each device
        tv.setOnOff(true);
        vcr.setOnOff(true);

        // put all devices in array
        SwitchedDevice3 device[] = new SwitchedDevice3[2];
        device[0] = tv;
        device[1] = vcr;

        // turn off all devices
        for(int i = 0; i < 2; ++i){
            device[i].setOnOff(false);
        }
    }
}
```

The example in Listing 3.29 illustrates the use of interface variables and combining interfaces. All interface variables are static public final by default. A new interface has been defined, VolumeDevice1. It is assumed that every volume device will also have a power switch, so the VolumeDevice1 interface extends the SwitchedDevice4 interface. This means that any class that implements the VolumeDevice1 interface is also required to implement the SwitchedDevice4 interface.

TV5 and VCR5 were changed to implement the VolumeDevice1 interface. Now TVs and VCRs can be turned on and off, and their volumes can be adjusted.

Listing 3.29 TV5 and VCR5 Classes (\msdev\samples\que\QueChap3.java)

```
interface SwitchedDevice4{
    void setOnOff(boolean bOn);
    public static final int DEVICE_TYPE_INPUT = 1;
    int DEVICE_TYPE_OUTPUT = 2; // default is public static final
}
interface VolumeDevice1 extends SwitchedDevice4{
    void setVolume(int volume);
}
class TV5 implements VolumeDevice1{
    boolean bOn;
    int volume;
```

continues

Part

I

Ch

3

Listing 3.29   Continued

```
        public void setOnOff(boolean bOn){ this.bOn = bOn; }
        public void setVolume(int volume){ this.volume = volume; }
}
class VCR5 implements VolumeDevice1{
        boolean bPower;
        int volume;
        public void setOnOff(boolean bPower){ this.bPower = bPower; }
        public void setVolume(int volume){ this.volume = volume; }
}
```

Interface variables are accessed in a manner similar to accessing class static variables (see Listing 3.30), through an object that implements the interface or through the interface name.

Listing 3.30   TV5 and VCR5 Test (\msdev\samples\que\QueChap3.java)

```
class Class3Interface2{
        static{
                TV5 tv = new TV5();
                VCR5 vcr = new VCR5();

                int n;

                //n = DEVICE_TYPE_INPUT;  //  error undefined variable
                //n = DEVICE_TYPE_OUTPUT; //  error undefined variable
                n = tv.DEVICE_TYPE_INPUT;
                n = vcr.DEVICE_TYPE_OUTPUT;
                n = SwitchedDevice4.DEVICE_TYPE_OUTPUT;
        }
}
```

Methods

In this section on methods you will learn about:

- Defining methods.
- Using methods.
- Overriding methods.
- Overloading methods.

Facts About Methods:

- Methods are called to perform operations on classes or objects.
- Methods are declared in classes and interfaces. An interface method has no body of statements.
- Methods are implemented in classes, except for `native` methods and `abstract` methods, which do not have bodies of statements.

- Method access is controlled by access specifiers `public`, `protected`, `private`, and the default.

- Every method must specify a return type of a simple data type, class object reference, or `interface` object reference. If a method does not return a value, then it must be declared `void`.

- A method may have a parameter list of comma-separated pairs of type, followed by an identifier. If a method has no parameters, then an empty list is specified. A parameter name must be specified with the type.

- Local variables in a method cannot "hide" parameter names, i.e., they cannot have the same name as a parameter. Parameter names can be the same as class or instance variables.

- Method *overloading* is supported. Method names can be reused with unique sequences of parameter lists. Return type is not considered in uniqueness of a method signature.

- Method *overriding* is supported.

The following example (see Listing 3.31) uses a simple TV class to illustrate the use of methods. The TV6 class has several different versions of the `setVolume` method. Each has a different parameter list, which makes it convenient and safer for a client to set the volume setting using different numeric data types. This is called method *overloading*.

The `SecureTV1` class extends the TV6 class by giving it security. The security consists of checking to see if the TV is being turned on during school hours on a weekday. The security check is implemented by *overriding* the `setOnOff` method.

Part

I

Ch

3

Listing 3.31   TV6 and VCR6 Classes
(\msdev\samples\que\QueChap3.java)

```java
class TV6{
    boolean bOn;
    int volume;
    public void setOnOff(boolean bOn){ this.bOn = bOn; }
    public void setVolume(int volume){ this.volume = volume; }
    public void setVolume(long volume){ this.volume = (int)volume; }
    public void setVolume(float volume){ this.volume = (int)volume; }
}
class SecureTV1 extends TV6{
    public void setOnOff(boolean bOn){
        // do not allow tv on during school hours
        if(bOn){
            Date date = new Date(); // get current date & time
            if( date.getDay() >= 1 && date.getDay() <=5)
                if( date.getHours() < 8 || date.getHours() < 4)
                    return;
        }
        super.setOnOff(bOn);
        //((TV6)this).setOnOff(bOn); // same as above      }
    }
}
```

Packages

In this section you will be introduced to Java *packages*. A package is a named collection of classes and interfaces. Packages are used to help structure and manage your source code.

Facts About Packages:

- The source code for a Java program, applet, or application, consists of one or more compilation units. A compilation unit is a Java source file with an extension of .java.

- A source file may begin with a single `package` statement to identify the package of the source file. If no `package` statement is specified, then the contents are placed in a default nameless package.

- After the optional `package` statement, the source file can contain zero or more `import` statements. `Import` statements bring the `public` contents of other packages into the name space of a source file. A source file automatically imports all classes and interfaces from its own package.

- After the `import` statements, the source file can contain zero or more type declarations, i.e., class and interface declarations.

- Only one "type," class or interface, per source file may be declared `public`. In addition, the name of the `public` type must be the same as the name of the source file, i.e., typename.java.

- There are two ways to import packaged classes and interfaces into a program:
  1) explicitly by qualifying the class name with the name of the package, or 2) implicitly by importing the class with an `import` statement.

The following examples (Listings 3.32 through 3.36) show how to install and use packages. Two packages are created: one as a subproject and one a global system class. The PackageDemo source file (see Listing 3.32) imports the global package named lonerock.quepack, which contains two classes, `QueClass1` and `QueClass2`. The PackageDemo source file uses a local subproject to manage a package called MyPackage. The MyPackage package contains two classes, `MyClass1` (see Listing 3.33) and `MyClass2` (see Listing 3.34). Each package class contains a method called display( ). Each class is in a separate source file.

Note the use of the `import` statements. You can import a class by name or using an asterisk (*) to import all the classes in a package. Class `QueClass1` (see Listing 3.35) is imported by the import statement. `QueClass2` (see Listing 3.36) is imported by the fully qualified package and class name.

Listing 3.32 is the client code which uses the "packaged" classes. `QueClass1` and `QueClass2` are installed as global classes, whereas the `MyClass1` and `MyClass2` classes are installed in subdirectories below the client project.

Listing 3.32 Package Example
(\msdev\samples\que\PackageDemo\PackageDemo.java)

```
import lonerock.quepack.QueClass1;
//import LoneRock.QuePackage.*; // this would work, too

import MyPackage.*;
//import MyPackage.MyClass1; // these two would work, too
//import MyPackage.MyClass2;

class PackageDemo {
    static public void main(String args[]) {
        System.out.println("PackageDemo!");

        MyClass1 x1 = new MyClass1();
        x1.display();
        MyClass2 x2 = new MyClass2();
        x2.display();

        QueClass1 q1 = new QueClass1();
        q1.display();

        lonerock.quepack.QueClass2 q2;
        q2 = new lonerock.quepack.QueClass2();
        q2.display();
    }
}
```

Part

I

Ch

3

Listing 3.33 shows the class MyClass1 in the local package MyPackage.

Listing 3.33 MyClass1 Package Example
(\msdev\samples\que\PackageDemo\MyPackage\MyClass1.java)

```
package MyPackage;
public class MyClass1{
    public void display(){
        System.out.println("MyPackage.MyClass1.display");
    }
}
```

Listing 3.34 shows the other class, MyClass2, in the local package MyPackage.

Listing 3.34 MyClass2 Package Example
(\msdev\samples\que\PackageDemo\MyPackage\MyClass2.java)

```
package MyPackage;
public class MyClass2{
    public void display(){
        System.out.println("MyPackage.MyClass2.display");
    }
}
```

Listing 3.35 shows the `QueClass1` class in the global package lonerock.quepack.

Listing 3.35   QueClass1 Package Example
(\msdev\classes\lonerock\quepack\QueClass1.java)

```
package lonerock.quepack;
public class QueClass1{
    public void display(){
        System.out.println("lonerock.quepack.QueClass1.display()");
    }
}
```

Listing 3.36 shows the `QueClass2` class in the global package lonerock.quepack. Notice the path to the class is in the global classpath because it is under the /MSDEV/CLASSES directory.

Listing 3.36   QueClass2 Package Example
(\msdev\classes\lonerock\quepack\QueClass2.java)

```
package lonerock.quepack;
public class QueClass2{
    public void display(){
        System.out.println("lonerock.quepack.QueClass2.display()");
    }
}
```

From Here...

As a C++ programmer, after learning the language, you were prepared to tackle the MFC libraries. Now that you have become familiar with many of the Java language basics, you are ready to learn about the standard Java packages. The following chapters will provide more information about using the Java packages.

- Chapter 8, "The Language and I/O classes," will show you how to use some of the more common language and I/O classes.

- Chapter 9, "The Utility and Network Classes," will show you how to use some of the network and utility classes.

Programming with Java

CHAPTER 4

Java Language Basics

by Clayton Walnum

Although it's closely based on C++, Java is unlike any language that you've seen before. This is because Java is mainly used to create executable content for the Internet—a task that previous languages didn't tackle. So, whereas Java's basic syntax may be familiar to C++ programmers, the way the language is used to construct programs is very different. In this chapter, you'll get an overview of the language, so that you'll be better prepared for the programming you'll do in the next part of the book. ∎

Learn how Java is similar to C++

As you know, Java's designers used C++ as the template for Java. It's no surprise then that the two languages have many similarities.

Discover how Java differs from C++

C++ programmers may have a head start when it comes to learning Java, but they have to watch out for some important differences between the two languages.

Learn about the many classes that comprise the Java system

The basic Java language is buttressed by a set of classes that make the language more powerful and easier to use.

Java versus C++

As you already know, Java is based on the C++ language. However, Java's designers scrutinized C++ closely before creating Java, looking for areas that they thought unnecessarily complicated the language. Over the course of this scrutiny, Java's designers removed some elements of C++ programming from Java's specification. The designers also added unique Java elements in order to round out the language and enable the language to handle the special situations that arise when programming for the Internet. Still, Java is more similar to C++ than to any other programming language. Some of the similarities are listed here.

- *Java uses C++ keywords.* Although not every C++ keyword can be found in Java, any C++ programmer can instantly understand most Java statements.

- *Java uses C++ operators.* C++'s rich set of powerful operators, which enable the programmer to manipulate data items and perform all types of comparisons, have always been a significant advantage of C++ programming. Java implements most of the C++ operators, allowing the construction of concise, yet powerful, statements.

- *Java uses C++ syntax.* For the most part, statements in a Java program are constructed just as they are in C++. This similarity is most evident in programming constructs like `for` and `while` loops, which feature the unique syntax first seen in C programs.

- *Java is object-oriented.* Like C++, Java supports object-oriented programming (OOP) by enabling the programmer to create classes that represent program objects. Encapsulation, inheritance, and polymorphism—the key elements of OOP—are all supported by Java.

- *Java is compiled.* All Java programs must be compiled before they are run. This is also true of C++ programs, although the compilation of a Java program results in a different type of file than a C++ compilation does.

As you can see, there are many important similarities between Java and C++. However, even the similar features are often implemented differently in Java. So, while Java is much like C++ in general, many of the details are different. Some of the important differences are listed here.

- *Java does not allow structures or unions.* The `struct` and `union` data types are not used in Java programming.

- *Java does not allow pointers.* Because Java must be heavily security-conscious, Java programs cannot create pointers. This ensures that a Java program can never obtain access to an area of memory for which it doesn't have access rights.

- *Java implements some operators differently from C++.* Although most C++ operators work as expected in Java programs, there are some important differences. For example, the C++ exponentiation operator (^) is used as an exclusive OR operator in Java. Java has no exponentiation operator.

- *Java performs automatic memory cleanup.* In a C++ program, if you allocate an object in memory, your program must also be sure to delete that object when the object is no longer needed. In Java programs, you never need to delete objects from memory. In fact, Java doesn't even support the `delete` keyword.

- *Java is strictly object-oriented.* All code in a Java program must be part of a class. This is unlike C++, which allows the programmer to ignore OOP if he so desires.

- *Java does not allow multiple inheritance.* C++ object-oriented programs can derive classes from multiple classes simultaneously. Java classes can have only a single base class (called a superclass in Java terminology). Java's interfaces, however, enable something similar to multiple inheritance.)

- *Java is interpreted.* This may seem like a direct contradiction to the fact that Java and C++ are both compiled languages. However, whereas C++ programs are compiled into an executable module (a program that the user can run directly), Java programs are compiled to an intermediate type of file called a byte-code. This byte-code file, although compiled, must then be executed by the Java interpreter. It is Java's compiled/interpreted nature that enables Java programs to run on any system that supports Java.

As you program in Java, you'll run into many other subtle differences between Java and C++. Those differences listed previously, however, are the most important. If you keep these differences in mind (assuming you're already familiar with C++), you'll have little difficulty moving from C++ to Java.

Parts of the Java Language

The Java language is implemented in several parts. First, there's the language itself, which is implemented according to the language's specifications. These specifications dictate how Java programs are written, including the supported keywords and the language's syntax. You'll learn about the basic language in this chapter. The basic language is supported by a set of classes that do everything from encapsulate data types to enable programs to connect to the Internet. These classes are organized into a set of packages, as listed below:

- lang
- io
- util
- net
- applet
- awt

The following sections will give you a brief introduction to each of these important packages and the classes they contain.

The *lang* Package

The lang package—which contains the classes that give Java much of its power—is automatically part of every Java program. Table 4.1 lists the commonly used classes included in the lang package. As you can see, Java provides a class wrapper for each data type it supports. Moreover, the Math class supports numerous mathematical functions, whereas the String and StringBuffer classes simplify the handling of text strings, which Java implements differently from C++. The `System` class is important in that it enables Java programs to make system-level function calls to perform simple I/O, get the current time, manipulate directories, get information about memory, and so on. You can learn more about the `lang` package in Chapter 8, "The Language and I/O Classes."

Table 4.1   Commonly Used Classes in the *java.lang* Package

Class	Description
Boolean	Represents the boolean data type.
Character	Represents the char data type.
Double	Represents the double data type.
Float	Represents the float data type.
Integer	Represents the int data type.
Long	Represents the long data type.
Math	Contains methods that implement mathematical functions.
Number	The superclass for all number-related classes, such as Float and Integer.
Object	The root of the entire class library. All Java classes can trace their ancestry back to Object.
String	Represents constant text strings.
StringBuffer	Represents a string buffer that can grow dynamically.
System	Contains methods for performing system-level function calls.
Thread	The superclass from which thread objects are derived.

The *io* Package

All programs must perform some sort of input/output. Java programs are unique in that the type of I/O they're allowed to perform depends on the type of program and, in the case of Internet programs, the security settings on the user's system. Java I/O streams are represented by classes, the simplest of which implement basic input and output streams. Java derives from the basic classes other classes that are more specifically oriented toward a certain type of input or output. All of these classes, listed in Table 4.2, can be found in the `io` package.

Besides the following classes, Java features two file-handling classes. These classes are `File`, which enables you to obtain information about a disk file, and `RandomAccessFile`, which represents a random-access disk file. You can learn more about the `io` package in Chapter 8, "The Language and I/O Classes."

Table 4.2   Classes in the *io* Package

Class	Description
InputStream	The basic input stream.
BufferedInputStream	A basic buffered input stream.
DataInputStream	An input stream for reading primitive data types.
FileInputStream	An input stream used for basic file input.
ByteArrayInputStream	An input stream whose source is a byte array.
StringBufferInputStream	An input stream whose source is a string.
LineNumberInputStream	An input stream that supports line numbers.
PushbackInputStream	An input stream that allows a byte to be pushed back onto the stream after the byte is read.
PipedInputStream	An input stream used for inter-thread communication.
SequenceInputStream	An input stream that combines two other input streams.
OutputStream	The basic output stream.
PrintStream	An output stream for displaying text.
BufferedOutputStream	A basic buffered output stream.
DataOutputStream	An output stream for writing primitive data types.
FileOutputStream	An output stream used for basic file output.
ByteArrayOutputStream	An output stream whose destination is a byte array.
PipedOutputStream	An output stream used for inter-thread communication.

Part
II

Ch
4

The *util* Package

The util package features classes that encapsulate useful data structures, including stacks, vectors, dates, dictionaries, hash tables, and bit fields. In addition, the util package provides a home for classes that perform special types of operations on data. For example, the StringTokenizer class extracts individual words from a string, whereas the Random class generates random numbers. The classes included in the java.util package are listed in Table 4.3, along with their descriptions. You can learn more about the util package in Chapter 9, "The Utility and Network Classes."

Table 4.3 Classes in the *java.util* Package

Class	Description
BitSet	Represents a collection of bits.
Date	Provides methods for manipulating dates and times.
Dictionary	Creates a keyed table of values.
Enumeration	Represents a list that can be enumerated (iterated through).
HashTable	Creates a table that is keyed through hash values.
Observable	Provides the base functionality for creating objects that, when changed, can notify other objects of the change.
Observer	An interface that represents objects that receive notices from objects of the `Observable` class.
Properties	A special type of `HashTable` that can be saved or loaded from a stream.
Random	Creates random numbers.
Stack	Creates a stack-like, data-storage object.
StringTokenizer	A class that can extract tokens (words or elements) from a string.
Vector	Represents a dynamic array (an array that can change size as needed).

The *net* Package

Java was designed for writing Internet applications, so the language includes a package of classes for handling online communications. To write programs with the network classes, however, requires familiarity with Internet client and server protocols. You'll get a chance to learn about Internet programming in Chapter 9, "The Utility and Network Classes." For now, look over the classes in the net package, which are listed in Table 4.4 along with their descriptions.

Table 4.4 Classes in the *java.net* Package

Class	Description
ContentHandler	An abstract class that handles MIME (Multipurpose Internet Multimedia Extensions) objects.
DatagramPacket	Handles datagrams being sent via a `DatagramSocket` object.
DatagramSocket	Provides a simple datagram connection.
InetAddress	Represents a host name, along with its IP (Internet Protocol) number.

Class	Description
ServerSocket	Represents the server side of a TCP connection.
Socket	Represents a TCP (Transmission Control Protocol) connection.
SocketImpl	An abstract class that is responsible for creating specific network connections.
URL	Represents an Internet URL (Uniform Resource Locator).
URLConnection	An abstract class that retrieves content represented by an URL object.
URLEncoder	Used mainly to encode CGI script arguments.
URLStreamHandler	A base class for objects that handle streams for various Internet protocols.

The *applet* Package

The most exciting aspect of Java programming is creating applets, which are small programs that can be embedded in HTML documents. Applets are represented by the four classes in the applet package: Applet, AppletContext, AudioClip, and AppletStub. The Applet class provides the basic functionality of all Java applets. The AppletContext class represents the environment under which an applet is run, which is usually a Web browser. The AudioClip class represents sounds that can be played from an applet. Finally, AppletStub is used to create applet viewers and is not normally used when programming applets. Because applets are such a huge part of Java programming, you'll learn a lot about them in the coming chapters.

The *awt* Package

Computers today do away with the clumsy text-based interfaces of yesteryear and instead use graphical user interfaces (GUIs) that enable the user to control the system with familiar, everyday objects such as buttons, pointers, lists, and windows. Because Java must run on many different platforms, it needs a way to support various user interfaces. Java's awt (Abstract Window Toolkit) package provides all the classes needed to run Java programs in a windowed environment such as Windows 95. These classes represent everything from windows and fonts to controls like buttons, text boxes, and menus. Table 4.5 lists some of the most commonly used classes in the awt package. You'll get a chance to use many of these classes throughout the book, as you create your own Java programs.

Table 4.5   Commonly Used Classes in the *awt* Package

Class	Description
Button	Represents a button control.
Canvas	Represents an area on which an applet can draw.

continues

Part

II

Ch

4

Table 4.5   Continued

Class	Description
Checkbox	Represents a checkbox control.
Choice	Represents a list of menu choices.
Dialog	Represents a dialog box.
Event	Represents a user or system action.
Font	Represents a font.
Frame	Represents an application's main window.
Graphics	Represents graphical functions that can be performed in a program.
Image	Represents a bitmap-type of image.
Label	Represents a static text label in a display.
LayoutManager	Represents different ways to organize the components of a display.
MenuBar	Represents a window's menu bar.
Menu	Represents a menu in a menu bar.
MenuItem	Represents a command in a menu.
Point	Represents a location in a display.
Polygon	Represents a multi-sided graphical object.
Rectangle	Represents a four-sided graphical object.
Scrollbar	Represents a scrollbar.
TextArea	Represents an editable paragraph of text.
TextField	Represents a single line of editable text.

From Here...

Now that you've taken a general look at the language, you can get started learning to program in Java. As you work through the chapters that make up the next part of the book, you'll not only learn the basic language, but also work with the many classes that were described in this chapter. For more information on related topics, please refer to the following:

- Chapter 5, "Loops, Conditionals, and Arrays," continues the Java programming tutorial by describing how to control program flow and how to handle arrays.
- Chapter 6, "Java and OOP," describes object-oriented programming, with an eye toward how OOP is implemented in Java.

- Chapter 7, "The Applet and Window Classes," covers the two packages that contain the classes that are most important to applet developers.
- Chapter 8, "The Language and I/O Classes," takes a closer look at the classes that give the basic Java language much of its power.
- Chapter 9, "The Utility and Network Classes," explores some more advanced classes and how they're used in Java programs.

Part
II

Ch
4

Loops, Conditionals, and Arrays

by Clayton Walnum

If programs had to be written so that each statement executed sequentially from the beginning to the end of the program, the world would have much bigger programs—and there'd be a lot of programmers in therapy. The ability to control what program statements are executed, as well as when they are executed, is a basic element of programming in almost every computer language.

Thankfully, Java is no different. You can easily control a program's flow of execution by using decision-making code comprised of if and switch statements, as well as incorporating while, do-while, and for loops into Java programs. In addition, Java's arrays enable you to store related data values into a data structure that's referenced by a single name. In this chapter, you not only learn how to control program execution, but also how to use arrays. ▪

How to use Java's if statement

The if statement is the simplest tool for program decision making. When combined with else clauses, the if statement becomes a powerful decision-maker.

Working with Java's switch statement

For some program decision-making, a switch statement is more appropriate than an if statement, although both the if and switch statements can be used to obtain identical results.

Programming while loops

Using while and do-while loops, a program can repeatedly execute a block of code until a specified condition becomes false.

Learn how to program for loops

The for loop enables you to specify exactly how many times the body of the loop executes. Java's for loops are identical to the for loops used in C and C++ programs.

Using Java's arrays

Arrays are a handy data structure that enable you to store related values under a single variable name.

The *if* Statement

Most conditional branching in a Java program occurs when the program executes an `if` statement. A simple `if` statement includes the keyword `if` followed by a logical expression, which is an expression that evaluates to either `true` or `false`. These expressions are surrounded by parentheses. You follow the parentheses with the statement that you want executed if the logical expression is true. For example, look at this `if` statement:

```
if (choice == 5)
    g.drawString("You chose number 5.", 30, 30);
```

In this case, if the variable `choice` is equal to 5, Java executes the call to `drawString()`. Otherwise, Java just skips the call to `drawString()`.

The syntax of languages such as Java is tolerant of the styles of various programmers, enabling programmers to construct programs that are organized in a way that's best suited to the programmer and the particular problem. For example, the Java language is not particular about how you specify the part of an `if` statement to be executed. The statement

```
if (choice == 1)
    num = 10;
```

could also be written like this:

```
if (choice == 1) num = 10;
```

In other words, although the parentheses are required around the logical expression, the code to be executed can be on the same line or the following line after the `if` statement.

In the case of an `if` statement that contains only one program line to be executed, you can choose to include or do away with the curly braces that usually mark a block of code. With this option in mind, you could rewrite the preceding `if` statement like Listing 5.1.

Listing 5.1   LST05_01.TXT: The *if* Statement with Braces

```
if (choice == 1)
{
    num = 10;
}
```

Another way you'll often see braces used with a Java `if` statement is shown here:

```
if (choice == 1) {
    num = 10;
}
```

In this case, the opening brace is on the `if` statement's first line.

N O T E   The if statement, no matter how complex it becomes, always evaluates to either `true` or `false`. If the statement evaluates to `true`, the second portion of the statement is executed. If the statement evaluates to `false`, the second portion of the statement is not executed. ▦

Multiple-Line *if* Statements

Listing 5.1 demonstrated the simplest if statement. This simple statement often fits your program's decision-making needs just fine. Sometimes, however, you want to perform more than one command as part of an if statement. To perform more than one command, enclose the commands within curly braces. Listing 5.2 uses this technique.

Listing 5.2   LST05_02.TXT: Multiple-Line *if* Statement

```
if (choice == 1)
{
    num = 1;
    num2 = 10;
}
```

The *else* Clause

The else keyword enables you to use a single if statement to choose between two outcomes. When the if statement evaluates to true, the second part of the statement is executed. When the if statement evaluates to false, the else portion is executed. (When the if statement evaluates to neither true nor false, it's time to get a new computer!) Listing 5.3 demonstrates how else works.

Listing 5.3   LST05_03.TXT: Using the *else* Clause

```
if (choice == 1)
{
    num = 1;
    num2 = 10;
}
else
{
    num = 2;
    num2 = 20;
}
```

In Listing 5.3, if choice equals 1, Java sets num to 1 and num2 to 10. If choice is any other value, Java executes the else portion, setting num to 2 and num2 to 20. As you can see, the else clause provides a default outcome for an if statement. A default outcome doesn't help much, however, if an if statement has to deal with more than two possible outcomes; that's the job of the else if clause. Listing 5.4 shows how to use the else if clause.

Listing 5.4   LST05_04.TXT: Using the *else if* Clause

```
if (choice == 1)
    num = 1;
else if (choice == 2)
```

Part
II

Ch
5

continues

Listing 5.4   Continued

```
    num = 2;
else if (choice == 3)
    num = 3;
```

If `choice` is 1 when Java executes the program code in Listing 5.4, Java looks at only the first `if` section and skips over both of the `else if` clauses. That is, Java sets `num` to 1 and then continues on its way to whatever part of the program follows the final `else if` clause. Note that, if `choice` doesn't equal 1, 2, or 3, Java must evaluate all three clauses in the listing, but doesn't do anything with `num`.

The *switch* Statement

Another way you can add decision-making code to your programs is with the `switch` statement. The `switch` statement enables a computer program to switch between different outcomes based on a given value. Similar to an `if` statement, a `switch` statement is more appropriate when you have many choices (rather than only a few) and on occasions when different sets of values require the same outcome. Look at the `if` statement in Listing 5.5.

Listing 5.5   LST05_05.TXT: A Typical *if* Statement

```
if (x == 1)
    y = 1;
if (x == 2)
    y = 2;
if (x == 3)
    y = 3;
else
    y = 0;
```

You could easily rewrite the preceding `if` statement as a `switch` statement, as shown in Listing 5.6.

Listing 5.6   LST05_06.TXT: Changing an *if* Statement to a *switch* Statement

```
switch(x)
{
    case 1:
        y = 1;
        break;
    case 2:
        y = 2;
        break;
    case 3:
        y = 3;
        break;
```

```
    default:
        y = 0;
}
```

The first line of a `switch` statement is the keyword `switch` followed by the variable whose value determines the outcome. This variable is called the control variable. Inside the main `switch` statement (which begins and ends with curly braces) are a number of `case` clauses, one for each possible value of the `switch` control variable (the x, in this case). In the above example, if x equals 1, Java jumps to the `case` 1 and sets y equal to 1. Then, the `break` statement tells Java that it should skip over the rest of the `switch` statement.

If x is 2, the same sort of program flow occurs, except Java jumps to the `case` 2, sets y equal to 2, and then breaks out of the `switch`. If the `switch` control variable is not equal to any of the values specified by the various `case` clauses, Java jumps to the `default` clause. The `default` clause, however, is optional. You can leave it out if you want, in which case Java will do nothing if there's no matching case for the control variable.

One tricky thing about `switch` statements is the various ways that you can use the `break` statement to control program flow. Look at Listing 5.7.

Listing 5.7   LST05_07.TXT: Using *break* to Control Program Flow

```
switch(x)
{
    case 1:
        y = 1;
    case 2:
        y = 2;
        break;
    case 3:
        y = 3;
        break;
    default:
        y = 0;
}
```

Part

II

Ch

5

Funny things happen in this example, depending on whether the control variable x equals 1 or 2. In the former case, Java first jumps to `case` 1 and sets y equal to 1. Then, because there is no `break` before the `case` 2 clause, Java continues executing statements, dropping through the `case` 2 and setting y equal to 2. The moral of the story is—make sure you have `break` statements in the right places.

If the outcome of Listing 5.7 was really what you wanted to happen, you'd probably rewrite the `switch` statement to look like Listing 5.8.

Listing 5.8   LST05_08.TXT: Rewriting Listing 5.7

```
switch(x)
{
    case 1:
    case 2:
        y = 2;
        break;
    case 3:
        y = 3;
        break;
    default:
        y = 0;
}
```

Here, just as in Listing 5.7, y ends up equal to 2 if x equals 1 or 2. This type of `switch` statement is very common in Java programs. If you're a C or C++ programmer, you've already seen a lot of this sort of thing, so you should feel right at home.

The *while* Loop

A `while` loop continues running until its control expression becomes `false`. The control expression is a logical expression, much like the logical expressions you use with `if` statements. In other words, you can use any expression that evaluates to `true` or `false` as a control expression for a `while` loop. Here's an example of a simple `while` loop:

```
num = 1;
while (num < 10)
    ++num;
```

Here the loop's control variable num is first set to 1. Then, at the start of the `while` loop, the program compares the value in num with 10. If num is less than 10, the expression evaluates to `true`, and the program executes the body of the loop, which in this case is a single statement that increments num. The program then goes back and checks the value of num again. As long as num is less than 10, the loop continues. But once num equals 10, the control expression evaluates to `false` and the loop ends.

N O T E   Notice how, in the previous example of a `while` loop, the program first sets the value of the control variable (num) to 1. Initializing your control variable before entering the `while` loop is extremely important. If you don't initialize the variable, you don't know what it might contain, and therefore the outcome of the loop is unpredictable. In the previous example, if num happened to be greater than 10, the loop wouldn't happen at all. Instead, the loop's control expression would immediately evaluate to `false`, and the program would branch to the statement after the curly braces. ■

Although the previous example has only a single program line in the body of the `while` loop, you can make a `while` loop do as much as you want. To add more program lines, you create a program block using braces. This program block tells Java where the body of the loop begins and ends. For example, suppose you want to create a loop that not only increments the loop control variable, but also displays a message each time through the loop. You might accomplish this task as shown in Listing 5.9.

Listing 5.9   LST05_09.TXT: Using a *while* Loop

```
num = 0;
while (num < 10)
{
    ++num;
    String s = String.valueOf(num);
    g.drawString("num is now equal to:", 20, 40);
    g.drawString(s, 20, 55);
}
```

CAUTION

Always initialize any variable used in a while loop's control expression. Failure to do so may result in your program skipping over the loop entirely. (Initializing a variable means setting it to its starting value. If you need a variable to start at a specific value, you must initialize it yourself.)

Also, be sure to increment or decrement the control variable, whichever is appropriate, in the body of a loop. Failure to do this could result in an infinite loop, which is when the loop conditional never yields a true result. Such a loop would execute endlessly.

The *do-while* Loop

Java also features do-while loops. A do-while loop is much like a while loop, except a do-while loop evaluates its control expression at the end of the loop rather than at the beginning. The body of the loop—the statements between the beginning and end of the loop—is always executed at least once; whereas in a while loop, the body of the loop may or may not ever be executed. Listing 5.10 shows how a do-while loop works.

Listing 5.10   LST05_10.TXT: Using a *do-while* Loop

```
num = 0;

do
    ++num;
while (num < 10);
```

The differences between a do-while loop and a while loop are readily apparent when you look at the listing. As you can see, the loop's conditional expression is at the end instead of the beginning; that is, in the example listing, num is always incremented at least once. After Java increments num, it gets to the while line and checks whether num is less than 10. If it is, program execution jumps back to the beginning of the loop, where num gets incremented again. Eventually, num becomes equal to 10; this causes the conditional expression to be false so that the loop ends.

Previously, you saw an example of a while loop whose body contained multiple statements. By using braces to mark off a program block, you can do the same thing with a do-while loop. Listing 5.11 shows how to create a multiple-line do-while loop.

Listing 5.11   LST05_11.TXT: A Multiple-Line *do-while* Loop

```
num = 0;

do
{
    ++num;
    String s = String.valueOf(num);
    g.drawString("num is now equal to:", 20, 40);
    g.drawString(s, 20, 55);
}
while (num < 10);
```

In Listing 5.11, num gets set to zero right before the loop starts. Then, the word do marks the beginning of the loop, after which the program increments num, creates a string from the current value of num, and displays the value on the screen. At the end of the loop, the program checks the value of num. If num is less than 10, the loop repeats; otherwise, the loop ends.

The *for* Loop

Probably the most often-used loop in programming is the for loop, which instructs a program to perform a block of code a specified number of times. There are many applications for a for loop, including tasks such as reading through a list of data items or initializing an array. (You learn about arrays later in this chapter, in the section "Arrays.") Here's an example of the first line of a for loop:

```
for (x=0; x<10; ++x)
```

The word for tells Java that you're starting a for loop. There are actually three elements inside the parentheses. The first part, x=0, is called the *initialization section*. The second part, x<10, is called the *condition*; the last part, ++x, is called the *increment*.

Separated by semicolons, all three sections of the for loop are references to the loop-control variable x. The loop-control variable, which can have any integer-variable name, is where Java stores the current loop count. Notice that the loop-control variable must be previously declared as an int (integer) variable. You can place this declaration as part of the initialization part of the command (although doing so will probably slow the loop down a little).

The initialization section of the for statement is used to initialize the loop-control variable that controls the action. The condition section represents a Boolean condition that should be equal to `true` for the loop to continue execution. Finally, the increment, which is the third part of the statement, is an expression describing how to increment the control variable. The statement after the `for` statement is executed each time the loop's conditional expression is found to be `true`.

The previous example of a `for` loop increments the loop counter by 1. But suppose you want a `for` loop that counts from 5 to 50 by fives. This could be useful if you need to use the loop counter to display a value that needs to be incremented by a different number. You can do this by changing the sections of the `for` loop, like this:

```
for (x=5; x<=50; x+=5)
```

This loop doesn't start counting at 1; rather, the loop variable begins with a value of 5. Thanks to the x+=5 statement, the loop variable is incremented by 5 each time through the loop. Therefore, x goes from 5 to 10, from 10 to 15, and so on up to 50, resulting in 10 loops.

You can also use a `for` loop to count backwards, like this:

```
for (x=50; x>=5; x-=5)
```

Notice that in the initialization part of the `for` statement, the higher value is used. Notice also that the increment clause uses a decrement operator; this causes the loop count to be decremented (decreased) rather than incremented.

Using Variables in Loops

Just as you can substitute variables for most numerical values in a program, you can also substitute variables for the literals in loops. In fact, you'll probably use variables in your loop limits as often as you use literals, if not more. Here's an example of how to use variables to control your `for` loops:

```
for (x=start; x<=end; x+=inc)
```

In this partial `for` loop, the loop control variable x starts off at the value of the variable start. Each time through the loop, Java increments x by the value stored in the variable inc. Finally, when x is greater than the value stored in end, the loop ends. As you can see, using variables with loops enables you to write loops that work differently based on the state of the program.

Expressions

To put it simply, an *expression* is a line of code that can be reduced to a value, or that assigns a value. Without a doubt, expressions are the main building blocks of a program. More importantly to this chapter, expressions are used as conditionals for `if` and `switch` statements, as well as for conditionals in all kinds of loops. There are so many different kinds of expressions that a majority of the source-code lines in a program end up being—you guessed it—expressions. There are expressions that result in numerical values. There are expressions that result in strings. There are simple expressions, complex expressions, and all manner of expressions in between.

For example, you know that the addition operator adds one expression to another, like this:

```
sum = expr1 + expr2;
```

In the preceding line, `expr1` can be something as simple as the variable x or as complex as `(4 + 5) * 2 * 5 / 7 + x / y`. The same goes for `expr2`, of course. And, in fact, the first example containing `expr1` and `expr2` is an expression itself!

But no matter how complicated, all expressions can be classified into one of three main categories:

- Numerical expressions combine numbers, variables, or constants using mathematical operators. An example is `2 + 3 / x`.
- Assignment expressions assign a value to a variable. An example is `num = 3`.
- Logical expressions are unique in that they result in a value of `true` or `false`. An example is `x < 3` (which reads "x is less than 3").

If you remember your high school math at all, you know that expressions often contain other simpler expressions. This is true for a Java expression, too. For example, look at the following assignment expression:

```
num = (5 - x) * (2 + y);
```

This is an assignment expression because it assigns a value to the variable `num`. However, the stuff on either side of the equals sign contains these other expressions:

```
num
(5 - x) * (2 + y)
```

Both of these lines are numerical expressions because they can be reduced to a numerical value (assuming that you know the values of `num`, x, and y).

But, wait a second—you're not done yet. You can still find more subexpressions. Look at the multiplication operation. Can you see that it's multiplying two expressions together? Those two expressions look like this:

```
(5 - x)
(2 + y)
```

And the simplified expressions contain yet more sub-expressions. Those expressions are:

```
5
x
2
y
```

Expressions are *recursive*, meaning that the definition of an expression keeps coming back on itself. An expression contains expressions that contain other expressions, which themselves contain other expressions. How deep you can dig depends on the complexity of the original expression. But, as you saw demonstrated, even the relatively simple expression `num = (5 - x) * (2 + y)` has four levels of depth.

Comparison Operators

Comparison operators are used to create comparison expressions, which result in a value of `true` or `false`. Table 5.1 lists the logical operators used in Java programming. C and C++ programmers will find these operators very familiar. Table 5.2 shows some comparison expressions and how they evaluate to `true` or `false`.

Table 5.1 Java's Comparison Operators

Operator	Description
==	Equal to
<	Less than
>	Greater than
<=	Less than or equal to
>=	Greater than or equal to
!=	Not equal to

Table 5.2 Examples of Comparison Expressions

Expression	Result
3 + 4 == 7	true
3 + 4 != 7	false
3 + 4 != 2 + 6	true
3 + 4 < 10	true
3 + 4 <= 10	true
3 + 4 == 4 + 4	false
3 + 4 > 10	false
3 + 4 >= 7	true
3 + 4 >= 8	false

Part
II

Ch
5

Logical Operators

The comparison operators enable you to compare two expressions. Logical operators supercharge comparison operators so that you can combine two or more comparison expressions into a more complex logical expression. Table 5.3 lists Java's logical operators and what they mean.

Table 5.3   Java's Logical Operators

Operator	Description
&&	AND
||	OR
^	Exclusive OR
!	NOT

The AND (&&) operator requires all expressions to be true for the entire expression to be true. For example, the expression

```
(3 + 2 == 5) && (6 + 2 == 8)
```

is true because the expressions on both sides of the && are true. However, the expression

```
(4 + 3 == 9) && (3 + 3 == 6)
```

is false because the expression on the left of the && is not true. Remember this when combining expressions with AND. If any expression is false, the entire expression is false.

The OR operator (\|\|) requires only one expression to be true for the entire expression to be true. For example, the expressions

```
(3 + 6 == 2) || (4 + 4 == 8)
```

and

```
(4 + 1 == 5) || (7 + 2 == 9)
```

are both true because at least one of the expressions being compared is true. Notice that in the second case both expressions being compared are true, which also makes an OR expression true.

The exclusive OR operator (^) is used to determine if one and only one of the expressions being compared is true. Unlike a regular OR, with an exclusive OR, if both expressions are true, the result is false (weird, huh?). For example, the expression

```
(5 + 7 == 12) ^ (4 + 3 == 8)
```

evaluates to `true`, whereas these expressions evaluate to `false`:

```
(5 + 7 == 12) ^ (4 + 3 == 7)
(5 + 7 == 10) ^ (4 + 3 == 6)
```

The NOT (!) operator switches the value of (or negates) a logical expression. For example, the expression

```
(4 + 3 == 5)
```

is false; however, the expression

```
!(4 + 3 == 5)
```

is true.

Like all operators, comparison and logical operators have an order of operations, or operator precedence. When you evaluate a complex expression, you must be sure to evaluate any sub-expressions in the correct order. As you learned in the previous example, however, you can use parentheses to group expressions so that they're easier to understand, or to change the order of operations. Table 5.4 lists the comparison and logical operators in order of precedence.

Table 5.4   Comparison and Logical Operators' Order of Operations

Operator	Description
!	NOT
< > <= >=	Relational
== !=	Equality
^	Exclusive OR
&&	Logical AND
||	Logical OR

Of course, you wouldn't write expressions such as

```
(4 + 5 == 9) && !(3 + 1 == 3)
```

in your programs. They would serve no purpose because you already know how the expressions evaluate. However, when you use variables you have no way of knowing in advance how an expression may evaluate. For example, is the expression

```
(num < 9) && (num > 15)
```

true or false? You don't know without being told the value of the numerical variable num. By using logical operators, though, your program can do the evaluation and, based on the result—true or false—take the appropriate action.

Arrays

Often in your programs, you'll want to store many values that are related in some way. Suppose you manage a bowling league, and you want to keep track of each player's average. A Java array would be the perfect data structure.

Simple Arrays

Suppose that you need an array that can hold 30 floating-point numbers. First, you'd declare the array like this:

```
float numbers[];
```

Another way to declare the array is to move the square brackets after the data type, like this:

```
float[] numbers;
```

After declaring the array, you need to create it in memory. Java lets you create arrays only using the new operator, like this:

```
numbers = new float[30];
```

The last step is to initialize the array, a task that you might perform using a for loop:

```
for (int x=0; x<30; ++x)
    numbers[x] = (float)x;
```

These lines of Java source code initialize the numbers[] array to the numbers 0.0 to 29.0. Notice how the loop only goes up to 29. This is because, although there are 30 elements in the numbers[] array, those elements are indexed starting with 0, rather than 1. That is, the subscript is always one less than the number of the element you're accessing. The first element has a subscript of 0, the second a subscript of 1, the third a subscript of 2, and so on.

> **CAUTION**
>
> Be careful not to try accessing a non-existent array element. For example, if you tried to access avg[3], you'd be beyond the boundaries of the array. Java will generate an exception when this happens, which means your applet may or may not perform the way you want it to. (You learn more about exceptions in Chapter 13, "Exceptions.")

Multidimensional Arrays

So far, you've looked at simple arrays that hold their data in a list. However, Java also supports *multidimensional arrays*, which are more like tables than lists. For example, take a look at Figure 5.1. The first array in the figure is a one-dimensional array, which is like the arrays you've used so far in this chapter. The next array is a two-dimensional example, which works like the typical spreadsheet type of table you're used to seeing.

FIG. 5.1
Arrays can have more than one dimension.

One-Dimensional Array

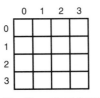

Two-Dimensional Array

Although Java doesn't support multidimensional arrays in the conventional sense, it does enable you to create arrays of arrays, which amount to the same thing. For example, to create a two-dimensional array of integers like the second array in Figure 5.1, you might use a line of code like this:

```
int table[][] = new int[4][4];
```

This line of Java code creates a table that can store 16 values—four across and four down. The first subscript selects the column and the second selects the row. To initialize such an array with values, you might use the lines shown in Listing 5.12, which would give you the array shown in Figure 5.2.

Listing 5.12   LST05_12.TXT: Initializing a Two-Dimensional Array

```
table[0][0] = 0;
table[1][0] = 1;
table[2][0] = 2;
table[3][0] = 3;
table[0][1] = 4;
table[1][1] = 5;
table[2][1] = 6;
table[3][1] = 7;
table[0][2] = 8;
table[1][2] = 9;
table[2][2] = 10;
table[3][2] = 11;
table[0][3] = 12;
table[1][3] = 13;
table[2][3] = 14;
table[3][3] = 15;
```

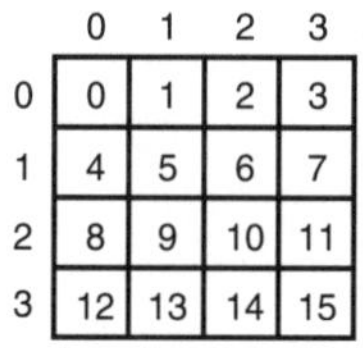

FIG. 5.2

Here's the two-dimensional array as initialized in Listing 5.12.

	0	1	2	3
0	0	1	2	3
1	4	5	6	7
2	8	9	10	11
3	12	13	14	15

You refer to a value stored in a two-dimensional array by using subscripts for both the column and row in which the value you want is stored. For example, to retrieve the value 11 from the `table[][]` array shown in Figure 5.2, you use a line like this:

```
int value = table[3][2];
```

A quick way to initialize a two-dimensional array is to use nested `for` loops, as shown in Listing 5.13.

Listing 5.13   LST05_13.TXT: Using Loops to Initialize a Two-Dimensional Array

```
for (int x=0; x<3; ++x)
{
    for (int y=0; y<3; ++y)
    {
        table[x][y] = 5;
    }
}
```

From Here...

Making decisions based on the state of data is an important part of a computer program. Java's `if` and `switch` statements enable you to program such decisions into your Java applets. In addition, by using `for`, `while`, and `do-while` loops, you can easily program your applets to perform repetitive operations.

Arrays are a powerful data structure that enable you to store many related values using the same variable name. A one-dimensional array is a lot like a list of values that you can access by telling Java the appropriate subscript (or index). But because array subscripts always start at 0, the subscript is always one less than the number of the associated element. You can also create multidimensional arrays (or, to be more precise, arrays of arrays). A two-dimensional array is organized much like a table. To access the elements of a two-dimensional array, you need two subscripts. The first subscript identifies the column of the table and the second identifies the row.

Refer to the following chapters for related topics:

- Chapter 4, "Java Language Basics," describes the basic elements of the Java language.
- Chapter 11, "Advanced Java Data Structures," describes some advanced ways to store and manipulate data.
- Chapter 15, "Building a Sample Applet," teaches you how to create applets with Visual J++.
- Chapter 21, "Using Visual J++ Debugging Tools," presents techniques for finding programming errors in your Java programs.

CHAPTER 6

Java and OOP

by Clayton Walnum

Programming languages, like their spoken-language kin, evolve over time. They are constantly refined and focused to meet the ever-changing needs of their users. Like other modern programming languages such as C++, Java is a mixture of all the techniques developed over the years. Therefore, you start exploring object-oriented programming (OOP) by briefly looking at the history of programming languages. Knowing where object-oriented ideas came from will help you to better understand why they are an important part of modern programming languages. Once you understand why OOP was developed, you learn exactly what makes a programming language object-oriented. ■

Why object-oriented programming was invented

Although object-oriented programming is more complex than procedural programming, it solves many problems inherent in previous types of programming.

About encapsulation, inheritance, and polymorphism

For all intents and purposes, once you understand the principles of encapsulation, inheritance, and polymorphism, you'll understand object-oriented programming.

How to create your own classes and subclasses

Java programs are comprised of classes that you write. Knowing how to apply object-oriented programming techniques is critical to learning how to write your own classes.

From Switches to Objects

Back in the dark ages of computing, technicians programmed computers by flipping banks of switches, with each switch representing a single bit of information. In those days, even the simple programs required agonizing patience and precision. As the need for more sophisticated programs grew, so to did the need for better ways to write these programs. The need to make computer programming quicker and simpler spurred the invention of assembly language and, shortly thereafter, high-level languages such as FORTRAN.

High-level languages enable programmers to use English-like commands in their programs, to be less concerned with the details of programming a computer and more concerned with the tasks that need to be completed. For example, in assembly language—a low-level language—it might take several instructions to display a line of text on the screen. In a high-level language, there's usually a single command, such as PRINT, that accomplishes this task.

With the advent of high-level languages, programming became accessible to more people; writing program code was no longer exclusively the domain of specially trained scientists. As a result, computing was used in increasingly complex roles. It was soon clear, however, that a more efficient way of programming was needed, one that would eliminate the obscure and tangled code that the early languages produced.

Programmers needed a new way of using high-level languages, one that would enable them to partition their programs into logical sections that represented the general tasks to be completed. Thus, the structured-programming paradigm was born. Structured programming encourages a top-down approach to programming whereby the programmer focuses on the general functions of a program rather than the details of how those functions are implemented. When programmers think and program in top-down fashion, they can more easily handle large projects without producing tangled code.

For example, consider an everyday task such as cleaning a house. Write out the steps needed to complete this task as follows.

Go to the living room.

Dust the coffee table.

Dust the end tables.

Vacuum the rug.

Go to the kitchen.

Wash the dishes.

Wipe the counters.

Clean the stove.

Wipe off the refrigerator.

Sweep the floor.

Go to the bedroom.

Make the bed.

Dust the bureau.

Vacuum the rug.

The preceding list of steps is similar, in theory, to how you'd program a computer without using a top-down approach. By using the top-down programming approach, you'd revise the "program" as follows:

TOP LEVEL

Clean the living room.

Clean the kitchen.

Clean the bedroom.

SECOND LEVEL

Clean the living room

START

   Go to the living room.

   Dust the coffee table.

   Dust the end tables.

   Vacuum the rug.

END

Clean the kitchen

START

   Go to the kitchen.

   Wash the dishes.

   Wipe the counters.

   Clean the stove.

   Wipe off the refrigerator.

   Sweep the floor.

END

Clean the bedroom

START

   Go to the bedroom.

   Make the bed.

   Dust the bureau.

   Vacuum the rug.

END

If you're only interested in seeing what the "program" does, you can glance at the top level and see that these are instructions for cleaning the living room, kitchen, and bedroom. If, however, you want to know exactly how to clean the living room, you can go down one level in the top-down structure and find the detailed instructions for cleaning the living room. While the top-down approach tends to make programs longer, it also adds clarity to the program because you can hide the details until you really need them.

Today, the need for efficient programming methods is more important than ever. The size of the average computer program has grown dramatically and now consists of hundreds of thousands of code lines. (It's rumored that Windows 95 comprises as much as 15 million lines of code.) With these huge programs, reusability is critical. Again, a better way of programming is needed—and that better way is object-oriented programming.

An Obvious, Yet Brilliant, Solution for Modern Programming

The world consists of many objects, most of which manipulate other objects or data. For example, a car is an object that uses speed and direction to transport people to a different location. This car object encapsulates all the functions and data that it needs to get its job done. It has a switch to turn it on, a wheel to control its direction, and brakes to slow it down. These functions directly manipulate the car's data, including direction, position, and speed.

When you travel in a car, however, you don't have to know the details of how these operations work. To stop a car, for example, you simply step on the brake pedal. You don't have to know how the pedal stops the car. You simply know that it works.

All these functions and data work together to define the object called a car. Moreover, all these functions work very similarly from one car to the next. You're not likely to confuse a car with a dishwasher, tree, or playground. A car is a complete unit—an object with unique properties.

You also can think of a computer program as consisting of objects. Instead of thinking of a piece of code that, for example, draws a rectangle on-screen, another piece of code that fills the rectangle with text, and still another piece of code that enables you to move the rectangle around on the screen, you can think of a single object: a window. This window object contains all the code that it needs in order to operate. It also contains all the data that it needs, including its size, location, and contents. This is the philosophy behind OOP.

Object-Oriented Programming

Object-oriented programming enables you to think of program elements as objects. In the case of a window object, you don't need to know the details of how it works, nor do you need to know about the window's private data fields. You need to know only how to call the various functions (called *methods* in Java) that make the window operate.

Consider the car object discussed in the previous section. To drive a car, you don't have to know the details of how a car works. You only need to know how to drive it. What's going on under the hood is none of your business. (And, if you casually try to make it your business, plan to face an amused mechanic who will have to straighten out your mess!)

But OOP is a lot more than just a way to hide the details of a program. To learn about OOP, you need to understand three main concepts that are the backbone of OOP. These concepts, which are covered in the following sections, are encapsulation, inheritance, and polymorphism.

Encapsulation

One major difference between conventional structured programming and object-oriented programming is a handy thing called encapsulation. *Encapsulation* enables you to hide both the data fields and the methods that act on that data inside the object. (In fact, data fields and methods are the two main elements of an object in the Java programming language.) After you do this, you can control access to the data, forcing programs to retrieve or modify data only through the object's interface. In strict object-oriented design, an object's data is always private to the object. Other parts of a program should never have direct access to that data.

How does this data-hiding differ from a structured-programming approach? After all, you can always hide data inside functions, just by making that data local to the function. A problem arises, however, when you want to make the data of one function available to other functions. The way to do this in a structured program is to make the data global to the program, which gives any function access to it. It seems that you could use another level of scope—one that would make your data global to the functions that need it—but still prevent other functions from gaining access. Encapsulation does just that. In an object, the encapsulated data members are global to the object's methods, yet they are local to the object. They are not global variables.

Classes as Data Types

An *object* is just an instance of a data type. For example, when you declare a variable of type int, you're creating an instance of the int data type. A *class* is like a data type in that it is the blueprint upon which an object is based. When you need a new object in a program, you create a class, which is a kind of template for the object. Then, in your program, you create an instance of the class. This instance is called an object.

Classes are really nothing more than user-defined data types. As with any data type, you can have as many instances of the class as you want. For example, you can have more than one window in a Windows application, each with its own contents.

Think again about the integer data type (int). It's absurd to think that a program can have only one integer. You can declare many integers, almost as many as you want. The same is true of classes. After you define a new class, you can create many instances of the class. Each instance (called an object) has full access to the class's methods and gets its own copy of the data members.

Part
II

Ch
6

Inheritance

Inheritance enables you to create a class that is similar to a previously defined class, but which still has some of its own properties. Consider a car-simulation program. Suppose that you have a class for a regular car, but now you want to create a car that has a high-speed passing gear. In a traditional program, you might have to modify the existing code extensively, which might introduce bugs into code that worked fine before your changes. To avoid these hassles, use the object-oriented approach: create a new class by inheritance. This new class inherits all the data and methods from the tested base class. (You can control the level of inheritance with the `public`, `private`, and `protected` keywords.) Now, you only need to worry about testing the new code you added to the derived class.

> **N O T E** The designers of OOP languages didn't pick the word *inheritance* out of a hat. Think of how children inherit many of their characteristics from their parents. But the children also have characteristics that are uniquely their own. In object-oriented programming, you can think of a base class as a parent and a derived class as a child.

Polymorphism

The last major feature of object-oriented programming is *polymorphism*. You can use polymorphism to create new objects that perform the same functions as the base object, but which perform one or more of these functions in a different way. For example, you may have a shape object that draws a circle on the screen. Using polymorphism, you can create a shape object that draws a rectangle instead. You do this by creating a new version of the method that draws the shape on the screen. Both the old circle-drawing and the new rectangle-drawing method have the same name (such as `DrawShape()`) but accomplish the drawing in a different way.

Using Encapsulation, Inheritance, and Polymorphism

Although you won't actually start using Java classes until later in this book, this is a good time to look at OOP concepts in a general way. As an example, the car analogy you read earlier in this chapter is extended.

In that section a car was described as an object having several characteristics (direction, position, and speed) and several means (steering wheel, gas pedal, and brakes) to act on those characteristics. In terms of constructing a class for a car object, you can think of direction, position, and speed as the class's data fields and the steering wheel, gas pedal, and brakes as representing the class's methods.

The first step in creating an object is to define its class. For now, use pseudocode to create a `Car` class. The base `Car` class might look like Listing 6.1.

Listing 6.1   LST06_01.TXT: The Pseudocode for a Base *Car* Class

```
class Car
{
    data direction;
    data position;
    data speed;

    method Steer();
    method PressGasPedal();
    method PressBrake();
}
```

In this base `Car` class, a car is defined by its `direction` (which way it's pointed), `position` (where it's located), and `speed`. These three data fields can be manipulated by the three methods `Steer()`, `PressGasPedal()`, and `PressBrake()`. The `Steer()` method changes the car's direction, whereas the `PressGasPedal()` and `PressBrake()` methods change the car's speed. The car's position is affected by all three methods, as well as by the direction and speed settings.

The data fields and methods are all encapsulated inside the class. Moreover, the data fields are private to the class, meaning that they cannot be directly accessed from outside of the class. Only the class's three methods can access the data fields. In short, Listing 6.1 not only shows what a class might look like, it also shows how encapsulation works.

Now, suppose you want to create a new car that has a special passing gear. To do this, you can use OOP inheritance to derive a new class from the `Car` base class. Listing 6.2 is the pseudocode for this new class.

Listing 6.2   LST06_02.TXT: Deriving a New Class Using Inheritance

```
Class PassingCar inherits from Car
{
    method Pass();
}
```

You may be surprised to see how small this new class is. It's small because it implicitly inherits all the data fields and methods from the `Car` base class. Not only does the `PassingCar` class have a method called `Pass()`, it also has the `direction`, `position`, and `speed` data fields, as well as the `Steer()`, `PressGasPedal()`, and `PressBrake()` methods. The `PassingCar` class can use all these data fields and methods exactly as if they were explicitly defined in Listing 6.2. This is an example of inheritance.

The last OOP concept that you apply to the car classes is polymorphism. Suppose that you now decide that you want a new kind of car that has all the characteristics of a `PassingCar`, except that its passing gear is twice as fast as `PassingCar`'s. You can solve this problem as shown in Listing 6.3.

Part

II

Ch

6

> **Listing 6.3   LST06_03.TXT: Using Polymorphism to Create a Faster Car**

```
class FastCar inherits from PassingCar
{
    method Pass();
}
```

The `FastCar` class looks exactly like the original `PassingCar` class. However, rather than just inheriting the `Pass()` method, it defines its own version. This new version makes the car move twice as fast as `PassingCar`'s `Pass()` method does (the code that actually implements each method is not shown). In this way, the `FastCar` class implements the same functionality as the `PassingCar()` class, but it implements that functionality a little differently.

N O T E   Because the `FastCar` class inherits from `PassingCar`, which itself inherits from `Car`, a `FastCar` also inherits all the data fields and methods of the `Car` class. There are ways that you can control how inheritance works (using the `public`, `protected`, and `private` keywords). ◼

Classes and Objects

In the previous sections, you learned that a class is the template for an object and that a class is a way to encapsulate both data (called *fields* in Java) and the functions (called *methods*) that operate on that data. You also learned about inheritance, which enables a class (called the *subclass*) to inherit the capabilities of a base class (called a *superclass* in Java). Finally, you discovered that polymorphism enables you to create methods that can be implemented differently in derived classes. In this section, you apply what you know about object-oriented programming toward creating Java classes.

Defining a Simple Class

As defined earlier, a class is sort of a template for an object. In this way, a class is equivalent to a data type such as `int`. The main difference is that Java already knows what an integer is. However, when you create a class, you must tell Java about the class's characteristics. You define a class by using the `class` keyword along with the class name, like this:

```
class MyClass
{
}
```

Believe it or not, the preceding lines are a complete Java class. If you save the lines in a file called MyClass.java, you could even compile the class into a .class file, although the file won't actually do anything if you try to run it. As you can see, the class definition begins with the keyword `class`, followed by the name of the class. The body of the class is marked off by curly braces just like any other program block. In this case, the class's body is empty.

Because its body is empty, this example class doesn't do anything. You can, however, compile the class and even create an object from it. To create an object from a class, type the class's name followed by the name of the object. For example, the line below creates an object from the MyClass class:

```
MyClass myObject = new MyClass();
```

Declaring Fields for a Class

The MyClass example class doesn't do much yet. In order to be useful it needs both data fields and methods. You declare fields for your class in much the same way you declare any variable in a program: by typing the data type of the field followed by the name of the field, like this:

```
int myField;
```

This line declares a data field of type integer. However, looking at the above line doesn't tell you much about how data fields are used with classes. To clear up this mystery, you can plug the above line into the MyClass class definition, as shown in Listing 6.4.

Listing 6.4   LST06_04.TXT: Adding a Data Field to a Class

```
class MyClass
{
    int myField;
}
```

Now you can see that myField is a data field of the MyClass class. Moreover, this data field is, by default, accessible only by methods in the same package. (For now, you can think of a package as a file.) You can change the rules of this access by using the public, protected, and private keywords. A public data field can be accessed by any part of a program, inside or outside of the class in which it's defined. A protected data field can only be accessed from within the class or from within a derived class (a subclass). A private data field cannot even be accessed by a derived class.

Defining a Constructor

You have now added a data field to MyClass. However, the class has no methods and so can do nothing with its data field. The next step in defining the class, then, is to create methods. One special type of method, called a *constructor*, enables an object to initialize itself when it's created. A constructor is a public method (a method that can be accessed anywhere in a program) with the same name as the class. Listing 6.5 shows the MyClass class with its constructor in place.

Listing 6.5   LST06_05.TXT: Adding a Constructor to a Class

```
class MyClass
{
    int myField;

    public MyClass(int value)
```

Part

II

Ch

6

continues

Listing 6.5   Continued

```
    {
        myField = value;
    }
}
```

As you can see, the class's constructor starts with the public keyword. This is important because you want to be able to create an object from the class anywhere in your program, and when you create an object, you're actually calling its constructor. After the public keyword comes the name of the constructor, followed by the constructor's arguments in parentheses. When you create an object of the class, you must also provide the required arguments.

For example, if you want to create an object from MyClass, you must supply an integer value that the class uses to initialize the myField data field. This integer is the MyClass constructor's single argument. You'd create an object of the class like this:

```
MyClass myObject = new MyClass(1);
```

This line not only creates an object of the MyClass class, but also initializes the myField data field to 1. The first word in the line tells Java that myObject is going to be an object of the MyClass class. The next word is the object's name. After the equals sign (an assignment operator, in this case) comes the keyword new and the call to the class's constructor.

Defining Methods

Other methods (functions that are part of a class) that you add to a class are just like the functions you've written in other programs you may have worked on. You just need to be sure to provide the proper type of access to your methods. Methods that must be called from outside the class should be defined as public; methods that must be callable only from the class and its derived classes should be defined as protected; and methods that must be callable only from within the class should be declared as private.

Suppose myField is defined as private, but you want to be able to set the value of myField from outside of the MyClass class. Because that data field is defined as private (accessible only from within the same class), you cannot access it directly by name. To solve this problem, you can create a public method that can set the value for you. You might also want to create a method that returns the value of the field as well, as shown in Listing 6.6.

Listing 6.6   LST06_06.TXT: Adding a Method to the Class

```
class MyClass
{
    private int myField;

    public MyClass(int value)
    {
        myField = value;
    }
```

```
    public void SetField(int value)
    {
        myField = value;
    }

    public int GetField()
    {
        return myField;
    }
}
```

N O T E According to the rules of strict object-oriented design, all class data fields should be declared as private. Some programmers would go so far as to say that you should not even provide access to data fields through public methods. However, you'll see these rules broken a lot, even by programmers in big companies like Microsoft, Borland, and Sun. As you become more familiar with object-oriented programming, you'll better understand why the rules were made and when it's appropriate to break them.

From Here...

Java is an object-oriented language, meaning it not only enables you to organize your program code into logical units called objects, it also enables you to take advantage of encapsulation, inheritance, and polymorphism. Learning OOP, however, can be a little tricky. Classes are the single biggest hurdle to jump when making the transition from normal procedural programming to object-oriented programming (OOP). Just think of classes as a way to provide another level of abstraction to your programs. In your non-OOP programs, you had program elements—called programs, files, and procedures—listed in the order of their level of abstraction. Now, you can add classes to the end of the list, right between files and procedures.

Refer to the following chapters for related topics:

- Chapter 4, "Java Language Basics," describes the basic elements of the Java language.
- Chapter 5, "Loops, Conditionals, and Arrays" extends the discussion of the Java language that began in Chapter 4.
- Chapter 7, "The Applet and Window Classes," shows how you can use Java's classes to create applets.

Part

II

Ch

6

The Applet and Window Classes

by Clayton Walnum

By far, some of the most important Java classes are found in the java.applet and java.awt packages. These classes not only enable you to create applets, but also to do everything from draw a simple line to add sophisticated controls to your programs. The awt package even contains classes that handle complex message-routing, ensuring that your Java program can interact with the user by responding to events. ■

Discover how to write a simple applet

Thanks to the Applet class, writing a basic applet requires only a few lines of Java source code.

Explore an applet's life cycle

Every applet's life cycle has four stages, each of which you can tap into to provide custom behavior.

Learn about drawing graphical shapes

Java's Graphics class contains a set of methods that enables your programs to draw just about any type of shape you need.

How to add images and sounds to an applet

Applets can handle vivid graphics and digital sound files, enabling you to create applets that keep people coming back for more.

About text and fonts

You can easily spice up your applets by displaying text with different fonts.

Add controls to an applet

Create the control and call a single method to add the control to the display.

Handling events in an applet

By handling events, your applets can respond to the user's actions.

The *java.applet* Package

Java can be used to create two types of programs: applets and stand-alone applications. An applet is simply part of a Web page, like an image or a line of text. Just as a browser takes care of displaying an image referenced in an HTML document, a Java-enabled browser locates and runs an applet. When your Java-capable Web browser loads the HTML document, the Java applet is also loaded and executed. It doesn't matter whether or not the applet is currently available on your hard drive. If necessary, your Web browser automatically downloads the applet before running it.

Applets are represented by the four classes in the applet package. These four classes are Applet, AppletContext, AudioClip, and AppletStub. Of these four classes, the Applet class provides the basic functionality of all Java applets. The AppletContext class represents the environment under which an applet is run, which is usually a Web browser. The AudioClip class represents sounds that can be played from an applet. Finally, AppletStub is used to create applet viewers and is not normally used when programming applets.

In this section, you get an introduction to the classes in the java.applet package, as well as learn how to write applets.

The Simplest Java Applet

The Java programming language and libraries enable you to create applets that are as simple or as complex as you like. In fact, you can write the simplest Java applet in only a few lines of code, as shown in Listing 7.1.

Listing 7.1   MyApplet.java—The Simplest Java Applet

```
import java.applet.*;
public class MyApplet extends Applet
{
}
```

The first line of Listing 7.1 tells the Java compiler that this applet will be using some or all of the classes defined in the applet package (the asterisk acts as a wild card, just as in DOS file names). All of the basic capabilities of an applet are provided for in these classes, which is why you can create a usable applet with so few lines of code.

The second line of code declares a new class called MyApplet. This new class is declared as public so that the class can be accessed when the applet is run in a Web browser or in the Appletviewer application. If you fail to declare the applet class as public, the code compiles fine, but the applet refuses to run. In other words, all applet classes must be public.

N O T E   As you can see, you take advantage of object-oriented programming (OOP) inheritance to declare your applet class by subclassing Java's Applet class. This inheritance works exactly the same as when you create your own class hierarchies. The only difference is that Applet is a class that's included with the Java Developer's Kit (JDK), rather than a class you created yourself. ▪

You can actually compile the applet shown in Listing 7.1. When you do, you'll have the MyApplet.class file, which is the byte-code file that can be executed by the Java system. To compile and run the applet, just follow the outlined procedure:

1. Select Visual J++'s File, Open command, and load the applet's source-code file.
2. Select the Build, Build command. A message box appears, asking whether you want to create a default project workspace for the program (see Figure 7.1).

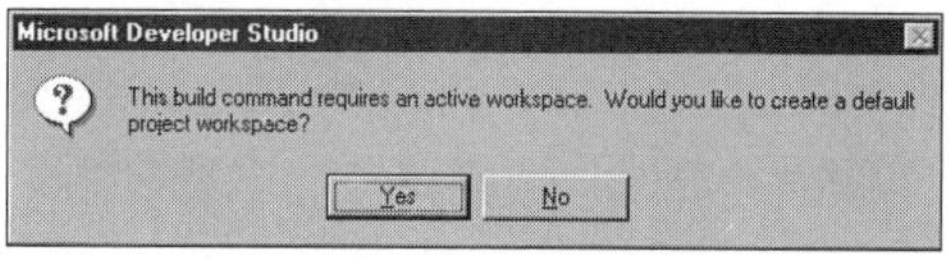

FIG. 7.1
You need to create a default project workspace for this applet.

3. Select the Yes button. Visual J++ creates the project workspace and compiles the applet.
4. When compilation is complete, select the Build, Execute command. The Information For Running Class dialog box appears.
5. Type the applet's main class name (in this case, **MyApplet**) into the Class File Name text box (see Figure 7.2) and click the OK button. Visual J++ creates a default HTML document for the applet and then loads the HTML document into Microsoft Explorer.

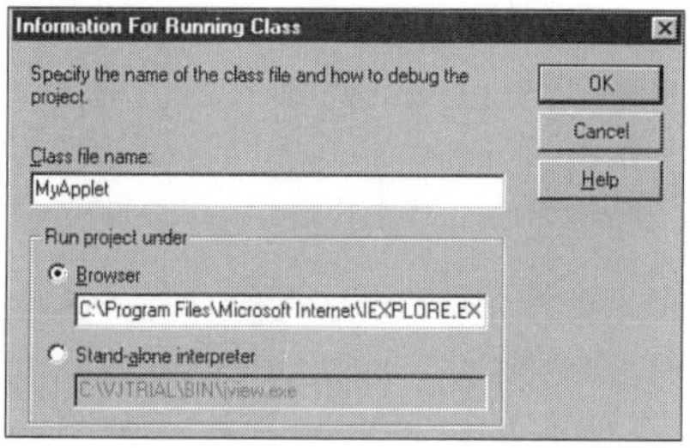

FIG. 7.2
You need to tell Visual J++ the name of the applet's main class.

If you were to run the MyApplet applet, however, you wouldn't see anything much. That's because the applet doesn't do anything visible. It just starts and runs, without displaying information in its display area. Soon, you will create an applet that actually does something. But first, you learn about an applet's life cycle.

The Four Stages of an Applet's Life Cycle

Every Java applet you create inherits a set of default behaviors from the Applet class. In most cases, these default behaviors do nothing, unless you override some of Applet's methods in order to extend the applet's basic functionality. However, although a simple applet might not seem to do much, a lot is going on in the background. Some of this activity is important to your understanding of applets, and some of it can stay out of sight and out of mind.

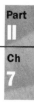

Part
II

Ch
7

Part of what goes on in a simple applet is the execution of the applet's life cycle. There are four parts to this cycle, each of which has a matching method that you can override to gain access to that cycle of the applet's life. The four stages of an applet's life cycle are listed here:

- *Initialization stage.* This is the part of an applet's life cycle in which the applet object is created and loaded. At this point, it's appropriate to create objects needed by the applet, as well as initialize values that must be valid when the applet runs. The initialization stage occurs only once in the applet's life cycle. You can tap into the initialization stage by overriding the `Applet` class's `init()` method.

- *Start stage.* This stage occurs when the system starts running the applet. The start stage can occur right after the initialization stage or when an applet is restarted. This usually happens when the user switches back to the applet's page after viewing a different page in his or her Web browser. Unlike the initialization stage, the start stage can occur several times over the life of the applet. To provide your own start code, override the `Applet` class's `start()` method.

- *Stop stage.* As you may have guessed, the stop stage is the counterpart to the start stage. Java executes this stage of the applet's life cycle when the applet is no longer visible on the screen, such as when the user switches to a different Web page. The default behavior for this cycle, however, is to keep the applet running in the background. If you want to handle the stop cycle differently, you should override the `Applet` class's `stop()` method.

- *Destroy stage.* This is the counterpart to the initialization stage and occurs when the system is about to remove the applet from memory. Like the initialization cycle, the destroy cycle occurs only once. If your applet has resources that need to be cleaned up before the applet exits, this is the place to do it. You tap into this cycle by overriding the `Applet` class's `destroy()` method.

N O T E   Although it's not official, there is a stage some like to call a paint stage, between the stop and start stages. This "paint stage" occurs whenever the applet's display must be drawn on the screen, which happens right after the applet's start stage, as well as whenever the applet's display must be restored or changed. This can happen when the applet is exposed from underneath another window, or when the program changes the applet's display in some way and explicitly repaints the applet. Every applet you write will have a `paint()` method, which is the method you override to provide your applet with its display. Actually, the `paint()` method isn't even defined in the `Applet` class. Rather, `Applet` inherits `paint()` from the `Component` class, a superclass in `Applet`'s long chain of inheritance, which goes from `Applet`, to `Panel`, to `Container`, and finally to `Component`.

All this talk about life cycles and overriding methods may have left you a little confused as to how all this actually applies to the applets you want to create. In the previous section, you managed to create an applet without dealing with most of this stuff because the `Applet` class, from which you derived your own applet class, handled the life-cycle methods in the default manner prescribed by the Java system. If you look at Listing 7.2, you see a small applet that overrides all the methods (including `paint()`) needed to provide custom behaviors for all the applet's life-cycle stages.

Listing 7.2   MyApplet2.java—Overriding the Applet Life-Cycle Methods

```java
import java.applet.*;
import java.awt.*;

public class MyApplet2 extends Applet
{
    public void init()
    {
        // Place initialization cycle code here.
    }

    public void start()
    {
        // Place start cycle code here.
    }

    public void paint(Graphics g)
    {
        // Place paint cycle code here.
    }

    public void stop()
    {
        // Place stop cycle code here.
    }

    public void destroy()
    {
        // Place destroy cycle code here.
    }
}
```

Notice that in order to override the `paint()` method, you must import the `java.awt.*` libraries, which contain information about the `Graphics` class. As you'll learn later in this chapter, in the section titled "The `java.awt` Package," the `Graphics` class enables you to display information and graphics in an applet's display area (or canvas, as the display area is sometimes called).

If you look for the previous methods in Java's source code, you'll discover that the default implementations of `init()`, `start()`, `paint()`, `stop()`, and `destroy()` do nothing at all. If you want your applet to do something in response to these cycles, you have to provide the code yourself by overriding the appropriate method.

An Applet that Draws on the Screen

Now that you know a little about applets, how about writing one that's more than just a skeleton program? Although most applets are fairly simple, there are a few things you need to know how to do in order to write your own applets. First, you must know how to draw your applet's display. This means using Java's `Graphics` class.

Part
II

Ch
7

Another important thing you must know is how to handle events. Just like any other program running in a windowed environment, Java applets receive a flood of messages from the system and the user. Your applet must handle the messages that are appropriate to the task it must complete. You learn about graphics and events later in this chapter, in the section "The java.awt Package." But for now, you'll write an applet that introduces you to the concepts you need to know in order to design your own applets.

Listing 7.3 is an applet called DrawApplet that enables you to use the mouse to draw on the screen. When you run DrawApplet with Visual J++ and Microsoft Explorer, you see a blank window. Click the mouse in the window to choose a starting point and then move the mouse around the window. Wherever the mouse pointer goes, it leaves a black line behind (see Figure 7.3). Although this is a very simple drawing program, it gives you some idea of how a full-fledged applet might work.

Listing 7.3   DrawApplet.java—The DrawApplet Applet

```
import java.awt.*;
import java.applet.*;
public class DrawApplet extends Applet
{
    Point startPoint;
    Point points[];
    int numPoints;
    boolean drawing;
    public void init()
    {
        startPoint = new Point(0, 0);
        points = new Point[1000];
        numPoints = 0;
        drawing = false;
        resize(400, 300);
    }
    public void paint(Graphics g)
    {
        int oldX = startPoint.x;
        int oldY = startPoint.y;
        for (int x=0; x<numPoints; ++x)
        {
            g.drawLine(oldX, oldY, points[x].x, points[x].y);
            oldX = points[x].x;
            oldY = points[x].y;
        }
    }
    public boolean mouseDown(Event evt, int x, int y)
    {
        if (!drawing)
        {
            drawing = true;
            startPoint.x = x;
            startPoint.y = y;
```

```
        }
        else
            drawing = false;
        return true;
    }
    public boolean mouseMove(Event evt, int x, int y)
    {
        if ((drawing) && (numPoints < 1000))
        {
            points[numPoints] = new Point(x, y);
            ++numPoints;
            repaint();
        }
        return true;
    }
}
```

FIG. 7.3
The DrawApplet applet responds to mouse movement and mouse-click messages.

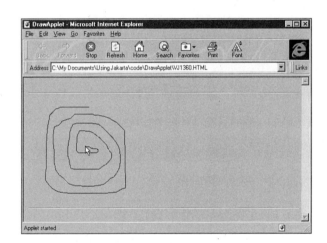

Understanding the DrawApplet Applet   Now that you're finished drawing masterpieces with DrawApplet, it's time to see how the applet works. The first two lines of source code tell Java that the applet uses the classes in the awt and applet packages:

```
import java.awt.*;
import java.applet.*;
```

The awt (Abstract Windowing Toolkit) package contains classes for drawing displays in a windowed environment. These classes give an applet access to methods for drawing on the screen, responding to events, manipulating controls like buttons and menus, and much more. (You learn more about the awt package soon.) The applet package, as you now know, contains the classes needed to create the basic applet.

The next line in the program derives DrawApplet from the Applet class, which Java defines in the applet package:

```
public class DrawApplet extends Applet
```

Part

II

Ch

7

TIP By deriving your own applet class from Java's `Applet` class, you take advantage of inheritance and automatically gain all the basic functionality of an applet. You need only add your own custom code in order to make the applet perform as you like.

Next in the program, you can see the applet's data members being declared, as shown in Listing 7.4.

Listing 7.4   DrawApplet's Data Members

```
Point startPoint;
Point points[];
int numPoints;
boolean drawing;
```

The `Point` class, which is defined as part of the awt package, represents a data structure that can hold the X, Y coordinates of a single point on the screen. The integer `numPoints` contains the number of points in the `Point` array, `points[]`, whereas the `boolean` value, `drawing`, tells the program whether the user is currently in drawing mode.

Exploring the *init()* Method   The `init()` member function is a method that's defined in the `Applet` class, but is overridden in `DrawApplet` to provide additional initialization for the applet. As you learned earlier, in the section "The Four Stages of an Applet's Life Cycle," `init()` represents the first part of an applet's life cycle. In the case of `DrawApplet`, `init()` first initializes a new `Point` object to hold the starting point of the drawing:

```
startPoint = new Point(0, 0);
```

The `new` operator creates a new object, just as it does in C++. In the above case, the new point will have the value 0 stored in its X and Y data members.

After creating the starting-point object, the program creates a new array of `Point` objects:

```
points = new Point[1000];
```

This array holds the coordinates of all the line segments that comprise the user's drawing. Here, the `new` operator is used again. However, this time the line has the number 1,000 in square brackets, which tells Java to create a `Point` array containing 1,000 points.

In the next two lines, the `init()` method initializes the two remaining data members:

```
numPoints = 0;
drawing = false;
```

Finally, in the last line of the method, the program sets the size of the applet:

```
resize(400, 300);
```

The two arguments accepted by the `resize()` method are the new width and height of the applet.

Exploring the *mouseDown()* Method   Applets, like any other windowed application, must respond to messages sent by the system. Often these messages are generated when the user triggers an event in the application. For example, when the user clicks the left mouse button, a mouse-button event gets passed to the applet, which is handled in the mouseDown() method. The mouseDown() method's parameters are an Event object, and the X and Y are coordinates of the mouse click. Here's the method's signature:

```
public boolean mouseDown(Event evt, int x, int y)
```

In DrawApplet's version of mouseDown(), the program first checks to see whether the user is currently in drawing mode:

```
if (!drawing)
```

If he isn't, the mouse-button click indicates that the user wants to start drawing. In this case, the program sets the drawing flag to true and initializes the drawing's starting point to the mouse pointer's coordinates at the time of the click:

```
drawing = true;
startPoint.x = x;
startPoint.y = y;
```

If the program is already in drawing mode (drawing = true), mouseDown()'s else clause simply sets the drawing flag to false:

```
else
    drawing = false;
```

As you see when you examine the paint() method, setting drawing to false stops all drawing operations.

Exploring the *mouseMove()* Method   Whenever the user moves the mouse over the applet's display area, the applet receives a stream of mouse-movement messages. Your applet can respond to these messages by overriding the mouseMove() method (which is defined in the awt package's Component class). The mouseMove() method's signature is very similar to mouseDown()'s, receiving exactly the same parameters:

```
public boolean mouseMove(Event evt, int x, int y)
```

If the user is currently in drawing mode, he expects the program to draw a line when he moves the mouse. So, mouseMove() first checks the drawing flag to see whether the user is currently in drawing mode. The program also checks that the number of drawing points generated by the user is still less than 1,000:

```
if ((drawing) && (numPoints < 1000))
```

If the user is drawing (and if there's still room in the points[] array for more points), the method adds the new point to the points[] array:

```
points[numPoints] = new Point(x, y);
++numPoints;
```

The program then calls the repaint() method:

```
repaint();
```

Part
II

Ch
7

The repaint() method forces the applet to redraw its display area, which, as you'll see in the next section, displays the user's drawing on the screen.

Exploring the *paint()* Method   An applet's paint() method is responsible for keeping the applet's display up-to-date. Usually, the code that draws to the applet's display area (or canvas, as the display area is sometimes called) is fully contained in the paint() method, which gets called whenever the applet needs to have its display redrawn. This might be when the applet first appears on the screen, when the applet has been revealed from under another window, or when the program implicitly calls paint() by calling the repaint() method, which you saw in the previous section.

The paint() method's signature looks like this:

```
public void paint(Graphics g)
```

N O T E   As you can see, the paint() method receives a Graphics object as a parameter. The Graphics object represents the graphical tasks, such as drawing shapes or setting fonts, that a Java program can handle. In DrawApplet, the program uses the Graphics object to draw lines on the screen. ▪

Inside DrawApplet's version of paint(), the applet first saves the starting point for the line:

```
int oldX = startPoint.x;
int oldY = startPoint.y;
```

Then, the method starts a for loop that iterates through the points[] array, using numPoints (the number of points stored in the array) as the loop-control variable:

```
for (int x=0; x<numPoints; ++x)
```

Inside the loop, the program draws a line from oldX and oldY to the next indexed point in the array:

```
g.drawLine(oldX, oldY, points[x].x, points[x].y);
```

The drawLine() function is a method of the Graphics class, so drawLine() can be accessed through g, which is the Graphics object passed into the paint() method as a parameter. The drawLine() method's four arguments are the X,Y coordinates of the line's starting point and the X,Y coordinates of the line's ending point.

After drawing the line, the program saves the end point of the current line to be used in the next iteration of the loop, as the starting point for the next line:

```
oldX = points[x].x;
oldY = points[x].y;
```

The loop continues until the entire drawing is reproduced in the applet's display area.

Now that you know how a basic applet works, it's time to learn how to add sounds to your Java programs.

Playing Sounds

There are two ways you can play sounds in an applet, one of which uses the `applet` package's `AudioClip` class. The easiest method, however, requires only that you call the applet's `play()` method. When it comes to applets, the only type of sound file you need to know about is audio files, which have the file extension AU. These types of sound files were popularized on UNIX machines and are the only type of sound file Java can currently load and play.

When you want to play a sound from beginning to end, you only have to call `getDocumentBase()` or `getCodeBase()` for the URL, and then call `play()` to play the sound. A call to `play()` looks like this:

```
play(baseURL, relLocation);
```

The `play()` method's two arguments are the URL returned from a call to `getDocumentBase()` or `getCodeBase()` and the relative location of the sound file.

Understanding *getDocumentBase()* and *getCodeBase()* The first step in playing a sound in your applet is to load the sound from disk. To do this, you need to create a URL object that holds the location of the sound file. You could just type the sound's URL directly into your Java source code. If you do this, however, you have to change and recompile the applet whenever you move the graphics file to a different directory on your disk.

A better way to create the image's URL object is to call either the `getDocumentBase()` or `getCodeBase()` method. The former returns the URL of the directory from which the current HTML file was loaded, whereas the latter returns the URL of the directory from which the applet was run. If you're storing your sounds in the same directory (or a subdirectory of that directory) as your HTML files, you should use `getDocumentBase()` to obtain an URL for a sound file.

Suppose you have your HTML documents in the C:/PUBLIC directory, and the sound you want, called SOUND.AU, is stored in a subdirectory of PUBLIC called SOUNDS. A call to `getDocumentBase()` will get you the appropriate base URL. That call looks like this:

```
URL url = getDocumentBase();
```

As you'll soon see, once you have the URL, you can load the file by using the URL along with the relative location of the sound, which in this case would be SOUNDS/SOUND.AU. The full URL to the file would then be FILE:/C:/PUBLIC/SOUNDS/SOUND.AU. If you decided to move your public files to a directory called MYHOMEPAGE, the call to `getDocumentBase()` gives you the URL for that new directory, without you having to change the applet's source code. Once you include the relative location of the sound file, this new URL would be FILE:/C:/MYHOMEPAGE/SOUNDS/SOUND.AU.

The `getCodeBase()` method works similarly to `getDocumentBase()`, except that it returns the URL of the directory from which the applet was loaded. If you're storing your sounds in the same directory (or a subdirectory of that directory) as your .CLASS files, you would want to call `getCodeBase()` to obtain an URL for a sound.

Part

II

Ch

7

Suppose you have your .CLASS files in the C:/CLASSES directory and the sound you want (still called SOUND.AU) is stored in a subdirectory of CLASSES called SOUNDS. A call to getCodeBase() gets you the base URL you need to load the image. That call looks like:

```
URL url = getCodeBase();
```

Again, once you have the URL, you can load the file by using the URL along with the relative location of the sound, which would still be SOUNDS/SOUND.AU. The full URL to the file would then be FILE:/C:/CLASSES/SOUNDS/SOUND.AU.

Suppose you have your .CLASS files in the directory C:/MYHOMEPAGE and your AU files in the directory C:/MYHOMEPAGE/AUDIO. The following lines then will load and play an audio file called SOUND.AU:

```
URL codeBase = getCodeBase();
play(codeBase, "audio/sound.au");
```

N O T E The getCodeBase() and getDocumentBase() methods are defined as part of the java.net package, so the line import java.net.* must be included at the top of any program that uses these methods. You learn more about the java.net package in Chapter 9, "The Utility and Network Classes." ▨

Playing a Sound in an Applet   Now get ready to write an applet that plays a sound file. Listing 7.5 is the applet in question, called SoundApplet. When you run the applet with Visual J++ and Microsoft Explorer, you see the window shown in Figure 7.4. Just click the button to hear the sound. Of course, you need to have a sound card properly installed on your system. You also must be sure that the SPACEMUSIC.AU sound file is in the same directory as the applet.

Listing 7.5   SoundApplet.java—An Applet that Plays a Sound File

```
import java.awt.*;
import java.applet.*;
import java.net.*;

public class SoundApplet extends Applet
{
    Button button;
    public void init()
    {
        BorderLayout layout = new BorderLayout();
        setLayout(layout);
        Font font = new Font("TimesRoman", Font.BOLD, 32);
        setFont(font);
        button = new Button("Play Sound");
        add("Center", button);
        resize(250, 250);
    }

    public boolean action(Event evt, Object arg)
    {
        if (evt.target instanceof Button)
```

```
    {
        URL codeBase = getCodeBase();
        play(codeBase, "spacemusic.au");
    }
    return true;
    }
}
```

FIG. 7.4

Click the button to hear the applet's sound file.

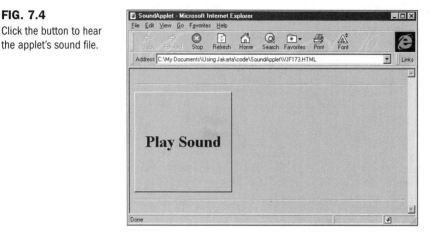

A lot of the code in Listing 7.5 is unfamiliar to you at this point. Specifically, you haven't learned anything about controls such as buttons, or about layouts, fonts, and events. You'll explore these important topics later in this chapter.

Using the *AudioClip* Class Although the applet's play() method is the easiest way to load and play sounds, it doesn't give you much control. You have only one option: play the sound from beginning to end. If you want a little more control over your sounds, you can create an AudioClip object and use the object's methods to control the sound. Unfortunately, even the AudioClip class doesn't give you much power, although you can play, stop, and loop the sound.

To create the AudioClip object, you call the getAudioClip() method, like this:

```
AudioClip audioClip = getAudioClip(baseURL, relLocation);
```

This method's two arguments are the sound file's base URL and relative location.

Once you have the AudioClip object created and loaded, you can call its methods to control the sound. There are only three from which to choose: play(), stop(), and loop(). The play() method plays the sound once from beginning to end, stop() stops the sound whether or not it has finished playing, and loop() causes the sound to keep repeating until it's stopped.

Although using audio clips is a little more complicated than simply loading and playing a sound using the applet's play() method, it's still a straightforward process. Listing 7.6 is an applet that creates an AudioClip object and enables the user to send commands to the object using

Part

II

Ch

7

the applet's command buttons. When you run the applet with Visual J++ and Microsoft Explorer, you see the window shown in Figure 7.5. To play the sound once from beginning to end, click the Play button. To stop the sound at any time, click the Stop button. Finally, to play the sound over and over, click the Loop button.

Listing 7.6 SoundApplet2.java—An Applet that Creates and Plays an *AudioClip* Object

```java
import java.awt.*;
import java.applet.*;
import java.net.*;

public class SoundApplet2 extends Applet
{
    AudioClip soundClip;
    public void init()
    {
        GridLayout layout = new GridLayout(1, 3, 10, 10);
        setLayout(layout);
        Font font = new Font("TimesRoman", Font.BOLD, 24);
        setFont(font);
        Button button = new Button("Play");
        add(button);
        button = new Button("Stop");
        add(button);
        button = new Button("Loop");
        add(button);
        URL codeBase = getCodeBase();
        soundClip = getAudioClip(codeBase, "spacemusic.au");
        resize(250, 250);
    }

    public boolean action(Event evt, Object arg)
    {
        if (arg == "Play")
            soundClip.play();
        else if (arg == "Stop")
            soundClip.stop();
        else if (arg == "Loop")
            soundClip.loop();
        return true;
    }
}
```

FIG. 7.5
This is Microsoft
Explorer running
SoundApplet2.

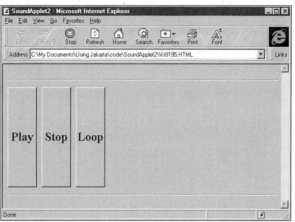

The *java.awt* Package

Java's awt (Abstract Window Toolkit) package provides all the classes needed to run Java programs in a windowed environment such as Windows 95. These classes represent everything from windows and fonts to controls like buttons, text boxes, and menus. In the following sections, you get an overview of how to use the many classes included in the awt package.

Drawing Graphics

Almost all applets must create some sort of display, whether that display is as simple as a line of text, or as sophisticated as an animation sequence. Because Windows is a graphical system, everything you see on the screen during a Windows session is displayed graphically. This is true even of text. Because of its graphical nature, a system like Java's must include the capability to handle device-independent graphics. In the following sections, you see not only how you can display various graphical shapes, but also how to query the system about the characteristics of the display.

The Applet's Canvas Every applet has an area of the screen, called the canvas, in which it creates its display. The size of an applet's canvas depends on the size of the applet, which is in turn controlled by the parameters included in an HTML document's <APPLET> tag. Generally, the larger the applet appears in the HTML document, the larger the applet's visible canvas. Anything that you try to draw outside of the visible canvas doesn't appear on the screen.

You draw graphical images on the canvas by using coordinates that identify pixel locations. Chances are good that you've had some sort of computer-graphics experience before Java, so you know that the coordinates that define pixel locations on a computer screen are organized in various ways. Windows, for example, supports a number of different mapping modes that determine how coordinates are calculated in a window.

Part
II

Ch
7

Thankfully, Java does away with the complications of displaying graphics in a window by adopting a single coordinate system. This coordinate system has its origin (point 0,0) in the upper-left corner, with the X-axis increasing to the right, and the Y-axis increasing downward, as shown in Figure 7.6.

FIG. 7.6

An applet's canvas uses the typical computer-display coordinate system.

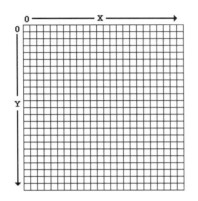

Java's `Graphics` class includes methods for drawing many different types of shapes, everything from straight lines to polygons. As you may have noticed in previous applets, a reference to a `Graphics` object is passed to the `paint()` method as its single argument. Because the `Graphics` class is part of the `awt` package, you have to include one of the following lines at the top of your applet's code to use the class:

```
import java.awt.Graphics
import java.awt.*
```

The first line imports only the `Graphics` class, whereas the second line imports all the classes included in the `awt` package. Table 7.1 lists the most commonly used drawing methods in the `Graphics` class.

Table 7.1   Drawing Methods of the *Graphics* Class

Method	Description
clearRect()	Erases a rectangular area of the canvas.
copyArea()	Copies a rectangular area of the canvas to another area.
drawArc()	Draws a hollow arc.
drawLine()	Draws a straight line.
drawOval()	Draws a hollow oval.
drawPolygon()	Draws a hollow polygon.
drawRect()	Draws a hollow rectangle.
drawRoundRect()	Draws a hollow rectangle with rounded corners.

Method	Description
drawString()	Displays a text string.
fillArc()	Draws a filled arc.
fillOval()	Draws a filled oval.
fillPolygon()	Draws a filled polygon.
fillRect()	Draws a filled rectangle.
fillRoundRect()	Draws a filled rectangle with rounded corners.
getColor()	Retrieves the current drawing color.
getFont()	Retrieves the currently used font.
getFontMetrics()	Retrieves information about the current font.
setColor()	Sets the drawing color.
setFont()	Sets the font.

To draw a shape in an applet's display area, you only need to call the appropriate method and supply the arguments required by the method. These arguments are based on the coordinates at which you want to draw the shape. For example, the following code draws a straight line from coordinate 5,10 to 20,30:

```
g.drawLine(5, 10, 20, 30);
```

The g in the preceding code line is the Graphics object passed to the paint() method. As you can see, the drawLine() method takes four arguments, which are X, Y coordinate pairs that specify the starting and ending points of the line.

TIP There may be times when you need to retrieve information about the system's currently set graphical attributes. Java's Graphics class supplies methods, like getColor(), getFont(), and getFontMetrics() to enable you to obtain this information.

Drawing Rectangles   Most of the shape-drawing methods are as easy to use as the drawLine() method is. Suppose that you want to write an applet that draws a filled rounded rectangle inside a hollow rectangle. You would then add calls to the Graphics class's fillRoundRect() and drawRect() to the applet's paint() method. Listing 7.7 is just such an applet. Figure 7.7 shows the applet running under Microsoft Explorer.

Listing 7.7   RectApplet.java—Drawing Rectangles

```
import java.awt.*;
import java.applet.*;

public class RectApplet extends Applet
{
```

Part

II

Ch

7

continues

Listing 7.7 Continued

```
public void paint(Graphics g)
{
    g.drawRect(35, 15, 125, 180);
    g.fillRoundRect(50, 30, 95, 150, 15, 15);
}
}
```

FIG. 7.7
This is RectApplet running under Microsoft Explorer.

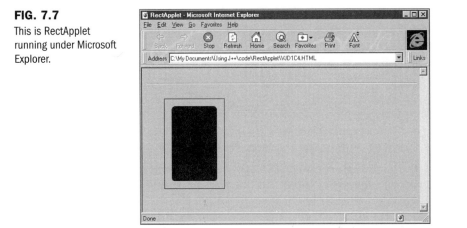

In RectApplet's `paint()` method, you can see the method call that produces the graphical display. The first line creates the outside rectangle. That method call looks like this:

```
g.drawRect(35, 15, 125, 200);
```

The `drawRect()` method's four arguments are the X, Y coordinates of the rectangle's upper-left corner and the width and height of the rectangle. The rounded filled rectangle is almost as easy to draw:

```
g.fillRoundRect(50, 30, 95, 170, 15, 15);
```

The first four arguments of the `fillRoundRect()` method are the same as those for the `drawRect()` method. The fifth and sixth arguments are the size of the rectangle that represents the rounded corners. Think of this rectangle as being placed on each corner of the main rectangle and a curved line drawn between its corners, as shown in Figure 7.8.

Some shapes you can draw with the `Graphics` class are more complex than others. For example, the `drawArc()` method requires six arguments in order to draw a simple curved line. Next, you create a new applet that enables you to experiment with the shape-drawing methods of the `Graphics` class to see how drawing other shapes works.

FIG. 7.8

The coordinates for the rounded corners are given as the width and height of the rectangle that encloses the rounded corner.

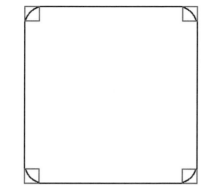

The ShapeApplet Applet   The graphics applet you'll create is ShapeApplet, which enables you to switch from one shape to another in the applet's display. Listing 7.8 is ShapeApplet's source code. Figure 7.9 shows what the applet looks like running under Microsoft Explorer. To change shapes, click the Next Shape button.

Listing 7.8   ShapeApplet.java—An Applet that Draws Various Shapes

```
import java.awt.*;
import java.applet.*;

public class ShapeApplet extends Applet
{
    int shape;
    Button button;

    public void init()
    {
        shape = 0;
        button = new Button("Next Shape");
        add(button);
    }

    public void paint(Graphics g)
    {
        int x[] = {35, 150, 60, 140, 60};
        int y[] = {50, 80, 110, 140, 170};
        int numPts = 5;

        switch(shape)
        {
            case 0:
                g.drawLine(35, 50, 160, 180);
                break;
            case 1:
                g.drawRect(35, 50, 125, 120);
                break;
```

continues

Part

II

Ch

7

Listing 7.8 Continued

```
            case 2:
                g.drawRoundRect(35, 50, 125, 120, 15, 15);
                break;
            case 3:
                g.drawOval(35, 50, 125, 120);
                break;
            case 4:
                g.drawArc(35, 50, 125, 120, 90, 180);
                break;
            case 5:
                g.drawPolygon(x, y, numPts);
                break;
            case 6:
                g.fillPolygon(x, y, numPts);
                break;
        }
    }

    public boolean action(Event event, Object arg)
    {
        ++shape;
        if (shape == 7)
            shape = 0;
        repaint();
        return true;
    }
}
```

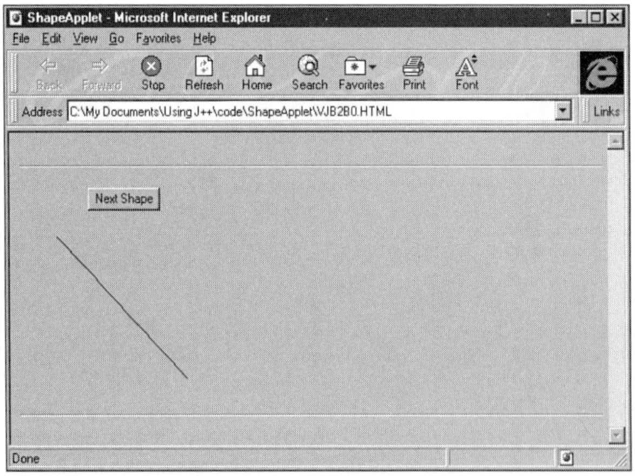

FIG. 7.9

This is what
ShapeApplet looks
like under Microsoft
Explorer.

You don't need to concern yourself at this point with the button control that ShapeApplet uses
to switch shapes, except to know that clicking the button causes Java to call the applet's
action() method. Java calls action() whenever the user performs some action with controls
in the applet. In this case, the action that action() responds to is the user clicking the Next

Shape button. In ShapeApplet, the action() method increments the shape counter, shape, and calls repaint(), which tells the applet to redraw itself. In the paint() method, the program uses the value of shape in a switch statement to determine which shape gets drawn.

Drawing Ovals   The real meat of this program is the calls to the Graphics object's various shape-drawing methods. You already know about the first three: drawLine(), drawRect(), and drawRoundRect(). The call to drawOval(), however, is new and looks like this:

```
g.drawOval(35, 50, 125, 120);
```

As you can see, this method, which draws ovals and circles, takes four arguments. These arguments are the X, Y coordinates, width, and height of a rectangle that can enclose the oval. Figure 7.10 shows how the resultant oval relates to its enclosing rectangle.

FIG. 7.10

An oval's coordinates are actually the coordinates of an enclosing rectangle.

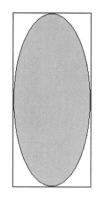

Drawing Arcs   Next in paint() is the drawArc() method, which is the most complicated (at least, from an understanding point of view) of the shape-drawing methods. The call to drawArc() looks like this:

```
g.drawArc(35, 50, 125, 120, 90, 180);
```

The first four arguments are the same as the arguments for drawOval(): the X and Y coordinates, width, and height of the enclosing rectangle. The last two arguments are the angle at which to start drawing the arc and the number of degrees around the arc to draw.

To understand all this angle nonsense, take a look at Figure 7.11, which shows how Java relates the arc's starting angle to the degrees of an oval. In the preceding example call to drawArc(), the fifth argument is 90, which means Java starts drawing the arc, within the arc's enclosing rectangle, at the 90-degree point. The sixth argument of 180 tells Java to draw around the arc 180 degrees (or halfway around the full 360 degrees). It doesn't mean that the ending point should be at the 180-degree point. Figure 7.12 shows the resultant arc.

Part

II

Ch

7

FIG. 7.11

The degrees of an oval start on the right side and travel counterclockwise around the arc.

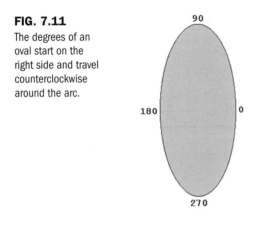

FIG. 7.12

The arc shown here starts at the 90-degree point and sweeps 180 degrees around the arc.

N O T E   Most of the shape-drawing methods come in two versions, one that draws a hollow shape, and one that draws a filled shape. The method that draws the filled shape has the same name as the one that draws the hollow shape, except you change the word `draw` in the name to `fill`. For example, because `drawArc()` draws a hollow arc, the method `fillArc()` draws a filled arc. ▪

Drawing Polygons   Polygons are simply many-sided shapes. For example, a triangle is a polygon (it is, in fact, the simplest polygon). Squares, rectangles, and hexagons are all polygons, as well. Because a polygon comprises many different lines, before you can draw a polygon in Java, you need to create arrays that contain the X, Y coordinates for each line in the polygon. In Listing 7.8, ShapeApplet defines those arrays like this:

```
int x[] = {35, 150, 60, 140, 60};
int y[] = {50, 80, 110, 140, 170};
int numPts = 5;
```

The first array, called x[], is the X coordinates for each X, Y pair, and the second array, called y[], is the Y coordinates for each X, Y pair. When you look at the values defined in the arrays, you can see that the first line gets drawn from 35,50 to 150,80. Because all the lines in a polygon are connected, Java can continue drawing lines by using the previous ending point (in this case, 150,80) and the next coordinate pair, which is 60,110. Java continues to work through the arrays until it uses all the given coordinates. The actual method call that draws the polygon looks like this:

```
g.drawPolygon(x, y, numPts);
```

The `drawPolygon()` method's three arguments are the array holding the X coordinates, the array holding the Y coordinates, and the number of points defined in the arrays. You can use a literal value for the third argument, but it's often handy to define a variable as shown in the example (`numPts`). Then, if you change the arrays, you can change the variable at the same time and not have to worry about correcting any method calls that use the arrays along with point count.

> **N O T E** If you need more control over your polygons, Java includes a `Polygon` class from which you can create polygon objects from the coordinate arrays. The `Polygon` class includes handy methods that enable you to add points to a polygon, determine whether a point is inside the polygon, and retrieve the polygon's bounding rectangle. You create a `Polygon` object with a line like `Polygon polygon = new Polygon(x, y, numPts)`. The arguments for the class's constructor are the same as those for the `drawPolygon()` method. The `Polygon` class's public methods are `addPoint(x, y)`, `getBoundingBox()` (which returns a `Rectangle` object), and `inside()` (which returns a Boolean value).

Graphical Text

Now that you know how to draw all kinds of shapes in your applets, it's time to see how to use text and text fonts, as well. By combining graphical text with other drawing methods, you can create attractive applets for your Web pages. In the following sections, you learn how to display text, as well as how to create fonts and retrieve information about those fonts.

Displaying Text in an Applet   The easiest thing to display is a line of text. But, because the text output is graphical, you need to use one of Java's graphical-text functions. The most commonly used is `drawString()`, which is part of the `Graphics` class contained in the `awt` package. You call `drawString()` like this:

```
g.drawString("Hello from Java!", 60, 75);
```

The arguments in the above call to `drawString()` tell Java to draw the text "Hello from Java!" at column 60 and row 75 of the display area. (The position is measured in pixels, not characters. A pixel is the smallest dot that can be displayed on the screen.) To display the text at a different location, just change the second and third arguments. Usually, you'll draw text in your applet's `paint()` method. As you know, Java calls `paint()` whenever the applet's display area needs to be redrawn. The `paint()` method always gets called when the applet first appears on the screen.

N O T E   The Java compiler is case-sensitive, meaning that it can differentiate between upper- and
lowercase letters. For this reason, you have to be extra careful to type method names
properly. For example, if you type `Paint()` instead of `paint()`, Java doesn't recognize the method
and won't call it when the applet needs to be redrawn. Java inherits its case-sensitive nature from the
C programming language. ▪

Getting Font Attributes   Every font that you can use with your Java applets is associated with
a group of attributes that determines the size and appearance of the font. The most important
of these attributes is the font's name, which determines the font's basic style. There is a big
difference, for example, between the Arial and Times Roman fonts as far as how they look.
When you're setting up a font for use, the first thing that you concern yourself with is the
name of the font.

You can easily get information about the currently active font. Start by calling the `Graphics`
object's `getFont()` method, like this:

```
Font font = g.getFont();
```

The `getFont()` method returns a `Font` object for the current font. Once you have the `Font`
object, you can use the `Font` class's various methods to obtain information about the font. Table
7.2 shows the most commonly used public methods of the `Font` class and what they do.

Table 7.2   The *Font* Class's Most Commonly Used Public Methods

Method	Description
getFamily()	Returns the family name of the font.
getName()	Returns the name of the font.
getSize()	Returns the size of the font.
getStyle()	Returns the style of the font, where 0 is plain, 1 is bold, 2 is italic, and 3 is bold italic.
isBold()	Returns a Boolean value indicating whether or not the font is bold.
isItalic()	Returns a Boolean value indicating whether or not the font is italic.
isPlain()	Returns a Boolean value indicating whether or not the font is plain.
toString()	Returns a string of information about the font.

As always, the best way to see how something works is to try it out yourself. With that end in
mind, Listing 7.9 is an applet that displays information about the currently active font using
many of the methods described in Table 7.2. Figure 7.13 shows the applet running under
Microsoft Explorer.

Listing 7.9 FontApplet.java—Getting Information About a Font

```java
import java.awt.*;
import java.applet.*;

public class FontApplet extends Applet
{
    public void paint(Graphics g)
    {
        Font font = getFont();
        String name = font.getName();
        String family = font.getFamily();

        int n = font.getStyle();
        String style;
        if (n == 0)
            style = "Plain";
        else if (n == 1)
            style = "Bold";
        else if (n == 2)
            style = "Italic";
        else
            style = "Bold Italic";

        n = font.getSize();
        String size = String.valueOf(n);
        String info = font.toString();

        String s = "Name: " + name;
        g.drawString(s, 50, 50);
        s = "Family: " + family;
        g.drawString(s, 50, 65);
        s = "Style: " + style;
        g.drawString(s, 50, 80);
        s = "Size: " + size;
        g.drawString(s, 50, 95);
        g.drawString(info, 20, 125);
    }
}
```

As you can see from Listing 7.9, using the Font class's method is straightforward. Just call the method, which returns a value that describes some aspect of the font represented by the Font object.

Part

II

Ch

7

FIG. 7.13

This is FontApplet running in Microsoft Explorer.

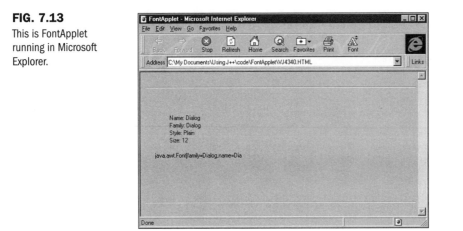

Creating Fonts   You may think an applet that always uses the default font is boring to look at. In many cases, you're right. An easy way to spruce up an applet is to use different fonts. Luckily, Java enables you to create and set fonts for your applet. You do this by creating your own font object, like this:

```
Font font = new Font("TimesRoman", Font.PLAIN, 20);
```

The constructor for the Font class takes three arguments: the font name, style, and size. The style can be any combination of the font attributes that are defined in the Font class. Those attributes are Font.PLAIN, Font.BOLD, and Font.ITALIC.

Although you can create fonts with the plain, bold, or italic styles, at times you may need to combine font styles. Suppose, for example, that you wanted to use both bold and italic styles. The line

```
Font font = new Font("Courier", Font.BOLD + Font.ITALIC, 18);
```

gives you an 18-point bold italic Courier font. (A point is a measurement of a font's height and is equal to 1/72 of an inch.)

After you've created the font, you have to tell Java to use the font. You do this by calling the Graphics (or Applet) class's setFont() method, like this:

```
g.setFont(font);
```

At this point, the next text you display in your applet uses the new font. However, when you request a certain type and size of font, you can't be sure of what you'll get. The system tries its best to match the requested font, but you still need to know at least the size of the font with which you ended up. You can get all the information you need by creating a FontMetrics object, like this:

```
FontMetrics fontMetrics = g.getFontMetrics(font);
```

To get the height of a line of text, call the FontMetrics object's getHeight() method, like this:

```
int height = fontMetrics.getHeight();
```

CAUTION

When creating a font, be aware that the user's system may not have a particular font loaded. In that case, Java chooses a default font as a replacement. This possible font substitution is a good reason to use methods like FontMetrics's getName() in order to see whether you got the font you wanted. You especially need to know the size of the font, so you can be sure to position your text lines properly.

You wouldn't create a font unless you had some text to display. Before you can display your text, you need to know at least the height of the font. Failure to consider the font's height may give you text lines that overlap or that are spaced too far apart. You can use the height returned from the FontMetrics class's getHeight() method as a row increment value for each line of text you need to print. Listing 7.10, which is the source code for the FontApplet2 applet, shows how this is done. Figure 7.14 shows what the applet looks like.

Listing 7.10 FontApplet2.java—Displaying Different-Sized Fonts

```
import java.awt.*;
import java.applet.*;

public class FontApplet2 extends Applet
{
    TextField textField;

    public void init()
    {
        textField = new TextField(10);
        add(textField);
        textField.setText("32");
    }

    public void paint(Graphics g)
    {
        String s = textField.getText();
        int height = Integer.parseInt(s);

        Font font = new Font("TimesRoman", Font.PLAIN, height);
        g.setFont(font);
        FontMetrics fontMetrics = g.getFontMetrics(font);
        height = fontMetrics.getHeight();

        int row = 80;
        g.drawString("First line.", 20, row);
        row += height;
        g.drawString("Second line.", 20, row);
        row += height;
        g.drawString("Third line.", 20, row);
```

Part

II

Ch

7

continues

Listing 7.10 Continued

```
        row += height;
        g.drawString("Fourth line.", 20, row);
    }

    public boolean action(Event event, Object arg)
    {
        repaint();
        return true;
    }
}
```

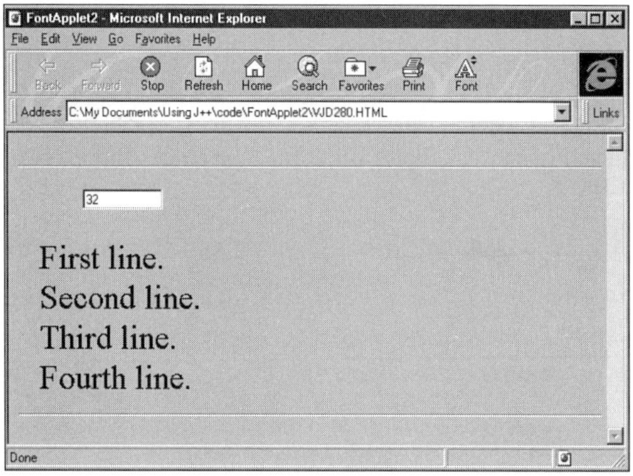

FIG. 7.14

This is FontApplet2 running in Microsoft Explorer.

When you run FontApplet2, you see the window shown in Figure 7.14. The size of the active font appears in the text box at the top of the applet, and a sample of the font appears below the text box. To change the size of the font, type a new value into the text box and press Enter.

The spacing of the lines is accomplished by first creating a variable to hold the vertical position for the next line of text:

```
int row = 80;
```

Here, the program not only declares the row variable, but also initializes it with the vertical position of the first row of text.

The applet then prints the first text line, using row for drawString()'s third argument:

```
g.drawString("This is the first line.", 20, row);
```

In preparation for printing the next line of text, the program adds the font's height to the row variable:

```
row += height;
```

Each line of text is printed, with row being incremented by the font's height in between, like this:

```
g.drawString("This is the second line.", 20, row);
row += height;
g.drawString("This is the third line.", 20, row);
```

Controls

Previously, you saw that applets are interactive applications that can handle messages generated by both the system and the user. Another way, besides the mouse, that you can enable user interaction is by including controls—such as buttons, menus, list boxes, and text boxes— in your applet's display. In this section, you get an introduction to controls, as you create an applet that can connect you to two Web sites on the Internet.

Listing 7.11 is the Java source code for the applet in question. Before running this applet, make your Internet connection. Then, when you run the applet, you see a window like Figure 7.15, which shows InternetApplet running in Microsoft Explorer. Just click one of the connection buttons, and you'll automatically log on to the Web site associated with the button.

Listing 7.11   InternetApplet.java—The InternetApplet Applet

```
import java.awt.*;
import java.applet.*;
import java.net.*;

public class InternetApplet extends Applet
{
    boolean badURL;

    public void init()
    {
        GridLayout layout = new GridLayout(2, 4, 10, 10);
        setLayout(layout);
        Font font = new Font("TimesRoman", Font.PLAIN, 24);
        setFont(font);
        Button button = new Button("Macmillan");
        add(button);
        button = new Button("CNet");
          add(button);
        badURL = false;
    }

    public void paint(Graphics g)
    {
        if (badURL)
            g.drawString("Bad URL!", 60, 130);
    }

    public boolean action(Event evt, Object arg)
    {
        String str;

        if (arg == "Macmillan")
            str = "http://www.mcp.com";
```

continues

Listing 7.11   Continued

```
        else
            str = "http://www.cnet.com";

        try
        {
            URL url = new URL(str);
            AppletContext context = getAppletContext();
            context.showDocument(url);
        }
        catch (MalformedURLException e)
        {
            badURL = true;
            repaint();
        }

        return true;
    }
}
```

FIG. 7.15

This is InternetApplet running in Microsoft Explorer.

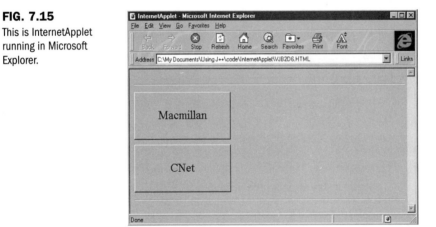

Now, take a look at the applet's source code. The first three lines enable the program to access the classes stored in Java's awt, applet, and net packages:

```
import java.awt.*;
import java.applet.*;
import java.net.*;
```

You're already familiar with the awt and applet packages. The net package, which you learn more about in Chapter 9, "The Utility and Network Classes," contains the classes needed to log on to the Internet.

The applet's main class, which is derived from Applet, begins in the next line:

```
public class InternetApplet extends Applet
```

InternetApplet then declares its single data member:

```
boolean badURL;
```

The `badURL` data member is used in the program to notify the applet that the currently selected URL is no good.

Next comes the familiar `init()` method, where the applet can perform whatever initialization it requires. In this case, the applet first declares and sets a layout manager:

```
GridLayout layout = new GridLayout(2, 4, 10, 10);
setLayout(layout);
```

Java programs use layout managers to control where components in the program will appear on the screen. Java offers many types of layout managers, each represented by its own class in the awt package. These layout managers include `FlowLayout`, `GridLayout`, `BorderLayout`, `CardLayout`, and `GridBagLayout`. If you don't create and set your own layout manager, Java uses the `FlowLayout` manager—which places components horizontally one after the other—by default. In InternetApplet, you're using a `GridLayout` manager, which organizes components into a grid. `GridLayout`'s constructor takes four arguments:

- Number of rows in the grid
- Number of columns in the grid
- Horizontal space between cells in the grid
- Vertical space between the cells

The latter two arguments have default values of 0 if you want to leave them off.

The `setLayout()` function is a member of the `Container` class, which is a superclass (a parent class in the class hierarchy) of the `Applet` class. Its single argument is a reference to a layout-manager object. After calling `setLayout()`, Java knows to use the new layout manager rather than the default one.

After setting the applet's layout manager, the program creates and sets the font that will be used for all text in the applet:

```
Font font = new Font("TimesRoman", Font.PLAIN, 24);
setFont(font);
```

The next task is to create, and add to the applet, the button controls used to select Web sites. Listing 7.12 shows the code that accomplishes this task.

Listing 7.12   LST04_12.TXT—Creating Button Controls

```
Button button = new Button("Macmillan");
add(button);
button = new Button("CNet");
add(button);
```

The Button class's constructor takes a single argument, which is the text label that appears in the button when it's displayed. The add() method adds the control to the next available cell in the GridLayout manager.

Finally, init() sets the badURL flag to false:

```
badURL = false;
```

Most user events caused in an applet can be handled by you overriding the action() method. The signature for the action() method looks like this:

```
public boolean action(Event evt, Object arg)
```

As you can see, action() receives two parameters—an Event object and an Object object. You learn more about these objects later in this chapter, in the section "Events." For now, it's enough to know that, in the case of a button control, arg will be the button's text label.

When the user clicks one of the applet's buttons, the action() method is called. As mentioned before, the arg parameter will be the text label of the button that was clicked, so it's pretty easy to determine which button the user selected. To do this, InternetApplet uses an if-else statement to check the button's label. When the program finds the button the user selected, it sets str, which is an object of Java's String class, to the selected URL, as shown in Listing 7.13.

Listing 7.13   LST04_13.TXT—Getting the Requested URL

```
String str;
if (arg == "Macmillan")
    str = "http://www.mcp.com";
else
    str = "http://www.cnet.com";
```

After obtaining the selected URL, the applet can connect to the Web site. Before doing this, though, the program must set up a try and catch program block, because the URL class's constructor throws a MalformedURLException exception, which must be caught by your program. The try program block attempts to create the URL object and connect to the Web site, as shown in Listing 7.14.

Listing 7.14   LST04_14.TXT—Connection to a Web Site

```
try
{
    URL url = new URL(str);
    AppletContext context = getAppletContext();
    context.showDocument(url);
}
```

In the try block, the program first tries to create an URL object from the URL text string. If the construction fails, the URL class throws a MalformedURLException exception, and program execution continues at the catch program block, which you look at soon. If the URL object gets constructed successfully, the program calls the `getAppletContext()` method to get a reference to the applet's `AppletContext` object. This object's `showDocument()` method is what connects the applet to the chosen URL.

If the `URL` class's constructor throws an exception, program execution jumps to the `catch` program block, which is shown in Listing 7.15.

Listing 7.15   LST04_15.TXT—The *catch* Program Block

```
catch (MalformedURLException e)
{
    badURL = true;
    repaint();
}
```

In the `catch` program block, the program simply sets the `badURL` flag to `true` and calls `repaint()` to display an error message to the user.

N O T E You create and add other types of controls similarly to how you created button controls in the previous applet. Just call the control's constructor to create it, and then call the `add()` method to add the control to the applet. Where the control ends up depends on the layout manager you're using. The controls you can use in your Java programs include push buttons, option buttons, text boxes, check boxes, scroll bars, list boxes, and more. ▪

Events

When you write applets or applications using Java, sooner or later you're going to run into events. Events represent actions that the user performs on your program, such as clicking a button or moving the mouse. As you'll soon see, there are several ways that your programs can handle events. This section gives you a look at the `Event` class and how it's used in your Java projects. You'll also learn about the different types of events your applets can receive.

The Event Class Under Java, events are actually objects of a class. This class, called appropriately enough `Event`, defines all the events to which a program can respond, as well as defines default methods for extracting information about the event. When all is said and done, `Event` is a complex class, as you'll soon see.

The `Event` class defines every event to which your Java program can respond. Those events are represented in the class by constants that name each event and associate that name with a value. When a Java program receives an event, the Java system can then match the event's value to one of the event-handling functions, which are defined in the `Component` class, from which all Java objects that can handle events are derived. Those functions are listed in Table 7.3.

Part

II

Ch

7

Table 7.3   Event-Handling Methods of the *Component* Class

Method	Description
action()	Responds to components that have action events.
deliverEvent()	Sends an event to the component.
handleEvent()	Routes events to the appropriate handler.
keyDown()	Responds to key-down events.
keyUp()	Responds to key-up events.
mouseDown()	Responds to mouse-down events.
mouseDrag()	Responds to mouse-drag events.
mouseEnter()	Responds to mouse-enter events.
mouseExit()	Responds to mouse-exit events.
mouseMove()	Responds to mouse-move events.
mouseUp()	Responds to mouse-up events.
postEvent()	Similar to deliverEvent().

In the Component class, event-handling methods like action(), mouseDown(), and keyDown() don't actually do anything except return false, which indicates to Java that the event hasn't yet been handled. These methods are meant to be overridden in your programs so that the program can respond to the event as is appropriate. For example, if you haven't overridden mouseDown() in an applet, the default version of mouseDown() returns false, which tells Java that the message will need to be handled further on down the line. In the case of a mouse-down event, Java probably returns the unhandled event to the system for default handling (meaning that the event is effectively ignored).

The applet in Listing 7.16 responds to mouse clicks by printing the word "Click!" wherever the user clicks in the applet. It does this by overriding the mouseDown() method and storing the coordinates of the mouse click in the applet's coordX and coordY data fields. The paint() method then uses these coordinates to display the word. Figure 7.16 shows MouseApplet running in Microsoft Explorer.

Listing 7.16   MouseApplet.java—Responding to Mouse Clicks in an Applet

```java
import java.awt.*;
import java.applet.*;

public class MouseApplet extends Applet
{
    int coordX, coordY;

    public void init()
```

```
    {
        coordX = -1;
        coordY = -1;

        Font font =
            new Font("TimesRoman", Font.BOLD, 24);
        setFont(font);

        resize(400, 300);
    }

    public void paint(Graphics g)
    {
        if (coordX != -1)
            g.drawString("Click!", coordX, coordY);
    }

    public boolean mouseDown(Event evt, int x, int y)
    {
        coordX = x;
        coordY = y;
        repaint();
        return true;
    }
}
```

FIG. 7.16
The MouseApplet applet responds to mouse clicks.

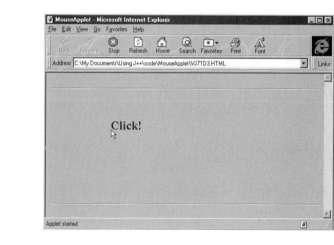

N O T E When you run MouseApplet, you'll discover that the applet window gets erased each time the paint() method is called. That's why only one "Click!" ever appears in the window. ■

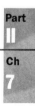

The Keyboard The keyboard has been around even longer than the mouse and has been the primary interface between humans and their computers for decades. Given the keyboard's importance, obviously there may be times when you'll want to handle the keyboard events. Java responds to two basic key events, which are represented by the KEY_PRESS and KEY_RELEASE constants. As you'll soon see, Java defines methods that make it just as easy to respond to the keyboard as it is to respond to the mouse.

Whenever the user presses a key when an applet is active, Java sends the applet a KEY_PRESS event. In your Java program, you can respond to this event by overriding the keyDown() method, whose signature looks like this:

```
public boolean keyDown(Event evt, int key)
```

As you can see, this method receives two arguments, which are an Event object and an integer representing the key that was pressed. This integer is actually the ASCII representation of the character represented by the key. In order to use this value in your programs, however, you must first cast it to a char value, like this:

```
char c = (char)key;
```

Some of the keys on your keyboard issue commands rather than generate characters. These keys include all the F keys, as well as keys like Shift, Ctrl, Page Up, Page Down, and so on. In order to make these types of keys easier to handle in your applets, Java's Event class defines a set of constants that represent these keys' values. Those constants are shown in Table 7.4.

Table 7.4 Keyboard Constants of the *Event* Class

Constant	Description
ALT_MASK	Alt (Alternate) key
CTRL_MASK	Ctrl key
DOWN	Down arrow key
END	End key
F1	F1 key
F10	F10 key
F11	F11 key
F12	F12 key
F2	F2 key
F3	F3 key
F4	F4 key
F5	F5 key
F6	F6 key
F7	F7 key
F8	F8 key
F9	F9 key
HOME	Home key
LEFT	Left arrow key

Constant	Description
META_MASK	A Meta key
PGDN	PageDown key
PGUP	PageUp key
RIGHT	Right arrow key
SHIFT_MASK	Shift key
UP	Up arrow key

The Event class also defines a number of constants for modifier keys that the user might press along with the basic key. These constants, which are also listed in Table 7.4, include ALT_MASK, SHIFT_MASK, and CTRL_MASK, which represent the Alt (or Alternate), Shift, and Ctrl (or Control) keys on your keyboard. The SHIFT_MASK and CTRL_MASK constants are used in the Event class's methods shiftDown() and controlDown(), each of which returns a boolean value indicating whether the modifier key is pressed. (There currently is no altDown() method.) You can also examine the Event object's modifiers field to determine whether a particular modifier key was pressed. For example, if you wanted to check for the Alt key, you might use a line of Java code like this:

```
boolean altPressed = (evt.modifiers & Event.ALT_MASK) != 0;
```

By ANDing the mask with the value in the modifiers field, you end up with a non-zero value if the Alt key was pressed, and a 0 if it wasn't. You convert this result to a boolean value by comparing the result with 0.

Images

If you've seen the applets that are floating around, you've undoubtedly noticed that many feature vivid graphics. When programming in a language such as C++, displaying graphics can be infamously difficult, thanks to the fact that these languages provide no direct support for handling these types of files. Even the Windows API, as immense as it is, provides little help when it comes to dealing with such graphical chores. Java, on the other hand, was designed to make creating applets as easy as possible. For that reason, Java's classes handle almost all the difficulties associated with displaying images (commonly called bitmaps). In this section, you use Java's power to add images to your applets.

Image Types   In the world of computers, there are many types of images, each of which is associated with a specific file format. These image types are usually identified by their file extensions, which include PCX, BMP, GIF, JPEG (or JPG), TIFF (or TIF), TGA, and more. Each of these file types was created by third-party software companies for use with their products, but many became popular enough to grow into standards. The PCX graphics file type, for example, began as the format for PC Paintbrush files, whereas BMP files are usually associated with the Windows graphical interface.

Part

II

Ch

7

If you were writing your Internet applications using a more conventional language like C++, you could choose to support whatever image type was most convenient for your use. This is because you would have to write all the file-loading code from scratch, anyway. Java, on the other hand, comes complete with classes that are capable of loading image files for you. This convenience comes with a small price, however, since Java can load only GIF and JPEG image file formats. In this chapter, you'll use GIF files, which are more common, although JPEG files are rapidly gaining a reputation, especially for high-resolution, true-color images.

Loading and Displaying an Image   The first step in displaying an image in your applet is to load the image from disk. To do this, you must create an object of Java's `Image` class. This is easy to do; however, in order to do so, you need to create a URL object that holds the location of the graphics file. You could just type the image's URL directly into your Java source code. If you do this, however, you have to change and recompile the applet whenever you move the graphics file to a different directory on your disk. A better way to create the image's URL object is to call either the `getDocumentBase()` or `getCodeBase()` method, as you did when you played sound effects earlier in this chapter.

Once you have the image's base URL, you're ready to load the image and create the `Image` object. You can complete both of these tasks at the same time, by calling your applet's `getImage()` method, like this:

```
Image image = getImage(baseURL, relLocation);
```

The `getImage()` method's two arguments are the URL returned by your call to `getCodeBase()` or `getDocumentBase()` and the relative location of the image. For example, assuming that you've stored your .CLASS files in the directory C:\CLASSES and your images in the directory C:\CLASSES\IMAGES, you would have a code that looks something like this:

```
URL codeBase = getCodeBase();
Image myImage = getImage(codeBase, "images/myimage.gif");
```

After Java has executed the above lines, your image is loaded into the computer's memory and is ready to display.

Displaying the image is a simple matter of calling the `Graphics` object's `drawImage()` method, like this:

```
g.drawImage(myImage, x, y, width, height, this);
```

This method's arguments are the image object to display, the X and Y coordinates at which to display the image, the width and height of the image, and the applet's `this` reference.

TIP When you want to display an image with its normal width and height, you can call a simpler version of the `drawImage()` method, which leaves out the width and height arguments, like this: `drawImage(image, x, y, this)`. This version of the method actually draws the image faster because it doesn't have to worry about reducing or expanding the image to the given width and height. It just blasts it onto the screen exactly as the image normally appears.

You may be wondering where you can get the width and the height of the image. As it turns out (no doubt thanks to careful consideration by Java's programmers over hundreds of cups of coffee), the Image class has two methods, getWidth() and getHeight(), that return the width and height of the image. The complete code for displaying the image, then, might look like this:

```
int width = image.getWidth(this);
int height = image.getHeight(this);
g.drawImage(image, x, y, width, height, this);
```

As you can see, the getWidth() and getHeight() methods require a single argument, which is the applet's this reference. (The this reference is a reference to the applet itself.)

Displaying an Image in an Applet   You're now ready to write an applet that can display images. Listing 7.17 is the Java source code for an applet called ImageApplet that displays a small image using the techniques described previously in this chapter. When you run the applet with Microsoft Explorer, you see the window shown in Figure 7.17. Make sure the SNAKE.GIF image is in the same directory as the ImageApplet.class file, because that's where the program expects to find it.

Listing 7.17   ImageApplet.java—An Applet that Displays an Image

```
import java.awt.*;
import java.applet.*;
import java.net.*;

public class ImageApplet extends Applet
{
    Image snake;

    public void init()
    {
        URL codeBase = getCodeBase();
        snake = getImage(codeBase, "snake.gif");
        resize(250, 250);
    }

    public void paint(Graphics g)
    {
        int width = snake.getWidth(this);
        int height = snake.getHeight(this);

        g.drawRect(52, 52, width+10, height+10);
        g.drawImage(snake, 57, 57, width, height, this);
    }
}
```

Part

II

Ch

7

FIG. 7.17

This is ImageApplet running in Microsoft Explorer.

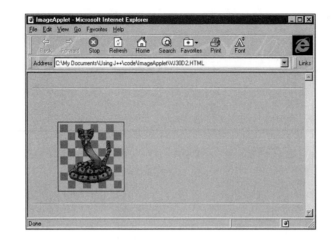

Notice how the applet imports the classes in the net package, which is where the URL class lives. If you fail to include this line at the top of the program, Java will be unable to find the URL class and the applet will not compile.

TIP By using different values for the drawImage() method's width and height arguments, you can display an image at any size you like. For example, to display an image at twice its normal size, just use 2*width and 2*height for the width and height arguments. To display the image at half its normal size, use width/2 and height/2.

From Here...

Learning about Java's applet and graphics classes is a big step toward mastering Java programming. With this knowledge, you should be able to write many different types of applets already. In upcoming chapters, you'll refine your knowledge of Java programming. You'll even run into sounds and images again when you learn about multimedia programming with Java.

For more information on related topics, please refer to the following chapters:

- Chapter 8, "The Language and I/O Classes," describes some of Java's other many useful classes, including classes for supporting disk I/O.

- Chapter 9, "The Utility and Network Classes," offers up useful programming tips, including how to make your applet Internet-aware.

- Chapter 18, "Multimedia," shows how to use sound and images to create animation in your applets.

The Language and I/O Classes

by Clayton Walnum

Although the applet and window classes that you learned about in the previous chapter hog all the glory, the Java language's nuts-and-bolts power comes from the classes in the java.lang and java.io packages. These classes not only determine to a great extent what Java is and how it works, but also enable you to handle anything from simple user input, to random-access files and inter-thread communication. ■

- **Learn about Java's data-type wrappers and the Math and System classes**

  The many classes that are defined as part of the java.lang package provide the Java language with much of its power.

- **Discover how to handle strings in Java programs**

  Java supplies two classes, String and StringBuffer, for dealing with strings in your programs.

- **Learn about performing simple user I/O in a Java program**

  Getting data to and from the user is an important part of interactive programming. Java's System class gives you the basic I/O tools you need.

- **Explore how Java's stream classes enable programs to read and write data**

  Streams are little more than flows of data. Still, it'd be tough to write a complete application without incorporating streams into the program.

- **Find out how to incorporate pipe streams into your programs**

  Pipes are a special type of stream that enable you to communicate between threads.

The *java.lang* Package

Although you may not have been aware of it, you've been using the lang package a lot. That's because this is the one package that Java automatically imports into every program. Without the lang package, you wouldn't be able to write Java programs; this package contains the libraries that make Java what it is. Table 8.1 is a list of the commonly used classes included in the lang package.

Table 8.1 Commonly Used Classes in the *java.lang* Package

Class	Description
Boolean	Represents the boolean data type.
Character	Represents the char data type.
Double	Represents the double data type.
Float	Represents the float data type.
Integer	Represents the int data type.
Long	Represents the long data type.
Math	Contains methods that implement mathematical functions.
Number	The superclass for all number-related classes, such as Float and Integer.
Object	The root of the entire class library. All Java classes can trace their ancestry back to Object.
String	Represents constant text strings.
StringBuffer	Represents a string buffer that can grow dynamically.
System	Contains methods for performing system-level function calls.
Thread	The superclass from which thread objects are derived.

Of these classes, the ones that are most useful to you at this time are the data-type wrappers—Boolean, Character, Double, Float, Integer, Long—as well as String, StringBuffer, Math, System, and Thread. The following sections provide general descriptions and usage tips for these classes.

The Data-Type Wrappers

The data-type wrapper classes enable you to perform various operations on values in your programs. For example, you can use the Integer.parseInt() method to convert strings containing digits to integer values, like this:

```
int value = Integer.parseInt(str);
```

Often, you can call static methods of the class, like `parseInt()`, to perform an operation on a value. But, you can also create objects of the class and operate directly on that object's value. To give you some idea of what you can do with the wrapper classes, Table 8.2 lists the methods of the `Integer` class.

Table 8.2   Methods of the *Integer* Class

Method	Description
Integer(int)	One of the class's constructors.
Integer(String)	One of the class's constructors.
doubleValue()	Returns the integer as a double value.
equals(Object)	Compares the integer to another object.
floatValue()	Returns the integer as a float value.
getInteger()	Gets a property of an integer.
hashCode()	Returns a hashcode for the integer.
intValue()	Returns the integer as an int value.
longValue()	Returns the integer as a long value.
parseInt(String, int)	Converts a string to an int value.
parseInt(String)	Converts a string to an int value.
toString(int, int)	Converts an integer to a string.
toString(int)	Converts an integer to a string.
toString()	Converts an integer to a string.
valueOf(String, int)	Creates an Integer object from a string.
valueOf(String)	Creates an Integer object from a string.

N O T E   Most of the data-type wrapper classes contain similar methods, so once you know how to use the methods for one class, you've got a huge head start on learning to use the other classes. ■

Suppose that you need an integer data field in a class, but you want to be able to use all of the `Integer` class's methods in order to manipulate that value. First, you declare an object of the `Integer` class and then call the class's constructor. Then, you can access the class's methods, as shown in Listing 8.1. Figure 8.1 shows the applet running under Microsoft Explorer.

Listing 8.1   IntApplet.java—Using the *Integer* Class

```java
import java.awt.*;
import java.applet.*;

public class IntApplet extends Applet
{
    public void paint(Graphics g)
    {
        Integer value = new Integer(125);

        long longValue = value.longValue();
        float floatValue = value.floatValue();

        String str = value.toString() + "     " +
            String.valueOf(longValue) + "     " +
            String.valueOf(floatValue);
        g.drawString(str, 50, 75);
    }
}
```

FIG. 8.1

This is IntApplet running in Microsoft Explorer.

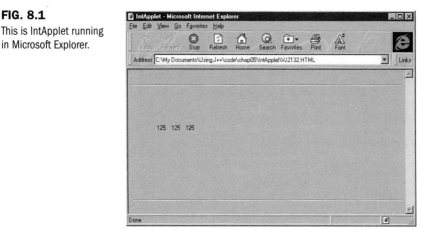

The *System* Class

The System class enables you to make system-level function calls to do things like perform simple I/O, get the current time, handle directories, copy arrays, get environment variables, get information about memory, and so on. You would use the class's I/O methods, for example, in a stand-alone applet in order to display text on the screen. Table 8.3 lists the more useful of the System class's methods and their descriptions.

N O T E   In addition to its many methods, the System class also defines standard input and output streams that you can use in your programs. For example, when you call the println() method, you're using an output stream. ▪

Table 8.3   The Most Useful Methods of the *System* Class

Method	Description
arraycopy()	Copies an array.
currentTimeMillis()	Gets the current time in milliseconds.
exit(int)	Ends the program.
getProperties()	Returns the current system properties.
getProperty()	Returns a specific property.
load()	Loads a dynamic library.
setProperties()	Sets the system properties.

Frequently, it's handy to know something about the system on which your application is running. That's why the System class makes it easy for you to find this information. Listing 8.2, for example, is a stand-alone application that displays Java's version, Java's class path, the OS name, and the OS version. Figure 8.2 shows the output from the program.

Listing 8.2   SystemApp.java—An Application that Displays System Information

```
public class SystemApp
{
    public static void main(String args[])
    {
        System.out.println("");
        System.out.println("----------------------------");

        String str = "Java Version: " +
            System.getProperty("java.version");
        System.out.println(str);

        str = "Java Class Path: " +
            System.getProperty("java.class.path");
        System.out.println(str);

        str = "OS Name: " +
            System.getProperty("os.name");
        System.out.println(str);

        str = "OS Version: " +
            System.getProperty("os.version");
        System.out.println(str);

        System.out.println("----------------------------");
    }
}
```

FIG. 8.2
The SystemApp
application displays
system properties.

N O T E The System class's getProperty() method accepts a string identifier for the property
you want. The strings you can use are file.separator, java.class.path,
java.class.version, java.home, java.vendor, java.vendor.url, java.version,
line.separator, os.arch, os.name, os.version, path.separator, user.dir, user.home,
and user.name. ■

The *Math* Class

If you need to do a lot of mathematical work in your applets and applications, you'll be glad to
have the Math class at your disposal. Using the Math class, you can perform many types of
calculations just by calling the appropriate methods. Table 8.4 lists the Math class's methods
and their descriptions:

Table 8.4   Methods of the *Math* Class

Method	Description
abs()	Returns the absolute value of a given number.
acos()	Returns the arc cosine of a value.
asin()	Returns the arc sine of a value.
atan()	Returns the arc tangent of a value.
atan2()	Converts rectangular coordinates to polar coordinates.
ceil()	Returns the smallest whole number greater than or equal to the given value.
cos()	Returns the cosine of an angle.
floor()	Returns the largest whole number less than or equal to the given value.
IEEEremainder()	Returns the remainder of a floating-point division.
log()	Returns the natural log of a value.
max()	Returns the greater of two values.

Method	Description
min()	Returns the smaller of two values.
random()	Returns a random number between 0.0 and 1.0.
round()	Rounds a floating-point or double number.
sin()	Returns the sine of an angle.
sqrt()	Returns the square root of a value.
tan()	Returns the tangent of an angle.

To call any of the math methods, reference them through the `Math` class, like this:

```
Math.Method()
```

For example, to get the square root of 10, you use this line:

```
double result = Math.sqrt(10);
```

The Java String Classes

If you've done any programming at all, you're no stranger to strings. You've probably used them in almost every program you've ever written. Java, however, has special classes you can use to store and manipulate text strings. Because these classes are so useful to a programmer, you'll take a look at them here. As you'll see, the `String` class is powerful, enabling you to manipulate string constants (strings that don't change) in more ways than you may have realized. The `StringBuffer` class, on the other hand, enables you to deal with dynamic strings. In this section, you get a look at both classes and how they're used.

The *String* Class   As said previously, Java's `String` class represents string constants, which are strings that never change. Although it may appear at times that the methods of this class are changing the contents of strings, what's really happening in these cases is that Java is creating a new string constant that contains the requested string. In other words, when you use the string class, you cannot change the contents of a string in any way. (Because of the way the class easily generates new strings, however, this distinction is almost invisible to the programmer.) Table 8.5 shows the most commonly used methods of the `String` class.

Table 8.5   Methods of the *String* Class

Method	Description
charAt()	Returns the character at the given string index.
compareTo()	Compares a string to another string.
concat()	Joins two strings.
copyValueOf()	Copies a character array to a string.
endsWith()	Checks a string for the given suffix.

continues

Table 8.5 Continued

Method	Description
equals()	Compares a string to another object.
equalsIgnoreCase()	Compares a string to another object with no regard for upper- or lowercase.
getBytes()	Copies selected characters from a string to a byte array.
getChars()	Copies selected characters from a string to a character array.
hashCode()	Returns a string's hashcode.
indexOf()	Finds the index of the first occurrence of a given character or substring in a string.
lastIndexOf()	Finds the index of the last occurrence of a given character or substring in a string.
length()	Returns the length of a string.
regionMatches()	Compares a portion of a string to a portion of another string.
replace()	Replaces all occurrences of a given character with a new character.
startsWith()	Checks a string for the given prefix.
substring()	Returns a substring of a string.
toCharArray()	Converts a string to a character array.
toLowerCase()	Converts all characters in the string to lowercase.
toUpperCase()	Converts all characters in the string to uppercase.
trim()	Removes whitespace characters from the beginning and end of a string.
valueOf()	Returns a string representation of an object.

Listing 8.3 is an applet that shows you how a few of the String methods work. When you run the applet with Visual J++, you see the window shown in Figure 8.3. The applet takes whatever text strings you type in the two text boxes and compares them for equality without considering upper- or lowercase. It then concatenates the strings and displays the new concatenated string along with its length.

Listing 8.3   StringApplet.java—An Applet that Manipulates Strings

```java
import java.awt.*;
import java.applet.*;

public class StringApplet extends Applet
{
    TextField textField1;
    TextField textField2;

    public void init()
    {
        textField1 = new TextField(20);
        textField2 = new TextField(20);

        textField1.setText("STRING");
        textField2.setText("String");

        add(textField1);
        add(textField2);
    }

    public void paint(Graphics g)
    {
        String str1 = textField1.getText();
        String str2 = textField2.getText();

        boolean equal = str1.equalsIgnoreCase(str2);
        if (equal)
            g.drawString("The strings are equal.", 70, 100);
        else
            g.drawString("The strings are not equal.", 70, 100);

        String newStr = str1.concat(str2);

        g.drawString("JOINED STRINGS:", 70, 130);
        g.drawString(newStr, 80, 150);

        g.drawString("STRING LENGTH:", 70, 180);
        int length = newStr.length();
        String s = String.valueOf(length);
        g.drawString(s, 80, 200);
    }

    public boolean action(Event evt, Object arg)
    {
        repaint();
        return true;
    }
}
```

FIG. 8.3
This is StringApplet
running under Microsoft
Explorer.

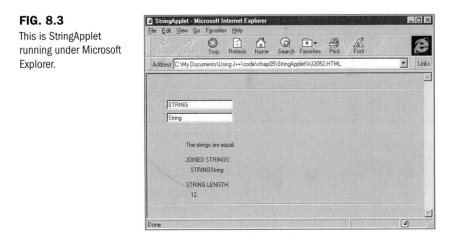

The *StringBuffer* Class   The StringBuffer class enables you to create string objects that can be changed in various ways, unlike the String class, which represents string constants. When you modify a string of the StringBuffer class, you're not creating a new string object, but rather operating directly on the original string itself. For this reason, the StringBuffer class offers a different set of methods than the String class, all of which operate directly on the buffer that contains the string.

The StringBuffer class offers several constructors that enable you to construct a StringBuffer object in various ways. Those constructors look like this:

```
StringBuffer()
StringBuffer(int length)
StringBuffer(String str)
```

These constructors create an empty StringBuffer, an empty StringBuffer of the given length, and a StringBuffer from a String object (or string literal), respectively.

Just as with regular strings, you might need to know the length of a string stored in a StringBuffer object. The class provides the length() method for this purpose. StringBuffer objects, however, also have a capacity() method that returns the capacity of the buffer. Simply put, a StringBuffer's length is the number of characters stored in the string, whereas capacity is the maximum number of characters that fit in the buffer. In the following code example, length is 2 and capacity is 17:

```
StringBuffer str = new StringBuffer("XX");
int length= str.length();
int capacity = str.capacity();
```

The StringBuffer class has two methods for extracting characters from a string. Those methods are charAt() and getChars(), both of which work similarly to the String versions. Here's an example of using charAt():

```
StringBuffer str = new StringBuffer("String buffer");
char ch = str.charAt(5);
```

And here's an example of using `getChars()`:

```
StringBuffer str = new StringBuffer("String buffer");
char ch[] = new char[20];
str.getChars(7, 10, ch, 0);
```

There are several ways you can modify the string that's stored in a `StringBuffer` object. Unlike with the string-modification methods in the `String` class, which create a new string, the methods in the `StringBuffer` class work directly on the buffer in which the original string is stored. The first thing you can do with a string buffer is set its length. You do this by calling the `setLength()` method:

```
StringBuffer str = new StringBuffer("String buffer");
str.setLength(40);
```

This method's single argument is the new length. If the new length is greater than the old length, both the string and buffer length are increased, with the additional characters being filled with zeroes (nulls). If the new length is smaller than the old length, characters are chopped off the end of the string, but the buffer size remains the same.

If you want to be guaranteed a specific buffer size, you can call the `ensureCapacity()` method, like this:

```
StringBuffer str = new StringBuffer("String buffer");
str.ensureCapacity(512);
```

The `ensureCapacity()` method's argument is the new capacity for the buffer.

You can change a character in the string buffer by calling the `setCharAt()` method:

```
StringBuffer str = new StringBuffer("String buffer");
str.setCharAt(3, 'X');
```

The `setCharAt()` method's arguments are the index of the character to change and the new character. In the previous example, the string buffer becomes "StrXng buffer."

N O T E　Just as in C, Java array indexes are zero-based. That is, the first array element has an index of 0, the second an index of 1, and so on. ▪

Finally, you can add characters to the end of the string with the `append()` method and insert characters anywhere in the string with the `insert()` method. Both of these methods come in several versions that enable you to handle many different types of data. For example, to add a character version of an integer to the end of the string, do something like this:

```
StringBuffer str = new StringBuffer("String buffer");
int value = 15;
str.append(value);
```

After this code executes, `str` contains "String buffer15." Similarly, you insert characters like this:

```
StringBuffer str = new StringBuffer("String buffer");
int value = 15;
str.insert(6, value);
```

This code results in a string of "String15 buffer." The two arguments in the previous version of `insert()` are the index at which to insert the characters and the data object to insert.

The I/O Classes

All computer programs must accept input and generate output. That is, after all, basically what a computer does. Obviously, every computer language must have a way of dealing with input and output. Otherwise, it would be impossible to write a program. Java features a rich set of classes that represent everything from a general input or output stream to a sophisticated random-access file. You'll now get a chance to experiment with these important classes, which are all part of the `java.io` package.

Learning About Streams

All data used with a computer system flows from the input, through the computer, to the output. It's this idea of data flow that leads to the term "stream." That is, a *stream* is really nothing more than a flow of data. There are *input streams*, which direct data from the outside world (usually from the keyboard) to the computer, and *output streams*, which direct data toward output devices, such as the computer screen or a file. Because streams are general in nature, a basic stream does not specifically define which devices the data flows from or to. Just like a wire carrying electricity that's being routed to a light bulb, a TV, or a dishwasher, a basic input or output stream can be directed to or from many different devices.

In Java, streams are represented by classes. The simplest of these classes represent basic input and output streams that provide general streaming abilities. Java derives from the basic classes other classes that are more specifically oriented toward a certain type of input or output. All of these classes, which are listed below, can be found in the `java.io` package.

- `InputStream`—The basic input stream.
- `BufferedInputStream`—A basic buffered input stream.
- `DataInputStream`—An input stream for reading primitive data types.
- `FileInputStream`—An input stream used for basic file input.
- `ByteArrayInputStream`—An input stream whose source is a byte array.
- `StringBufferInputStream`—An input stream whose source is a string.
- `LineNumberInputStream`—An input stream that supports line numbers.
- `PushbackInputStream`—An input stream that allows a byte to be pushed back onto the stream after the byte is read.
- `PipedInputStream`—An input stream used for inter-thread communication.
- `SequenceInputStream`—An input stream that combines two other input streams.
- `OutputStream`—The basic output stream.
- `PrintStream`—An output stream for displaying text.
- `BufferedOutputStream`—A basic buffered output stream.

■ `DataOutputStream`—An output stream for writing primitive data types.

■ `FileOutputStream`—An output stream used for basic file output.

■ `ByteArrayOutputStream`—An output stream whose destination is a byte array.

■ `PipedOutputStream`—An output stream used for inter-thread communication.

Besides the previous classes, Java provides two classes specially designed for manipulating files. These classes are `File`, which enables you to obtain information about a disk file, and `RandomAccessFile`, which represents a random-access disk file. A *random-access file* is one that can be read from, or written to, any location in the file.

Obviously, there are too many stream classes to be covered thoroughly in a single chapter. An entire book could be written on Java I/O alone. For that reason, this chapter will cover the most useful of the stream classes, concentrating on basic input and output, as well as file handling. You'll begin with a brief introduction to the classes, after which sample programs will demonstrate how the classes work.

The Basic Input and Output Classes

As with any well-developed class hierarchy, the more specific Java stream classes like `FileInputStream` and `ByteArrayOutputStream` rely upon the general base classes `InputStream` and `OutputStream` for their basic functionality. Because `InputStream` and `OutputStream` are abstract classes, you won't use them directly. However, all of Java's stream classes have `InputStream` or `OutputStream` in their family tree, so you should know what these classes have to offer.

The *InputStream* Class   As mentioned, the `InputStream` class represents the basic input stream. As such, it defines a set of methods that all input streams need. These methods are listed in Table 8.6 below:

Table 8.6   Methods of the *InputStream* Class

Method	Description
read()	Reads data into the stream.
skip()	Skips over bytes in the stream.
available()	Returns the number of bytes immediately available in the stream.
mark()	Marks a position in the stream.
reset()	Returns to the marked position in the stream.
markSupported()	Returns a Boolean value indicating whether or not the stream supports marking and resetting.
close()	Closes the stream.

The read() method is overloaded in the class, providing three methods for reading data from the stream. The methods' signatures look like this:

```
int read()
int read(byte b[])
int read(byte b[], int off, int len)
```

The first version of read() simply reads single bytes as integers from the input stream, returning -1 if there is no data left to read. The second version reads multiple bytes into a byte array, returning the number of bytes actually read; whereas the third version also reads data into a byte array, but enables you to specify an offset (off) in the array at which to start storing characters, as well as to indicate the maximum number of bytes to read (len).

The signatures for the remaining methods look like this:

```
long skip(long n)
int available()
void close()
void mark(int readlimit)
void reset()
boolean markSupported()
```

The *OutputStream* Class   The counterpart to InputStream is the OutputStream class, which provides the basic functionality for all output streams. The methods defined in the OutputStream class are listed, along with their descriptions, in Table 8.7.

Table 8.7   Methods of the *OutputStream* Class

Method	Description
write()	Writes data to the stream.
flush()	Flushes all data from the stream.
close()	Closes the stream.

As is the case with the InputStream class's read() method, OutputStream's write() method comes in several versions, the signatures for which are shown below:

```
void write(int b)
void write(byte b[])
void write(byte b[], int off, int len)
```

The first version of the write() method simply writes a single byte to the stream, whereas the second version writes all the bytes contained in the given byte array. Finally, the third version enables your program to write data from a byte array, specifying a starting offset (off) for the write and the number of bytes to write (len).

The signatures for the flush() and close() look exactly as they're shown in Table 8.7.

The *System.in* and *System.out* Objects   In order to support the standard input and output devices (usually the keyboard and screen, respectively), Java defines two stream objects (in the java.lang package) that you can use in your programs without having to create stream objects of your own. The System.in object (instantiated from the InputStream class) enables your programs to read data from the keyboard, whereas the System.out object (instantiated from the PrintStream class) routes output to the computer's screen. You can use these stream objects directly in order to handle standard input and output in your Java programs, or you can use them as the basis for other stream objects you may want to create.

For example, Listing 8.4 is a Java application that accepts a line of input from the user and then displays the line on the screen. Figure 8.4 shows the application running in a DOS window.

Listing 8.4   IOApp.java—Performing Basic User Input and Output

```java
import java.io.*;

class IOApp
{
    public static void main(String args[])
    {
        byte buffer[] = new byte[255];
        System.out.println("\nType a line of text: ");

        try
            System.in.read(buffer, 0, 255);
        catch (Exception e)
        {
            String err = e.toString();
            System.out.println(err);
        }

        System.out.println("\nThe line you typed was: ");
        String inputStr = new String(buffer, 0);
        System.out.println(inputStr);
    }
}
```

FIG. 8.4

Java's *System* class provides for standard IO.

The *PrintStream* Class   You probably noticed in Listing 8.4 a method called println(), which is not a part of the OutputStream class. In order to provide for more flexible output on the standard output stream, the System class derives its out output-stream object from the

PrintStream class, which provides for printing values as text output. Table 8.8 lists the methods of the PrintStream class, along with their descriptions.

Table 8.8 Methods of the *PrintStream* Class

Method	Description
write()	Writes data to the stream.
flush()	Flushes data from the stream.
close()	Closes the stream.
checkError()	Flushes the stream, returning errors that occurred.
print()	Prints data in text form.
println()	Prints a line of data (followed by a newline character) in text form.

As with many of the methods included in the stream classes, the write(), print(), and println() methods come in several versions. The write() method can write single bytes or whole byte arrays, whereas the print() and println() methods can display almost any type of data on the screen. The various method signatures look like this:

```
void write(int b)
void write(byte b[], int off, int len)
void print(Object obj)
void print(String s)
void print(char s[])
void print(char c)
void print(int i)
void print(long l)
void print(float f)
void print(double d)
void print(boolean b)
void println()
void println(Object obj)
void println(String s)
void println(char s[])
void println(char c)
void println(int i)
void println(long l)
```

```
void println(float f)

void println(double d)

void println(boolean b)
```

Handling Files

Now that you've had an introduction to the stream classes, you can put your knowledge to work. Perhaps the most common use of I/O, outside of retrieving data from the keyboard and displaying data on the screen, is file I/O. Any program that wants to retain its status (including the status of any edited files) must be capable of loading and saving files. Java provides several classes—including `File`, `RandomAccessFile`, `FileInputStream`, and `FileOutputStream`—for dealing with files. In this section, you'll examine these classes and get a chance to see how they work. But first, a word from the guys in the security department.

File Security   When you start reading and writing to a disk from a networked application, you have to consider security issues. Because the Java language was designed especially for creating Internet-based applications, security is even more important. No user wants to worry that the Web pages he's currently viewing are capable of uncontrolled reading from and writing to his hard disk. For this reason, the Java system was designed such that the user can set system security from within his Java-compatible browser, and so determine which files and directories are to remain accessible to the browser and which are to be locked up tight.

In most cases, the user will disallow all file access on his local system, thus completely protecting his system from unwarranted intrusion. Because of this, virtually no applet relies on being able to create, read, or write files. This tight security is vital to the existence of applets because of the way they are automatically downloaded onto a user's system behind the user's back, as it were. No one would use Java-compatible browsers if they feared that such use would open their system to the tampering of nosy corporations and sociopathic programmers.

Java stand-alone applications, however, are a whole different story. Java applications are no different than any other application on your system. They cannot be automatically downloaded and run the way applets are. For this reason, stand-alone applications can have full access to the file system on which they are run. The file-handling examples in this chapter, then, are incorporated into Java stand-alone applications.

Using the *FileInputStream* Class   If your file-reading needs are relatively simple, you can use the `FileInputStream` class, which is a simple input-stream class derived from `InputStream`. This class features all the methods inherited from the `InputStream` class. To create an object of the `FileInputStream` class, you call one of its constructors, of which there are three, as shown below:

```
FileInputStream(String name)
FileInputStream(File file)
FileInputStream(FileDescriptor fdObj)
```

The first constructor above creates a `FileInputStream` object from the given file name, name. The second constructor creates the object from a `File` object, and the third creates the object from a `FileDescriptor` object.

Listing 8.5 is a Java application that reads its own source code from disk and displays the code on the screen. Figure 8.5 shows the application's output in a DOS window.

Listing 8.5   FileApp.java—An Application that Reads its Own Source Code

```java
import java.io.*;

class FileApp
{
    public static void main(String args[])
    {
        byte buffer[] = new byte[2056];

        try
        {
            FileInputStream fileIn =
                new FileInputStream("fileapp.java");
            int bytes = fileIn.read(buffer, 0, 2056);
            String str = new String(buffer, 0, 0, bytes);
            System.out.println(str);
        }
        catch (Exception e)
        {
            String err = e.toString();
            System.out.println(err);
        }
    }
}
```

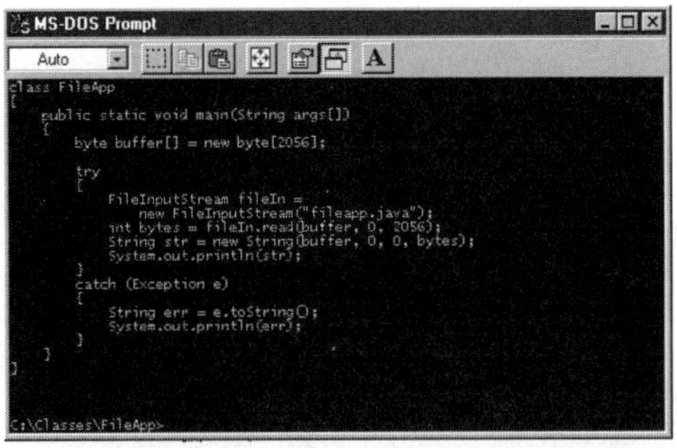

FIG. 8.5

The FileApp application reads and displays its own source code.

Using the *FileOutputStream* Class   As you may have guessed, the counterpart to the FileInputStream class is FileOutputStream, which provides basic file-writing capabilities. Besides FileOutputStream's methods, which are inherited from OutputStream, the class features three constructors, whose signatures look like this:

```java
FileOutputStream(String name)
FileOutputStream(File file)
FileOutputStream(FileDescriptor fdObj)
```

The first constructor creates a `FileOutputStream` object from the given file name, name, whereas the second constructor creates the object from a `File` object. Finally, the third constructor creates the object from a `FileDescriptor` object.

Listing 8.6 is a Java application that reads a line of text from the keyboard and saves it to a file. When you run the application, type a line and press Enter. Then, at the system prompt, type **TYPE LINE.TXT** to display the text in the file, just to prove it's really there. Figure 8.6 shows a typical program run.

Listing 8.6 FileApp2.java—An Application that Saves Text to a File

```java
import java.io.*;

class FileApp2
{
    public static void main(String args[])
    {
        byte buffer[] = new byte[80];

        try
        {
            System.out.println
                ("\nEnter a line to be saved to disk:");
            int bytes = System.in.read(buffer);

            FileOutputStream fileOut =
                new FileOutputStream("line.txt");
            fileOut.write(buffer, 0, bytes);
        }
        catch (Exception e)
        {
            String err = e.toString();
            System.out.println(err);
        }
    }
}
```

FIG. 8.6

The FileApp2 application saves user input to a file.

Using the *File* Class   If you need to obtain information about a file, you should create an object of Java's `File` class. This class enables you to query the system about everything from the file's name to the time it was last modified. You can also use the `File` class to make new directories, as well as to delete and rename files. You create a `File` object by calling one of the class's three constructors, whose signatures are listed below:

```
File(String path)
File(String path, String name)
File(File dir, String name)
```

The first constructor above creates a `File` object from the given full path name (i.e., c:\classes\myapp.java). The second constructor creates the object from a separate path and a file, and the third creates the object from a separate path and file name, with the path being that associated with another `File` object.

The `File` class features a full set of methods that give your program lots of file-handling options. Table 8.9 lists these methods along with their descriptions.

Table 8.9   Methods of the *File* Class

Method	Description
getName()	Gets the file's name.
getPath()	Gets the file's path.
getAbsolutePath()	Gets the file's absolute path.
getParent()	Gets the file's parent directory.
exists()	Returns true if the file exists.
canWrite()	Returns true if the file can be written to.
canRead()	Returns true if the file can be read.
isFile()	Returns true if the file is valid.
isDirectory()	Returns true if the directory is valid.
isAbsolute()	Returns true if the file name is absolute.
lastModified()	Returns the time the file was last changed.
length()	Returns the length of the file.
mkdir()	Makes a directory.
renameTo()	Renames the file.
mkdirs()	Creates a directory tree.
list()	Gets a list of files in the directory.
delete()	Deletes the file.

Method	Description
hashCode()	Gets a hash code for the file.
equals()	Compares the file object with another object.
toString()	Gets a string containing the file's path.

Using the *RandomAccessFile* Class   You may think, at this point, that Java's file-handling abilities are scattered through a lot of different classes, making it difficult to obtain the basic functionality you need to read, write, and otherwise manage a file. But Java's creators are way ahead of you. They created the RandomAccessFile class for those times when you really need to get serious about your file handling. Using this class, you can do just about everything you need to do with a file.

You create a RandomAccessFile object by calling one of the class's two constructors, whose signatures are shown below:

```
RandomAccessFile(String name, String mode)
RandomAccessFile(File file, String mode)
```

The first constructor creates a RandomAccessFile object from a string containing the file name and another string containing the access mode ("r" for read, and "rw" for read and write). The second constructor creates the object from a File object and the mode string.

Once you have the RandomAccessFile object created, you can call upon the object's methods to manipulate the file. Those methods are listed in Table 8.10.

Table 8.10   Methods of the *RandomAccessFile* Class

Method	Description
close()	Closes the file.
getFD()	Gets a FileDescriptor object for the file.
getFilePointer()	Gets the location of the file pointer.
length()	Gets the length of the file.
read()	Reads data from the file.
readBoolean()	Reads a Boolean value from the file.
readByte()	Reads a byte from the file.
readChar()	Reads a char from the file.
readDouble()	Reads a double floating-point value from the file.
readFloat()	Reads a float from the file.
readFully()	Reads data into an array, completely filling the array.

continues

Table 8.10 Continued

Method	Description
readInt()	Reads an int from the file.
readLine()	Reads a text line from the file.
readLong()	Reads a long int from the file.
readShort()	Reads a short int from the file.
readUnsignedByte()	Reads an unsigned byte from the file.
readUnsignedShort()	Reads an unsigned short int from the file.
readUTF()	Reads a UTF string from the file.
seek()	Positions the file pointer in the file.
skipBytes()	Skips over a given number of bytes in the file.
write()	Writes data to the file.
writeBoolean()	Writes a Boolean to the file.
writeByte()	Writes a byte to the file.
writeBytes()	Writes a string as bytes.
writeChar()	Writes a char to the file.
writeChars()	Writes a string as char data.
writeDouble()	Writes a double floating-point value to the file.
writeFloat()	Writes a float to the file.
writeInt()	Writes an int to the file.
writeLong()	Writes a long int to the file.
writeShort()	Writes a short int to the file.
writeUTF()	Writes a UTF string.

Listing 8.7 is a Java application that reads and displays its own source code using a `RandomAccessFile` object.

Listing 8.7 FileApp3.java—Using a *RandomAccessFile* Object

```
import java.io.*;

class FileApp3
{
    public static void main(String args[])
    {
        try
```

```
    {
        RandomAccessFile file =
            new RandomAccessFile("fileapp3.java", "r");

        long filePointer = 0;
        long length = file.length();
        while (filePointer < length)
        {
            String s = file.readLine();
            System.out.println(s);
            filePointer = file.getFilePointer();
        }
    }
    catch (Exception e)
    {
        String err = e.toString();
        System.out.println(err);
    }
}
}
```

Using Pipes

Normal stream and file handling under Java isn't all that different than under any other computer language. The Java stream classes provide all the functions you're used to using to handle streams. However, Java also supports *pipes*, a form of data stream with which you may have little experience. Basically, pipes are a way to transfer data directly between different threads. One thread sends data through its output pipe, and another thread reads the data from its input pipe. By using pipes, you can share data between different threads without having to resort to things like temporary files.

Introducing *PipedInputStream* and *PipedOutputStream* As you may have guessed, Java provides two special classes for dealing with pipes. The first class, PipedInputStream, represents the input side of a pipe (the side of the pipe from which a program inputs data). The second, PipedOutputStream represents the output side of the pipe (the side of the pipe into which a program outputs data). These classes work together to provide a piped stream of data in much the same way a conventional pipe provides a stream of water. If you were to cap off one end of a conventional pipe, the flow of water would stop. The same is also true of piped streams. If you don't have both an input and output stream, you've effectively sealed off one or both of the ends of the data pipe.

To create a piped stream, you first create an object of the PipedOutputStream class. Then, you create an object of the PipedInputStream class, handing it a reference to the piped output stream, like this:

```
pipeOut = new PipedOutputStream();
pipeIn = new PipedInputStream(pipeOut);
```

By giving the PipedInputStream object a reference to the output pipe, you've effectively connected the input and output into a stream through which data can flow in a single direction.

Data that's pumped into the output side of the pipe can be received by another thread that has access to the input side of the pipe, as shown in Figure 8.7.

FIG. 8.7
The output stream and input stream act as two ends on a one-way pipe.

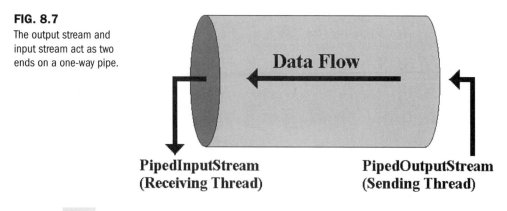

PipedInputStream
(Receiving Thread)   **PipedOutputStream**
                                                          (Sending Thread)

N O T E It may seem a little weird that the output side of the pipe is the side into which data is pumped, and the input side is the side from which the data flows. You have to think in terms of the threads that are using the pipe, rather than of the pipe itself. That is, the thread supplying data sends its output into the piped output stream, and the thread inputting the data takes it from the piped input stream. ■

Once you have the pipe created, you can read and write data just as you would with a conventional file. In the next section, you get a chance to see pipes in action.

The PipeApp Application   Listings 8.8 through 8.10 are the source code for an application called PipeApp that uses pipes to process data. The application has three threads, the main thread plus two secondary threads that are started by the main thread. The program takes a file that contains all X's, and, using pipes to transfer data, first changes the data to all Y's and finally changes the data to all Z's, after which the program displays the modified data on the screen. Note that no additional files, beyond the input file, are created. All data is manipulated using pipes. Figure 8.8 shows a program run.

FIG. 8.8
The PipeApp application uses pipes to share data with three threads.

Listing 8.8   PipeApp.java—The Main PipeApp Application

```java
import java.io.*;

class PipeApp
{
    public static void main(String[] args)
    {
        PipeApp pipeApp = new PipeApp();

        try
        {
            FileInputStream XFileIn = new FileInputStream("input.txt");
            InputStream YInPipe = pipeApp.changeToY(XFileIn);
            InputStream ZInPipe = pipeApp.changeToZ(YInPipe);

            System.out.println();
            System.out.println("Here are the results:");
            System.out.println();

            DataInputStream inputStream = new DataInputStream(ZInPipe);

            String str = inputStream.readLine();
            while (str != null)
            {
                System.out.println(str);
                str = inputStream.readLine();
            }

            inputStream.close();
        }
        catch (Exception e)
            System.out.println(e.toString());
    }

    public InputStream changeToY(InputStream inputStream)
    {
        try
        {
            DataInputStream XFileIn = new DataInputStream(inputStream);
            PipedOutputStream pipeOut = new PipedOutputStream();
            PipedInputStream pipeIn = new PipedInputStream(pipeOut);
            PrintStream printStream = new PrintStream(pipeOut);

            YThread yThread = new YThread(XFileIn, printStream);
            yThread.start();
            return pipeIn;
        }
        catch (Exception e)
            System.out.println(e.toString());

        return null;
    }

    public InputStream changeToZ(InputStream inputStream)
    {
```

continues

Listing 8.8 Continued

```
        try
        {
            DataInputStream YFileIn = new DataInputStream(inputStream);
            PipedOutputStream pipeOut2 = new PipedOutputStream();
            PipedInputStream pipeIn2 = new PipedInputStream(pipeOut2);
            PrintStream printStream2 = new PrintStream(pipeOut2);

            ZThread zThread = new ZThread(YFileIn, printStream2);
            zThread.start();
            return pipeIn2;
        }
        catch (Exception e)
            System.out.println(e.toString());

        return null;
    }
}
```

Listing 8.9 YThread.java—The Thread that Changes the Data to Y's

```
import java.io.*;

class YThread extends Thread
{
    DataInputStream XFileIn;
    PrintStream printStream;

    YThread(DataInputStream XFileIn, PrintStream printStream)
    {
        this.XFileIn = XFileIn;
        this.printStream = printStream;
    }

    public void run()
    {
        try
        {
            String XString = XFileIn.readLine();
            while (XString != null)
            {
                String YString = XString.replace('X', 'Y');
                printStream.println(YString);
                printStream.flush();
                XString = XFileIn.readLine();
            }

            printStream.close();
        }
        catch (IOException e)
            System.out.println(e.toString());
    }
}
```

Listing 8.10   ZThread.java—The Thread that Changes the Data to All Z's

```java
import java.io.*;

class ZThread extends Thread
{
    DataInputStream YFileIn;
    PrintStream printStream;

    ZThread(DataInputStream YFileIn, PrintStream printStream)
    {
        this.YFileIn = YFileIn;
        this.printStream = printStream;
    }

    public void run()
    {
        try
        {
            String YString = YFileIn.readLine();
            while (YString != null)
            {
                String ZString = YString.replace('Y', 'Z');
                printStream.println(ZString);
                printStream.flush();
                YString = YFileIn.readLine();
            }

            printStream.close();
        }
        catch (IOException e)
            System.out.println(e.toString());
    }
}
```

Exploring the *main()* Method   Seeing the PipeApp application work and understanding why it works are two very different things. So, in this section, you'll examine the program line by line in order to see what's going on. The PipeApp.java file is the main program thread, so you'll start your exploration there. This application contains three methods: the `main()` method, which all applications must have, and the `changeToY()` and `changeToZ()` methods, which start two additional threads.

Inside `main()`, the program first creates an application object for the program:

```java
PipeApp pipeApp = new PipeApp();
```

This is necessary in order to be able to call the `ChangeToY()` and `ChangeToZ()` methods, which don't exist until the application class has been instantiated. One way around this would be to make all the class's methods static, rather than just `main()`. Then, you could call the methods without creating an object of the class.

After creating the application object, the program sets up a `try` program block, because streams require that `IOException` exceptions be caught in your code. Inside the `try` block, the program creates an input stream for the source text file:

```
FileInputStream XFileIn = new FileInputStream("input.txt");
```

This new input stream is passed to the `changeToY()` method so that the next thread can read the file:

```
InputStream YInPipe = pipeApp.changeToY(XFileIn);
```

The `changeToY()` method creates the thread that changes the input data to all Y's (you'll see how this method works soon) and returns the input pipe from the thread. The next thread can use this input pipe to access the data created by the first thread. So, the input pipe is passed as an argument to the `changeToZ()` method:

```
InputStream ZInPipe = pipeApp.changeToZ(YInPipe);
```

The `changeToZ()` method starts the thread that changes the data from all Y's to all Z's. The main program uses the input pipe returned from `changeToZ()` in order to access the modified data and print it on the screen.

After the program gets the `ZInPipe` piped input stream, it prints a message on the screen:

```
System.out.println();
System.out.println("Here are the results:");
System.out.println();
```

Then, the program maps the piped input stream to a `DataInputStream` object, which enables the program to read the data using the `readLine()` method:

```
DataInputStream inputStream = new DataInputStream(ZInPipe);
```

Once the input stream is created, the program can read the data in, line by line, and display it on the screen, as shown in Listing 8.11.

Listing 8.11   LST05_11.TXT—Reading and Displaying the Data Line by Line

```
String str = inputStream.readLine();
while (str != null)
{
    System.out.println(str);
    str = inputStream.readLine();
}
```

Finally, after displaying the data, the program closes the input stream:

```
inputStream.close();
```

Exploring the *changeToY()* Method   Inside the `changeToY()` method is the first place in the program you really get to see pipes in action. Like `main()`, the `changeToY()` method does most of its processing inside a `try` program block in order to catch `IOException` exceptions. The method first maps the source input stream (which was passed as the method's single parameter) to a `DataInputStream` object. This enables the program to read data from the stream using the `readLine()` method:

```
DataInputStream XFileIn = new DataInputStream(inputStream);
```

Next, `changeToY()` creates the output pipe and input pipe:

```
PipedOutputStream pipeOut = new PipedOutputStream();
PipedInputStream pipeIn = new PipedInputStream(pipeOut);
```

Then, in order to be able to use the `println()` method to output text lines to the pipe, the program maps the output pipe to a `PrintStream` object:

```
PrintStream printStream = new PrintStream(pipeOut);
```

At this point, the method has four streams created. The first (`XFileIn`) represents the data that will be read from the file, the second and third (`pipeOut` and `printStream`, which you can think of as the same stream, if you like) are the output end of the pipe into which the new thread will output its data. The fourth (`pipeIn`) is the input side of the pipe from which the next thread will input its data. Figure 8.9 illustrates this situation.

FIG. 8.9
These are the streams created in the *changeToY()* method.

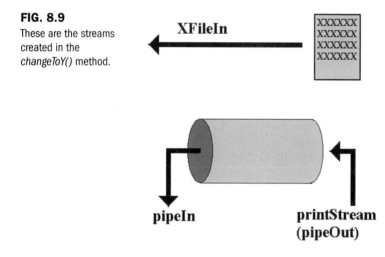

Now the program can create the thread that will change the data from X's to Y's. That thread is an object of the `YThread` class, whose constructor is passed the input file (`XFileIn`) and the output pipe (now called `printStream`) as arguments:

```
YThread yThread = new YThread(XFileIn, printStream);
```

After creating the thread, the program starts it:

```
yThread.start();
```

As you'll soon see, the `YThread` thread reads data in from `XFileIn`, changes the data from X's to Y's, and outputs the result into `printStream`, which is the output end of the pipe. Because the output end of the pipe is connected to the input end (`pipeIn`), the input end will contain the data that the `YThread` thread changed to Y's. The program returns that end of the pipe from the changeToY() method so that it can be used as the input for the changeToZ() method. Figure 8.10 shows the changeToY() portion of the chain.

FIG. 8.10

The *changeToY()* method reads X's and sends Y's into the pipe.

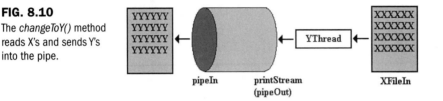

pipeIn   printStream   XFileIn
                (pipeOut)

Exploring the *changeToZ()* Method

The changeToZ() method works similarly to the changeToY() method. However, because the way each method accesses its streams is important to the understanding of the PipeApp application, you'll examine changeToZ() line by line, too. The changeToZ() method starts by mapping its input stream (which is the input end of the pipe returned from changeToY()) to a DataInputStream object, so that the program can read from the stream using the readLine() method:

```
DataInputStream YFileIn = new DataInputStream(inputStream);
```

The program then creates a new pipe:

```
PipedOutputStream pipeOut2 = new PipedOutputStream();
PipedInputStream pipeIn2 = new PipedInputStream(pipeOut2);
```

This new pipe will route data from the third thread (counting the main thread) back to the main program.

After creating the pipe, the program maps the output end to a PrintStream object so that data can be sent into the pipe using the println() method:

```
PrintStream printStream2 = new PrintStream(pipeOut2);
```

Next, the program creates a thread from the ZThread class, providing the input pipe created by changeToY() and the new output pipe (mapped to printStream2) as arguments to the class's constructor:

```
ZThread zThread = new ZThread(YFileIn, printStream2);
```

The next line starts the thread:

```
zThread.start();
```

The ZThread thread reads data from the input pipe created by changeToY() that was stuffed with data by the YThread thread, changes the data to Z's, and finally outputs the data to the output pipe called printStream2. The changeToZ() method returns the input half of this pipe (pipeIn2) from the method, where the main program prints the stream's contents on the screen. You now have a stream scenario like that illustrated in Figure 8.11.

FIG. 8.11
The data travels a long path as it's changed from all X's to all Z's.

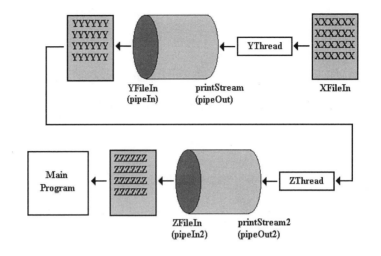

YFileIn (pipeIn) — printStream (pipeOut) — XFileIn

ZFileIn (pipeIn2) — printStream2 (pipeOut2)

Exploring the *YThread* Class You now should have a basic understanding of how the pipes work. The last part of the puzzle is the way that the secondary threads, YThread and ZThread, service the pipes. Because the two threads work almost identically, you'll examine only YThread.

YThread's constructor receives two parameters, the input file and the output end of the first pipe. The constructor saves these parameters as data members of the class:

```
this.XFileIn = XFileIn;
this.printStream = printStream;
```

With its streams in hand, the thread can start processing the data, which it does in its run() method. First the thread reads a line from the input file, then it starts a while loop that will process all the data in the file. The first line read from the file before the loop begins ensures that XString will not be null, which would prevent the loop from executing:

```
String XString = XFileIn.readLine();
while (XString != null)
```

Inside the loop, the thread first changes the newly read data to all Y's:

```
String YString = XString.replace('X', 'Y');
```

It then outputs the modified data to the output end of the pipe:

```
printStream.println(YString);
printStream.flush();
```

Next, the thread reads another line of data for the next iteration of the loop:

```
XString = XFileIn.readLine();
```

Finally, when the loop completes, the thread closes the piped output stream:

```
printStream.close();
```

And that's all there is to it. To put it simply, the thread does nothing more than read lines from the input file, change the characters in the lines to Y's, and ship the changed data into the pipe, from which it will be retrieved from the next thread.

The ZThread thread works almost exactly the same, except its input stream is the input end of the pipe into which YThread outputs its data. Finally, the input end of ZThread's pipe feeds the main program as the program reads the text lines and displays them on the screen.

From Here...

As you've now discovered, the classes included in the language and input/output classes make it easier to write powerful applets quickly. For example, the Math class enables you to manipulate numbers in many sophisticated ways, whereas the string-related classes, String and StringBuffer, make text handling almost as easy as popping a balloon with a grenade. Java even provides you with comprehensive file-handling classes, which, while they can rarely be used in applets, give Java stand-alone applications complete I/O capabilities.

For more information on related topics, please refer to the following chapters:

- Chapter 7, "The Applet and Window Classes," provides important information that you need in order to write any Java applet.
- Chapter 9, "The Utility and Network Classes," describes advanced programming techniques, including how to make your applet Internet-aware.

The Utility and Network Classes

by Clayton Walnum

The last classes you'll examine in this section of the book are those that provide useful complex data structures for your Java programs, as well as those that enable you to connect your applets and applications to the Internet. You'll find the classes in question in the `java.util` and `java.net` classes. However, whereas the utility classes are fairly easy to use, the networking classes require a good background in Internet programming. This chapter will give you an introduction to this complex subject, but you should refer to a book specifically geared toward writing Java Internet applications for more information. ■

Learn about the many classes in the `java.util` package

The classes that make up the `java.util` package enable you to do everything from get the current date to create and manage stacks, hash tables, and dictionaries.

Explore how to use the `Date` class in your programs

The `Date` class provides a convenient way to manipulate dates and times in your programs.

Learn about tokenizing strings

The `StringTokenizer` class extracts individual words (or tokens) from a text string.

Discover how to generate random numbers

If you want to write game applets, you'll almost certainly need to use random numbers. Java's `Random` class handles this important task.

Learn how to write simple Internet-capable applets

Java's `URL` class provides the easiest pathway to Internet connections.

The *java.util* Package

The java.util package is a grab bag of helpful classes that represent frequently used data structures, including stacks, vectors, dates, dictionaries, hash tables, and bit fields. This package also features classes for performing special types of operations on data. For example, the StringTokenizer class enables you to extract individual words from a string, and the Random class enables you to create random numbers for your game applets. The classes included in the java.util package are listed in Table 9.1, along with their descriptions.

Table 9.1   Classes in the *java.util* Package

Class	Description
BitSet	Represents a collection of bits.
Date	Provides methods for manipulating dates and times.
Dictionary	Creates a keyed table of values.
Enumeration	Represents a list that can be enumerated (iterated through).
HashTable	Creates a table that is keyed through hash values.
Observable	Provides the base functionality for creating objects that, when changed, can notify other objects of the change.
Observer	An interface that represents objects that receive notices from objects of the Observable class.
Properties	A special type of HashTable that can be saved or loaded from a stream.
Random	Creates random numbers.
Stack	Creates a stack-like, data-storage object.
StringTokenizer	A class that can extract tokens (words or elements) from a string.
Vector	Represents a dynamic array (an array that can change size as needed).

Many of the classes and interfaces in the java.util package are closely related. For example, the Stack class is derived from Vector, whereas StringTokenizer implements the Enumeration interface and HashTable is derived from Dictionary. In the following sections, you get a chance to experiment with a few of the classes in the java.util package.

The *Date* Class

If you looked over Table 9.1, you know that the Date class represents dates and times. If you've been programming for a while, you've probably written many programs that needed to manipulate dates and times in some way. The Date class makes handling this special type of data more convenient than working with it directly.

To create a Date object that represents the current date and time, you just call the class's constructor, like this:

```
Date date = new Date();
```

When you've created the Date object, you can manipulate it using the class's methods, the most useful of which are listed with their descriptions in Table 9.2.

Table 9.2 Most Useful Methods of the *Date* Class

Method	Description
parse()	Returns the time value represented by a string.
getYear()	Returns the year after 1900.
setYear()	Sets the year.
getMonth()	Returns the month.
setMonth()	Sets the month.
getDate()	Returns the day of the month.
setDate()	Sets the day of the month.
getDay()	Returns the day of the week.
getHours()	Returns the hour.
setHours()	Sets the hour.
getMinutes()	Returns the minute.
setMinutes()	Sets the minute.
getSeconds()	Returns the second.
setSeconds()	Sets the second.
getTime()	Returns the milliseconds since the epoch.
setTime()	Sets the milliseconds since the epoch.
before()	Returns true if the date comes before a given date.
after()	Returns true if the date comes after a given date.
equals()	Returns true if the objects are equal.
toString()	Returns a string representation of the date.

Listing 9.1 is a short applet that demonstrates how to use a Date object. The program creates the Date object and then calls various methods of the class to extract information about the current date. Figure 9.1 shows the applet running in Microsoft Explorer.

Listing 9.1   DateApplet.java—An Applet that Displays Information About the Current Date

```
import java.awt.*;
import java.applet.*;
import java.util.Date;

public class DateApplet extends Applet
{
    int year, month, date, day;
    int hour, minute, second;
    String dateString;

    public void init()
    {
        Date currentDate = new Date();
        year = currentDate.getYear();
        month = currentDate.getMonth();
        date = currentDate.getDate();
        day = currentDate.getDay();
        hour = currentDate.getHours();
        minute = currentDate.getMinutes();
        second = currentDate.getSeconds();
        dateString = currentDate.toString();
    }

    public void paint(Graphics g)
    {
        Font font = g.getFont();
        int height = font.getSize();
        String s = "Year: " + String.valueOf(year);
        g.drawString(s, 50, height*2);
        s = "Month: " + String.valueOf(month);
        g.drawString(s, 50, height*3);
        s = "Date: " + String.valueOf(date);
        g.drawString(s, 50, height*4);
        s = "Day: " + String.valueOf(day);
        g.drawString(s, 50, height*5);
        s = "Hour: " + String.valueOf(hour);
        g.drawString(s, 50, height*6);
        s = "Minute: " + String.valueOf(minute);
        g.drawString(s, 50, height*7);
        s = "Second: " + String.valueOf(second);
        g.drawString(s, 50, height*8);
        g.drawString(dateString, 50, height*9);
    }
}
```

FIG. 9.1
DateApplet displays
information about the
current date.

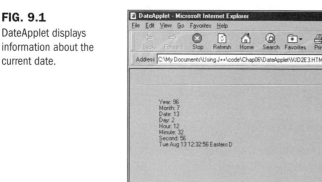

Although the previous applet showed how to create a Date object for the current date, there
are several other ways you can construct Date objects. The signatures of the various constructors look like this:

```
public Date()
public Date(long date)
public Date(int year, int month, int date)
public Date(int year, int month, int date, int hrs, int min)
public Date(int year, int month, int date, int hrs, int min, int sec)
public Date(String s)
```

As you can see, you can create a Date object for a specific date. Moreover, the date can be
represented in a number of ways.

The *StringTokenizer* Class

If you've been using your computer for a while, you may remember the old-fashioned text
adventure games where you'd enter a command from the keyboard such as **GET KEY AND
OPEN DOOR**, and the computer would follow your instructions. Programs like these had to
parse a text string and separate the string into separate words. These words are called *tokens*,
and you may run into times when you'd like to extract tokens from a text string. Java provides
the StringTokenizer class for just this purpose.

Because StringTokenizer is not part of the java.lang package as the String and
StringBuffer classes are, you must include the correct package in your applet. That package
is java.util, and you import it like this:

```
import java.util.StringTokenizer;
```

Or, if you want to import the entire util package, you could write this:

```
import java.util.*;
```

You can construct a StringTokenizer object in several ways, but the easiest is to supply the string you want to tokenize as the constructor's single argument, like this:

```
StringTokenizer tokenizer =
    new StringTokenizer("One Two Three Four Five");
```

This type of StringTokenizer uses space characters as the separators (called delimiters) between the tokens. To get a token, you call the nextToken() method:

```
String token = tokenizer.nextToken();
```

Each time you call nextToken(), you get the next token in the string. Usually, you extract tokens using a while loop. To control the while loop, you call the hasMoreTokens() method, which returns true as long as there are more tokens in the string. A typical tokenizing loop might look like this:

```
while (tokenizer.hasMoreTokens())
    String token = tokenizer.nextToken();
```

You can also determine how may tokens are in the string by calling the countTokens() method:

```
StringTokenizer tokenizer =
    new StringTokenizer("One Two Three Four Five");
int count = tokenizer.countTokens();
```

In this example, count will equal 5.

Listing 9.2 is an applet that tokenizes any string you enter. When you run the applet, enter a string into the first text box. Then, click the Tokenize button to get a list of tokens in the string (see Figure 9.2).

Listing 9.2   TokenApplet.java—An Applet that Tokenizes Strings

```
import java.awt.*;
import java.applet.*;
import java.util.StringTokenizer;

public class TokenApplet extends Applet
{
    TextField textField1;
    Button button1;

    public void init()
    {
        textField1 = new TextField(30);
        add(textField1);
        button1 = new Button("Tokenize");
        add(button1);
        resize(300, 300);
    }

    public void paint(Graphics g)
    {
```

```
        String str = textField1.getText();
        StringTokenizer tokenizer =
            new StringTokenizer(str);
        int row = 110;
        while (tokenizer.hasMoreTokens())
        {
            String token = tokenizer.nextToken();
            g.drawString(token, 80, row);
            row += 20;
        }
    }

    public boolean action(Event evt, Object arg)
    {
        if (arg == "Tokenize")
        {
            repaint();
            return true;
        }
        else
            return false;
    }
}
```

Part

II

Ch

9

FIG. 9.2
TokenApplet can extract
Individual words from a
string.

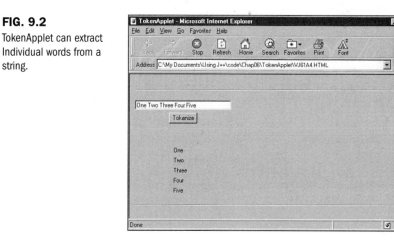

The *Random* Class

If you want to write game applets, you'll almost certainly need to generate random numbers.
Luckily, Java features the Random class, which makes handling random numbers easy. Table 9.3
shows the methods of the Random class.

Table 9.3 Methods of the *Random* Class

Method	Description
setSeed()	Sets the seed value for the random-number generator.
nextInt()	Gets the next random integer.
nextLong()	Gets the next random long integer.
nextFloat()	Gets the next random float (between 0.0 and 1.0).
nextDouble()	Gets the next random double (between 0.0 and 1.0).
nextGaussian()	Gets the next random Gaussian value.

Creating an object of the Random class is as easy as calling one of the class's constructors, like this:

```
Random random = new Random();
```

After you create the Random object, you call one of the class's methods to retrieve the type of random number you need.

Listing 9.3 is an applet that demonstrates using random numbers. When you run the applet using Visual J++, you see the window shown in Figure 9.3. At this point, the applet has chosen a random number between 1 and 100. Your task is to guess the number. To do this, enter a value into the text box and then press Enter. The program then compares your input with the number the program selected and displays a message indicating whether the value you entered was high, low, or right on the money. After you guess the random number, you can play again by clicking the Play Again button.

Listing 9.3 RandomApplet.java—A Number-Guessing Game that Uses Random Numbers

```java
import java.awt.*;
import java.applet.*;
import java.util.Random;

public class RandomApplet extends Applet
{
    Random random;
    int number;
    TextField textField;
    String displayString;
    Button button;

    public void init()
    {
        random = new Random();
        InitGame();
        textField = new TextField(20);
```

```
        add(textField);
        button = new Button("Play Again");
        add(button);
    }

    public void paint(Graphics g)
    {
        g.drawString(displayString, 30, 100);
    }

    public boolean action(Event event, Object arg)
    {
        if (event.target instanceof TextField)
        {
            String s = textField.getText();
            int selectedNumber = Integer.parseInt(s);

            if (selectedNumber < number)
                displayString = "Your number is too low.";
            else if (selectedNumber > number)
                displayString = "Your number is too high.";
            else
                displayString = "You guessed it!";

            repaint();

            return true;
        }
        else if (arg == "Play Again")
        {
            InitGame();
            return true;
        }
        else
            return false;
    }

    protected void InitGame()
    {
        number = random.nextInt();
        number = Math.abs(number % 100 + 1);
        displayString = "Guess a number from 1 to 100.";
        repaint();
    }
}
```

Of special importance in RandomApplet is how the program generates a random number between 1 and 100. First, in init(), the program creates the Random object:

```
random = new Random();
```

Then, the program calls InitGame(), which actually generates the random number. First, InitGame() gets the next random number in the series:

```
number = random.nextInt();
```

FIG. 9.3

RandomApplet is a number-guessing game.

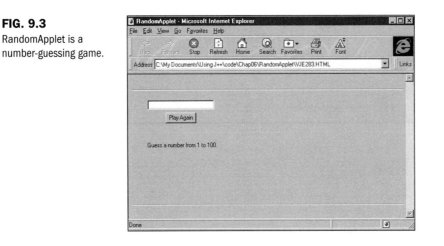

Then the program uses a formula to limit the returned integer to the desired range:

```
number = Math.abs(number % 100 + 1);
```

In the above line, Java divides the random number by 100 using the module operator. This results in the remainder of the division, yielding a number between 0 and 99. Adding 1 to the result brings the value into the desired range of 1 to 100. Notice that the entire calculation is enclosed in a call to the `Math` package's `abs()` method. That's because the returned integer could be negative, as well as positive. The `abs()` method ensures that you get only positive results.

After calculating the random number, `InitGame()` sets the string that will be displayed in the applet's window:

```
displayString = "Guess a number from 1 to 100.";
```

Finally, a call to `repaint()` causes the applet to repaint its display area, which causes the new display string to appear:

```
repaint();
```

A generalized Java formula for retrieving a random integer within a specific range is as follows:

```
int number = Math.abs(random.nextInt() % numValues + lowValue);
```

Here, `numValues` is the number of values included in the desired range and `lowValue` is the lowest value in the range. So, if you wanted a range of random integers from 30 to 75, you'd use this code line:

```
int number = Math.abs(random.nextInt() % 46 + 30);
```

The *java.net* Package

Because Java was designed mainly for writing Internet applications, it's no surprise that the language includes a package of classes for dealing with online communications. You got a brief look at writing Internet-capable applets in Chapter 7, "The Applet and Window Classes," where you had a chance to work with URL objects. The other classes in the java.net package are listed in Table 9.4 along with their descriptions.

Table 9.4   Classes of the *java.net* Package

Class	Description
ContentHandler	An abstract class that handles MIME (Multiple Internet Mail Extensions) objects.
DatagramPacket	Handles datagrams being sent via a DatagramSocket object.
DatagramSocket	Provides a simple datagram connection.
InetAddress	Represents a host name, along with its IP (Internet Protocol) number.
ServerSocket	Represents the server side of a TCP connection.
Socket	Represents a TCP (Transmission Control Protocol) connection.
SocketImpl	An abstract class that is responsible for creating specific network connections.
URL	Represents an Internet URL (Uniform Resource Locator).
URLConnection	An abstract class that retrieves content represented by a URL object.
URLEncoder	Used mainly to encode CGI script arguments.
URLStreamHandler	A base class for objects that handle streams for various Internet protocols.

As you can see from the table, to fully understand the classes in the java.net package, you must be well-versed in the ways of the Internet. Unfortunately, this chapter cannot provide such extensive background. The good news, though, is that you can get started with Java network programming fairly quickly. In the following sections, you'll see how.

Simple Internet Communications

Writing an applet or application that can connect to WWW pages is fairly easy when you use the URL class. To do this, you usually construct a URL object, using as the constructor's argument a string that represents the URL to which the user wants to connect. You then get the applet context (which represents the browser in which the applet is running), and finally call the context's showDocument() method.

Listing 9.4 is a simple applet that enables the user to type an URL into a text box and then connect to the URL by clicking a button. If the URL represents an actual Web site, the browser makes the connection and shows the site's contents. If the URL is incorrectly formatted, the applet displays an error message in the browser's status bar. Figure 9.4 shows the applet running, after the user has entered the URL to which he wants to connect. Figure 9.5 shows the browser after the connection has been made.

Listing 9.4   URLApplet.java—An Applet that Connects to Any URL the User Requests

```java
import java.awt.*;
import java.applet.*;
import java.net.*;

public class URLApplet extends Applet
{
    TextField textField;

    public void init()
    {
        Label label = new Label("Type an URL:");
        add(label);
        textField = new TextField(20);
        add(textField);
        Button button = new Button("Connect");
        add(button);
    }

    public boolean action(Event evt, Object arg)
    {
        String str;
        String error;

        if (arg == "Connect")
        {
            str = textField.getText();

            try
            {
                URL url = new URL(str);
                AppletContext context = getAppletContext();
                showStatus("Connecting to: " + str);
                context.showDocument(url);
            }
            catch (MalformedURLException e)
            {
                error = e.getMessage();
                showStatus(error);
            }
            catch (Exception e)
            {
                error = e.getMessage();
                showStatus(error);
```

```
            }
        }

        return true;
    }
}
```

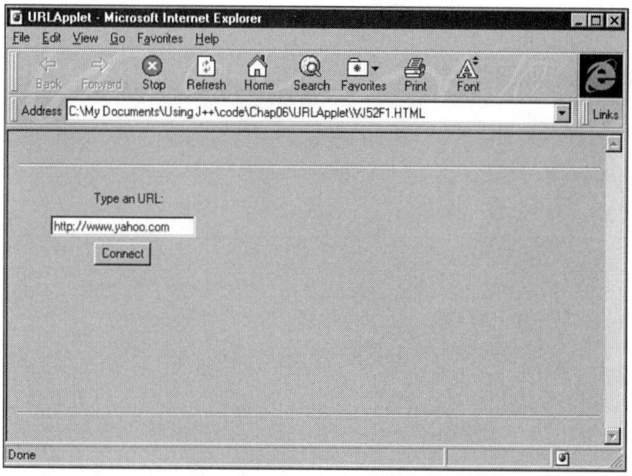

FIG. 9.4

The user can enter a URL into the applet's text box.

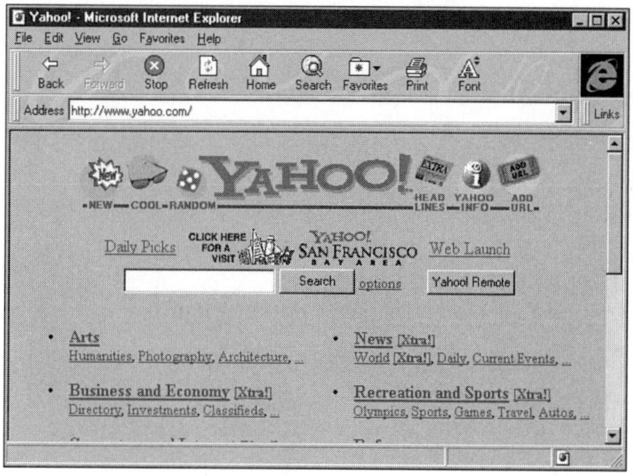

FIG. 9.5

The applet connects to whatever URL the user requests.

Understanding URLApplet

Although the URLApplet applet is small, there's a lot going on. In order to be sure that you understand all these goings on, you'll need to examine the program line by line. First, at the top of the source code, the applet imports the classes it needs:

```
import java.awt.*;
import java.applet.*;
import java.net.*;
```

If you remember, the `java.awt` package contains the classes that enable you to create a user interface, the `java.applet` contains the classes that represent a basic applet, and the `java.net` package contains the networking classes.

Next, the program declares `URLApplet` to be a subclass of the `Applet` class:

```
public class URLApplet extends Applet
```

As you learned previously, in Chapter 7, "The Applet and Window Classes," the applet class features the basic functionality of all applets. When you derive your applet from this class, your new class inherits this basic applet functionality.

After declaring the class, the program declares a single data member:

```
TextField textField;
```

This data member is an object of the `TextField` class, which represents a control into which the user can type a line of text. The control is declared as a data member of the class because you need to reference the control throughout the program, requiring it to be global to the class.

Next comes the `init()` member function, which is called when the applet first starts up. (For more information on `init()`, see the section "The Four Stages of an Applet's Life Cycle" in Chapter 7, "The Applet and Window Classes.") In the `init()` method, the program first adds a `Label` control to the applet's display:

```
Label label = new Label("Type an URL:");
add(label);
```

A `Label` control is nothing more than a line of text that cannot be edited by the user.

After adding the label to the applet, the program creates and adds the `TextField` object:

```
textField = new TextField(20);
add(textField);
```

The user will use this `TextField` object to enter the URL to which he wants to connect.

Another control the applet needs is the button that tells the applet to make its connection. That button is created and added to the applet like this:

```
Button button = new Button("Connect");
add(button);
```

N O T E   Notice that the `Label` and `Button` controls are local to the `init()` method. This means that when `init()` ends, the variable's `label` and `button` go out of scope and are no longer accessible. In the case of these particular controls, this isn't a problem. You don't need to reference the `Label` control anywhere else in the program, and you can check to see if the button was pressed by using its label "Connect." The important thing to know is that, even though the local variables for these objects exist only within `init()`, the controls themselves remain a part of the applet until the applet terminates. ▪

After `init()` exits, the applet is running and waiting for the user to do something with the controls. When the user types the URL, the `TextField` control handles all the user interaction related to editing. If the user presses Enter after typing text into the `TextField` control, Java calls the `action()` method. However, in this program, the `action()` method doesn't respond to events generated by the `TextField` control. It responds only to button clicks.

When the user clicks the Connect button, Java calls the applet's `action()` method. Inside this method, the applet first declares a couple of local strings:

```
String str;
String error;
```

The first string is used for handling the URL, and the second string is used to display error messages if the applet should generate an exception.

After declaring the local variables, the applet checks whether the button control caused the current event:

```
if (arg == "Connect")
```

If so, the program extracts the text from the `TextField` control:

```
str = textField.getText();
```

The program then enters a `try` program block in which it will attempt to create a `URL` object from the string and connect to the URL. If any of these actions generate an exception, the exception will be handled in the `catch` program blocks that follow the `try` program block.

Inside the `try` block, the program creates a `URL` object from the string that was extracted from the `TextField` control:

```
URL url = new URL(str);
```

The above line could generate a `MalformedURLException` exception if the user typed an improperly formatted URL. In this case, program execution will jump to the `catch` block that handles that exception.

If the URL is created successfully, the program gets the applet's context, which represents the browser in which the applet is running:

```
AppletContext context = getAppletContext();
```

The program then displays a message in the browser's status bar, telling the user that it's about to connect to the requested URL:

```
showStatus("Connecting to: " + str);
```

Finally, the applet performs the connection by calling the `AppletContext` object's `showDocument()` method:

```
context.showDocument(url);
```

If any method call in the `try` block generates an exception, the `catch` program blocks handle the exception. The first `catch` block specifically handles `MalformedURLException` exceptions, while the second `catch` block handles any other exception. In both cases, the program extracts the error message string from the exception object and displays it in the browser's status bar:

```
error = e.getMessage();
showStatus(error);
```

From Here...

Using only the URL class, you can create many different types of Internet-capable Java programs. However, the remaining classes in the `java.net` package enable you to perform more specific Internet tasks. Unfortunately, there isn't enough room in this book to provide a useful tutorial on Internet communications. Your local bookstore, however, should have several volumes that can help you learn more about this complex subject.

For more information on related topics, please refer to the following chapters:

■ Chapter 2, "Java and Visual J++," discusses network security issues that are important to Java programs.

■ Chapter 14, "Getting Started with Visual J++," includes information about other network topics such as HTML, VRML, plug-ins, and ActiveX controls.

CHAPTER 10

Packages and Interfaces

by Clayton Walnum

As you write more and more Java source code, you're going to start having a hard time finding the snippets of code you need for your current project. You may, for example, have a number of classes that are related in some way, yet are scattered in separate files making it difficult to determine exactly what you have. One solution to this problem is *packages*, which enable you to organize your classes into logical groups.

You may also have a number of classes that contain capabilities that you'd like to use in a newly derived class. However, Java does not allow *multiple inheritance*, which is deriving a single class directly from two or more classes simultaneously. To get around this deliberate limitation, Java uses something called *interfaces*, which enable the programmer to define capabilities for classes without implementing those capabilities until the classes that use the interface are defined. In this chapter, you study both *packages* and *interfaces*. ■

See how Java implements its own packages

All of Java's classes are organized into packages.

Learn about creating your own custom packages

When you create a set of related classes, you can organize them into a package, just as Java does with its own classes.

Discover how a package's `import` line reveals the directory structure under which the package is stored

When you import a package into a program, you're not only telling Java you want to use the package. You're also telling Java where to find the package.

Learn how to create interfaces

Although Java doesn't support multiple inheritance, you can get similar results by using Java's interfaces.

Packages

You may not realize it, but you've been using Java packages since the first applet you created. That's because all of the Java Developer's Kit's classes are organized into packages. You've been importing those packages into your source code with code similar to this:

```
import java.awt.*;
import java.applet.*;
```

If you examine either of these lines, you'll see that each starts with the word java followed by a package name and an asterisk, each element being separated by a dot. The use of the different names separated by the dots illustrates the hierarchy that Java's creators used when they created the Java packages. This hierarchy is used not only as a way of referring to class names in source code, but also as a way to organize the .class files that comprise a class library.

If you've ever installed the original Java Developer's Kit and looked in your Java\Lib folder, you found the Java folder, within which were the Awt and Applet folders. In the Awt and Applet folders were the .class files for the awt and applet packages. You can see that the import lines indicate the directory structure under which the package source-code files are stored. When Java's compiler runs into such import lines, it expects the directory structure to match the package's hierarchy.

In the preceding two sample import lines, the asterisks mean that Java should import all of the classes of the awt and applet packages into the applet you're writing. If you wanted to, you could streamline the import process by importing exactly the classes used in your source code. (When doing this, keep in mind that Java is case-sensitive.) You would do this by replacing the asterisk with the name of the class you want to import. For example, to import only the Button class from the awt package, you use this line:

```
import java.awt.Button;
```

However, because you frequently need to access more than a single class in a package, it's often more convenient to import all of the classes at once.

N O T E If you like, you can do without import statements. To do this, you need to use fully qualified package names when referring to a Java class. For example, to create a new button object, you could write java.awt.Button button = new java.awt.Button(label). As you can see, however, such program lines become unwieldy, which is why Java supports the import statement. ▨

Your Own Packages

As you write your own classes, you're going to want to organize the related classes into packages just as Java does. You do this by organizing your classes into the same sort of hierarchy. For example, you may want to start with a folder called MyPackages where you'll store the .class files comprising your class libraries. This folder should be in the folder where your main source-code files are located. You might use a folder called Classes for this purpose.

To add a class to a package, you put the following line at the top of the class's source code:

```
package PackageName;
```

Here, the keyword `package` tells Java that you want to add this class to a package. The name of this package will be `PackageName`. The package line must be the first line in the class's source code (except for blank lines or comments).

Creating a Simple Package

Suppose that you want to create a class called `DisplayClass` that returns a test string to be displayed in an applet. You want this class to be part of a package called Display. Listing 10.1 shows the source code for the `DisplayClass` class:

Listing 10.1   DisplayClass.java: The *DisplayClass* Class

```
package MyPackages.Display;

public class DisplayClass
{
    public String GetDisplayText()
    {
        return "Display Text";
    }
}
```

Part

II

Ch

10

N O T E   When you examine Listing 10.1, you may wonder how `DisplayClass` can reference Java's `String` class without including an `import` line at the top of the listing. The class gets away with this because Java automatically imports the java.lang package, where the `String` class is defined. ■

The first line of Listing 10.1 determines not only the name of the package, but also the way it must be stored on your hard drive. That is, the DisplayClass.class file must end up in a folder called Display, which itself must be in a folder called MyPackages. To compile DisplayClass.java, follow these steps:

1. Create a Classes folder on your hard drive's root directory. This is where Visual J++ will create the folders needed by each of the packages you create.

2. Type in Listing 10.1 and save it in the Classes folder, under the name DisplayClass.java. (If you don't want to type, you can copy the file from this book's CD-ROM.)

3. Select the File, Open command from Visual J++'s menu bar. Find and open the DisplayClass.java file, as shown in Figure 10.1.

FIG. 10.1

Load the DisplayClass.java file.

4. Select the <u>B</u>uild, <u>B</u>uild command from the menu bar. When Visual J++ asks whether you want to create a default project workspace (see Figure 10.2), select <u>Y</u>es.

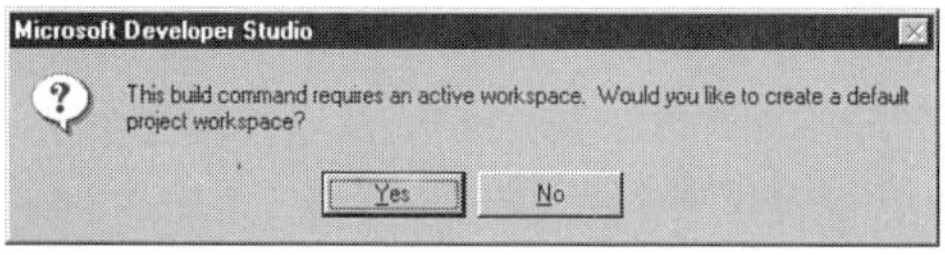

FIG. 10.2

You must create a default project workspace for the file.

If you now look in your Classes folder, you'll have not only the original source code file for the DisplayClass class, but also the DisplayClass.class file, which is the class's byte-code representation that Java can understand. Moreover, Visual J++ has created the folders that represent the package hierarchy. Specifically, your Classes folder now contains the MyPackages\Display folder hierarchy. Congratulations! You've just created your first package.

Using the New Package

Now that you've created a package, you'd probably like to use it in an applet. To do this, you must first import the class into the applet's source code file. You can then use the class in exactly the same way you've been using Java's classes throughout this book. Listing 10.2 is an applet, called PackageApplet, that demonstrates how to use your new package.

Listing 10.2   PackageApplet.java: An Applet that Uses Your New Package

```
import java.awt.*;
import java.applet.*;
import MyPackages.Display.DisplayClass;

public class PackageApplet extends Applet
{
    public void paint(Graphics g)
    {
        Font font = new Font("TimesRoman", Font.PLAIN, 24);
        g.setFont(font);
```

```
        DisplayClass myClass = new DisplayClass();
        String s = myClass.GetDisplayText();

        g.drawString(s, 60, 80);
    }
}
```

Notice how the third line in Listing 10.2 imports the `DisplayClass` class from the `Display` package. You also could have used the line `import MyPackages.Display.*`, as you did with the Java packages in the first two lines of the listing. Because there is currently only one class in the package, using the asterisk achieves exactly the same results as specifying the class's name in the `import` line. However, when you add other classes to the package, the asterisk will tell Java to include those classes as well.

To see how all this package material works with the PackageApplet applet, follow these steps:

1. Type in Listing 10.2, and save it in your Classes folder (the same folder that contains your new MyPackages folder). If you prefer, you can copy the listing from this book's CD-ROM.

2. Copy the DisplayClass.class file from the Classes directory to the Classes\MyPackages\Display directory, where the compiler will expect to find it.

3. Select the File, Open command from Visual J++'s menu bar. Find and open the PackageApplet.java file.

4. Select the Build, Build command from the menu bar. When Visual J++ asks whether you want to create a default project workspace, select Yes.

5. Select the Build, Execute command from the menu bar. When Visual J++ asks for the class file name, type **PackageApplet**, as shown in Figure 10.3.

FIG. 10.3

You must give Visual J++ the applet's name.

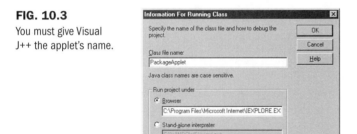

When you run the applet, you see the window shown in Figure 10.4. The text that's displayed in the applet is acquired by the call to the `DisplayClass` class's `GetDisplayText()` method. This class is part of your new `Display` class. When you run the applet, Java knows where to find the `Display` class because of the hierarchy of folders that mirror the MyPackages\Display\DisplayClass.class hierarchy.

FIG. 10.4
PackageApplet displays the text string obtained from a class defined in your new Display package.

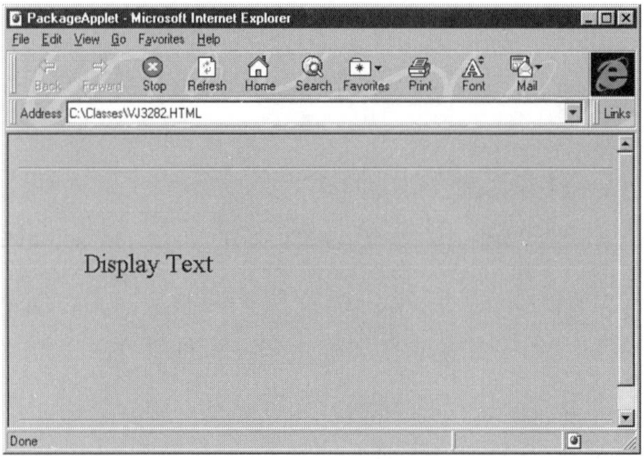

Extending the Package

Now that you have the package started, you can extend it simply by creating new classes that have the line package MyPackages.Display at the top of the source code. Thanks to the folder hierarchy you've developed (and that Java insists upon), the compiler can expect to find all the class files in the Display folder. You could have one or a hundred.

You can add new packages to your growing library by creating and compiling new classes and then storing the resultant .class files in the Display folder. Suppose, for example, that you want to start a new package called Shapes. The classes you want to add to this package are called Star, Hexagon, and Triangle. You'd then follow the steps given here:

1. Create the Star, Hexagon, and Triangle classes in separate source-code files, being sure to place the line package MyPackages.Shapes at the top of each file.

2. Compile each class as described previously.

3. Move the .class files into the Shapes folder that the compiler created.

4. Write the source code for the applet that uses your new Shapes package, storing the file in the Classes directory. Remember to put the line import MyPackages.Shapes.*; at the top of the file. The asterisk ensures that all classes in the Shapes package are imported into the program.

Interfaces

Whether supplied with Java or created by a programmer like yourself, packages are fairly easy to understand. They are little more than a way to organize related classes. Interfaces, on the other hand, are a bit harder to grasp. To really understand Java's interfaces, you have to know about something called *multiple inheritance*, which is not allowed in Java, but is often used in other object-oriented languages.

Multiple inheritance means creating a new class that inherits behavior directly from more than one superclass. To make this concept a little clearer, look at how you derive classes from superclasses in Java. For example, every applet you've created so far has been derived from Java's `Applet` class, like this:

```
public class AppletName extends Applet
```

The preceding line tells Java that you want to create a new class that inherits the data fields and methods of the `Applet` class. This is a sample of *single inheritance*. Now, suppose that you had a class of your own, called `MyClass`, that implemented some capabilities that you also want your new applet to inherit. In a language like C++, you simply add the class to a list of superclasses, like this:

```
public class AppletName extends Applet, MyClass
```

This would be an example of multiple inheritance if Java allowed such a thing. However, for many reasons, Java's designers decided that multiple inheritance was too cumbersome and unpredictable to be useful. They still liked the idea, though, of being able to declare a set of behaviors that can be inherited by one or more classes. So, they came up with *interfaces*.

The Basic Interface

An *interface* is very much like a class—with one important difference. None of the methods declared in an interface are implemented in the interface itself. Instead, these methods must be implemented in any class that uses the interface. In short, interfaces describe behaviors but do not detail how those behaviors will be carried out.

Interfaces are so much like classes, in fact, that they are declared in almost exactly the same way. You just replace the `class` keyword with the `interface` keyword, like this:

```
interface MyInterface
{
}
```

The preceding example is a complete interface, meaning that it can be compiled, after which other Java programs can reference it. You compile an interface exactly the same way you compile a class. First, you save the interface's source code in a file with the .java extension. Then you use Visual J++ to compile the source code into byte-code form. Just like a normal class, the byte-code file will have the .class extension.

Missing from the preceding sample interface are the methods that describe the interface's behaviors. In the sections that follow, you'll learn how to add this important element to an interface.

Creating an Interface

Suppose that instead of creating a full-fledged class out of your `Display` package's `DisplayClass` class, you want to make it an interface. (Yes, just like classes, you can make interfaces part of a package.) Listing 10.3 shows how the source code would be modified.

Part
II
Ch
10

Listing 10.3   DisplayInterface.java: Creating an Interface

```
package MyPackages.Display;

public interface DisplayInterface
{
    public String GetDisplayText();
}
```

The first line in Listing 10.3 is exactly like the first line in Listing 10.1, which shows the original class. The first line specifies that this interface is to be part of the MyPackages.Display package. The second line declares the interface. The only difference here is the use of the interface keyword in place of class and the new name, DisplayInterface.

Now, the real difference between a class and an interface becomes evident. Although Listing 10.4 declares the GetDisplayText() method, it doesn't actually implement the method. That is, you can see from the interface that GetDisplayText() is supposed to return a String object, but there isn't a clue as to how that String object is created or what it contains. Those details are left up to any class that decides to implement the interface.

But before you worry about implementing the interface in a class, you have to compile the interface source code. To do that, follow these steps:

1. Type in Listing 10.4 and save it in your Classes folder, under the name DisplayInterface.java. (If you don't want to type, you can copy the file from this book's CD-ROM.)

2. Select the File, Open command from Visual J++'s menu bar. Find and open the DisplayInterface.java file.

3. Select the Build, Build command from the menu bar. When Visual J++ asks whether you want to create a default project workspace, select Yes.

4. Copy the DisplayInterface.class file to the Classes\MyPackages\Display directory. When you write Java programs that use the interface, the compiler will expect to find the .class file in the Display directory.

Implementing an Interface

Now that you have your new interface compiled, you can implement it in a class. This means not only telling Java that you'll be using the interface, but also implementing the interface within the new class. That is, every method that is listed in the interface's declaration must be defined in the class's source code. Listing 10.4 is a new applet, called InterfaceApplet, that shows how to implement the DisplayInterface interface. When you compile and run this applet, you see exactly the same display as that produced by the original version, PackageApplet. Notice how the listing uses the implements keyword to tell Java that the applet will be implementing the DisplayInterface interface.

Listing 10.4   InterfaceApplet.java: An Applet that Implements the *DisplayInterface* Interface

```
import java.awt.*;
import java.applet.*;
import MyPackages.Display.DisplayInterface;

public class InterfaceApplet extends Applet
    implements DisplayInterface
{
    public void paint(Graphics g)
    {
        Font font = new Font("TimesRoman", Font.PLAIN, 24);
        g.setFont(font);

        String s = GetDisplayText();

        g.drawString(s, 60, 80);
    }

    public String GetDisplayText()
    {
        return "Display Text";
    }
}
```

Part

II

Ch

10

T I P   A class can implement as many interfaces as it needs to. To implement multiple interfaces, just list the interfaces after the `implements` keyword, separating each interface name from the others with a comma. Remember, however, that you must implement in your new class all the methods declared in all the interfaces you implement.

N O T E   There's quite a lot to learn about interfaces. However, due to the skill level of this book and the fact that you probably won't have to worry about interfaces until you're an experienced Java programmer, only the basics have been presented here. Chances are good that you won't have to create interfaces at all. It's just good to know they're there in case you need them. ■

From Here...

Packages are a great way to create and organize class libraries. The more Java code you write, the more you'll appreciate the ability to create your own packages. Although you may not need to use interfaces right away, interfaces are a unique element of the Java programming language. Although other object-oriented languages such as C++ allow multiple inheritance, only Java supports the idea of interfaces, which can be powerful tools when they're needed. For more information on related topics, please see the following:

- Chapter 4, "Java Language Basics," describes the basic elements of the Java language.

- Chapter 5, "Loops, Conditionals, and Arrays" extends the discussion of the Java language that began in Chapter 4.

- Chapter 7, "The Applet and Window Classes," shows how you can use Java's classes to create applets.

- Chapter 14, "Getting Started with Visual J++," gives you an overview of the Visual J++ programming environment.

- Chapter 16, "Creating an Applet with AppletWizard," shows you how to get a new applet started with only a few mouse clicks.

CHAPTER 11

Advanced Java Data Structures

by Clayton Walnum

Back in Chapter 9, "The Utility and Network Classes," you learned about some of the more useful classes within Java's util package. These classes included the Date, StringTokenizer, and Random classes. As you discovered, the util package also features a number of classes representing data structures that you might find useful in your Java programs. These data structures include dictionaries, hash tables, stacks, vectors, and bitsets, which are represented in Java by the Dictionary, Hashtable, Stack, Vector, and BitSet classes. In this chapter, you explore these advanced data-structure classes. ■

How to program stacks and vectors with Java

Java's Stack and Vector classes give you all the power you need to create and manipulate these useful data structures.

Learn about bitsets

Represented by Java's BitSet class, bitsets enable you to easily manage a group of Boolean values.

Discover how hash tables work

Java's Hashtable class can store a large number of elements and retrieve an element almost instantly by using a mathematical calculation.

How to design and create custom dictionary classes

A dictionary is a list of items, each item of which is associated with a key. A hash table is one type of dictionary, but you can create your own types, too.

Learn to use and write enumerators

Enumerators return, one by one, all the elements stored in a data structure.

Using the *Stack* Class

Stack is one of the easiest of the data-structure classes to use. As you may already know, a stack is a storage area arranged so that data can be accessed in a last-in/first-out order. That is, you can think of the stack data structure as a literal stack of objects placed one on top of the other, like a stack of dishes. In order to get to the dishes at the bottom of the stack, you have to remove the ones that you placed on top.

Creating a *Stack* Object

To create a Stack object, you first must be sure that you've included the class's definition in your program. Typically, that's done by including the entire util package, like this:

```
import java.util.*;
```

The util package also contains the other classes and interfaces you'll examine in this chapter. In other words, the util package must be included in a program that uses any of the special data structures covered in this chapter.

When you've imported the util package into your program, you can create the Stack object by calling the class's constructor:

```
Stack stack = new Stack();
```

The constructor creates an empty stack and requires no arguments.

Manipulating a *Stack* Object

Data is placed onto a stack using the push() method. The pop() method removes the top element from a stack. The Stack class also features a few other helpful methods, as shown in Table 11.1.

Table 11.1   Methods of the *Stack* Class

Method	Description
empty()	Returns true if the stack is empty.
peek()	Gets the object on the top of the stack without removing the object.
pop()	Removes an object from the stack.
push()	Places an object on the stack.
search()	Finds an object in the stack, returning the object's position in the stack.

Listing 11.1 is a simple applet that demonstrates how to use a Stack object. When you run the program with Visual J++, you see the window shown in Figure 11.1. The applet window shows the objects currently on the stack. To remove objects one-by-one from the stack, click the Pop Stack button. The popped object disappears from the stack and appears in the upper left of the applet's display (see Figure 11.2).

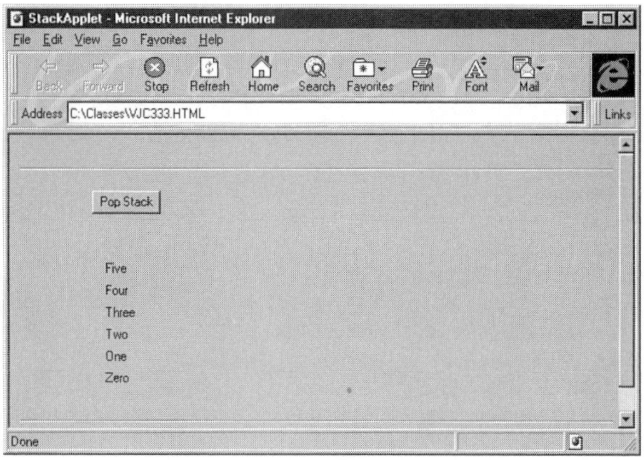

FIG. 11.1
The StackApplet applet displays the contents of its Stack object.

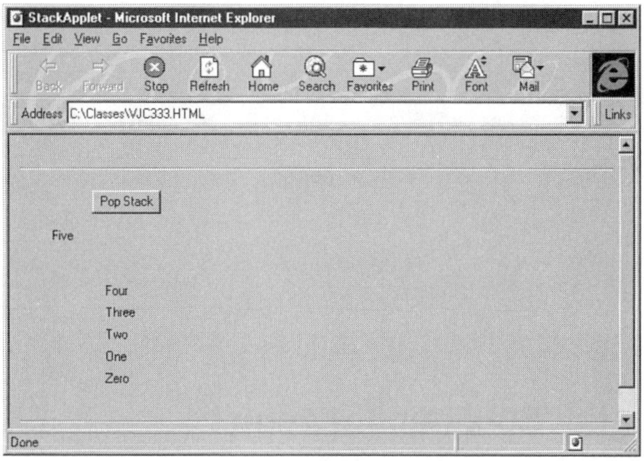

FIG. 11.2
Clicking the applet's button pops an object from the stack.

Listing 11.1 StackApplet.java—An Applet that Manipulates a *Stack* Object

```java
import java.applet.*;
import java.awt.*;
import java.util.*;

class StackApplet extends Applet
{
    Stack stack;
    String element;

    public void init()
    {
        stack = new Stack();
        stack.push("Zero");
        stack.push("One");
        stack.push("Two");
        stack.push("Three");
```

continues

Listing 11.1 Continued

```
        stack.push("Four");
        stack.push("Five");
        Button button = new Button("Pop Stack");
        add(button);
        element = "";
    }

    public void paint(Graphics g)
    {
        g.drawString(element, 30, 50);

        int row = 180;
        for (Enumeration enum = stack.elements(); enum.hasMoreElements();)
        {
            String str = (String) enum.nextElement();
            g.drawString(str, 80, row);
            row += -20;;
        }
    }

    public boolean action(Event event, Object arg)
    {
        element = (String) stack.pop();
        repaint();

        return true;
    }
}
```

Understanding the StackApplet Applet

The StackApplet is easy to understand. The applet declares a `Stack` object as a data field of the `StackApplet` class:

```
Stack stack;
```

The applet then creates the `Stack` object in its `init()` method:

```
stack = new Stack();
```

Once the `Stack` object is created, the applet can add items to the stack, which it does by calling the `Stack` object's `push()` method, as shown in Listing 11.2:

Listing 11.2 LST11_02.TXT—Adding Data to the Stack

```
stack.push("Zero");
stack.push("One");
stack.push("Two");
stack.push("Three");
stack.push("Four");
stack.push("Five");
```

In order to display the objects contained in the stack, the applet's `paint()` method creates an `Enumeration` object for the stack and displays the stack as shown in Listing 11.3.

Listing 11.3 LST11_03.TXT—Using the Stack's *Enumeration* Object

```
int row = 180;
for (Enumeration enum = stack.elements(); enum.hasMoreElements();)
{
    String str = (String) enum.nextElement();
    g.drawString(str, 80, row);
    row += -20;;
}
```

An `Enumeration` object enables you to read through the contents of a data structure. To get an `Enumeration` object for a stack, you call the stack's `elements()` method, which the class inherits from the `Vector` class (from which `Stack` is derived). You then use the enumerator's `hasMoreElements()` and `nextElement()` methods to read through the data structure. The `hasMoreElements()` returns `true` if the data structure contains more elements, whereas the `nextElement()` method returns the next object stored in the data structure. You'll learn how to create your own `Enumeration` objects later in this chapter, in the section titled "Writing the Enumeration Class."

When the user wants to pop an item off from the top of the stack, he clicks the Pop Stack button. This causes Java to call the applet's `action()` method, in which the applet pops an item from the stack:

```
element = (String) stack.pop();
```

The `element` object is a `String` data field of the class. The string contained in `element` is displayed on the screen in the applet's `paint()` method. To ensure that the string is displayed immediately, the `action()` method calls `repaint()` after changing the contents of the `element` string.

Part
II

Ch
11

Using the *Vector* Class

The `Vector` class represents nothing more than an array that can grow dynamically. That is, when you use the `Vector` class to create an array for your program, you don't have to worry about whether the array is large enough. If the `Vector` object runs out of space, it automatically enlarges itself to accommodate the new data.

Creating a *Vector* Object

To create a `Vector` object, call the class's constructor:

```
Vector vector = new Vector(10, 5);
```

This constructor takes two arguments. The first argument is the initial size of the array. The second argument is the number of elements that should be added to the array each time the array needs more space. The preceding example creates an array that holds 10 items before it overflows. When the array overflows, it automatically adds five additional elements to accommodate the data that didn't fit in the array.

Manipulating a *Vector* Object

To add new elements to a `Vector` object, you call the class's `addElement()` method, which adds the new element to the next available position in the array. You can also add elements using the `insertElementAt()` method, which places the element at the given location, pushing the following elements down in the array in order to make space. There are also several ways to remove or locate elements of the array. Table 11.2 lists the methods of the `Vector` class, along with their descriptions.

Table 11.2 Methods of the *Vector* Class

Method	Description
addElement()	Adds an element to the vector.
capacity()	Returns the capacity of the vector.
clone()	Creates a copy of the vector.
contains()	Returns `true` if the given object is in the vector.
copyInto()	Copies the contents of the vector into a conventional array.
elementAt()	Gets the element at the given index.
elements()	Returns an `Enumeration` object for the vector's elements.
ensureCapacity()	Increases the vector's size in order to ensure that the vector can hold a given number of elements.
firstElement()	Gets the first element of the vector.
indexOf()	Gets the index of the first occurrence of the given element in the vector.
insertElementAt()	Inserts an element at the given vector index.
isEmpty()	Returns `true` if the vector is empty.
lastElement()	Gets the last element in the vector.
lastIndexOf()	Gets the index of the last occurrence of the given element in the vector.
removeAllElements()	Removes all elements from the vector.
removeElement()	Removes the given element from the vector.
removeElementAt()	Removes the element at the given index.
setElementAt()	Sets the value of the element at the given index.

Method	Description
setSize()	Sets the size of the vector.
size()	Returns the size of the vector.
toString()	Returns a string representation of the Vector object.
trimToSize()	Sets the vector's capacity to its current size.

Listing 11.4 is an applet that demonstrates how to use a Vector object. When you run the program with Visual J++, you see the window shown in Figure 11.3. The applet window shows the objects currently stored in the vector. The first value is the index, and the second is the value stored at that index in the vector. To access an element in the vector, enter its index in the text box and press Enter. The selected element appears in the upper left of the applet's display (see Figure 11.4).

FIG. 11.3

The VectorApplet applet demonstrates how to use vectors.

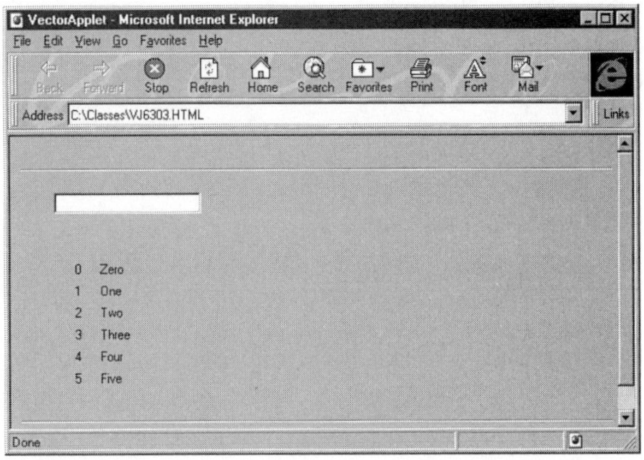

FIG. 11.4

Type an index to select an element in the vector.

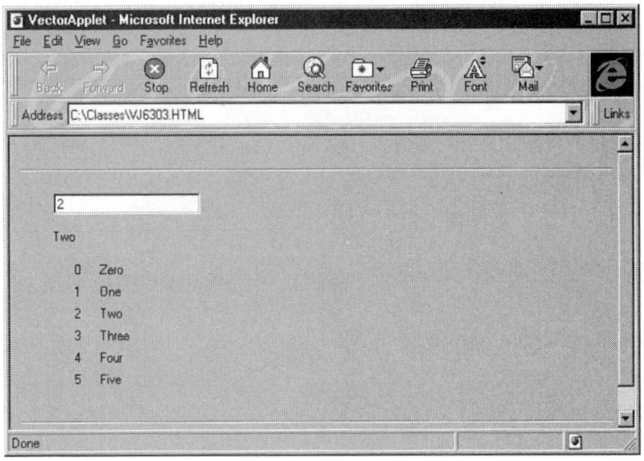

Listing 11.4 VectorApplet.java—An Applet that Demonstrates Vectors

```java
import java.applet.*;
import java.awt.*;
import java.util.*;

class VectorApplet extends Applet
{
    Vector vector;
    TextField textField;
    String element;

    public void init()
    {
        vector = new Vector(10, 10);
        vector.addElement("Zero");
        vector.addElement("One");
        vector.addElement("Two");
        vector.addElement("Three");
        vector.addElement("Four");
        vector.addElement("Five");
        textField = new TextField(20);
        add(textField);
        element = "";
    }

    public void paint(Graphics g)
    {
        g.drawString(element, 30, 50);

        int index = 0;
        for (Enumeration enum = vector.elements(); enum.hasMoreElements();)
        {
            String str = String.valueOf(index);
            str += "     " + (String) enum.nextElement();
            g.drawString(str, 50, 80+index*20);
            ++index;
        }
    }

    public boolean action(Event event, Object arg)
    {
        String str = textField.getText();
        int index = Integer.parseInt(str);

        try
        {
            element = (String) vector.elementAt(index);
        }
        catch (Exception e)
        {
            element = "No such element!";
        }

        repaint();
```

```
        return true;
    }
}
```

Understanding the *VectorApplet* Applet

Now that you've had a chance to experiment with the program, it's time to see how it works. The applet creates its `Vector` object, which is declared as a data field of the class, in the applet's `init()` method:

```
vector = new Vector(10, 10);
```

This vector will start out with a capacity of 10. If it should need to automatically increase its size, it will do so 10 elements at a time.

After creating the vector, the applet adds six elements, as shown in Listing 11.5.

Listing 11.5 LST11_05.TXT—Adding Elements to a Vector

```
vector.addElement("Zero");
vector.addElement("One");
vector.addElement("Two");
vector.addElement("Three");
vector.addElement("Four");
vector.addElement("Five");
```

In order to display the objects contained in the vector, the applet's `paint()` method creates an `Enumeration` object for the vector and displays the vector's elements as shown in Listing 11.6:

Listing 11.6 LST11_06.TXT—Using a Vector's *Enumeration* Object

```
int index = 0;
for (Enumeration enum = vector.elements(); enum.hasMoreElements();)
{
    String str = String.valueOf(index);
    str += "        " + (String) enum.nextElement();
    g.drawString(str, 50, 80+index*20);
    ++index;
}
```

When the user types an index into the text box and presses Enter, Java calls the applet's `action()` method, where the program retrieves the requested vector element by calling the `elementAt()` method with the given index. Notice that, as shown in Listing 11.7, the call to `elementAt()` is enclosed in a `try` program block, which enables the program to respond to an exception in the matching `catch` block. The exception will occur if the user requests an element at a nonexistent index.

Listing 11.7   LST11_07.TXT—Retrieving a Vector Element

```
try
{
    element = (String) vector.elementAt(index);
}
catch (Exception e)
{
    element = "No such element!";
}
```

Using the *BitSet* Class

There may be times when you need to keep track of a group of settings in a program. When these settings are Boolean in nature (that is, the settings can be only on or off), you can use a BitSet object in order to store the values of the settings. A BitSet object represents a set of single bits, each of which represents a single Boolean value. Using single bits to represent settings is memory efficient, and makes it easier to pass related settings between methods as a single data object.

Creating a *BitSet* Object

To create a BitSet object, you call the class's constructor, like this:

```
BitSet bitSet = new BitSet();
```

The constructor requires no arguments, creating an initial bitset containing 64 elements, all of which are initialized to false. There is also a form of the constructor that enables you to specify the number of bits in the bitset. However, the BitSet class creates bitsets with bit counts that are a multiple of 64, so specifying an initial number of bits is only necessary when you need more than 64 bits (pretty unlikely). Moreover, if you were to specify something like 96 bits, you'd end up with 128.

Manipulating a *BitSet* Object

Setting and clearing bits are the basic operations you perform on a bitset. You can accomplish these actions by calling the class's set() and clear() methods. You can retrieve the value of a bit by calling the get() method. However, the class also provides a number of methods for manipulating bits in various ways. Table 11.3 shows the BitSet class's methods, along with their descriptions.

Table 11.3   Methods of the *BitSet* Class

Method	Description
and()	Logically ANDs the bitset with a given bitset.
clear()	Clears the given bit.

Method	Description
clone()	Creates a copy of the bitset.
equals()	Returns `true` if the bitset is equal to the given bitset.
get()	Gets the value of a bit in the bitset.
hashCode()	Gets a hash code for the bitset.
or()	Logically ORs the bitset with a given bitset.
set()	Sets a bit in the bitset.
size()	Gets the size of the bitset.
toString()	Returns a string representation of the bitset.
xor()	Exclusively ORs the bitset with a given bitset.

Listing 11.8 is an applet that demonstrates how to use a `BitSet` object. When you run the program with Visual J++, you see the window shown in Figure 11.5. The applet window shows the values currently stored in the bitset. The first value in the display is the index, and the second is the Boolean value stored at that index in the bitset. To change an element in the bitset, enter its index in the text box and press Enter. When you do, the selected element toggles from `true` to `false`, or vice versa.

Part

II

Ch

11

FIG. 11.5

The BitSetApplet applet demonstrates how to use `BitSet` objects.

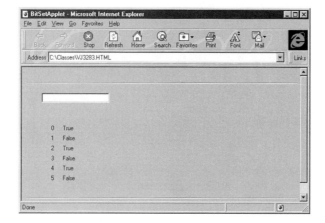

Listing 11.8   BitSetApplet.java—An Applet that Demonstrates *BitSet* Objects

```
import java.applet.*;
import java.awt.*;
import java.util.*;
```

continues

Listing 11.8   Continued

```java
class BitSetApplet extends Applet
{
    BitSet bitSet;
    TextField textField;

    public void init()
    {
        bitSet = new BitSet();
        bitSet.set(0);
        bitSet.clear(1);
        bitSet.set(2);
        bitSet.clear(3);
        bitSet.set(4);
        bitSet.clear(5);
        textField = new TextField(20);
        add(textField);
    }

    public void paint(Graphics g)
    {
        for (int index=0; index<6; ++index)
        {
            String str = String.valueOf(index) + "        ";
            boolean bit = bitSet.get(index);

            if (bit)
                str += "True";
            else
                str += "False";

            g.drawString(str, 50, 80+index*20);
        }
    }

    public boolean action(Event event, Object arg)
    {
        String str = textField.getText();
        int index = Integer.parseInt(str);

        boolean bit = bitSet.get(index);
        if (bit)
            bitSet.clear(index);
        else
            bitSet.set(index);

        repaint();

        return true;
    }
}
```

Understanding the *BitSetApplet* Applet

As with other applets in this chapter, BitSetApplet creates its data-structure object, which is declared as a data field of the class, in the applet's `init()` method:

```
bitSet = new BitSet();
```

This bitset will start out with 64 bits, although the program only uses a few of them.

After creating the bitset, the applet sets or clears six elements, as shown in Listing 11.9.

Listing 11.9   LST11_09.TXT—Setting and Clearing Bits in a Bitset

```
bitSet.set(0);
bitSet.clear(1);
bitSet.set(2);
bitSet.clear(3);
bitSet.set(4);
bitSet.clear(5);
```

In order to display the values of the bits contained in the bitset, the applet's `paint()` method loops through the bitset and displays the elements, as shown in Listing 11.10.

Listing 11.10   LST11_10.TXT—Displaying the Bitset's Values

```
for (int index=0; index<6; ++index)
{
    String str = String.valueOf(index) + "      ";
    boolean bit = bitSet.get(index);

    if (bit)
        str += "True";
    else
        str += "False";

    g.drawString(str, 50, 80+index*20);
}
```

When the user types an index into the text box and presses Enter, Java calls the applet's `action()` method, where the program toggles the requested bit by calling the `set()` or `clear()` method, depending on the current value of the bit, as shown in Listing 11.11.

Listing 11.11   LST11_11.TXT—Retrieving a Vector Element

```
boolean bit = bitSet.get(index);
if (bit)
    bitSet.clear(index);
else
    bitSet.set(index);
```

Part

II

Ch

11

Using the *Hashtable* Class

Hash tables are a great way to organize a large number of data elements so that any element can be retrieved almost instantly. For example, a customer database could use a hash table in order to locate customer records quickly. The great thing about a hash table is that the size of the table hardly affects how fast you can locate any particular record. This is because the table uses a set of mathematically generated keys. To locate a record almost instantly, the hash table only needs to reproduce the key mathematically in order to generate the index at which the item is located. Java uses the Hashtable class to implement this type of fast-search data storage.

Creating a *Hashtable* Object

As you've no doubt surmised, to create a Hashtable object, you call the class's constructor:

```
Hashtable hashtable = new Hashtable();
```

This constructor requires no arguments and creates an empty hash table. There is also a form of the constructor that enables you to specify the table's initial capacity.

Manipulating a *Hashtable* Object

As with most tables, the most important functions are the ability to store and retrieve objects to and from the table. The Hashtable class features the put() and get() methods for these important actions. The class also features a full set of methods that enable you to do everything from search for objects to remove objects from the table. Table 11.4 lists the methods of the Hashtable class.

Table 11.4 Methods of the *Hashtable* Class

Method	Description
clear()	Clears the hash table.
clone()	Makes a copy of the hash table.
contains()	Returns true if the given key represents a value in the table.
containsKey()	Returns true if the table contains the given key.
elements()	Returns an Enumerator object for the table's elements.
get()	Gets the table value associated with the given key.
isEmpty()	Returns true if the hash table is empty.
keys()	Returns an Enumerator object for the table's keys.
put()	Adds an item to the hash table.
remove()	Removes an element and its key from the table.
size()	Returns the table's size.

Method	Description
toString()	Returns a string representation of the table.

Listing 11.12 is an applet that demonstrates how to use a `Hashtable` object. When you run the program with Visual J++, you see the window shown in Figure 11.6. The applet window shows the values currently stored in the table. The first value in the display is the key, and the second is the `String` value associated with that key in the table. To retrieve an element from the table, enter its key in the text box and press Enter. When you do, the selected element appears in the upper-left portion of the applet (see Figure 11.7).

N O T E Notice that the items in the table are listed in a different order than the order in which they were added to the table. This is because the hash table performs a mathematical function (called a *hash function*) on the keys to determine where they'll be placed in the table. ■

FIG. 11.6

HashtableApplet demonstrates the use of Java's `Hashtable` class.

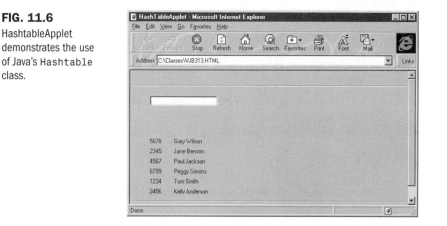

FIG. 11.7

You access the table by typing an item's key.

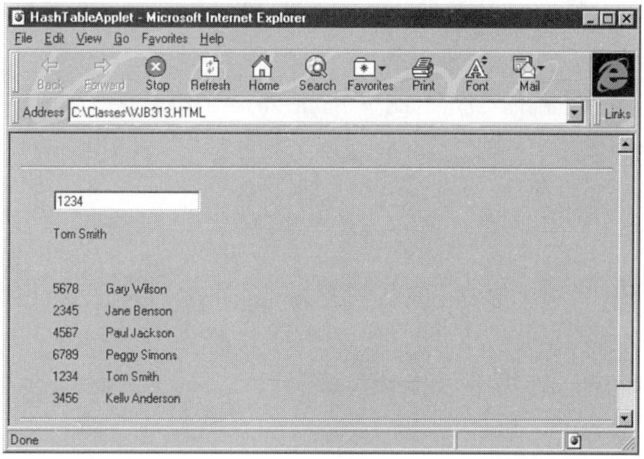

Listing 11.12 HashtableApplet.java—An Applet that Demonstrates Hashtable Objects

```java
import java.applet.*;
import java.awt.*;
import java.util.*;

class HashtableApplet extends Applet
{
    Hashtable hashtable;
    TextField textField;
    String element;

    public void init()
    {
        hashtable = new Hashtable();
        hashtable.put("1234", "Tom Smith");
        hashtable.put("2345", "Jane Benson");
        hashtable.put("3456", "Kelly Anderson");
        hashtable.put("4567", "Paul Jackson");
        hashtable.put("5678", "Gary Wilson");
        hashtable.put("6789", "Peggy Simons");
        textField = new TextField(20);
        add(textField);
        element = "";
    }

    public void paint(Graphics g)
    {
        g.drawString(element, 30, 50);

        int row = 100;
        for (Enumeration enum = hashtable.keys(); enum.hasMoreElements();)
        {
            String key = (String) enum.nextElement();
            g.drawString(key, 30, row);
            row += 20;
        }

        row = 100;
        for (Enumeration enum = hashtable.elements(); enum.hasMoreElements();)
        {
            String element = (String) enum.nextElement();
            g.drawString(element, 80, row);
            row += 20;
        }
    }

    public boolean action(Event event, Object arg)
    {
        String str = textField.getText();

        try
        {
            element = (String) hashtable.get(str);
        }
```

```
catch (NoSuchElementException e)
{
    element = "No such element!";
}

repaint();

return true;
    }
}
```

Understanding the *HashtableApplet* Applet

HashtableApplet creates its `Hashtable` object, which is declared as a data field of the class, in the applet's `init()` method:

```
hashtable = new Hashtable();
```

After creating the hash table, the applet adds six items to the table, as shown in Listing 11.13.

Listing 11.13   LST11_13.TXT—Adding Elements to the Hash Table

```
hashtable.put("1234", "Tom Smith");
hashtable.put("2345", "Jane Benson");
hashtable.put("3456", "Kelly Anderson");
hashtable.put("4567", "Paul Jackson");
hashtable.put("5678", "Gary Wilson");
hashtable.put("6789", "Peggy Simons");
```

The `put()` method's two arguments are a key and the value to be associated with that key. The object that you use as a key (in this case, a `String` object) must have implemented a `hashCode()` method that returns hash codes for the object. All of Java's data classes implement a `hashCode()` method, which is why strings work well as keys. When the `Hashtable` object adds an item to the table, it calls the key's `hashCode()` method and then uses the value returned from `hashCode()` to generate an index for the item in the table.

In order to display the keys and their associated values in the table, the applet's `paint()` method gets two enumerators from the table, one for the keys and one for the elements. The applet then uses these enumerators in order to display a table of keys and values, as shown in Listing 11.14:

Listing 11.14   LST11_14.TXT—Displaying the *Hashtable* Object's Keys and Values

```
int row = 100;
for (Enumeration enum = hashtable.keys(); enum.hasMoreElements();)
{
    String key = (String) enum.nextElement();
```

continues

Part

II

Ch

11

Listing 11.14   Continued

```
        g.drawString(key, 30, row);
        row += 20;
    }

    row = 100;
    for (Enumeration enum = hashtable.elements(); enum.hasMoreElements();)
    {
        String element = (String) enum.nextElement();
        g.drawString(element, 80, row);
        row += 20;
    }
```

When the user types a key into the text box and presses Enter, Java calls the applet's `action()` method, where the program calls the hash table's `get()` method to retrieve the value associated with the requested key, as shown in Listing 11.15.

Listing 11.15   LST11_15.TXT—Retrieving a *Hashtable* Element

```
try
{
    element = (String) hashtable.get(str);
}
catch (NoSuchElementException e)
{
    element = "No such element!";
}
```

Using the *Dictionary* Class

In a way, you've already used the `Dictionary` class in this chapter. Where? When you created hash tables in the previous section. The `Hashtable` class is derived from Java's abstract `Dictionary` class. The key word in the previous sentence is "abstract." The `Dictionary` class is an abstract class, which means that it declares a set of methods, but implements none of them. If you derive a class from `Dictionary`, you must be sure to implement all of `Dictionary`'s abstract methods. In practice, this is similar to using a Java interface, which also declares methods but doesn't implement them. The difference is that, while any class can implement as many interfaces as it likes, `Dictionary` can be used only as a superclass.

But what exactly is a dictionary? Simply, a dictionary is a table of keys and associated values. Think of an English language dictionary: The keys are the words, and the associated values are the words' definitions. A Java dictionary works exactly the same way, although you can use it for many other things. The hash table you used in the previous section is a dictionary, even though that dictionary's keys are organized mathematically rather than in numerical or alphabetical order.

Deriving a Class from *Dictionary*

As stated previously, `Dictionary` is an abstract class. In order to derive your own class from `Dictionary`, you have to implement in the new subclass all the abstract methods declared in the superclass. Java declares the `Dictionary` class as shown in Listing 11.16 (comments have been removed from the listing):

Listing 11.16   LST11_16.TXT—The Declaration of the *Dictionary* Class

```
package java.util;

public abstract
class Dictionary {
    abstract public int size();
    abstract public boolean isEmpty();
    abstract public Enumeration keys();
    abstract public Enumeration elements();
    abstract public Object get(Object key);
    abstract public Object put(Object key, Object value);
    abstract public Object remove(Object key);
}
```

So, to create your own dictionary class, you have to write implementations for the `size()`, `isEmpty()`, `keys()`, `elements()`, `get()`, `put()`, and `remove()` methods. Table 11.5 lists these methods and what they need to do. Notice that two of the methods—`keys()` and `elements()`— return enumerators, which means you also have to implement the `Enumeration` interface.

Table 11.5   Abstract Methods of the *Dictionary* Class

Method	Description
size()	Returns the size (number of elements) of the dictionary.
isEmpty()	Returns `true` if the dictionary is empty.
keys()	Returns an enumerator object for the dictionary's keys.
elements()	Returns an enumerator object for the dictionary's elements.
get()	Gets the value associated with a given key.
put()	Puts a new value in the dictionary.
remove()	Removes a key and element from the dictionary.

Suppose that you want to create a class called `CustomerDictionary` that uses customer IDs as keys and customer names as values. This is similar to what you used a hash table for. (In fact, remember that a hash table is a special type of dictionary.) Listing 11.17 shows how you might write the `CustomerDictionary` class.

Part

II

Ch

11

Listing 11.17   CustomerDictionary.java—A Class Derived from Dictionary

```java
import java.util.*;

class CustomerDictionary extends Dictionary
{
    Vector keyVector;
    Vector elementVector;

    public CustomerDictionary()
    {
        keyVector = new Vector(10, 10);
        elementVector = new Vector(10, 10);
    }

    public int size()
    {
        return keyVector.size();
    }

    public boolean isEmpty()
    {
        return keyVector.isEmpty();
    }

    public Enumeration keys()
    {
        return new CustomerDictionaryEnumerator(keyVector);
    }

    public Enumeration elements()
    {
        return new CustomerDictionaryEnumerator(elementVector);
    }

    public Object get(Object key)
    {
        int index = keyVector.indexOf(key);
        if (index != -1)
            return elementVector.elementAt(index);
        else
            throw new NoSuchElementException("CustomerDictionary");

    }

    public Object put(Object key, Object value)
    {
        if ((key == null) || (value == null))
            return new Integer(-1);
        keyVector.addElement(key);
        elementVector.addElement(value);
        return new Integer(keyVector.indexOf(key));
    }

    public Object remove(Object key)
    {
```

```
        int index = keyVector.indexOf(key);
        if (index != -1)
        {
            keyVector.removeElementAt(index);
            elementVector.removeElementAt(index);
        }
        return new Integer(index);
    }
}
```

Deciding on a Type of Storage

When writing the CustomerDictionary class, the first thing you must decide is how you're going to store the values that make up the dictionary. If you look at the top of the class's listing, you'll see that the class has two data fields declared like this:

```
Vector keyVector;
Vector elementVector;
```

The class will use two Vector objects—one for storing keys and one for storing values. The keys and values will be stored in the same order, so that an index in one vector matches up with the entry in the other vector at the same index. The program creates the two vectors in the class's constructor, like this:

```
keyVector = new Vector(10, 10);
elementVector = new Vector(10, 10);
```

Implementing *size()* and *isEmpty()*

Now, the size() and isEmpty() methods are easy to implement. In the case of size(), the class only needs to return the size of one of the vectors:

```
return keyVector.size();
```

In the case of isEmpty(), the class can return the result of a call to the vector's isEmpty() method:

```
return keyVector.isEmpty();
```

Implementing *keys()* and *elements()*

Implementing the keys() and elements() methods is just a matter of returning an enumerator object for the key vector and the element vector, respectively. The program returns the key enumerator like this:

```
return new CustomerDictionaryEnumerator(keyVector);
```

And the program returns the element enumerator like this:

```
return new CustomerDictionaryEnumerator(elementVector);
```

What's a CustomerDictionaryEnumerator? Ah! Now you've discovered the tricky part. In order to return an enumerator for your custom dictionary class, you have to write the class that

Part

II

Ch

11

implements the enumerator. You'll learn how to do this later in the chapter, in the section called "Writing the Enumerator Class." For now, just know that `keys()` and `elements()` both return `CustomerDictionaryEnumerator` objects.

Implementing *get()*

The `get()` method enables a program to retrieve an element from the dictionary given the element's key. The method returns the element as an `Object` and its single parameter is the key as an `Object`. The method's signature looks like this:

```
public Object get(Object key)
```

Obviously, how you implement the `get()` method depends on how you've chosen to store data in your dictionary. In the case of `CustomerDictionary`, the program must find the index of the given key in the vector that holds the keys, `keyVector`. That index can then be used with the vector that holds the matching elements, `elementVector`, to retrieve the requested element. In `CustomerDictionary`, the code that gets the index looks like this:

```
int index = keyVector.indexOf(key);
```

Thanks to the `Vector` class, getting the key's index is just a matter of calling the class's `indexOf()` method. If the index comes back as -1, the requested key doesn't exist. In that case, `CustomerDictionary` throws an exception:

```
throw new NoSuchElementException("CustomerDictionary");
```

With the index in-hand, the program can now get the associated element by calling the `elementVector` object's `elementAt()` method, like this:

```
return elementVector.elementAt(index);
```

Implementing *put()*

The `put()` method enables a program to add an element to the dictionary given the element's key and value. The method returns the element's index as an `Object` (in this case, an `Integer` object), and its parameters are the key and the value as `Objects`. The method's signature looks like this:

```
public Object put(Object key, Object value)
```

Again, how you implement the `put()` method depends on how you've chosen to store data in your dictionary. In the case of `CustomerDictionary`, the program must add the given key to the `keyVector` object and must add the given value to the `elementVector` object.

First, if either the key or value is null, the program returns -1 as the index:

```
if ((key == null) || (value == null))
    return new Integer(-1);
```

If both the key and value are not null, `CustomerDictionary` can add the key and element to the appropriate vector objects by calling the vectors' `addElement()` methods:

```
keyVector.addElement(key);
elementVector.addElement(value);
```

Because the addElement() method adds the new items to the end of a vector, the key and value indexes will be the same, something that CustomerDictionary relies upon to locate values based on the key.

The CustomerDictionary put() method finally returns the index used to store both the key and the value:

```
return new Integer(keyVector.indexOf(key));
```

The program can check the value returned from put() to ensure that the new entry was added successfully.

Implementing *remove()*

The last method CustomerDictionary must implement is remove(), which enables a program to remove an element from the dictionary given the element's key. The method returns the element's old index as an Integer. Its single parameter is the key of the element to remove. The method's signature looks like this:

```
public Object remove(Object key)
```

To remove an element, CustomerDictionary must find the index of the given key, which it does by calling keyVector's indexOf() method:

```
int index = keyVector.indexOf(key);
```

If the returned index isn't -1, the vector found the requested key. CustomerDictionary can then use the returned index to locate and remove the key and element from the vectors:

```
keyVector.removeElementAt(index);
elementVector.removeElementAt(index);
```

The method then returns the old index:

```
return new Integer(index);
```

The user can examine the returned index to see whether the item was successfully removed from the dictionary. A value of -1 indicates a failure.

Writing the *Enumerator* Class

At this point, you have your custom dictionary class written. However, you may recall that two of the methods in that class—keys() and elements()—must return enumerator objects. Specifically, these methods must return objects of the CustomerDictionaryEnumerator class—a class you've yet to write.

Don't sweat it, though. The enumeration class is easier to write than you might suspect, if for no other reason than that you have to implement only two methods. The enumerator class must implement the Enumeration interface, which is shown in Listing 11.18. (All comments have been removed from the listing for the sake of clarity and brevity.)

Part II

Ch 11

Listing 11.18   LST11_18.TXT—The Enumeration Interface

```
package java.util;

public interface Enumeration {
    boolean hasMoreElements();
    Object nextElement();
}
```

As you can see from the listing, to create your enumerator class, you only need to implement the `hasMoreElements()` and `nextElement()` methods. The `hasMoreElements()` method returns `true` if the object that's being enumerated has more elements to enumerate, and the `nextElement()` method returns the next element in the object. You saw how these methods worked when you enumerated objects back in the section titled "Manipulating a Hashtable Object." Listing 11.19 is the code for the `CustomerDictionaryEnumerator` class.

Listing 11.19   CustomerDictionaryEnumerator.java—A Custom *Enumerator* Class

```
import java.util.*;

class CustomerDictionaryEnumerator implements Enumeration
{
    int index;
    Vector vector;

    CustomerDictionaryEnumerator(Vector vector)
    {
        CustomerDictionaryEnumerator.vector = vector;
        index = 0;
    }

    public boolean hasMoreElements()
    {
        if (index < vector.size())
            return true;
        return false;
    }

    public Object nextElement()
    {
        if (index < vector.size())
            return vector.elementAt(index++);
        else
            throw new NoSuchElementException
                        ("CustomerDictionaryEnumerator");
    }
}
```

The `CustomerDictionaryEnumerator` class contains two data fields, `index` and `vector`. The `index` field, which is an integer, holds the index of the current element in the vector. The vector field, which is an object of the `Vector` class, holds the vector being enumerated. This vector can be `CustomerDictionary`'s keys or elements vector, depending upon which is currently being enumerated.

The `hasMoreElements()` method simply returns `true` if the current index is less than the vector's size. The `nextElement()` method returns the currently indexed element and then increments the index. That's all there is to it!

Using the Custom Dictionary Class

Now that you've gone through all the work of designing and implementing a custom dictionary class, you'll want to see your labor yield results. Listing 11.20 is an applet that puts together the dictionary and enumerator classes with a test applet called DictionaryApplet. When you run the applet, you see the window shown in Figure 11.8. The display shows the dictionary's enumerated keys and elements. Type a key into the text box, and press Enter. The selected element appears in the upper left of the applet's display (see Figure 11.9).

FIG. 11.8
DictionaryApplet uses the custom dictionary class to manage a simple customer database.

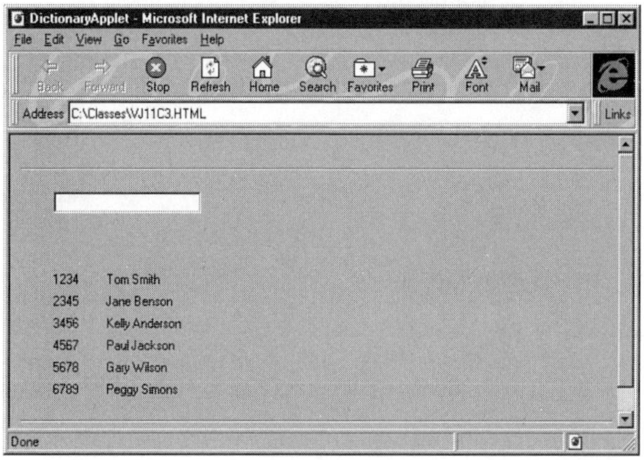

Part II

Ch 11

FIG. 11.9
The applet can retrieve any element given the element's key.

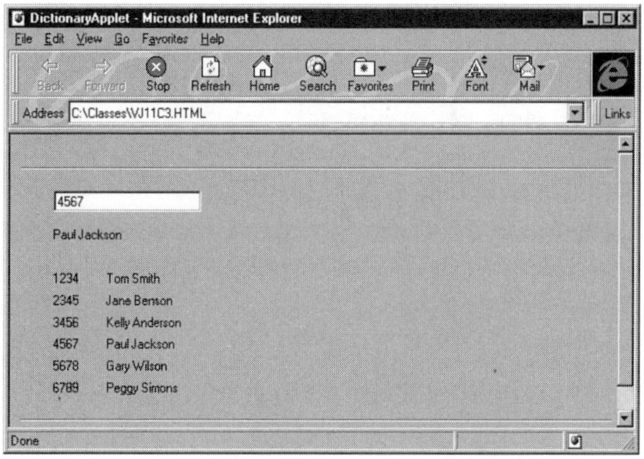

Listing 11.20   DictionaryApplet.java—An Applet that Uses the Custom Dictionary Class

```java
import java.applet.*;
import java.awt.*;
import java.util.*;

class DictionaryApplet extends Applet
{
    CustomerDictionary customerDictionary;
    TextField textField;
    String element;

    public void init()
    {
        customerDictionary = new CustomerDictionary();
        customerDictionary.put("1234", "Tom Smith");
        customerDictionary.put("2345", "Jane Benson");
        customerDictionary.put("3456", "Kelly Anderson");
        customerDictionary.put("4567", "Paul Jackson");
        customerDictionary.put("5678", "Gary Wilson");
        customerDictionary.put("6789", "Peggy Simons");
        textField = new TextField(20);
        add(textField);
        element = "";
    }

    public void paint(Graphics g)
    {
        g.drawString(element, 30, 50);

        int row = 90;
        for (Enumeration enum = customerDictionary.keys();
                enum.hasMoreElements();)
        {
            String key = (String) enum.nextElement();
            g.drawString(key, 30, row);
            row += 20;
        }

        row = 90;
        for (Enumeration enum = customerDictionary.elements();
                enum.hasMoreElements();)
        {
            String element = (String) enum.nextElement();
            g.drawString(element, 80, row);
            row += 20;
        }
    }

    public boolean action(Event event, Object arg)
    {
        String str = textField.getText();
```

```
        try
        {
            element = (String) customerDictionary.get(str);
        }
        catch (NoSuchElementException e)
        {
            element = "No such element!";
        }

        repaint();

        return true;
    }
}

class CustomerDictionary extends Dictionary
{
    Vector keyVector;
    Vector elementVector;

    public CustomerDictionary()
    {
        keyVector = new Vector(10, 10);
        elementVector = new Vector(10, 10);
    }

    public int size()
    {
        return keyVector.size();
    }

    public boolean isEmpty()
    {
        return keyVector.isEmpty();
    }

    public Enumeration keys()
    {
        return new CustomerDictionaryEnumerator(keyVector);
    }

    public Enumeration elements()
    {
        return new CustomerDictionaryEnumerator(elementVector);
    }

    public Object get(Object key)
    {
        int index = keyVector.indexOf(key);
        if (index != -1)
            return elementVector.elementAt(index);
        else
            throw new NoSuchElementException("CustomerDictionary");

    }
```

Part

II

Ch

11

continues

Listing 11.20   Continued

```java
    public Object put(Object key, Object value)
    {
        if ((key == null) || (value == null))
            return new Integer(-1);
        keyVector.addElement(key);
        elementVector.addElement(value);
        return new Integer(keyVector.indexOf(key));
    }

    public Object remove(Object key)
    {
        int index = keyVector.indexOf(key);
        if (index != -1)
        {
            keyVector.removeElementAt(index);
            elementVector.removeElementAt(index);
        }
        return new Integer(index);
    }
}

class CustomerDictionaryEnumerator implements Enumeration
{
    int index;
    Vector vector;

    CustomerDictionaryEnumerator(Vector vector)
    {
        CustomerDictionaryEnumerator.vector = vector;
        index = 0;
    }

    public boolean hasMoreElements()
    {
        if (index < vector.size())
            return true;
        return false;
    }

    public Object nextElement()
    {
        if (index < vector.size())
            return vector.elementAt(index++);
        else
            throw new NoSuchElementException
                        ("CustomerDictionaryEnumerator");
    }

}
```

From Here...

Now that you know more about Java's powerful data-structure classes, you're ready to manage data in new and wonderful ways. Each of the discussed data structures has its own special use. With a little experience, you'll be using Java data structures like a true Java guru. For more information on related topics, please refer to the following chapters:

- Chapter 4, "Java Language Basics," describes the basic elements of the Java language.

- Chapter 5, "Loops, Conditionals, and Arrays," describes how Java arrays, another important data structure, behave.

- Chapter 9, "The Utility and Network Classes," describes a few other classes you'll find in the util package.

- Chapter 14, "Getting Started with Visual J++," gives you an overview of the Visual J++ programming environment.

- Chapter 16, "Creating an Applet with AppletWizard," shows you how to get a new applet started with only a few mouse clicks.

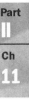

Part

II

Ch

11

CHAPTER 12

Threads

by Clayton Walnum

As you know, Windows 95 (and other modern operating systems) can run several programs simultaneously. This ability is called *multitasking*. What you may not know is that many of today's operating systems also allow threads—separate processes that are a step down from a complete application.

A thread is similar to a subprogram. An applet can create several threads—several different flows of execution—and run them concurrently. This is basically multitasking inside multitasking: the user knows that he or she can run several applications at a time; and the programmer knows that each application can run several threads at a time. In this chapter, you'll learn how to create and manage threads in your own applets. ■

Learn about the two techniques for creating threads

There are two ways you can create additional threads from your applets: by converting an existing class, or by writing a new class derived from Java's Thread class.

See how to manage threads in an applet

Threads must be initialized, started, and stopped, depending on what part of the applet's life cycle is executing.

Discover how multiple threads can share resources

When two or more threads are accessing the same resources, the threads must be carefully synchronized.

Two Kinds of Threads

In Java, you can create threads in two ways. The simplest way is to take an existing class and turn it into a thread. You do this by modifying the class so that it implements the Runnable interface, which declares the run() method required by all types of threads. (The run() method contains the code to be executed by a thread.) In Chapter 10, "Packages and Interfaces," you learned how interfaces in Java enable you to add capabilities to classes simply by implementing the interface in that class. Now, you get a chance to apply this knowledge to concrete situations.

The second way to create a thread is to write a completely separate class derived from Java's Thread class. Because the Thread class itself implements the Runnable interface, it already contains a run() method. However, Thread's run() method doesn't do anything. You usually have to override the method in your own class in order to create the type of thread you want.

Converting a Class to a Thread

As mentioned in the preceding section, the first way to create a thread is to convert a class to a thread. To do this, you must perform several steps, as listed here:

1. Declare the class as implementing the Runnable interface.
2. Implement the run() method.
3. Declare a Thread object as a data field of the class.
4. Create the Thread object and call its start() method.
5. Call the thread's stop() method to destroy the thread.

The following sections look at each of these steps in detail.

Declaring the Class as Implementing the *Runnable* Interface

As you can see in Step 1 in the preceding section, to create a thread from a regular class, the class must first be declared as implementing the Runnable interface. For example, if your class is declared as

```
public class MyApplet extends Applet
```

you must change that declaration to

```
public class MyApplet extends Applet
    implements Runnable
```

Implementing the *run()* Method

Now, because you've told Java you're about to implement an interface, you must implement every method in the interface. In the case of Runnable, that's easy because there's only one method, run(), the basic implementation of which looks like this:

```
public void run()
{
}
```

When you start your new thread, Java calls the thread's run() method, so it is in run() where all the action takes place. The preceding example of the run() method is the minimum you need to compile the new source code for the thread. However, in a real program, you'll add code to run() so that the thread works how you want.

Declaring a *Thread* Object

The next step is to declare a Thread object as a data field of the class, like this:

```
Thread thread;
```

The thread object will hold a reference to the thread with which the applet is associated. You will be able to access the thread's methods through this object.

Creating and Starting the *Thread* Object

Now it's time to write the code that creates the thread and gets it going. Assuming that your new threaded class is an applet, you'll often want to create and start the thread in the applet's start() method, as shown in Listing 12.1.

Listing 12.1   LST12_01.TXT: Creating and Starting a *Thread* Object

```
public void start()
{
    thread = new Thread(this);
    thread.start();
}
```

N O T E Back in Chapter 7, "The Applet and Window Classes," you learned that start() is the method that represents the applet's second life-cycle stage. Java calls your applet's life-cycle methods in this order: init(), start(), stop(), and destroy(). Java calls the start() method whenever the applet needs to start running, usually when it's first loaded or when the user has switched back to the applet from another Web page. ▓

Look at the call to the Thread constructor in Listing 12.1. Notice that the constructor's single argument is the applet's this reference. This is how Java knows with which class to associate the thread. After the call to the constructor, the applet calls the Thread object's start() method, which starts the thread running. Java then calls the thread's run() method, where the thread's work gets done.

Stopping the Thread

When the thread's run() method ends, so does the thread. However, because threads tend to run for quite a while, controlling things like animation in the applet, the user is likely to switch away from your applet before the thread stops. In this case, it's up to your applet to stop the thread. Because Java calls an applet's stop() method whenever the user switches away from the applet, the stop() method is a good place to stop the thread, as shown in Listing 12.2.

Listing 12.2 LST12_02.TXT: Stopping a Thread

```
public void stop()
{
    thread.stop();
}
```

Using a Thread in an Applet

To understand about threads, you really have to dig in and use them. In this section, you'll put together an applet that associates itself with a `Thread` object and runs the thread to control a very simple animated display. The animation in this case is not of your Saturday morning cartoon variety, but rather only a changing number that proves that the thread is running. Listing 12.3 is the applet in question, which is called ThreadApplet. Figure 12.1 shows the applet running under Internet Explorer 3.0.

Listing 12.3 ThreadApplet.java: Using a Thread in an Applet

```
import java.awt.*;
import java.applet.*;

public class ThreadApplet extends Applet
  implements Runnable
{
    Thread thread;
    int count;
    String displayStr;
    Font font;

    public void start()
    {
        font = new Font("TimesRoman", Font.PLAIN, 72);
        setFont(font);

        count = 0;
        displayStr = "";

        thread = new Thread(this);
        thread.start();
    }

    public void stop()
    {
        thread.stop();
    }

    public void run()
    {
        while (count < 1000)
        {
```

```
            ++count;
            displayStr = String.valueOf(count);
            repaint();

            try
            {
                thread.sleep(100);
            }
            catch (InterruptedException e)
            {
            }
        }
    }

    public void paint(Graphics g)
    {
        g.drawString(displayStr, 50, 130);
    }
}
```

FIG. 12.1
ThreadApplet uses
a thread to count
to 1,000.

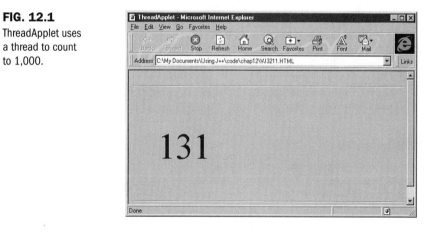

There are a couple of interesting things in ThreadApplet that you should be aware of. First, notice that in run(), the thread loops one thousand times, after which the while loop ends. When the while loop ends, so does the run() method. This means that when you run ThreadApplet, if you let it count all the way to one thousand, the thread ends on its own. However, what if you switch to a different Web page before ThreadApplet has counted all the way to one thousand? Then, Java calls the applet's stop() method, which ends the thread by calling the thread's stop() method.

The next point of interest is what's going on inside run(). At the beginning of the loop, the program increments the counter, converts the counter's value to a string, and then repaints the applet so that the new count value appears in the window. But what's all that nonsense after the call to repaint()? That's where the thread not only times the animation, but also relinquishes the computer so that other threads get a chance to run. Simply, the call to the thread's sleep() method suspends the thread for the number of milliseconds given as its single argument. In this case, the sleep time is 100 milliseconds, or one-tenth of a second. If you want the animation to run faster, change the 100 to a smaller value. To count slower, change the 100 to a larger value.

> **CAUTION**
>
> It's important that your threads not dominate the computer's processor for longer than necessary. This is because other threads and processes are probably in competition for the processor at the same time. If your thread will be running for a while, you should call the sleep() or yield() methods in order to give other processes a chance to run. This is more important on some systems than others, but because you can't know for sure which system your applet will be running on, be a considerate thread programmer.

Notice that the call to sleep() is enclosed in a try block and followed by a catch block that's watching for InterruptedException exceptions. You have to catch this exception because the sleep() method throws it. If you fail to catch the exception, your program will not compile.

Deriving a Class from *Thread*

The second way to create a thread is to derive a new class from Thread. Then, in your applet's class, you create and start a thread object of your thread class. This leaves you with two processes going simultaneously—the applet and the thread object created in the class. By giving the thread class access to data and methods in the applet, the thread can easily communicate with the applet in order to perform whatever tasks it was written for.

Creating a Thread Class

Suppose that you want to write the same sort of applet as that shown in Listing 12.3, but now you want a separate thread to control the counting process. Listing 12.4 shows how you might write the new class for the thread. (Don't try to compile this code yet. You'll use it in the next example in this chapter.)

Listing 12.4   MyThread.java: A Class Derived from *Thread*

```
public class MyThread extends Thread
{
    ThreadApplet2 applet;
    int count;

    MyThread(ThreadApplet2 applet)
    {
        this.applet = applet;
    }

    public void run()
    {
        count = 0;
        while (count < 1000)
        {
```

```
        ++count;
        applet.displayStr = String.valueOf(count);
        applet.repaint();

        try
        {
            sleep(100);
        }
        catch (InterruptedException e)
        {
        }
    }
  }
}
```

The first thing to notice in this thread class is that its constructor takes as a single argument a reference to a ThreadApplet2 object—the applet from which you'll be running this thread. The thread needs this reference to communicate with the applet.

Next, look at run(). The thread still counts from zero to one thousand, but now it accesses the applet object to create the display string and repaint the applet. In the original version of the program, the thread was directly associated with the class, rather than a completely separate process.

Now that you have a new thread class, you'll want to call it up for active duty. You'll do that in the next example.

Using a Separate Thread in an Applet

Now, you'll put that new thread class to work. To do this, you must have an applet that creates an object from the new thread class and calls that object's start() method to get the thread running. Listing 12.5 shows just such an applet, called ThreadApplet2. When you run the applet under Appletviewer, you'll see the same display that was created in the original version of the applet (ThreadApplet); but now the counting animation is controlled by a separate thread class.

N O T E   To compile Listing 12.5, make sure you have both the MyThread.java and ThreadApplet2.java files in the same folder. Visual J++ will compile both files when you compile ThreadApplet2.java. ▪

Listing 12.5   ThreadApplet2.java: An Applet that Creates a Separate Thread

```
import java.awt.*;
import java.applet.*;
import MyThread;

public class ThreadApplet2 extends Applet
{
```

continues

Listing 12.5 Continued

```
    MyThread thread;
    String displayStr;
    Font font;

    public void start()
    {
        font = new Font("TimesRoman", Font.PLAIN, 72);
        setFont(font);

        displayStr = "";

        thread = new MyThread(this);
        thread.start();
    }

    public void stop()
    {
        thread.stop();
    }

    public void paint(Graphics g)
    {
        g.drawString(displayStr, 50, 150);
    }
}
```

Synchronizing Multiple Threads

There may be times when you have several threads going, each competing for the same resources. This type of resource competition can be deadly for threads. For example, what if one
thread tries to read from a string while another thread is still writing to that string? Depending
on the situation, you'll get strange results. You can avoid these problems by telling Java where
synchronization problems may occur, so that Java can keep an eye out for unhealthy thread
competition.

To put Java on guard, you use the `synchronized` keyword when you define a method (or even a
code block). When you mark a method as synchronized, Java creates a monitor object for the
class. The first time a thread calls the synchronized method, Java gives the monitor object to
that thread. As long as the thread holds the monitor object, no other thread can enter the
synchronized section of code. You can think of the monitor object as a key. Unless a thread is
holding the key, it can't unlock the door to the synchronized method.

Using a Synchronized Method

Using synchronized methods makes sense only when more than one thread is vying for an
applet's resources. For that reason, you need to create two threads to demonstrate thread
synchronization. Listing 12.6 is a thread class, called MyThread2, that can count either forward

or backward, depending upon the values you give to the class's constructor. By creating two thread objects from this class, you can experiment with thread synchronization.

N O T E To compile Listings 12.6 and 12.7, make sure you have both the MyThread2.java and ThreadApplet3.java files in the same folder. Visual J++ will then compile both files when you compile ThreadApplet3.java. ▪

Listing 12.6   MyThread2.java: A Double-Duty Thread

```java
public class MyThread2 extends Thread
{
    ThreadApplet3 applet;
    boolean forward;
    int count;
    int increment;
    int end;
    int position;

    MyThread2(ThreadApplet3 applet, boolean forward)
    {
        this.applet = applet;
        this.forward = forward;
    }

    public void run()
    {
        InitCounter();
        DoCount();
    }

    protected void InitCounter()
    {
        if (forward)
        {
            count = 0;
            increment = 1;
            end = 1000;
            position = 120;
        }
        else
        {
            count = 1000;
            increment = -1;
            end = 0;
            position = 180;
        }
    }

    protected void DoCount()
    {
```

continues

Listing 12.6 Continued

```
        while (count != end)
        {
            count = count + increment;
            String str = String.valueOf(count);
            applet.SetDisplayStr(str, position);

            try
                sleep(100);
            catch (InterruptedException e)
            {
            }
        }
    }
}
```

When you construct a MyThread2 thread object, you must pass two values as parameters: a reference to the applet and a boolean value indicating whether the thread should count forward or backward. The thread uses the boolean value in its InitCounter() method to set the values needed to accomplish the counting. These values are the starting count value (count), the counting increment (increment), the target count (end), and the position at which to display the count in the applet (position). Notice that the increment variable can be either 1 or -1. When the increment gets added to the count, a positive increment increases the count by one, whereas a negative increment decreases the count by one.

In its run() method, the thread calls the applet's SetDisplayStr() method which, as you'll soon see, is the synchronized method. In other words, if the thread isn't holding the monitor object for SetDisplayStr(), it cannot enter the method. This prevents two running instances of the MyThread2 thread from trying to change the display string at the same time.

Now it's time to look at the applet that's in charge of the threads. Listing 12.7 is the applet, which is called ThreadApplet3. This applet creates two objects of the MyThread2 class: one that counts forward and one that counts backward. The applet's SetDisplayStr() method is where the synchronization comes into play because both threads will be trying to access this method.

When you run the applet, you'll see that when the first thread can display its count, the string will appear closer to the top of the display area. The second thread, however, displays its count below the first thread's. For this reason, you can sit back and watch the two threads battle over the SetDisplayStr() method.

Listing 12.7 ThreadApplet3.java: An Applet that Uses Thread Synchronization

```
import java.awt.*;
import java.applet.*;
import MyThread2;

public class ThreadApplet3 extends Applet
{
```

```
MyThread2 thread1;
MyThread2 thread2;
String displayStr;
Font font;
int position;

public void init()
{
    font = new Font("TimesRoman", Font.PLAIN, 72);
    setFont(font);

    displayStr = "";
    position = 120;

    thread1 = new MyThread2(this, true);
    thread2 = new MyThread2(this, false);
}

public void start()
{
    if (thread1.isAlive())
        thread1.resume();
    else
        thread1.start();

    if (thread2.isAlive())
        thread2.resume();
    else
        thread2.start();
}

public void stop()
{
    thread1.suspend();
    thread2.suspend();
}

public void destroy()
{
    thread1.stop();
    thread2.stop();
}

public void paint(Graphics g)
{
    g.drawString(displayStr, 50, position);
}

synchronized public void SetDisplayStr(String str, int pos)
{
    displayStr = str;
    position = pos;
    repaint();
}
}
```

Understanding ThreadApplet3

The ThreadApplet3 applet is unique with regard to other applets in this chapter because it takes full advantage of the applet's life-cycle stages. In the `init()` method, the applet creates the two threads. The different `boolean` values given as the constructor's second argument cause the first thread to count forward and the second thread to count backward.

In the `start()` method, the applet calls each thread's `isAlive()` method (defined in Java's `Thread` class) to determine whether the thread has been started yet. The first time `start()` gets called, the threads have been created in `init()`, but haven't been started. In this case, `isAlive()` returns `false`, and the applet calls each thread's `start()` method to get the threads rolling. If `start()` is not being called for the first time, it's because the user has switched back to the applet from another Web page. In this case, `isAlive()` returns `true`. The applet knows that it must call the threads' `resume()` method rather than `start()`.

When the user switches to another Web page, the applet calls the `stop()` method and suspends, rather than stops, the threads. The threads remain suspended until the applet calls their `resume()` methods.

Finally, when Java calls the `destroy()` method, the applet is being deleted. The threads follow suit, with the applet calling each thread's `stop()` method.

Be Aware of Deadlock

When programming threads, you always have to watch out for a condition known as *deadlock*. Deadlock occurs when two or more threads are waiting to gain control of a resource, but for one reason or another, the threads rely on conditions that can't be met to control the resource. To understand this situation, imagine that you have a pencil in your hand, and someone else has a pen. Now, assume that you can't release the pencil until you have the pen, and the other person can't release the pen until she has the pencil. Deadlock! A more computer-oriented example would be when one thread must access Method1 before it can release its hold on Method2, but the second thread must access Method2 before it can release its hold on Method1. Because these are mutually exclusive conditions, the threads are deadlocked and cannot run.

From Here...

Threads enable you to break an applet's tasks into separate flows of execution. These subprograms seem to run concurrently thanks to the task-switching that occurs in multitasking systems. You can create a thread from a class by implementing the `Runnable` interface in the class. However, you can also create a separate class for your threads by deriving the class from `Thread`.

Depending on how you want to use the threads, you can create and start your threads in the applet's `start()` method and stop the threads in the `stop()` method. If you want your threads to retain their state when the user switches to and from your Web page, you should create the threads in `init()`, start or resume the threads in `start()`, suspend the threads in `stop()`, and stop the threads in `destroy()`. Remember that if there's a chance that two or more threads may compete for a resource, you need to protect that resource using thread synchronization.

For more information on related topics, please see the following chapters:

- Chapter 4, "Java Language Basics," describes the basic elements of the Java language.
- Chapter 5, "Loops, Conditionals, and Arrays," extends the discussion of the Java language that began in Chapter 4.
- Chapter 7, "The Applet and Window Classes," tells you more about creating applets.
- Chapter 16, "Creating an Applet with AppletWizard," describes how Visual J++'s source-code generator supports multithreaded applets.

Part

II

Ch

12

CHAPTER 13

Exceptions

by Clayton Walnum

When you write applets or applications using Java, sooner or later you're going to run into exceptions. An *exception* is a special type of error object that is created when something goes wrong in a program. After Java creates the exception object, it sends it to your program, an action called *throwing an exception*. It's up to your program to *catch* the exception. You do this by writing the exception-handling code. In this chapter, you get the inside info on these important error-handling objects. ■

How to catch exceptions

There are several types of exceptions that Java insists you handle in your program. To do this, you must catch the exception and then perform some action.

How to throw exceptions

If you want to handle an exception somewhere other than where the exception occurred, you can throw the exception back up the method hierarchy.

Creating your own exceptions

Java's Exception class enables you to create custom exception objects. You can create and throw these custom exception objects in your programs.

Learn about Java's error classes

Besides its exception classes, Java defines many error classes that represent serious errors in a program.

Java's Exceptions

In Chapter 9, "The Utility and Network Classes," you got a quick look at exceptions and how they are handled in a program. Specifically, you had to be prepared to handle an exception when you created an URL object from a text string. This is because the text string may not use the proper syntax for an URL, making it impossible to create the URL object. In this case, the URL constructor throws an exception object called MalformedURLException. Listing 13.1 shows the code segment that handles this exception.

Listing 13.1   LST13_01.TXT: Handling an Exception

```
try
{
    URL url = new URL(str);
    AppletContext context = getAppletContext();
    showStatus("Connecting to: " + str);
    context.showDocument(url);
}
catch (MalformedURLException e)
{
    error = e.getMessage();
    showStatus(error);
}
```

As you can see from the listing, you place the code that may cause the exception in a try program block, whereas the exception-handling code goes into a catch program block. In this case, the first line of the try block attempts to create an URL object from the string given in the variable str. If the string is not properly formatted for an URL, the URL constructor throws a MalformedURLException. When this happens, Java ignores the rest of the code in the try block and jumps to the catch block, where the program handles the exception. On the other hand, if the URL object gets created okay, Java executes all the code in the try block and skips the catch block.

N O T E The catch program block does more than direct program execution. It actually catches the exception object thrown by Java. For example, in Listing 13.1, you can see the exception object being caught inside the parentheses following the catch keyword. This is very similar to a parameter being received by a method. In this case, the type of the "parameter" is MalformedURLException and the name of the parameter is e. If you need to, you can access the exception object's methods through the e object. ▪

Java defines many exception objects that may be thrown by the methods in Java's classes. How do you know which exceptions you have to handle? First, if you write an applet that calls a method that may throw an exception, Java insists that you handle the exception in one way or another. If you fail to do so, your applet will not compile. Instead, you'll receive an error message indicating where your program may generate the exception. You can also discover whether a method throws an exception by looking up the method in Visual J++ online documentation. Figure 13.1 shows the Visual J++ documentation for the URL class's constructor, which throws the MalformedURLException exception.

FIG. 13.1
Visual J++'s online documentation tells you which methods throw which exceptions.

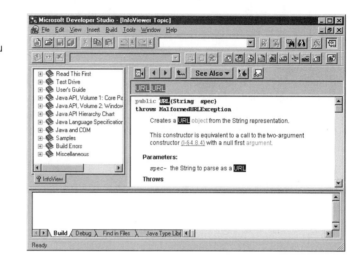

Throwing an Exception

One handy thing about exceptions is that you don't have to handle them in the same method in which the exception is generated. For example, in Listing 13.1, the applet tries to create an URL object. If the URL creation fails, the URL constructor throws an exception that the event() method handles in its catch block. But what if, for some reason, you don't want to handle the exception in the same method in which you call the URL constructor? You can simply pass the buck, so to speak, by throwing the exception on up the method hierarchy. Listing 13.2 shows one way you might do this with the MalformedURLException exception.

Part
II

Ch
13

Listing 13.2   LST13_02.TXT: Throwing an Exception

```java
public boolean action(Event evt, Object arg)
{
    try
        GetURL();
    catch (MalformedURLException e)
    {
        badURL = true;
        repaint();
    }

    return true;
}
```

continues

Listing 13.2   Continued

```
protected void GetURL() throws MalformedURLException
{
    String str = textField.getText();
    URL url = new URL(str);
    AppletContext context = getAppletContext();
    context.showDocument(url);
}
```

In this listing, the call to the URL class's constructor has been moved to a method called GetURL(). However, GetURL() does not directly handle the MalformedURLException exception. Instead, it passes the exception back to the action() method. Java knows that GetURL() wants to pass the exception, because GetURL() adds the phrase throws MalformedURLException to its signature. Throwing the exception, however, doesn't relieve you from handling it eventually. Notice that in Listing 13.2, the exception still gets handled in the action() method.

In short, you can handle an exception in two ways. The first way is to write try and catch program blocks exactly where you call the function that may generate the exception. The second way is to declare the method as throwing the exception, in which case you must write the try and catch program blocks in the method that calls the "throwing" method, as shown in Listing 13.2.

Types of Exceptions

Java defines many different exception objects. Some of these you must always handle in your code if you call a function that may throw the exception. Others are generated by the system when something like memory allocation fails, an expression tries to divide by zero, a null value is used inappropriately, and so on. You can choose to watch for this second kind of exception or let Java deal with them.

Just as with programming before exceptions existed, you should always be on the lookout for places in your program where an exception could be generated. These places are usually associated with user input, which can be infamously unpredictable. However, programmers, too, have been known to make mistakes in their programs that lead to exception throwing. Some common exceptions you may want to watch out for at appropriate places in your applet are listed in Table 13.1.

Table 13.1   Common Java Exceptions

Exceptions	Description
ArithmeticException	Caused by math errors such as division by zero.
ArrayIndexOutOfBounds Exception	Caused by bad array indexes.
ArrayStoreException	Caused when a program tries to store the wrong type of data in an array.

Exceptions	Description
FileNotFoundException	Caused by an attempt to access a nonexistent file.
IOException	Caused by general I/O failures, such as inability to read from a file.
NullPointerException	Caused by referencing a null object.
NumberFormatException	Caused when a conversion between strings and numbers fails.
OutOfMemoryException	Caused when there's not enough memory to allocate a new object.
SecurityException	Caused when an applet tries to perform an action not allowed by the browser's security setting.
StackOverflowException	Caused when the system runs out of stack space.
StringIndexOutOfBoundsException	Caused when a program attempts to access a nonexistent character position in a string.

T I P You can catch all types of exceptions by setting up your catch block for exceptions of type Exception, like this: catch (Exception e). Call the exception's getMessage() method (inherited from the Throwable superclass) to get information about the specific exception that you've intercepted.

All of Java's exceptions are organized into a class hierarchy. At the root of this hierarchy is the Throwable class, to which all exception and error objects can trace their ancestry. (You learn about error objects later in this chapter, in the section "Java's Error Classes.") The Throwable class defines three useful methods that you can call to get information about an exception:

- getMessage(). Gets a string that details information about the exception.
- toString(). Converts the object to a string that you can display on-screen.
- printStackTrace(). Displays the hierarchy of method calls that leads to the exception.

Next in the hierarchy after Throwable is the Exception class. That is, Exception is derived directly from Throwable (as is Error). However, the Exception class provides no useful methods beyond its constructors; it is the base class for all exception classes in the Java system.

After Exception, the hierarchy divides into three main categories:

- Exception classes that are directly derived from Exception
- Runtime exception classes
- I/O exception classes

Java's many exception classes are shown in the following list as they appear in the class hierarchy. The package in which a class is defined is shown in parentheses after the class name.

Part
II

Ch
13

Throwable (java.lang)

Exception (java.lang)

AWTException (java.awt)

NoSuchMethodException (java.lang)

InterruptedException (java.lang)

InstantiationException (java.lang)

ClassNotFoundException (java.lang)

CloneNotSupportedException (java.lang)

IllegalAccessException (java.lang)

IOException (java.io)

EOFException (java.io)

FileNotFoundException (java.io)

InterruptedIOException (java.io)

UTFDataFormatException (java.io)

MalformedURLException (java.net)

ProtocolException (java.net)

SocketException (java.net)

UnknownHostException (java.net)

UnknownServiceException (java.net)

RuntimeException (java.lang)

ArithmeticException (java.lang)

ArrayStoreException (java.lang)

ClassCastException (java.lang)

IllegalArgumentException (java.lang)

IllegalThreadStateException (java.lang)

NumberFormatException (java.lang)

IllegalMonitorStateException (java.lang)

IndexOutOfBoundsException (java.lang)

ArrayIndexOutOfBoundsException (java.lang)

StringIndexOutOfBoundsException (java.lang)

NegativeArraySizeException (java.lang)

NullPointerException (java.lang)

SecurityException (java.lang)

EmptyStackException (java.util)

NoSuchElementException (java.util)

Determining the Exceptions to Handle

Experienced programmers usually know when their code may generate an exception of some sort. However, when you first start writing applets with exception-handling code, you may not be sure what type of exceptions to watch out for. One way to discover this information is to see what exceptions get generated as you test your applet. Listing 13.3, for example, is an applet called ExceptionApplet that divides two integer numbers obtained from the user and displays the integer result (dropping any remainder). Because the applet must deal with user input, the probability of disaster is high. ExceptionApplet, however, contains no exception-handling code.

Listing 13.3 ExceptionApplet.java: An Applet with no Exception Handling

```java
import java.awt.*;
import java.applet.*;

public class ExceptionApplet extends Applet
{
    TextField textField1, textField2;
    String answerStr;

    public void init()
    {
        textField1 = new TextField(15);
        add(textField1);
        textField2 = new TextField(15);
        add(textField2);
        answerStr = "Undefined";
    }

    public void paint(Graphics g)
    {
        Font font = new Font("TimesRoman", Font.PLAIN, 24);
        g.setFont(font);

        g.drawString("The answer is:", 50, 100);
        g.drawString(answerStr, 70, 130);
    }

    public boolean action(Event evt, Object arg)
    {
        String str1 = textField1.getText();
        String str2 = textField2.getText();
        int int1 = Integer.parseInt(str1);
        int int2 = Integer.parseInt(str2);
        int answer = int1 / int2;
        answerStr = String.valueOf(answer);
        repaint();
        return true;
    }
}
```

Part

II

Ch

13

You'll use this applet as the starting point for a more robust applet. When you run the applet using Visual J++, you'll see the window shown in Figure 13.2. Enter a number into each of the two text boxes and then press Enter. The program then divides the first number by the second number and displays the result (see Figure 13.3).

FIG. 13.2

This is ExceptionApplet running under Visual J++.

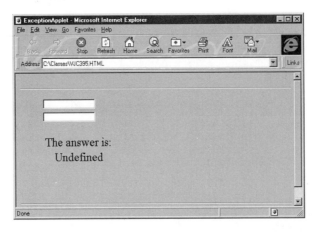

FIG. 13.3

ExceptionApplet divides the first number by the second.

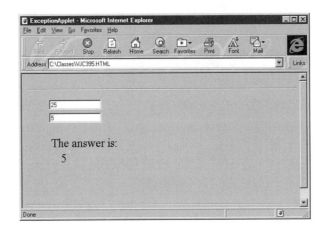

As long as the user enters valid numbers into the text boxes, the program runs perfectly. What happens, though, if the user presses Enter when either or both of the text boxes are empty? Java immediately throws a NumberFormatException when the action() method attempts to convert the contents of the text boxes to integer values. The user can't see this happening, but he will notice that, when he presses Enter, the applet does not respond to the input.

Catching a Runtime Exception

You now know that the user can cause a NumberFormatException if he or she leaves one or more text boxes blank or enters an invalid numerical value, like the string one. In order to ensure that your applet will not be caught by surprise, you now need to write the code that will handle this exception. Follow these steps to add this new code:

1. Load ExceptionApplet into Visual J++.

2. Replace the action() method with the new version shown in Listing 13.4.

Listing 13.4   LST13_04.TXT: Handling the *NumberFormatException* Exception

```
public boolean action(Event evt, Object arg)
{
    String str1 = textField1.getText();
    String str2 = textField2.getText();

    try
    {
        int int1 = Integer.parseInt(str1);
        int int2 = Integer.parseInt(str2);
        int answer = int1 / int2;
        answerStr = String.valueOf(answer);
    }
    catch (NumberFormatException e)
    {
        answerStr = "Bad number!";
    }

    repaint();
    return true;
}
```

3. In the class declaration line, change the name of the class to ExceptionApplet2.

4. Save the new applet under the name ExceptionApplet2.java.

In Listing 13.4, the action() method now uses try and catch program blocks to handle the NumberFormatException gracefully. Figure 13.4 shows what happens now when the user leaves the text boxes blank. When the program gets to the first call to String.valueOf(), Java generates the NumberFormatException exception, which causes program execution to jump to the catch block. In the catch block, the program sets the display string to Bad number! The call to repaint() ensures that this message to the user gets displayed on the screen.

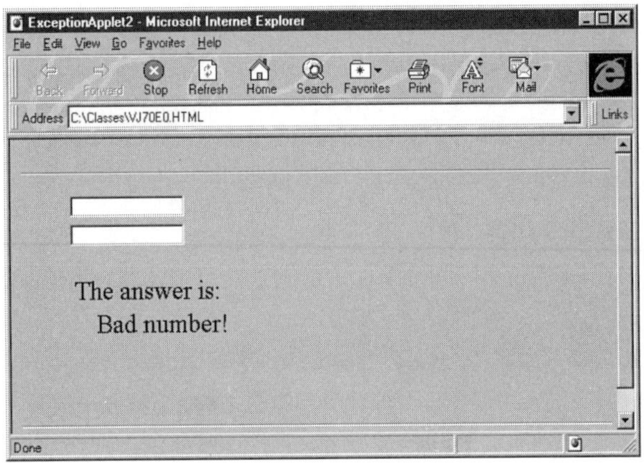

FIG. 13.4
ExceptionApplet2
handles the
NumberFormatException
exception.

Handling Multiple Exceptions

So, here you are, having a good time entering numbers into ExceptionApplet2's text boxes and getting the results. Without thinking, you enter a zero into the second box, Java tries to divide the first number by the zero, and *pow!* you've got yourself an ArithmeticException exception. What to do? You're already using your catch block to grab NumberFormatException; now, you've got yet another exception to deal with.

The good news is that you're not limited to only a single catch block. You can, in fact, create catch blocks for any exceptions you think the program may generate. To see how this works with your new applet, follow these steps:

1. Load ExceptionApplet2 into Visual J++.

2. Replace the action() method with the new version shown in Listing 13.5.

Listing 13.5 LST13_05.TXT: Handling Multiple Exceptions

```java
public boolean action(Event evt, Object arg)
{
    String str1 = textField1.getText();
    String str2 = textField2.getText();

    try
    {
        int int1 = Integer.parseInt(str1);
        int int2 = Integer.parseInt(str2);
        int answer = int1 / int2;
        answerStr = String.valueOf(answer);
    }
    catch (NumberFormatException e)
    {
        answerStr = "Bad number!";
    }
```

```
        catch (ArithmeticException e)
        {
            answerStr = "Division by 0!";
        }

        repaint();
        return true;
    }
```

3. In the class declaration line, change the name of the class to ExceptionApplet3.

4. Save the new applet under the name ExceptionApplet3.java.

If you examine Listing 13.5, you'll see that the action() method now defines two catch program blocks, one each for the NumberFormatException and ArithmeticException exceptions. In this way, the program can watch for both potential problems from within a single try block. Figure 13.5 shows what ExceptionApplet3 looks like when the user attempts a division by zero. If you discovered another exception that your program may cause, you can add yet another catch block.

FIG. 13.5

ExceptionApplet3 catches division-by-zero exceptions.

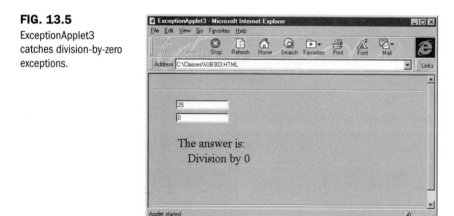

N O T E Although handling exceptions is a powerful tool for creating crash-proof programs, you should use them only in situations where you have little control over the cause of the exception, such as when dealing with user input. If your applet causes an exception because of a program bug, you should track down and fix the problem rather than try to catch the exception. ■

T I P There may be times when you want to be sure that a specific block of code gets executed whether or not an exception is generated. You can do this by adding a finally program block after the last catch. The code in the finally block gets executed after the try block or catch block finishes its task. Listing 13.6 shows an example.

Listing 13.6 LST13_06.TXT: Using the *Finally* Program Block

```
try
{
    // The code that may generate an exception goes here.
}
catch (Exception e)
{
    // The code that handles the exception goes here.
}
finally
{
    // The code here is executed after the try or
    // catch blocks finish executing.
}
```

Creating Your Own Exception Classes

Although Java provides exception classes for just about every general error you can imagine, the designers of the language couldn't possibly know what type of code you're going to write and what kinds of errors that code may experience. For example, you may write a method that sums two numbers within a specific range. If the user enters a value outside of the selected range, your program could throw a custom exception called something like NumberRangeException.

To create and throw your own custom exceptions, you must first define a class for the exception. Usually, you derive this class from Java's Exception class. Listing 13.7 shows how you might define the aforementioned NumberRangeException class.

Listing 13.7 NumberRangeException.java: The *NumberRangeException* Class

```
public class NumberRangeException extends Exception
{
    public NumberRangeException(String msg)
    {
        super(msg);
    }
}
```

As you can see, defining a new exception requires little work. In fact, you can get by with just creating a constructor for the class. Notice that the NumberRangeException class's constructor receives a String parameter. This string is the detail message that the class returns if you call its getMessage() method (which the class inherits from Throwable through Exception). Inside the constructor, this string is passed on up to NumberRangeException's superclass (Exception), which itself passes the string on up to the Throwable class where it is stored as a data member of the class. Now, inside your program, wherever you determine that your custom-exception condition has occurred, you can create and throw an object of your exception class.

Listing 13.8 is an applet that puts the new NumberRangeException to the test. When you run the applet, type a number into each text box. If you follow the directions, typing two numbers within the range 10-20, the applet sums the numbers and displays the results. Otherwise, the applet generates a NumberRangeException exception and displays an error message, as shown in Figure 13.6.

 TIP When you compile the ExceptionApplet4 applet, make sure the NumberRangeException.java file is in the same directory as the applet's source code. Otherwise, the Visual J++ compiler may not be able to find it.

Listing 13.8   ExceptionApplet4.java: An Applet that Incorporates a Custom Exception Class

```java
import java.awt.*;
import java.applet.*;
public class ExceptionApplet4 extends Applet
{
    TextField textField1, textField2;
    String answerStr;
    public void init()
    {
        textField1 = new TextField(15);
        add(textField1);
        textField2 = new TextField(15);
        add(textField2);
        answerStr = "Undefined";
        resize(500, 200);
    }

    public void paint(Graphics g)
    {
        Font font = new Font("TimesRoman", Font.PLAIN, 24);
        g.setFont(font);
        g.drawString("Enter numbers", 30, 80);
        g.drawString("from 10 to 20.", 30, 100);
        g.drawString("The answer is:", 40, 130);
        g.drawString(answerStr, 40, 150);
    }

    public boolean action(Event evt, Object arg)
    {
        try
        {
            int answer = CalcAnswer();
            answerStr = String.valueOf(answer);
        }
        catch (NumberRangeException e)
        {
            answerStr = e.getMessage();
        }
```

continues

Part

II

Ch

13

Listing 13.8   Continued

```
            repaint();
            return true;
    }

    public int CalcAnswer() throws NumberRangeException
    {
        int int1, int2;
        int answer = -1;
        String str1 = textField1.getText();
        String str2 = textField2.getText();
        try
        {
            int1 = Integer.parseInt(str1);
            int2 = Integer.parseInt(str2);
            if ((int1 < 10) || (int1 > 20) ||
                (int2 < 10) || (int2 > 20))
            {
                NumberRangeException e = new NumberRangeException
                    ("Out of range.");
                throw e;
            }
            answer = int1 + int2;
        }
        catch (NumberFormatException e)
        {
            answerStr = e.toString();
        }
        return answer;
    }
}
```

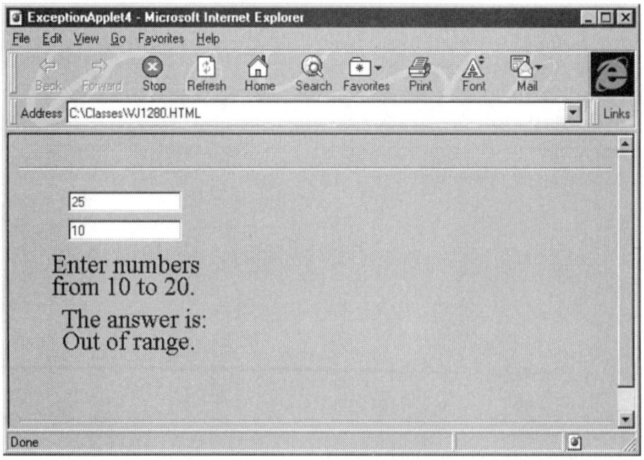

FIG. 13.6

This applet catches
NumberRangeException
custom exceptions.

In the ExceptionApplet4 applet's action() method, the program calls the local CalcAnswer() method. The action() method must enclose this method call in try and catch program blocks because CalcAnswer() throws a NumberRangeException exception (the exception class you just created). In `CalcAnswer()`, the program extracts the strings the user typed into the text boxes and converts the returned strings to integers. Because the `parseInt()` method calls can throw `NumberFormatException` exceptions, `CalcAnswer()` encloses the calls to `parseInt()` within a `try` program block. In the `try` block, the program not only converts the strings to integers, but also checks whether the integers fall within the proper range of values. If they don't, the program creates and throws an object of the `NumberRangeException` class.

Java's *Error* Classes

So far, you've had a look at the exception classes that you can handle in your own programs. Java also defines a set of `Error` classes that are really little more than special types of exceptions. Like the class `Exception`, the class `Error` is derived from `Throwable`. However, the more specific error classes that are derived from `Error` represent serious errors, such as internal errors or problems with a class, that your program shouldn't fool with. The Java system handles these errors for you.

The following is a list of the `Error` classes organized into their inheritance hierarchy. The package in which a class is defined is shown in parentheses after the class's name. (All but one are defined in java.lang.)

Throwable (java.lang)

  Error (java.lang)

    AWTError (java.awt)

    ThreadDeath (java.lang)

    LinkageError (java.lang)

      ClassCircularityError (java.lang)

      ClassFormatError (java.lang)

      NoClassDefFoundError (java.lang)

      UnsatisfiedLinkError (java.lang)

      VerifyError (java.lang)

      IncompatibleClassChangeError (java.lang)

        AbstractMethodError (java.lang)

        IllegalAccessError (java.lang)

        InstantiationError (java.lang)

        NoSuchFieldError (java.lang)

        NoSuchMethodError (java.lang)

    VirtualMachineError (java.lang)

      InternalError (java.lang)

      OutOfMemoryError (java.lang)

      StackOverflowError (java.lang)

      UnknownError (java.lang)

Part

II

Ch

13

From Here...

A good applet doesn't give the user nasty surprises. It's up to the programmer to check for potential problem spots in programs and guard against program failure. One tool the programmer can use is exceptions, which are objects created by Java when a program encounters a serious error. After Java creates an exception object, it throws the exception and expects some other part of the program to catch the exception.

The `try` and `catch` program blocks enable you to test for exceptions and respond to them as appropriate. Some types of exceptions must be handled in your program before the Java compiler will compile the program. Other exceptions—those that may be generated at runtime by more unpredictable problems like referencing a null pointer or dividing by zero—don't have to be handled in your program. However, a good programmer will design his or her applet so that common exceptions are handled where appropriate.

For more information on related topics, please see the following:

- Chapter 4, "Java Language Basics," describes the basic elements of the Java language.
- Chapter 5, "Loops, Conditionals, and Arrays," extends the discussion of the Java language that began in Chapter 4.
- Chapter 7, "The Applet and Window Classes," shows how you can use Java's classes to create applets.
- Chapter 21, "Using Visual J++ Debugging Tools," offers techniques for locating programming errors.

Introducing Visual J++

CHAPTER 14

Getting Started with Visual J++

by Mark Culverhouse

Visual J++ is for Java developers using the Windows 95 or Windows NT platform to produce Java language applets and applications. The compiled applets and applications can run over the Internet through Java-enabled Web browsers or as downloaded applications. Visual J++ offers many features, but before describing the features using programming examples, this section will give you an overview of some of the miscellaneous Visual J++ tools. ■

Installation

Installation requirements and options are presented.

Toolbars

Toolbars are tools you will use every minute in Visual J++. Learn how to use them early.

Search tools

Find, Replace, and Find In Files tools find text or patterns of text in a file or directory of files.

Bookmarks

Learn how to use named, unnamed, and InfoViewer bookmarks.

Configuration

Before writing code, review the configuration option settings.

About Visual J++

Visual J++ 1.0 is the first release of Microsoft's Windows-based programming tool for the Java language. Visual J++ uses the same integrated development environment as Microsoft's Visual C++. All of the advancements made to Developer Studio to support the object-oriented C++ language are now available for use by the first generation language, Java. The ability to develop and manage Java projects has increased significantly with the availability of Visual J++.

The Developer Studio includes:

- Source code editor
- Java compiler
- Java AppletWizard
- Java ResourceWizard
- Menu editor
- Dialog editor

Developer Studio is only one of several Visual J++ programs. Part of the Visual J++ installation for Windows 95 is the creation of a file folder containing shortcuts to the programs that make up Visual J++, including Developer Studio. These shortcuts are listed in Table 14.1. The name of the folder is Microsoft Visual J++ 1.0 (see Figure 14.1). It is created under your user name in WINDOWS\Profiles in the \Start Menu\Programs\ folder. Because this folder is in the \Start Menu\Programs\ folder, its contents also show up in the Start menu on the taskbar (see Figure 14.2). Visual J++ comes with other programs that are invoked from within Developer Studio. These will be discussed in the following chapters.

Table 14.1   Visual J++ Programs

Program Name	Shortcut
Microsoft Developer Studio	C:\MSDEV\BIN\MSDEV.EXE
Java Compiler	C:\MSDEV\BIN\JVC.EXE
Java Type Library Utility	C:\MSDEV\BIN\JAVATLB.EXE
Java Registration Utility	C:\MSDEV\BIN\JAVAREG.EXE
Java Type Library Wizard	C:\MSDEV\BIN\JT.EXE
Control Registration Utility	C:\MSDEV\BIN\REGSVR32.EXE
OLE Object Viewer	C:\MSDEV\BIN\OLE2VW32.EXE

FIG. 14.1
The Explorer view of the
Visual J++ group icons.

FIG. 14.2
Here is the view of
the Visual J++ task-
bar menu from the
Start button.

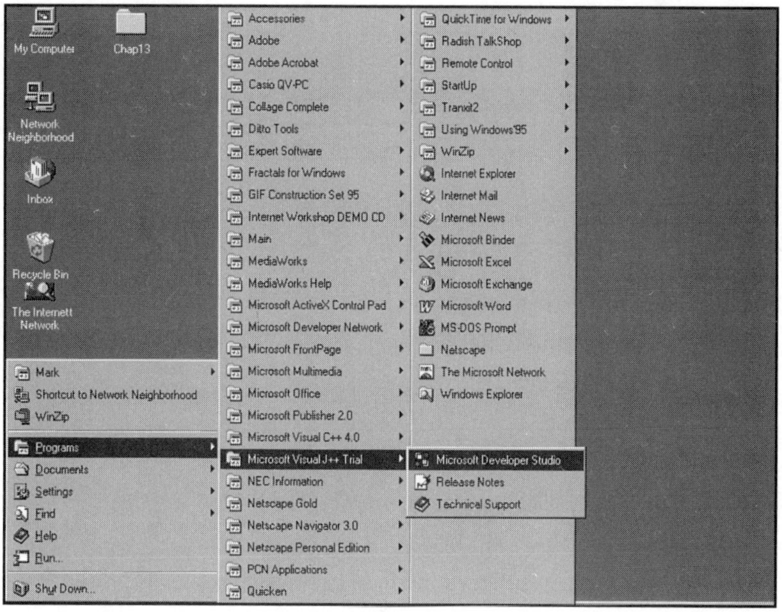

System Requirements

Visual J++ needs the following minimum requirements for installation and operation:

- A personal computer with a 486 or higher processor.
- A Windows 95 or Windows NT 4.0 or later operating system.
- A VGA monitor (Microsoft recommends a Super VGA monitor).
- Memory: 16M (Microsoft recommends 20M); 8M (12 M recommended) for Windows 95.
- A CD-ROM drive.
- A mouse or compatible pointing device.
- Hard disk space: A typical Visual J++ installation may require 20M. A minimum installation requires 14M. The maximum space required to install all tools and information on CD-ROM is 50M.

Installing Visual J++

Installing Visual J++ is a simple process. Insert the Visual J++ CD-ROM into your CD-ROM drive. Choose Start, Run; click Browse, then navigate to the root of the CD-ROM drive. Choose Setup.exe in the Browse dialog box, and click Open and OK to run it (see Figure 14.3).

FIG. 14.3

Running Setup.exe from the Visual J++ CD-ROM.

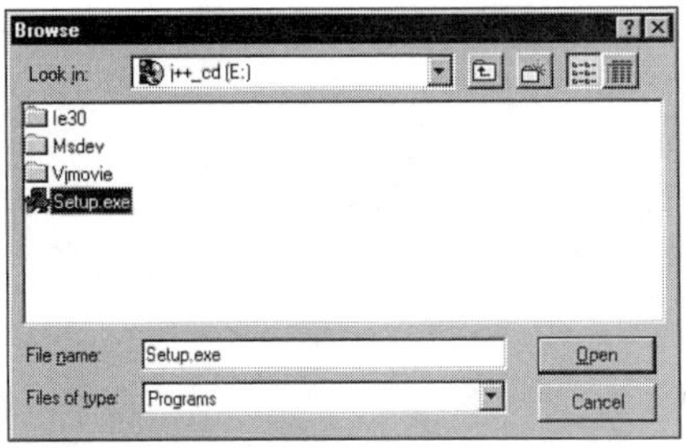

The Visual J++ 1.0 Master Setup dialog box provides you with a choice of applications to install (see Figure 14.4). The choices are:

- Install Visual J++ 1.0

  Choose this to install all or part of the Visual J++ development environment.

- Install IE 3.0

  Install the Java-enabled Internet Explorer browser application.

- Introducing Visual J++

  A really cool multimedia tour of Visual J++.

- Explore the CD

  Opens an explorer window to browse the contents of the CD-ROM.

Click Install Visual J++ 1.0 to start the installation of Visual J++.

The first dialog box in the Visual J++ installation process (see Figure 14.5) is the Welcome screen, which informs you that you can install or modify your installation in the future. Click Next to continue.

The next dialog box (see Figure 14.6) displays the End-User License Agreement (EULA) from Microsoft. Click Yes to continue. If you choose No, then the program returns to the Master Setup dialog box.

TIP   There is a French version at the bottom of the EULA document.

The next dialog box (see Figure 14.7) is the Registration screen, which allows you to enter your User Name, Organization, and the 10-digit key from the CD-ROM case. This information is saved in the system Registry. Click Next to continue.

FIG. 14.4

The Visual J++ 1.0 Master Setup dialog box supports installing Visual J++ and components.

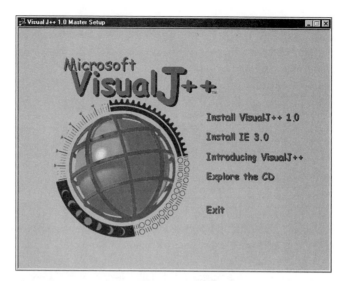

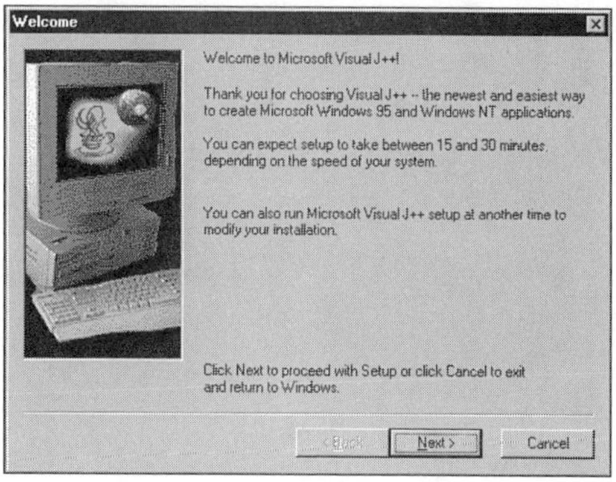

FIG. 14.5

The Visual J++ Welcome dialog box.

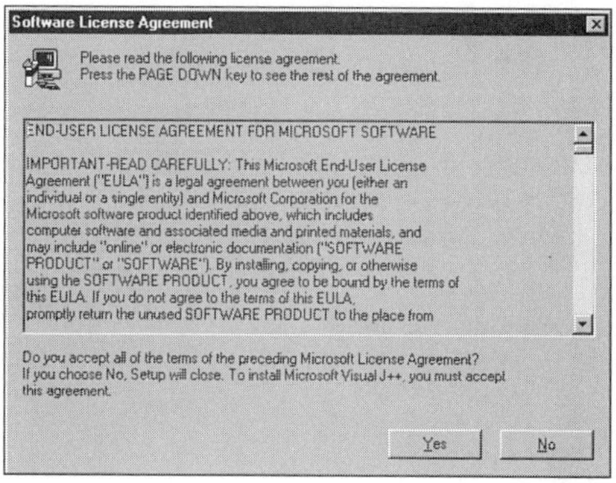

FIG. 14.6

The Software License Agreement dialog box describes terms for you to accept.

Part

III

Ch

14

FIG. 14.7

The Registration dialog box is used to specify User Name and Organization.

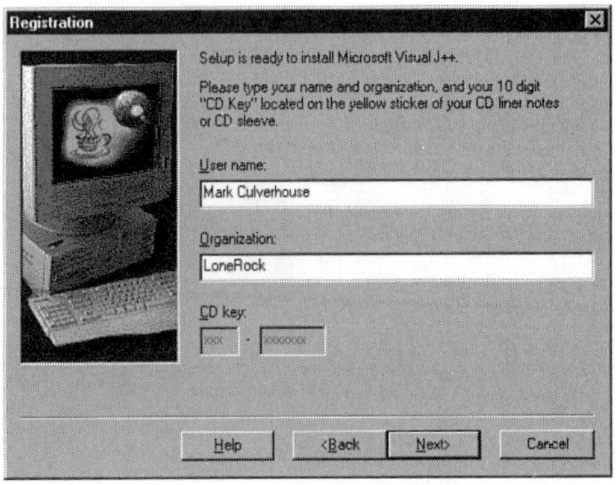

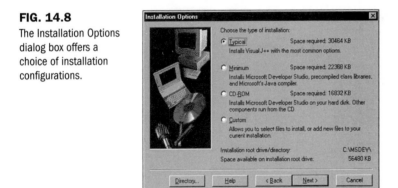

The Installation Options dialog box (see Figure 14.8) allows you to choose from four different installation configurations. Choose another option or accept the default, Typical. You can always run Setup.exe again and change your installation options. Before continuing, click Directory if you want to change the folder used to install files (see Figure 14.9) or click Next to continue.

FIG. 14.8

The Installation Options dialog box offers a choice of installation configurations.

FIG. 14.9

The Change Directory dialog box is used to change the installation location.

The Microsoft Visual J++ Setup dialog box (see Figure 14.10) is the last dialog box of the installation process. Click Next to continue.

FIG. 14.10

The Microsoft Visual J++ Setup (ready to install) dialog box.

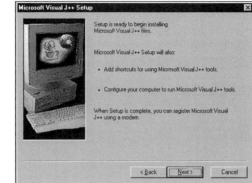

If you chose <u>C</u>ustom in the Installation Options dialog box, then the Microsoft Visual J++ Setup dialog box is displayed (see Figure 14.11). Browse through the components and their details to become more familiar with the contents of Visual J++.

Select the Java Class Libraries entry and click <u>D</u>etails to display the Java Class Libraries dialog box (see Figure 14.12).Click OK to accept any changes and return to Installation Options. Or, click Cancel to reject any changes and return to Installation Options.

FIG. 14.11

The next Microsoft Visual J++ Setup dialog box allows adding or removing of components.

FIG. 14.12

The Java Class Libraries dialog box lets you install Java files now or later.

Part

III

Ch

14

Select the Database Options entry from the Microsoft Visual J++ Setup box and click Details to display the Database Options dialog box (see Figure 14.13). Click OK to accept any changes and return to Installation Options. Or, click Cancel to reject any changes and return to Installation Options.

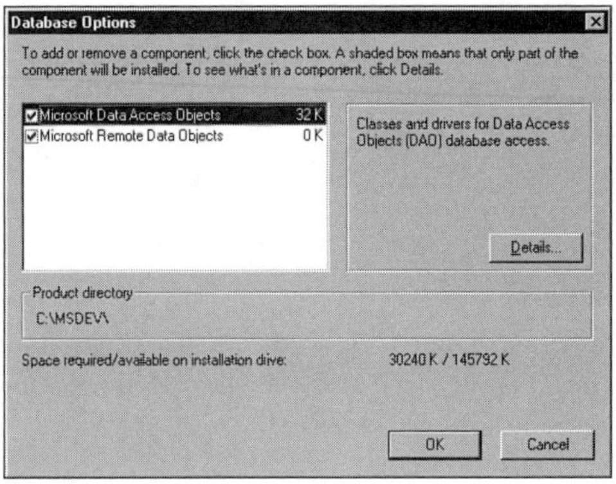

FIG. 14.13
The Database Options dialog box provides a selection of database components.

Using Visual J++ Toolbars

Toolbars are convenient to organize sets of commands. Toolbar use can enhance your productivity and understanding of Visual J++ capabilities. Developer Studio has eight standard predefined toolbars (see Table 14.2). You can also create new toolbars.

Table 14.2   Visual J++ Toolbars

Toolbar	Description
Standard	File, Edit, Search, ClassWizard, and Project Workspace commands.
Project	Build, Project, Debug, and Resource commands.
Resource	Same Resource commands as Project, plus Resource Symbols.
Edit	Bookmark, Window sizing, and Indent commands.
Debug	Start, Go, Step, and Watch commands.
Browse	Goto, Class Browser, and Call graphs.
InfoViewer	Query and Bookmark commands.
InfoView Contents	Define subset of contents to search.

You can customize toolbars in various ways. To show or hide a toolbar, right-click it to display the pop-up menu (see upper-right corner of Figure 14.14) that contains the names of the eight toolbars. A check appears to the left of the toolbar name if it is currently visible. Choose the desired toolbar item to show or hide it.

Another method is to choose Toolbars from the pop-up menu to display the Toolbars dialog box (see lower-right corner of Figure 14.14). Check or uncheck a toolbar in the Toolbars list box to show or hide the toolbar. The Toolbars dialog box can be displayed by selecting View, Toolbars from the main menu.

FIG. 14.14

Here are the eight standard Visual J++ toolbars, the Toolbars dialog box, and the toolbar pop-up menu.

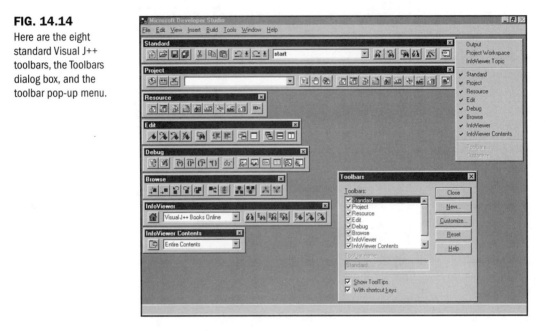

Toolbars are dockable along the four sides of the project workspace (see Figure 14.15). Double-click a toolbar to dock or undock it. You can also drag a toolbar to dock or undock it. Drag a toolbar along the four sides. Its outline changes size to indicate where it will dock when it is dropped. If you want to cancel the resizing of a dockable toolbar, just press Esc.

To customize a toolbar, choose Customize from the pop-up menu in Figure 14.14, displayed by right-clicking any toolbar or menu. This displays the Customize dialog box (see Figure 14.16), or choose Tools, Customize. When the Customize dialog box is displayed, the existing toolbars are in edit mode. You can delete a toolbar button by dragging it off the toolbar and dropping it. To add a command button, drag it from the Customize dialog box and drop it on a toolbar. Close the Customize dialog box to exit toolbar edit mode.

Part
III

Ch
14

FIG. 14.15
Toolbars can be docked to any side of the Developer Studio window.

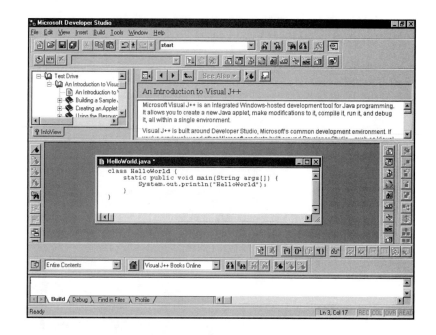

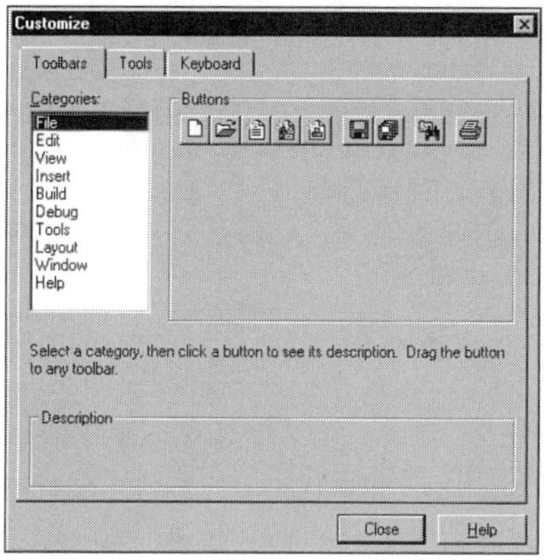

FIG. 14.16
The Customize toolbar dialog box is used to configure toolbars, tool menu entries, and keyboard shortcut assignments.

Using Search Tools

Developer Studio has several tools related to searching files. These tools include:

- Find dialog box
- Replace dialog box
- Find In Files dialog box
- Go To dialog box

Each of the above search tool's dialogs contains a Fi<u>n</u>d What drop-down list box. This is where you enter the string or regular expression that will be used to find matches. Each dialog also has a Regular <u>E</u>xpression check box. If it's not checked, then the contents of Fi<u>n</u>d What are treated as an exact string. If it is checked, then the contents of Fi<u>n</u>d What are treated as a regular expression.

A *regular expression* is a pattern of special characters that is used to find matching strings on lines of files. The Fi<u>n</u>d What control of the search dialogs also has a menu button to the right of it. Clicking the menu button will display a menu containing valid special characters (see Figure 14.17). When one of the menu items is selected, the special pattern character is inserted into the Fi<u>n</u>d What control and the Regular <u>E</u>xpression check box is checked.

T I P For more information on each special character, search Visual J++ Books Online for regular expressions. Browse the article "Using Regular Expressions with Developer Studio."

In addition to the Regular <u>E</u>xpression check box, there are two other check boxes that are shared by the search tools. These further refine the search matching process. The other common search controls are:

- Match <u>W</u>hole Word Only check box—Find only whole words delimited by white space characters.
- Match <u>C</u>ase check box—Make the search upper/lowercase sensitive.

FIG. 14.17
The Find dialog box has a button to display the Regular Expression Special Character menu.

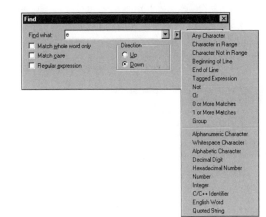

Using the Find Tool

The Find tool is used to search a string or a regular expression in the current active file. To use the Find tool, put the cursor in a text file and choose <u>E</u>dit, <u>F</u>ind to display the Find dialog box (see Figure 14.18).

In the Fi<u>n</u>d What box, enter the string or expression to be searched for in the active open file. Check Regular <u>E</u>xpression if you manually enter special characters of a pattern. To start the search click <u>F</u>ind Next or <u>M</u>ark All.

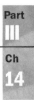

Find Next finds the next occurrence in the file of the string or regular expression. Mark All will search the entire file for matches and mark them with bookmarks. To go to the next bookmark press F2, to go to the previous bookmark press Shift F2. Bookmarks are discussed in the next section.

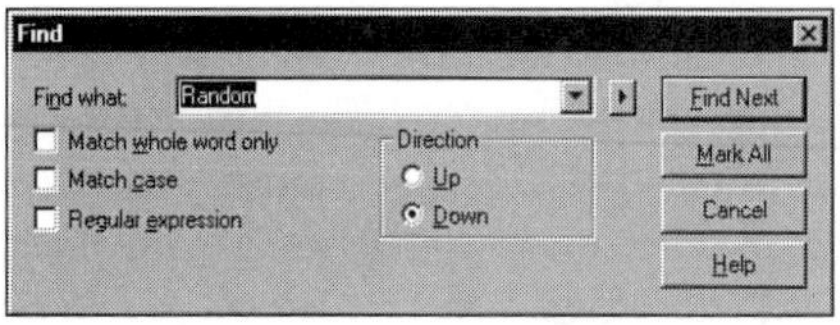

FIG. 14.18

The standard Find dialog box is a frequently used search tool.

Using the Replace Tool

The Replace tool finds and replaces a string or a regular expression in the current active file. To use the Replace tool, put the cursor in a text file and choose Edit, Replace to display the Replace dialog box (see Figure 14.19). Replace also supports defining replacement text in terms of what the current string or matching text to a regular expression is. The replacement text can contain references to the current match or tagged expressions within the regular expression.

Figure 14.20 shows the menu displayed when the menu button to the right of Replace With is selected. In the Replace With menu, the Find What Text item will insert a code to be substituted with the current value of Find What. Tagged expressions are defined in the Find What regular expressions. When a tagged expression is inserted in the Replace With text box, then that fragment of the Find What value is substituted. A tagged expression is a fragment of the Find What text that is delimited by /(and /). The first tagged expression fragment can be referred to as /1, the second, /2, and so on.

FIG. 14.19

The Replace dialog box is used to change text strings and support finding regular expressions.

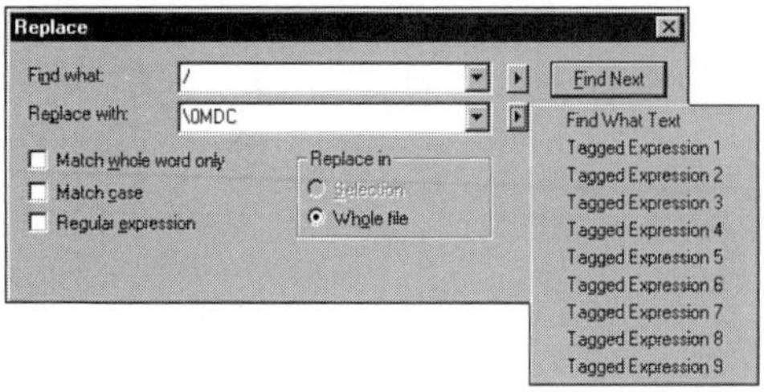

FIG. 14.20

The Replace dialog box has a button to display tagged expression menu options.

Using the Find In Files Tool

The Find In Files tool finds a string or a regular expression in one or more files in a folder and its subfolders. Use Find In Files to scan folders of files. To use the Find In Files tool, put the cursor in a text file and choose File, Find In Files to display the Find In Files dialog box (see Figure 14.21).

The Find In Files dialog box in Figure 14.21 is displaying the Advanced portion at the bottom of the dialog box. The bottom two-thirds of the dialog are displayed as a result of clicking Advanced (which then changes text to Advanced). Click Advanced again to hide the advanced options. The Advanced option allows specifying additional folders to be searched together with the In Folder entry.

To start the search click Find. A Save As dialog box will prompt you for a text file name to save the search results. If you click Cancel, then the Developer Studio Output window is used for output of the search results. Figure 14.22 shows the results of a Find In Files search.

FIG. 14.21

The Find In Files dialog box lets you search for text in multiple files in multiple directories.

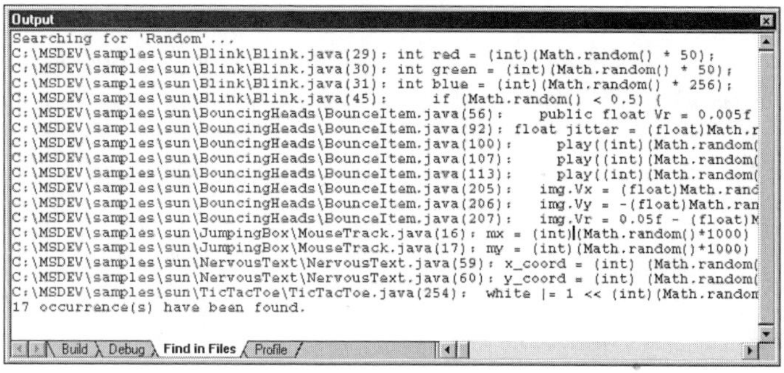

FIG. 14.22

The Find In Files results are displayed in the Output window.

Part

III

Ch

14

Using Bookmarks

Bookmarks are a useful tool for maintaining anchors to lines in files. There are two types of bookmarks in Visual J++, named and unnamed. Named bookmark definitions are persistent. They are stored between Visual J++ sessions. Unnamed bookmarks are temporary and exist only while the file is open.

To create an unnamed bookmark, open a file, place the cursor on a line, and press Ctrl+F2 to toggle a bookmark on and off. To go to the next unnamed bookmark press F2. Press Shift+F2 to go to the previous bookmark in the active file.

To use named bookmarks, select Edit, Bookmark to display the Bookmark dialog box (see Figure 14.23). If your cursor is in an open file, then you can enter a Name to enable the Add button. Click Add to create a new named bookmark.

Named bookmarks store the file name and the line number. You can close Developer Studio, start it again tomorrow, and the bookmarks will still be there. As you edit files within Developer Studio, your named bookmarks will be adjusted to reflect inserts and deletes.

The Bookmark dialog box has a Go To button. To go to a bookmark whether the file is open or not, select the name of the bookmark and click Go To.

FIG. 14.23

The Bookmark dialog box allows you to manage your bookmarks.

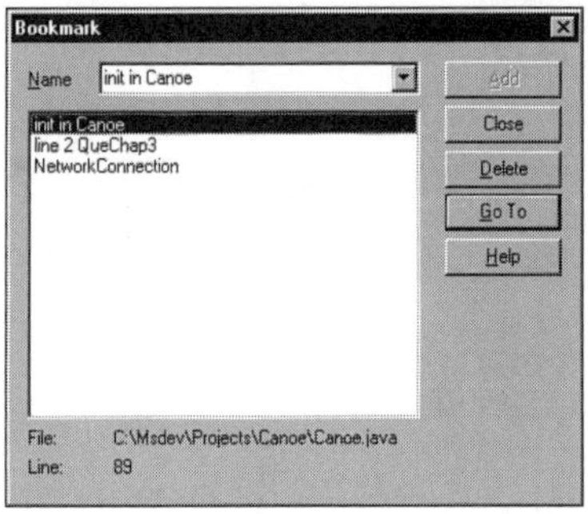

The InfoViewer has its own bookmarks. To use InfoViewer bookmarks select Edit, InfoViewer Bookmarks to display the InfoViewer Bookmarks dialog box (see Figure 14.24). If your cursor was in the InfoViewer topic window before displaying the InfoViewer Bookmarks dialog box, the Add button will be enabled. Click Add to create a bookmark using the dialog.

To go to an InfoViewer Bookmark, select the bookmark in the table and click Display. The bookmarks can be sorted by name or book by clicking the title bars in the bookmark table.

T I P The toolbar in the InfoViewer Topic window (see Figure 14.26) contains a button to Add A Bookmark (Ctrl+Shift+B) to the InfoViewer Bookmarks.

FIG. 14.24

The InfoViewer
Bookmarks dialog
box manages the
InfoViewer bookmarks.

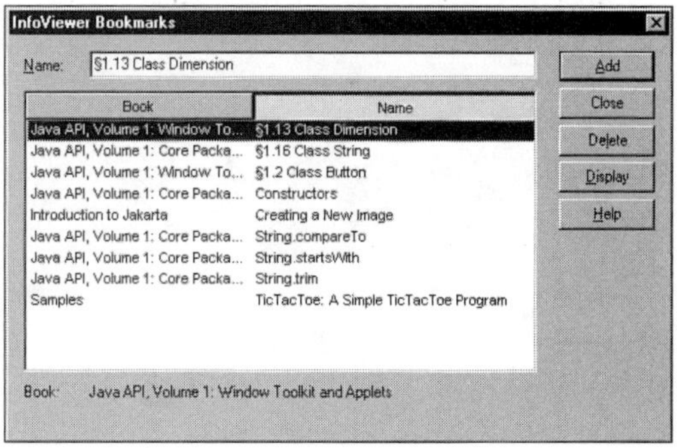

Using the Go To Tool

The Go To tool is a single dialog box that provides an interface to select and go to various anchors supported by Visual J++. Named bookmarks, InfoViewer Bookmarks, and other target anchors are accessible from the Go To dialog box.

To display the Go To dialog box, select Edit, Go To (see Figure 14.25).

FIG. 14.25

The Go To dialog box
lets you jump to any of
the different kinds of
bookmarks supported
by Developer Studio
components.

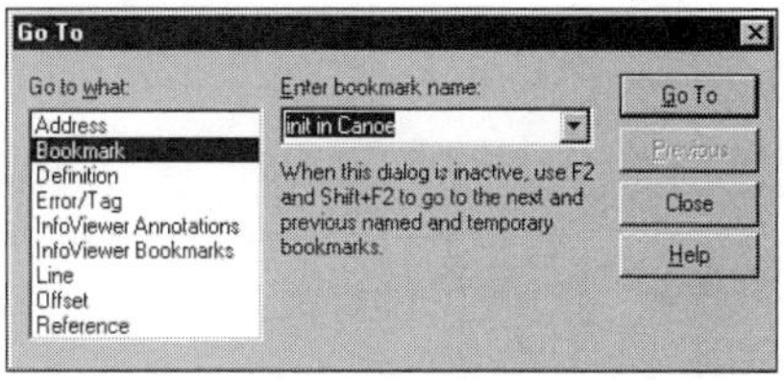

Using the InfoViewer Online Help System

Visual J++ has an integrated online help system that consists of the Project Workspace window, the InfoViewer Topic window, and the InfoViewer and InfoViewer Contents toolbars (see Figure 14.26). The topic outline is displayed in the InfoView tab of the Project Workspace window. Double-clicking a topic in the InfoView tab will display that topic's content in the InfoViewer Topic window.

Part

III

Ch

14

FIG. 14.26

The InfoViewer online help system components include the InfoViewer and InfoViewer Contents toolbars, and the Project Workspace and InfoViewer Topic windows.

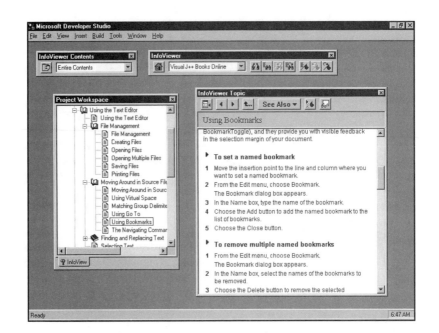

The InfoViewer toolbar contains a Search button. Clicking the Search button will display the InfoViewer Search dialog box (see Figure 14.27).

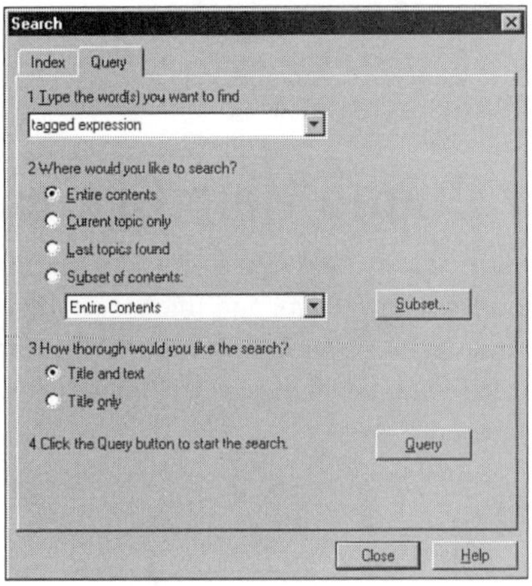

FIG. 14.27

The InfoViewer Search dialog box is used to specify keyword searches of InfoViewer topics.

The InfoViewer Search dialog box is used to search for topics containing a search string. Click Query to perform the search. The results of the search are displayed in the Query Results dialog box (see Figure 14.28).

To redisplay the last Query Results dialog box, select View, InfoViewer Query Results.

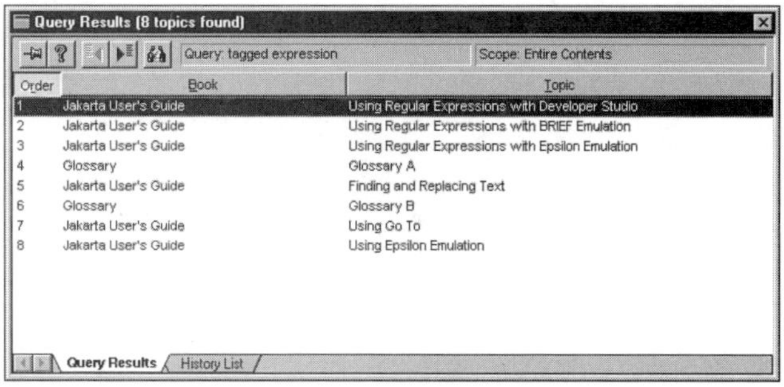

FIG. 14.28
The Query Results dialog box contains the results of the last search.

Configuring Visual J++

Before building projects with Visual J++, browse the configuration options to change the settings to meet your needs. Select Tools, Options to display the Options dialog box (see Figure 14.29). Ctrl+Tab through the tabbed dialogs to review all of the options available.

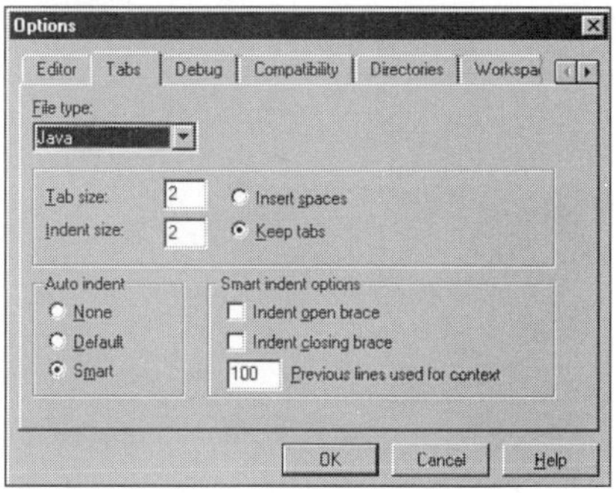

FIG. 14.29
The Options dialog box is used to specify global options that may affect all projects.

From Here...

In this chapter you learned about installing Visual J++ and using some of its useful tools. In the next two chapters, you will begin to build and execute Java projects.

- In Chapter 15, "Building a Sample Applet," you will build your first J++ project using the code that comes with the J++ sample projects.

- Learn how to use the AppletWizard to create a new Java applet in Chapter 16, "Creating an Applet with AppletWizard."

Part
III

Ch
14

Building a Sample Applet

by Mark Culverhouse

The first part of this book introduced you to the Java language. The previous chapter introduced you to Visual J++. In this chapter, you will build your first J++ project using the code that comes with the J++ sample projects. Before writing your own code in the following chapters, you can get acquainted with using Visual J++ by building a project using existing sample code. You probably will want to build many of the sample projects in order to examine their features.

The Visual J++ samples are each complete, pre-built Visual J++ projects. In the first section, you will install, build, and execute a complete sample project. In the following sections, you will create, configure, build, and execute a new project using only the *.java source file(s) from a sample project.

The process of creating a project using only *.java files is the same process you would use to migrate your existing Sun JDK Java projects into the Visual J++ development environment. Also, by learning this process, you will better understand how Visual J++ projects work.

The final section in this chapter discusses each sample and shows each applet running. ■

Create the J++ project files

Learn how to create a Visual J++ project to build an existing source.

Include the files containing Java classes into the J++ project

Use Visual J++ to manage your classes with the ClassView and FileView windows.

Build the new project by compiling the classes

When a project is properly configured, it can be built.

Run the applet using a browser

Use Visual J++ to start a browser to run your applet.

Test the applet by using a debug-generated HTML page with parameter values

Visual J++ will generate HTML to pass your test values through applet parameters.

Installing a Java Sample Applet Project

In this section, you will install, build, and execute a Visual J++ sample project. This is a very simple process because the sample projects are already complete Visual J++ projects with all of the configuration options already specified.

The first step is to select one of the sample Java applets that come with Visual J++. These samples include the original Sun JDK samples and a new set of Microsoft J++ sample projects. The Sun JDK samples have been upgraded to Visual J++ projects. In most cases, the actual Java source files (*.java) have not been changed from their release with the Sun JDK. In this chapter, the Sun BarChart sample applet will be used to build a J++ project.

The files associated with a Visual J++ Sun Java Development Kit sample can be copied to an existing or a new directory using the InfoView window. Follow these steps:

1. Insert your Visual J++ CD-ROM.
2. Open the Visual J++ Books Online entry in the Open Information Title drop-down list box on the InfoViewer toolbar.
3. Activate the InfoView tab on the Project Workspace toolbar.
4. Open the first-level Samples entry by clicking the "+" or double-clicking Samples.
5. Open the Sun Samples entry by clicking the "+" or double-clicking Sun Samples.
6. Double-click the entry marked BarChart: Demonstrates Chart Drawing. This will display the InfoViewer Topic toolbar containing the BarChart sample.
7. Select the Click to Open or Copy the BarChart Project Files button to display the Sample Application dialog box (see Figure 15.1).
8. Click the Copy All button to display the Copy dialog box (see Figure 15.2).
9. Click OK to accept the default c:\msdev\samples\sun\barchart.

    If a new directory needs to be created, you will be prompted to allow it.

The Sun sample files are now in the project directory. The next step is to use Visual J++ to create a Developer Studio project in the same directory.

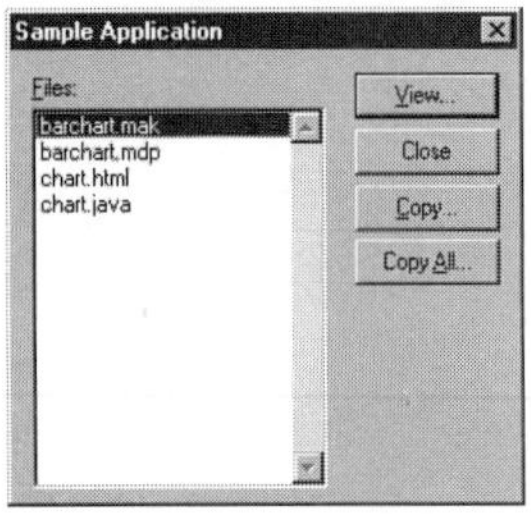

FIG. 15.1

The Sample Application files dialog box is used to properly copy Visual J++ sample project files.

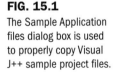

FIG. 15.2

The Copy dialog box is used to specify the target directory, new or old, to copy sample project files.

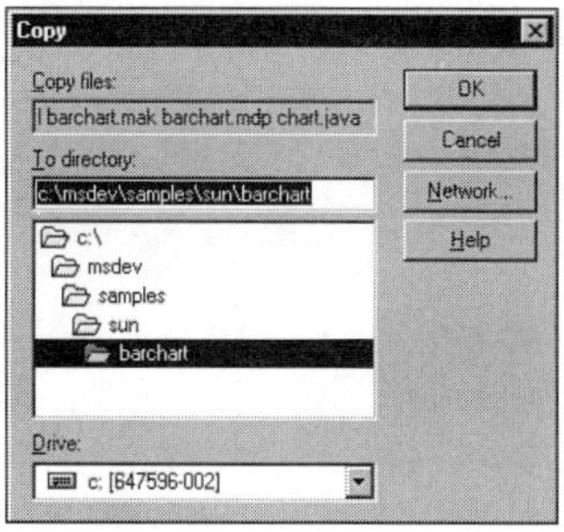

A directory now exists containing the sample project files. The next step is to open the sample project.

To open the BarChart project, select File, Open Workspace to display the Open Project Workspace dialog box. Navigate to the sample project directory, in this case Drive\msdev\samples\Sun\samples\barchart, select the barchart.mdp file and click Open (see Figure 15.3).

FIG. 15.3

The Open Project Workspace dialog box is used to open an existing project file (*.mdp).

After opening the project file, you should see the Developer Studio window containing the BarChart project. The project name, BarChart, should appear in the main window's title. You should also see the ClassView window showing a collapsed list of the classes in the BarChart project.

To see the Java classes in the BarChart project, click the "+" to the left of BarChart classes in the ClassView window (see Figure 15.4). This expands the ClassView to show a single class called chart.

To see the methods and variables defined in the chart class, click the "+" to the left of the chart class in the ClassView window. You should see two methods, init and paint. You should also see a dozen or so class variables beginning with a variable named barSpacing.

Finally, to see the source code for the init method, double-click init in the chart class method list in the ClassView window. This will cause the source file that contains the chart.init method to be opened and positioned to the init method within the file (see Figure 15.4).

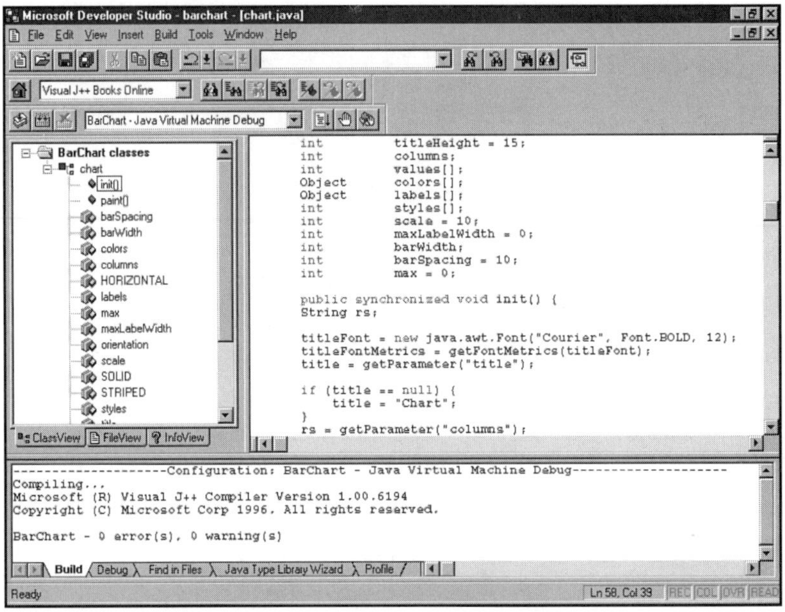

FIG. 15.4

The BarChart Project windows after a build with build messages in the Output window at the bottom.

The next step is to build the project. Select Build, Build BarChart to start the build. The project should build successfully in a few seconds. See the Output window at the bottom of Figure 15.4 for the build messages.

When the project is built, you are ready to execute the project's applet. Select Build, Execute chart to execute the BarChart applet using the current project settings. You may be prompted to enter the name of the class to be used when running the applet. If the Information For Running Class dialog box (see Figure 15.5) is displayed, then enter the name of the project's applet class, in this case **chart**, into the Class File Name field. Make sure you enter the correct upper- and lowercase letters for the class name. Click OK to continue. The value will be saved with the project settings, so you will not be prompted subsequently for the same information.

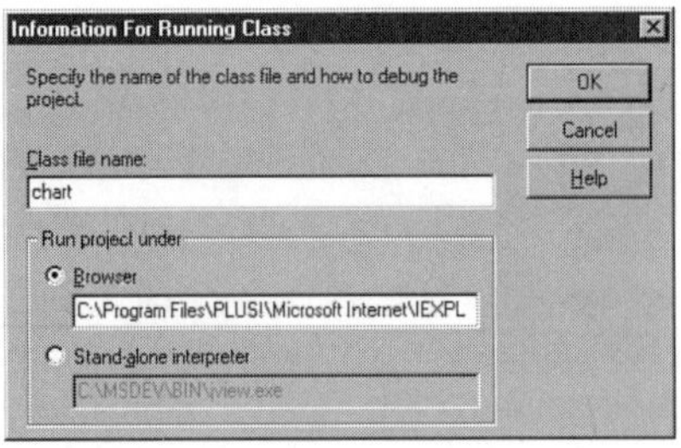

FIG. 15.5

Use the Information For Running Class dialog box to activate a browser or stand-alone interpreter to be used.

At this point, Internet Explorer should have been started with C:\MSDEV\samples\sun\barchart\chart.html as its initial page to be displayed (see Figure 15.6).

FIG. 15.6
Internet Explorer is shown running the Bar Chart sample applet.

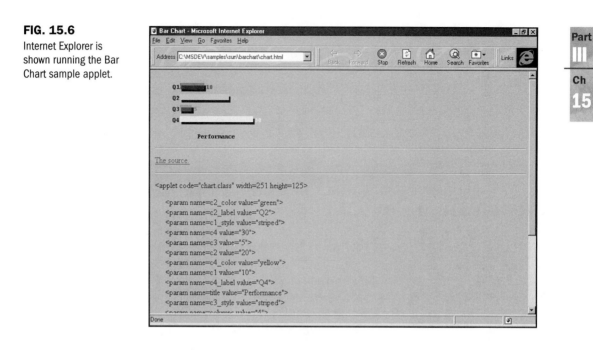

That is all there is to installing the Sun BarChart sample project. The other Sun and Microsoft samples are just as easy. The last section of this chapter contains an overview of each sample.

Building a J++ Project from Java Source Files Only

In the previous section, you installed a pre-existing sample Visual J++ project. Many project settings were predefined and saved in the project definition and make files. All you had to do was install the project files and build it.

However, what if you have your own Java projects created using the Sun JDK and/or other Java programmer tools? How do you easily migrate your programs into Visual J++? If you have existing applet code, then one of your first tasks using Visual J++ will be to migrate an existing project.

In this section, you will create a directory containing a single Java source file and a single HTML file. In the following sections of this chapter, you will learn about each step necessary to turn these two files into a Visual J++ project.

The sample Java and HTML files that will be used in this example will be the chart.java and chart.html files from the Sun BarChart sample. The BarChart sample was the same one used in the previous section. Note the barchart.mdp and barchart.mak files will not be used. The contents of these files will be created by the steps described in the following sections.

The first step is to create the \MSDEV\SAMPLES\SAMPLES\SUN\BarChart directory containing two files, chart.java and chart.html. If you have installed the BarChart sample project in the previous section, then delete every file in that directory except for the chart.java and chart.html files.

If you did not install the BarChart sample yet, then follow the instructions in the previous section. Except instead of clicking Copy All (refer to Figure 15.1), select chart.java and chart.html in the Files list box. Then click Copy to create the directory and copy the two files into it.

Now, you are ready to continue to the next step. In this chapter you are using files from the BarChart sample project. You may want to follow along in the next sections using your own project instead.

Creating Java Project Files

A directory now exists containing the sample files. The next step is to create a new project in the same directory. Select File, New to display the New dialog box (see Figure 15.7).

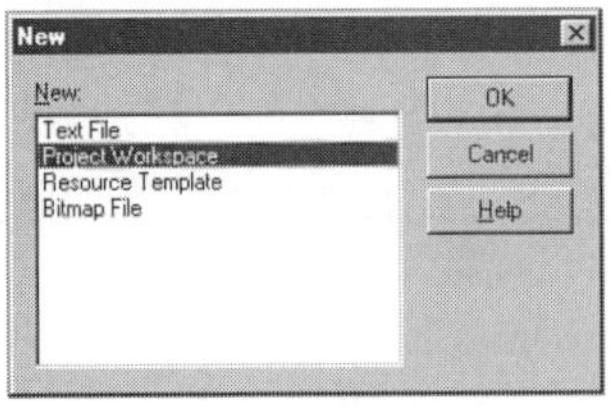

FIG. 15.7
The New dialog box is used to create new files and projects.

Select Project Workspace in the New list box. Click OK to display the New Project Workspace dialog box shown in Figure 15.8. In the New Project Workspace dialog box, scroll the Type list box and select the Java Workspace entry. Because the directory already exists, click the Browse button to select the *parent* directory of the sample project, or enter the full name of the *parent* directory in the Location control, for example, C:\MSDEV\samples\sun. You *must* enter the subdirectory name into the Name control. The Name control cannot be blank. As you type in the Name box, each character is appended to the path in Location which is why you should not enter the project name in the Location field. Click Create to create the files that define the Visual J++ project.

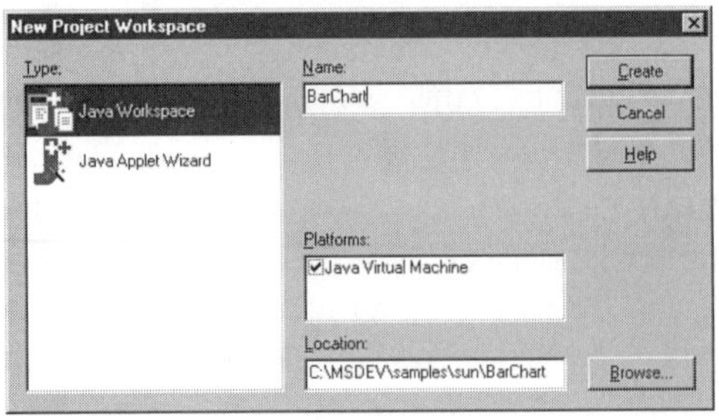

FIG. 15.8
The New Project Workspace dialog box is used to create a new empty project workspace or a new working applet.

As a result of creating the new Java Project Workspace, two new files were added to the BarChart directory, BarChart.mak and BarChart.mdp.

Adding Class Files to a Project

Use the Project Workspace toolbar to view the ClassView and FileView windows to see that the BarChart project has no classes and no files yet. The BarChart sample files that we started with include chart.java, which is the single Java source file in this sample JDK project. This file needs to be added to the BarChart project workspace so that it will be compiled when the project is built.

To add a file to a project, select the Insert, Files into Project menu item to display the Insert Files into Project dialog box (see Figure 15.9). You want to add both files, chart.java and chart.html, to the project. First, choose All Files(*.*) in the Files of type drop-down list box. Next, select the chart.java and chart.html files by holding down the Ctrl key while clicking those entries. Finally, click the Add button. Now, revisit the ClassView and FileView windows to see the results of inserting the chart.java and chart.html files into the project.

FIG. 15.9

The Insert Files into Project dialog box.

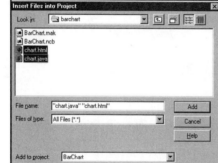

The Project Workspace window's FileView tab shows the list of all files currently part of the project. By right-clicking the file name in the FileView, you can display a menu of commands that may be performed on the file (see Figure 15.10). For example, you can open a file. If the file is a Java source file, then the source editor will open the file. However, because Java source files contain classes, and classes are best viewed using the ClassView window, Java source files are usually opened from the ClassView window. The chart.html file can also be easily opened for editing by double-clicking the file name in the FileView. This is the main advantage of adding HTML files to the project.

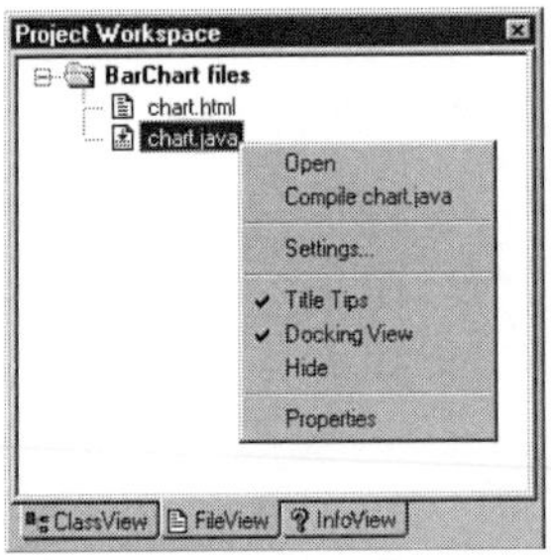

FIG. 15.10

The Project Workspace FileView tab displays files that can be right-clicked to display the properties menu.

The last command in the file's pop-up menu is Properties. Select the Properties menu item to display the Source File Properties dialog box (see Figure 15.11).

Activate the Inputs tab of the Source File Properties dialog box by clicking the Inputs tab or pressing Ctrl+Tab until it is active. The Source File Properties dialog box with the Inputs tab selected shows which tools use the file as an input source (see Figure 15.12). In the case of the chart.java file, the Java Compiler tool uses the chart.java file as input.

FIG. 15.11

The Source File Properties dialog box is shown with the Inputs tab activated.

The Source File Properties dialog box with the Outputs tab selected (see Figure 15.12) shows which tools produce output files from the source. In this case, the Java compiler produces a chart.class file and a chart.dep file.

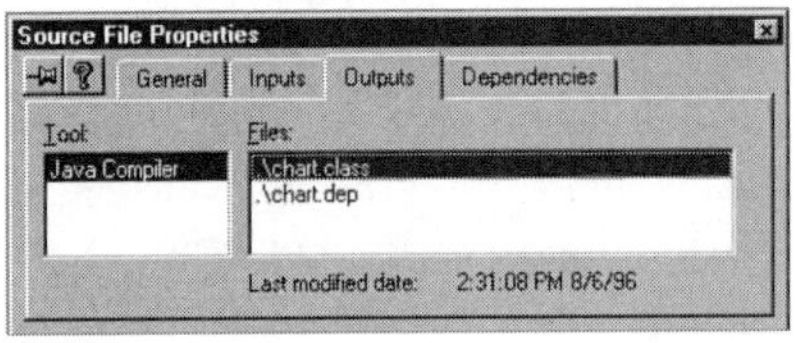

FIG. 15.12

The Source File Properties Outputs tab dialog box shows which files are produced when chart.java is compiled.

The Project Workspace ClassView tab is used to view your project's contents as Java classes. The classes can be expanded to display a list of their components such as variables and methods. Right-click a class name to see the pop-up menu that contains commands to execute on the class object (see Figure 15.13). For example, you can create a new class, or add a new variable or method to a class.

FIG. 15.13
The Project Workspace window's ClassView tab displays a project's classes and their respective variables and methods.

As you can see, simply adding a Java source file to a project also adds default relationships to invoke tools to create other files that make up the results of building the project.

Building the Project

The project is now ready to be built. Select Build, Build BarChart to build the current debug project. Figure 15.14 shows the results of a successful build in the Output window. The project is ready to be run.

FIG. 15.14
The Output window at the bottom of the Developer Studio window displays the build status.

Running the Applet

After a successful build, the BarChart project is ready to be executed. There are two settings to be made so that the Visual J++ Developer Studio can properly execute the BarChart applet. Two settings changes must be made: 1) the HTML page to load must be specified, and 2) the name of the class to debug.

To change the HTML page to be used by the debug build, select Build, Settings to display the Project Settings dialog box (see Figure 15.15). Select the Debug tab. Select Browser in the Category text box, and enter chart.html in the HTML page control. Select Use Parameters From HTML Page.

FIG. 15.15

The Project Settings dialog box with the Debug tab activated and Browser category selected.

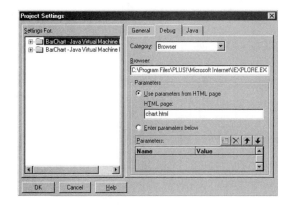

Don't click OK yet because the other setting change is on this same dialog box.

The second setting to change is the name of the class to debug. Select the General category (not the General tab!) from the Category drop-down list box. Enter **class** in the Class For Debugging Session field (see Figure 15.16). Now, click OK to save the settings.

The project settings are now set for the Internet Explorer browser to use the chart.html file to run the applet. To run the applet, select Build, Execute. An instance of the Internet Explorer is started with the chart.html file opened (refer to Figure 15.6).

The compiled chart.class can be executed by any Java-enabled browser or applet viewer. For example, open another Web browser, like Netscape Navigator. Use the File, Open File command to open the chart.html file directly. Figure 15.17 shows the same compiled applet running under the Netscape browser. Of course, you can change the project settings so that another browser is invoked by Developer Studio.

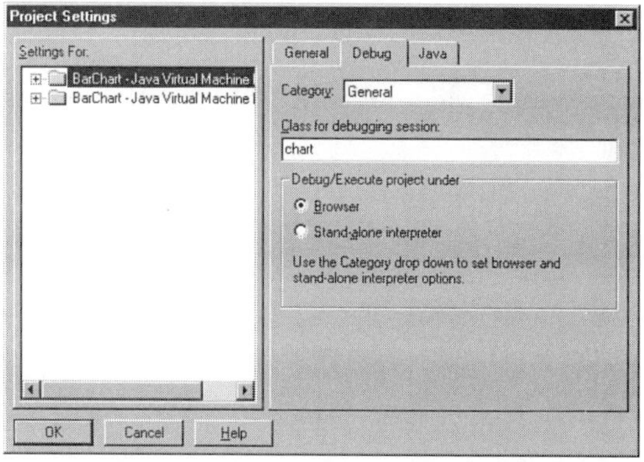

FIG. 15.16
Change another setting here in the Project Settings dialog box with the Debug tab and General category selected.

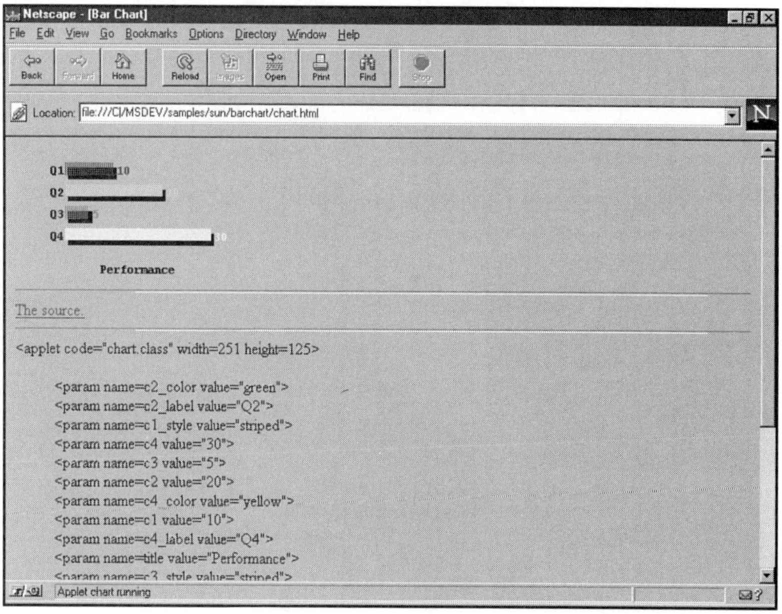

FIG. 15.17
The Bar Chart sample applet running in Netscape Navigator.

Testing the Applet

Most Java applets have parameters that allow the user to pass in values that are used to customize the applet. The applet can define its own parameters. During development, running the applet with different parameter values is necessary to test the applet thoroughly. Visual J++ will allow you to enter values for the applet parameters; and it will then generate an HTML file to use for testing the changed parameter values.

Earlier in this chapter, you changed the project settings to test the applet using the chart.html file. The content of chart.html is shown in Listing 15.1 as follows. Each <param> tag contains an applet-defined parameter name and a user-specified parameter value.

Listing 15.1 Default chart.html

```
<title>Bar Chart</title>
<applet code="chart.class" width=251 height=125>
<param name=c2_color value="green">
<param name=c2_label value="Q2">
<param name=c1_style value="striped">
<param name=c4 value="30">
<param name=c3 value="5">
<param name=c2 value="20">
<param name=c4_color value="yellow">
<param name=c1 value="10">
<param name=c4_label value="Q4">
<param name=title value="Performance">
<param name=c3_style value="striped">
<param name=columns value="4">
<param name=c1_color value="blue">
<param name=c1_label value="Q1">
<param name=c3_color value="magenta">
<param name=c3_label value="Q3">
<param name=c2_style value="solid">
<param name=orientation value="horizontal">
<param name=c4_style value="solid">
<param name=scale value="5">
</applet>
<hr>
<a href="chart.java">The source.</a>
<hr>
&lt;applet code="chart.class" width=251 height=125&gt;<p>
<blockquote>
&lt;param name=c2_color value="green"&gt;<br>
&lt;param name=c2_label value="Q2"&gt;<br>
&lt;param name=c1_style value="striped"&gt;<br>
&lt;param name=c4 value="30"&gt;<br>
&lt;param name=c3 value="5"&gt;<br>
&lt;param name=c2 value="20"&gt;<br>
&lt;param name=c4_color value="yellow"&gt;<br>
&lt;param name=c1 value="10"&gt;<br>
&lt;param name=c4_label value="Q4"&gt;<br>
&lt;param name=title value="Performance"&gt;<br>
&lt;param name=c3_style value="striped"&gt;<br>
&lt;param name=columns value="4"&gt;<br>
&lt;param name=c1_color value="blue"&gt;<br>
&lt;param name=c1_label value="Q1"&gt;<br>
&lt;param name=c3_color value="magenta"&gt;<br>
&lt;param name=c3_label value="Q3"&gt;<br>
&lt;param name=c2_style value="solid"&gt;<br>
&lt;param name=orientation value="horizontal"&gt;<br>
&lt;param name=c4_style value="solid"&gt;<br>
&lt;param name=scale value="5"&gt;<br>
```

```
    </blockquote>
    &lt;/applet&gt;
```

To let Developer Studio manage invoking the applet with your specified values, select Build, Settings to display the Project Settings dialog box (see Figure 15.18). Activate the Debug tab. Choose the Enter Parameters Below option in the Parameters group box.

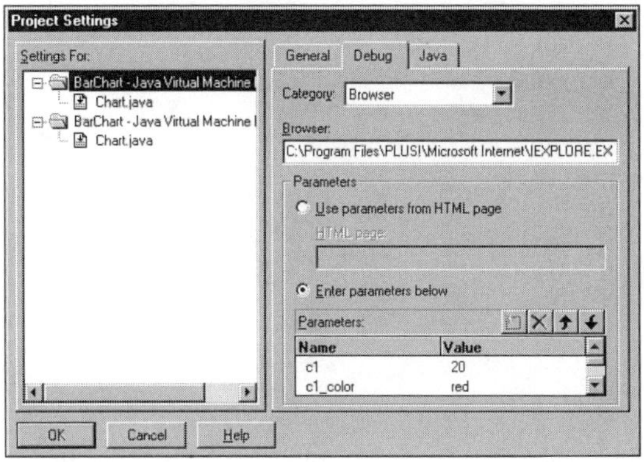

FIG. 15.18
The Project Settings dialog box with the Debug tab selected.

In the Parameters list box, enter the name and value of each applet parameter to be used. In this example, the BarChart parameters in chart.html are entered in alphabetical order with slightly different values.

Now the project is ready to be tested with the new parameter values. From the Build menu select Execute.

Developer Studio will generate an HTML file (the file name begins with VJ and is followed by four digits. For example, VJ3045.HTML) to call the applet with the specified parameters and values. The contents of the generated HTML file are shown in Listing 15.2 as follows.

Listing 15.2   The Visual J++ Generated HTML Test File: VJ3045.HTML

```
<html>
<head>
<title>chart</title>
</head>
<body>
<hr>
<applet
code=chart
width=200
height=200>
<param name=c1 value=20>
<param name=c1_color value=red>
<param name=c1_label value=Q1>
<param name=c1_style value=stripped>
```

continues

Listing 15.2   Continued

```
<param name=c2 value=5>
<param name=c2_color value=yellow>
<param name=c2_label value=Q2>
<param name=c2_style value=solid>
<param name=c3 value=28>
<param name=c3_color value=green>
<param name=c3_label value=Q3>
<param name=c3_style value=striped>
<param name=c4 value=5>
<param name=c4_color value=white>
<param name=c4_label value=Q4>
<param name=c4_style value=solid>
<param name=columns value=4>
<param name=orientation value=horizontal>
<param name=scale value=5>
<param name=title value="Performance Plus">

</applet>
<hr>
</body>
</html>
```

Figure 15.19 shows the applet running under Internet Explorer from within the above VJ3045.HTML file.

FIG. 15.19

Applet running with test-generated parameters.

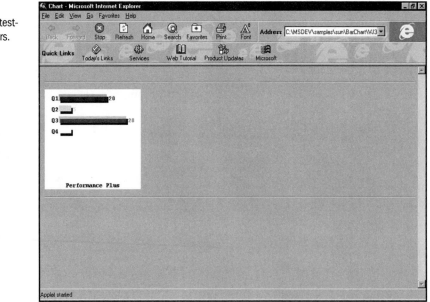

You have learned how to build a sample applet in the above sections. The next section will give you a convenient overview of the other sample applets that are a part of Visual J++.

An Overview of the Visual J++ Sun Sample Applets

This section is a collection of figures showing each of the Visual J++ Sun JDK sample applets executing. Table 15.1 shows the list of the Sun JDK samples that come with Visual J++. A screen shot of each applet is provided for quick review of the visual aspect of the sample. With each screen shot is a short description of the applet, its parameters, and the Java Class Library classes that are used in the applet code.

Table 15.1   List of Sun JDK Samples Included with Visual J++

Sample Name	Description
Animator	Demonstrates animation
Arc Test	Demonstrates arc drawing
Bar Chart	Demonstrates chart drawing
Blink	Demonstrates blinking text
Bouncing Heads	Demonstrates animation and audio
Dithering Test	Demonstrates color dithering
Draw Test	A line drawing program
Fractal	A fractal drawing program
Graphics Test	Demonstrates graphics primitives
Image Test	Demonstrates images manipulation
Jumping Box	Demonstrates mouse tracking
NervousText	Demonstrates text animation
ScrollingImages	Demonstrates scrolling
Simple Graph	Demonstrates graphing
SpreadSheet	A simple spreadsheet program
TicTacToe	A simple tictactoe program
Tumbling Duke	Demonstrates animation
WireFrame	Demonstrates 3-D modeling

Figure 15.20 shows "Duke Waving," the first of the three example pages of the Animator sample applet. The main HTML file, animator.html, contains links to "Duke waving," "Light-house," and "Duke waving, plus 'loading images.'"

The applet has parameters that allow specification of sets of images to display iteratively, and sounds to be played. The <applet> tag for example1.html is shown in Listing 15.3.

Animator uses `java.util.Hashtable`, `java.util.Vector`, `java.awt.Image`, and the `java.applet.AudioClip` interface.

Listing 15.3 Applet Tag from example1.html

```
<applet code=animator.class width=200 height=200>
<param name=imagesource value="images/Duke">
<param name=endimage value=10>
<param name=soundsource value="audio">
<param name=soundtrack value=spacemusic.au>
<param name=sounds value="1.au|2.au|3.au|4.au|5.au|6.au|7.au|8.au|9.au|0.au">
<param name=pause value=200>
</applet>
```

FIG. 15.20

The Animator sample applet is running.

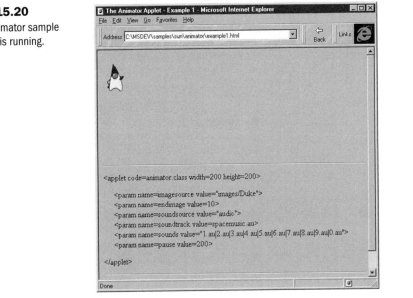

Figure 15.21 shows the Arc Test applet running. The applet draws or fills an arc starting at angle, S, and for a rotation of E degrees. The drawing of the arc is done with the java.awt.Graphics class methods fillArc and drawArc. In addition, the java.awt.Canvas class is extended to implement the painting of the grid and arc.

FIG. 15.21

The Arc Test sample applet is running.

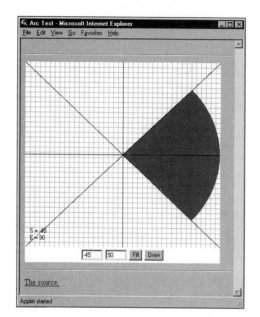

The following code (see Listing 15.4) is from arctest.java. It shows how the arc is drawn or filled. The labels startAngle and endAngle (as well as the S and E labels painted) are a little confusing. The fillArc and drawArc methods use the startAngle and the arcAngle, in other words, the angle of rotation to begin the arc and the number of degrees of arc to sweep out. The arc ends at startAngle + arcAngle.

Listing 15.4   Arc Drawing Code from arctest.java

```
if (filled) {
    g.fillArc(0, 0, r.width - 1, r.height - 1, startAngle, endAngle);
} else {
    g.drawArc(0, 0, r.width - 1, r.height - 1, startAngle, endAngle);
}
```

Other java.awt.Graphics methods used in Arc Test include: drawArc, fillArc, drawLine, drawString, setColor, and setFont.

The Bar Chart sample applet was discussed earlier in this chapter. It is shown executing in Figure 15.22. The bar chart can be configured using applet parameters.

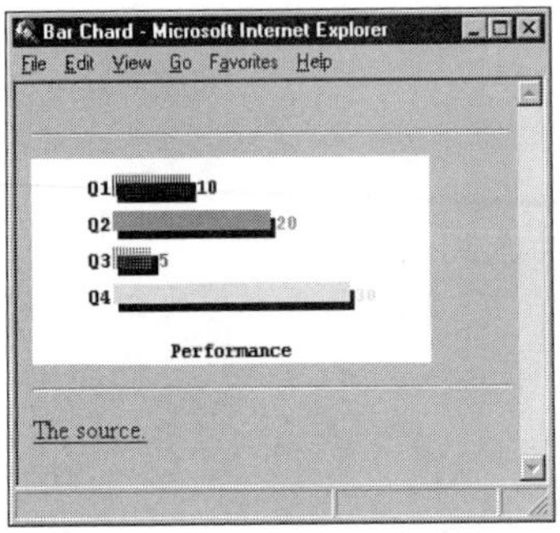

FIG. 15.22

The Bar Chart sample applet is executing.

Bar Chart illustrates use of the `java.awt.Font` and `java.awt.FontMetrics` classes.

The Blink applet (see Figure 15.23) has parameters to receive a string and a speed. The string is parsed using the `java.util.StringTokenizer` class. Each word is randomly drawn (or not drawn) with a varying font color. The speed parameter is the millisecond sleep time between painting for the applet. Blink also uses the `java.awt.FontMetrics` class.

FIG. 15.23

The Blink sample applet is executing.

The Bouncing Heads applet is shown in Figure 15.24. The head rotates and moves within the applet window. A set of sounds is played.

Bouncing Heads uses `java.applet.getAudioClip`, `java.awt.Graphics.drawRect`, `java.lang.Thread.sleep`, and `java.lang.Math.random`.

FIG. 15.24

The Bouncing Heads
sample applet is
executing in a browser.

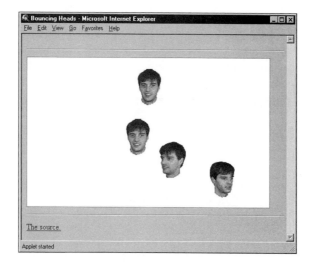

The Dithering Test applet (see Figure 15.25) creates and draws a two-dimensional dithered
image of color ranges mapped on the horizontal and vertical axes. The color image is created
using an array of pixels and `java.awt.Component.createImage`. Also used are
`java.awt.image.MemoryImageSource` and `java.awt.image.ColorModel`.

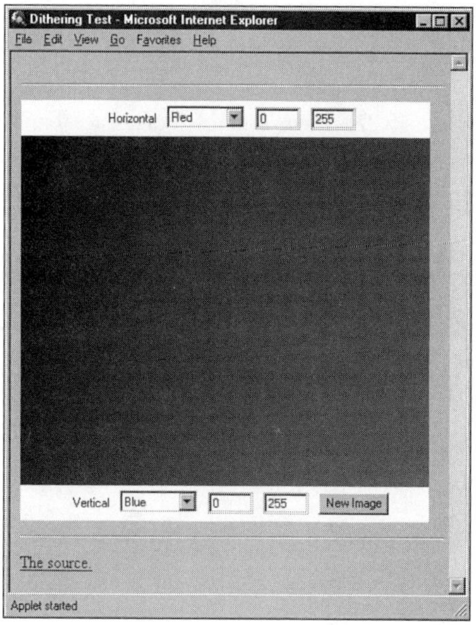

FIG. 15.25

The Dithering Test
sample applet is
running.

Draw Test (see Figure 15.26) is a simple line and point drawing program. Select a pen color and a line drawing mode, line, or point, and click and drag lines. Draw Test uses `java.util.Vector` class objects to store the list of points and colors used for painting. In addition, `java.awt.Graphics.setXORMode` and `java.awt.Graphics.setPaintMode` are used.

FIG. 15.26

The Draw Test sample applet is executing in Internet Explorer.

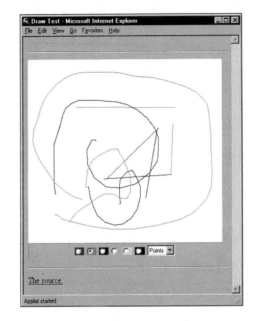

The Fractal sample (see Figure 15.27) draws one third of a fractal known as Triadic Koch Island or Snowflake by Ernest Cesaro as described by Benoit Mandelbrot in his book *The Fractal Geometry of Nature*.

FIG. 15.27

The Fractal sample applet is running.

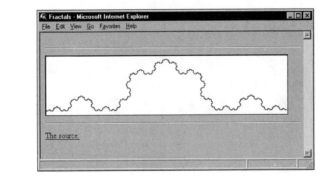

The Graphics Test sample applet is shown in Figure 15.28. This applet demonstrates graphics drawing capabilities. The go to: Choice component (i.e., drop-down list box) contains the different drawing modes: Arc, Oval, Polygon, Rect, and RoundRect. The methods used include: java.awt.Graphics.drawArc, fillArc, drawPolygon, and fillPolygon.

FIG. 15.28

The Graphics Test sample applet is shown running in a browser.

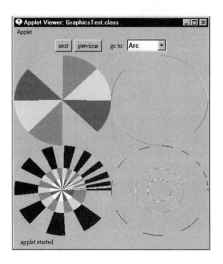

The Image Test applet displays images as shown in Figure 15.29. The applet uses the java.awt.image.DirectColorModel and java.awt.image.RGBImageFilter classes and the java.awt.image.ImageObserver interface.

FIG. 15.29

The Image Test sample applet is shown executing.

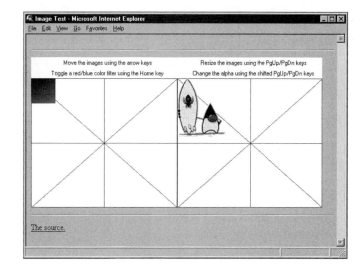

The Jumping Box applet, shown in Figure 15.30, has a box that moves away from the mouse pointer. When you click the mouse, the coordinates are displayed. The code is similar to the Image Test sample applet.

FIG. 15.30

The Jumping Box sample applet is shown executing.

The NervousText sample applet is shown in Figure 15.31. It is similar to the Blink sample, but instead of blinking words, the NervousText applet jiggles the placement of each character in the message. The `Math.random` method is used to randomize the coordinates of each character. The `java.awt.Graphics.drawChars` method is used to draw the characters.

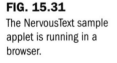

FIG. 15.31

The NervousText sample applet is running in a browser.

The ScrollingImage applet is shown in Figure 15.32. A set of images is loaded and scrolled to the right. The `java.awt.Graphics` methods used include: `fillRect`, `clipRect`, `draw3DRect`, and `copyArea`.

The Simple Graph applet is shown in Figure 15.33. The applet is very simple, consisting of fewer than 10 lines of code. It draws a continuous harmonic curve using `java.awt.Graphics.drawLine`, `java.lang.Math.cos`, and `java.lang.Math.sin`.

FIG. 15.32

The ScrollingImage sample applet is executing.

FIG. 15.33

The Simple Graph sample applet is running.

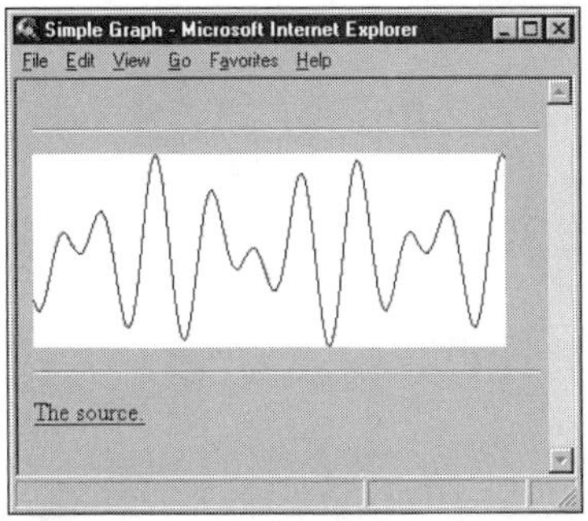

The SpreadSheet applet, shown in Figure 15.34, is a working spreadsheet. The row and column headings, and cell values can be specified using the applet parameters. You can enter a value (v) or a formula (f) into a cell while running. Click a cell to see the current value of the formula assigned. Press backspace to delete characters of a value and type in new characters. To enter a numeric value the first character should be "v." To enter a formula the first character should be "f." Cell labels use uppercase letters, A1, B2, and so on. When you press Enter, the formulas are recalculated. Once a formula is entered into a cell it cannot be changed.

FIG. 15.34

The SpreadSheet sample applet is executing in Internet Explorer.

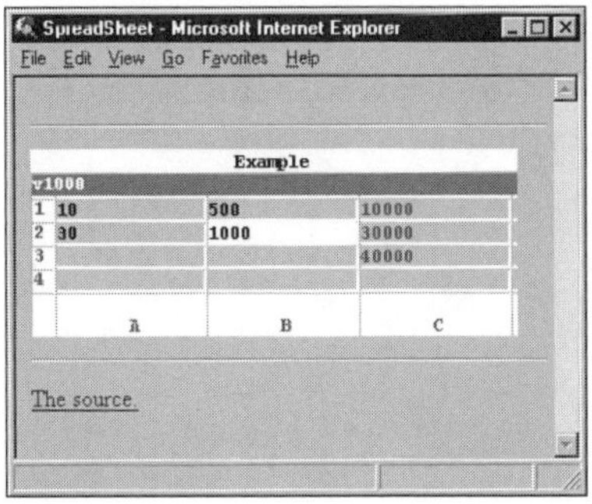

The TicTacToe applet is shown in Figure 15.35. It is a working game. You start the game by clicking the first "X." The applet makes the next move automatically. When the game is over, start a new game by clicking the applet.

FIG. 15.35
The TicTacToe sample applet is shown executing.

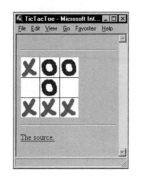

The Tumbling Duke applet is shown in Figure 15.36. It displays a series of 17 images of the Duke tumbling.

FIG. 15.36
The Tumbling Duke sample applet is running.

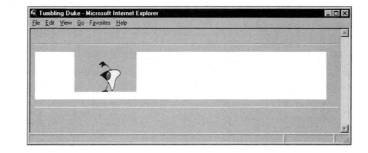

The WireFrame applet is shown in Figure 15.37. There are four example HTML files that show four different wireframe models. The examples are a cube, a dinosaur, a helicopter, and a ship. Each model can be dragged to rotate it in 3-D. The `java.util.StringTokenizer` class is used.

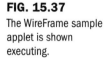

FIG. 15.37
The WireFrame sample
applet is shown
executing.

From Here...

You have learned how to build a sample project in this chapter. The following chapters will
provide more information related to creating new applets and applications, enhancing the user
interface, and adding new classes and methods. Whether building a sample application or
converting your existing JDK project to a Visual J++ project, Visual J++ allows specification of
many project settings to build and execute your project with the minimum number of changes.

- Chapter 16, "Creating an Applet with AppletWizard," will show you how to create a new
  applet or application using the Java Applet Wizard.
- Chapter 17, "Using AppStudio," will show you how to use the resource editor to add
  dialogs, controls, menus, and other resources to your project.
- Chapter 21, "Using Visual J++ Debugging Tools," will show you how to use the various
  debugging tools.

Creating an Applet with AppletWizard

by Mark Culverhouse

In the previous chapter, "Building a Sample Applet," you learned how to build a project from existing Java code. In this chapter, you will learn how to use the AppletWizard to create a new Java applet based on configuration options you specify through the wizard dialog boxes.

The AppletWizard uses the following user-specified options to build a project with source code:

- The name of your applet class.
- Generate stand-alone Java application execution capability.
- Generate Explanatory and/or To Do comments in the source code.
- Generate a sample HTML page to test the applet.
- The initial size in pixels of the applet display space.
- Multithreading support.
- Generate support for painting a rotating globe animation.
- Generate mouse event handlers.
- Define applet parameters to be used on an HTML page. The code to parse these parameters is also generated.
- Define applet information to generate override of Applet.getAppletInfo method.

Create a new Java project

Use AppletWizard to create a running Java applet. Configure your applet with the five-step AppletWizard dialogs.

Build the new project

Configure Visual J++ project settings to control the build process and then build the program.

Run the project as an applet

Test your new applet from Developer Studio using two Java-enabled Web browsers, Internet Explorer, and Netscape.

Run the project as an application

Reconfigure the project to be executed as an application. Test the applet from Developer Studio as an application running under a runtime interpreter.

Examine the AppletWizard-generated code

The generated code for each AppletWizard feature is analyzed independently. Learn about AppletWizard and Java.

In this chapter, you will build a sample applet project with most options selected. The generated project with its source code is then examined. Each AppletWizard feature is looked at in isolation to better understand how Java applets and applications work. ■

Creating a Project Using the AppletWizard

In Chapter 15, "Building a Sample Applet," the \MSDEV\SAMPLES\ directory was used to create a subdirectory to contain the sample applet project. In this section, you use the Java AppletWizard to create a subdirectory under \MSDEV\PROJECTS\CHAP16 to contain the generated applet project. The name of the project in this example is "MyJavaApp."

To invoke the AppletWizard, select File, New to display the New dialog box (see Figure 16.1). Select Project Workspace in the list box and click OK.

FIG. 16.1

Create a new Project Workspace with the New dialog box.

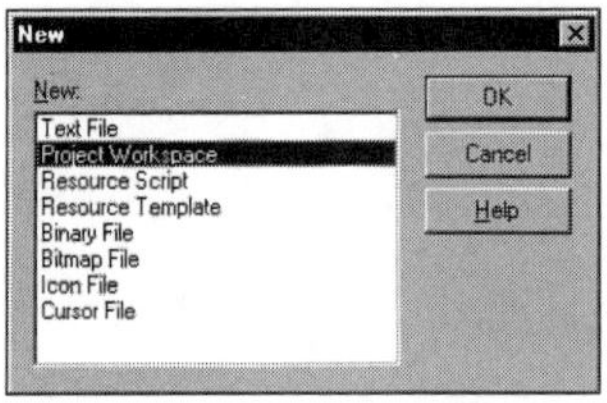

In the New Project Workspace dialog box (see Figure 16.2), select Java AppletWizard in the Type list box. Enter **\MSDEV\PROJECTS\CHAP09** into the Location field. Type **MyJavaApp** into the Name text box. Finally, click Create to start the AppletWizard.

FIG. 16.2

Use the New Project Workspace dialog box to name a new project and its location.

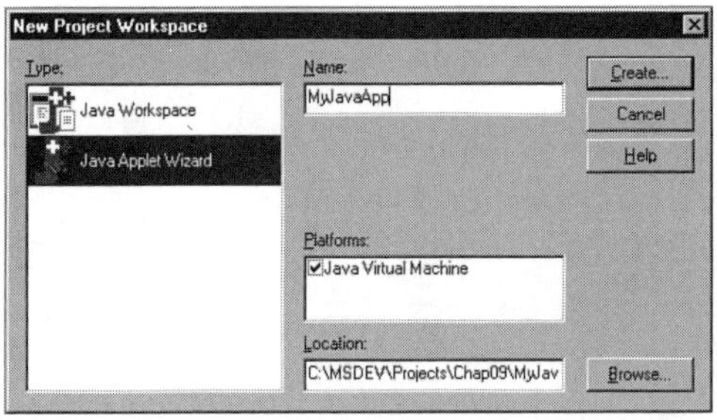

In the AppletWizard's Step 1 dialog box (see Figure 16.3), select As An Applet And As An Application. This causes code to be generated to run the applet as a stand-alone application. Leave What You Would Like To Name Your Applet Class as MyJavaApp. Check the Explanatory and TODO Comments options. Click the Next button.

In the AppletWizard's Step 2 dialog box (see Figure 16.4), select Yes, Please for an HTML sample file. Accept the default applet Width in Pixels and Height in Pixels. Click the Next button.

FIG. 16.3

Step 1 of the Java Applet Wizard is to specify your applet class name and comment style.

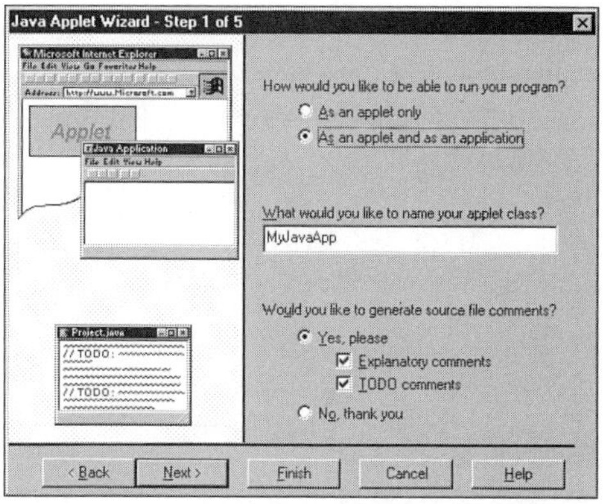

Part
III

Ch

16

FIG. 16.4

Step 2 of the Java Applet Wizard controls the HTML page and applet size.

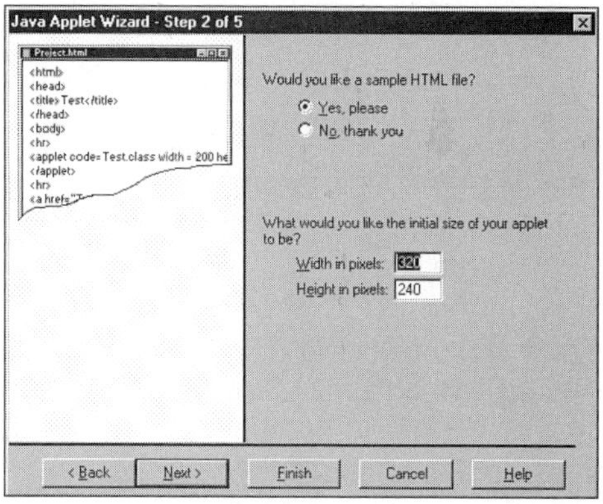

In the AppletWizard's Step 3 dialog box (see Figure 16.5), select Yes, Please for multithread support. Select Yes, Please for animation. Select the mouseDown event handler. The mouseDown selection also generates a mouseUp event handler method. Click the Next button.

FIG. 16.5

Step 3 of the Java Applet Wizard controls multithreading, animation, and mouse event handlers.

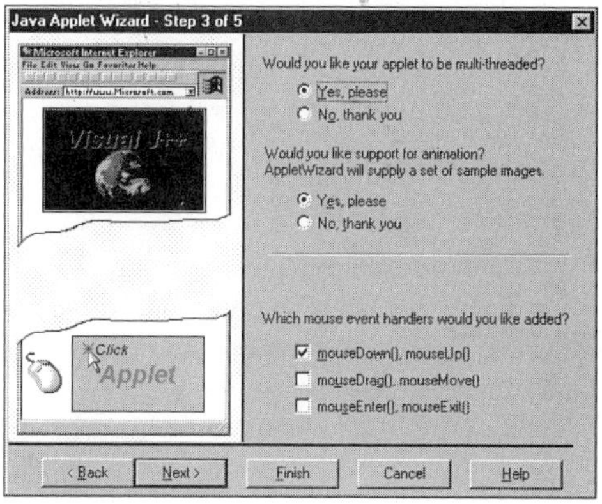

In the AppletWizard's Step 4 dialog box (see Figure 16.6), enter the description of two applet parameters. Code is generated to access the values of the HTML parameter values at runtime. Click the empty row in the Parameter box and begin to type in the Name of the first parameter. Continue to click the Member, Type, Def-Value, and Description fields, and fill in their values. The example defines a String and Boolean parameter. Click the Next button.

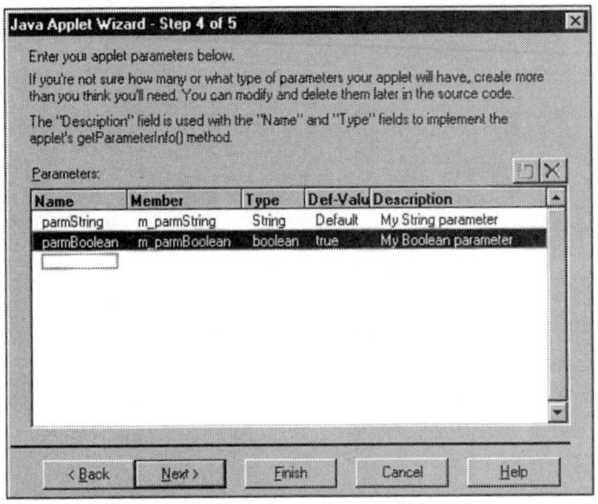

FIG. 16.6

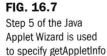

Step 4 of the Java Applet Wizard defines applet parameters and default values.

In the AppletWizard's Step 5 dialog box (see Figure 16.7), you can enter information to be returned by the getAppletInfo method. The AppletWizard creates MyJavaApp.getAppletInfo method to override the default version, Applet.getAppletInfo. The getAppletInfo method should return information about the applet's author, version, and copyright. Click the Finish button.

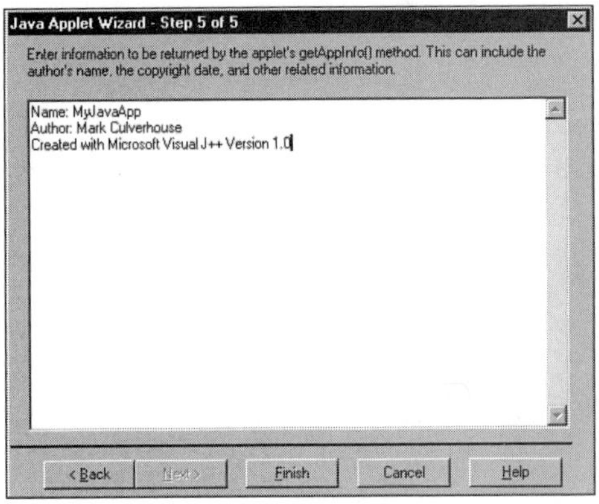

FIG. 16.7

Step 5 of the Java Applet Wizard is used to specify getAppletInfo data.

The New Project Information dialog box (see Figure 16.8) summarizes the specifications of the project that will be generated based on the project options. Click OK to generate the project files. Click Cancel to go back and review or change options.

FIG. 16.8

The New Project Information dialog box summarizes all specified options.

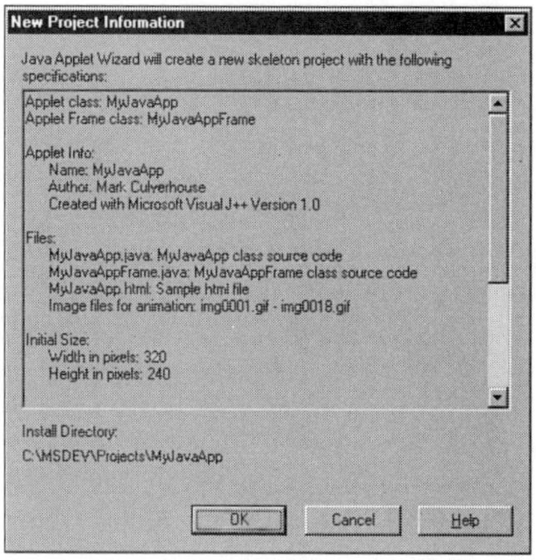

The contents of the Program Information list box are shown in Listing 16.1. The list summarizes all of the options you specified using the AppletWizard dialog boxes.

Listing 16.1   Contents of the Program Information List Box

```
Applet class: MyJavaApp
Applet Frame class: MyJavaAppFrame

Applet Info:
     Name: MyJavaApp
     Author: Mark Culverhouse
     Created with Microsoft Visual J++ Version 1.0

Files:
     MyJavaApp.java: MyJavaApp class source code
     MyJavaAppFrame.java: MyJavaAppFrame class source code
     MyJavaApp.html: Sample html file
     Image files for animation: img0001.gif - img0018.gif

Initial Size:
     Width in pixels: 320
     Height in pixels: 240

Features:
     + Can run as a standalone application
     + User Comments
     + TODO Comments
     + Multi Threaded
     + Simple Animation
     + Mouse Down/Up interaction

Parameters: (Name, Type, Default Value, Description)
     parmString, String, "Default", "My String parameter"
     parmBoolean, boolean, true, "My Boolean parameter"     + Simple Animation
```

Building the Project

You have now created the project files. The next step is to build the project and see the applet in action. Before building the project, you should review your project settings. Select Build, Settings to display the Project Settings dialog box (see Figure 16.9).

On the General property page, you see the Output Directory text control. You can set the directory that should contain the files created by the build process. You can enter no subdirectory, which puts all output files in the project directory. If you want to maintain separate directories for the output files of each subproject, enter a different output directory for each subproject.

By default, the Debug subproject and the Release subproject specify no subdirectory, so the output files all go to the project directory. You could specify JavaDbg and JavaRel as the respective subdirectories for the Debug and Release targets.

To test from these subdirectories, you must make some changes. You can copy the HTML file into each subdirectory, or you can add the codebase parameter to the applet tag.

FIG. 16.9
The Project Settings
General dialog box can
be used to browse the
project setting.

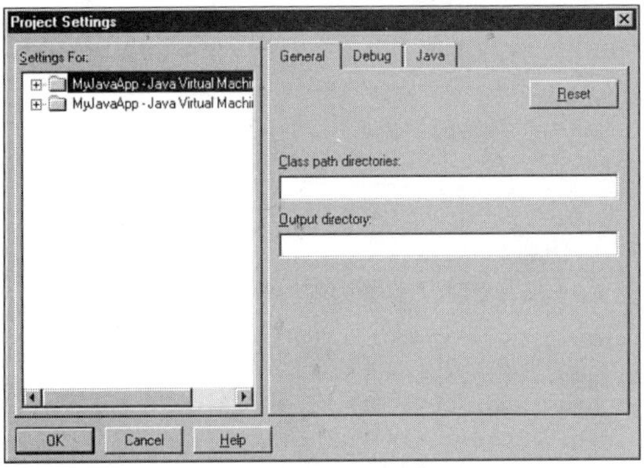

In Listing 16.2, the generated HTML file does not have a codebase applet parameter. If you wanted this HTML file to load the applet *.class files from the JavaDbg subdirectory, then the following line would be added after the code= statement: codebase=JavaDbg.

**Listing 16.2   Listing of the MyJavaApp.html File
(msdev\projects\chap16\MyJavaApp\MyJavaApp.html)**

```
<html>
<head>
<title>MyJavaApp</title>
</head>
<body>
<hr>
<applet
    code=MyJavaApp.class
```

```
width=320
    height=240 >
</applet>
<hr>
<a href="MyJavaApp.java">The source.</a>
</body>
</html>
```

If you specified an output directory, Developer Studio creates that subdirectory and builds the Java class files in it. To build the project, select Build, Rebuild All. Figure 16.10 shows the result of a successful build.

Part

III

Ch

16

FIG. 16.10
The Output window displays the status of your project as it builds.

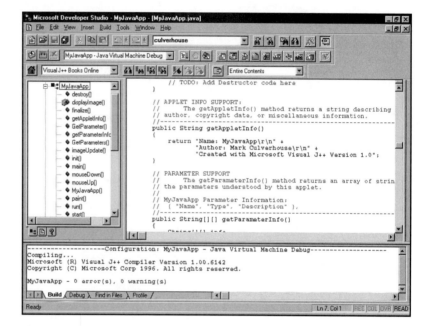

Running the Applet

After you have successfully built the project, you can execute the applet. If you have generated an applet to run only as an applet on an HTML page, you must execute the applet using a Java-enabled browser application such as Microsoft's Internet Explorer or Netscape's Navigator. You can also open the HTML file with the browser directly.

To execute your applet in an HTML file within a browser application from within Visual J++, you must change some project settings. Select Build, Settings to display the Project Settings dialog box, and select the Debug property tab. Select the General Category; then select the Browser radio button (see Figure 16.11). Don't click OK just yet! There is another setting on this dialog tab that needs changing.

This tells Developer Studio to use a browser to execute this project. The next step is to specify which browser application to use.

FIG. 16.11

The General Category of the Debug tab in the Project Settings dialog box specifies the class to debug.

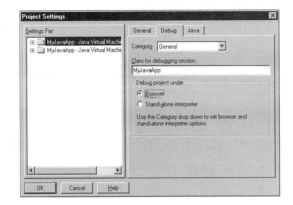

Select Browser from the Category list box (see Figure 16.12). Enter the name of the browser for Developer Studio to use. The Microsoft browser is named IEXPLORE.EXE. Select Use Parameters From HTML Page. Now you can click OK to configure Developer Studio to use the Internet Explorer browser when executing the project.

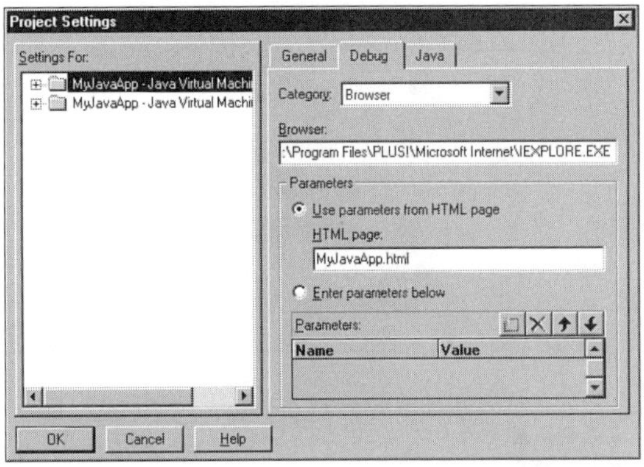

FIG. 16.12

Use the Browser Category of the Debug Project Settings dialog box to specify Internet Explorer as the project browser.

To execute your project with the current settings, select Build, Execute MyJavaApp. The Internet Explorer browser is started with your application running (see Figure 16.13).

To set your project to run your applet using Netscape Navigator, select Build, Settings, Debug tab, Category Browser, and enter the Navigator program path and file name in the Browser text box (see Figure 16.14). Click OK to save changed settings.

FIG. 16.13

Your Java AppletWizard applet is shown running in Internet Explorer.

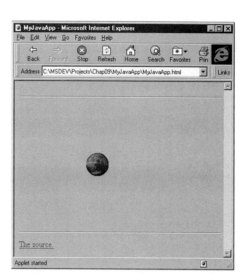

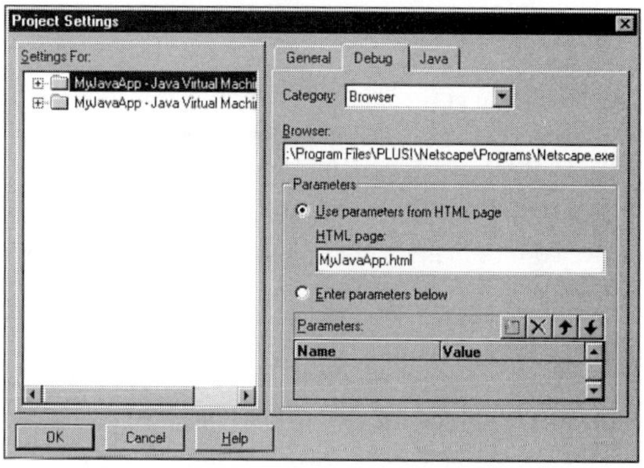

FIG. 16.14

Use the Debug tab on the Project Settings dialog box to specify Netscape Navigator as the project browser.

Select Build, Execute MyJavaApp to execute your applet using Netscape Navigator (see Figure 16.15). It is always useful to test your applets with different browsers because there are always slight differences in rendering HTML pages.

In this section, you learned how to run your applet from a browser. In the next section, you learn to run the same project as a stand-alone application.

FIG. 16.15

Here is the Java Applet Wizard applet running in Netscape Navigator.

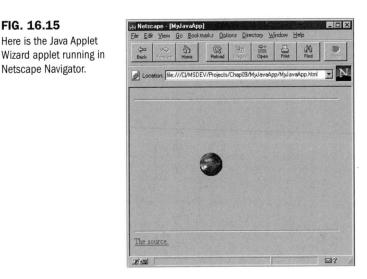

Running the Application

In this section, you learn how to run your applet as an application without a browser. One of the biggest reasons to run an applet using a stand-alone interpreter instead of a browser is security. Under a browser, Java applets are restricted by the security manager of the browser from performing certain operations. These include reading and writing files on the client's system, and accessing resources over the Internet from hosts other than the applet's.

The following steps are necessary to run your applet project as an application:

1. Specify that the project is to run as a stand-alone application.
2. Specify the name of the virtual machine (VM) on which to run the application.
3. Run the VM with parameters to start the application.

To execute your applet as a stand-alone application from within Visual J++, you must change some project settings. Select Build, Settings to display the Project Settings dialog box. Select the Debug property tab; then select the General Category (see Figure 16.16).

Select Stand-Alone Interpreter. This tells Developer Studio to use a stand-alone interpreter to execute this project. The class to pass the interpreter is your applet class, MyJavaApp, which is the default. The next step is to specify which stand-alone interpreter to use. Don't click OK yet.

Select Stand-Alone Interpreter from the Category list box (see Figure 16.17). Enter the name of the interpreter for Developer Studio to use in the Stand-Alone Interpreter text box. The Microsoft interpreter is named JView.EXE.

The Stand-Alone Interpreter Arguments control is used to enter command line options for the specified interpreter. For example, the sidebar contains the description of the JView command obtained by running JView with no parameters.

FIG. 16.16
Use the General
Category of Debug
Project Settings dialog
box to run the stand-
alone interpreter.

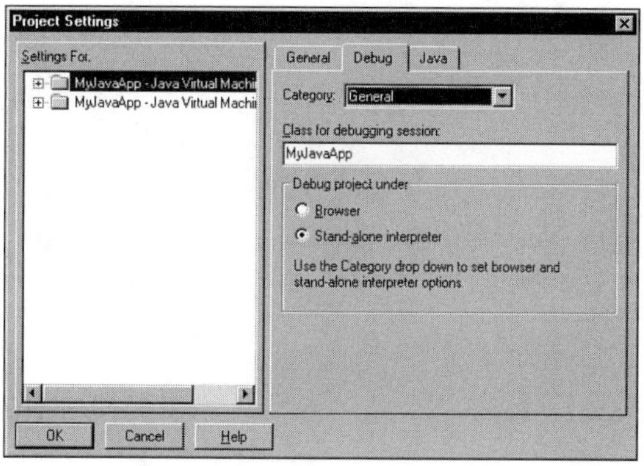

Click OK and you are ready to execute your application.

JView Command Usage

Run JView with no parameters to display its Help on parameter usage:

```
Microsoft (R) Visual J++ Command-line Interpreter Version 1.00.6194
Copyright (C) Microsoft Corp 1996. All rights reserved.

Usage: JView [options] <classname> [arguments]

Options:
    /?               displays usage text
    /cp <classpath>  set class path
    /cp:p <path>     prepend path to class path
    /cp:a <path>     append path to class path

Classname:
    .CLASS file to be executed.

Arguments:
    command-line arguments to be passed on to the class file
```

TIP During testing with Developer Studio, you can run JView by using the Build, Execute menu command. To run your applet as an application independent of Developer Studio, you can run JView from a command line. JView needs all paths to classes specified explicitly, including your project directory, even if you invoke JView from that directory.

Therefore, the command to run MyJavaApp using JView from the command line within the MyJavaApp directory would be:

JView /cp:a .\MyJavaApp MyJavaApp

This assumes that your CLASSPATH environment variable is set to \windows\java\classes. If it is not, you can use the following command to explicitly list all class paths:

JView /cp:a c:\windows\java\classes /cp:a .\MyJavaApp MyJavaApp

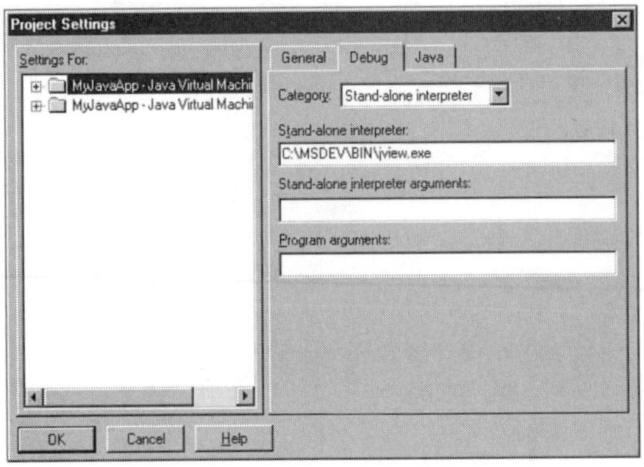

FIG. 16.17
Use the Stand-alone
interpreter category of
the Debug Project
Settings dialog box to
specify the project
interpreter.

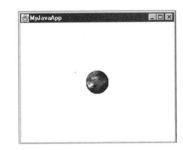

To execute MyJavaApp with the new project settings, select the Build, Execute MyJavaApp
menu item. Figure 16.18 shows the applet running within JView as an application because it is
not using a browser.

FIG. 16.18
Here is your Java applet
running as an
application using
JView.exe.

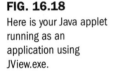

Understanding AppletWizard-Generated Code

The sample project you generated, MyJavaApp, contains most of the features offered by the
AppletWizard. In this section, you learn about these features and how they are implemented by
the AppletWizard. Before looking at the code generated for the MyJavaApp project, you examine other smaller and simpler projects generated by AppletWizard.

AppWizard0: The Simplest Applet

The first example is AppWizard0. This example shows how a simple applet runs. This project is
generated with the "run program as applet only" feature. There is no multithreading, no animation or painting, and no application support.

An applet on an HTML page is usually created by the browser application or an applet viewer.
AppWizard0 is a Java class that extends the java.applet.Applet class (see Listing 16.3).

The AppletWizard created the following AppWizard0 methods, which override the
java.applet.Applet versions: init, destroy, start, and stop.

When the applet is run, the following events occur:

- With the browser, the user opens the HTML page containing the applet for the first time.
- An AppWizard0 object is created, which causes the constructor AppWizard0 to be called.
- The AppWizard0.init, AppWizard0.start, and AppWizard0.paint methods are called. (Throughout the following steps, the paint method may be called several times but is not noted from here on.)
- With the browser's Back command, the user goes back to the previous page.
- In response to the Back command, the AppWizard0.stop and AppWizard0.start methods are called.
- The user resizes the browser's window.
- In response to the resize, the AppWizard0.stop and start methods are called.
- The user reopens the same HTML file.
- In response, the AppWizard0's stop method is called for the existing AppWizard0 instance. Then, a new AppWizard0 instance is created. The new AppWizard0 instance's AppWizard0 constructor, init, and start methods are called.
- With the browser's Refresh command, the user refreshes the applet's HTML page.
- In response to the Refresh command, the AppWizard's stop and start methods are called.

As you can see from the above scenario, many events can cause the init, start, and stop methods of the Applet class to be called. Different browsers may implement these calls in slightly different ways.

The init method is usually called once each time the HTML page is "opened," either with the File Open command or by clicking Enter in the address control of the browser. Notice that a browser Back or Refresh command may not be the same as an Open command.

The AppletWizard inserted a call to resize in the init method. This is the correct method to place the call to resize because between the calls to the start and stop methods, the size of the applet window does not change.

The start method is called when the same applet is displayed for the first or subsequent times. Notice that in the browser scenario, when the user changes the size of the browser window, the stop and start methods are called.

The stop method is called whenever the applet goes out of view—that is, it is replaced by another page. The stop method should "stop" anything "started" in the start method. After the stop method is called, the start method might be called again or the destroy method might be called.

The destroy method is called when the browser is about to destroy the AppWizard0 object. The destroy method should release any resources acquired in the init method. It is unpredictable when the destroy method will be called.

The finalize method may or may not be called. The paint method does nothing in this applet.

**Listing 16.3 AppWizard0 Class
(\msdev\project\AppWizard0\AppWizard0.java)**

```
import java.applet.*;
import java.awt.*;

public class AppWizard0 extends Applet
{

    public AppWizard0()
    {
    }

    public void finalize()
    {
    }

    public String getAppletInfo()
    {
        return "Name: AppWizard0\r\n" +
            "Author: Mark Culverhouse\r\n" +
            "Created with Microsoft Visual J++ Version 1.0";
    }

    public void init()
    {
        resize(320, 240);
    }

    public void destroy()
    {
    }

    public void paint(Graphics g)
    {
    }

    public void start()
    {
    }

    public void stop()
    {
    }
}
```

AppWizard1: Adding Multithreading

The next example project generated by AppletWizard is called AppWizard1 (see Listing 16.4). AppWizard1 is the same as AppWizard0 except that multithreading support is turned on but animation is still turned off.

This lets you look at what the AppletWizard means by multithreading support. The code for the AppWizard `constructor`, `finalize`, `init`, `destroy`, and `getAppletInfo` methods is unchanged from the previous example.

The new code generated to support multithreading includes:

- The `AppWizard1` class is defined to implement the Runnable interface.
- There is a new instance variable `m_AppWizard1` of type `Thread`.
- The `paint` method outputs a string with a random number.
- The `start` and `stop` methods create and destroy a thread.
- A new method `run` is defined.

Part
III

Ch
16

The Runnable interface is defined in java.lang.Runnable. It consists of a single method called `run` that has no parameters and returns void. The `run` method generated by AppletWizard contains an infinite loop that calls `repaint` and goes to sleep for 50 milliseconds (ms). But how does the `run` method get called to begin with?

The `AppWizard1.start` method now has code to create a new `Thread` object and call its `start` method, as long as one does not already exist. Notice that the `m_AppWizard1` is created by passing this as a parameter to the `Thread` constructor. The `java.lang.Thread` class does not have a constructor that accepts an instance of the Applet class but it does have a constructor that accepts an object that implements the Runnable interface.

That `Thread` constructor in turn calls the `Runnable.run` method of the object, which in this case is `AppWizard1.run`. Note that the `AppWizard1.run` method runs under the `m_AppWizard1` `Thread` object's thread. So when it calls sleep(50 ms), it is the `m_AppWizard1` `Thread` object that goes to sleep and not the `AppWizard1` applet object.

The `AppWizard1.stop` method now has code to destroy the thread created in the `AppWizard1.start` method. When the m_AppWizard1 reference is set to null, the `Thread` object is relegated to the garbage collector.

Therefore, the behavior of this applet when it is displayed or redisplayed is to create a thread that calls the `run` method to paint a random number every 50 ms. When the applet goes out of view, the `stop` method destroys the `Thread` object until the applet comes into view again and the `start` method is called again.

Listing 16.4   AppWizard1 Class
(\msdev\project\AppWizard1\AppWizard1.java)

```
import java.applet.*;
import java.awt.*;

public class AppWizard1 extends Applet implements Runnable
{
```

continues

Listing 16.4 Continued

```
Thread       m_AppWizard1 = null;
public void paint(Graphics g)
{
    g.drawString("Running: " + Math.random(), 10, 20);
}

public void start()
{
    if (m_AppWizard1 == null)
    {
        m_AppWizard1 = new Thread(this);
        m_AppWizard1.start();
    }
}

public void stop()
{
    if (m_AppWizard1 != null)
    {
        m_AppWizard1.stop();
        m_AppWizard1 = null;
    }
}

public void run()
{
    while (true)
    {
        try
        {
            repaint();
            Thread.sleep(50);
        }
        catch (InterruptedException e)
        {
            stop();
        }
    }
}
public AppWizard1(). . .
public void finalize() . . .
public void init()(). . .
public void destroy()(). . .
public String getAppletInfo()(). . .
}
```

AppWizard2: Adding Application Support

The next sample project generated by AppletWizard is called AppWizard2. AppWizard2 is the same as AppWizard1, except that support to run as an application and an applet is turned on but animation is still turned off.

This lets you look at what the AppletWizard does so your applet code can run unchanged as an application. The code for the AppWizard `constructor`, `finalize`, `getAppletInfo`, `init`, `destroy`, `paint`, `start`, `stop`, and `run` methods are unchanged from the previous example.

The new code generated to support running the applet as an application includes:

- A new class and file are created called `AppWizard2Frame`.
- A new Boolean instance variable is defined to indicate that the applet is running as a stand-alone application.
- A new static method, `main`, is created.

Part
III

Ch
16

A new import statement is added to import the new `AppWizard2Frame` class (see Listing 16.5). `AppWizard2Frame` extends the `java.awt.Frame` class. The `Frame` class represents a top-level window with title bar, menu bar, icon, and cursor.

When an applet runs under a browser or applet viewer, a window is created for the applet to use. When the applet runs as an application, it must create its own window to run in. That is what the `AppWizard2Frame` class is used for.

A new `Boolean` instance variable, `m_fStandAlone`, is created. It is initially `false` and is set `true` when the applet is run as an application. This flag, `m_fStandAlone`, is used by AppletWizard generated to code to test if the applet is running as an application and not an applet.

For example, applet and application parameters and image loading are handled differently. As you enhance your applet/applications, you may also need to use this flag in special circumstances.

A new static method named `main` is created. The `public static main` method is what is started by stand-alone interpreters.

The `main` method must perform the tasks that a browser or applet viewer would perform. Because AppWizard2 is already a complete running applet, it just needs to be "started."

First, an `AppWizard2Frame` object is created for the applet to draw itself. Next, a new `AppWizard2` object is created. The new applet object is added to the frame as "Center" so it takes over the entire client area of the frame.

The `m_fStandAlone` flag is set, and the applet `init` and `start` methods are called. Because this is not a browser in which another page might replace this page, there is no need to call `stop` or, in fact, to do anything more.

Listing 16.5 AppWizard2 Class
(\msdev\project\AppWizard2\AppWizard2.java)

```
import java.applet.*;
import java.awt.*;
import AppWizard2Frame;
```

continues

Listing 16.5 Continued

```
public class AppWizard2 extends Applet implements Runnable
{
    Thread      m_AppWizard2 = null;

    // STANDALONE APPLICATION SUPPORT:
    //          m_fStandAlone will be set to true if applet is run standalone
    //--------------------------------------------------------------------

    boolean m_fStandAlone = false;

    public static void main(String args[])
    {
        AppWizard2Frame frame = new AppWizard2Frame("AppWizard2");

        // Must show Frame before we size it so insets() will return valid
        ➥values
        //--------------------------------------------------------------------

        frame.show();
        frame.resize(frame.insets().left + frame.insets().right  + 320,
                     frame.insets().top  + frame.insets().bottom + 240);

        AppWizard2 applet_AppWizard2 = new AppWizard2();

        frame.add("Center", applet_AppWizard2);
        applet_AppWizard2.m_fStandAlone = true;
        applet_AppWizard2.init();
        applet_AppWizard2.start();
    }

    public AppWizard2() . . .
    public void finalize(). . .
    public String getAppletInfo(). . .
    public void init(). . .
    public void destroy(). . .
    public void paint(Graphics g) . . .
    public void start(). . .
    public void stop(). . .
    public void run(). . .
}
```

The AppletWizard also creates a new class that extends the Frame class. The AppWizard2Frame class (see Listing 16.6) is used as the container of the applet object. There is not much to the Frame class yet. In handleEvent, the WINDOW_DESTROY event is necessary to exit the Java interpreter. Without it, the system close command would not work.

That is, clicking the application's close button or selecting Close from the system menu would be ignored and the application would continue to run. In fact, you have to end the task rather ungracefully.

**Listing 16.6   AppWizard2Frame Class
(\msdev\project\AppWizard2\AppWizard2Frame.java)**

```java
import java.awt.*;

class AppWizard2Frame extends Frame
{
    public AppWizard2Frame(String str)
    {
        super (str);
    }

    public void finalize()
    {
    }

    public boolean handleEvent(Event evt)
    {
        switch (evt.id)
        {
            case Event.WINDOW_DESTROY:
                dispose();
                System.exit(0);
                return true;

            default:
                return super.handleEvent(evt);
        }
    }
}
```

AppWizard3: Adding Animation

The next sample project generated by AppletWizard is called AppWizard3. AppWizard3 is the same as AppWizard2 except that animation is turned on. This additional application feature adds code to load and continuously paint a series of images of a rotating globe.

The new code generated to support running the applet as an application includes:

- A new "images" subdirectory is created within the directory of each target. A set of images that represent snapshots of a rotating globe are copied to the new images directory. These image files are also added to the project.
- There are seven new variables to store image information.
- The paint and run methods are the only methods that changed from corresponding AppWizard2 methods.
- There are two new methods to support painting the images: imageUpdate and displayImage. The constructor, main, finalize, getAppletInfo, init, destroy, start, and stop methods are not changed by adding the animation support.

In the new images subdirectory, there are eighteen GIF files named img0001.gif through img0018.gif. These images are loaded into memory and drawn by the applet's paint method.

The seven new variables are shown below. They are used to store and paint the loaded image files.

```
Graphics m_Graphics;
Image     m_Images[];
int       m_nCurrImage;
int       m_nImgWidth  = 0;
int       m_nImgHeight = 0;
boolean   m_fAllLoaded = false;
final int NUM_IMAGES = 18;
```

The only methods from AppWizard2 that change in AppWizard3 are paint and run. The paint method contained a single drawString statement that displayed a random number.

The new paint method (see Listing 16.7) is still simple: it checks to see if all images have been loaded. If they are all loaded, it clears the rectangle that needs painting and calls one of the new methods, displayImage, to do the actual image drawing. If the images are not yet loaded, a "Loading images" string is displayed instead. The Graphics object parameter to paint is similar to a Windows device context.

Listing 16.7   AppWizard3.paint Method
(\msdev\project\AppWizard3\AppWizard3.java)

```
public void paint(Graphics g)
    {
        // ANIMATION SUPPORT:
        //          The following code displays a status message until all the
        // images are loaded. Then it calls displayImage to display the
        ➥current
        // image.
        //-------------------------------------------------------------
        if (m_fAllLoaded)
        {
            Rectangle r = g.getClipRect();

            g.clearRect(r.x, r.y, r.width, r.height);
            displayImage(g);
        }
        else
            g.drawString("Loading images...", 10, 20);

    }
```

The run method (see Listing 16.8) has the most new code to handle loading all the images. The previous run method had an infinite loop that would sleep for 50 milliseconds and then call repaint. The new run method must first load all images into memory.

The java.awt.Component.getGraphics method returns the graphics context of the applet. The graphics context is used for drawing images. The nCurrImage variable is used to control indexing through the array of images when drawing. m_Images is the array that stores the loaded images.

The for construct starts the loading of each image by constructing its name, including the images subdirectory name. Here is an instance of using the m_fStandAlone flag to normalize a difference between applets and applications.

Loading images is a catch-22 situation. The getDocumentBase method only works when you are running under a browser because applications have no document or HTML page.

The Toolkit.getDefaultToolkit.getImage call does not work under an applet because its String parameter specifies a file name instead of a URL name. Therefore, applets cannot use this because it would result in a security exception when the file is read. In either case, though, an Image object is returned.

When the first image is loaded, its width and height are obtained and used for the group of images that are assumed to all be the same size. As the AppletWizard comments describe, the java.awt.Image getWidth and getHeight methods return -1 until the image dimensions are known. The code sleeps in a loop until the width and height are known from the first image.

At the end of the for construct's body is a call to drawImage with coordinates off the screen. The last parameter takes an object that implements the ImageObserver. For the Applet class, this is the Component superclass. The ImageObserver interface contains the imageUpdate method, which is called when the image passed to drawImage is completely loaded. Because this is passed as the ImageObserver parameter, the new imageUpdate method in AppWizard3 will be called.

After the for construct, which starts the loading of each image, the while(!m_AllLoaded) loop waits until all images have been loaded. The m_AllLoaded flag is set in the imageUpdate method, discussed next. Once all images are loaded, a call to repaint is done to force painting.

The while loop in the run method sleeps, calls displayImage to paint the current image, and then increments the image index and sleeps again.

Listing 16.8   AppWizard3.run Method
(\msdev\project\AppWizard3\AppWizard3.java)

```
public void run()
    {
        repaint();

        m_Graphics = getGraphics();
        m_nCurrImage   = 0;
        m_Images    = new Image[NUM_IMAGES];

        String strImage;
```

continues

Listing 16.8 Continued

```
         // For each image in the animation, this method first constructs a
         // string containing the path to the image file; then it begins
     ➡loading
         // the image into the m_Images array.  Note that the call to getImage
         // will return before the image is completely loaded.
         //-------------------------------------------------------------
         for (int i = 1; i <= NUM_IMAGES; i++)
         {
             strImage = "images/img00" + ((i < 10) ? "0" : "") + i + ".gif";
             if (m_fStandAlone)
                 m_Images[i-1] =
Toolkit.getDefaultToolkit().getImage(strImage);
             else
                 m_Images[i-1] = getImage(getDocumentBase(), strImage);
             if (m_nImgWidth == 0)
             {
                 try
                 {
                     // The getWidth() and getHeight() methods of the Image
                     ➡    class
                     // return -1 if the dimensions are not yet known. The
                     // following code keeps calling getWidth() and
                     ➡    getHeight()
                     // until they return actual values.
                     // NOTE: This is only executed once in this loop, since
                     ➡    we
                     //       are assuming all images are the same width and
                     //       height.  However, since we do not want to
                     ➡    duplicate
                     //       the above image load code, the code resides in
                     ➡    the
                     //       loop.
                     //-------------------------------------------------------------
                     while ((m_nImgWidth = m_Images[i-1].getWidth(null)) <
                     ➡    0)
                         Thread.sleep(1);

                     while ((m_nImgHeight = m_Images[i-1].getHeight(null)) <
                     ➡    0)
                         Thread.sleep(1);
                 }
                 catch (InterruptedException e)
                 {
                 }
             }
             m_Graphics.drawImage(m_Images[i-1], -1000, -1000, this);
         }

         while (!m_fAllLoaded)
         {
             try
             {
```

```
        {
            Thread.sleep(10);
        }
        catch (InterruptedException e)
        {
        }
    }

    repaint();

    while (true)
    {
        try
        {
            displayImage(m_Graphics);
            m_nCurrImage++;
            if (m_nCurrImage == NUM_IMAGES)
                m_nCurrImage = 0;

            Thread.sleep(50);
        }+
        catch (InterruptedException e)
        {
            stop();
        }
    }
}
}
```

Below is the imageUpdate method of AppWizard3 (see Listing 16.9), which overrides the version in the Component superclass of Applet. When the ALLBITS flag is true, the number of completed images counter, m_nCurrImage, is incremented. When all images are completed, m_fAllLoaded is set to true and m_nCurrImage is reset to zero to get ready for painting.

Listing 16.9 AppWizard3.imageUpdate Method
(\msdev\project\AppWizard3\AppWizard3.java)

```
public boolean imageUpdate(Image img, int flags, int x, int y, int w, int h)
    {
        if (m_fAllLoaded)
            return false;

        if ((flags & ALLBITS) == 0)
            return true;

        if (++m_nCurrImage == NUM_IMAGES)
        {
            m_nCurrImage = 0;
            m_fAllLoaded = true;
        }

        return false;
    }
```

The drawImage method (see Listing 16.10) is simple. It uses the Graphics.drawImage method to draw the image in the center of the applet.

Listing 16.10 AppWizard3.displayImage Method (\msdev\project\AppWizard3\AppWizard3.java)

```
void displayImage(Graphics g)
{
    if (!m_fAllLoaded)
        return;

    g.drawImage(m_Images[m_nCurrImage],
                (size().width - m_nImgWidth)   / 2,
                (size().height - m_nImgHeight) / 2, null);
}
```

AppWizard4: Adding Parameters

The next sample project generated by AppletWizard is called AppWizard4. AppWizard4 is the same as AppWizard3 except that two parameters are defined. This application feature adds code to read and store the HTML applet parameters and/or the application command line arguments.

Parameters pass values from the user to the running applet. By providing parameters, an applet can become more useful, giving the user more control over an applet's behavior.

The AppWizard4 sample is generated with two parameters defined: a String parameter named "parm1" and an int parameter named "parm2." Figure 16.19 shows the definition of the parameters, including data type and initial values.

FIG. 16.19

The Java Applet Wizard Step 4 of 5 Applet Parameters dialog box is used to define applet parameters.

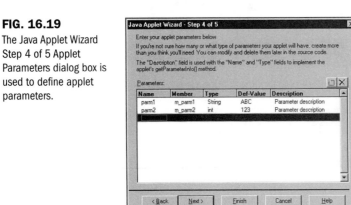

The new code generated to support applet and application parameters includes the following:

- Two new applet parameters are added to the AppWizard4.html file. These parameters pass in the initial values given to the AppletWizard.

- Four new instance variables are created for the two parameters. For each parameter, two variables are defined. One variable stores the data value of the parameter; it has the data type of the parameter. The other variable is a String instance that is used to store the name of the parameter.

- Two existing methods have been changed: `main` and `init`.

- Three new methods are created to support parameters: `GetParameters`, `GetParameter`, and `getParameterInfo`.

Part
III

Ch
16

The AppWizard4.html file in Listing 16.11 shows the `parm1` and `parm2` applet parameters. They are set with the initial values but can be changed to cause the applet to alter its behavior.

**Listing 16.11   AppWizard4.html File
(\msdev\project\AppWizard4\AppWizard4.html)**

```
<html>
<head>
<title>AppWizard4</title>
</head>
<body>
<hr>
<applet
    code=AppWizard4.class
    width=320
    height=240 >
    <param name=parm1 value="ABC">
    <param name=parm2 value=123>
</applet>
<hr>
<a href="AppWizard4.java">The source.</a>
</body>
</html>
```

The new instance variables `m_parm1` and `m_parm2` are used to store the value of the parameters. They are initialized with the initial values specified in Step 4 of the AppletWizard. The "m_parm1" name is the default name generated by AppletWizard by concatenating "m_" and the parameter name "parm1."

The instance variables that hold the names of the parameters `PARAM_parm1` and `PARAM_parm2` are final because they do not change during execution of the applet.

```
String m_parm1 = "ABC";
    int m_parm2 = 123;
```

```
// Parameter names.  To change a name of a parameter, you need only make
// a single change.  Simply modify the value of the parameter string below.
//--------------------------------------------------------------------
final String PARAM_parm1 = "parm1";
final String PARAM_parm2 = "parm2";
```

The main method (see Listing 16.12) is run only when the program is run as an application. A single line is added that calls the new GetParameters method. GetParameters is passed the args String array. Notice that the AppWizard4.init method is called next.

Listing 16.12   AppWizard4.main Method (\msdev\project\AppWizard4\AppWizard4.java)

```
public static void main(String args[])
{
    AppWizard4Frame frame = new AppWizard4Frame("AppWizard4");

    // Must show Frame before we size it so insets() will return valid
    ➥values
    //-----------------------------------------------------------------
    frame.show();
    frame.resize(frame.insets().left + frame.insets().right  + 320,
                 frame.insets().top  + frame.insets().bottom + 240);

    AppWizard4 applet_AppWizard4 = new AppWizard4();

    frame.add("Center", applet_AppWizard4);
    applet_AppWizard4.m_fStandAlone = true;
    applet_AppWizard4.GetParameters(args);
    applet_AppWizard4.init();
    applet_AppWizard4.start();
}
```

The init method of the AppWizard4 applet class is called from main when the program runs as an application and from the browser when run as an applet. GetParameters is called with a null parameter only if init is running as an applet in a browser. If init is running as a stand-alone application, main has already called GetParameters with the application's args String array.

The details of sorting out the differences in processing applet and application parameters are left to GetParameters: it gets either the args String array or null if running as an applet.

```
public void init()
    {
        if (!m_fStandAlone)
            GetParameters(null);
        resize(320, 240);
    }
```

GetParameters (see Listing 16.13) gets an args String array and passes it down to GetParameter along with the name of the parameter. GetParameters is responsible for converting the String parameter value returned from GetParameter to the same data type as the defined parameter. The details of sorting out the differences in processing applet and application parameters are left to GetParameter.

Listing 16.13   AppWizard4.GetParameters Method (\msdev\project\AppWizard4\AppWizard4.java)

```java
public void GetParameters(String args[])
{
    String param;

    param = GetParameter(PARAM_parm1, args);
    if (param != null)
        m_parm1 = param;

    param = GetParameter(PARAM_parm2, args);
    if (param != null)
        m_parm2 = Integer.parseInt(param);
}
```

Part III

Ch 16

GetParameter (see Listing 16.14) has to return the String value of the parameter specified by name. If args is null, assume that the method is running as an applet. An applet gets the value of its applet parameters using the java.awt.Applet.getParameter method, which returns the string value specified in the HTML file.

If the args reference is not null, it is an array of strings of keyword and value pairs parsed from the command line. The args array of strings is searched. Each string is checked to see if it starts with the keyword name followed by an "=." If it does, the rest of the string is skimmed for the value.

Listing 16.14   AppWizard4.GetParameter Method (\msdev\project\AppWizard4\AppWizard4.java)

```java
public String GetParameter(String strName, String args[])
{
    if (args == null)
    {
        return getParameter(strName);
    }

    int     i;
    String strArg     = strName + "=";
    String strValue = null;

    for (i = 0; i < args.length; i++)
    {
        if (strArg.equalsIgnoreCase(args[i].substring(0, strArg.length())))
```

continues

Listing 16.14 Continued

```
        {
            // Found matching parameter on command line, so extract its
            ➥value.
            // If in double quotes, remove the quotes.
            //-----------------------------------------------------------
            strValue= args[i].substring(strArg.length());
            if (strValue.startsWith("\""))
            {
                strValue = strValue.substring(1);
                if (strValue.endsWith("\""))
                    strValue = strValue.substring(0, strValue.length()
        ➥    - 1);
            }
        }
    }

    return strValue;
}
```

The final new method is `getParameterInfo` (see Listing 16.15), which overrides `java.applet.Applet.getParameterInfo` to provide more useful information.

Listing 16.15 AppWizard4.getParameterInfo Method
(\msdev\project\AppWizard4\AppWizard4.java)

```
public String[][] getParameterInfo()
{
    String[][] info =
    {
        { PARAM_parm1, "String", "Parameter description" },
        { PARAM_parm2, "int", "Parameter description" },
    };
    return info;
}
```

In this section, you learned about adding support for parameters for applets and applications using the AppletWizard. Now that you understand the AppletWizard-generated code, you can add new parameters to your applets in the future.

AppWizard5: Adding Event Handlers

The next example project generated by AppletWizard is called AppWizard5. AppWizard5 is the same as AppWizard4, except that three mouse events options have been selected. This application feature adds code to handle common mouse events.

The mouse event handlers are selected from three pairs mouseDown/mouseDown, mouseDrag/mouseMove, and mouseEnter/mouseExit (see Listing 16.16). The code generated for each pair of events is a pair of methods that are called whenever the respective mouse event occurs. These mouse event handlers are overrides of the applet's corresponding java.awt.Component methods. The event handlers are called by handleEvent. Rather than writing switch-like code in your handleEvent method, you can call the default handleEvent and let it call your overridden method.

In addition to mouse event handlers, other event handler methods called by java.awt.Component.handleEvent are:

- action
- gotFocus
- lostFocus
- keyDown
- keyUp

Part III

Ch 16

Listing 16.16 AppWizard5 Mouse Event Methods (\msdev\project\AppWizard5\AppWizard5.java)

```java
public boolean mouseDown(Event evt, int x, int y)
{
        return true;
}

public boolean mouseUp(Event evt, int x, int y)
{
        return true;
}

public boolean mouseDrag(Event evt, int x, int y)
{
        return true;
}

public boolean mouseMove(Event evt, int x, int y)
{
        return true;
}

public boolean mouseEnter(Event evt, int x, int y)
{
        return true;
}

public boolean mouseExit(Event evt, int x, int y)
{
        return true;
}
```

From Here...

In this chapter, you learned about the AppletWizard and the code that it generates in response to configuration options. You also learned how to build and execute the generated programs.

In the next chapter, you learn to use AppStudio and the Java ResourceWizard to create menus and dialog boxes, and to integrate them into the AppletWizard-generated projects.

■ Chapter 17, "Using AppStudio," will show you how to use the resource editor to add dialogs, controls, menus, and other resources to your AppletWizard-generated project.

Using AppStudio

by Mark Culverhouse

In the previous chapter, "Creating An Applet with AppletWizard," you learned how to generate a Java project. In this chapter, you will learn to use AppStudio to customize your project's user interface by adding menus and dialogs.

Java does *not* support "resource" files, which are familiar to Windows and Macintosh programmers. The process of compiling, linking, and running resource files is similar to the process of compiling, loading, and running Java classes. Perhaps in the spirit of eliminating redundant features for simplicity, or simply because Java is a 1.0 product, resource files were left out of Java.

Visual J++ allows you to use AppStudio to graphically design menus and dialogs and save them in a new file format called RCT for resource template file. This template file of menus and dialogs is input to the ResourceWizard, which generates Java classes to implement the menus and dialogs defined in the RCT.

You must then add code to your project classes to create and initialize the menus and dialogs. ▪

Creating an RCT, resource template file

An RCT is used to store menus and dialogs that are used as templates to generate Java classes to implement.

Adding a new menu template to the RCT file

Use AppStudio to design menus for your Java applet frame windows.

Adding a new dialog to the RCT file

A dialog box template becomes a Frame extended class when input to ResourceWizard.

Adding controls to the dialog template

Learn which Windows controls are supported by Java ResourceWizard.

Using ResourceWizard to generate Java classes from the RCT file

Java only has classes; ResourceWizard converts resource template objects to Java classes.

Connecting the new Java classes to your project classes

Integrate the newly created Java classes for menus and dialog into your applet. Learn more about Java event handlers and ResourceWizard output.

Windows Resource Files

Windows applications have resource files (*.RC) that contain user interface components like menus and dialogs. These files are "compiled" by a resource compiler into compiled resource files (*.RES). The RES file is then added to the application's executable file (*.EXE), where it can be referenced at run time. The resource can be changed, recompiled, and relinked with the unchanged executable.

Creating Resource Templates (RCT File)

Menu and dialog templates are stored in an RCT file. To create an RCT file, select File, New to display the New dialog box. Select Resource Template from the list box and click OK (see Figure 17.1).

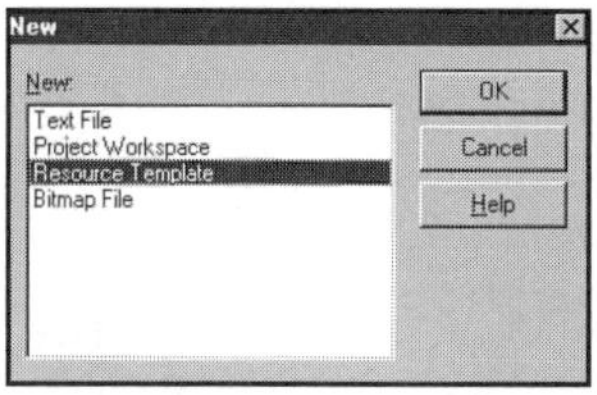

FIG. 17.1

The New dialog box is used to create a new Resource Template.

A new window will appear in the project workspace to represent the new template file. Its name will start with "Templ." You can change this name later when you save the file.

Adding a Menu Template

The new template file is empty. First add a new menu template. The new menu will be a single pop-up menu named File, and a single menu item named Exit. To add a new menu, click the right mouse button over the folder icon that represents the template file. Choose Insert from the pop-up menu (see Figure 17.2) to display the Insert Resource dialog box (see Figure 17.3).

FIG. 17.2

The Resource Template property menu is displayed by right-clicking the folder icon.

In the Insert Resource dialog box (see Figure 17.3), select Menu and click OK. The project workspace will now contain a new menu editor window with an empty menu.

FIG. 17.3

The Insert Resource dialog box is used to create new resources, i.e., a menu.

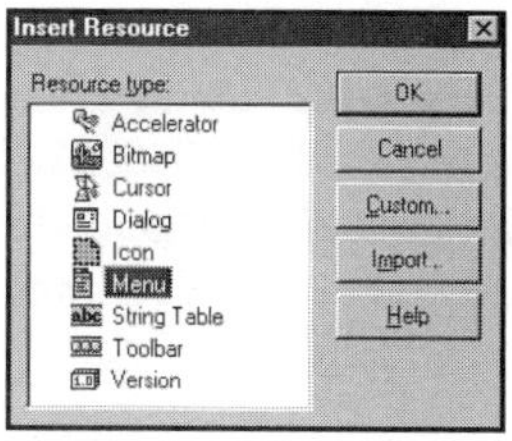

TIP You will notice that the Cursor and Dialog entries have subentries. These default templates are contained in \Msdev\Template\Mfc.rct, which was installed with Visual J++. When you save an RCT file for the first time, the \Msdev\Template\ directory is offered as the default directory to save your template. You may save the RCT file here or within your project directory. If you save it in /Msdev/ Template/, then each resource within the RCT file will appear as subentries in the Insert Resource dialog box for all projects. When you select one of these default templates, your new component will be a copy of the template version.

Before creating the File pop-up menu, you should name your menu. To name the menu, display the Menu Properties dialog box by double-clicking the menu bar (see Figure 17.4). You can also right-click the menu bar and select Properties from the menu.

The default name may be something like IDR_MENU1. This is an example of Visual C++/MFC naming conventions which may not be appropriate if you are using Java naming conventions. The IDR_MENU label is capitalized because in Visual C++, menu resources are identified by a constant integer value.

In the case of your Java menu resources, the name you use as the menu resource ID will be used by the ResourceWizard as the name of a Java class. Therefore, you should use a menu name that is appropriate for use as a class name. In this example, the name MyMenu is used. Later you will see that the ResourceWizard allows you to enter a class name to override the ID you specify here. However, if you enter the proper class name now, you will not have to manually overwrite it later each time you refresh the resource template file. This could also be error-prone because you might forget the manual step.

Close the Menu Properties dialog box by clicking its close button, pressing the Esc key, or by activating any other window.

FIG. 17.4

The Menu Properties dialog box is displayed by right-clicking the menu bar to the right of any menu items. Use it to change the menu ID.

Part
III

Ch
17

Next, create the File menu on the menu bar by clicking the empty menu item highlighted in the Menu Editor window. Typing **&File** directly into the menu will display the Menu Item Properties dialog box with the text, &File, entered into the Caption field (see Figure 17.5). The "&" in the caption text will cause the following character to be underlined as the keyboard accelerator for the menu or menu item. Because the File menu item is menu on the menu bar, there is no ID assigned.

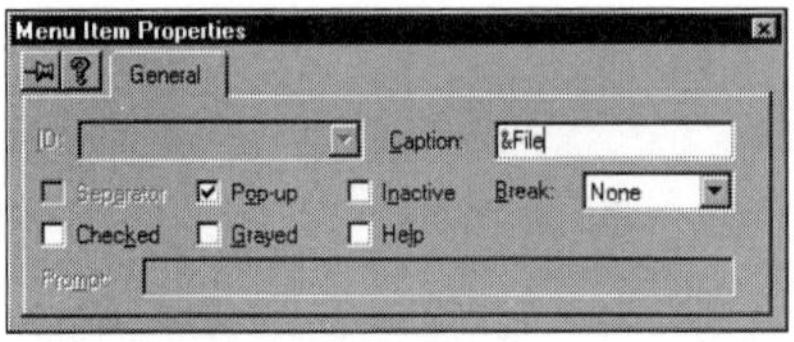

FIG. 17.5
The Menu Item
Properties dialog box
shows the properties of
the File menu.

Next, create the Exit menu item by clicking the empty menu item below the File menu. In the Menu Item Properties dialog box for the Exit menu item, enter **E&xit** as the Caption and enter **menuItemExit** as the ID symbol (see Figure 17.6). To finish, close the dialog box.

As with the menu resource name, MyMenu, the ID of the menu item is used by the ResourceWizard as the name of a class to represent the menu resource. Enter a name appropriate for a program instance of the MenuItem class.

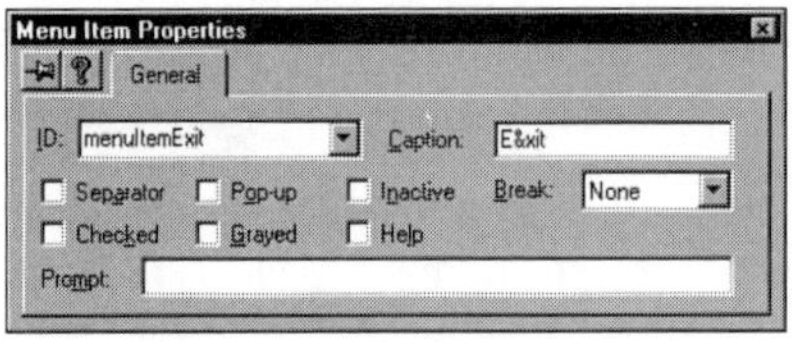

FIG. 17.6
The Menu Item
Properties dialog box
shows the properties for
the Exit menu item.

You have now successfully created a menu resource template. In the next section you will add a dialog resource template to the resource template file.

Adding a Dialog Template

In this section you will add a simple dialog template to the resource template file containing the menu created in the previous section.

In this example, you will add several common controls to a dialog template. Later, this dialog of controls will be created as the applet window. Remember that there is the spinning globe in the center of the applet window. The controls that will be added in this section will allow control of the globe's spinning.

The controls created in this example are listed in Table 17.1.

Table 17.1 MyDialog Controls

Java Class Name	ID	Description
Checkbox	checkTurn	Checkbox to start and stop globe turning.
Checkbox	radioRight	Radio button to spin globe to the right.
Checkbox	radioLeft	Radio button to spin globe to the left.
Button	buttonReverse	Click button to reverse the spin of the globe.
List	listDemo	List box with entries: Stop, Right, and Left.
Label	staticSleep	"Sleep" label for scrollbar and text edit.
Scrollbar	scrollSpeed	Horizontal scrollbar for sleep time between images.
TextField	editSpeed	Text control displays value of scrollbar.

To create a new dialog, again right-click the folder representing the template resource file, and select Insert from the pop-up menu, or select Insert, Resource to display the Insert Resource dialog box (see Figure 17.7). Select the Dialog entry in the list box, and click OK.

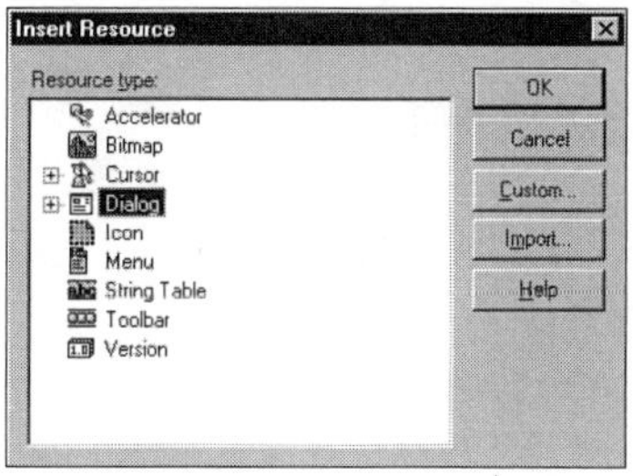

FIG. 17.7

The Insert Resource dialog box is used to create a dialog resource.

A new dialog editor window is displayed containing the new dialog box. First, name the dialog box resource by double-clicking the dialog background to display the Dialog Properties dialog box (see Figure 17.8). Enter the ID value to be used as the name of a class to represent the dialog. This example uses MyDialog. The caption is the value of the dialog's window title.

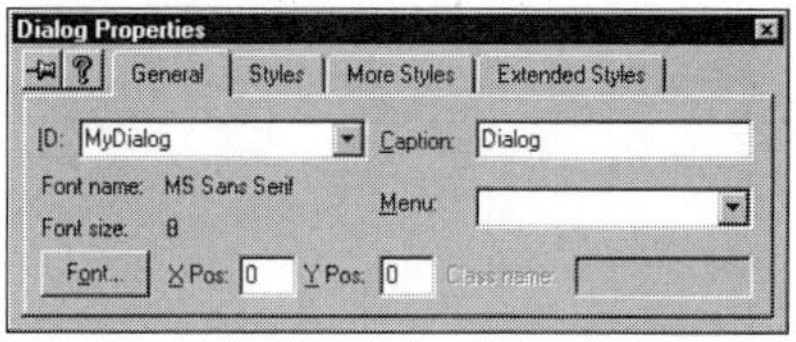

FIG. 17.8

The Dialog Properties dialog box has several tabs used to manage dialog box properties.

Part

III

Ch

17

You can size the dialog box by selecting it, and then dragging on the size buttons on the edges and corners of the dialog window.

You can add controls to the dialog by using the Controls tool palette to add a static text, text edit, check box, radio button, push button, list box, or scrollbar control. Note that all controls on the tool palette are not supported by the Java ResourceWizard, even though you can add them to your resource template dialog. The ResourceWizard ignores any unsupported resource controls.

Add a Reverse push button control to the dialog template by selecting the push button tool on the Controls tool palette, and then click and drag a button onto the dialog background. Type **R&everse** into the new push button which will cause the Push Button Properties dialog box to appear.

Figure 17.9 illustrates the use of the Push Button Properties dialog box to assign the push button an ID of buttonReverse and a Caption of Reverse.

FIG. 17.9

Here is the Push Button Properties dialog box.

The tool palette is used to create and customize the properties of the remaining controls. The final result is shown in Figure 17.10.

FIG. 17.10

The completed MyDialog dialog box template is shown in the Dialog Editor.

Now that the dialog and menu resource templates are created, you must save the resource template file by selecting File, Save. Select the directory and name of your resource template file (see Figure 17.11). In the example, the name of the project is used, MyJavaApp.rct. Click Save to create the resource file.

FIG. 17.11

The Save As dialog box is used to save your resource template file.

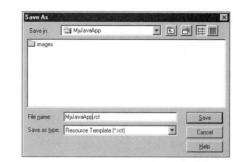

Generating Java Code Using ResourceWizard

The resource template file, MyJavaApp.rct, now contains your new menu and dialog resources. The next step is to generate Java classes from the RCT file. To generate Java classes from the resource file, use the ResourceWizard by selecting Tools, Java Resource Wizard. This will cause the first in a series of Wizard option dialog boxes to be displayed.

In the first Java Resource Wizard dialog box (see Figure 17.12) you must select your RCT file. Enter the name of the RCT file, MyJavaApp.rct, or click the Browse button to select the file with a file open dialog. After entering the RCT file name, click the Next button.

Part

III

Ch

17

FIG. 17.12

The Java Resource Wizard - Step 1 of 2 dialog box is used to specify the *.rct or *.res file to read.

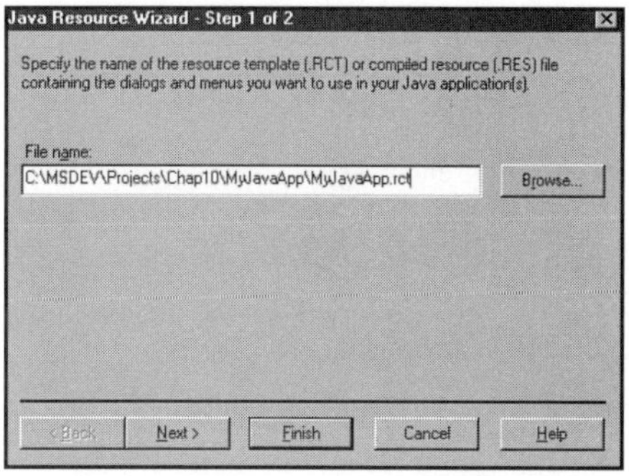

The second Java Resource Wizard dialog box allows you to change the name of the Java classes and class files that will be created (see Figure 17.13). The Class Name by default is the same as the Resource name. In this example, the class names MyMenu and MyDialog were entered originally as the name of the resources. These are the names you want as class names; therefore, no changes are necessary. As long as these names are used unchanged, it will be easier to update your resource files in the future without breaking existing code. Finally, click Finish to cause the Resource Wizard to generate the class files.

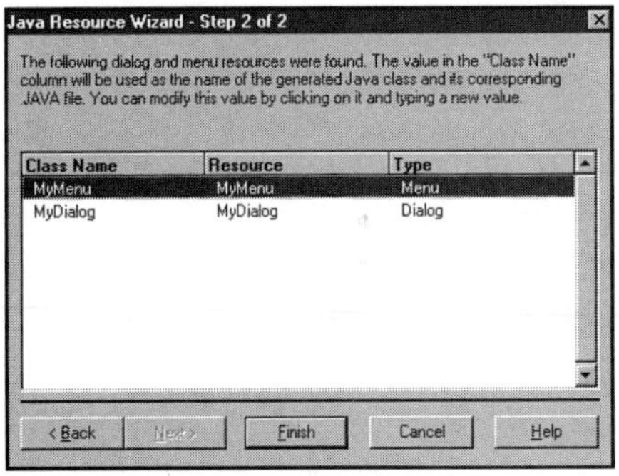

FIG. 17.13

The Java Resource
Wizard - Step 2 of 2
dialog box displays a list
of resources. You can
only modify the class
name.

After the Java class files have been created by the Java Resource Wizard, a message box is displayed listing the names of the *.java files that were created (see Figure 17.14). You should note the names of these files, as they will be needed later.

Note that if these files already exist, they are overwritten without warning. If you had made changes to code in any of these files, they have been lost. It is best to not modify these files.

Table 17.2 lists the files created by the Java Resource Wizard and the Java classes that are implemented in each file.

Table 17.2   The Java Resource Wizard-Generated File Contents

File Name	Contents
MyMenu.java	Generated class, MyMenu
MyDialog.java	Generated class, MyDialog
DialogLayout.java	Generated class, DialogLayout

FIG. 17.14

The Java Resource
Wizard message box
displays the files that
were successfully
created.

TIP The classes that the Java ResourceWizard generates should not be modified unless you do not plan to use AppStudio again to modify the menus and dialogs. Each time you use AppStudio to modify an RCT file, you must run the ResourceWizard to generate new class files. These new files will overwrite the old ones. If you have made changes to these files then those changes will be lost. You will have to manage those changes outside the Developer Studio. This chapter demonstrates how to integrate the ResourceWizard classes without modifying them.

Next, add the new Java source files to the project. This will cause these files to be compiled when the project is built.

To add files to your project, select Insert, Files into Project to display the Insert Files into Project dialog box (see Figure 17.15). Select the three new .java files to be added to the project. By depressing the Ctrl key while selecting the three file names, you can select them all and add them at once. Click Add to insert the files and close the dialog box.

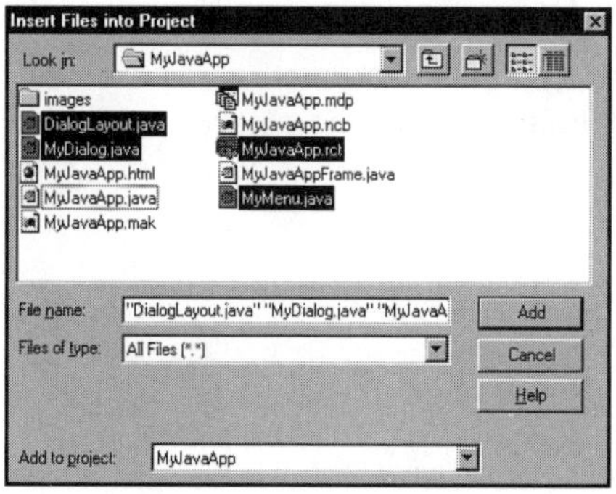

FIG. 17.15

The Insert Files into Project dialog box is used to add the Resource Wizard-generated files to the project.

TIP You might want to add your *.RCT files into your project as well. This makes it easy to open these files later by double-clicking them in the FileView. You added your *.java files to the project because the Developer Studio will compile them automatically when you build the project. However, Developer Studio does *not* automatically generate new *.java files when the *.RCT files in the project have changed.

Connecting Resources to Your Project

The ResourceWizard has generated Java classes to implement the dialogs and menus contained in the resource template file. The files were added to the project. These files and the classes they implement must still be integrated into your existing applet and frame classes. The menu bar must be added to the frame window, and the applet dialog controls must get created. Also, the dialog controls must be connected to code in order to control the globe when dialog control events occur.

In this section you will learn how to:

- Connect a ResourceWizard-generated menu bar to a Frame window.
- Connect ResourceWizard-generated dialog box controls to an applet.

Connecting a Menu Resource to a Frame

All of the source code changes needed to connect MyMenu to MyJavaAppFrame are made to the MyJavaAppFrame.java file. No changes are made to any Java Resource Wizard-generated files, i.e., MyMenu.java.

The steps to integrate a menu are:

1. Update the MyJavaAppFrame.java file to import the new `MyMenu` class.
2. Add a `MyMenu` reference variable to the `MyJavaAppFrame` class.
3. Update the `MyJavaAppFrame` constructor to create and initialize a menu instance.
4. Add `MyJavaAppFrame.action()` method to process the Exit menu item command.

These steps are described in detail later. An attempt has been made to describe the typical mouse and keyboard use of the Developer Studio interface to accomplish common tasks. Rather than describing every menu item to be used, other more useful, but less apparent user interface elements are used.

Step 1: Update the MyJavaAppFrame.java file to import the new `MyMenu` class.

The `MyMenu` class will be used in the MyJavaAppFrame. The Java `import` statement is used to import classes.

Add an `import` statement to `MyJavaAppFrame` for the `MyMenu` class (see Listing 17.1). Edit the top of the MyJavaAppFrame.java file by activating the ClassView tab of the Project Workspace window, and then select the MyJavaAppFrame.java file by double-clicking the class name. Or right-click the class name, `MyJavaAppFrame`, and select Go To Definition. This will open the file and position it at the top where the import statements are. Insert the line with the comment `//add this`. This statement will make the `MyMenu` class visible to the classes in the MyJavaAppFrame file.

**Listing 17.1 MyJavaAppFrame Imports
(\msdev\projects\Chap17\MyJavaApp\MyJavaAppFrame.java)**

```
//******************************************************************************
// MyJavaAppFrame.java:
//
//******************************************************************************
import java.awt.*;
import MyMenu;          // add this
```

> **TIP** If you want to go to the source code for an imported Java class, try right-clicking the import statement and choose the Open menu item. For instance, when you right-click the line Import MyMenu, the pop-up menu will contain a menu item named Open MyMenu.java.

Step 2: Add a MyMenu reference variable to the MyJavaAppFrame class.

To use the menu class, you need to declare an instance. The MyMenu class creates the menu and its items, and adds them to a specified frame window. You could define a local instance of MyMenu to use to initialize the frame's menu, but a class variable is used instead. The reason is that a MyMenu object also contains MenuItem instances defined with the resource ID values that you entered in the Menu Item Properties dialog box earlier. Because these reference values are used to identify menu item events, it is useful to reference them through the MyMenu object.

To add a variable to a class, right-click the class name, MyJavaAppFrame, in the ClassView tab of the Project Workspace window. This will display the Add Variable dialog box (see Figure 17.16). Enter:

- **MyMenu** as the Variable type.
- **m_Menu** as the Variable name.
- **null** as the Initial value.

After clicking OK, the m_Menu variable declaration is added to the class definition (see Listing 17.2).

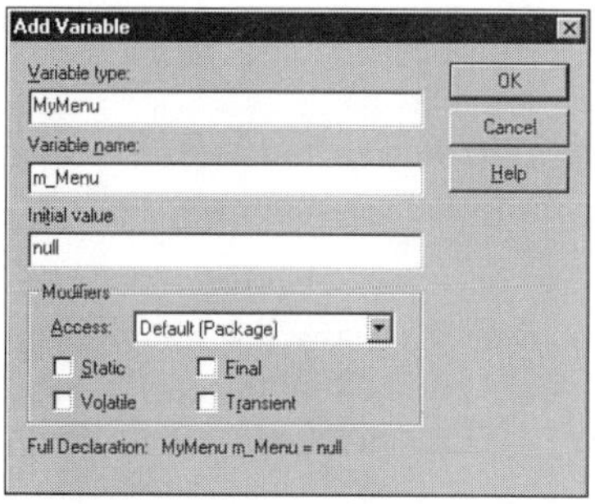

FIG. 17.16
The Add Variable dialog box is used to create a new class variable.

Listing 17.2   MyJavaAppFrame Variables (\msdev\projects\Chap17\MyJavaApp\MyJavaAppFrame.java)

```
//===============================================================================
// STANDALONE APPLICATION SUPPORT
//     This frame class acts as a top-level window in which the applet appears
// when it's run as a standalone application.
//===============================================================================
class MyJavaAppFrame extends Frame
{
        MyMenu m_Menu = null;
```

Step 3: Update the MyJavaAppFrame constructor to create and initialize a menu instance.

Because the menu is part of the frame, the menu is created and initialized in the frame's constructor. Edit the constructor by activating the ClassView tab in the Project Workspace window, then select the source code for the MyJavaAppFrame constructor by double-clicking the constructor name. This will bring the source into view in the Project Workspace window.

Add the two lines with the comments, **// add this** (see Listing 17.3). This connects your MyMenu class instance with your MyJavaAppFrame class instance. The call to CreateMenu causes the menu and each menu item to be created and added to the frame. This will cause the menu to be displayed with the frame window when the applet is run as an application.

Listing 17.3   MyJavaAppFrame Constructor (\msdev\projects\Chap17\MyJavaApp\MyJavaAppFrame.java)

```
public MyJavaAppFrame(String str)
{
    // TODO: Add additional construction code here
    super (str);

    m_Menu = new MyMenu( this );// add this
    m_Menu.CreateMenu();// add this
}
```

Step 4: Add MyJavaAppFrame.action() method to process the Exit menu item command.

When a menu item is selected by the user, the Frame's action method is called. (Note action is a method of the Component class.) This method can be overridden to intercept and process the menu command.

To create a new method in a class, activate the ClassView window, then right-click the MyJavaAppFrame class name. Select Add Method from the pop-up menu. This will display the Add Method dialog box (see Figure 17.17). To define the action method enter:

- **boolean** for the Return type.
- **action(Event evt, Object arg)** for the Method declaration.
- **Public** for Access.

When you click OK in the Add Method dialog box, an empty method will be added to the MyJavaAppFrame class. You must manually enter the following statements to the method (see Listing 17.4). If the action event occurred for the menuItemExit menu item, then the System.exit method is called. This method will shut down the application.

Listing 17.4 MyJavaAppFrame Action Method (\msdev\projects\Chap17\MyJavaApp\MyJavaAppFrame.java)

```java
public boolean action(Event evt, Object arg)
{
    if(evt.id == Event.ACTION_EVENT)
    {
        if(evt.target == m_Menu.menuItemExit)
            System.exit(0);
        return true;
    }
    return false;
}
```

FIG. 17.17

Use the Add Method dialog box to create a new method in a class.

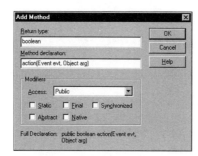

This completes the process of adding a menu to a frame. Before testing the menu, add the dialog to the application in the next section.

Connecting a Dialog Resource to an Applet

All of the source code changes needed to add the dialog resource to MyJavaApp are made to the MyJavaApp.java file. No changes are made to the Java Resource Wizard-generated file, MyDialog.java, or DialogLayout.java.

The steps to integrate a dialog resource are:

1. Update the MyJavaApp.java file to import the new MyDialog class.
2. Add a MyDialog reference variable to the MyJavaApp class.
3. Update MyJavaApp.init() to create and initialize a MyDialog instance.
4. Add MyJavaApp.setTurn() and setRight() helper methods.
5. Add MyJavaApp.action() method to process dialog control action events.
6. Add MyJavaApp.handleEvent() method to process dialog control events.
7. Update MyJavaApp.displayImage to support stopping globe spinning and changing direction.
8. Update MyJavaApp.run to support speed of globe spinning.

Step 1: Update the MyJavaApp.java file to import the new `MyDialog` class.

Add an import statement into `MyJavaApp` for the `MyDialog` class. Edit the MyJavaApp.java file by activating the ClassView window, then select the MyJavaApp.java file by double-clicking the class name. Or right-click the class name, `MyJavaApp`, and select Go To Definition. This will open the file and position it at the top where the `import` statements are. Insert the line (see Listing 17.5) with the comment `// add this`. This statement will make the `MyDialog` classes visible to the MyJavaApp file.

Listing 17.5   MyJavaApp Imports
(\msdev\projects\Chap17\MyJavaApp\MyJavaApp.java)

```
//**************************************************************************
// MyJavaApp.java:     Applet
//
//**************************************************************************
import java.applet.*;
import java.awt.*;
import MyJavaAppFrame;
import MyDialog;        // add this
```

Step 2: Add a `MyDialog` reference variable to the `MyJavaApp` class

To use the dialog class you need to declare an instance. The `MyDialog` class contains named instances of each dialog control. Because these objects need to be accessed later, the MyDialog instance is defined as a class instance variable named, `m_Dialog`.

To add a variable to a class, right-click the class name, MyJavaApp, in the ClassView window. This will display the Add Variable dialog box. Enter:

- **MyDialog** as the Variable type.
- **m_Dialog** as the Variable name.
- **null** as the Initial value.

After clicking OK, the `m_Dialog` variable declaration is added to the `MyJavaApp` class definition (see Listing 17.6).

Listing 17.6   MyJavaApp Constructor
(\msdev\projects\Chap17\MyJavaApp\MyJavaApp.java)

```
public class MyJavaApp extends Applet implements Runnable
{
      MyDialog m_Dialog = null;
```

Step 3: Update `MyJavaApp.init()` to create and initialize a MyDialog instance.

Select the `MyJavaApp.init()` method source code by double-clicking the method name in the ClassView window. Add the lines after the comment `// TODO:` (see Listing 17.7). This connects your `MyJavaApp` class with your `MyDialog` class instance, `m_Dialog`. The call to `CreateControls` causes each control to be created and added to the applet container.

The references to the controls created are stored in reference variables in `m_Dialog`. The names were the names you entered into the control property dialog ID field when using the AppStudio dialog resource editor.

The control initialization includes:

- Adding three items to the list box.
- Setting the current, page amount, minimum, and maximum values of the scrollbar.
- Setting the text of the edit control to be the current value of the scrollbar.
- Calling helper methods `setTurn` and `setRight`, which are created in the next step.

Part

III

Ch

17

Listing 17.7 MyJavaApp init Method
(\msdev\projects\Chap17\MyJavaApp\MyJavaApp.java)

```java
public void init()
{
    if (!m_fStandAlone)
        GetParameters(null);
    resize(220, 240);

    // TODO: Place Addition Initialization code here
    // add this
    m_Dialog = new MyDialog( this );
    m_Dialog.CreateControls();

    m_Dialog.listDemo.addItem("Stop");
    m_Dialog.listDemo.addItem("Right");
    m_Dialog.listDemo.addItem("Left");

    m_Dialog.scrollSpeed.setValues(50, 10, 0, 200);

m_Dialog.editSpeed.setText(
Integer.toString(
m_Dialog.scrollSpeed.getValue()));

    setTurn(true);

    setRight(false);

}
```

Step 4: Add `MyJavaApp.setTurn()` and `setRight()` helper methods.

`MyJavaApp.setTurn` is a helper method called to set the state of the globe turning. `MyJavaApp.setRight` is a helper method called to set the state of the direction that the globe turns.

To create the new `setTurn` method, activate the ClassView tab in the Project Workspace window, then right-click the `MyJavaApp` class name to display the pop-up menu. Select Add Method from the pop-up menu. This will display the Add Method dialog box. To define the `setTurn` method enter:

- **void** for the Return type.
- **setTurn(boolean bTurn)** for the Method declaration.
- **Default** for Access.

When you click OK in the Add Method dialog box, an empty method will be added to the `MyJavaApp` class. Manually add the following lines (see Listing 17.8). The state of the globe turning is saved in the check box state and the list box selection.

Listing 17.8   MyJavaApp setTurn Method
(\msdev\projects\Chap17\MyJavaApp\MyJavaApp.java)

```
void setTurn(boolean bTurn)
{
    m_Dialog.checkTurn.setState(bTurn); // add this

    m_Dialog.listDemo.select(!bTurn ? 0 :
        (m_Dialog.radioRight.getState() ? 1 : 2));// add this
}
```

To create the new `setRight` method, Activate the ClassView window, then right-click the `MyJavaApp` class name. Select Add Method from the pop-up menu. This will display the Add Method dialog box. To define the `setRight` method enter:

- **void** for the Return type.
- **setRight(boolean bRight)** for the Method declaration.
- **Default** for Access.

When you click OK in the Add Method dialog box, an empty method will be added to the `MyJavaApp` class. Manually add the following lines as shown in Listing 17.9. The state of the direction of the globe turning is saved in radio button state and the list box selection through the call to `setTurn`.

> **Listing 17.9   MyJavaApp setRight Method**
> **(\msdev\projects\Chap17\MyJavaApp\MyJavaApp.java)**

```
void setRight(boolean bRight)
{
    m_Dialog.radioRight.setState(bRight); // add this
    m_Dialog.radioLeft.setState(!bRight); // add this

    setTurn(true);
}
```

Step 5: Add `MyJavaApp.action()` method to process dialog control action events.

The default `handleEvent` method will call a component's `action` method for the `ACTION_EVENT`. If you only want to process a component's `ACTION_EVENT`, then a convenient way to do it is by overriding the `action` method. If you need to handle more than just the `ACTION_EVENT` event, then override the `handleEvent` method. If you use the `ACTION_EVENT` and other events of a component, you should keep all of the event handling together in `handleEvent`. Some of the controls in this example are handled with the `action` method, while others require that `handleEvent` be overridden.

To create the `MyJavaApp.action` method, right-click the `MyJavaApp` class name in the ClassView window. Select Add Method from the pop-up menu. This will display the Add Method dialog box. To define the `action` method, enter the same values used in the `MyMenu.action` method:

- **boolean** for the Return type.
- **action (Event evt, Object arg)** for the Method declaration.
- **Public** for Access.

When you click OK in the Add Method dialog box, an empty method will be added to the `MyJavaApp` class. You must manually enter the following statements (see Listing 17.10) to the method. The processing in the `action` method includes:

- When the push button is pressed, the direction of the globe is reversed by complementing the current value, which is obtained from the state of the Right radio button.
- If the Turn check box is checked, the value of the globe turning is set using the current setting of the check box.
- If the Right or Left radio buttons is checked then the helper function `setRight` is called to set the new direction using the state of the Right radio button.

Listing 17.10 MyJavaApp Action Method
(\msdev\projects\Chap17\MyJavaApp\MyJavaApp.java)

```
public boolean action(Event evt, Object arg)
{
    if(evt.target == m_Dialog.buttonReverse)
    {
        setRight(! m_Dialog.radioRight.getState());
    }
    else if(evt.target == m_Dialog.checkTurn)
    {
        setTurn(m_Dialog.checkTurn.getState());
    }
    else if(evt.target == m_Dialog.radioRight ||
        evt.target == m_Dialog.radioLeft)
    {
        setRight(m_Dialog.radioRight.getState());
    }
    else
        return false;

    return true;
}
```

Step 6: Add `MyJavaApp.handleEvent()` method to process dialog control events.

In the `handleEvent` method you can handle all of the events of a component, not just the `ACTION_EVENT` as with the `action` method. To create the `MyJavaApp.handleEvent`, right-click the `MyJavaApp` class name in the ClassView window. Select Add Method from the pop-up menu. This will display the Add Method dialog box. To define the `action` method enter the same values used in the `MyMenu. handleEvent` method:

- **boolean** for the <u>R</u>eturn type.
- **handleEvent (Event evt)** for the <u>M</u>ethod declaration.
- **Public** for <u>A</u>ccess.

When you click OK in the Add Method dialog box, an empty method will be added to the `MyJavaApp` class. You must manually enter the following statements (see Listing 17.11) to the method. The processing in the `handleEvent` includes:

- When a list box entry is clicked (`LIST_SELECT`) or double-clicked (`ACTION_EVENT`), the state of the globe is changed depending on the list box entry selected.
- When any event occurs with the scrollbar, the edit control is updated to reflect the current scrollbar value. Scrollbars have many events besides `ACTION_EVENT`. There are events that correspond to the user actions on a scrollbar such as, `SCROLL_LINE_UP`, `SCROLL_LINE_DOWN`, `SCROLL_PAGE_UP`, `SCROLL_PAGE_DOWN`, and `SCROLL_ABSOLUTE`. Because the same processing is done for all changes to a scrollbar, `handleEvent` was used, and all events were used to update the text control.

■ Only certain events for the list box and scrollbar are to be processed by the MyJavaApp version of handleEvent. The rest should be handled as if you had not overridden the default version. This is accomplished by calling the default version of handleEvent through the super reference.

**Listing 17.11   MyJavaApp handleEvent Method
(\msdev\projects\Chap17\MyJavaApp\MyJavaApp.java)**

```
public boolean handleEvent(Event evt)
{
    if(evt.target == m_Dialog.listDemo)
    {
        switch (evt.id)
        {
        case Event.ACTION_EVENT:
        case Event.LIST_SELECT:
            switch(m_Dialog.listDemo.getSelectedIndex())
            {
            case 0:
                setTurn(false);
                break;
            case 1:
                setRight(true);
                break;
            case 2:
                setRight(false);
                break;
            }
            return true;
        }
    }
    else if(evt.target == m_Dialog.scrollSpeed)
    {
        m_Dialog.editSpeed.setText(
Integer.toString(
m_Dialog.scrollSpeed.getValue()));
return true;
    }
    return super.handleEvent(evt);
}
```

Step 7: Update MyJavaApp.displayImage to support stopping globe spinning and changing direction.

The spinning globe needs to have a stopped state where it does not spin. If the globe is not spinning, then only the first image in the array of globe images is used to paint the globe. Because the same image is painted, the globe does not spin. Also, the globe has to spin to the right or to the left. This is implemented by "reversing" the index to the globe image array before drawing, depending on the spin direction.

To update the `displayImage` method, double-click the `displayImage` method name in the ClassView window. Change the code to match that displayed as follows (see Listing 17.12). The state of the check box, `checkTurn`, is used to see if no spinning is allowed. If not, then the first element in `m_Images` is displayed and the method returns.

A local variable `nCurrImage` is introduced to hold the "reversed" image array index. It should be changed in the first parameter to `drawImage`, as well.

Listing 17.12   MyJavaApp displayImage Method (\msdev\projects\Chap17\MyJavaApp\MyJavaApp.java)

```java
void displayImage(Graphics g)
{
    if (!m_fAllLoaded)
        return;

    if (! m_Dialog.checkTurn.getState())// add this
    {
        g.drawImage(m_Images[0],
                        (size().width - m_nImgWidth)    / 2,
                        (size().height - m_nImgHeight) / 2, null);
        return;
    }

    // use m_Dialog.radioRight.getState() to control the order
    // of cycling image array
    int nCurrImage;
    if(m_Dialog.radioRight.getState())
        nCurrImage = m_nCurrImage;
    else
        nCurrImage = NUM_IMAGES - m_nCurrImage - 1;


    // Draw Image in center of applet
    //-----------------------------------------------------------------
    g.drawImage(m_Images[nCurrImage], // change this!
                (size().width - m_nImgWidth)    / 2,
                (size().height - m_nImgHeight) / 2, null);
}
```

Step 8: Update MyJavaApp.run to support speed of globe spinning.

The speed of the globe spinning is controlled by the value of the scrollbar. The value of the scrollbar is used for the length of time to sleep between drawing the globe images. The minimum and maximum range values for the scrollbar are 0 and 200. The current value of the scrollbar is used each time the thread is put to sleep. The unit of time for the `Thread.sleep()` method is milliseconds.

To update the `run` method, use the ClassView window to double-click the `run` method name "run" in the MyJavaApp class. Change the code to match that displayed in Listing 17.13.

Change the parameter to the Thread.sleep method call. The more the scrollbar is scrolled, the higher the sleep value will be, and the slower the globe will spin.

Listing 17.13   MyJavaApp run Method
(\msdev\projects\Chap17\MyJavaApp\MyJavaApp.java)

```
public void run()
.  .  .
    repaint();

    while (true)
    {
        try
        {
            // Draw next image in animation
            //-------------------------------------------------------------
            displayImage(m_Graphics);
            m_nCurrImage++;
            if (m_nCurrImage == NUM_IMAGES)
                m_nCurrImage = 0;

            // TODO:  Add additional Thread specific code here
            Thread.sleep( m_Dialog.scrollSpeed.getValue() ); // change this
        }
.  .  .
```

That completes the changes to the MyJavaApp project. It is now time to build the project and run it.

Running the Applet

Because all of the new Java source files have been added to the project and all the connecting code written, all that needs to be done now is to build the project and run the applet. When using the Java Applet Wizard to create the MyJavaApp project, you specified that it would run as an applet and as an application. In this section you will run the applet using three different environments:

- Running the applet within the Microsoft Internet Explorer browser application.
- Running the applet within the Netscape Navigator browser application.
- Running the applet as a stand-alone application under Microsoft's JView program.

First, run the applet by loading the project's HTML page using the Internet Explorer browser. If your project settings are set to run as an applet using Internet Explorer, then select Build, Execute MyJavaApp. Otherwise, change your project settings or open the HTML file from the running browser.

Figure 17.18 shows the project running in Internet Explorer. Try clicking the different controls to test the effects on the globe.

FIG. 17.18

MyJavaApp with the new controls is shown running under Internet Explorer.

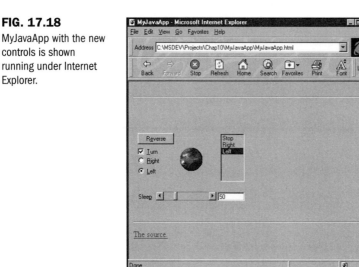

Figure 17.19 shows the same compiled MyJavaApp class files running in Netscape Navigator browser. Though there may be slight differences, the applets run the same compiled bytecode.

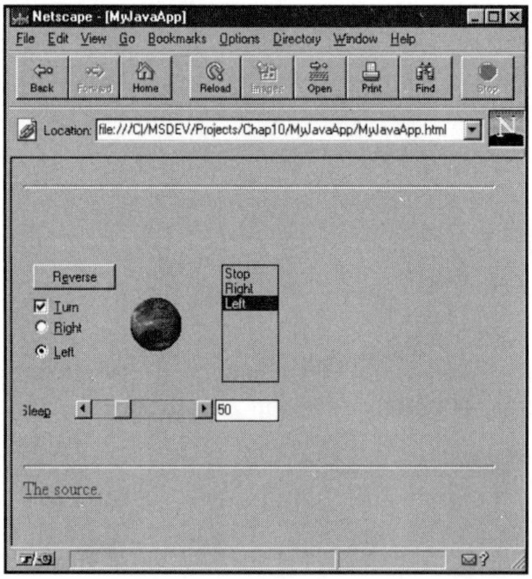

FIG. 17.19

MyJavaApp is running unchanged under Netscape Navigator browser.

The MyJavaApp applet can also be run as an application, outside a browser. Figure 17.20 shows MyJavaApp running in JVIEW.EXE. Notice the File menu, which did not appear in the browser examples above. The menu only appears when MyJavaApp is executed as an application because it is then that the MyJavaAppFrame is created. The frame contains the menu. When run as an application, the applet's main window is a MyJavaAppFrame instance created in the static MyJavaApp.main method, which is called by JView.

This applet should run correctly on many different computer platforms.

FIG. 17.20
MyJavaApp running as a stand-alone application under JView.exe stand-alone interpreter.

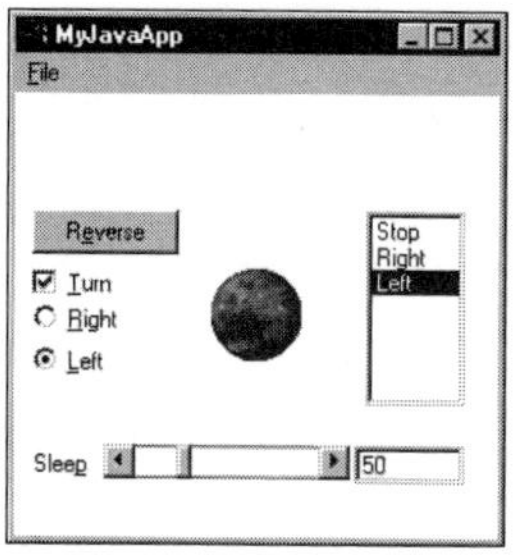

From Here...

In this chapter you learned to add menus and dialogs to your project. The AppStudio tools were used to lay out menu and dialog resources. The Developer Studio tools were used to integrate the menu and dialog resources into the project to control the applet's behavior.

The following chapters will cover additional challenging topics:

- In Chapter 21, "Using Visual J++ Debugging Tools," you will learn how to use the various debugging tools to test your applet's code.

- In Chapter 23, "Calling an ActiveX Object from Java," learn how your Java applets can control ActiveX components.

Part
III

Ch
17

Programming with Visual J++

Multimedia

by Clayton Walnum

Under Java, your ability to program multimedia is limited. In fact, using the word "multimedia" to describe a Java applet is an overstatement. The truth is that a Java applet's multimedia abilities are mostly limited to displaying images and playing sound files. The good news is that an applet has powerful graphical abilities. When these graphical abilities are combined with sound, your applets can do everything from perform a slide show to display a mini-cartoon.

The secrets to performing complex graphical tasks in an applet are found buried in the Image and MediaTracker classes. In this chapter, you'll get a look at these important classes as you explore Java multimedia. ▓

Load a single image without flicker

Normally, Java displays images a chunk at a time. You can force your applet to display an image only after it's fully loaded.

Load multiple images without flicker

Using Java's MediaTracker class, you can keep track of the loading status of many different images at once.

Use multiple threads to perform animation

A multithreaded applet can perform animation concurrently with its regular duties.

Synchronize animation and sound

You can easily add sound effects to your animation sequences.

Use transparent colors and double-buffering when creating animation

Transparent colors and double-buffers give you all the power you need to create just about any kind of animation sequence.

Performing Slideshow Animation

An applet that uses slideshow animation is much like one of those flip books that you can get in a box of Cracker Jacks. You hold the flip book so that you can see the bottom page, and then you bend the rest of the pages up and let them flip rapidly past your thumb. The images on each page of the book are drawn so that flipping by them creates the illusion of animation. Slideshow animation is similar in that the animation is created by displaying many images, one after another, on the screen.

Of course, you can use the slideshow technique to create an actual slideshow, rather than an animation sequence. To do this, you just slow down the speed at which the images are displayed so that images remain on the screen longer. In either case, though, Java doesn't ordinarily display images smoothly enough to implement a good slideshow program. So, the first task when programming Java multimedia applets is to smooth out the image-loading process.

Normally, you can display an image simply by loading the image (which associates the image with an object of the Image class) and drawing the image. You learned how to do this in Chapter 7, "The Applet and Window Classes." In this chapter, you'll learn to refine that process.

Normal Image Display

As said previously, loading and displaying an image is an easy process when you're not concerned with how the image appears on-screen. For example, by the way of review, take a look at Listing 18.1, which is the ImageApplet applet that you programmed back in Chapter 7.

Listing 18.1 ImageApplet.java—An Applet that Loads and Displays an Image

```java
import java.awt.*;
import java.applet.*;
import java.net.*;

public class ImageApplet extends Applet
{
    Image snake;

    public void init()
    {
        URL codeBase = getCodeBase();
        snake = getImage(codeBase, "snake.gif");
        resize(250, 250);
    }

    public void paint(Graphics g)
    {
        int width = snake.getWidth(this);
        int height = snake.getHeight(this);

        g.drawRect(52, 52, width+10, height+10);
        g.drawImage(snake, 57, 57, width, height, this);
```

```
        }
}
```

When you run this applet, watch the screen closely. You'll notice that the image appears in chunks rather than all at once. This is because Java uses a secondary thread to load the image and updates the display after each chunk of the image is loaded. This type of image display is fine for a normal Web page, because it enables the applet's main thread to keep working, while at the same time displaying as much of the page's graphics as possible at any given time. However, when programming animation, displaying pictures a chunk at a time is not an option.

The SlideShowApplet Applet, Version 1

There may be times (especially when programming animation), when you want to display an image all at once rather than a chunk at a time. This smoother image-displaying is accomplished by overriding your applet's imageUpdate() method (inherited from the Component class), which Java calls every time it's ready to display an image chunk. The default version of imageUpdate() calls repaint() whenever the image that's being loaded changes. However, you can supply your own version that calls repaint() only when the image is fully loaded, and so display the image all at once.

In the next few sections, you'll create an applet called SlideShowApplet. When completed, the applet will be able to smoothly display a series of images given as parameters in the applet's HTML document. To create the first version of SlideShowApplet, follow the steps listed:

1. Create a new Java workspace using the Java Applet Wizard. Call the new workspace **SlideShowApplet**, as shown in Figure 18.1.

FIG. 18.1

Create a new Java workspace called SlideShowApplet.

2. Select the options displayed in the wizard pages as shown:

    Step 1 of 5—Keep defaults.

    Step 2 of 5—Keep defaults.

    Step 3 of 5—Select "No, Thank You" for multithreading and animation.

    Step 4 of 5—Create a string parameter called **image1** with a member name of **m_image1**, a default value of **snake.gif,** and a description of **Image file name** (see Figure 18.2).

    Step 5 of 5—Keep defaults.

Part
IV
Ch
18

FIG. 18.2

Create a parameter called image1.

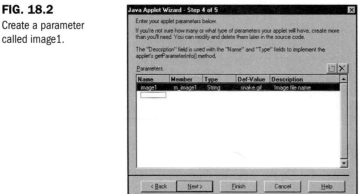

FIG. 18.3

The New Project Information dialog box for SlideShowApplet.

3. Select Finish. When the New Project Information dialog box appears (see Figure 18.3), select OK. Visual J++ creates the files for the new project.

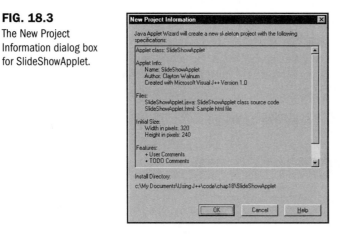

4. Load the SlideShowApplet.java file and add the following line near the top of the file, right after the line `import java.awt.*` that's already there:

```
import java.net.*;
```

By importing the `java.net` package, the applet will be able to access the URL class.

5. Add the following line right after the opening brace in the class's definition, before the PARAMETER SUPPORT comment:

```
Image image;
```

6. Add the following lines to the `init()` method, right after the `TODO: Place additional initialization code here` comment:

```
URL codeBase = getCodeBase();
image = getImage(codeBase, m_image1);
```

7. Replace the lines in the paint() method with those shown in Listing 18.2:

Listing 18.2 LST18_02.TXT—Code for the *paint()* Method

```
int width = image.getWidth(this);
int height = image.getHeight(this);
g.drawRect(52, 52, width+10, height+10);
g.drawImage(image, 57, 57, width, height, this);
```

8. Add the method shown in Listing 18.3 to the SlideShowApplet class, right after the
   TODO: Place additional applet code here comment:

Listing 18.3 LST18_03.TXT—The *imageUpdate()* Method

```
public boolean imageUpdate(Image img, int flags,
    int x, int y, int w, int h)
{
    int picLoaded = flags & ALLBITS;
    int error = flags & ERROR;

    if (picLoaded != 0)
    {
        repaint();
        return false;
    }

    return error == 0;
}
```

9. Copy the file SNAKE.GIF from the CHAP18\SLIDESHOWAPPLET directory of this
   book's CD-ROM to your SLIDESHOWAPPLET project directory.

How SlideShowApplet, Version 1, Works

You can now compile the new applet and run it. When you do, the window shown in Figure 18.4 appears. Watch how the program displays the image on the screen. Now, instead of appearing in several quick chunks, the image appears all at once. This is because you've taken over control of the imageUpdate() method, calling repaint() only when the entire image is loaded.

The imageUpdate() method receives six parameters, which are the image being loaded, a set of status flags, the image's X,Y coordinates, and the image's width and height. The flags parameter is used to communicate the status of the image-loading process and can contain one or more of the values shown in Table 18.1.

Part
IV

Ch
18

FIG. 18.4
SlideShowApplet
displays its image.

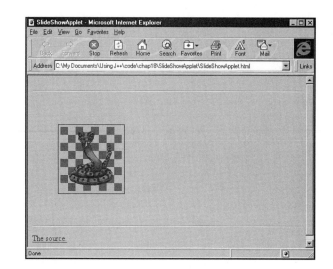

Table 18.1   Flag Values Used in *imageUpdate()*

Value	Description
ABORT	The image was aborted.
ALLBITS	The image is fully loaded.
ERROR	The image-loading process encountered an error.
FRAMEBITS	A frame in a multi-frame image is ready.
HEIGHT	The image's height is available.
PROPERTIES	The image's properties are available.
SOMEBITS	Information about a scaled version of the image is available.
WIDTH	The image's width is available.

The `imageUpdate()` function should return `true` if the image requires more processing, and should return `false` if the image is fully loaded or if an error occurs. That is, returning a value of `false` from `imageUpdate()` tells Java not to call `imageUpdate()` again. SlideShowApplet's version of `imageUpdate()` uses the AND operator to get the values of the `ALLBITS` and `ERROR` flags, like this:

```
int picLoaded = flags & ALLBITS;
int error = flags & ERROR;
```

If the `ALLBITS` flag is set, the image is fully loaded, so the program calls `repaint()` to draw the image and returns `false` in order to prevent further calls to `imageUpdate()`, as shown in Listing 18.4.

Listing 18.4 LST18_04.TXT—Checking for a Fully Loaded Image

```
if (picLoaded != 0)
{
    repaint();
    return false;
}
```

If ALLBITS is not set, the program checks whether the ERROR flag is set. If it is, the method returns false; otherwise, if ERROR is not set, the method returns true:

```
return error == 0;
```

The SlideShowApplet Applet, Version 2

Overriding the imageUpdate() method is all you have to do to obtain smoother image loading and displaying. Now that that task is accomplished, the next step is to load a series of images and display them in a loop. To create version 2 of SlideShowApplet, perform the following steps:

1. Load SlideShowApplet.java, and change the line public class SlideShowApplet extends Applet to the following:

   ```
   public class SlideShowApplet extends Applet implements Runnable
   ```

   By implementing the Runnable interface, the applet can create a secondary thread.

2. Near the top of the file, change the line Image image to the following:

   ```
   Image images[];
   int imageNum;
   Thread imageThread;
   ```

3. After the line private String m_image1 = "snake.gif" add the following lines:

   ```
   private String m_image2 = "snake2.gif";
   private String m_image3 = "snake3.gif";
   ```

4. After the line private final String PARAM_image1 = "image1" add the following lines:

   ```
   private final String PARAM_image2 = "image2";
   private final String PARAM_image3 = "image3";
   ```

5. In the getParameterInfo() method, add the following lines after the line { PARAM_image1, "String", "Image file name" } that's already there:

   ```
   { PARAM_image2, "String", "Image 2 file name" },
   { PARAM_image3, "String", "Image 3 file name" },
   ```

6. Add the lines shown in Listing 18.5 to the init() method, right after the line m_image1 = param that's already there.

Part IV

Ch

18

Listing 18.5 LST18_05.TXT—New Code for the *init()* Method

```
param = getParameter(PARAM_image2);
if (param != null)
    m_image2 = param;
```

continues

Listing 18.5   Continued

```
param = getParameter(PARAM_image3);
if (param != null)
    m_image3 = param;
```

7. Still in init(), replace the line image = getImage(codeBase, m_image1) with the lines shown in Listing 18.6.

Listing 18.6   LST18_06.TXT—New Lines for the *init()* Method

```
imageNum = 0;
images = new Image[3];
images[0] = getImage(codeBase, m_image1);
images[1] = getImage(codeBase, m_image2);
images[2] = getImage(codeBase, m_image3);
```

8. Replace the code in the paint() method with the lines shown in Listing 18.7.

Listing 18.7   LST18_07.TXT—New Code for the *paint()* Method

```
int width = images[imageNum].getWidth(this);
int height = images[imageNum].getHeight(this);
g.drawRect(52, 52, width+10, height+10);
g.drawImage(images[imageNum], 57, 57, width, height, this);
```

9. Add the following lines to the start() method, right after the TODO: Place additional applet start code here comment:

```
imageThread = new Thread(this);
imageThread.start();
```

10. Add the following lines to the stop() method:

```
if (imageThread != null)
    imageThread.stop();
```

11. Add the method shown in Listing 18.8 to the end of the class, right after the imageUpdate() method you placed there previously.

Listing 18.8   LST18_08.TXT—The Thread's *run()* Method

```
public void run()
{
    while(true)
    {
        ++imageNum;
        if (imageNum > 2)
            imageNum = 0;
        repaint();

        try
```

```
        {
            Thread.sleep(100);
        }
        catch (Exception e)
        {
        }
    }
}
```

12. Load SlideShowApplet.html and add the following lines right after the line `<param
    name=image1 value="snake.gif">` that's already there:

    ```
    <param name=image2 value="snake2.gif">
    <param name=image3 value="snake3.gif">
    ```

13. Copy the SNAKE2.GIF and SNAKE3.GIF files from the CHAP18\SLIDESHOWAPPLET
    directory of this book's CD-ROM to your SlideShowApplet project directory.

Now that you've completed the second version of the program, you can go ahead and compile
it. After the program compiles, run it. The program loads all three images and rapidly displays
them one after the other, which gives the snake image a cool flickering background.

How SlideShowApplet, Version 2, Works

The main difference between version 1 of SlideShowApplet and version 2 is that version 2 loads
three image files and uses a secondary thread to display the images one after the other. Because the program displays these images quickly, the snake's background flickers different
colors, a simple animation effect that can add a lot of pizzazz to a Web page.

The three images used by the program are specified as parameters in the applet's HTML document, like this:

```
<param name=image1 value="snake.gif">
<param name=image2 value="snake2.gif">
<param name=image3 value="snake3.gif">
```

The applet then reads the parameters as shown in Listing 18.9.

Listing 18.9   LST18_09.TXT—Reading the Image File-Name Parameters

```
param = getParameter(PARAM_image1);
if (param != null)
    m_image1 = param;

param = getParameter(PARAM_image2);
if (param != null)
    m_image2 = param;

param = getParameter(PARAM_image3);
if (param != null)
    m_image3 = param;
```

Part

IV

Ch

18

Finally, the program uses the file names represented by the parameters to load the three images into an array of Image objects, as shown in Listing 18.10.

Listing 18.10   LST18_10.TXT—Loading the Images

```
URL codeBase = getCodeBase();
imageNum = 0;
images = new Image[3];
images[0] = getImage(codeBase, m_image1);
images[1] = getImage(codeBase, m_image2);
images[2] = getImage(codeBase, m_image3);
```

In order to handle the image-display tasks, the applet starts a secondary thread in its start() method, like this:

```
imageThread = new Thread(this);
imageThread.start();
```

This thread's run() method comprises an infinite loop. The loop first increments the number of the next image to display:

```
++imageNum;
if (imageNum > 2)
        imageNum = 0;
```

The loop then calls repaint() to force the applet to display the next image. In order to time the slideshow, the last thing run() does in its loop is to call the Thread class's sleep() method, which suspends the thread for the given number of milliseconds:

```
Thread.sleep(100);
```

In this case, the thread sleeps for 100 milliseconds (a tenth of a second) before cycling through the loop again.

TIP You can add a parameter to the program that enables the applet's user to control the thread's sleep time from the HTML document. The HTML document would then have four parameters: the file names of the three images and the speed of the slideshow.

The paint() method in this version of SlideShowApplet is much like version 1's. The only difference is that the method accesses the new images[] array rather than the single image data member, as shown in Listing 18.11.

Listing 18.11   LST18_11.TXT—Changes to *paint()*

```
int width = images[imageNum].getWidth(this);
int height = images[imageNum].getHeight(this);
g.drawRect(52, 52, width+10, height+10);
g.drawImage(images[imageNum], 57, 57, width, height, this);
```

The SlideShowApplet Applet, Version 3

If you were paying close attention when you ran SlideShowApplet, Version 2, you noticed that although the first image gets loaded and displayed smoothly, the other images sometimes get only partially displayed until all three images are completely loaded. Is all that work to get images smoothly loaded and displayed wasted? No. Overriding `imageUpdate()` to load an image works great for single images. However, the second version of SlideShowApplet needs to keep track of three images, which can be a bit tricky for `imageUpdate()`. The solution is to use the `MediaTracker` class, which you do in the third version of SlideShowApplet. Perform the steps below to build this new version of the applet:

1. Load SlideShowApplet.java, and add the following line to the `Init()` method, right after the `TODO: Place additional initialization code here` comment:

   ```
   MediaTracker mediaTracker = new MediaTracker(this);
   ```

2. Add the following line after the line `images[0] = getImage(codeBase, m_image1)`:

   ```
   mediaTracker.addImage(images[0], 0);
   ```

3. Add the following line after the line `images[1] = getImage(codeBase, m_image2)`:

   ```
   mediaTracker.addImage(images[1], 0);
   ```

4. Add the lines shown in Listing 18.12 after the line `images[2] = getImage(codeBase, ↪m_image3)`.

Listing 18.12   LST18_12.TXT—New Lines for the *init()* Method

```
mediaTracker.addImage(images[2], 0);

try
{
    mediaTracker.waitForAll();
}
catch (InterruptedException e)
{
}
```

5. Delete the `imageUpdate()` method from the SlideShowApplet class.

6. Add the method shown in Listing 18.13 to the SlideShowApplet class, right after the `run()` method near the end of the file.

Listing 18.13   LST18_13.TXT—The New *update()* Method

```
public void update(Graphics g)
{
    paint(g);
}
```

You've now completed the third version of the SlideShowApplet applet. Compile and run the applet. In this version, the slideshow animation doesn't start until all three images are loaded, preventing partial images from appearing in the applet's display area. Moreover, the animation is now smoother, without the slight flickering that you may have noticed in the previous version of the applet.

How SlideShowApplet, Version 3, Works

In version 3 of SlideShowApplet, it's the MediaTracker object that's responsible for ensuring that all the images are loaded before the slideshow begins. To implement this image-loading technique, the program first creates a MediaTracker object:

```
MediaTracker mediaTracker = new MediaTracker(this);
```

The MediaTracker class's constructor takes the applet's this reference as its single argument. This single argument is a reference to an object derived directly or indirectly from the Component class and is the component upon which the images will be drawn.

Once the MediaTracker object is created, the program must register with the object the images that the object should track. To do this, the program loads an image and then calls the MediaTracker object's addImage() method, like this:

```
images[0] = getImage(codeBase, m_image1);
mediaTracker.addImage(images[0], 0);
```

The addImage() method's two arguments are the image to be added and the image's ID. In SlideShowApplet, the program doesn't use the image IDs for anything. You can, however, use the IDs to organize images into groups, giving each image in a group the same ID. The SlideShowApplet applet organizes its images into a single group, all images of which have an ID of 0.

When all the images have been registered with the MediaTracker object, a call to the object's waitForAll() method ensures that all the images will be loaded before program execution continues:

```
mediaTracker.waitForAll();
```

The last thing of interest in this version of SlideShowApplet is the smoother animation, which is accomplished by overriding the applet's update() method. Because the default version of update() erases the applet's display area every time the display is redrawn, version 2 of SlideShowApplet had a slight flicker problem. In version 3 of the applet, you've overridden the applet's update() method. The overriding method calls paint() without bothering to erase the applet's display area. By removing the erase cycle, the slideshow animation is completely flicker-free.

The SlideShowApplet Applet, Version 4

Because this is supposed to be a chapter about multimedia (at least, multimedia as it applies to Java applets), it might be nice to add some sound to the slideshow animation you created in the previous sections. You already learned how to play audio files, way back in Chapter 7,

"The Applet and Window Classes." With that knowledge under your belt, adding sound to SlideShowApplet is a snap. First, add the following lines to the beginning of the `paint()` method:

```
URL codeBase = getCodeBase();
play(codeBase, "chirp1.au");
```

Then, copy the CHIRP1.AU (borrowed from the Java Developer's Kit) file from the CHAP18\SLIDESHOWAPPLET directory of this book's CD-ROM to your SlideShowApplet project directory. Finally, compile the new version of the program and run it.

Now, every time the applet draws a new image, it also produces a chirp sound, an interesting effect at first, but darn annoying after a minute or two!

You've now completed the SlideShowApplet applet. Listing 18.14 shows the complete applet for your reference. In the next section, you'll learn about another animation method that uses a technique called double-buffering.

Listing 18.14 SLIDESHOWAPPLET.JAVA—The Complete SlideShowApplet Applet

```java
//********************************************************************
// SlideShowApplet.java:    Applet
//
//********************************************************************
import java.applet.*;
import java.awt.*;
import java.net.*;


//====================================================================
// Main Class for applet SlideShowApplet
//
//====================================================================
public class SlideShowApplet extends Applet implements Runnable
{
    Image images[];
    int imageNum;
    Thread imageThread;

    // PARAMETER SUPPORT:
    //         Parameters allow an HTML author to pass information to
    // the applet; the HTML author specifies them using the <PARAM>
    // tag within the <APPLET> tag.  The following variables are
    // used to store the values of the parameters.
    //-------------------------------------------------------------

    // Members for applet parameters
    // <type>         <MemberVar>     = <Default Value>
    //-------------------------------------------------------------
    private String m_image1 = "snake.gif";
    private String m_image2 = "snake2.gif";
    private String m_image3 = "snake3.gif";
```

continues

Part

IV

Ch

18

Listing 18.14   Continued

```
// Parameter names.  To change a name of a parameter, you need
// only make a single change.  Simply modify the value of the
// parameter string below.
//----------------------------------------------------------------
private final String PARAM_image1 = "image1";
private final String PARAM_image2 = "image2";
private final String PARAM_image3 = "image3";

// SlideShowApplet Class Constructor
//----------------------------------------------------------------
public SlideShowApplet()
{
    // TODO: Add constructor code here
}

// APPLET INFO SUPPORT:
//        The getAppletInfo() method returns a string describing
// the applet's author, copyright date, or miscellaneous
// information.
//----------------------------------------------------------------
public String getAppletInfo()
{
    return "Name: SlideShowApplet\r\n" +
           "Author: Clayton Walnum\r\n" +
           "Created with Microsoft Visual J++ Version 1.0";
}

// PARAMETER SUPPORT
//        The getParameterInfo() method returns an array of
// strings describing the parameters understood by this applet.
//
// SlideShowApplet Parameter Information:
//   { "Name", "Type", "Description" },
//----------------------------------------------------------------
public String[][] getParameterInfo()
{
    String[][] info =
    {
        { PARAM_image1, "String", "Image file name" },
        { PARAM_image2, "String", "Image 2 file name" },
        { PARAM_image3, "String", "Image 3 file name" },
    };
    return info;
}

// The init() method is called by the AWT when an applet is first
// loaded or reloaded.  Override this method to perform whatever
// initialization your applet needs, such as initializing data
// structures, loading images or fonts, creating frame windows,
// setting the layout manager, or adding UI components.
//----------------------------------------------------------------
public void init()
{
```

```
    // PARAMETER SUPPORT
    //          The following code retrieves the value of each
    // parameter specified with the <PARAM> tag and stores it in
    // a member variable.
    //----------------------------------------------------------
    String param;

    // image1: Image file name
    //----------------------------------------------------------
    param = getParameter(PARAM_image1);
    if (param != null)
        m_image1 = param;

    param = getParameter(PARAM_image2);
    if (param != null)
        m_image2 = param;

    param = getParameter(PARAM_image3);
    if (param != null)
        m_image3 = param;

    // If you use a ResourceWizard-generated "control creator"
    // class to arrange controls in your applet, you may want to
    // call its CreateControls() method from within this method.
    // Remove the following call to resize() before adding the
    // call to CreateControls();
    // CreateControls() does its own resizing.
    //----------------------------------------------------------
    resize(320, 240);

    // TODO: Place additional initialization code here

    MediaTracker mediaTracker = new MediaTracker(this);

    URL codeBase = getCodeBase();
    imageNum = 0;
    images = new Image[3];
    images[0] = getImage(codeBase, m_image1);
    mediaTracker.addImage(images[0], 0);
    images[1] = getImage(codeBase, m_image2);
    mediaTracker.addImage(images[1], 0);
    images[2] = getImage(codeBase, m_image3);
    mediaTracker.addImage(images[2], 0);

    try
    {
        mediaTracker.waitForAll();
    }
    catch (InterruptedException e)
    {
    }
}

// Place additional applet clean up code here.  destroy() is
// called when your applet is terminating and being unloaded.
```

continues

Listing 18.14   Continued

```
//-----------------------------------------------------------------
public void destroy()
{
    // TODO: Place applet cleanup code here
}

// SlideShowApplet Paint Handler
//-----------------------------------------------------------------
public void paint(Graphics g)
{
    URL codeBase = getCodeBase();
    play(codeBase, "chirp1.au");

    int width = images[imageNum].getWidth(this);
    int height = images[imageNum].getHeight(this);
    g.drawRect(52, 52, width+10, height+10);
    g.drawImage(images[imageNum], 57, 57, width, height, this);
}

//        The start() method is called when the page containing
// the applet first appears on the screen. The AppletWizard's
// initial implementation of this method starts execution of the
// applet's thread.
//-----------------------------------------------------------------
public void start()
{
    // TODO: Place additional applet start code here

    imageThread = new Thread(this);
    imageThread.start();
}

//        The stop() method is called when the page containing
// the applet is no longer on the screen. The AppletWizard's
// initial implementation of this method stops execution of the
// applet's thread.
//-----------------------------------------------------------------
public void stop()
{
    if (imageThread != null)
        imageThread.stop();
}


// TODO: Place additional applet code here

public void run()
{
    while(true)
    {
        ++imageNum;
```

```
            if (imageNum > 2)
                imageNum = 0;
            repaint();

            try
            {
                Thread.sleep(100);
            }
            catch (Exception e)
            {
            }
        }
    }

    public void update(Graphics g)
    {
        paint(g);
    }
}
```

Performing Double-Buffered Animation

One thing that may have occurred to you as you worked with SlideShowApplet is that it always displays rectangular images that are the same size. In other words, the next image in the animation sequence always fits exactly on top of the previous image, relieving the applet of having to do any kind of erasing. Moreover, because all the images are rectangular, you didn't have to worry about an image's background messing up what's already on the screen.

Suppose, however, that such limitations are not acceptable for an animation sequence on which you're working. Specifically, suppose that you want to write an animation sequence in which you need to place an irregularly shaped object on top of a background. To do this, you need to know about transparent colors and double-buffered graphics.

Using Transparent Colors

Computers have a major handicap when it comes to displaying graphics on the screen. The truth is that computers can display only rectangular images. This works fine as long as the image you want to display fits exactly inside the rectangle that the computer will display. For example, in SlideShowApplet, the images you displayed on the screen were all rectangular, as well as all the same size. What happens when you want to display an object that is irregularly shaped? You might, for example, want to place an image of a creature on top of a background image. When you do this normally, you end up with something like Figure 18.5.

As you can see in the figure, because computers can display only rectangular images, the area around the leopard blots out the background, making for an unrealistic scene. You need a way to draw only the leopard on the screen and not the white area surrounding the leopard. This is done by converting the background of the leopard image into a transparent color. Then, even though the computer still has to work with a rectangular image, it knows enough not to display the pixels that are drawn in the transparent color, giving a scene like that shown in Figure 18.6. Much better!

FIG. 18.5
Irregularly shaped images can be trouble to display.

FIG. 18.6
Transparent colors fix the leopard display.

But what exactly is a transparent color? Simply, a transparent color is a color that the computer ignores when it displays the image. The transparent color can be any color you like, but it's up to you to choose the color and save the image file with the transparent-color information. The GIF file format handles transparent colors nicely, if you use the 89a version of the GIF format. To be sure your GIF files are saved in the correct format, you must use a paint program that supports GIF files with transparent colors. For Windows 95 and NT users, one popular shareware paint program is PaintShop Pro. (Point your Web browser to **http://www.jasc.com**.) The following steps illustrate how to create a GIF file with a transparent color using PaintShop Pro:

1. Load PaintShop Pro. The program's main window appears.

2. Select the File, Open command, and load the GIF file you want to convert. The GIF file appears in its own window (see Figure 18.7).

3. Set PaintShop Pro's background color to the color you want to be transparent. To do this, double-click the background-color square (see Figure 18.8), and select the color from the dialog box that appears.

4. Select the Fill tool from the Paint toolbox, and right-click the picture's background to fill with the background color (see Figure 18.9). (Make sure you right-click, rather than left-click.)

5. Select PaintShop Pro's File, Save As command. The Save As dialog box appears.

6. Set the File Sub-Format box to Version 89a—Non-interlaced, as shown in Figure 18.10.

7. Click the Save As dialog box's Options button. The GIF Transparency Options dialog box appears.

8. Select the Set The Transparency Value To The Background Color option (see Figure 18.11), and click OK.

9. Use the Save As dialog box's <u>D</u>irectory box to choose where to save the file, and then click OK.

FIG. 18.7
PaintShop Pro displays a GIF image.

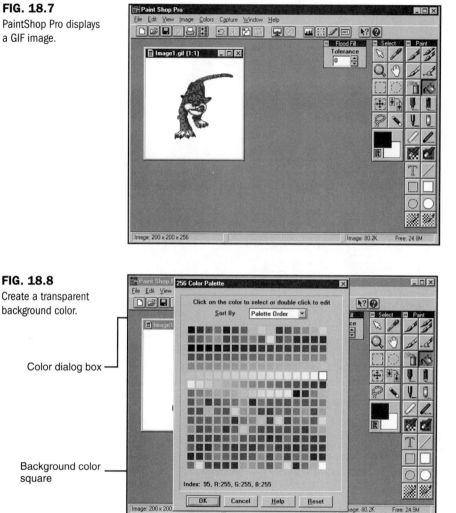

FIG. 18.8
Create a transparent background color.

Color dialog box ——

Background color square ——

FIG. 18.9
Right-click to fill the picture with the background color.

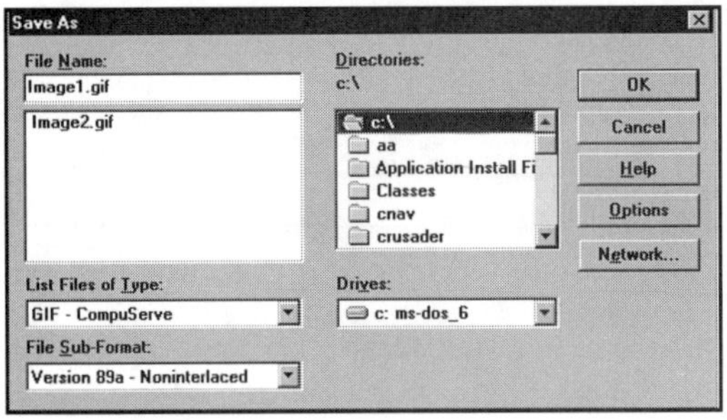

Image background

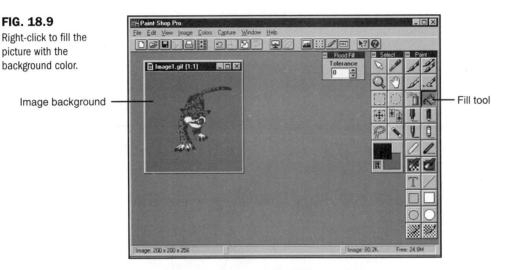

Fill tool

FIG. 18.10
The Save As dialog box enables you to choose a sub-format.

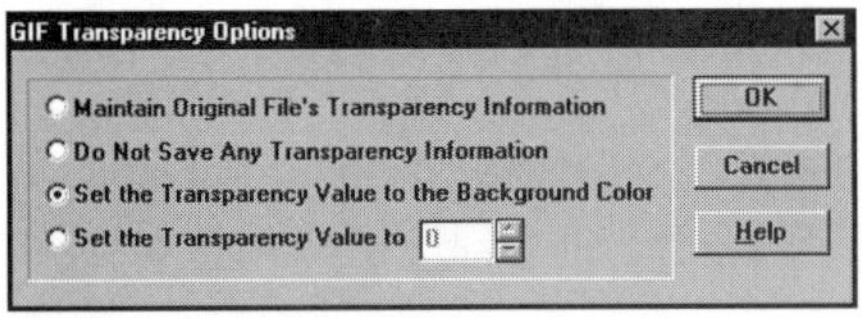

FIG. 18.11
Setting the transparency option ensures that the background color is saved properly.

Double-Buffered Graphics

Using double-buffering, you can create scenes for your applet in the computer's memory and then blast the completed scene all at once onto the display. By preparing the scenes out of sight of the user, you avoid the flicker that occurs when you build an animation frame on the screen.

For example, the next sample program you'll create displays an animated dungeon scene. The program first loads the images that will be used to create each frame of the animation. Then, the program creates an off-screen image buffer that it uses to assemble a frame of animation.

To assemble this frame, the program first copies the background image to the off-screen image buffer. Then, the program copies the next needed creature image onto the background, taking advantage of the transparent background color to avoid blotting out the dungeon scene behind the creature. Finally, the program displays the assembled scene on the applet's display surface.

After the assembled image is displayed, the process starts all over again for the next frame of animation. The background image is recopied to the off-screen image buffer, the next creature image is added to the scene, and the new scene is displayed. This process repeats again and again until the user exits the applet. In the next section, you get to see how all this double-buffering stuff works as you build the DoubleBufferApplet applet.

The DoubleBufferApplet Applet

As you now know, using double-buffering, you can create effective animation sequences for your applets. Under Java, you incorporate double-buffering into an applet by using the `createImage()` method to create an empty image in memory. You then use this empty image as the off-screen image buffer. To see how this works, perform the following steps to create the DoubleBufferApplet applet:

1. Create a new Java workspace using the Java Applet Wizard. Call the new workspace **DoubleBufferApplet**.

2. Select the options displayed in the wizard pages as listed:

   Step 1 of 5—Keep defaults.

   Step 2 of 5—Set the width and height to 320 and 300, respectively.

   Step 3 of 5—Select Yes, Please for multithreading and No, Thank You for animation.

   Step 4 of 5—Create four string parameters called **image1**, **image2**, **image3**, and **backgrnd**, as shown in Figure 18.12.

   Step 5 of 5—Keep defaults.

FIG. 18.12
Create these parameters for DoubleBufferApplet.

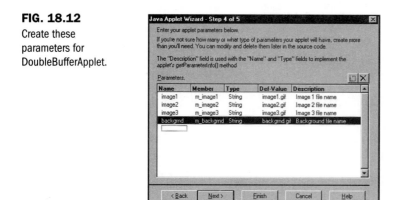

3. Select Finish. When the New Project Information dialog box appears, select OK. Visual J++ creates the files for the new project.

4. Load the DoubleBufferApplet.java file and add the following line near the top of the file, right after the line `import java.awt.*` that's already there:

```
import java.net.*;
```

5. Add the lines shown in Listing 18.15 right after the opening brace in the class's definition, before the THREAD SUPPORT comment.

Listing 18.15 LST18_15.TXT—Data Members of the *DoubleBufferApplet* Class

```
Image images[];
int imageNum;
Image imageBuffer;
Image backImageObj;
Graphics bufferGraphics;
int imageSequence[] = {0,1,0,1,0,1,2};
int sequenceNum;
```

6. Add the lines shown in Listing 18.16 to the init() method, right after the TODO: Place additional initialization code here comment.

Listing 18.16 LST18_16.TXT—New Code for the *init()* Method

```
MediaTracker mediaTracker = new MediaTracker(this);

URL codeBase = getCodeBase();
imageNum = 0;
sequenceNum = 0;
images = new Image[3];
images[0] = getImage(codeBase, m_image1);
mediaTracker.addImage(images[0], 0);
images[1] = getImage(codeBase, m_image2);
mediaTracker.addImage(images[1], 0);
images[2] = getImage(codeBase, m_image3);
mediaTracker.addImage(images[2], 0);
backImageObj = getImage(codeBase, m_backgrnd);
mediaTracker.addImage(backImageObj, 0);

try
{
    mediaTracker.waitForAll();
}
catch (InterruptedException e)
{
}

imageBuffer = createImage(240, 240);
bufferGraphics = imageBuffer.getGraphics();
```

7. Replace the lines in the paint() method with the lines shown as follows:

```
bufferGraphics.drawImage(backImageObj, 0, 0, this);
bufferGraphics.drawImage(images[imageNum], 20, 60, this);
g.drawImage(imageBuffer, 0, 0, this);
```

8. Replace the lines in the `run()` method with the lines shown in Listing 18.17.

Listing 18.17   LST18_17.TXT—Lines for the *run()* Method

```
while(true)
{
    ++sequenceNum;
    if (sequenceNum > 6)
        sequenceNum = 0;
    imageNum = imageSequence[sequenceNum];

    repaint();

    try
    {
        Thread.sleep(500);
    }
    catch (Exception e)
    {
    }
}
```

9. Add the method shown in Listing 18.18 near the end of the DoubleBufferApplet.java file, right before the file's closing brace.

Listing 18.18   LST18_18.TXT—The *update()* Method

```
public void update(Graphics g)
{
    paint(g);
}
```

10. Copy the files IMAGE1.GIF, IMAGE2.GIF, IMAGE3.GIF, and BACKGRND.GIF from the CHAP18\DOUBLEBUFFERAPPLET directory of this book's CD-ROM to your DoubleBufferApplet project directory.

You've now completed the DoubleBufferApplet applet. To compile the applet, choose Visual J++'s Build, Build command. After the application finishes compiling, run it. When you do, you see the window shown in Figure 18.13. What the figure doesn't show is the animation sequence. The leopard twitches its tail and then lunges for an attack (see Figure 18.14).

How DoubleBufferApplet Works

The program handles its parameters and the loading of its images much like SlideShowApplet did. However, DoubleBufferApplet loads four images, one of which is the dungeon background and three of which comprise the animated leopard (see Figure 18.15). Only the three leopard images are loaded into the `Image` array `images[]`. The background image is kept separate from the other images.

Part

IV

Ch

18

FIG. 18.13
This leopard looks like trouble.

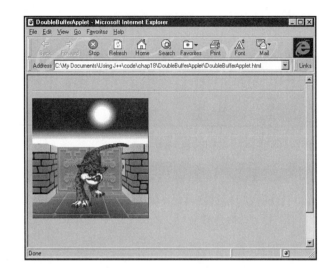

FIG. 18.14
At the end of each animation sequence, the leopard attacks.

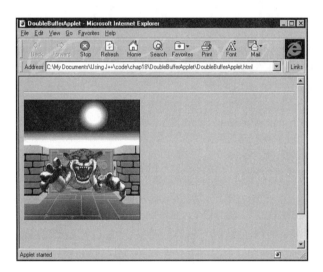

FIG. 18.15

The four images used by DoubleBufferApplet comprise an animation sequence.

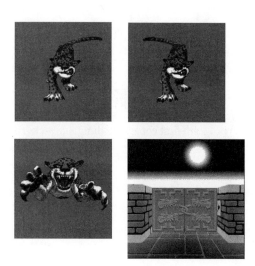

With the images loaded, the program creates an off-screen image buffer, like this:

```
imageBuffer = createImage(240, 240);
```

The `createImage()` method returns a reference to an `Image` object. The method's two arguments are the width and height of the image. The empty image created by the call to `createImage()` is tucked away in memory out of sight of the user. Any drawing the program does on this image will be unseen by the applet's user.

In order to manipulate the off-screen image, the program needs access to the image's `Graphics` object. A call to the image's `getGraphics()` method returns the `Graphics` object:

```
bufferGraphics = imageBuffer.getGraphics();
```

As with SlideShowApplet, DoubleBufferApplet's animation takes place in a secondary thread. In the thread's `run()` method is an infinite `while` loop that keeps the animation going until the user exits the applet and so destroys the thread. Within the loop, the program increments the sequence number:

```
++sequenceNum;
if (sequenceNum > 6)
    sequenceNum = 0;
```

The sequence number is an index into the `imageSequence[]` array, which holds the order in which the images should be displayed. That array is defined like this:

```
int imageSequence[] = {0,1,0,1,0,1,2};
```

The numbers in the array are indexes into the `images[]` array. That is, the above array specifies that images 0 and 1 will be displayed alternatively three times and then image 2 will be displayed. To change the order in which the images are displayed, just change the numbers in this array.

Part

IV

Ch

18

After calculating the next sequence number, the program uses the sequence number to index the `imageSequence[]` array and so gets the index of the next image to display:

```
imageNum = imageSequence[sequenceNum];
```

After getting the next image number, the `run()` method calls `repaint()` and then sleeps for 500 milliseconds, just as the similar thread in SlideShowApplet did.

In the `paint()` method, the program first copies the dungeon-background image to the off-screen image buffer, like this:

```
bufferGraphics.drawImage(backImageObj, 0, 0, this);
```

As you can see, the `drawImage()` function is called through the reference to the buffer's `Graphics` object.

After copying the background, the program copies the next creature image in the animation sequence to the buffer:

```
bufferGraphics.drawImage(images[imageNum], 20, 60, this);
```

Because the creature images define a transparent color, their backgrounds don't wipe out the dungeon background scene.

Finally, the program displays the assembled image on the applet's display area:

```
g.drawImage(imageBuffer, 0, 0, this);
```

When the animation sequence reaches the end, it loops back to the start, performing the same animation sequence repeatedly until the user exits the applet. For your reference, Listing 18.19 shows the complete source code for the DoubleBufferApplet applet.

Listing 18.19   DoubleBufferApplet.java—Source Code for DoubleBufferApplet

```java
//*******************************************************************
// DoubleBufferApplet.java:     Applet
//
//*******************************************************************
import java.applet.*;
import java.awt.*;
import java.net.*;


//===================================================================
// Main Class for applet DoubleBufferApplet
//
//===================================================================
public class DoubleBufferApplet extends Applet implements Runnable
{
    Image images[];
    int imageNum;
    Image imageBuffer;
    Image backImageObj;
    Graphics bufferGraphics;
    int imageSequence[] = {0,1,0,1,0,1,2};
```

```
    int sequenceNum;

    // THREAD SUPPORT:
    //      m_DoubleBufferApplet is the Thread object for the applet
    //---------------------------------------------------------------
    Thread    m_DoubleBufferApplet = null;

    // PARAMETER SUPPORT:
    //      Parameters allow an HTML author to pass information to
    // the applet; the HTML author specifies them using the <PARAM>
    // tag within the <APPLET> tag.  The following variables are used
    // to store the values of the parameters.
    //---------------------------------------------------------------

    // Members for applet parameters
    // <type>       <MemberVar>   = <Default Value>
    //---------------------------------------------------------------
    private String m_image1 = "image1.gif";
    private String m_image2 = "image2.gif";
    private String m_image3 = "image3.gif";
    private String m_backgrnd = "backgrnd.gif";

    // Parameter names.  To change a name of a parameter, you need
    // only make a single change.  Simply modify the value of the
    // parameter string below.
    //---------------------------------------------------------------
    private final String PARAM_image1 = "image1";
    private final String PARAM_image2 = "image2";
    private final String PARAM_image3 = "image3";
    private final String PARAM_backgrnd = "backgrnd";

    // DoubleBufferApplet Class Constructor
    //---------------------------------------------------------------
    public DoubleBufferApplet()
    {
        // TODO: Add constructor code here
    }

    // APPLET INFO SUPPORT:
    //      The getAppletInfo() method returns a string describing
    // the applet's author, copyright date, or miscellaneous
    // information.
    //---------------------------------------------------------------
    public String getAppletInfo()
    {
        return "Name: DoubleBufferApplet\r\n" +
               "Author: Clayton Walnum\r\n" +
               "Created with Microsoft Visual J++ Version 1.0";
    }

    // PARAMETER SUPPORT
    //      The getParameterInfo() method returns an array of
    // strings describing the parameters understood by this applet.
    //
    // DoubleBufferApplet Parameter Information:
```

continues

Listing 18.19 Continued

```
//   { "Name", "Type", "Description" },
//------------------------------------------------------------
public String[][] getParameterInfo()
{
    String[][] info =
    {
        { PARAM_image1, "String", "Image 1 file name" },
        { PARAM_image2, "String", "Image 2 file name" },
        { PARAM_image3, "String", "Image 3 file name" },
        { PARAM_backgrnd, "String", "Background file name" },
    };
    return info;
}

// The init() method is called by the AWT when an applet is first
// loaded or reloaded.  Override this method to perform whatever
// initialization your applet needs, such as initializing data
// structures, loading images or fonts, creating frame windows,
// setting the layout manager, or adding UI components.
//------------------------------------------------------------
public void init()
{
    // PARAMETER SUPPORT
    //        The following code retrieves the value of each
    // parameter specified with the <PARAM> tag and stores it in
    // a member variable.
    //--------------------------------------------------------
    String param;

    // image1: Image 1 file name
    //--------------------------------------------------------
    param = getParameter(PARAM_image1);
    if (param != null)
        m_image1 = param;

    // image2: Image 2 file name
    //--------------------------------------------------------
    param = getParameter(PARAM_image2);
    if (param != null)
        m_image2 = param;

    // image3: Image 3 file name
    //--------------------------------------------------------
    param = getParameter(PARAM_image3);
    if (param != null)
        m_image3 = param;

    // backgrnd: Background file name
    //--------------------------------------------------------
    param = getParameter(PARAM_backgrnd);
    if (param != null)
        m_backgrnd = param;
```

```
    // If you use a ResourceWizard-generated "control creator"
    // class to arrange controls in your applet, you may want to
    // call its CreateControls() method from within this method.
    // Remove the following call to resize() before adding the
    // call to CreateControls();
    // CreateControls() does its own resizing.
    //----------------------------------------------------------
    resize(320, 300);

    // TODO: Place additional initialization code here

    MediaTracker mediaTracker = new MediaTracker(this);

    URL codeBase = getCodeBase();
    imageNum = 0;
    sequenceNum = 0;
    images = new Image[3];
    images[0] = getImage(codeBase, m_image1);
    mediaTracker.addImage(images[0], 0);
    images[1] = getImage(codeBase, m_image2);
    mediaTracker.addImage(images[1], 0);
    images[2] = getImage(codeBase, m_image3);
    mediaTracker.addImage(images[2], 0);
    backImageObj = getImage(codeBase, m_backgrnd);
    mediaTracker.addImage(backImageObj, 0);

    try
    {
        mediaTracker.waitForAll();
    }
    catch (InterruptedException e)
    {
    }

    imageBuffer = createImage(240, 240);
    bufferGraphics = imageBuffer.getGraphics();
}

// Place additional applet clean up code here.  destroy() is
// called when your applet is terminating and being unloaded.
//----------------------------------------------------------
public void destroy()
{
    // TODO: Place applet cleanup code here
}

// DoubleBufferApplet Paint Handler
//----------------------------------------------------------
public void paint(Graphics g)
{
    // TODO: Place applet paint code here

    bufferGraphics.drawImage(backImageObj, 0, 0, this);
    bufferGraphics.drawImage(images[imageNum], 20, 60, this);
    g.drawImage(imageBuffer, 0, 0, this);
```

Part

IV

Ch

18

continues

Listing 18.19 Continued

```
}

//       The start() method is called when the page containing
// the applet first appears on the screen. The AppletWizard's
// initial implementation of this method starts execution of the
// applet's thread.
//--------------------------------------------------------------
public void start()
{
    if (m_DoubleBufferApplet == null)
    {
        m_DoubleBufferApplet = new Thread(this);
        m_DoubleBufferApplet.start();
    }
    // TODO: Place additional applet start code here
}

//       The stop() method is called when the page containing
// the applet is no longer on the screen. The AppletWizard's
// initial implementation of this method stops execution of the
// applet's thread.
//--------------------------------------------------------------
public void stop()
{
    if (m_DoubleBufferApplet != null)
    {
        m_DoubleBufferApplet.stop();
        m_DoubleBufferApplet = null;
    }

    // TODO: Place additional applet stop code here
}

// THREAD SUPPORT
//       The run() method is called when the applet's thread is
// started. If your applet performs any ongoing activities
// without waiting for user input, the code for implementing that
// behavior typically goes here. For example, for an applet that
// performs animation, the run() method controls the display of
// images.
//--------------------------------------------------------------
public void run()
{
    while(true)
    {
        ++sequenceNum;
        if (sequenceNum > 6)
            sequenceNum = 0;
        imageNum = imageSequence[sequenceNum];

        repaint();

        try
```

```
            {
                Thread.sleep(500);
            }
            catch (Exception e)
            {
            }
        }
    }


    // TODO: Place additional applet code here

    public void update(Graphics g)
    {
        paint(g);
    }
}
```

From Here...

Now, you have all the tools you need to create snazzy multimedia sequences for your Java applets. Using double-buffering, especially, you can create sophisticated displays that'll delight the viewers of your Web pages. For information on related topics, please refer to these chapters:

Part

IV

Ch

18

- ■ Chapter 3, "The Java Language," describes how to use the Java language.
- ■ Chapter 7, "The Applet and Window Classes," describes the basics of programming graphics with Java.

CHAPTER 19

Advanced Java Graphics

by Clayton Walnum

In the previous chapter, you began creating dynamic applets. Through images, sounds, and even animation, you can now create Web pages to entice even the most discerning of Internet users. Java boasts a host of other advanced graphics features that you can add to your programming repertoire. You'll learn about many of these other advanced techniques in this chapter. ■

Learn about image producers and image consumers

Java's image producers feed image data to image consumers.

Discover how to create in-memory images

Most images reside somewhere on disk. However, Java enables you to create images directly in memory.

Understand how an array of integers can represent an image

You can create images from an array of integers, each element of which contains the alpha, red, green, and blue color values for each pixel in the image.

Create your own image filters

Image filters enable you to modify images in various ways.

Programming sprites in order to create more dynamic applets

Sprites are animated objects that move around an applet's display. Thanks to Java's object-oriented nature, sprites are easier to implement than you might think.

Image Producers and Consumers

Before you can understand many of the advanced graphics techniques in this chapter, you have to know about Java's image producers (based on the `ImageProducer` class) and image consumers (based on the `ImageConsumer` class). Basically, an image producer is charged with loading and preparing an image to ship off to an image consumer. The image consumer associates itself with the image producer and receives the image's data when the producer is ready to send it.

For example, Java features a method called `createImage()` (defined in the `Component` class) that—you guessed it—creates images. This method can be used in two ways: to create an image of a given size for use in double-buffering, or to create an image from an image producer. In the latter usage, the `createImage()` method takes the image producer as its single argument. Internally, the method then creates an image consumer to which the image producer feeds the image's data. You'll see all this in action in the following section, where you learn to create in-memory images.

Creating In-Memory Images

In Chapter 7, "The Applet and Windows Classes," and in Chapter 18, "Multimedia," you learned how to load and display images. The images you worked with in these chapters were stored on disk in the .GIF file format. In order to display the image, you first had to load it from disk. What you may have not known is that Java images are much more versatile than that. In fact, you can actually create your own images directly in memory, without ever loading data from disk.

Creating an Image Producer

The first step in creating an in-memory image is to construct an image producer. You can create an image producer that is not associated with a disk file or an URL, but rather manages an image stored only in the computer's memory. To create such an image producer, you construct an object of the `MemoryImageSource` class, which Java derives from `ImageProducer`:

```
MemoryImageSource producer =
    new MemoryImageSource(width, height, imageBits, offset, lineWidth);
```

Here, `width` is the width of the image, `height` is the height of the image, `imageBits` is an array of color values that represent the image, `offset` is the index of the first image pixel in the array, and `lineWidth` is the number of pixels in each line of the image.

For example, look at this line:

```
MemoryImageSource producer =
    new MemoryImageSource(300, 200, imageBits, 0, 200);
```

This line creates an image producer that can supply an in-memory image whose dimensions are 300x200. The color of each pixel in the image is stored in the `imageBits` array. The image's pixels start at the very first element of the array and require 200 pixels per line.

Creating the Image

After creating the image producer, you pass the producer on to the `createImage()` method:

```
Image image = createImage(producer);
```

The `createImage()` method manages the interaction between the image producer and the image consumer, returning a reference to an image that you can display just as you displayed .GIF images loaded from disk:

```
g.drawImage(image, 0, 0, this);
```

Defining the Pixel Array

You probably have an important question right about now: Exactly what values does the pixel array need to contain in order to create the image properly? The easy answer is that the array contains color values for each pixel in the image. The complicated, and more helpful, answer is that the array contains integer values for each pixel in the image, each integer of which contains the alpha, red, green, and blue values for the pixel. The alpha value is in the upper byte, with the remaining bytes containing the red, green, and blue values—in that order—as shown in Figure 19.1.

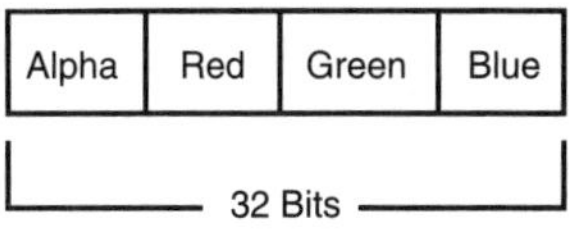

FIG. 19.1
The color values for
each pixel are stored
as integers containing
RGBA values.

Alpha	Red	Green	Blue

└─────── 32 Bits ───────┘

Because the alpha, red, green, and blue values are each allotted one byte, they can each be a value between 0 and 255. What's an alpha value? You'll learn about these values later in the chapter, in the section "Working with Alpha Values." For now, just know that the alpha value determines how the background and the image are blended. An alpha value of 255 ensures that the pixel appears with no background blending.

The pixels in the array are arranged as if you laid each row of the image one after the other in memory. That is, if the image is 100 pixels wide, the first row of pixels would be in the array elements 0 through 99, the second row in 100 through 199, the third row in 200 through 299, and so on, up to the height of the image.

So, suppose you want to create an in-memory image that contains a red square. You'd probably initialize the pixel array as shown in Listing 19.1.

Listing 19.1 LST19_01.TXT—Initializing the Pixel Array to All Red

```
for (int i = 0; i < WIDTH*HEIGHT; ++i)
{
    int red = 255;
    int green = 0;
```

continues

Listing 19.1   Continued

```
    int blue = 0;
    int alpha = 255;
    imageBits[i] = (alpha << 24) ¦ (red << 16) ¦ (green << 8) ¦ blue;
}
```

In Listing 19.1, a for loop iterates through the array one element at a time, stuffing the appropriate color into each pixel value. The red pixel value is created with a red value of 255, a green value of 0, a blue value of 0, and an alpha value of 255. The program first shifts the bits in each RGBA value into the correct position using Java's left-shift operator (<<). The resultant values are then ORed together into the final 32-bit color value. Figure 19.2 illustrates the shifting process for the color red. The other shifts work similarly, placing the color values in their correct positions. The OR performed using Java's OR operator (¦) then merges the four color values into one 32-bit value.

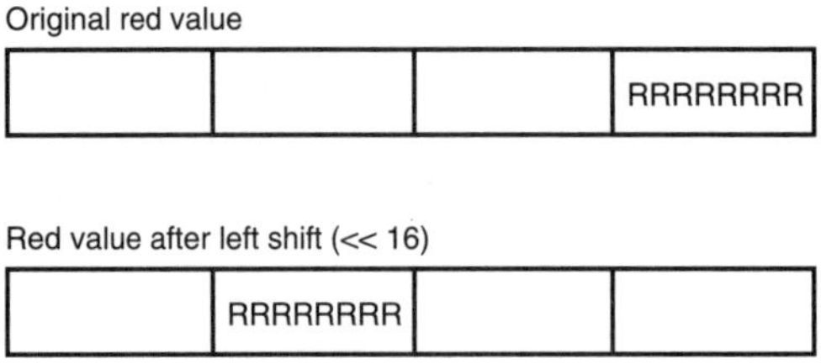

FIG. 19.2

The left-shifting process places color values in their correct positions.

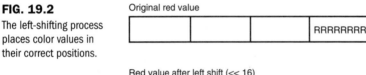

Original red value

Red value after left shift (<< 16)

Introducing the ImageApplet2 Applet

To test all of these in-memory image items, this chapter includes a sample applet called ImageApplet2, the code for which is shown in Listing 19.2. When you run the applet, you see the window in Figure 19.3. Although it's hard to tell with the black-and-white figure, the image in the window comprises 256 rows of green, starting from the darkest green at the top and going to the brightest green at the bottom.

FIG. 19.3

ImageApplet2 displays an image created in memory.

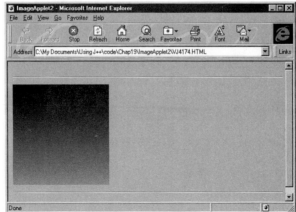

Listing 19.2   ImageApplet2.java—Creating an In-Memory Image

```java
import java.applet.*;
import java.awt.*;
import java.awt.image.MemoryImageSource;

public class ImageApplet2 extends Applet
{
    Image backImage;
    final int WIDTH = 256;
    final int HEIGHT = 256;

    public void init()
    {
        int imageBits[] = new int[WIDTH * HEIGHT];

        for (int row = 0; row < HEIGHT; ++row)
        {
            int red = 0;
            int green = (row * 255) / (HEIGHT - 1);
            int blue = 0;
            int alpha = 255;
            for (int col = 0; col < WIDTH; ++col)
            {
                int index = row * WIDTH + col;
                imageBits[index++] =
                    (alpha << 24) | (red << 16) | (green << 8) | blue;
            }
        }

        MemoryImageSource producer = new MemoryImageSource
            (WIDTH, HEIGHT, imageBits, 0, WIDTH);
        backImage = createImage(producer);
    }

    public void paint(Graphics g)
    {
        g.drawImage(backImage, 0, 0, this);
    }
}
```

Part
IV

Ch
19

Understanding Image Filters

In most cases, when you display an image in an applet, you want the image to look exactly as it was created. However, by using image filters, you can do many clever things with your images, such as tinting them different colors or causing them to fade in and out. An image filter is a special object that processes each pixel of an image, changing the image whatever way you like.

Writing an *ImageFilter* Class

Image filters are derived from Java's `ImageFilter` class, which is a type of image consumer (that is, `ImageFilter` implements the `ImageConsumer` interface). You can derive your own custom image filters from `ImageFilter`, but for most filtering needs, you'll probably find that Java's `RGBImageFilter` class is the best superclass to use. `RGBImageFilter` is an abstract class that defines most of its methods, but leaves one abstract method for you to define. This means that, in order to create an `RGBImageFilter` for your applet, you need to derive a new class that implements the abstract `filterRGB()` method. Listing 19.3 shows how you might derive your own class from `RGBImageFilter`.

Listing 19.3   ColorFilter.java—Creating an Image Filter Class

```java
import java.awt.image.*;
class ColorFilter extends RGBImageFilter
{
    int color;
    final int RED = 0;
    final int GREEN = 1;
    final int BLUE = 2;

    public ColorFilter(int color)
    {
        ColorFilter.color = color;
        canFilterIndexColorModel = true;
    }

    public int filterRGB(int x, int y, int rgb)
    {
        int newRGB;

        if (color == RED)
            newRGB = (rgb & 0xff00ffff) | (255 << 16);
        else if (color == GREEN)
            newRGB = (rgb & 0xffff00ff) | (255 << 8);
        else if (color == BLUE)
            newRGB = (rgb & 0xffffff00) | (255);
        else
            newRGB = rgb;

        return newRGB;
    }
}
```

The `ColorFilter` class shown in Listing 19.3 enables a program to add a red, green, or blue tint to the image being filtered. When constructing a `ColorFilter` object, you pass the constructor the value 0 for red tint, 1 for green tint, or 2 for blue tint. The class's constructor then saves the tint selection in its data field `color`. The constructor also sets `canFilterIndexColorModel` to true. `ColorFilter` inherits the `canFilterIndexColorModel` field from the `RGBImageFilter` class. Setting this field to `true` (its default value is `false`) indicates that you will be ignoring the x and y parameters sent to the `filterRGB()` method.

And speaking of `filterRGB()`, this is the abstract method that has to be defined in any class derived from `RGBImageFilter`. Java calls this method for every pixel in the image, giving you a chance to tweak each pixel as needed. In the case of `ColorFilter`, the `filterRGB()` method sets either the red, green, or blue color content of each pixel to its maximum value (255) in order to tint the image as requested when the image-filter object was constructed. The method returns the modified pixel value.

Using an *ImageFilter* Class

To use the `ColorFilter` class, you must follow several steps. First, you must load the image you want to filter:

```
Image origImage = getImage(getDocumentBase(), imageName);
```

Then, you need to get a reference to the image's image producer, like this:

```
ImageProducer origProducer = origImage.getSource();
```

Next, you create a `ColorFilter` object:

```
ColorFilter colorFilter = new ColorFilter(RED);
```

In this case, the image filter will tint the image red (assuming that RED is defined as 0 somewhere in the program).

With the image filter created, you can now create an image producer for the filtered image, like this:

```
FilteredImageSource filterProducer =
    new FilteredImageSource(origProducer, colorFilter);
```

The `FilteredImageSource` class creates an image producer from another producer and an image filter. That is, you can think of the previous line as causing the image producer for the original image to feed the image through the image-filter class to the next image producer in the chain. This second image producer will then be able to feed the filtered image to an image consumer.

The last step is to create the actual image, by calling `createImage()`, like this:

```
Image filteredImage = createImage(filterProducer);
```

As you can see, `createImage()`'s single argument is the image producer that manages the filtered image. After `createImage()` executes, you can display the resultant image. Now, however, the image will have been filtered by the `ColorFilter` image filter.

Introducing the FilterApplet Applet

Listing 19.4 is an applet, called FilterApplet, that puts the `ColorFilter` class to the test. When you run the applet, you see the screen shown in Figure 19.4. The applet's display starts off displaying the original image. When you click either the Red, Green, or Blue button, the image gets filtered and redisplayed. Click the Original button whenever you want to go back to the original, unfiltered image.

FIG. 19.4

FilterApplet enables you
to tint an image using
an image-filter object.

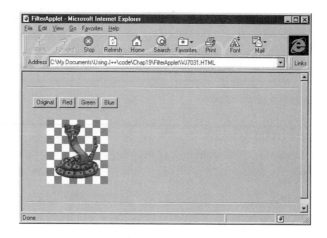

Listing 19.4   FilterApplet.java—An Applet that Displays Filtered Images

```java
import java.awt.*;
import java.applet.*;
import java.awt.image.*;

public class FilterApplet extends Applet
{
    Image origImage;
    Image redImage;
    Image greenImage;
    Image blueImage;
    Image curImage;
    final int RED = 0;
    final int GREEN = 1;
    final int BLUE = 2;

    public void init()
    {
        origImage = getImage(getDocumentBase(), "snake.gif");

        ImageProducer origProducer = origImage.getSource();
        ColorFilter colorFilter = new ColorFilter(RED);
        FilteredImageSource filterProducer =
            new FilteredImageSource(origProducer, colorFilter);
        redImage = createImage(filterProducer);

        colorFilter = new ColorFilter(GREEN);
        filterProducer =
            new FilteredImageSource(origProducer, colorFilter);
        greenImage = createImage(filterProducer);

        colorFilter = new ColorFilter(BLUE);
        filterProducer =
            new FilteredImageSource(origProducer, colorFilter);
        blueImage = createImage(filterProducer);
```

```
        curImage = origImage;

        Button button = new Button("Original");
        add(button);
        button = new Button("Red");
        add(button);
        button = new Button("Green");
        add(button);
        button = new Button("Blue");
        add(button);
    }

    public void paint(Graphics g)
    {
        g.drawImage(curImage, 40, 50, this);
    }

    public boolean action(Event event, Object arg)
    {
        if (arg == "Red")
            curImage = redImage;
        else if (arg == "Green")
            curImage = greenImage;
        else if (arg == "Blue")
            curImage = blueImage;
        else
            curImage = origImage;

        repaint();
        return true;
    }
}

class ColorFilter extends RGBImageFilter
{
    int color;
    final int RED = 0;
    final int GREEN = 1;
    final int BLUE = 2;

    public ColorFilter(int color)
    {
        ColorFilter.color = color;
        canFilterIndexColorModel = true;
    }

    public int filterRGB(int x, int y, int rgb)
    {
        int newRGB;

        if (color == RED)
            newRGB = (rgb & 0xff00ffff) ¦ (255 << 16);
        else if (color == GREEN)
            newRGB = (rgb & 0xffff00ff) ¦ (255 << 8);
```

continues

Listing 19.4 Continued

```
        else if (color == BLUE)
            newRGB = (rgb & 0xffffff00) | (255);
        else
            newRGB = rgb;

        return newRGB;
    }
}
```

N O T E You can find the SNAKE.GIF image file on this book's CD-ROM, in the chap19\FilterApplet folder. ■

Understanding the FilterApplet Applet

There's really not much new in FilterApplet. You already know how the `ColorFilter` class works. The rest of the action takes place in the applet's `init()` method. There, the applet loads the original image, and then creates three new versions of the image, using three different `ColorFilter` objects. The three new images will be tinted red, green, and blue, respectively. When the user clicks one of the applet's buttons, the `action()` method determines which button was clicked and displays the requested version of the image.

Working with Alpha Values

Earlier in this chapter, in the section titled "Defining the Pixel Array," you looked briefly at alpha values. You learned that the alpha value determines how a background and an image are blended. Specifically, the alpha value determines how much of the background shows through the image. This gives the image a transparent quality. The lower the alpha value, the more the background shows through and the more transparent the image appears to be. An alpha value of 0 means that the image area will show only the background, whereas an alpha value of 255 means that no background will show through at all. As you already know, you use an alpha value of 255 when you want to display the image normally.

You can create interesting visual effects with alpha values, one of which is causing an image to fade in rather than appear all at once. There are many other times when being able to make an image look transparent would be handy. You could, for example, create objects that appear to be made out of glass.

Introducing the AlphaApplet Applet

Listing 19.5 is an applet called AlphaApplet that lets you experiment with alpha values. When you run the applet, you see the window shown in Figure 19.5. At startup, the applet's display shows the familiar snake image drawn on top of a multicolored background. Type a value between 0 and 255 into the text box and press Enter. When you do, the program filters the snake image using the number you entered as an alpha value. The smaller the number, the more transparent the snake image becomes (see Figure 19.6).

FIG. 19.5
AlphaApplet enables you to apply different alpha values to the displayed snake image.

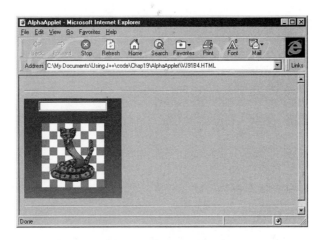

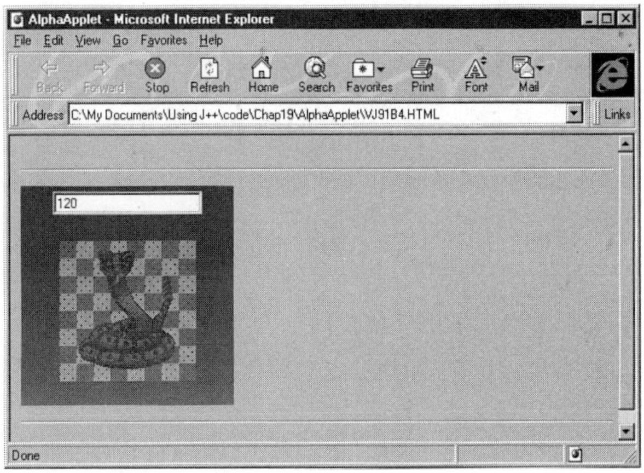

FIG. 19.6
The lower the alpha value, the more transparent the snake image becomes.

Part
IV

Ch
19

Listing 19.5 AlphaApplet.java—An Applet that Demonstrates how Alpha Values Work

```java
import java.awt.*;
import java.applet.*;
import java.awt.image.*;

public class AlphaApplet extends Applet
{
    Image origImage;
    Image backImage;
    Image filteredImage;
    TextField textField;
    final int WIDTH = 256;
    final int HEIGHT = 256;
```

continues

Listing 19.5   Continued

```java
public void init()
{
    origImage = getImage(getDocumentBase(), "snake.gif");
    filteredImage = origImage;
    backImage = createBackImage();
    textField = new TextField(20);
    add(textField);
}

public void paint(Graphics g)
{
    g.drawImage(backImage, 0, 0, this);
    g.drawImage(filteredImage, 36, 50, this);
}

public boolean action(Event event, Object arg)
{
    try
    {
        String str = textField.getText();
        int alpha = Integer.parseInt(str);
        ImageProducer origProducer = origImage.getSource();
        AlphaFilter alphaFilter = new AlphaFilter(alpha);
        FilteredImageSource filterProducer =
            new FilteredImageSource(origProducer, alphaFilter);
        filteredImage = createImage(filterProducer);
    }
    catch (Exception e)
    {
    }

    repaint();
    return true;
}

public Image createBackImage()
{
    int imageBits[] = new int[WIDTH * HEIGHT];

    for (int row = 0; row < HEIGHT; ++row)
    {
        int red = (row * 255) / (HEIGHT - 1);
        int green = 50;
        int blue = 100;
        int alpha = 255;
        for (int col = 0; col < WIDTH; ++col)
        {
            int index = row * WIDTH + col;
            imageBits[index++] =
                (alpha << 24) | (red << 16) | (green << 8) | blue;
        }
    }
```

```
        MemoryImageSource producer = new MemoryImageSource
            (WIDTH, HEIGHT, imageBits, 0, WIDTH);

        return createImage(producer);
    }
}

class AlphaFilter extends RGBImageFilter
{
    int alpha;

    public AlphaFilter(int alpha)
    {
        AlphaFilter.alpha = alpha;
        canFilterIndexColorModel = true;
    }

    public int filterRGB(int x, int y, int rgb)
    {
        int newRGB = (rgb & 0x00ffffff) | (alpha << 24);
        return newRGB;
    }
}
```

Understanding the AlphaApplet Applet

There's not a lot to say about Listing 19.5. Everything in it should be familiar to you by now. It's all just used in a slightly different way. For example, the image filter, called `AlphaFilter`, changes the alpha values of each pixel, rather than the color tint. It's exactly the same idea as in the `ColorFilter` class, but you get a very different result, showing just how versatile image filters can be.

Programming Sprites

In the previous chapter, "Multimedia," you saw how to use images, threads, and double-buffering to create animated scenes. For many applications, the methods discussed in that chapter work fine. However, it's often handy to have a self-contained object that can be moved and animated on the screen. By self-contained, I mean that the animated object itself keeps track of which animation frame to display, where the object is currently located on the display, and other information that is related to the object itself. Such an object is called a *sprite* and is often used in game programs.

Most of what you learned in the previous chapter can be applied to the creation and managing of sprites. The main difference is that sprites aren't only animated; they also move around on the screen. Another important difference is that sprites are usually programmed as an object of a class. By creating a class to represent a sprite, you can easily handle multiple sprites without having to overly complicate your main program.

Writing the *Sprite* Class

Look at Listing 19.6, which contains a simple class for creating sprites. There are a zillion ways you could write such a class, depending upon how the sprites are to be used. The `Sprite` class sticks to only the very basics in order to more easily illustrate how a sprite class might be developed.

Listing 19.6   Sprite.java—A Sprite Class

```java
import java.awt.*;
class Sprite
{
    Image images[];
    Point position;
    int curImage;
    int minX, maxX;
    int minY, maxY;

    Sprite(Image image1, Image image2,
        int minX, int maxX, int minY, int maxY)
    {
        curImage = 0;
        Sprite.minX = minX;
        Sprite.maxX = maxX;
        Sprite.minY = minY;
        Sprite.maxY = maxY;
        position = new Point(minX, minY);
        images = new Image[2];
        images[0] = image1;
        images[1] = image2;
    }

    public Point changeHorPosition(int x)
    {
        position.x += x;
        if (position.x > maxX)
            position.x = minX;
        if (position.x < minX)
            position.x = maxX;

        return position;
    }

    public Point changeVerPosition(int y)
    {
        position.y += y;
        if (position.y > maxY)
            position.y = minY;
        if (position.y < minY)
            position.y = maxY;
```

```
        return position;
    }

    public Image nextImage()
    {
        int nextImage = curImage;
        ++curImage;
        if (curImage == 2)
            curImage = 0;
        return images[nextImage];
    }
}
```

The Sprite class starts off by declaring seven data fields. Those fields and how they're used in the class are listed below:

Field	How it's Used
images[]	An array that holds the sprites' images.
position	The sprite's current position on the screen.
curImage	The index of the currently displayed sprite image.
minX	The minimum X coordinate at which the sprite can appear in the display.
maxX	The maximum X coordinate at which the sprite can appear in the display.
minY	The minimum Y coordinate at which the sprite can appear in the display.
maxY	The maximum Y coordinate at which the sprite can appear in the display.

The class also defines several methods, including a constructor, that enable a program to create and manipulate a sprite. Those methods and their descriptions are listed below:

Method	Description
Sprite()	Constructs a Sprite object.
changeHorPosition()	Changes the sprite's horizontal location.
changeVerPosition()	Changes the sprite's vertical position.
nextImage()	Returns the next image in the sprite's animation sequence.

Part IV

Ch 19

Using the *Sprite* Class

To create an object of the Sprite class, you call the class's constructor like this:

```
Sprite sprite = new Sprite(image1, image2, minX, maxX, minY, maxY);
```

The constructor's arguments are the two images that make up the animation sequence and the minimum and maximum X and Y coordinates. The class's constructor stores all this information in its data fields for future use. The class's constructor also sets the sprite's starting position to the minimum X and Y coordinates, as well as sets the curImage index to 0, which is the index of the first image in the images[] array.

To display the sprite on the screen, call the sprite object's `nextImage()` method, which returns the image to display. You can then display this image just as you would any other image. To move the sprite around the screen, you first change its position by calling `changeHorPosition()` or `changeVerPosition()`. Both of these methods return a `Point` object containing the sprite's new position. Just draw the sprite on the screen using the X and Y coordinates stored in the `Point` object.

N O T E The `changeHorPosition()` and `changeVerPosition()` methods use the minimum and maximum X and Y coordinates in order to ensure that the sprite stays within the given bounds. Whenever the sprite moves beyond one of these boundaries, the method wraps the sprite's position around. For example, when the sprite's X position goes past `maxX`, the sprite gets set back to `minX`. ▓

Building the SpriteApplet Applet

A little confused? No problem. In this section, you'll build an applet that uses the `Sprite` class. This applet takes the animated leopard from the previous chapter, and gives him a spinning tail that helicopters him around the display. Just follow the steps below to create the applet.

1. Create a new Java workspace using the Java Applet Wizard. Call the new workspace **SpriteApplet**, as shown in Figure 19.7.

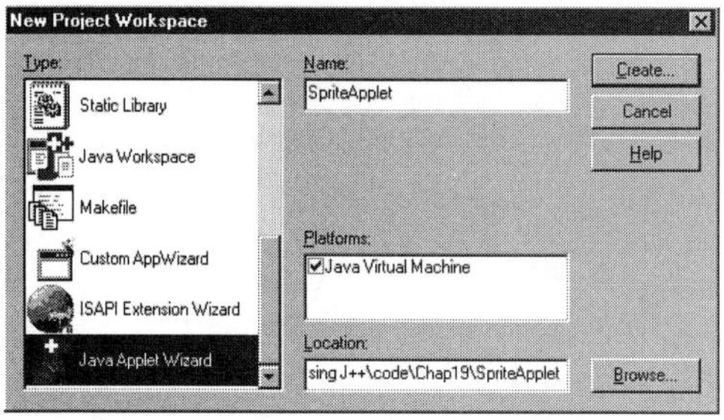

FIG. 19.7
Use AppletWizard to create the SpriteApplet workspace.

2. Select the options displayed in the wizard pages as shown below:

Step 1 of 5—Keep defaults

Step 2 of 5—Keep defaults

Step 3 of 5—Select Yes, Please for multithreading and No, Thank You for animation (see Figure 19.8).

Step 4 of 5—Keep defaults (no applet parameters)

Step 5 of 5—Keep defaults

3. Click Finish. When the New Project Information dialog box appears (see Figure 19.9), click OK. Visual J++ creates the files for the new project.

FIG. 19.8

SpriteApplet needs multithreading, but you'll add your own animation.

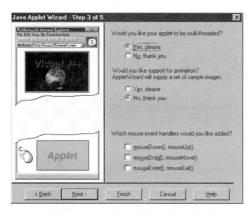

FIG. 19.9

This is the New Project Information dialog box for SpriteApplet.

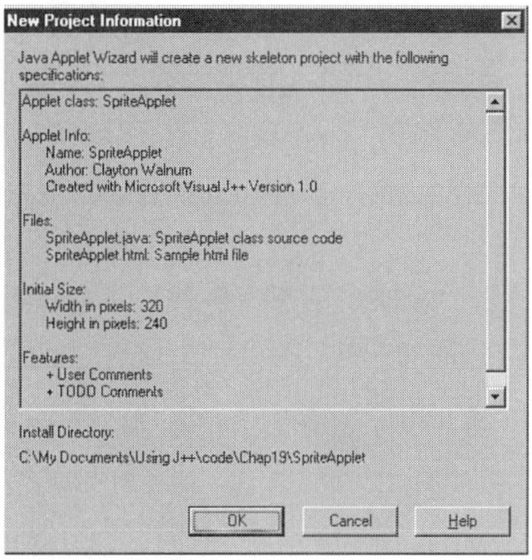

Part
IV

Ch
19

4. Load the SpriteApplet.java file and add the lines shown in Listing 19.7 to the beginning of the SpriteApplet class's definition, right after the class's opening brace.

Listing 19.7   LST19_07.TXT—Data Fields for the Class

```
Sprite sprite;
Image spriteImage;
Point spritePos;
Image imageBuffer;
Image backImageObj;
Graphics bufferGraphics;
```

5. Add the lines shown in Listing 19.8 to the init() method, right after the TODO: Place additional initialization code here comment.

Listing 19.8   LST19_08.TXT—Code for the *init()* Method

```
MediaTracker mediaTracker = new MediaTracker(this);
backImageObj = getImage(getCodeBase(), "backgrnd.gif");
mediaTracker.addImage(backImageObj, 0);
Image image1 = getImage(getCodeBase(), "image1.gif");
mediaTracker.addImage(image1, 0);
Image image2 = getImage(getCodeBase(), "image2.gif");
mediaTracker.addImage(image2, 0);

try
{
    mediaTracker.waitForAll();
}
catch (InterruptedException e)
{
}

imageBuffer = createImage(240, 240);
bufferGraphics = imageBuffer.getGraphics();
sprite = new Sprite(image1, image2, 0, 60, 0, 60);
```

6. Replace the lines in the paint() method with those shown in Listing 19.9.

Listing 19.9   LST19_09.TXT—Code for the *paint()* Method

```
bufferGraphics.drawImage(backImageObj, 0, 0, this);
bufferGraphics.drawImage(spriteImage,
    spritePos.x, spritePos.y, this);
g.drawImage(imageBuffer, 0, 0, this);
```

7. Replace the code in the run() method with the lines shown in Listing 19.10.

Listing 19.10   LST19_10.TXT—Code for the *run()* Method

```
while(true)
{
    spriteImage = sprite.nextImage();
    spritePos = sprite.changeHorPosition(4);
    if (spritePos.x == 0)
        spritePos = sprite.changeVerPosition(20);

    repaint();

    try
    {
        Thread.sleep(50);
    }
    catch (Exception e)
    {
    }
}
```

8. Add the lines shown in Listing 19.11 to the end of the `SpriteApplet` class, right after the `TODO: Place additional applet code here` comment.

Listing 19.11   LST19_11.TXT—The *update()* Method

```
public void update(Graphics g)
{
    paint(g);
}
```

9. Add the lines shown in Listing 19.12 to the end of the file, outside of the `SpriteApplet` class's definition.

Listing 19.12   LST19_12.TXT—The Code for the *Sprite* Class

```
class Sprite
{
    Image images[];
    Point position;
    int curImage;
    int minX, maxX;
    int minY, maxY;

    Sprite(Image image1, Image image2,
        int minX, int maxX, int minY, int maxY)
    {
        curImage = 0;
        Sprite.minX = minX;
        Sprite.maxX = maxX;
        Sprite.minY = minY;
        Sprite.maxY = maxY;
        position = new Point(minX, minY);
        images = new Image[2];
        images[0] = image1;
        images[1] = image2;
    }

    public Point changeHorPosition(int x)
    {
        position.x += x;
        if (position.x > maxX)
            position.x = minX;
        if (position.x < minX)
            position.x = maxX;

        return position;
    }

    public Point changeVerPosition(int y)
    {
        position.y += y;
        if (position.y > maxY)
```

Part

IV

Ch

19

continues

Listing 19.12 Continued

```
            position.y = minY;
        if (position.y < minY)
            position.y = maxY;

        return position;
    }

    public Image nextImage()
    {
        int nextImage = curImage;
        ++curImage;
        if (curImage == 2)
            curImage = 0;
        return images[nextImage];
    }
}
```

10. Copy the BACKGRND.GIF, IMAGE1.GIF, and IMAGE2.GIF files from the Chap19\SpriteApplet directory of this book's CD-ROM to your SpriteApplet project directory.

You've now completed the SpriteApplet applet. Select the Build, Build command to compile the applet, and then select Build, Execute to run it. When you do, you'll see that strange leopard with the helicopter tail flying around your applet (see Figure 19.10).

FIG. 19.10
Now the leopard is a sprite rather than a stationary animation.

Understanding the SpriteApplet Applet

Given the previous discussion of the Sprite class, you should already know how the class works. In this section, you'll look over the main program. SpriteApplet loads all three images (the background image and the two animation frames) in its init() method, using a

`MediaTracker` object to ensure that the images are completely loaded before the program continues, as shown in Listing 19.13.

Listing 19.13 LST19_13.TXT—Loading the Images

```
MediaTracker mediaTracker = new MediaTracker(this);
backImageObj = getImage(getCodeBase(), "backgrnd.gif");
mediaTracker.addImage(backImageObj, 0);
Image image1 = getImage(getCodeBase(), "image1.gif");
mediaTracker.addImage(image1, 0);
Image image2 = getImage(getCodeBase(), "image2.gif");
mediaTracker.addImage(image2, 0);
```

The `init()` method also creates the memory image that'll be used for double-buffering, gets a `Graphics` object for the buffer, and creates a `Sprite` object:

```
imageBuffer = createImage(240, 240);
bufferGraphics = imageBuffer.getGraphics();
sprite = new Sprite(image1, image2, 0, 60, 0, 60);
```

Each time through the main loop in the thread's `run()` method, the program gets the next sprite image to display:

```
spriteImage = sprite.nextImage();
```

Then the applet changes the sprite's current position:

```
spritePos = sprite.changeHorPosition(4);
```

If, after changing the horizontal position, the sprite's X coordinate is 0, the sprite has wrapped around from its maximum X position to its minimum X position. When that happens, the program changes the sprite's Y position in order to move it down on the display:

```
if (spritePos.x == 0)
    spritePos = sprite.changeVerPosition(20);
```

A call to `repaint()` then gets the current sprite image displayed in its new position. Meanwhile, the thread sleeps for 50 milliseconds:

```
Thread.sleep(50);
```

The thread's sleep time is what controls the animation's speed. To make the sprite move faster, decrease the sleep time. To slow the sprite down, increase the sleep time.

It is, of course, the `paint()` method that draws the new sprite image on the display. First `paint()` copies the background image to the memory image buffer:

```
bufferGraphics.drawImage(backImageObj, 0, 0, this);
```

Then, `paint()` draws the current sprite image on the buffer image, using the new sprite coordinates:

```
bufferGraphics.drawImage(spriteImage,
    spritePos.x, spritePos.y, this);
```

Part

IV

Ch

19

Finally, `paint()` draws the newly constructed scene onto the visible display:

```
g.drawImage(imageBuffer, 0, 0, this);
```

From Here...

You now have a whole new array of graphics techniques to apply to your applet programming projects. Remember, the World Wide Web is an intensely graphical place. The more interesting and dynamic you make your applets and Web pages, the more people are going to want to visit your Web site or use your applets in their own Web pages.

For more information on related topics, please see the following:

- Chapter 4, "Java Language Basics," describes the basic elements of the Java language.
- Chapter 5, "Loops, Conditionals, and Arrays" extends the discussion of the Java language that began in Chapter 4.
- Chapter 7, "The Applet and Window Classes," introduces you to Java's basic graphical abilities.
- Chapter 12, "Threads," shows you how to create and program multithreaded applets.
- Chapter 18, "Multimedia," teaches how to create double-buffered applets, how to use `MediaTracker` objects, and how to create images with transparent backgrounds.

CHAPTER 20

Using Native Methods and Libraries

by Clayton Walnum

In most cases, in spite of its interpreted nature, Java chugs along at a zippy clip. That is, most Java applets have little trouble doing what they need to do without being too sluggish. However, there may be times when you need a method in your applet to run faster than what is possible using Java code. Or, you may need to implement a feature that is not directly supported by the Java language. In these cases, you can create *native methods*, which are functions written in a language other than Java (usually C or C++) and then called from within your Java program. In this chapter, you'll see how to create native methods using C. ■

Using native methods

Using native methods, you can enhance Java applets and applications.

Encapsulate your native methods into a Java class

Declaring your native methods in a Java class enables you to more easily incorporate the methods into your other Java programs.

Use Java tools to create supporting files for your native methods

In order to link your Java code with the C or C++ code used to implement native methods, you need C header and stub files.

Create the C or C++ code that implements your native methods

To create native methods in C or C++, you have to learn a few new techniques.

Call native methods from your Java programs

Once you have created your native methods, you still need to know how to use them.

Introducing Native Methods

Java enables you to call functions, called native methods, that are written in other languages. As you might imagine, the process of creating native methods can be a little tricky. However, if you have the right tools and a little know-how, you can have your native methods up and running in no time.

> **CAUTION**
>
> Because native methods are written in a language other than Java, they are platform dependent. That is, a native method will run only on the platform (IBM, Macintosh, and so on) for which it was developed.

How do native methods work? The native method's implementation (written in C or C++) lives in a library file. When you write a Java program that uses the native method, you declare the method using the `native` keyword, but you don't implement the method in the class. You don't need to implement the method in the class, because it's already implemented in the library file. Here's an example of a native-method declaration:

```
public native void MyNativeMethod();
```

The `native` keyword tells Java not to bother looking for the method's implementation in the class. Rather, Java needs to find the method elsewhere. When the Java class containing the native method runs, the class loads the library file containing the native method's implementation. When the program calls the native method, the system finds the function in the loaded library and runs it.

Basically, to create and use a native method, you need to complete five steps. These steps are listed here:

1. Write and compile the Java class that represents the native method.
2. Use the javah tool to create header and stub files from the Java class.
3. Write the C++ function that implements the native method.
4. Compile the C++ function into LIB and DLL files.
5. Write and compile the Java program that calls the native method.

In the following sections, you'll take a closer look at each of these steps, as you create a sample Java stand-alone application that uses native methods. Along the way, you will be creating three programs:

- The Java class that represents the native methods.
- The C program that implements the native methods.
- The Java test application that uses the native methods.

NOTE Because Visual J++ does not directly support the Java tools used to create native methods, you must have the Java Developer's Kit (JDK) installed in order to complete the samples in this chapter. This chapter assumes you have performed the default Java installation, with the JDK ending up in a directory called C:\JAVA.

Write and Compile the Java Class

When you create native methods for your Java programs, you create a class that will hold the methods' declarations. Listing 20.1 shows the native-method class you'll use in this chapter's sample program.

Listing 20.1   NativeMethods.java—A Class for Native Methods

```
class NativeMethods
{
    // Class data members.
    protected String message;

    // Class methods.
    public native void setMessage(String msg);
    public native void printMessage();

    // Class implementation.
    static {
        System.loadLibrary("NativeMethodsImp");
    }
}
```

If you examine Listing 20.1, you'll see that the `NativeMethod` class declares two methods called `setMessage()` and `printMessage()`. The `native` keyword tells Java that these methods will be implemented in another language, rather than part of the `NativeMethod` class.

Below the native-method declarations, you can see a static program block. A static program block runs automatically when a class is run. Because the code in the block has no method name, you can't call it from your program. It runs only once, when the class is run. In the case of Listing 20.1, the static program block calls Java's `loadLibrary()` method, which is defined in the `System` class. The method's single argument is the name of the library to load. In this case, the name of the library is `NativeMethodsImp`. The `NativeMethodsImp` library will contain the implementations of the `setMessage()` and `printMessage()` native methods.

Now that you have developed the `NativeMethods` class, you can type and compile it. To do this, perform the following steps:

1. Type Listing 20.1 (or copy it from this book's CD-ROM), and save the file in a directory called C:\Classes\NativeMethods.

2. Run Visual J++.

3. Select Visual J++'s File, Open command. The Open dialog box appears.

4. Use the dialog box to load the NativeMethods.java file, as shown in Figure 20.1.

5. Select Visual J++'s Build, Build command. The Microsoft Developer Studio dialog box appears (see Figure 20.2).

6. Select the Yes button in order to create a default project and compile the `NativeMethods` class.

Part

IV

Ch

20

FIG. 20.1

The Open dialog box enables you to load source-code files.

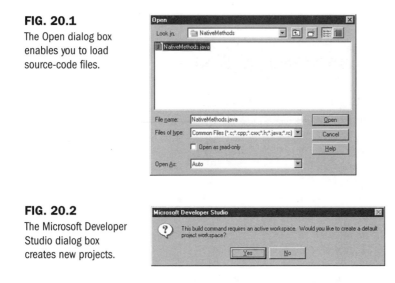

FIG. 20.2

The Microsoft Developer Studio dialog box creates new projects.

Create Header and Stub Files

When you complete the native-method implementations, you're going to have both Java and C source code. To make native methods work, you have to link these two languages together somehow so that they can communicate. The first step in completing this task is to create header and stub files.

The header file contains information about the Java class that the C native-method implementation can use. This information includes the class's data members and the C function names for the native-method implementations. The stub file contains machine-generated C code that is pretty strange looking to all but C gurus. Luckily, you don't have to understand the stub file in order to create native methods.

To create the header and stub files for this chapter's sample program, follow the steps here:

1. Select the Start, Programs, MS-DOS Prompt command from Windows 95's Start menu. A DOS window appears.

2. Type **SET CLASSPATH=C:\JAVA\LIB\CLASSES.ZIP; C:\CLASSES\NATIVEMETHODS** and press Enter (see Figure 20.3). The system sets the CLASSPATH variable so that Java's tools can find the classes being used in the program.

3. Type **PATH=C:\ JAVA\BIN** and press Enter (see Figure 20.4). The system sets your path so that it can find the JDK's executables.

4. Type **CD C:\CLASSES\NATIVEMETHODS** in order to switch to the directory containing the NativeMethods.java file.

FIG. 20.3

You must be sure that the CLASSPATH system variable is properly set.

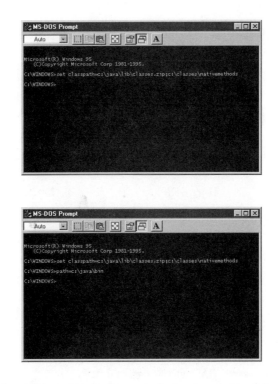

FIG. 20.4

It's also helpful to have the JAVA\BIN directory in your path.

5. Type **javah NativeMethods** to run the javah tool. (Don't forget that Java tools are case-sensitive. File names have to be typed in both upper- and lowercase.) The javah tool creates the NativeMethods.h header file.

6. Type **javah -stubs NativeMethods** to run the javah tool again. This time, thanks to the -stubs parameter, the javah tool creates the NativeMethods.c stubs file.

Now that you've created the header and stub files, take a look at them. Listing 20.2 is the NativeMethods.h file. The header file has two main parts. The first is the ClassNativeMethods structure that links the C source code to the data members of the Java class. You may remember that the Java class had a single data member called message. You can see that data member listed in the structure. The Hjava_lang_String is a special data type that links C-style strings with objects of Java's String class. Table 20.1 shows other special data types that are used in C native-method header and implementation files.

Part
IV

Ch
20

Table 20.1 Native Method Data Types

Java Type	Native Type
boolean	long
boolean[]	HArrayOfInt*

continues

Table 20.1 Continued

Java Type	Native Type
char	unicode
char[]	HArrayOfChar*
double	double
double[]	HArrayOfDouble*
float	float
float[]	HArrayOfFloat*
int	int64_t
int[]	HArrayOFInt*
long	long
long[]	HArrayOfLong*
short	short
short[]	HArrayOfShort*
String	struct Hjava_lang_String*
String[]	HArrayOfString*

The second main part of the header file is where the native methods are declared. As you can see, javah has given the C functions different names from the Java methods they represent. The C function NativeMethods_setMessage() matches up with the NativeMethods class's setMessage() method, and the C function NativeMethods_printMessage() is the printMessage() method's counterpart. In the next section, you'll write the C code for the NativeMethods_setMessage() and NativeMethods_printMessage() functions.

Listing 20.3 shows the stub file javah created. (The file has been edited for line length.) As you can see, it's a good thing that you don't have to decipher the code contained in NativeMethods.c. However, you can easily see that both of the native methods that you're going to implement in C are represented in the NativeMethods.c file. Beyond that, you can just let the compiler figure it out!

Listing 20.2 NativeMethods.h—The Header File Created by Javah

```
/* DO NOT EDIT THIS FILE - it is machine generated */
#include <native.h>
/* Header for class NativeMethods */

#ifndef _Included_NativeMethods
#define _Included_NativeMethods
struct Hjava_lang_String;
```

```
typedef struct ClassNativeMethods {
    struct Hjava_lang_String *message;
} ClassNativeMethods;
HandleTo(NativeMethods);

#ifdef __cplusplus
extern "C" {
#endif
extern void NativeMethods_setMessage(struct HNativeMethods *,
                                     struct Hjava_lang_String *);
extern void NativeMethods_printMessage(struct HNativeMethods *);
#ifdef __cplusplus
}
#endif
#endif
```

Listing 20.3 NativeMethods.c—The Stub File Created by Javah

```
/* DO NOT EDIT THIS FILE - it is machine generated */
#include <StubPreamble.h>

/* Stubs for class NativeMethods */
/* SYMBOL: "NativeMethods/setMessage()V",
           Java_NativeMethods_setMessage_stub */
__declspec(dllexport) stack_item
           *Java_NativeMethods_setMessage_stub(stack_item
           *_P_,struct execenv *_EE_) {
    extern void NativeMethods_setMessage(void *);
    (void) NativeMethods_setMessage(_P_[0].p);
    return _P_;
}
/* SYMBOL: "NativeMethods/printMessage()V",
           Java_NativeMethods_printMessage_stub */
__declspec(dllexport) stack_item
           *Java_NativeMethods_printMessage_stub(stack_item
           *_P_,struct execenv *_EE_) {
    extern void NativeMethods_printMessage(void *);
    (void) NativeMethods_printMessage(_P_[0].p);
    return _P_;
}
```

Write the C Functions

At this point, you're ready to write the native methods' implementations. This means that you're going to have to crank up your C or C++ compiler. In this section, you use Visual C++ 4.2 to create and compile the native-method implementations. If you use a different compiler, you'll probably have to change the steps somewhat. The code for the functions' implementations is shown in Listing 20.4.

Listing 20.4   NativeMethodsImp.c—Implementation File for the Native Methods

```
#include "NativeMethods.h"
#include <stdio.h>

void NativeMethods_setMessage(struct HNativeMethods* this,
                              struct Hjava_lang_String* msg)
{
    ClassNativeMethods* data = unhand(this);
    data->message = msg;
}

void NativeMethods_printMessage(struct HNativeMethods* this)
{
    ClassNativeMethods* data = unhand(this);
    javaStringPrint(data->message);
}
```

Follow the steps below to create and compile the native-function C implementations:

1. Type Listing 20.4 (or copy it from this book's CD-ROM), and store it in your C:\Classes directory, under the name NativeMethodsImp.c. (The "Imp" in the name stands for "Implementation.")

2. Start Visual C++.

3. Select Visual C++'s File, New command. The New dialog box appears.

4. Select Project Workspace and click OK. The New Project Workspace dialog box appears.

5. Create a Dynamic-Link Library (DLL) project called NativeMethodsImp, as shown in Figure 20.5.

FIG. 20.5

Create a DLL project called NativeMethodsImp.

6. Copy the NativeMethods.h, NativeMethods.c, and NativeMethodsImp.c files into the new NativeMethodsImp project directory.

7. Select Visual C++'s Insert, Files into Project command. The Insert Files into Project dialog box appears (see Figure 20.6).

FIG. 20.6

The Insert Files into Project dialog box adds files to projects.

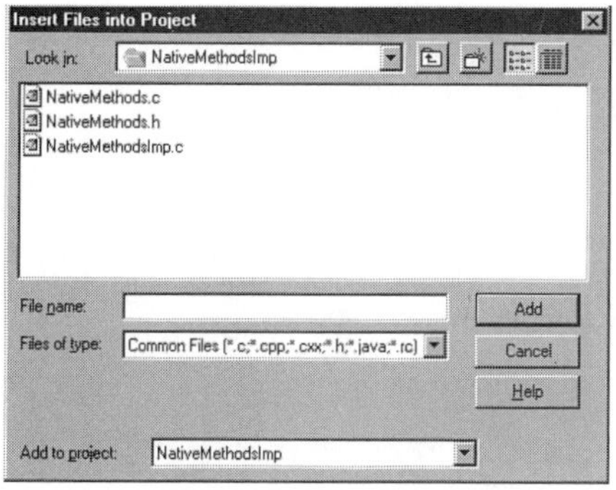

Insert Files into Project

Look in: NativeMethodsImp

NativeMethods.c
NativeMethods.h
NativeMethodsImp.c

File name: Add
Files of type: Common Files [*.c;*.cpp;*.cxx;*.h;*.java;*.rc]   Cancel
                                               Help

Add to project: NativeMethodsImp

8. Add the NativeMethods.c and NativeMethodsImp.c files to the project.

9. Using the Insert Files into Project dialog box, add the JAVAI.LIB file to the project. (You'll find JAVAI.LIB in the C:\JAVA\LIB directory.)

10. Select Visual C++'s Tools, Options command. The Options property sheet appears, as shown in Figure 20.7. Select the Directories tab.

FIG. 20.7

The Options property sheet enables you to set various project options.

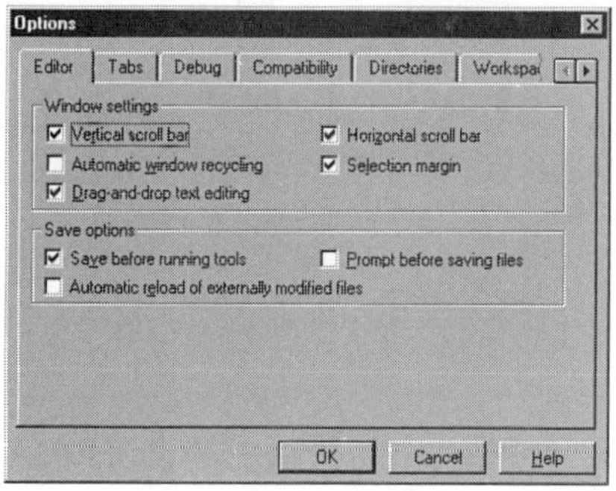

Options

Editor | Tabs | Debug | Compatibility | Directories | Workspac

Window settings
☑ Vertical scroll bar   ☑ Horizontal scroll bar
☐ Automatic window recycling   ☑ Selection margin
☑ Drag-and-drop text editing

Save options
☑ Save before running tools   ☐ Prompt before saving files
☐ Automatic reload of externally modified files

OK   Cancel   Help

11. Add **c:\java\include** and **c:\java\include\win32** to the directory list, as shown in Figure 20.8.

12. In Visual C++'s project toolbar, change the project target from Win32 Debug to Win32 Release (see Figure 20.9).

13. Select Visual C++'s Build, Build command to build the DLL.

In your project's Release folder, you now have a file called NativeMethodsImp.dll. This is the Dynamic-Link Library that contains the C implementations of your native methods. But before you write the Java program that calls the native methods, examine the DLL's source code (the file NativeMethodsImp.C, found in the NativeMethodsImp directory), which probably looks a bit strange to you.

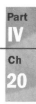

Part
IV

Ch
20

FIG. 20.8

You have to add Java directories to your project.

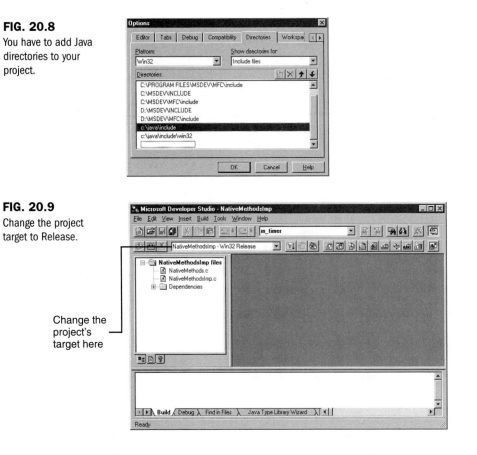

FIG. 20.9

Change the project target to Release.

Change the project's target here

At the top of Listing 20.4, the program includes the header files it needs:

```
#include "NativeMethods.h"
#include <stdio.h>
```

The NativeMethods.h file is the header file that you created with javah. The stdio.h file gives the program access to the `printf()` function.

Next, the program begins the definition of the `setMessage()` native method, which has a different name from its Java declaration:

```
void NativeMethods_setMessage(struct HNativeMethods* this,
                              struct Hjava_lang_String* msg)
```

The C name for the method, as well as the data types for the parameters, are found in the NativeMethods.h file. When you write the implementations of your native methods, check the header file created by javah for the C function signatures.

Next, the program gets the address of the structure that contains the native-method Java class's data members:

```
ClassNativeMethods* data = unhand(this);
```

As you can see, to get the pointer to the data structure, you call the unhand() function, passing the function the pointer that was received as the function's first parameter.

With the pointer in hand, you can easily access the String data member message and set it to the String value msg, which was passed to setMessage() by the calling method:

```
data->message = msg;
```

The printMessage() method's C implementation begins like this:

```
void NativeMethods_printMessage(struct HNativeMethods* this)
```

Just as with setMessage(), the signature of the C version of the method can be found in the header file created by javah.

Inside the method, the program gets a pointer to the structure that contains the Java class's data members:

```
ClassNativeMethods* data = unhand(this);
```

Then, the program calls the javaStringPrint() method to display the message String object on the screen:

```
javaStringPrint(data->message);
```

The javaStringPrint() function is one of many functions defined in the JAVAI.LIB library that you included in the NativeMethodsImp project. Other string-related functions you can call include javaStringLength(), makeJavaString(), makeCString(), allocCString(), javaString2unicode(), and javaString2CString(). These functions are declared in the JavaString.H file found in the INCLUDE directory of your Java installation.

Use the Native Methods

Congratulations! Most of the hard stuff is now out of the way. You've written and compiled your native methods (both the Java class and the DLL), so you're all ready to actually use them. In this section, you write a test program that incorporates the NativeMethods class. The test program will call both of the native methods you created. To create the Test program, follow these steps:

1. Create a folder called Test in your Classes directory, and save Listing 20.5 in this folder. (You can either type the listing or copy it from this book's CD-ROM.)

Part

IV

Ch

20

Listing 20.5   Test.java—The Test Program for the *NativeMethods* Class

```
class Test
{
    public static void main(String args[])
    {
        NativeMethods nativeMethods = new NativeMethods();
        nativeMethods.setMessage("A new message!");
        nativeMethods.printMessage();
    }
}
```

2. Copy the NativeMethods.class file into the Test directory. NativeMethods.class is the compiled version of the Java class that declares the native methods. You can find the file in your NativeMethods directory.

3. Start Visual J++ and select the File, Open command. Load the Test.java file.

4. Select Visual J++'s Build, Build command. When asked if you want to create a default project, select Yes. Visual J++ compiles the Test program.

You should now have a file called Test.class in your Test folder. This is the compiled Test application. Because Test is a non-windowed stand-alone application, you must run it from the DOS prompt. To do this, bring up a DOS window and switch to the C:\Classes\Test directory. Type the following command line (all on one line) in order to place the Test directory into the CLASSPATH variable:

```
SET CLASSPATH=C:\JAVA\LIB\CLASSES.ZIP;
    C:\CLASSES\NATIVEMETHODS;C:\CLASSES\TEST
```

If you've started a new DOS session, you may also have to add the JAVA\BIN directory to your path like this:

```
PATH=C:\JAVA\BIN
```

Because the Test program calls the native methods you've just created, Test has to have the DLL containing the native methods' implementations available to it. To make the DLL (called NativeMethodsImp.dll and found in your NativeMethodsImp\Release directory) available, simply copy it to your Test directory.

Finally, you can run the test program by typing the following command:

```
java Test
```

When you run the Test program, the message "A new message!" should appear on the screen. And you thought using native methods was difficult!

From Here...

Native methods give Java programs a lot of versatility. However, there's one serious caveat of which you must be aware: *Because native methods are implemented with a language other than Java, they are platform-dependent.* For example, the native methods you created in this chapter run under Windows 95 and NT, but they will not run under other operating systems. Because one of the main advantages of Java is platform-independence—the ability to run Java programs on any machine—you should think long and hard about using native methods, should you be tempted to.

For more information on related topics, please see the following chapters:

■ Chapter 1, "Why Java Is Hot," explains why Java applets are system-independent.

■ Chapter 14, "Getting Started with Visual J++," reviews how to use the various tools that come with the Visual J++ development environment.

■ Chapter 27, "Scripting Client Applets," describes techniques, other than using native methods, for improving the performance of your Java programs.

CHAPTER 21

Using Visual J++ Debugging Tools

by Mark Culverhouse

In this chapter, the Visual J++ integrated debugging tools are introduced. The tools come in the forms of commands, menus, toolbars, and windows. They are integrated because they work together intelligently to make debugging Java programs manageable. There are many explicit and implicit dynamic links between the debugging tools.

To review debugging-related commands, select Tools, Customize to display the Customize dialog box. Activate the Keyboard tab. The Debug and View categories contain debugging-related commands. ■

Debugging session

Learn about steps to prepare a debugging session and how to start debugging.

Debugging commands

Learn about the debugging commands: keyboard, menus, and toolbars.

Watch variables

Learn the various ways to watch variable and expression values: QuickWatch, Local watch, this watch, and Auto watch.

Debugging windows

Review the special debugging windows: Call Stack, Variables, Source, Exceptions, and Threads.

Breakpoints

Learn to set breakpoints using the mouse, menu, and toolbar commands, and centrally manage breakpoints.

Starting a Debugging Session

Tables 21.1 and 21.2 list the commands and their standard descriptions. These commands can be used to configure the development environment to your personal specifications.

Table 21.1   Keyboard Commands for Debug Category

Command	Shortcut Key	Description
DebugBreak	none	Stops program execution; breaks into the debugger.
DebugDisableAll Breakpoints	none	Disables all breakpoints.
DebugEnableBreakpoint	Ctrl+Shift+F9	Enables or disables a breakpoint.
DebugExceptions	none	Edits debug actions taken when an exception occurs.
DebugGo	F5	Starts or continues the program.
DebugHexadecimalDisplay	Alt+F9	Toggles between decimal and hexadecimal format.
DebugMemoryNextFormat	Alt+F7	Switches the memory window to the next display format.
DebugMemoryPrevFormat	Alt+Shift+F7	Switches the memory window to the previous display format.
DebugQuickWatch	Shift+F9	Performs immediate evaluation of variables and expressions.
DebugRemoveAllBreakpoints	none	Removes all breakpoints.
DebugRestart	Shift+F5	Restarts the program.
DebugRunToCursor	F7	Runs the program to the line containing the cursor.
DebugSetNextStatement	Ctrl+Shift+F7	Sets the instruction pointer to the line that contains the cursor.
DebugStepInto	F8	Steps into the next statement.
DebugStepOut	Shift+F7	Steps out of the current function.

Command	Shortcut Key	Description
DebugStepOver	F10	Steps over the next statement.
DebugStepOverSource	Ctrl+F10	Steps over the next source level statement.
DebugStopDebugging	Alt+F5	Stops debugging the program.
DebugThreads	none	Sets the debuggee's thread attributes.
DebugToggleBreakpoint	F9	Inserts or removes a breakpoint.
DebugToggleMixedMode	Ctrl+F7	Switches between the source view and the disassembly view for this instruction.

Table 21.2   Debug-Related Keyboard Commands for View Category

Command	Shortcut Key	Description
ToggleCallStackWindow	none	Shows or hides the Call Stack window.
ToggleDisassemblyWindow	none	Shows or hides the Disassembly window.
ToggleOutputWindow	none	Shows or hides the Output window.
ToggleVariablesWindow	none	Shows or hides the Variables window.
ToggleWatchWindow	none	Shows or hides the Watch window.
ViewCallStackWindow	Alt+7, Ctrl+K	Activates the Call Stack window.
ViewDisassemblyWindow	Alt+8	Activates the Disassembly window.
ViewOutputWindow	Alt+2	Activates the Output window.
ViewVariablesWindow	Alt+4	Activates the Variables window.
ViewWatchWindow	Alt+3	Activates the Watch window.

Part

IV

Ch

21

Before starting a debugging session, you must have a debug project built. This chapter uses the /MSDEV/SAMPLES/MICROSOFT/JAVABEEP sample project. After installing the sample code Build, select Rebuild All from the Build menu to rebuild the project. In the example project, the project by default uses the Internet Explorer browser for testing. The Build menu (see Figure 21.1) is a starting point for debugging. Select Build, Debug, Go (or press F5) to start debugging.

FIG. 21.1

This view of the Build menu shows the debug commands to start a debug session.

When starting to debug the default javabeep project, the Information For Debugging Class dialog box (see Figure 21.2) is displayed to obtain the name of the class to debug. This will occur if the Class For Debugging Session is not set in the Project Settings dialog box (see Figure 21.3). Once you set the class in the Information For Debugging Class dialog box, it sets the project settings for you, so you will only see the dialog box the first time you debug the project. Click OK and the browser will start the program.

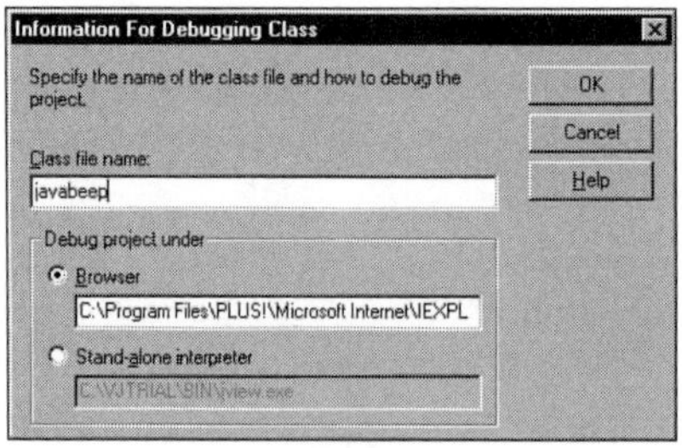

FIG. 21.2

The Information For Debugging Class dialog box prompts for the class name to debug if not already specified.

The Debug tab of the Project Settings dialog box allows you to specify that the project be executed under a browser or a stand-alone interpreter. If Stand-alone Interpreter is selected on the Project Settings Debug tab in the General Category (see Figure 21.3), then JView.exe must be specified as the interpreter in the Debug Category. Figure 21.4 shows the javabeep application running under the Visual J++ interpreter, JView.exe.

FIG. 21.3

The General Category on the Debug tab of the Project Settings dialog box is where the debug class name and the debugging execute option is specified.

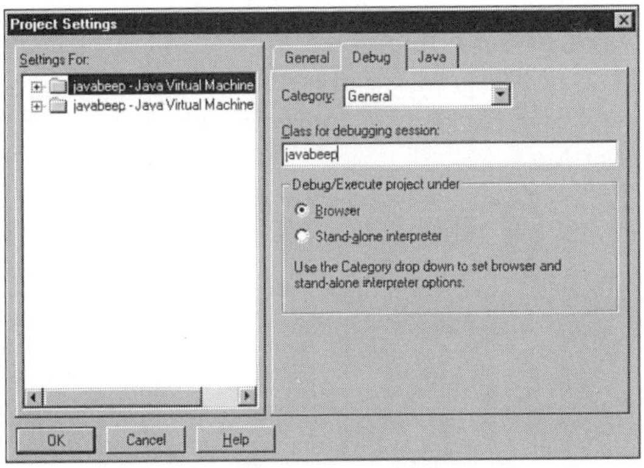

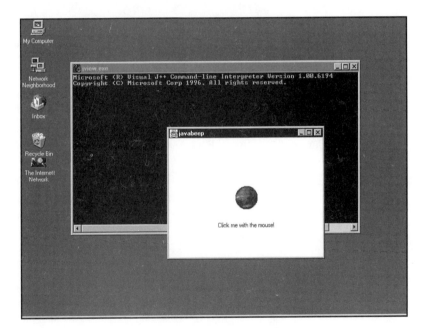

FIG. 21.4

The javabeep applet is shown running under JView.exe, the stand-alone interpreter.

Using the Debug Menu Commands

The Debug menu (see Figure 21.5) is only displayed when debugging. The Debug menu replaces the Build menu. After the Stop Debugging command is executed, the Build menu again replaces the Debug menu. Table 21.3 shows a brief overview of the Debug menu commands.

Part
IV

Ch
21

Table 21.3   Debug Menu Commands

Command	Shortcut Key	Description
Go	F5	Runs the program associated with the current project.
Restart	Shift+F5	Reloads a program and restarts execution.
Stop Debugging	Alt+F5	Ends the debugging session.
Break	none	Halts program execution and returns control to the debugger without ending the program.
Step Into	F8	Single-steps through each program line.
Step Over	F10	Single-steps through each program line, but executes functions without entering them.
Step Out	Shift+F7	Runs the program to the first statement after the current function call.
Run to Cursor	F7	Runs the program until it reaches the insertion point.
Exceptions	none	Lets you set what debug actions are triggered for microprocessor and C++ exception handling.
Threads	none	Controls which thread is the current thread when debugging multi-threaded applications.
Settings	none	Displays the breakpoints associated with a program and lets you clear and set breakpoints.
QuickWatch	Shift+F9	Opens the QuickWatch window to add, view the value of, or alter the value of a watched variable.

FIG. 21.5

The Debug menu is only available during a debugging session. Shown here is the javabeep project being debugged.

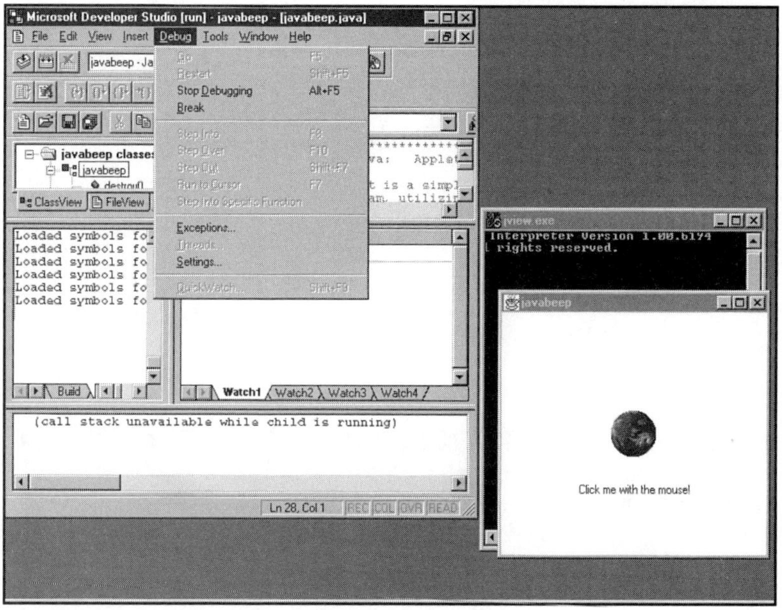

Many of the debugging commands have buttons on existing toolbars. Figure 21.6 shows the Project and Debug toolbars. The Project and Debug toolbar commands are listed as follows.

TIP Toolbars can be floating windows or they can be docked on any side of the project workspace by being dragged. Toolbars are fully customizable. You can add, delete, and rearrange the toolbar buttons. You can create your own new toolbars, and reassign keyboard shortcuts. See Chapter 14 "Getting Started with Visual J++" and the section "Using Toolbars" for more information.

Project Toolbar Commands

Compile (Ctrl+F8)

Build (Shift+F8)

Stop Build

Select Default Project Configuration

Go (F5)

Insert/Remove Breakpoint(F9)

Remove All Breakpoints

Debug Toolbar Commands

Restart (Shift+F5)

Stop Debugging (Alt+F5)

Step Into (F8)

Part
IV

Ch
21

Step Over (F10)

Step Out (Shift+F7)

Run to Cursor (F7)

QuickWatch (Shift+F9)

Watch

Variables

Registers

Memory

Call Stack

Disassembly

FIG. 21.6

The Project and Debug toolbars are used for debugging.

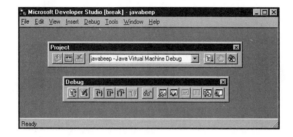

Using the Debugging Windows

Visual J++ has a set of windows that is integrated into debugging. Table 21.4 lists the special debugging windows and their contents. In addition, source code editor windows have debugging capabilities.

There are several ways to control the showing and hiding of the debugging windows. The View menu (see Figure 21.7) has commands to control debugging windows. The View menu items are listed in Table 21.5. The Debug toolbar (refer to Figure 21.6) has buttons to control the debugging windows. If the window's Docking View is on, then the window name will appear in the pop-up menu of the menu bars. The window name can be shown and hidden by checking and unchecking this menu item.

Table 21.4   Debugging Windows

Window	Contents
Output	The Build tab shows information from the build process including programs, such as the compiler, linker, and Custom Build Commands.
	The Debug tab shows messages from class loading, unhandled exceptions, and thread and program termination.

Window	Contents
Watch	The names and current values of selected variables and expressions.
Variables	The names and values of variables, parameters, and *this,* which are within scope in the current breakpoint context.
Call Stack	The current stack of calling methods with the breakpoint at the top.
Disassembly	Code bytes for each line of source code.

Table 21.5   The View Menu's Debug-Related Commands

Command	Shortcut Key	Description
Output	Alt+2	Activates the Output window.
Watch	Alt+3	Activates the Watch window.
Variables	Alt+4	Displays parameters, local and auto variables in scope.
Call Stack	Alt+7	Displays the Call Stack of methods not yet returned.
Disassembly	Alt+8	Activates window showing code bytes of source statement with focus.

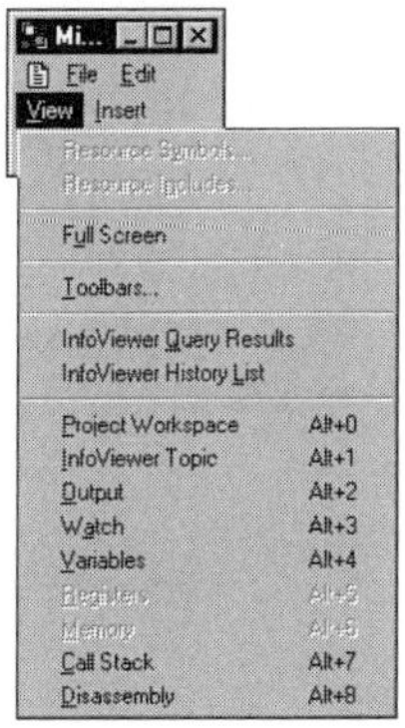

FIG. 21.7

The View menu is used to control many of the debug-related windows.

Select Tools, Options to display the Options dialog box (see Figure 21.8). Activate the Debug tab to see some options that pertain to debugging windows such as Disassembly, Call Stack, and Variables.

Part

IV

Ch

21

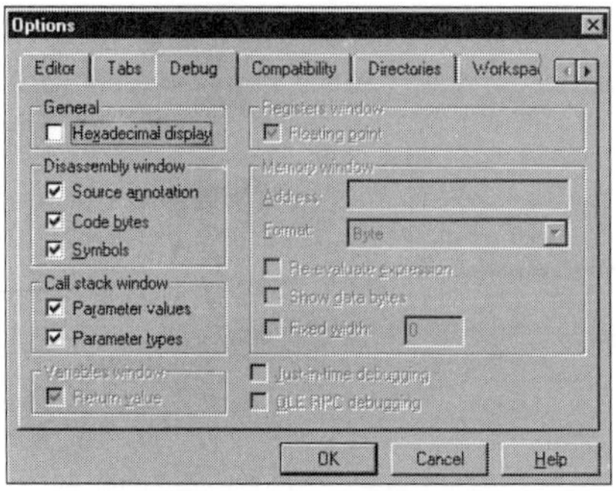

FIG. 21.8

The Debug tab of
the Options dialog
box is used to specify
debug configuration
options that apply to
all projects.

Output Window

The Output window (see Figure 21.9) manages output from various sources using different views selected by clicking tabs at the bottom of the Output window. The Build and Debug tabs are related to debugging. The Build tab displays build information from the compiler, linker, and Custom Build Commands. The Debug tab shows messages from class loading, unhandled exceptions, and thread and program termination.

Right-clicking the Output window will cause a pop-up menu to be displayed as in Figure 21.9. The Go To Error/ Tag item is used in the Build tab to cause the focus to go to a window displaying the offending line in the source file. The Go To Error/Tag command can also be executed by double-clicking the line.

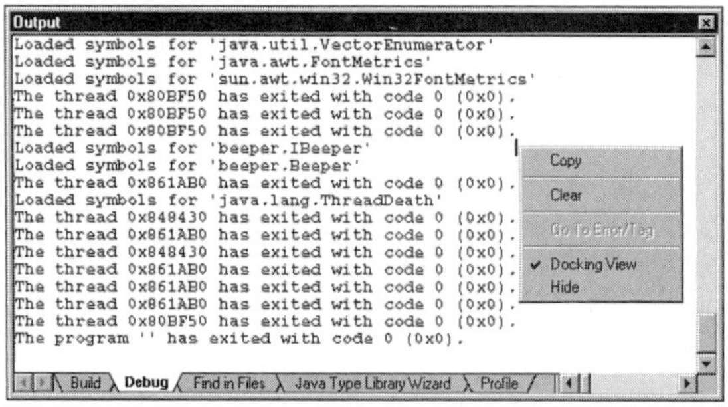

FIG. 21.9

This is the Output
window after right-
clicking it to display the
pop-up menu.

Watch Window

The Watch window (see Figure 21.10) can display *multiple* watch variables and/or expressions during debugging. You can create an entry in the spreadsheet window in several ways:

- By typing a new expression into the empty cell in the Name column.
- By Dragging and dropping an expression onto the Watch window.
- By clicking the Add Watch button in the QuickWatch dialog box (see Figure 21.11). The QuickWatch dialog box is discussed as follows.

The Watch window always displays the current values for all entries. The Watch window is like a spreadsheet because you can have variables x and y, and then define an expression entry for x + y. When the value of x or y is changed, the value of the entry x + y will also change.

The Watch window has tabs Watch1 through Watch4. You can group your watches using the tabs. Watch1 in this example shows the *this* reference to the javabeep class which extends the Applet class. Objects show their superclasses, the classes from which they have been extended, as indented objects. The class variables appear at the first level under *this*. Values of variables, but not expressions, can be changed.

The pop-up menu item Hexadecimal Display toggles the *default* format between hexadecimal and decimal for *all* numeric items in the Watch window. The format of each individual entry can be specified by appending a comma and one or more formatting symbols to the variable or expression. Table 21.6 lists the different formatting symbols.

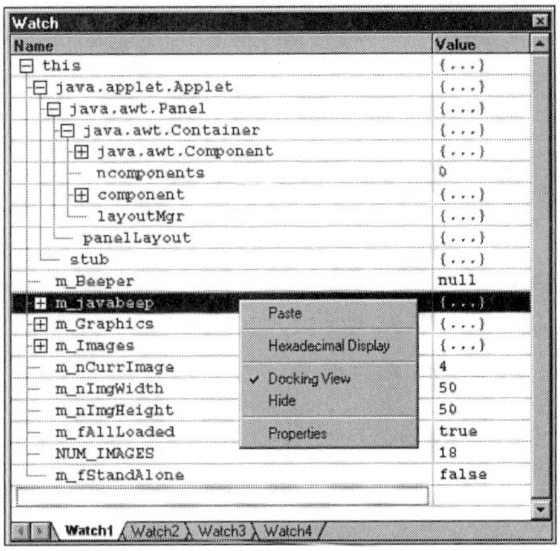

FIG. 21.10
The Watch window is shown with its right-click pop-up menu.

Table 21.6 Watch Variable Formatting Symbols

Symbol	Format
d,i	signed decimal integer
u	unsigned decimal integer
o	unsigned octal integer
x,X	hexadecimal integer
l,h	long or short prefix for: d, i, u, o, x, X
f	signed floating-point
e	signed scientific notation
g	signed floating-point or signed scientific notation, whichever is shorter

Part
IV

Ch
21

continues

Table 21.6 Continued	
c	single character
s	string
su	unicode string

The QuickWatch modal dialog box (see Figure 21.11) can be invoked using the Debug, QuickWatch menu item (refer to Figure 21.5) or the Debug toolbar (refer to Figure 21.6). The QuickWatch dialog box can be used to enter and recalculate the value of any single variable or expression.

QuickWatch uses the same spreadsheet window that the Watch window uses, except there is only a single entry in the QuickWatch dialog box. The use of expressions is the same between QuickWatch and the Watch window. Click the Add Watch button to add the expression to the Watch window's list of expressions. These also appear in the Expression drop-down list in the QuickWatch dialog box.

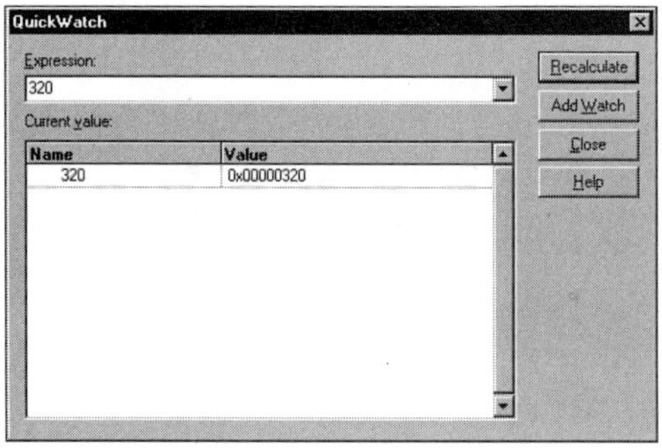

FIG. 21.11

The QuickWatch dialog box can display an expression temporarily.

Variables Window

The Variables window (see Figure 21.12) is similar to the Watch window except you cannot add entries. Instead, the entries are controlled for you by the Variables window and the debugging context. You can change the value of a variable as in the Watch window. The contents are divided into three tabs:

- Auto displays variables referenced at the current breakpoint and the previous line.
- Locals displays all method parameters, local variables, and *this*.
- this is *this*.

When you are stepping through a method, the Auto tab is useful to browse active variables. For a broader view of all local variables and parameters, the Locals tab is useful. Because each tab maintains its own display state, the *this* tab is useful for setting up the browsing of the current object.

The example Variables window in Figure 21.12 shows the Auto tab. The source window shows the breakpoint and current stop markers. The contents of the Variables window are determined by the current and previous lines.

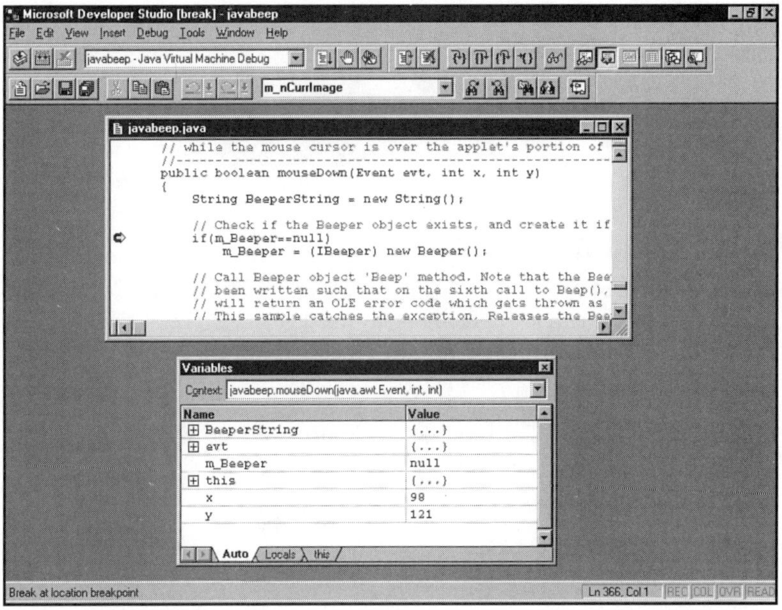

FIG. 21.12
The Variables window displays variable values at the current breakpoint.

Using the Call Stack Window

When stopped at a breakpoint, the Call Stack window (see Figure 21.13) displays a list of methods that have not yet returned to their callers. The most recent method is at the top of the list. This is the method in which the debugger is waiting.

The pop-up menu contains the Go To Code command, which is the same as double-clicking a Call Stack list entry. The Go To Code command will activate the source code of the method line if it is available. The Insert/Remove Breakpoint item will toggle the breakpoint at the corresponding line of the method. This is useful if you want to break in a method somewhere down the stack.

TIP When you are stopped at a breakpoint and forget where you are, how do you find out where the program is stopped? Use the Call Stack window. The top of the stack is where the program is currently stopped. Double-click it and you will be looking at the source line with the breakpoint marker sitting right where you left it.

Part
IV

Ch
21

FIG. 21.13

The Call Stack window shows the current method and its calling methods. Right-click to display the pop-up menu.

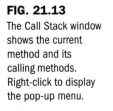
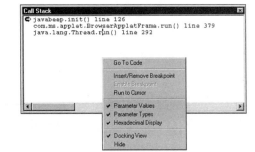

Source Window

The Source window (see Figure 21.14) is used for editing, but is also integrated into the debugging environment. There are many implicit and explicit links back to a source document window during debugging. Table 21.7 lists some of the links to source windows.

Table 21.7   List of Links to Source Windows

Window	Command
Output	Go To Error/Tag
ClassView	Go To Definition
Call Stack	Go To Code
Breakpoints	Edit Code
Disassembly	Go To Source

The Source window pop-up menu has an item to Go To Disassembly window. Notice that when right-clicking over a variable, the menu has an item to call QuickWatch with the name of the variable. The pop-up menu also contains items to insert/remove or enable/disable breakpoints.

FIG. 21.14

The Java Source window with pop-up menu shows the javabeep.java file opened.

To manage your breakpoints centrally, use the Breakpoints dialog box. Select Edit, Breakpoints to display the Breakpoints dialog box (see Figure 21.15). Breakpoints can be deleted and edited. Go to the source code by clicking the Edit Code button. During debugging, click Condition to display the Breakpoint Condition dialog box.

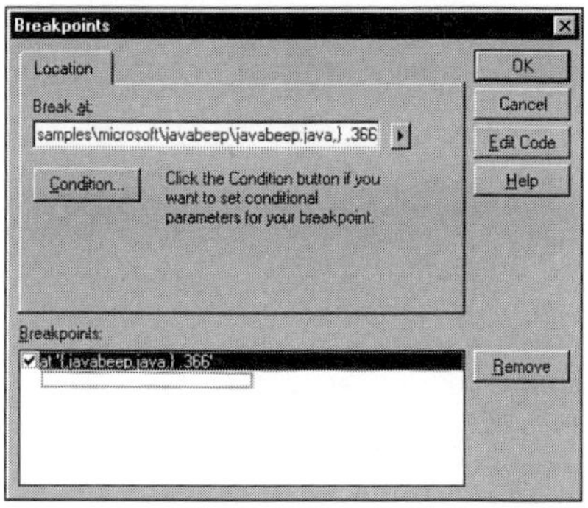

FIG. 21.15

The Breakpoints dialog box allows management of breakpoints.

The Breakpoint Condition dialog box (see Figure 21.16) allows you to assign conditions for breaking at that point. You can assign an expression to be evaluated to determine if the break should occur. You can specify the number of times to skip the breakpoint before actually stopping.

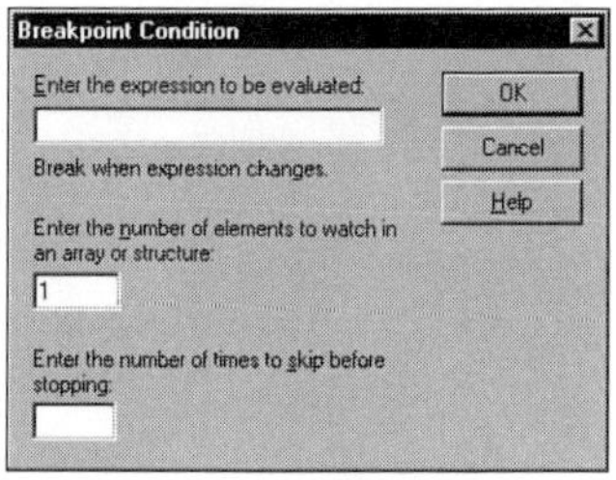

FIG. 21.16

The Breakpoint Condition dialog box is used to make stopping at a breakpoint conditional on the value of an expression.

Disassembly Window

To show the Disassembly window (see Figure 21.17) during debugging, select View, Disassembly or use the Source window pop-up menu command Go To Disassembly. The Disassembly window always shows the disassembled code bytes of the statement where the program is stopped at currently, and a few statements before and after it.

The pop-up menu item Source Annotation controls the display of the source statements. The Code Bytes item controls the display of the byte values of the byte code operators and operands.

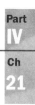

Part
IV

Ch
21

FIG. 21.17

The Disassembly window with pop-up menu shows the source code along with Java byte codes.

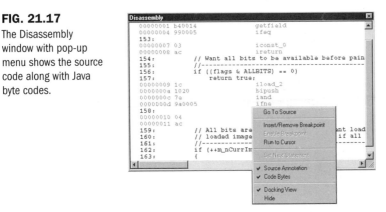

Exceptions Window

Select Debug, Exceptions to display the Exceptions dialog box (see Figure 21.18). The Exceptions dialog box does not appear to work with Java exceptions.

FIG. 21.18

The Exceptions dialog box shows which exceptions should be handled during debugging.

Threads Window

Select Debug, Threads to display the Threads dialog box (see Figure 21.19). The Threads dialog box is used to manage individual threads. The *focus* can be set to which thread you want to be debugged. Threads can be suspended and resumed. Double-clicking a thread entry in the Threads dialog box will cause the focus to go to the source file for the thread.

FIG. 21.19

The Threads dialog box allows you to manage the threads in your applet.

From Here...

In this chapter, you have been introduced to Visual J++ debugging tools. In the chapters ahead, you will be using Java in many different ways. Your familiarity with the debugging tools will help get you past any roadblocks.

The following chapter will explore how J++ can be used with ActiveX technology:

■ In Chapter 23, "Calling an ActiveX Object from Java," learn how your Java applets can control ActiveX components.

Part

IV

Ch

21

Database Programming

by Nelson Howell and Chris Lester

Storing information has effectively plagued the computer industry since before the rise of the Information Age. Sometimes we are left wondering if this problem will simply go away, frustrated from dealing with the information overload. Little has changed since E.F. Codd conceived of the relational data model. We still need faster access, and more manageable interfaces for the data we oversee. We now have at our disposal relational databases, object-oriented databases, and emerging from both, a hybrid relational object-oriented database. However, because the current technologies interact best with relational databases, these are the ones we will cover in this chapter. ■

Learn about relational databases

Relational databases are composed of tables with unique keys.

Discover SQL

Structured Query Language is the means of communication with a relational database.

Find out about ODBC

Open Database Connectivity is an API that enables us to write applications without worrying about the specific database behind it.

Learn about the Microsoft DAO

Data Access Objects are COM objects originally designed to access the Microsoft Jet database engine.

Learn about the Microsoft RDO

Remote Data Objects are designed for the client/server world of database programming.

Understanding Relational Databases

The effectiveness of any database can be measured by the ease with which we can manipulate the data. To enhance our capability to manipulate data, Structured Query Language was created. SQL has greatly eased this process because it has been standardized to the point that most SQL statements will be correct with any Relational Database Management System or RDBMS.

The rise of client/server computing has separated the application from the relational database engine. In a client/server model, the client sends a SQL (pronounced sequel) statement to the database engine, and the database engine sends back the data that was requested.

Although SQL has been standardized, most relational database engines use slightly different versions of SQL, and each will have their own APIs. This created a need for a middleware layer that serves as a translator. This translator stands between the client and the database engine and translates any nuances of the SQL dialect from the standard SQL statements issued by the client into the dialect used by the RDBMS API.

Two such translators are Microsoft's Open Database Connectivity (ODBC) and Sun Microsystem's Java Database Connection (JDBC), which resembles ODBC. Both are based on the same X/OPEN-SQL 92 standard. JDBC can use ODBC to interface to some databases. JDBC is not currently supported by Microsoft Visual J++.

Visual J++ provides us with two interfaces between Java and databases. The first is the Microsoft Data Access Object (DAO). This set of high-level objects provides insulation from the details of working with databases.

The second option is the Remote Data Object (RDO), which works through ODBC. This also eliminates much of the detail in working with databases; however, it has been tuned for accessing remote databases where DAO is used mainly for local access.

Several sections of this chapter justify their own book or books. The goal is to give you a basic understanding of the structure and functions in Microsoft DAO and RDO. The sections of this chapter covering relational databases, SQL, and ODBC contain background information for those of you who are new to these subjects.

Using Relational Databases

A relational database stores data tables. A table is made up of rows and columns and each table has a name. If you wanted to create a table composed of data concerning frequently used phone numbers, the information collected would include at a minimum, first name, last name, and phone number. The table can be given any name. In this case, the table is named PhoneList. The entry, John Smith 555-1212, comprises a row. All the first names constitute a column, as do the last names and phone numbers. A table looks like a spreadsheet as shown in Figure 22.1.

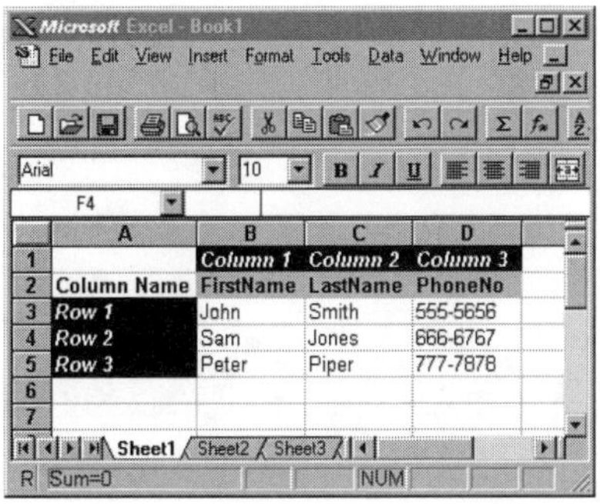

FIG. 22.1

The organization of the data in this Microsoft Excel spread sheet is similar to a database table.

A relational database depends on some part of the data being unique to each row. This data is referred to as *primary key*. The database engine uses the primary key to link tables, and ensure that we can control the output of a query. A primary key can contain one or more columns of data to ensure it is unique. One that does contain multiple columns is normally referred to as a *concatenated key*.

Suppose, for example, there are two people named John Smith at the phone number 555-5656. In the example in Figure 22.1, the records would be identical. In this case, a new column would be added to differentiate the two people. This column can contain a number or perhaps the person's middle initial. The primary key can be the combination of all the columns in a table. In Figure 22.2, an expanded table is shown with an added column to serve as the primary key.

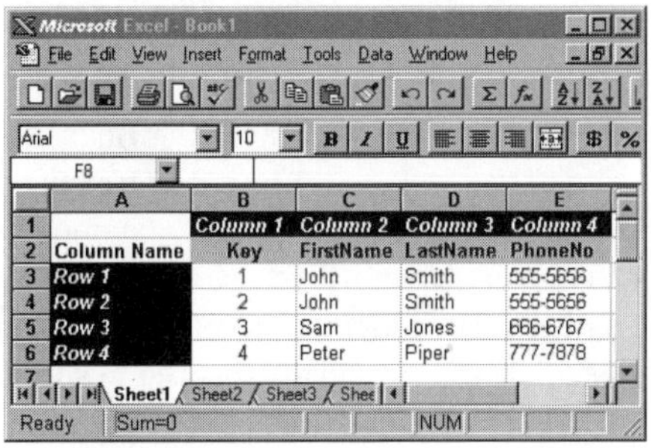

FIG. 22.2

Using a number as the primary key is a very useful technique in the design of databases.

Most databases consist of many tables. In the next example, we create a table named CallList to record the calls made to each of these phone numbers. We will record the time and date the call started, and the time and date the call ended. Now that we have the data where we can deal with it, getting what we want from it will be a breeze.

We can now retrieve the duration of each call, or even better, calculate the total time for each number. You might also want to know to whom the call was made. We can achieve this by creating all the necessary columns in the current table (for example, Name, Address, and so on), or we can use what is called a *lookup table*. Because storing all that information in a single table leads to significant duplication of data, we'll create a lookup table named PhoneList for this. This will centralize all the changes to the data, and keep space requirements to a minimum. Notice the primary key of the PhoneList table is also in the CallList table; this is referred to as a *foreign key*. Simply put, a foreign key comes from some other table. Most foreign keys will be used like this, to provide a way to link several tables together. Figure 22.3 shows an example of the CallList table.

FIG. 22.3
The key from the PhoneList table is called a foreign key when it is used in the CallList table.

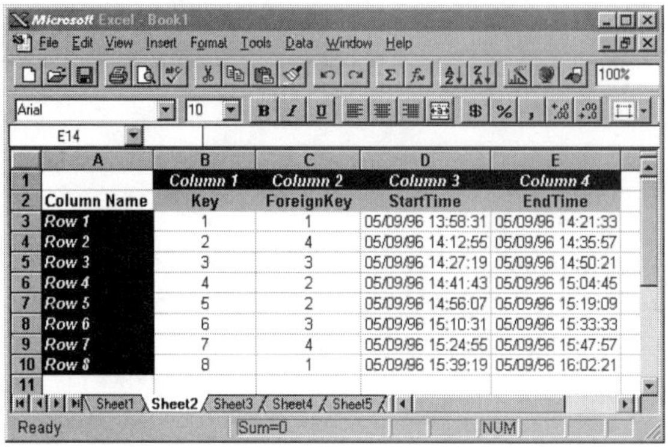

	A	B	C	D	E
1		Column 1	Column 2	Column 3	Column 4
2	Column Name	Key	ForeignKey	StartTime	EndTime
3	Row 1	1	1	05/09/96 13:58:31	05/09/96 14:21:33
4	Row 2	2	4	05/09/96 14:12:55	05/09/96 14:35:57
5	Row 3	3	3	05/09/96 14:27:19	05/09/96 14:50:21
6	Row 4	4	2	05/09/96 14:41:43	05/09/96 15:04:45
7	Row 5	5	2	05/09/96 14:56:07	05/09/96 15:19:09
8	Row 6	6	3	05/09/96 15:10:31	05/09/96 15:33:33
9	Row 7	7	4	05/09/96 15:24:55	05/09/96 15:47:57
10	Row 8	8	1	05/09/96 15:39:19	05/09/96 16:02:21
11					

Speaking SQL

Whole books are devoted to the subject of SQL, so only a few examples will be covered here. When a SQL statement is passed to a Relational Database Management System (RDBMS) engine, the engine will respond to the statement. This response is called a results set.

SELECT Statement

If there is a SQL statement to tattoo to your forehead, it's this one: The `SELECT` statement is used for nearly every transaction. If you want to retrieve data from a SQL database, you'll do it with the `SELECT` statement. Joining a table? Use the `SELECT` statement. Throwing a party? Well, you get the idea. The `SELECT` statement is really pretty simple, although you can make it complex through nesting several of them. The different pieces of a `SELECT` statement are referred to as *clauses*. In the following example the `FROM` clause is used to specify which database we want to query.

```
SELECT Key, FirstName, LastName, PhoneNo FROM PhoneList
```

Each of the parts of this very English-like statement has a specific function:

- *SELECT.* In its simplest form, this statement performs an action (or group of actions) on a database specified in the `FROM` clause.
- *Key, FirstName, LastName, PhoneNo.* These are the columns that will be retrieved from the table.
- *FROM.* This is the name of the table or tables from which to pull the data.
- *PhoneList.* This is the name of the table from which we want data.

In this case, we will select all the rows from the table. The result set will look like Table 22.1.

Table 22.1   The Result Set from the *SELECT* Statement

Key	FirstName	LastName	PhoneNo
1	John	Smith	555-5656
2	John	Smith	555-5656
3	Sam	Jones	666-6767
4	Peter	Piper	777-7878

If you want to retrieve only those records where the last name is Smith, we can use the WHERE clause. The modified SELECT statement is shown in the following example.

```
SELECT * FROM PhoneList

WHERE LastName = "Smith"
```

Notice a wildcard was used for the column names this time. This allows us to choose all columns in a table or group of tables easily. What we have done with the WHERE clause is narrow our *result set* to names ending in "Smith." Table 22.2 shows the result set.

Table 22.2   The Result Set from the *SELECT* Statement

Key	FirstName	LastName	PhoneNo
1	John	Smith	555-5656
2	John	Smith	555-5656

Joins

When the database containing the two tables PhoneList and CallList was designed, the key of the PhoneList table was included in the CallList table as a foreign key. We can use this foreign key in an operation called a *join*. A *join* is the combining of the data from two tables to respond to one SELECT statement. There are many types of joins; the inner join will be illustrated here. In the following SELECT statement, the goal is to retrieve the rows from the CallList table that represent calls that were made to the phone numbers of anyone with a last name of Jones.

```
SELECT CallList.StartTime, CallList.EndTime FROM PhoneList, CallList

WHERE CallList.ForeignKey = PhoneList.Key AND PhoneList.LastName = 'Jones'
```

Examining the SQL statement item by item, you see:

- *SELECT.* This tells the database engine what it is going to do.
- *CallList.StartTime, CallList.EndTime.* These are the columns we're wanting to retrieve.

- *FROM PhoneList, CallList.* This names the two tables that will be used in the SELECT statement.
- *WHERE.* This tells us there will be a search argument for the rows to be selected.
- *CallList.ForeignKey = PhoneList.Key.* This is the inner join for the SELECT statement.
- *AND.* We use this to tack on additional conditions to the search criteria.
- *PhoneList.LastName = 'Jones'.* This is the second condition.

The result set created by this SELECT statement is shown in Table 22.3. Refer to Figure 22.3 to see the complete table.

Table 22.3   The Result Set from the *SELECT* Statement Using an Inner Join

StartTime	EndTime
05/09/96 14:27:19	05/09/96 14:50:21
05/09/96 15:10:31	05/09/96 15:33:33

We used the CallList.[Column Name] statement to show how to SELECT columns when multiple databases have column names in common. In this case, we could have left off the prefix because they are unique to the CallList table. The PhoneList.Key and CallList.Foreign columns were used to choose only data that exists in both tables.

INSERT Statement

The INSERT statement is used to add a new row or record to the table. The most important requirement for an INSERT is that the primary key must be unique. If you attempt to insert a record with a duplicate primary key, the database engine will refuse to perform the operation. The following example is an INSERT statement.

```
INSERT INTO PhoneList (Key, FirstName, LastName, PhoneNo) VALUES (5, 'Harold',
'Lloyd' '888-8989')
```

Examining this SQL statement element by element, you see:

- *INSERT INTO.* This tells the database engine the type of action.
- *PhoneList.* This names the table into which the record is being inserted.
- *(Key, FirstName, LastName, PhoneNo).* This names the columns into which data is being inserted.
- *VALUES (5, 'Harold', 'Lloyd' '888-8989').* This contains the values to be inserted into the table.

Our return value from this operation should be "1 row inserted."

UPDATE Statement

When using the UPDATE statement, be careful to include a WHERE clause. An UPDATE statement will be accepted without one, and will promptly update *all* columns to the same value. Now wouldn't that be fun to watch replicate from one server to another? The following example shows an UPDATE statement.

```
UPDATE PhoneList SET LastName = 'Floyd' WHERE LastName = 'Lloyd'
```

In this case, we corrected a misspelling using the UPDATE statement. The last name was misspelled—Lloyd was entered instead of Floyd. The result set of "1 row updated" informs you that the action was completed.

DELETE Statement

The DELETE statement, like the UPDATE statement, should also include a WHERE clause, unless you've accomplished your career goals. The WHERE clause determines which rows are to be deleted. The database engine will also blithely execute a DELETE statement without one, in which case all rows in the table will be deleted. A DELETE statement is shown in the following example.

```
DELETE FROM PhoneList WHERE LastName = 'Floyd'
```

This DELETE statement removed the record that we added with the INSERT statement and changed with the UPDATE statement. The result set will be "1 row deleted," informing you that the action has been completed.

N O T E A common error that new users of SQL make is the assumption that an empty result set indicates an error. When you use a SELECT statement with a WHERE clause, the result set will return only those columns we asked for in the SELECT statement. There are times when our search results in no matches. This will result in an empty result set, which is a perfectly valid result. ■

N O T E Database client/server computing in the Java world raises some additional issues that need to be kept in mind. With Java, the client executes on the user's machine, either as an applet or an application. This can be a problem for a developer of the application, as the data access software (ODBC or JDBC drivers for example) must be installed and configured on the user's machine for the application to work properly. ■

Using ODBC

Microsoft Open Database Connectivity is a set of APIs that provides an interface between the client and the database. ODBC Drivers can be accessed with the same set of API calls regardless of the type of database engine they connect to. This eases the process of developing robust data applications and secures the investment you've put into your code.

ODBC Drivers can be written for nearly any type of database, not only relational, allowing developers to harness the power of object-oriented databases with their existing applications.

ODBC Administrator

The ODBC Administrator is used to manage the ODBC Drivers (discussed in the next section "ODBC Drivers") and create and maintain the ODBC data sources. The ODBC Administrator is opened by choosing Start, Settings, Control Panel and double-clicking the ODBC icon as shown in Figure 22.4. The ODBC Data Sources dialog box is opened as shown in Figure 22.5.

FIG. 22.4

If both 16-bit and 32-bit ODBC drivers are installed on your system, there will be two ODBC icons in the Control Panel. This is the 32-bit administrator.

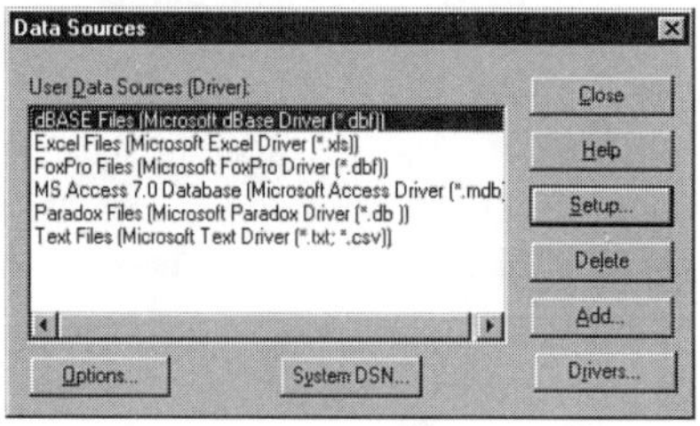

FIG. 22.5

When a database is registered here as an ODBC data source, it can be accessed using ODBC.

Creating an ODBC data source will provide a quick tour through the ODBC Administrator.

1. With the ODBC data source dialog open, click Add. The Add Data Source dialog box appears as shown in Figure 22.6. All ODBC drivers installed on the system are listed here. Select an ODBC Driver by selecting it and clicking OK.

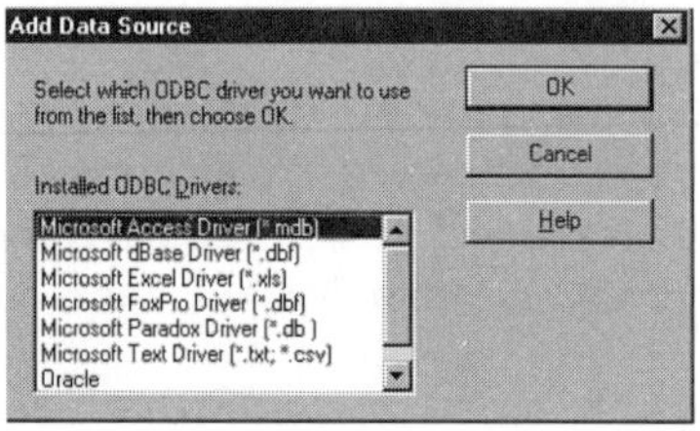

FIG. 22.6

Each driver has a Setup dialog that collects the information required.

2. Enter the data source name in the data source Setup dialog box as shown in Figure 22.7. In this case, SimpleSelect is the name that has been chosen for the data source.

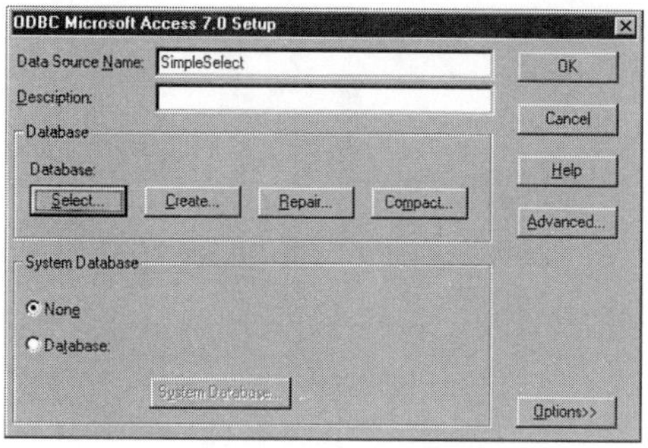

FIG. 22.7

A new empty Microsoft Access database can be created with the Setup dialog by clicking Create.

3. Click Select and the Select Database dialog box appears as shown in Figure 22.8. Select the database, in this case SimpleTest.Mdb, and click OK.

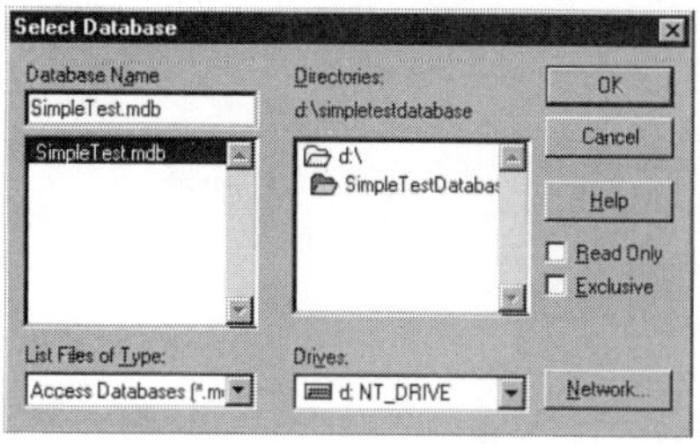

FIG. 22.8

In the Select Database dialog box, the Read Only and Exclusive check boxes should usually be left unchecked.

4. You will now see the database in the ODBC Setup dialog as shown in Figure 22.9. Click OK.

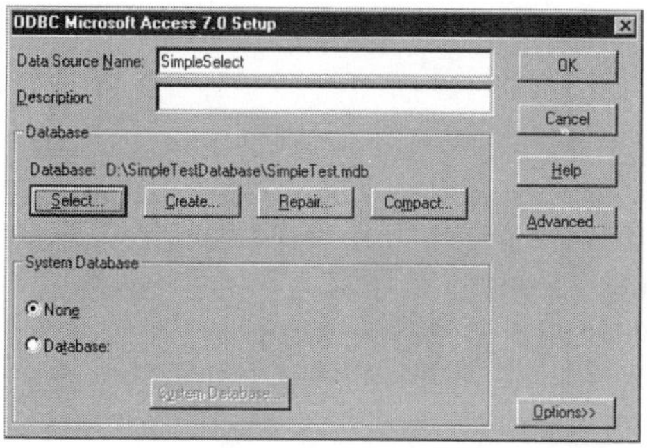

FIG. 22.9

The path for the data source database is shown above the Select button.

5. You now see the data source listed in the ODBC Data Source dialog box as shown in Figure 22.10. Click Close.

FIG. 22.10

This dialog can also be used to delete data sources.

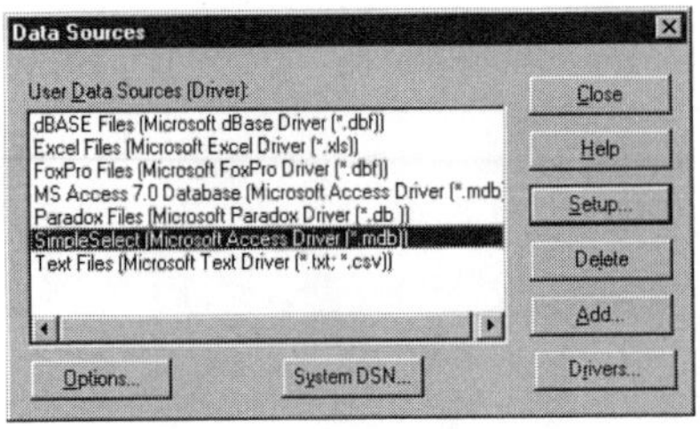

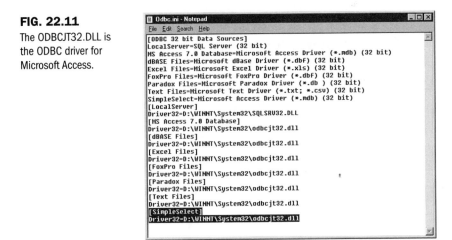

The setup of the ODBC data source created an entry in the ODBC.INI file, located in the \WINNT directory. This entry tells ODBC which ODBC driver to use when the data source is accessed, as shown in Figure 22.11.

FIG. 22.11

The ODBCJT32.DLL is the ODBC driver for Microsoft Access.

ODBC Drivers

ODBC drivers are DLLs that are much like printer drivers in concept, in that they take care of converting the ODBC calls to their native database APIs. This enables us to use the best database for our particular needs without worrying about the specter of a code rewrite. There are hundreds of drivers for almost every database engine in the market today, allowing you a freedom of choice previously unknown to the database developer. These drivers are given a set of standards they must conform to.

When troubleshooting a problem, the manufacturer and version of the ODBC driver can be very important. To check the version, choose Start, Settings, Control Panel and double-click the ODBC icon. With the ODBC Data sources dialog box open, click the Drivers button. This opens a list of the ODBC drivers installed on the system. Select a driver, click the About button, and the information about the driver will be displayed as shown in Figure 22.12.

FIG. 22.12
If an ODBC driver is not performing as it should, there may be a newer version that fixes the problem or enhances its functionality.

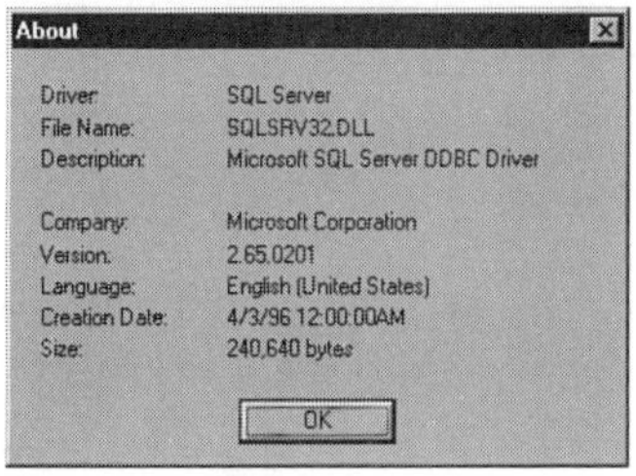

About	
Driver:	SQL Server
File Name:	SQLSRV32.DLL
Description:	Microsoft SQL Server ODBC Driver
Company:	Microsoft Corporation
Version:	2.65.0201
Language:	English (United States)
Creation Date:	4/3/96 12:00:00AM
Size:	240,640 bytes

ODBC drivers are divided into two categories: desktop drivers and multiple tier drivers.

Desktop Drivers The desktop ODBC drivers are also called single tier drivers. A desktop driver also serves the function of the database engine. ODBCJT32.DLL is the desktop driver supplied by Microsoft. It provides the driver function for MS Access 7.0; MS Excel versions 3.0, 4.0, 5.0, and 7.0; MS FoxPro versions 2.0, 2.5, and 2.6; dBase versions III, IV, and 5.0; Paradox versions 3.X, 4.X, and 5.X; and delimited text files.

Text files are not thought of as databases; however, they can be used as one by simply overloading the I\O streams to handle object persistence and using Linked Lists or Binary Trees to keep track of the data structures (keep in mind these aren't easy tasks).

Multiple Tier Drivers The multiple tier ODBC driver stands between the client application and the server database engine. The ODBC driver accepts requests for service in the form of SQL statements. The SQL statement is then translated into the particular dialect of SQL used by the server database engine. The driver submits the translated SQL statement to the database engine. The database engine creates the result set and passes it back to the ODBC driver. The ODBC driver performs any formatting and passes the data back to the client.

Because the client application and server database engine are never directly connected, it is possible to change the database engine without rewriting the client application simply by choosing a new driver for the data source.

TIP When a UI client program establishes a connection to a database through ODBC, three items of information are required in addition to the SQL statements. These are the DSN or Data Source Name, the UID or User ID, and the PWD or password.

Installing DAO in Visual J++

Installing DAO is fairly simple; just enable database support when installing Visual J++. When the installation is finished, run the Java Type Library Wizard to create the Java class files for the Microsoft Data Access Objects 3.0. A summary.txt file will be created in your <%Windir%>\java\trustlib\dao3032, which will contain detailed information on what the public interfaces are for the DBEngine object.

Working with Microsoft DAO

Data Access Objects were first introduced with Microsoft Access as a way to enable users of other development environments to use the Jet Database Engine to enhance their applications. While it has remained close to the Jet database engine, DAO has become a very rich interface into ISAM databases such as FoxPro or Oracle (and quite a few others).

The DAO Structure

DAO is basically a group of objects with the DBEngine object being at the top of the hierarchy. Under the DBEngine there is what is known as a Workspace object, used to manage existing sessions or create new ones. It is very similar to the MAPI Session object if you are familiar with Microsoft's Messaging APIs. Once we have created a Workspace, we can define databases, set security permissions, and generally do whatever we need to. See Figure 22.13 for a complete view of DAO's objects and collections.

FIG. 22.13
This is the DAO object hierarchy.

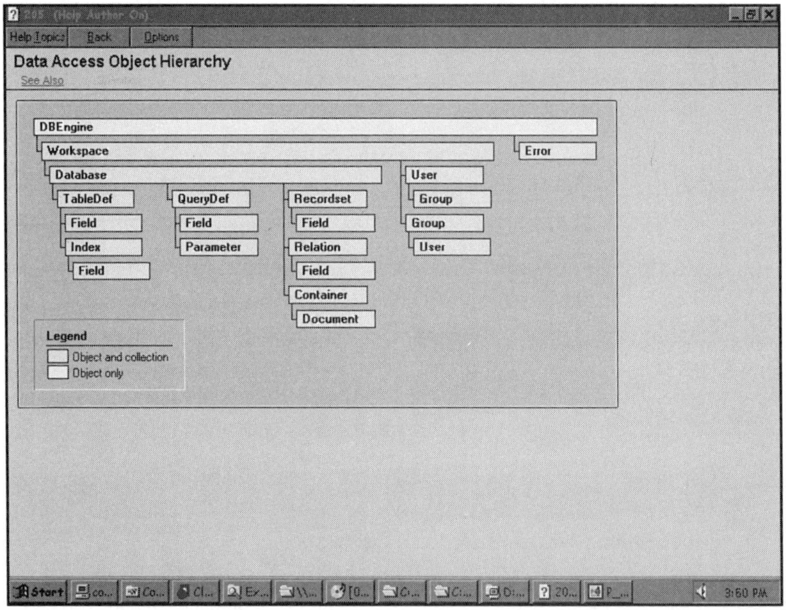

Exploring the DAO These objects can be combined to present a quite powerful interface for database programming. With the inclusion of ODBC Direct in the latest version, we are beginning to see DAO catch up to RDO in terms of interoperability with other data sources. We're going to take a tour of the DAO object library and give some sample code for the objects we use most often. However, the objects will not be discussed in depth, as several hundred books cover this subject thoroughly.

The *DBEngine*

DBEngine is the one object from which all DAO objects are derived. From it, we can create Workspaces, encrypt databases, and register new datasources. This is quite similar to the rdoEngine object we'll be covering in the section on RDO.

The *Workspace* Object

Workspaces are analogous to a workbench. It is a simple place to put all of our stuff while we work on it. Let's go ahead and create a DBEngine object and Workspace object now, as shown in Listing 22.1. We'll open the database later.

Listing 22.1   Creating the *DBEngine* and *Workspace* Objects

```
DBEngine db_engine = (_DBEngine) new DBEngine();

Workspace workspace = db_engine.CreateWorkspace("Overworked","Me","");
```

The *Databases* Object

From here the horizon grows. We use this object to create the table definitions and temporary views on the data source, as well as define relations between objects, and define queries and record sets. To illustrate some of the code required, see Listing 22.2.

Listing 22.2   Connecting to a Database

```
Variant flExclusive = new Variant();

Varaint flReadOnly = new Variant();

flExclusive.putBoolean(false);

flReadOnly.putBoolean(false);



Database db;

Db = db_engine.OpenDatabase("SomeDatabase.mdb", flExclusive, flReadOnly)
```

Some of the elements of the previous listing are described here:

- *flExclusive*. The second argument to OpenDatabase, specifying whether we want exclusive access or not.
- *flReadOnly*. The third argument in OpenDatabase that allows us to open the database as read-only if we want.
- *db_engine.OpenDatabase*. Creates a database object.

The User and Group Objects

Security is of growing importance to most of us, and these objects enable us to set user and group permissions for our data. We can then secure our record sets, tables, and query definitions by specifying access by group or user.

TableDefs

This object enables us to view the internal structure of the table, as well as the indexes into the table.

Querydefs

Think of these as a table of stored SQL statements, and you will be very close. However, this object also allows for configuring the properties of the query, such as timeout and replication. In ODBC terms, this is much like a table of prepared statements that we can execute and modify at will.

The *RecordSet* Object

This is the one doing the work. You've run across record sets before; they are really just ODBC cursor types. There are three of them.

Table-type Table-type record sets are solely for use with the Microsoft Jet Engine databases. This record set can only return data from a single table (hence its name). We don't have the capability to execute queries on this object either, but given an index, this will return the data to us in an ordered fashion.

Dynaset This type of query is perhaps the most common, because it enables us to dynamically update the data as it is changed. This is what most RDBMS's would call a "view." You can combine data from several sources into a single updateable record set. This eases the problem of synchronizing tables and presenting a single view to the end user.

Snapshot Think of this one as a static query; the data will never change, even if we update the table. This is used mainly for read-only queries that a search engine would return.

Let's open recordset on the PhoneList database. We'll open it as read-only with a Snapshot and then move through the rows in the database (See Listing 22.3).

Listing 22.3 Using the *Recordset* Object

```
Recordset rset;

Variant flOpenAs = new Variant();

Variant flAccess = new Variant();

flOpenAs.putShort(Constants.dbReadOnly);
```

```
flAccess.putShort(Constants.dbOpenTable);

rset = db.OpenRecordset("SomeTableName",flAccess, flOpenAs);
```

- **■** *Constants.dbReadOnly.* A flag specifying this database will be opened read-only.
- **■** *Constants.dbOpenSnapshot.* We wanted a Snapshot type record set.
- **■** *db.OpenRecordset.* Opens a record set on a specific database.

Relation

With the `Relation` object, we can get information about the current relations between tables, the foreign keys, and enforce business rules during changes to the base tables (but not on queries or attached tables).

Container

This enables us to query for information on any object stored in the `DBEngine` hierarchy. We can then get, or set, the owner permissions, or set security information on the object.

Installing RDO Support in Visual J++

When installing Visual J++ you are given an option to enable database support; choose this option. Then run the Java Type Library Wizard and select the Microsoft Remote Data Object 1.0. This will generate a class called `msrdo32`. In order to use this in our applications, simply specify the import statement with `msrdo32`:

```
Import msrdo32.*;
```

There will be a summary.txt file in the <%Windir%>\java\trustlib\msrdo32 directory, which will contain detailed information on what the public interfaces are for the `rdoEngine` object.

Working with Microsoft RDO

Remote Data Objects were designed as an OLE alternative to coding to the ODBC APIs in C or C++. With RDO, developers of other languages could finally have a chance at designing real world distributed data systems. Using this new interface, we can now create our own queries, set up parameterized statements, select from a wide variety of cursors, and generally have our way with the ODBC world. We're going to get into these topics and more in the next section, but first we'll look at the RDO object model in a little more detail.

Building an RDO Application

As with DAO, the `rdoEngine` object sits atop the pile of objects at RDO's feet. Most of these objects will seem familiar; that's because RDO is a very thin layer above the ODBC API. Before we delve into the methods, let's learn this the easy way—by building a small application to open a database and return some result to us. Let's start with getting access to the `rdoEngine` object itself. This is the representation of the actual data source:

```
_rdoEngine Sample_Engine = (_rdoEngine) new _rdoEngine();
```

Notice that we need to cast the rdoEngine object to the rdoEngine interface. Next we'll open an environment to work in (see Listing 22.4).

Listing 22.4   Creating the Environment Using *rdoCreateEnvironment()*

```
rdoEnvironment Sample_environ;

Sample_environ = Sample_engine.rdoCreatEnvironment
➥("name","user_id","password");
```

Unlike most methods, the rdoCreateEnvironment method of the rdoEngine object requires all three parameters to be given.

- ■ *rdoEngine.rdoCreateEnvironment.* This creates an environment session.
- ■ *"name".* This parameter sets the name for the environment so we can refer to it later.
- ■ *"user_id".* Our user account to use. This can be " ".
- ■ *"password".* Password for the user account. This, too, can be " ".

If we do not supply the user name or password arguments, a value of " " is assumed. Also, when a remote data object is accessed for the first time, a default environment is created automatically and is named "Default_Environment" with both user name and password set to " ".

Here's what we just accomplished. We created an environment session to host various connections we are going to make to our database.

Now that we have an environment, let's open a connection to our database. We'll use the OpenConnection method of the rdoEnvironment object we just created (see Listing 22.5).

Listing 22.5   Making a Connection to an Existing Database Using the *OpenConnection* Method

```
Variant flPrompt = new Variant();

Variant flAccess = new Variant();

Variant Connect = new Variant();

flPrompt.putInt(PromptConstants.rdDriverNoPrompt())

lflAccess.putBoolean(true);     //Use false if you want to open for read\write
                                ➥access

Connect.putString("");          //Leaving this emtpy accepts the user name &
                                ➥password of Sample_environ

Sample_connection = Sample_environ.OpenConnection("Data Source Name",
➥flPrompt, flAccess, Connect)
```

- *PromptConstants.rdoDriverNoPrompt.* A flag we pass to `OpenConnection` specifying we don't want to be prompted with a connect dialog.
- *Sample_environ.OpenConnection().* A method used to open a connection with a data source.
- *Data Source Name.* The name of the data source to connect to.
- *flPrompt.* Use this to decide whether we want to display a connection dialog.
- *flAccess.* The second argument in this statement, used to specify the type of access wanted, such as read-only.
- *flConnect.* Use this argument if you have any driver-specific information, like a user name and password.

Now, let's see what kind of damage we've done. Our use of `OpenConnection` here was pretty basic; after all, this is a sample. If we wanted to, we could have placed driver-specific information in the `Connect` argument, perhaps squeezing extra functionality from it. Had we needed to change the database, we could have requested read\write access with the `flAccess` argument.

Okay, we've got a connection, so let's play with it. We'll open a result set requesting everything in the database. `OpenResultset` has several different ways to do this, so we'll keep it simple and actually tell it the SQL commands. We could, if we had need of a SQL command that we used often, create what is known as a Parametered Query. Doing so would enable us to use variables in place of the SQL columns, tables, or search criteria and prove very useful. Alright, take a look at what's involved in using `OpenResultset` (see Listing 22.6).

Listing 22.6 Using the *OpenResultset* Method

```
String query = new String("Select * FROM  PhoneList");

Variant flCursor = new Variant();

Variant flLockType = new Variant();

Variant flOption = new Variant();


flCursor.putInt(ResultsetTypeConstants.rdOpenStatic);

flLockType.putInt(LockTypeConstants.rdConcurReadOnly);

flOption.putInt(OptionsConstants.rdAsyncEnable);

rdoResultset Sample_set = new rdoResultset();

Sample_set = Sample_connection.OpenResultset
➥(query,flCursor,flLockType,flOption);
```

- *ResultsetTypeConstants.rdOpenStatic.* This argument creates a static cursor for our query.
- *LockTypeConstants.rdConcurReadOnly.* Pretty much what it says; opens a read-only result set.

■ *OptionsConstants.rdAsyncEnable.* We've told `rdoEngine` to do this asynchronously, giving us back control immediately.

■ *Sample_connection.OpenResultset.* Returns a result set with the information we asked for.

Notice that we asked for an asynchronous query. This way, we can get back to our user without waiting for the method to return. Using the `OptionsConstants` we could also have executed a `rdExecDirect`, which would not create a temporary table before executing, and may increase the performance.

T I P   When asking for a cursor, keep in mind that the Forward Only cursor, while being the fastest cursor, does not have the capability to scroll backwards. So in applications where static data is needed, use a Static cursor unless you do not need backward movement through the result set.

RDO is a very powerful interface made to ease designing large data warehouses or enterprise distributed data systems. The simple examples here show the basics of what is needed to open a data source and acquire a result set.

The Remote Data Object Model

We have seen some part of this model, the `rdoEngine`, the `rdoEnvirnment`, `rdoConnections` and the `rdoResultset`. These are only a few of the objects made available to us with RDO. In this section we'll take a quick look at the entire model from a top-down perspective.

rdoEngine   This is the mother of all RDO objects. The `rdoEngine` object is essentially a representation of the data source. When we create an `rdoEngine` object we can then find out many things about this particular data source. Among other things, we can find out what the default cursor is, retrieve and set the login timeout, find out what environments are active, and register a new data source with `rdoRegisterDataSource`.

rdoEnvironment   We can create this object by calling the `CreateEnvironment` method of the `rdoEngine` object. The `rdoEnvironment` object is responsible for determining the default user account and password used to connect to the data sources. It also provides us with a means to differentiate between simultaneous transactions, as well as the methods to begin, commit, and roll back those transactions. Using the `rdoEnvironment`, we can find out information on the current connections using the `getrdoConnections`. We can also open new connections with the `rdoEnvironment` object's `OpenConnection` method.

rdoError   The `rdoError` object enables us to perform some intelligent error-handling and find out about the operation that caused the error.

rdoConnection   `RdoConnection` is our primary workhorse for RDO operations. Using this object we can find out information on our open result set, the prepared statements we've created, what tables we have open, and the capability to create prepared statements and result sets. This object gives us a way to find out if the data source supports transactions as well, providing a means of creating an application that can take advantage of upsizing without being rebuilt.

rdoResultset This is where we'll send the SQL query, or prepared statement, to the data source. Setting the cursors and access is also done with the `rdoResultset` object. In fact, most of our interaction with the data source is with `rdoResultset`.

rdoTable The `rdoTable` object is the representation of our table in memory. This object is useful mostly for discovering *metadata*, or information about the information in the table, such as the number of columns or rows, and the data type.

rdoPreparedStatement This object enables us to create the prepared statement before executing the `OpenResultset` method. If we don't specify a prepared statement in our `OpenResultset` call, one is created for us. This can slow things down in a heavy environment, thus the need for the prepared statement.

rdoColumn This object is simply a good interface to information about the column, as well as defining a method for copying the structure of a database.

rdoParameter When creating a prepared statement, this object enables us to submit individual parameters, such as the direction, name, and value of the statement.

From Here...

Database programming with Java is an area that is undergoing rapid growth and development. New tools and techniques can be expected in the near future. Database interfaces expand the capability of Java for major application development and the use of Java in enterprise level applications on intranets.

- Chapter 21, "Using Visual J++ Debugging Tools," reviews techniques for testing your Java applications and applets.
- Chapter 25, "Code Signing Java with Authenticode," examines keeping your database safe.

CHAPTER 23

Calling an ActiveX Object from Java

by Mark Culverhouse

Java supports objects; Microsoft supports the Component Object Model, COM, objects. Can Java objects interact with COM objects? The answer is definitely. There are two sides to the Java-COM interface: Java objects calling COM objects, and COM objects calling Java objects. The former topic is covered in this chapter, which introduces you to the underlying concepts of Java to COM integration. This chapter explains some of the details of the interface between a Java program and a DLL-based COM class. To the Java program, the COM object appears as just another Java class. You will learn about the tools and procedures necessary to expose a COM class to a Java program.

The ActiveX interface illustrated in this chapter should be considered useful for a "lightweight" COM-server object. That is, the functionality is limited to calling methods and accessing properties. If a user interface is necessary, then other interfaces should be considered.

There are potentially many existing ActiveX controls and automation objects that could provide service to Java programs through the Java-to-COM interface. Perhaps you have written some of your own. Even if you are not familiar with OLE, COM, or ActiveX, this chapter will still be useful to you as a Java programmer.

ON THE WEB

http://www.microsoft.com/intdev/sdk   The ActiveX SDK including the ActiveX Template Library can be downloaded from this address. ■

Integration of Java and COM

Windows programmers have witnessed the evolution of programming object interfaces, from dialog editor extensions, to custom controls through VBX, OLE1, OLE2, Automation, OCX, containers, and so on. The evolution of Windows software is driven by making increasing functionality easier to use. But the basic programmer tools have not been getting simpler. As underlying APIs swell, programming complexity increases to make life simpler for the end user. Wizards help programmers get where they want to go more easily. Unfortunately, programmers often end up in the middle of a swamp full of dangerous and murky details.

Java offers some hope for Windows programmers. The integration of Java and COM may be a good example of Java's influence on the future of Windows programming. The complexity of COM was driven by the needs and convenience of "battleship-class" desktop applications. Recently, the Internet, with its download-software-on-demand-over-a-wire paradigm, has helped to put smaller-sized executables back in fashion.

The integration of Java and COM can be summarized as: "Java simple, COM COMplex." The complexity of COM is almost totally hidden from the Java language because low-level COM APIs map to single Java language constructs. COM is an API to implement a system of objects in *any* language, including non-object-oriented languages. Therefore, the COM API exposes many low-level object management details that are normally subsumed by object-oriented languages. No new keywords were added to Java to support COM. Look at the code below. Can you tell if Beeper is a COM object or a Java object? All the lines are from the JavaBeep sample discussed in the next section. Beeper is a COM object in beeper.dll.

```
import beeper.*;
public class javabeep extends Applet implements Runnable
{
     IBeeper m_Beeper=null;
...
     if(m_Beeper==null)
          m_Beeper = (IBeeper) new Beeper();
     m_Beeper.Beep();

     String BeeperString = new String();
     for(int i=1;i<=m_Beeper.getCount();i++)
     {
          // Build a message string from the strings that getItem returns
          BeeperString+=m_Beeper.getItem(i)+" ";
     }
```

The COM APIs to Java feature mappings include the following:

- ■ IUnknown interface
- ■ Reference counting

- `QueryInterface`
- Return values and error handling

Every COM object must implement an interface known as IUnknown. The `IUnknown` interface consists of three functions: `QueryInterface`, `AddRef`, and `Release`.

COM objects use reference counting to track object deletions. Each object has a reference count. The `IUnknown AddRef` function increments the reference count. The `IUnknown Release` function decrements the reference count. Clients of COM objects must call `AddRef` and `Release` correctly. To delete the object, its reference count is decremented. If the count is zero, the object is destroyed, otherwise it is not until the count is zero. There is a set of complicated rules to be followed when dealing with COM-object pointers and reference counting.

Of course in Java things are simpler, and they are simpler for COM objects as well. First of all, Java does not have pointers, it has garbage collection instead. The J++ Java VM handles all of the details of mapping COM reference counting into Java garbage collection. There is no need for a Java programmer to have access to a COM object's `AddRef` or `Release` function.

COM objects support multiple interfaces that are similar to Java interfaces, a collection of functions or methods. COM programmers must call the COM object's `IUnknown` `QueryInterface` function to get an interface from an object. Then that interface is used to call a function. Java classes support Java interfaces. Java interfaces are objects themselves. The Java language supports casting any object's interface to an interface object. This Java language feature of casting interface objects is the same mechanism implemented by the `IUnknown` `QueryInterface`, with a lot fewer details involved for the programmer.

Every COM function must return an HRESULT. HRESULT can be `S_OK`, the default value for success, or one of a variety of standard error codes. When a call to a COM object fails, the error codes must be interpreted. COM does not support exceptions. COM IDL supports a `retval` keyword which distinguishes an output parameter as the return value. Java, on the other hand, supports methods that can return a value and exceptions. Therefore, COM HRESULT codes are handled through an exception class: `com.ms.com.ComException`. Every COM object method imported into Java has an implicit throws (`com.ms.com.ComException`) clause added to its definition. The `ComException` class has a `getHResult` method to return the HRESULT value.

The rest of this chapter uses two sample projects that work together to demonstrate working examples of Java to COM integration. Using COM objects in Java is as natural as using Java objects; Java simplifies the use of COM objects.

Installing the JavaBeep Sample Project

The Visual J++ JavaBeep sample from Microsoft uses the Java Type Library Wizard to create special Java class files that are used to interact with an ActiveX object, Beeper. The Beeper ActiveX class is implemented by beeper.dll, which comes with the JavaBeep sample. The beeper.dll contains a type library that is accessed by the Java Type Library Wizard to generate corresponding Java class files.

The first step to installing the JavaBeep sample project is to copy the sample project files to a new project directory (see Figure 23.1). The sample is installed using the InfoViewer and Visual J++ Books Online. Select the Visual J++ Books Online entry in the Open Information Title combo box on the InfoViewer toolbar. In the Project Workspace window, activate the InfoView tab to display the contents of Visual J++ Books Online. Expand the Samples.Microsoft Samples and double-click JavaBeep: Java calling a COM Object.

In the InfoViewer Topic window, select the Click to open or copy the JavaBeep project files button, which will display the Sample Application dialog box. Click the Copy All button in the Sample Application dialog box to display the Copy dialog box. Specify the directory, new or existing, where you want the files to be copied. The example uses the \MSDEV\SAMPLES\MICROSOFT\JavaBeep directory. Click OK to optionally create the directory and copy the files.

The names and descriptions of the files that were copied into the JavaBeep directory are listed in Table 23.1.

Table 23.1   List of JavaBeep Sample Project Files

File Name	Description
beeper.dll	ActiveX Beeper class
javabeep.html	Test page for javabeep applet
Javabeep.java	Java source for applet
Javabeep.mak	Make file
Javabeep.mdp	Microsoft project workspace
javabeepframe.java	Application frame class
Images/img00??.gif	Globe graphic image files

Next, open the new project by selecting File, Open Workspace. Open the javabeep.mdp file in the newly created JavaBeep project directory. Rebuild the project by selecting Build, Rebuild All. Figure 23.2 shows the output from the build process. This output and the build process that produced it will be discussed in detail later. Before that, however, run the applet to see what JavaBeep does from the user's point of view.

To run the project, select Build, Execute JavaBeep. The first time you execute or debug the new project you will be prompted for the class name to use for executing or debugging. Enter **javabeep** and click OK. The JavaBeep project was initially created using the Java AppletWizard. It is a spinning globe application like the ones built in Chapter 16, "Creating an Applet with AppletWizard."

A new feature of JavaBeep is that when you click the applet, it beeps and displays the string "Hello World From Beeper" where the cursor was. Figure 23.3 shows the JavaBeep applet running after being clicked several times.

FIG. 23.1

The Using Visual J++ Books Online topics are seen in the Project Workspace InfoView window. The JavaBeep sample is installed through a series of dialog boxes.

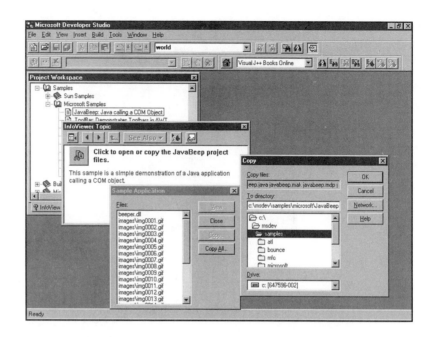

FIG. 23.2

The Output window shows the output from the steps of the JavaBeep Rebuild All command.

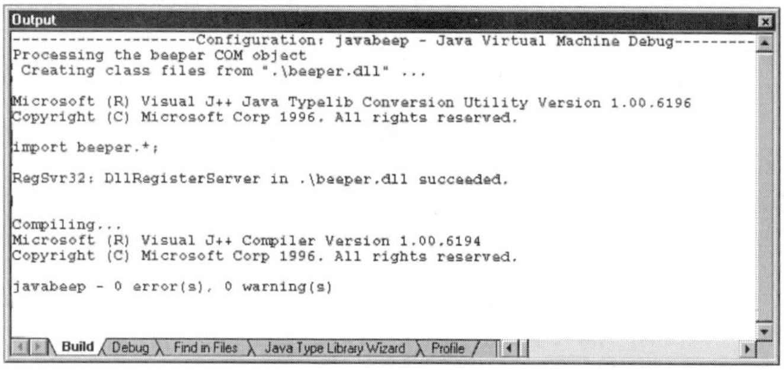

The beeping is done from within the beeper.dll in a method named Beep. The text displayed, "Hello World From Beeper," is also obtained from the beeper.dll. A list of words is maintained by beeper.dll which provides two methods to access the list, the methods getCount and getItem. getCount return the number of strings beeper.dll has. getItem returns a specified string. These methods are examined next.

FIG. 23.3

Here the JavaBeep
Applet is shown drawing
the beeper.dll string
each time it is clicked.

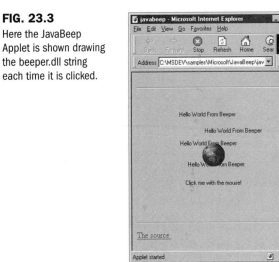

Importing A COM Object into Java

The changes to JavaBeep occur in the beginning of javabeep.java and in the mouseDown method. Listing 23.1 shows the beginning of the javabeep.java file. Notice the import beep.* statement. This imports the definition of the classes implemented in beeper.dll. The syntax is exactly the same as importing a Java package. Next notice the declaration of the IBeeper m_Beeper variable in the last line of Listing 23.1. A reference to an object implementing the IBeeper interface is declared using the same syntax as a reference to an object implemented in Java.

Note that an import statement is not necessary to use the classes under \WINDOWS\JAVA\LIB\. The import statement allows you to refer to the Beeper class and IBeeper interface without the fully qualified "beeper." prefixing the names. In other words, you could remove the import beeper.* statement and use explicit references to the beeper.Beeper class and the beeper.IBeeper interface.

Listing 23.1   Beginning of javabeep.java(\msdev\samples\ Microsoft\javabeep.java.)

```
//****************************************************************************
// javabeep.java:      Applet
//
//     This applet is a simple demonstration of calling a COM object in a
//     Java program, utilizing the ActiveX runtime for Java. The COM object
//   is the Beeper sample from the ActiveX Template Library (ATL). ATL is
//     a Template based Visual C++ 4.x add on that contains a custom AppWizard
//     and various header files to generate a skeleton ActiveX Control. For
//     more information on ATL, including the source code to the beeper.dll
//     COM object, please visit the Microsoft web site at:
//
//                     http://www.microsoft.com/visualc/v42/atl
```

```
//
//    Most of the code of interest can be found in the javabeep.mouseDown()
//    method
//***************************************************************************
import java.applet.*;
import java.awt.*;
import javabeepframe;

// Import the class files that JavaTLB generates from beeper.dll
import beeper.*;

//==============================================================================
// Main Class for applet javabeep
//
//==============================================================================
public class javabeep extends Applet implements Runnable
{
    // Beeper COM Interface variable
    IBeeper m_Beeper=null;
...
```

Listing 23.2 shows the mouseDown method in the JavaBeep class. When you click the applet, a beep sound is generated and a string displayed. The mouseDown method does this by using a Beeper object. A new Beeper object is created and its reference is cast and stored as a reference to an IBeeper interface object. The Beeper Java class implements a Java interface named IBeeper. This will be explained later. The Beep() method of the IBeeper interface is called to sound the beep. The call to Beep is done within a try block. The catch parameter com.ms.com.ComException is the first indication that Beeper is not just another Java class.

Next, the string is built from the list of words maintained by the IBeeper interface of the Beeper object. getCount is used to determine how many times to call getItem to concatenate each word in a string to be displayed. The count is four. The four words returned by IBeeper.getItem are "Hello," "World," "From," and "Beeper."

Listing 23.2   Listing of javabeep.mouseDown Method (\msdev\samples\Microsoft\javabeep.java)

```
public boolean mouseDown(Event evt, int x, int y)
    {
        String BeeperString = new String();

        // Check if the Beeper object exists, and create it if necessary
        if(m_Beeper==null)
            m_Beeper = (IBeeper) new Beeper();

        // Call Beeper object 'Beep' method. Note that the Beep object has
        // been written such that on the sixth call to Beep(), the Beep object
        // will return an OLE error code which gets thrown as a Java
        ➥exception.
        // This sample catches the exception, Releases the Beeper object,
        // creates a new Beeper object, and continues
```

continues

Listing 23.2   Continued

```
try
{
    m_Beeper.Beep();
}
catch(com.ms.com.ComException e)
{
    // Release the Beeper object by setting m_Beeper=null
    m_Beeper=null;
    // Create a new Beeper object
    m_Beeper = (IBeeper) new Beeper();
    m_Beeper.Beep();
}

// Call the Beepers getCount and getItem methods
for(int i=1;i<=m_Beeper.getCount();i++)
{
    // Build a message string from the strings that getItem returns
    BeeperString+=m_Beeper.getItem(i)+" ";
}

// Display the string
m_Graphics.drawString(BeeperString,x,y);

return true;
}
```

Using Custom Build Commands

Now you have seen how the Beeper class implements an interface IBeeper, which has three methods: Beep, getCount, and getItem. But you have not seen the Java source code that implements the Beeper class or IBeeper interface. That is because there isn't any. As mentioned above, the Beeper object is implemented in beeper.dll. So, right now you should be thinking, "What does import beeper.* do if there are no Java classes?" Well, there are Java classes, such as *.class files, but there is no Java source code.

To understand where the Beeper.class and IBeeper.class files are and where they come from, you must go back to the output of the build of JavaBeep (refer to Listing 23.1). Listing 23.3 shows the first eight lines from the output of the build of JavaBeep. The first line is output by Visual J++. The next two lines are echoed from the Custom Build commands for beeper.dll. the last lines are output by the Java Type Library utility program, javaTLB.exe.

Listing 23.3   Listing of Java Typelib Conversion Utility Output for JavaBeep Build

```
-------------------Configuration: javabeep - Java Virtual Machine Debug--------
-----------
Processing the beeper COM object
 Creating class files from ".\beeper.dll" ...
```

```
Microsoft (R) Visual J++ Java Typelib Conversion Utility Version 1.00.6196
Copyright (C) Microsoft Corp 1996. All rights reserved.

import beeper.*;
```

The Java Typelib utility was invoked because a Custom Build command was created as part of the sample JavaBeep project. To view the Custom Build commands for the beeper.dll file, select Build, Settings to display the Project Settings dialog box. Expand the project to display the files, and select the beeper.dll file name in the Settings For list box. Activate the Custom Build tab on the right (see Figure 23.4). Listing 23.4 shows the text from each entry in the Build command(s) list box for the beeper.dll file. An explanation for each command in the list follows:

Part

IV

Ch

23

- The first echo command displays the "Creating class" message in the Output window.
- The second command resolves to "JavaTLB.\beeper.dll." This command causes the IDL information in the beeper.dll to be used to create *.class files under the \WINDOWS\JAVA\LIB\BEEPER directory.
- The third command resolves to "RegSvr32 /s /c .\beeper.dll." This command causes the DllRegisterServer exported function in beeper.dll to be called. DllRegisterServer registers the Beeper object, the IBeeper interface, and the Beeper type library in the system Registry.
- The last command echoes "finished!" to a file named javabeep.trg in the target directory of the subproject. The javabeep.trg file ("$(OutDir)"\javabeep.trg) is also the Output file(s) for beeper.dll. So the Build command will cause the Custom Build commands for the beeper.dll file to be executed when the last modified date of beeper.dll is later than that of javabeep.trg.

Listing 23.4   beeper.dll Custom Build Commands

```
echo Creating class files from "$(Inputpath)" ...
JavaTLB "$(InputPath)"
RegSvr32 /s /c "$(InputPath)"
echo finished! > "$(OutDir)"\javabeep.trg
```

TIP When using the Project Settings dialog box to change Custom Build commands for a DLL (or any file), select each DLL file entry in each project before editing the commands. With all instances of the file entry selected, you will change the settings for all of them at one time. Select multiple, noncontiguous entries by pressing the Ctrl key while selecting entries with your mouse.

FIG. 23.4

The Custom Build tab in the Project Settings dialog box shows the Build commands for the beeper.dll file.

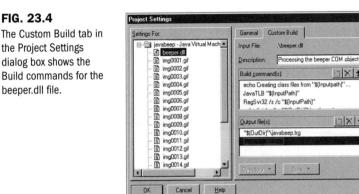

Using the Java Type Library Utility

The Java Type Library utility, JavaTLB.exe, accepts an input "typelib" file name as its parameter. The file can be a *.TLB, *.OLB, *.OCX, *.DLL, or *.EXE file that contains type library information. JavaTLB creates *.class files for each class and interface in a directory under \WINDOWS\JAVA\LIB\ (or (\WINNT\JAVA\LIB\ for Windows NT users) with the name of the file without its extension.

In the case of the JavaBeep project JavaTLB created two files in \WINDOWS\JAVA\LIB\BEEPER\, Beeper.class and IBeeper.class. The Java compiler can only find these class files if \WINDOWS\JAVA\LIB is in the Class files path specified in your project. Select Tools, Options to display the Options dialog box, then activate the Directories tab (see Figure 23.5). Select the Class files entry in the Show Directories drop-down box. Verify that the \WINDOWS\JAVA\CLASSES and \WINDOWS\JAVA\LIB directories are in the Directories list box. If you need to add an entry to the Directories list box, double-click the empty entry at the bottom of the list. An edit control is displayed with a button containing "…" at the right. You can enter the path of the directory directly, or click the "…" button to use a file open dialog to navigate to the directory. After entering the new entry, click OK to save the changed settings. This setting will affect all J++ projects.

JavaTLB also displays in the Output window the import statement that can be used to import the contained entities. In Listing 23.1 of the output from the JavaBeep build, the import statement displayed was: "import beeper.*;". This is the same syntax as importing the contents of a Java package. Individual classes can be imported explicitly as well, for example, import beeper.Beeper; and import beeper.IBeeper;.

TIP The classes in the *.class files created by JavaTLB have a flag set to indicate that they are COM wrapper classes. The Java browser or run-time interpreter looks for this flag and automatically handles mapping the Java method calls to COM function calls. Because of this flag, certain Java utilities may not work properly with these *.class files.

The Beeper class and the IBeeper interface were defined in the beeper.dll type library information. This came from the Beeper project that created the DLL. The Beeper project will be examined later.

FIG. 23.5

The Directories tab of the Tools Options dialog box is used to set the list of directories to search for Class files.

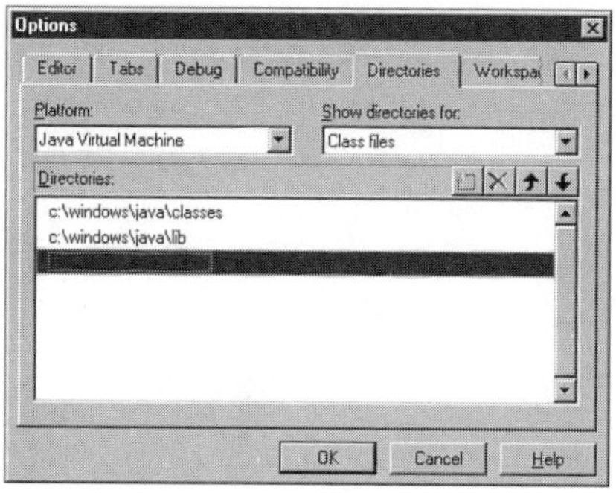

Using the Java Type Library Wizard

The JavaBeep sample project calls JavaTLB.exe from a Custom Build Command to build the wrapper classes for beeper.dll. You can also create the wrapper classes directly for any registered type library by using the Java Type Library Wizard. The Java Type Library Wizard can also produce wrapper classes for any file that contains type library information, including files with the following extensions: *.TLB, *.OLB, *.OCX, *.DLL, *.EXE.

The Java Type Library Wizard, JT.exe, is shown in Figure 23.6. To display the Java Typelib Wizard dialog box, select Tools, Java Type Library Wizard. The Java Type Library Wizard displays all entries in the system Registry under \HKEY_CLASSES_ROOT\TypeLib.

By checking objects from this list and clicking OK, the wizard will call JavaTLB.exe for each selected object. This will cause a directory under \WINDOWS\JAVA\LIB\ to be created for each library selected. Each directory will contain the compiled *.class files for the Java wrapper classes. You need to rebuild these only after the COM object has changed.

FIG. 23.6

The Java Type Library Wizard dialog box displays a list of registered type libraries.

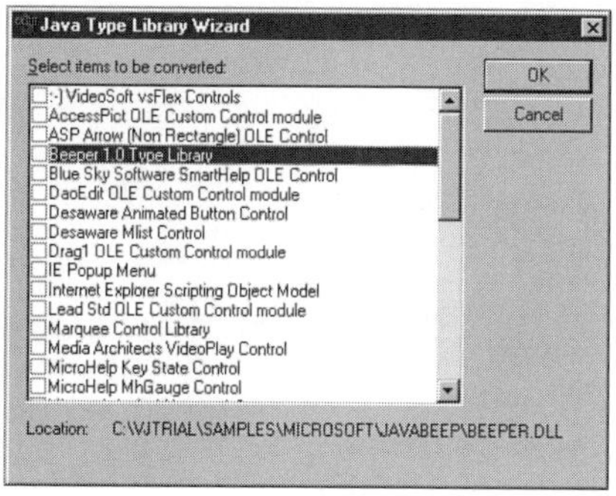

JavaTLB translates the type library information into Java *.class files. COM objects are mapped to Java classes and Java interfaces. ODL data types used by COM objects are mapped to Java data types. Table 23.2 and Table 23.3 below define the mappings used by JavaTLB.

Table 23.2 Mapping of COM/ODL Entities to Java Entities

Java	COM
class	COM classes: `coclass`
interface	Custom interface: v-table-based
interfaces	Dispatch interface: `dispinterface`
interface	Dispatch interface: property*
class	Structure: `typedef`
n/a	Module: module

* For COM interface properties a get\<PropertyName\> and put\<PropertyName\> method is created in the Java interface.

Table 23.3 Mapping of ODL Types to Java Data Types

ODL Type	Java Data Type
boolean	boolean
char	char
double	double
int	int
float	float
long	int
short	short
unsigned char	byte
wchar_t	short
BSTR	class java.lang.String
CURRENCY	long
DATE	double
SCODE/HRESULT	int
VARIANT	class com.ms.com.Variant
IDispatch *	class java.lang.Object

ODL Type	Java Data Type
IUnknown *	class java.lang.Object
SAFEARRAY(<typename>)	array of <typename>
<typename> *	one-element array of <typename>
void	void
LPSTR	class java.lang.String

Using the OLE Object View Tool

The OLE 2 Object View tool is displayed by selecting Tools, OLE Object View. The tool can be used to display more information about registered objects including type libraries. Figure 23.7 shows the Object View tool open with the Beeper Type Library selected. By double-clicking the entry, the ITypeLib dialog box is displayed with detailed information about the type library.

The Beeper 1.0 Type Library contains two types: a Beeper object and an IBeeper interface. Notice that the IBeeper interface contains a function named Count. Its invkind=PROPERTYGET implies that the Java wrapper class for IBeeper will have a method getCount.

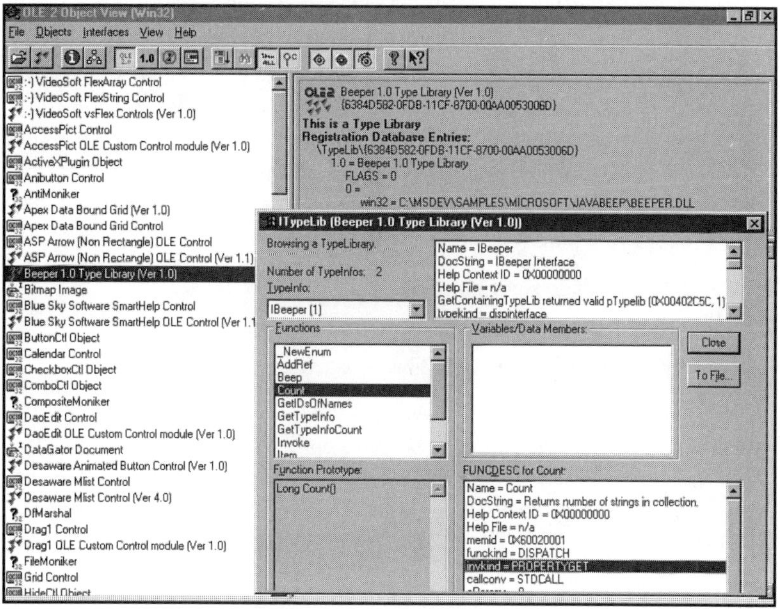

FIG. 23.7

The OLE Object View tool allows you to explore the attributes of registered objects including the Beeper Type Library.

Using the Control Registration Utility

The Custom Build Commands for beeper.dll included a command to call RegSvr32.exe., the Control Registration utility. The command that was executed during the build of JavaBeep was: RegSvr32 /s /c .\beeper.dll. Listing 23.5 shows the usage of the RegSvr32 command. By default RegSvr32 registers the objects (CLSIDs and type library IDs) supported by the beeper.dll. It does this by calling the `DllRegisterServer` function in beeper.dll.

When the /u option is specified, the objects registered during registration are unregistered by a call to the beeper.dll function `DllUnregisterServer`.

Listing 23.5   Listing of RegSvr32.exe Usage

```
RegSvr32 [/u][/s] dllname
/u - Unregister server
/s - Silent; display no message boxes
/c = Console output
```

Examining the Beeper ActiveX COM Object

The JavaBeep sample contains the beeper.dll file. From the dll file the type library information is used to make the Java wrapper classes so that Java programs can interact with the Beeper object as if it was a Java object. To further understand how the JavaBeep program interacts with the Beeper COM object, the Beeper project is examined in closer detail.

The Beeper project is a sample project that comes with the ActiveX Template Library (ATL). The ActiveX Template Library is a library of C++ templates. The purpose of the ATL is to facilitate the construction of lightweight, small, and fast COM servers. These servers are actually candidates for downloading and running as clients on Web pages. That is why they must be as small as possible. The goals of the ATL are to:

- Eliminate static libraries: *.LIB or *.DLL files.
- Eliminate MFC, the Microsoft Foundation Classes for C++.
- Eliminate C run-time library startup code.

Beeper is a Visual C++ project. All Developer Studio figures are of Visual C++, not Visual J++. You can easily get confused because both products share many of the same features. If you only have Visual J++ you will not be able to build Beeper, however, reviewing its components will help understand JavaBeep and Beeper. The files in the project are listed in Table 23.4.

Table 23.4 Beeper Sample Project Files

File Name	Description
Beeper.clw	ClassWizard information
Beeper.cpp	DLL Functions: DllMain, DllCanUnloadNow, DllGetClassObject, DllRegisterServer, DllUnregisterServer
Beeper.def	Exports: DllCanUnloadNow, DllGetClassObject, DllRegisterServer, DllUnregisterServer
Beeper.frm	Visual Basic Form
Beeper.ico	Icon
Beeper.idl	Beeper Interface Definition Language
Beeper.mak	Project Make file
Beeper.rc	Resource file
Beeper.vbp	Visual Basic project file
Beepobj.cpp	CBeeper methods: Beep, get_Count, get_Item, get_NewEnum
Beepobj.h	CBeeper class declaration
Resource.h	Developer Studio generated file for Beeper.rc
Stdafx.cpp	For precompiled headers
Stdafx.h	For precompiled headers

Using the MIDL Compiler

The output from the build process can be seen in Listing 23.7. Figure 23.8 shows the Custom Build Commands for the beeper.idl file in the Beeper project. The single command is MIDL `beeper.idl`. The output files are: beeper.h, beeper_i.c, and beeper.tlb. Another file, beeper_p.c, is also created because this is an OLE interface.

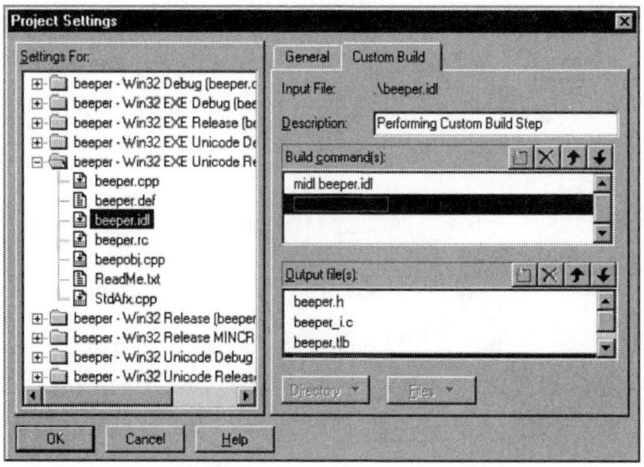

FIG. 23.8

The Custom Build tab of the Project Settings dialog box shows the build commands for the beeper.idl file.

MIDL is the Microsoft Interface Definition Compiler. Its input file is beeper.idl, which is listed in Listing 23.6. The `object` attribute in the interface attribute list of the IDL file tells MIDL that this is a custom OLE interface. When MIDL encounters a library block in its input IDL file, it generates a type library file. The files created by MIDL are described below in Table 23.5.

Listing 23.6 is the Beeper.idl file, which contains the Interface Definition Language (IDL) description of the `Beeper` class and `IBeeper` interface. You can see the definition of the IBeeper interface and its methods `Beep`, and the properties `Count` and `Item`.

Listing 23.6 Beeper.idl Usage

```
// This is a part of the ActiveX Template Library.
// Copyright (C) 1996 Microsoft Corporation
// All rights reserved.
//
// This source code is only intended as a supplement to the
// ActiveX Template Library Reference and related
// electronic documentation provided with the library.
// See these sources for detailed information regarding the
// ActiveX Template Library product.

#define DISPID_NEWENUM -4
[
    object,
    uuid(6384D584-0FDB-11cf-8700-00AA0053006D),
    dual,
    helpstring("IBeeper Interface"),
    pointer_default(unique)
]
interface IBeeper : IDispatch
{
    import "oaidl.idl";
        [helpstring("Play the current sound")]
            HRESULT Beep();
        [propget, helpstring("Returns number of strings in collection.")]
        HRESULT Count([out, retval] long* retval);

        [propget, id(0),
        helpstring("Given an index, returns a string in the collection")]
        HRESULT Item([in] long Index, [out, retval] BSTR* pbstr);

        [propget, restricted, id(DISPID_NEWENUM)]    // Must be propget.
        HRESULT _NewEnum([out, retval] IUnknown** retval);
};

[
    uuid(6384D582-0FDB-11cf-8700-00AA0053006D),
    helpstring("Beeper 1.0 Type Library"),
    version(1.0)
]
library BeeperLib
{
```

```
        importlib("stdole32.tlb");

        //  Class information
        [ uuid(6384D586-0FDB-11cf-8700-00AA0053006D), helpstring("Beeper Object") ]
        coclass Beeper
        {
            [default] interface IBeeper;
        };

};
```

Table 23.5   MIDL Created Files

File Name	Description
beeper.h	The interface header file. This public header file contains a C interface to the OLE custom interface for use in C or C++ programs.
beeper.tlb	Beeper type library.
beeper_i.c	The interface UUID file contains the IIDs and CLSIDs constants generated for Beeper.
beeper_p.c	The interface proxy file contains proxy stub code for creating proxy DLL.

Listing 23.7   Beeper Build Output

```
------------------Configuration: beeper - Win32 Release------------------
Performing Custom Build Step
Microsoft (R) MIDL Compiler Version 3.00.15
Copyright (c) Microsoft Corp 1991-1995. All rights reserved.
Processing .\beeper.idl
beeper.idl
Processing C:\MSDEV\INCLUDE\oaidl.idl
oaidl.idl
Processing C:\MSDEV\INCLUDE\objidl.idl
objidl.idl
Processing C:\MSDEV\INCLUDE\unknwn.idl
unknwn.idl
Processing C:\MSDEV\INCLUDE\wtypes.idl
wtypes.idl
Compiling resources...
Compiling...
StdAfx.cpp
Compiling...
beepobj.cpp
beeper.cpp
Generating Code...
```

continues

Listing 23.7 Continued

```
Linking...
    Creating library Release/beeper.lib and object Release/beeper.exp
Registering OLE Server...
RegSvr32: DllRegisterServer in .\Release\beeper.dll succeeded.


beeper.dll - 0 error(s), 0 warning(s)
```

The interface header file, beeper.h, contains the type and function definitions generated from the definitions in the beeper.idl file. This file is included by source files to build the proxy DLL, and by the calling client program source.

The interface UUID file contains the constants for the registered Beeper classes and interfaces. Beeper services are accessed by clients through the UUID constants.

The interface proxy file, beeper_p.c, implements client proxy and object server stub routines for RPC use. The proxy and stub implementations perform parameter value marshaling necessary for remoting object interfaces. A client proxy first marshals parameters, then sends a message to the object server, and finally unmarshals the results into output parameters and return values. Conversely, an object server stub first unmarshals parameters received from the client proxy, then calls the actual method on the object, and finally marshals any results to be sent back to the client proxy interface.

> **T I P** Starting with MIDL version 3.00.15, you no longer must maintain ODL and IDL files. MIDL supports ODL files. The MKTYPLIB utility was used to produce type libraries.

Another way to access the Custom Build information about the beeper.idl file is to select it in the Project Workspace FileView window, then right-click the entry to display the pop-up menu. Select Properties from the menu to display the Source File Properties dialog box (see Figure 23.9). Activate the Inputs and Outputs tabs to view the Custom Build Command information.

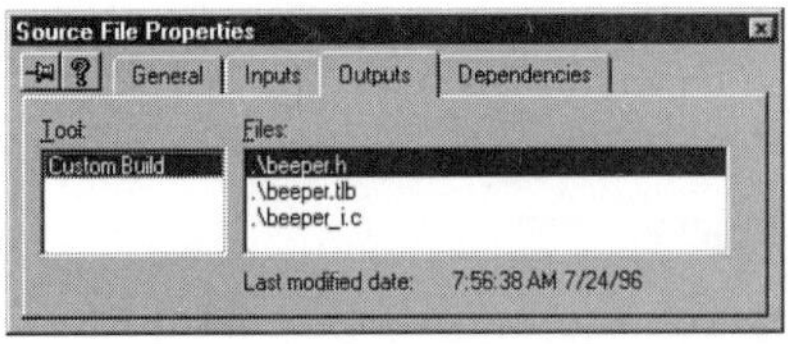

FIG. 23.9
The Outputs tab of the Source File Properties dialog box shows the output files affected by commands for beeper.idl.

Figure 23.10 shows the Custom Build Commands for beeper.dll. Notice that you must select the project target in the Settings For list box, in order to access the Custom Build dialog for the target project's DLL file. The beeper.dll Custom Build Commands include a call to RegSvr32 to register itself.

Remember that RegSvr32 calls `DllRegisterServer` to register itself. Beeper's `DllRegisterServer` function does not use the beeper.tlb file that is created by MIDL. Instead, beeper.tlb is included in beeper.dll. This is done by the inclusion of a TYPELIB statement in the beeper.rc file (see Listing 23.8). The type library file becomes a resource of the DLL file. This helps simplify packaging and distribution of objects by eliminating an extra file.

Listing 23.8 Partial Listing of beeper.rc TYPELIB Statements

```
...
#ifdef APSTUDIO_INVOKED
...
3 TEXTINCLUDE DISCARDABLE
BEGIN
    "1 TYPELIB ""beeper.tlb""\r\n"
    "\0"
END
...
#ifndef APSTUDIO_INVOKED
/////////////////////////////////////////////////////////////////////////////
//
// Generated from the TEXTINCLUDE 3 resource.
//
1 TYPELIB "beeper.tlb"

/////////////////////////////////////////////////////////////////////////////
#endif    // not APSTUDIO_INVOKED

#endif    // APSTUDIO_INVOKED
```

Part
IV
Ch
23

FIG. 23.10

The Custom Build tab of the Project Settings dialog box for beeper.dll shows its Build commands.

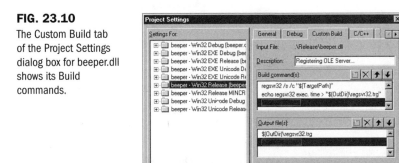

Using The Registry Editor

The Registry Editor (see Figure 23.11) can be used to browse the Registry entries. To start the Registry Editor in Windows 95, from the Start menu, select Run. In the Open control, type **regedit.exe** and Click OK. Select Edit, Find to display the Find dialog box. Enter **beeper** as the string to find, click Find Next to find the first entry. Press F3 to find the following occurrences of the beeper string in the table below. You will find many of the entries created for Beeper. Table 23.6 lists some of the keys and values of entries related to Beeper.

FIG. 23.11

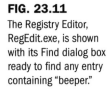

The Registry Editor, RegEdit.exe, is shown with its Find dialog box ready to find any entry containing "beeper."

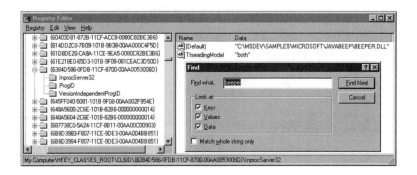

Table 23.6 Some Beeper System Registry Entries

Key	Value
\HKEY_CLASSES_ROOT\Acme.Beeper	Acme Beeper 1.0 Object
\HKEY_CLASSES_ROOT\Acme.Beeper\CLSID	{6384D586-0FDB-11CF-8700-00AA0053006D}
\HKEY_CLASSES_ROOT\Acme.Beeper.1	Acme Beeper 1.0 Object
\HKEY_CLASSES_ROOT\Acme.Beeper.1\CLSID	{6384D586-0FDB-11CF-8700-00AA0053006D}
\HKEY_CLASSES_ROOT\CLSID\	{6384D586-0FDB-11CF-8700-00AA0053006D} Acme Beeper 1.0 Object
\HKEY_CLASSES_ROOT\CLSID\	{6384D586-0FDB-11CF-8700-00AA0053006D}\InprocServer32 C:\MSDEV\SAMPLES\MICROSOFT\JAVABEEP\BEEPER.DLL
\HKEY_CLASSES_ROOT\Interface\	{6384D584-0FDB-11CF-8700-00AA0053006D}\InprocServer32 IBeeper
\HKEY_CLASSES_ROOT\Interface\	{6384D584-0FDB-11CF-8700-00AA0053006D}\Typelib {6384D582-0FDB-11CF-8700-00AA0053006D}
\HKEY_CLASSES_ROOT\Typelib\	{6384D582-0FDB-11CF-8700-00AA0053006D}\Typelib (value not set)

Viewing the Beeper Functions

In this section some of the source files will be examined to show more details of how the functionality is implemented. The beepobj.h file (see Listing 23.9) shows the C++ class definitions for Beeper. You can see that these classes are derived from other classes found in the ActiveX Template Library. The ATL will be examined in more detail in another chapter.

Part

IV

Ch

23

Listing 23.9   Listing beepobj.h

```
// beepobj.h : main header file for BEEPER.DLL
//
// This is a part of the ActiveX Template Library.
// Copyright (C) 1996 Microsoft Corporation
// All rights reserved.
//
// This source code is only intended as a supplement to the
// ActiveX Template Library Reference and related
// electronic documentation provided with the library.
// See these sources for detailed information regarding the
// ActiveX Template Library product.

#include "resource.h"        // main symbols

/////////////////////////////////////////////////////////////////////////////
// Beeper

class CBeeper;

class CBeeper2 :
    public CComISupportErrorInfoImpl<&IID_IBeeper>,
    public CComTearOffObjectBase<&CLSID_Beeper, CBeeper>
{
public:
    CBeeper2() {}

BEGIN_COM_MAP(CBeeper2)
    COM_INTERFACE_ENTRY(ISupportErrorInfo)
END_COM_MAP()

};

class CBeeper :
    public CComDualImpl<IBeeper, &IID_IBeeper, &LIBID_BeeperLib>,
    public CComObjectBase<&CLSID_Beeper>
{
public:
    CBeeper();
    BEGIN_COM_MAP(CBeeper)
        COM_INTERFACE_ENTRY(IDispatch)
        COM_INTERFACE_ENTRY(IBeeper)
        COM_INTERFACE_ENTRY_TEAR_OFF(IID_ISupportErrorInfo, CBeeper2)
    END_COM_MAP()
    DECLARE_NOT_AGGREGATABLE(CBeeper)
```

continues

Listing 23.9   Continued

```
// IBeeper
public:
    STDMETHOD(Beep)();
    STDMETHOD(get_Count)(long* retval);
    STDMETHOD(get_Item)(long Index, BSTR* pbstr);
    STDMETHOD(get__NewEnum)(IUnknown** retval);
private:
    int m_nCnt;
    CComVariant var[4];
};
```

The `DllRegisterServer` (see Listing 23.10) is called to have the DLL register itself in the system Registry. It is called by RegSvr32.exe, which registers the contained type library by default.

**Listing 23.10   DllRegisterServer Function
(\MSDEV\SAMPLES\ATL\BEEPER\beeper.cpp)**

```
/////////////////////////////////////////////////////////////////////////////
// DllRegisterServer - Adds entries to the system registry
STDAPI DllRegisterServer(void)
{
    HRESULT hRes = S_OK;
#ifdef _MERGE_PROXYSTUB
    hRes = PrxDllRegisterServer();
    if (FAILED(hRes))
        return hRes;
#endif
    // registers object, typelib and all interfaces in typelib
    hRes = _Module.UpdateRegistry(TRUE);
    return hRes;
}
```

The `DllUnregisterServer` (see Listing 12.11) is called to have the DLL unregister itself. All entries created by `DllRegisterServer` should be unregistered (if possible). It is called by RegSvr32.exe when the `/u` parameter specified.

**Listing 23.11   DllUnregisterServer Function
(\MSDEV\SAMPLES\ATL\BEEPER\beeper.cpp)**

```
/////////////////////////////////////////////////////////////////////////////
// DllRegisterServer - Adds entries to the system registry

STDAPI DllUnregisterServer(void)
{
    HRESULT hRes = S_OK;
    _Module.RemoveRegistry();
```

```
#ifdef _MERGE_PROXYSTUB
    hRes = PrxDllUnregisterServer();
#endif
    return hRes;
}
```

The Beep function (see Listing 23.12) is called when the IBeeper.Beep() method is called. It sounds a beep by calling MessageBeep. An error is returned after the first four beeps. This is for testing purposes.

Listing 23.12   CBeeper::Beep Function
(\MSDEV\SAMPLES\ATL\BEEPER\beepobj.cpp)

```
STDMETHODIMP CBeeper::Beep()
{
    if (m_nCnt++ == 5)
    {
        m_nCnt = 0;
        return Error(L"Too many beeps");
    }
    MessageBeep(0);
    return S_OK;
}
```

The get_Count function is called when the IBeeper.getCount() method is called from JavaBeep. It returns the count of the number of words supported by Beeper. The Java method name exposed for get_Count (see Listing 23.13) is "getCount" This name is formed by appending "get" with the property name that is defined in the IDL (refer to Listing 23.6, "Beeper.idl Usage") as "Count."

Listing 23.13   CBeeper::get_Count
(\MSDEV\SAMPLES\ATL\BEEPER\beepobj.cpp)

```
STDMETHODIMP CBeeper::get_Count(long* retval)
{
    *retval = 4;
    return S_OK;
}
```

The get_Item function (see Listing 23.14) is called when the IBeeper.getItem method is called from JavaBeep. It returns the zero-based word from the work array. Notice the global character array, arr, used to store the word list.

**Listing 23.14   CBeeper::get_Item Functions
(\MSDEV\SAMPLES\ATL\BEEPER\beepobj.cpp)**

```
...
unsigned short* arr[] = {L"Hello", L"World", L"From", L"Beeper"};
...
STDMETHODIMP CBeeper::get_Item(long Index, BSTR* pbstr)
{
    if (Index > 4)
        *pbstr = NULL;
    *pbstr = SysAllocString(arr[Index-1]);
    return S_OK;
```

Putting It All Together

This chapter has covered a lot of territory. The purpose was to expose many pieces of the puzzle and thus explain how a Java program can call a COM object.

As an exercise, the last word of beeper was changed from "Beeper" to "NewBeeper" in beepobj.cpp. The beeper project was then rebuilt. The JavaBeep.html page was loaded into the browser without rebuilding the JavaBeep project. The result of three mouse clicks on JavaBeep is shown in Figure 23.12. Notice that "Hello World From Beeper" is now "Hello World From NewBeeper."

Nothing in the JavaBeep project has changed, but the \MSDEV\SAMPLES\MICROSOFT\JAVABEEP\beeper.dll is no longer being called. Instead the \MSDEV\SAMPLES\ATL\BEEPER\beeper.dll is being called. The reason is that the new beeper registered itself using the same UUIDs used by the beeper.dll in the JavaBeep project. It overrode the existing definitions created when the JavaBeep project was built.

The \WINDOWS\JAVA\LIB\BEEPER*.class files are bound to these UUID constants and not any file names. The Registry entries can change without affecting other compiled objects. A new version of an ActiveX object can be installed that uses new UUID values, without affecting the working of the existing versions.

When the Internet Explorer browser loaded the Beeper.class and IBeeper.class files, it could tell from a flag that they were COM wrapper classes. Using the UUID information, the Java Virtual Machine did the rest of the work to make the Beeper class and IBeeper interface work in a compatible manner with the Java language.

FIG. 23.12

Here is JavaBeep running unchanged, but a newly registered Beeper is being called and returning the NewBeeper String.

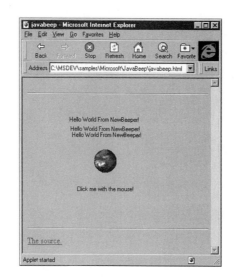

From Here...

In this chapter you have been introduced to the capabilities (and complexities) made possible by the integration of COM and Java. This introduction dealt with Java calling ActiveX objects. There are still more important related topics ahead such as:

- In Chapter 27, "Scripting Client Applets," you learn to call Java applets from JavaScript and Visual Basic scripts, and use the Internet Explorer scripting Object Model to control the browser.

CHAPTER 24

Working with Internet Information Server

by Nelson Howell

For the creation of a Java applet or application, Visual J++ requires Windows NT 4.0 or later, or Windows 95. Visual J++ does not require Microsoft Internet Information Server or any other Web server for the creation of Java applets. The execution of a Visual J++ applet or application requires either a Java-enabled Web browser or another Java-interpreting virtual machine. Why then should you spend your valuable time learning about an Internet server? This description of Microsoft Internet Information Server is included to illustrate the functions of a Web server. Understanding the server environment will enhance your ability to effectively design your Visual J++ Java applets. ■

What servers do and how they communicate with the browser

The server is listening on Port 80.

How to install Microsoft Internet Information Server

The Installation of Microsoft Internet Information Server is all but automatic.

How to explore your Web site

Exploring the Web site created by MS IIS is easy.

Where the pages and files should be on the server

Understand Home, Root, and Virtual directories.

Security issues

You want to keep your users properly under control when they are visiting your Web site.

What the server logs can tell you

Are your Java applets putting a large load on the server?

How to make your applet work on a Web site

Where should your applet be located? How does HTML call your applet?

Listening on Port 80

A Well Known Port is one that has become standardized for a specific function. For the World Wide Web and its Web servers, this is Port 80.

When a World Wide Web client/browser wants to connect to a Web server, it sends a request for service in the form of a URL (Uniform Resource Locator), like this:

```
http://www.yourserver.com
```

When the browser sends the request for service, the URL is used to generate an Internet IP address. A Domain Name Server translates the portion of the URL (yourserver.com) into a 32-bit IP address that looks like 127.1.1.0. The http part of the URL indicates that the client is using the Hypertext Transport Protocol. WWW indicates that it will log on to a World Wide Web server.

When the server receives the request for service in the preceding form, the server transmits the HTML document default.htm if the server is MS IIS and is at its default settings. Actually, the default document can have any name because this is a parameter that can be set in MS IIS. If the server is not MS IIS, the usual default is to transmit the document named index.html.

> **CAUTION**
>
> Microsoft Internet Information Server is provided only with Windows NT 4.0 Server. Windows NT 4.0 WorkStation provides the Personal Web Server which is much like the IIS.

For more information on Microsoft Internet Information Server, *Special Edition Using Microsoft Internet Information Server* published by Que should help.

The document may have other files such as graphics that it includes. The browser begins to interpret the HTML document and requests these files. A well-designed browser maintains a cache of files and documents recently received. If the file that is requested already exists in the browser cache, then the file does not have to be transmitted; it will be loaded from the cache. Of course, one of the files that may be called for can be a Java applet.

The default.htm HTML document usually has hyperlinks to other documents in the particular Web site and/or on other Web sites. Because a hyperlink is a URL pointing to another Web page, the URL may point to a page on the local server or elsewhere on the Internet. If the document is on the current Web site, the URL is relative to the current document location. If the hyperlink is to a document on another Web site, the process begins with the DSN translation of the domain name into an IP address.

The URL occasionally contains information after the domain name. This information is the name of a file, a directory, or parameters. The following is an example of such a URL:

http://www.yourserver.com/somedirectory/somepage.htm

In this case, the request is directed to a specific file and the default.htm page will not be transmitted. If the address had a directory specified but no file name, then there would need to be a default.htm file in that directory.

Installing Microsoft Internet Information Server

The installation of Microsoft Internet Information Server is easy and straightforward. The installation programs are on the Windows NT 4.0 CD-ROM. To install Microsoft Internet Information Server follow these steps:

1. Choose Start, Run and enter the path *Drive:\Platform*\inetsrv\inetstp.exe as shown in Figure 24.1.

2. Simply click OK or press the Enter key to continue as shown in Figure 24.2.

FIG. 24.1
When Windows NT 4.0 is installed, you are offered the choice to install MS IIS.

FIG. 24.2
MS IIS can be reinstalled or removed from this setup program.

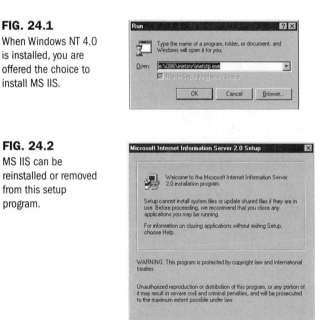

3. Select the services that you want installed as shown in Figure 24.3. At a minimum, you need the Internet Service Manager, World Wide Web Service, and the Help & Sample Files.

4. The default installation location is \WINNT\SYSTEM32\INETSRV as shown in Figure 24.4.

FIG. 24.3

If you do not install a service, it can be added later.

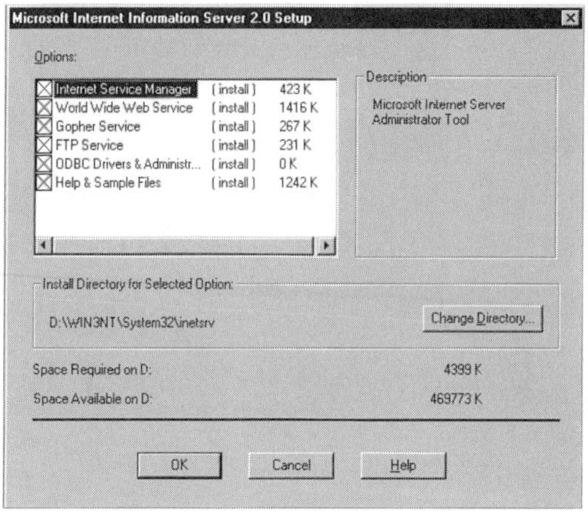

FIG. 24.4

Click Yes to continue or No to change the directory.

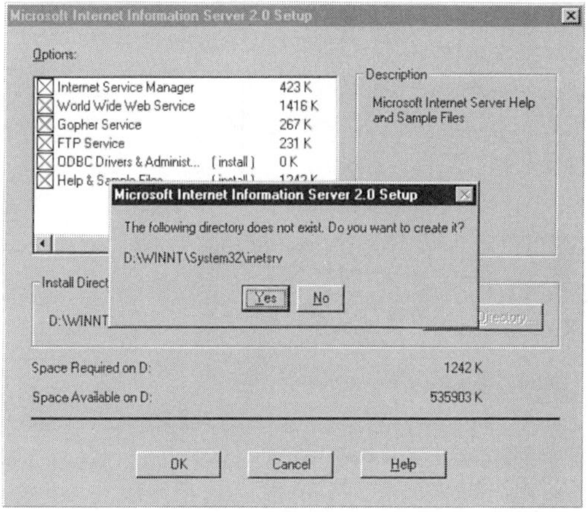

5. You must select the location of the home directories for the Internet publishing services being installed as shown in Figure 24.5. Click OK to continue.

6. You are given the chance to accept the default locations or change the directories as shown in Figure 24.6.

7. If you chose to install ODBC Drivers and Administration, you need to select the drivers to be installed as shown in Figure 24.7. The installation program's automatic version check ensures that you do not overwrite a newer version with an older version.

8. You have successfully installed Microsoft Internet Information Server as shown in Figure 24.8.

FIG. 24.5

You are shown only the services that you have chosen to install.

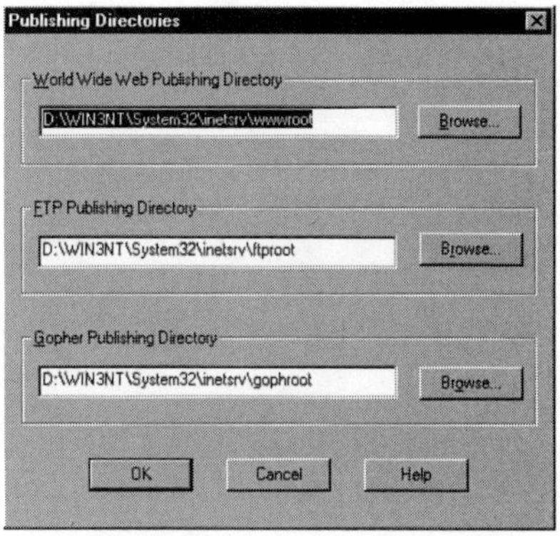

FIG. 24.6

Click Yes to accept the defaults and continue.

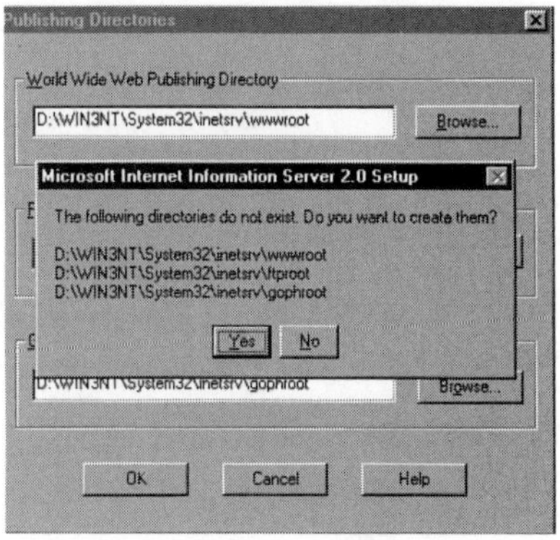

FIG. 24.7

Select the driver or drivers to be installed.

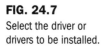

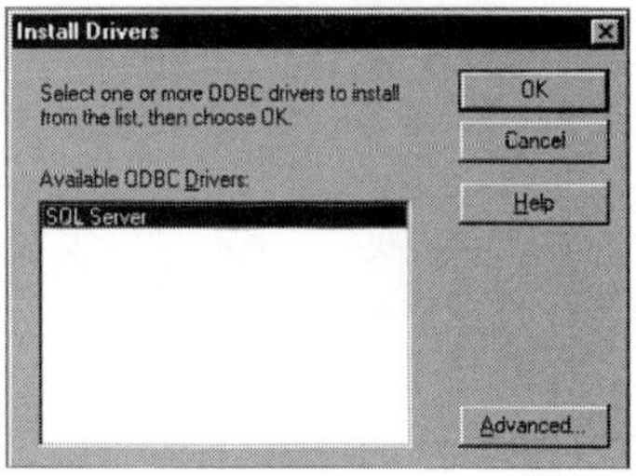

FIG. 24.8

Click OK to finish the installation process.

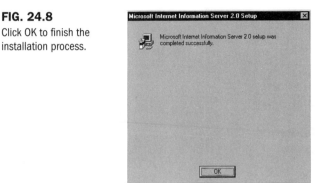

At the end of the installation process, you will have a functional Web site. All that is required is to open your Web browser to your server name as shown in Figure 24.9. If you look at the directories using the Windows NT Explorer, you will see default.htm located in \WINNT\SYSTEM32\INETSRV\WWWROOT.

FIG. 24.9

Enter **http:// yourservername** in the Address field to view your new Web site.

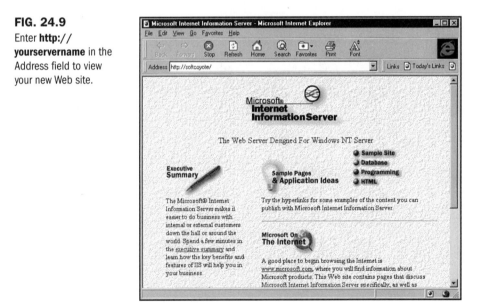

Surfing Your Web Site

Investigating the samples and information within the Microsoft Internet Information Server will reveal tools and techniques to enhance your Internet knowledge. When you see a Web page that you like, you can look behind the presentation of the Web browser by choosing View, Source to see how it was accomplished in HTML. This one feature of the World Wide Web contributes to the sharing of techniques. You always have the opportunity to view the source document in Notepad. On your tour of your Web site, you should look under the covers at some Web pages.

1. Open your Web browser and set the Address to **http://*yourservername*** as shown in Figure 24.10.

FIG. 24.10

The page displayed is the default page, default.htm, located at wwwroot which is the World Wide Web home directory.

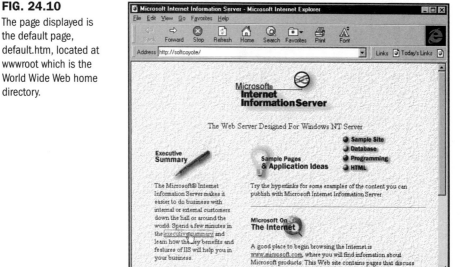

2. Also in Figure 24.10 notice that when the mouse is over a hyperlink, the cursor turns into a hand. In the status bar at the bottom you also see that the link points to a file named bendrill.htm.

3. To see how this is created in HTML, press Alt, View, Source (Alt+V+C) to display the source HTML in Notepad as shown in Figure 24.11. The path shown is a relative path that starts with the wwwroot directory.

FIG. 24.11

The path to the bendrill.htm file is /samples/tour/ bendrill.htm.

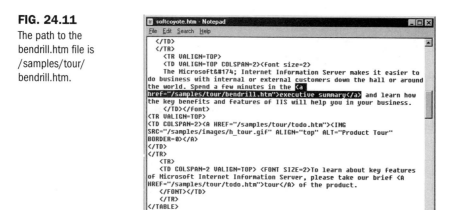

4. Click the hyperlink executive summary to open the page bendrill.htm as shown in Figure 24.12.

FIG. 24.12

This is the bendrill.htm page.

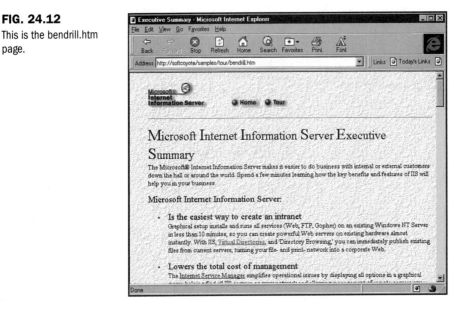

5. Continue to explore the sample Web site by repeating the steps above on other Web pages.

The technique of looking under the covers works on any Web page that you have opened with your Web browser.

Understanding Home, Root, and Virtual Directories

Understanding how MS IIS deals with directories is critical to understanding the limits of where files and directories are placed.

WWW Home or Root Directory

For a Microsoft Internet Information Server, there is only one "Home" directory for the World Wide Web publishing service. The default installation creates this directory as \WINNT\SYSTEM32\INETSRV\WWWROOT. It is also called the WWW root directory. When a WWW client submits a request for service to a MS IIS Web server, by default it sees the WWW home directory, as the root or lowest level directory. MS IIS confines the Web client to the WWW home directory, and the client is unable to see any file not located in the WWW home directory or one of its subdirectories. Figure 24.13 shows the directories in the World Wide Web publishing service. The directory dialog of the WWW publishing service is opened by choosing Start, Programs, Microsoft Internet Server (Common), Internet Service Manager.

Select the Computer Name by the WWW service, press Alt, Properties, Service Properties, (Alt+P+S), and click the Directories tab. The other directories not labeled <Home> are virtual directories that are discussed in the next section.

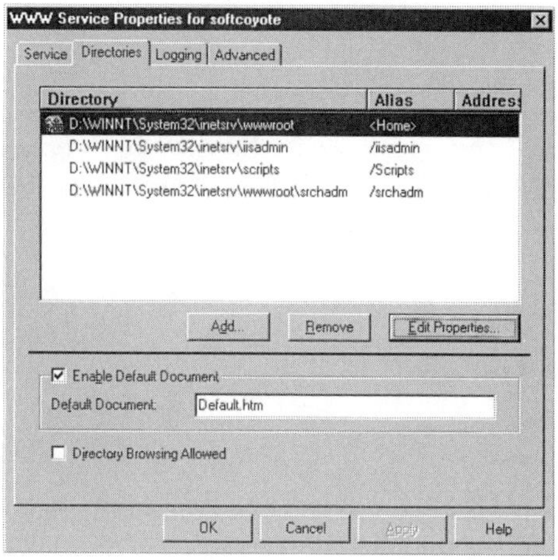

FIG. 24.13

There is only one and can be only one "Home" directory for the World Wide Web publishing service.

Virtual Directories

Virtual directories are directories that are located logically in the WWW Home or Root directory but not located physically in the WWW Home directory. These directories can be located on the local computer drive or on any computer in the same Windows NT domain. The alias is the relative path from the WWW Home directory. In Figure 24.14, both the physical and relative, or alias, paths are shown.

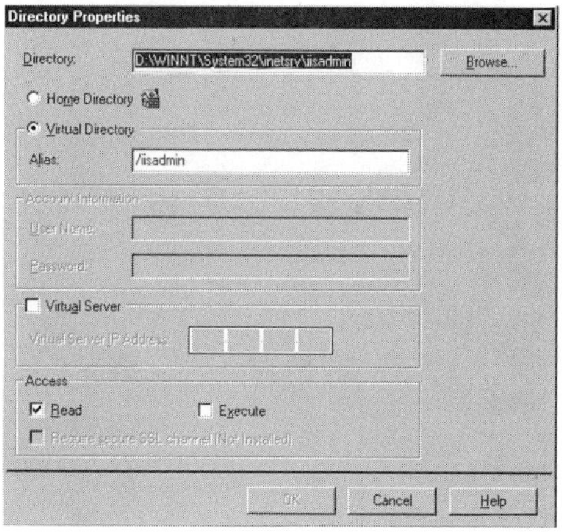

FIG. 24.14

The URL Address to a virtual directory is **http://servername/ alias**. This is different from the physical path that is shown.

Securing Your Web Site

Windows NT provides part of the Web site security and is further complemented by the security features of MS IIS.

Windows NT Security

The majority of users accessing the World Wide Web are anonymous. For Windows NT to allow this access, an account is set up for all anonymous WWW connections. The default name for this account is IUSR_SERVERNAME. The rights of this account and the rights of the groups to which this account belongs will provide Windows NT limitations on what a Web client can do.

It is also strongly recommended that the disk volumes on the Windows NT server use NTFS. This will provide file and directory level security.

MS IIS Security

There are four settings in the MS IIS that affect the Web site security. The settings are seen by choosing Start, Programs, Microsoft Internet Server (Common), Internet Service Manager. Select the server name by WWW and choosing Properties, Service Properties. Clicking the appropriate tab of the Service Properties dialog box will open the following property sheets.

■ *Password Authentication properties.* This setting is displayed by clicking the Service tab of the Service Properties dialog in the Internet Service Manager as seen in Figure 24.15.

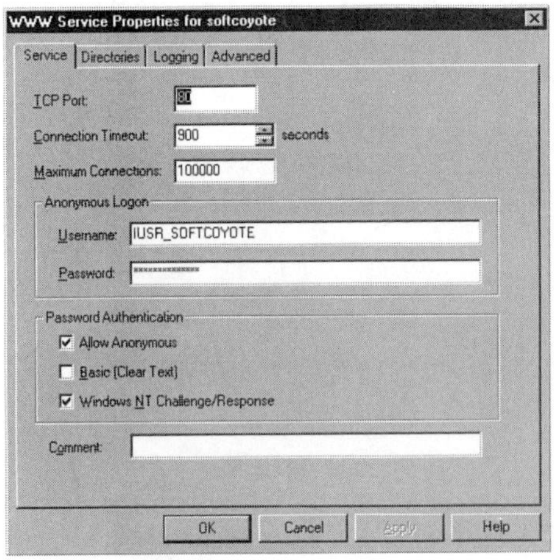

FIG. 24.15
The Windows NT Challenge/Response option determines whether passwords and user IDs are encrypted during transmission.

■ *Directory Browsing Allowed setting.* This setting is displayed by clicking the Directories tab of the Service Properties dialog in the Internet Service Manager as seen in Figure 24.16.

FIG. 24.16
If the Directory Browsing Allowed option is checked, the user will be able to see the contents of the directory.

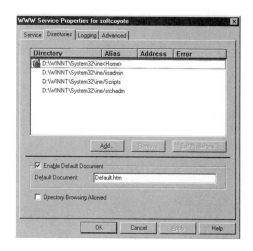

■ *Directory Access settings.* These settings are displayed by clicking the Directories tab of the Service Properties dialog, selecting a directory, and clicking the Edit Properties button (see Figure 24.17).

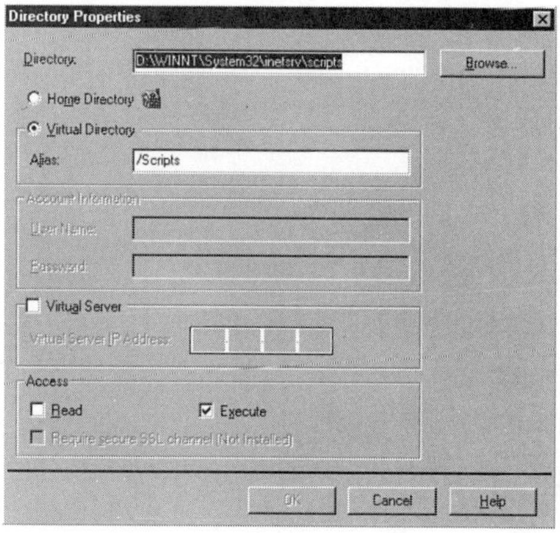

FIG. 24.17
Only scripts and executables that will be executed on the server should be set to Execute. All others should be set to Read.

■ *Advanced Properties.* These properties are displayed by clicking the Advanced tab of the Service Properties dialog in the Internet Service Manager as seen in Figure 24.18. This dialog box allows for the inclusion or exclusion of computers by IP address. Either all computers except those listed are allowed access, or no computers are allowed access except those listed.

FIG. 24.18

The logic of this dialog box is that everything except those computers listed are either allowed or denied access.

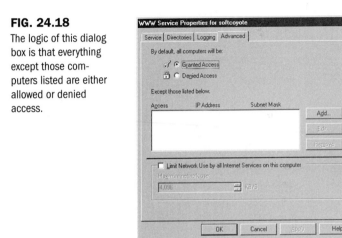

The combination of the Windows NT security and the MS IIS security allows for a very secure Web site. It should resist penetration by all but the most skillful and dedicated hacker.

Reading the Log

One question that may arise is how much load does the Java applet place on the server. The Microsoft Internet Information Server logs each request for service by a client and the response.

The log file will usually be located in the directory \WINNT\SYSTEM32\LOGFILES. The default log file will be named inyymmdd.Log where the log file name is determined by the settings in the logging options as shown in Figure 24.19. You can open the dialog box shown in Figure 24.19 by choosing Start, Programs, Microsoft Internet Server (Common), Internet Service Manager, double-clicking the Computer Name next to the WWW Service, and clicking the Logging tab.

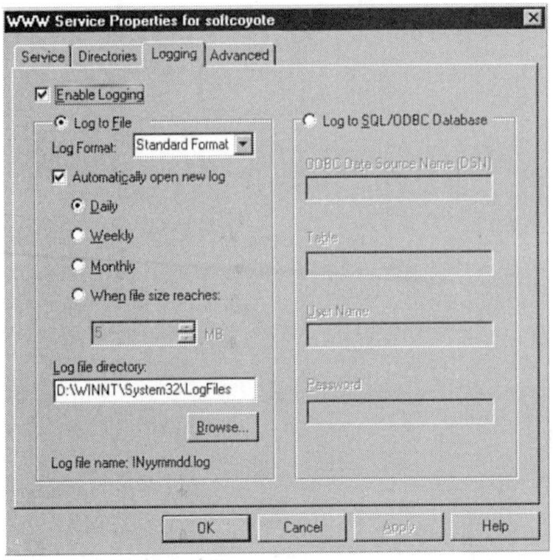

FIG. 24.19

The option of using an ODBC database may also be used with MS IIS.

N O T E Other Web servers also log the request for service and response by the server. These are usually in the Common Log File format which is different than the MS IIS logging format. MS IIS can also log to an ODBC SQL database. If the MS IIS installation that you are working with is using this option, you will need to consult the database documentation for information on how to retrieve data.

The information found in the MS IIS log file (see Figure 24.20 for an example of the log file shown in Notepad) contains the following comma-delimited fields:

FIG. 24.20

The selected area shows a Java applet being transferred with a size of 2086 bytes.

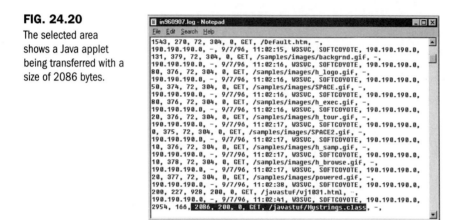

- ■ *Client's IP address.* 190.190.190.0
- ■ *Client's username.* This will be blank for anonymous WWW and Gopher connections and will show anonymous for FTP anonymous connections. For non-anonymous connections, a username will be shown.

  \- (A hyphen acts as a place holder if there is no value as is the case in Figure 24.20.)
- ■ *Date of the transfer.* 9/7/96
- ■ *Time of the transfer.* 11:02:41
- ■ *MS IIS service that created the entry.* W3SVC   This is the WWW Publishing Service.
- ■ *Computer name of the server.* SOFTCOYOTE
- ■ *IP address of the server.* 190.190.190.0
- ■ *Processing time in milliseconds.* 2954
- ■ *Bytes received.* 166   This is the request for the applet file.
- ■ *Bytes sent.* 2086   This is the applet file.
- ■ *Service status code.* 200   This is a successful transfer.
- ■ *Windows NT status code.* 0   This is a success.
- ■ *Name of the operation.* GET

■ *Target of the operation*. This field will also contain any parameters for the operation if required.

/javastuf/Mystrings.class—the path is relative to the WWW Home directory.

After loading the file into a usage statistics program or using a spreadsheet such as Microsoft Excel, the processing time for the transfer of .class files and the bytes transferred can be calculated as a percentage of the total activity for the server.

Getting Your Applet to Work with the Server

Getting a Java applet to run from the MS IIS Web server is very easy. The first thing required is a HTML page that will call the applet. In Figure 24.21 notice a Java applet named MyStrings.class running in a HTML page named String.html. MyStrings is a Java applet that was created as one of the sample applets in this book. The HTML page was placed in a directory /javastuf and the applet was placed in a directory /javacode.

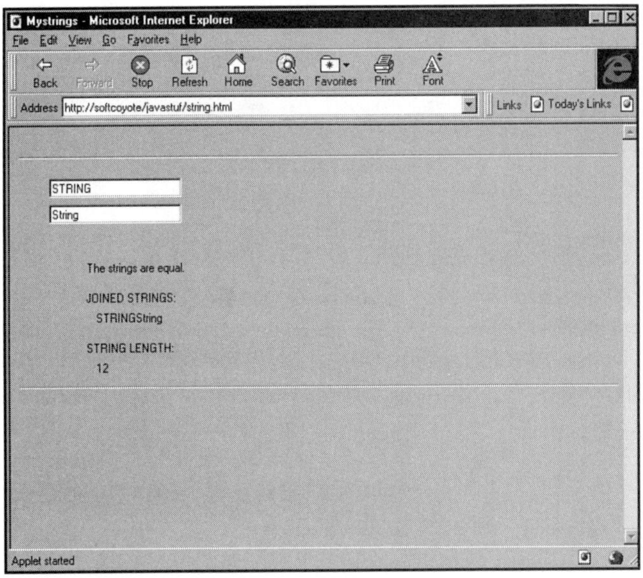

FIG. 24.21
The status bar at
the bottom of the
browser window
informs you that the
applet has started.

In Figure 24.22, the HTML code in Strings.HTML is shown. The HTML that runs the Java applet is shown in Listing 24.1.

**Listing 24.1   HTML—The HTML Required to Call the Java Applet
MyStrings**

```
<applet codebase="/javacode"
code=Mystrings
width=200
height=200>
</applet>
```

FIG. 24.22

The code is shown here by choosing View, Source on the Web browser.

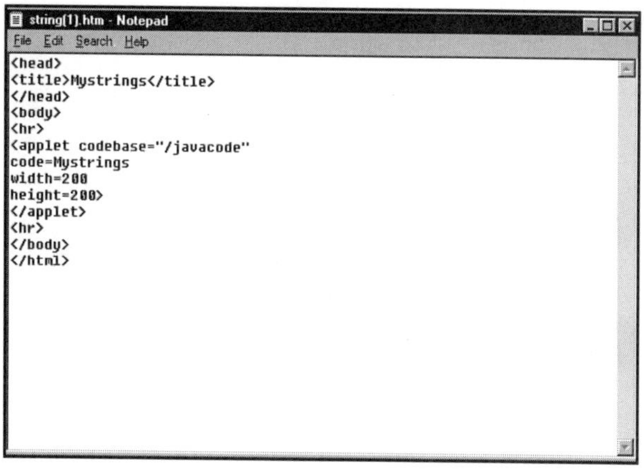

```
string(1).htm - Notepad
File  Edit  Search  Help
<head>
<title>Mystrings</title>
</head>
<body>
<hr>
<applet codebase="/javacode"
code=Mystrings
width=200
height=200>
</applet>
<hr>
</body>
</html>
```

The line `codebase ="/javacode"` gives the relative path for the directory containing the Java applet Mystrings.class.

The line `code=Mystrings` gives the name of the applet to be run.

The next two lines give the height and width of the palette for the applet.

From Here...

Understanding the Web server environment is one important piece of the puzzle that you must understand to create Java applets that perform as you want. A review and understanding of HTML is also useful in preparing to create Java applets. Java is one of the more innovative new technologies for the Internet and for the computer industry in general. It has the promise of delivering the platform independence that for years has been the quest of many developers. The following chapters present related information about topics discussed in this chapter:

- Chapter 1, "Why Java Is Hot," reviews some browser issues.
- Chapter 2, "Java and Visual J++," explores the issues of the Internet and how your server relates to it.
- Chapter 3, "The Java Language," takes you on a trip through the fascinating world of Java and Visual J++.
- Chapter 15, "Building a Sample Applet," helps you create an applet to begin your Web server experimentation.

CHAPTER 25

Code Signing Java with Authenticode

by Mark Culverhouse

Microsoft has introduced support for a security framework for the Internet. Digital IDs are issued to individuals and companies by a trusted third-party certification authority. The Digital IDs uniquely identify each individual and each company.

The Internet is designed to deliver software on demand to the user. But there are so many individuals and corporate software publishers on the Internet; who can you trust? Software downloaded today from the Internet is anonymous. It would be nice to tell your browser to download and install any software that comes from say, Microsoft Corporation, without warning. When any software from Microsoft is downloaded, you also want it checked to make sure it really came from Microsoft. Digital IDs make this possible.

There are many potential uses for Digital IDs. A company might issue employee certificates that identify individuals as company employees, and then deploy applications that allow access only to certified employees.

Of course, a certification authority can revoke certificates before they expire. If a software publishing company or individual is shown to be distributing destructive code, then their IDs can be revoked to prevent any more authorized downloading of their signed code. ■

Microsoft's Authenticode security framework for the Internet

Authenticode is part of the ActiveX SDK. It contains utilities used to digitally sign files including CAB files.

CAB technology

"Cabinet" technology has been used for installing software packages. It has been enhanced to support distributing signed code including Java *.class files.

How to package Java classes in CAB files

Internet Explorer supports the downloading of Java class files packaged as CAB files.

How to digitally sign Java applet code

Signed CAB files containing Java applet class files can be downloaded and run *outside* the applet security manager.

How to digitally sign Java class libraries

Digitally signed CAB files containing libraries of Java class files can be downloaded, installed with a CLSID made from a generated GUID (globally unique identifier), accessed by applets, and run *outside* the applet security manager.

Microsoft's Internet Explorer 3.0 supports Digital IDs issued by VeriSign, Inc. Individuals can obtain a Class 1 Digital ID (**http://digitalid.verisign.com/**) that uniquely identifies that individual. Digital IDs are used by client authentication software to verify the identity of parties in a transaction. The Microsoft/VeriSign Digital IDs are compatible with ISO X.509 certificates and PKCS #7 signature blocks.

Microsoft's client authentication support for Digital IDs is built into Internet Explorer 3.0, with plans to integrate support into Windows NT server through Secure Sockets Layer (SSL). The CryptoAPI 2.0 will also support certificates.

ON THE WEB

http://www.microsoft.com/intdev/sdk/   Microsoft ActiveX SDK

http://www.microsoft.com/workshop/java/cab-f.htm   CAB technology

http://www.microsoft.com/intdev/signcode/   How software publishers can use Authenticode technology

http://digitalid.verisign.com/   VeriSign Digital ID Center

http://microsoft.com/intdev/security/misf8-f.htm   Microsoft Authenticode technology

http://www.winzip.com   WinZip by Nico Mak Computing, Inc.

When you begin working with Authenticode and Cabinet, you will need all the documentation you can find. Most of the important information is scattered about in different places and different formats. Table 25.1 lists the files with the primary detailed technical information that you will need to get started.

Table 25.1   Other CAB and ActiveX/Authenticode SDK Must-Read Documentation

File	Description
\CabSDK\README.txt	README for CABinet Development Kit.
\CabSDK\overview.htm	Reducing download times with cabinet files.
\CabSDK\diamond.doc	Diamond: A compression and disk layout tool.
\INetSDK\Readme.txt	Release notes for the Microsoft ActiveX Development Kit.
\INetSDK\bin\Readme.txt	Signing code for download.
\INetSDK\bin\Reg.txt	WinVerifyTrust, root certificates, and wvtston/off.reg.

This chapter uses programming samples to show how code signing tools work. The files for these samples are on the companion CD-ROM. The files are in directories under \msdev\projects\chap25\. The directories and their descriptions are listed in Table 25.2. The samples start out simple and progress step-by-step.

Table 25.2   Contents of \msdev\projects\chap25\ Subdirectories

Directory	Description
Cabinet0	Files shared by other projects.
Cabinet1	Java States applet project packaged in CAB.
Cabinet2	Cabinet1 project packaged in signed CAB.
Cabinet3	Java States Library project in signed CAB.
Cabinet4	Cabinet3 zipped project packaged in signed CAB.
Cabinet5	MyStates project signed applet calls libraries.

Packaging a Java Applet in a CAB File

In this section, we start out by learning how to put Java applet classes into a CAB file. Why is this so important? Because CAB files are the files that get digitally signed. Digitally signed CAB files are what browsers like Internet Explorer 3.0 are designed to detect. When Internet Explorer detects a signed CAB file, it will get permission from the user before installing it. But once installed, the signed code can run outside the applet security manager.

Microsoft has stated its support for the goal of getting rid of anonymous code on the Internet. In the near future, the default settings of most Web browsers will be to deny any unsigned code.

Instead of anonymous code, software publishers and users will execute digitally secured contracts by exchanging digital IDs over the Web. The software publisher warrants the signed and published software. Users obtain secure software automatically only from selected and trusted secure software publishers.

Code signing is part of an exciting beginning for the application of cryptography to products for the global mass market. So let's see what new tools are available to apply this new technology now.

Updating the *States* Applet

In Chapter 21, "Using Visual J++ Debugging Tools," the section "Using Forms" introduces and explains the order.html file. This HTML order form will be used in this chapter to illustrate how to use code signing and its security implications. The order.html file (\msdev\projects\Chap21\Forms\order.html) is a simple form to order chocolate truffles. A simple Java applet, States.class, is called during validation of the entered U.S. states.

The States class uses a list of valid states as a program literal string. The first enhancement to be made to the States class is to have it read a file of states from the *client's* disk drive. A Java applet running within a browser is subject to the applet security rules implemented by the browser. Normally, a Java applet running in a browser can only read from the host from which it was downloaded. This provides a level of security for the user whose browser is constantly downloading anonymous Java applet code. Applet code can be run as an application outside a browser and with none of the constraints of a browser's security manager, or "outside the security sandbox." But an application must be installed by the user who presumably *trusts* the author of the software.

Internet Explorer extends the Java security model to incorporate Java code stored in CAB files that are signed with digital IDs. Java code downloaded in signed CAB can run within a browser, but *outside* the applet security manager. This chapter discusses some of the many ways to configure signed Java classes. This section will first introduce the new States class that is used in the remaining sections of this chapter. The actual signing of the States code will be done in the next section. First, let's see what is new with the States class.

TIP

When running an applet on an HTML page opened through Visual J++'s debugger, the applet runs *without* applet security violations. That is how we can test the modified States class that reads a file on the user's disk without actually signing the code. If the same applet page is opened directly by Internet Explorer, it will fail with a security exception.

The original States class is very simple as shown in Listing 25.1. A static string is initialized with the two-letter abbreviations for 10 U.S. states. The States.isStates method is called to search the list of states.

Listing 25.1 Source of the Original *States* Class
(\msdev\projects\chap21\Forms\States.java)

```
import java.applet.*;
import java.awt.*;

final public class States extends Applet
{
    final static String states = "AL,AK,AR,CA,HA,IO,NJ,NY,WI,WY";
    public States()
    {
    }

    final public boolean isState(String state)
    {
        if(state.length != 2)
            return false;
        String st = new String(state.toUpperCase());
        if(-1 != states.indexOf(st))
            return true;
        return false;
    }
}
```

Listing 25.2 shows the updated States applet class and a new helper class named USStates. This version reads a file containing two-letter U.S. state abbreviations separated by commas. The file name is a file on the *client's* disk drive.

The applet works as follows: A static class initializer is used to create a USStates object and call the USStates.getStates method to obtain the list of states read from the file.

The USStates constructor has a file name as its parameter. The first line of the text file needs to be read and saved in a static String variable named states. The static variable states is returned by the public method getStates. The caller of this method is a VBScript of JavaScript statement.

Because a line of text needs to be read, the DataInputStream class has been chosen because it provides the readLine method. The readLine method reads a line from a stream and returns it as a String.

The DataInputStream class has a constructor that requires an InputStream object, which is provided by the FileInputStream class. The FileInputStream class extends the InputStream class and takes the file name in its constructor.

Listing 25.2 Source of the New *States* Class (\msdev\projects\chap25\Cabinet1\States.java)

```java
import java.applet.*;
import java.io.*;

final public class States extends Applet
{
    static String states;
    static{
        USStates usStates;
        usStates =
            new USStates
            ➥("C:\\msdev\\projects\\chap16\\cabinet0\\statesx.txt");

        states = usStates.getStates();
        if(states == null)
            states = new String("AL,AK,AR,CA,HA,IO,NJ,NY,WI,WY");
    }

    public States()
    {
    }

    final public boolean isState(String state)
    {
        if(state.length() != 2)
            return false;
        String st = new String(state);
        st = st.toUpperCase();
        if(-1 != states.indexOf(st))
            return true;
        return false;
    }
}
```

Part

IV

Ch

25

continues

Listing 25.2 Continued

```
final class USStates
{
    String states;

    public  USStates(String fileName)
    {
        FileInputStream stream;
        try{
            stream = new FileInputStream(fileName);
        }
        catch(FileNotFoundException e){
            return;
        }
        DataInputStream data;
          if(null == (data = new DataInputStream(stream)))
            return;

        try{
            states = data.readLine();
        }
        catch(IOException e){
            states = null;
        }
        try{
            data.close();
        }
        catch(IOException e){
        }
    }
    final public String getStates()
    {
        return states;
    }
}
```

When the `DataInputStream` has successfully been created, the `readLine` method is called to read the first line in the file. The line is saved for later use by the `getStates` method. The contents of the statesx.txt file are shown in Listing 25.3.

The states.txt file contains some state names used for testing applets in this chapter. This file is supposed to be installed on the client's disk when the applet is run.

**Listing 25.3 Valid States Text File
(\msdev\projects\chap25\Cabinet0\Statesx.txt)**

```
WI,CA,XX
```

The new `States` applet is designed to read a file from the client's disk. If you run this applet with a browser, the applet will fail because of a security violation. Figure 25.1 shows the applet after attempting to open it directly from the browser by opening the order1.html file in the Cabinet1 directory. Notice the error message in the status bar at the bottom of the browser window. More information about this security violation is contained in the Java log. The log file for this event is shown in Listing 25.4.

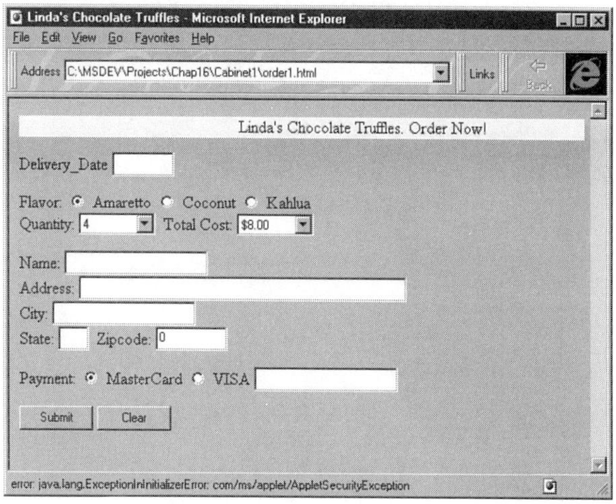

FIG. 25.1

The applet running in order1.html has failed because of a security violation when trying to read a file.

Listing 25.4   The Java Log File Shows the Security Exception Caused by
readLine **(C:\WINDOWS\JAVA\javalog.txt)**

```
*** Security Exception: file.read:C:\msdev\projects\chap16\cabinet0\statesx.txt
***
com.ms.applet.AppletSecurityException: security.file.read:
C:\msdev\projects\chap25\cabinet0\statesx.txt
        at com/ms/applet/AppletSecurity.checkRead
        at com/ms/applet/AppletSecurity.checkRead
        at java/io/FileInputStream.<init>
        at USStates.<init>
        at States.<clinit>
        at java/lang/Class.newInstance
        at com/ms/applet/BrowserAppletFrame.run
        at java/lang/Thread.run
java.lang.ExceptionInInitializerError: com/ms/applet/AppletSecurityException
        at java/lang/Class.newInstance
        at com/ms/applet/BrowserAppletFrame.run
        at java/lang/Thread.run
```

You can still debug this application because Visual J++ does not enforce security rules when an applet is run under the debugger. The Visual J++ configuration settings for the sample Cabinet project have been set to use the order1.html file and the States class for debugging. Figure 25.2 shows the order1.html page running under the debugger. The form has been filled in and the Submit button pressed. The applet has been stopped at a breakpoint set in the isStates method. The Watch window shows the value of the states variable.

T I P   In Figure 25.2, notice the value of the `st` variable being displayed in a pop-up window: `st = {"WI"}`. This pop-up window appears when the cursor is left over a variable name in a source code window when stopped for a breakpoint.

FIG. 25.2

The applet is shown stopped at a breakpoint during initialization.

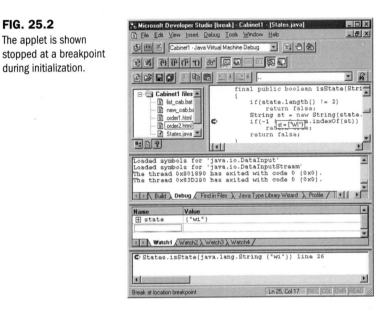

When the applet runs successfully, it will display a message box thanking the user for placing their order (see Figure 25.3). The value of the state entered is validated against the list of states in the statesx.txt file.

FIG. 25.3

The order form running under the debugger is shown filled in and validated.

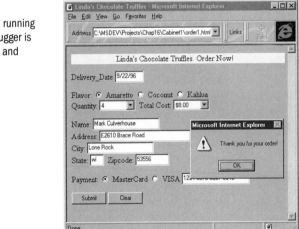

Installing the Cabinet SDK

The next step in allowing the updated States applet to run in a browser without violating security is to put its classes into a CAB file. A CAB or Cabinet file is used for packaging software for distribution. Its use has been extended to support code signing, as well as downloading and installing Java class files on a client machine.

ON THE WEB

The tools used to create a CAB file are contained in Microsoft's *CABinet Development Kit*. The latest version of the CAB SDK is available on the Internet at

http://www.microsoft.com/workshop/java/cab-f.htm

http://www.microsoft.com/windows/software/powertoy.htm   A free extension for Internet Explorer treats CAB files like folders, including dragging files in and out of CABs.

A newsgroup is available for more information from users at:

news://msnews.microsoft.com/microsoft.public.internetexplorer.java

news://msnews.microsoft.com/microsoft.public.internetexplorer.java.cabdevkit

To install the CAB SDK, download the self-extracting cabdevkt.exe file and run it. The files in the CAB SDK are described in Table 25.3.

Part
IV

Ch
25

Table 25.3   List of CABinet SDK Installed Files

File Name	Description
cabarc.exe	Diamond cabinet archive helper tool
README.txt	Read this file before installing
ClassPck.ddf	Diamond Directive File (DDF) template for class files
master.ddf	DDF template for creating download file
master.inf	Template for CAB installation instructions
overview.htm	Reducing download times with cabinet files
outline.gif	Good graphic (not loaded due to bad <img src=> in overview.htm)
diamond.exe	Diamond cabinet builder
diamond.doc	Diamond: A compression and disk layout tool

TIP   The downloaded ActiveX SDK self-extracting activex.exe file contains the \INetSDK\bin\Cabdevkt.exe file. This is the CABinet SDK self-extracting file. It is not executed as part of the ActiveX installation. You can download the CABinet SDK separately from the Internet from **http://www.microsoft.com/workshop/java/cab-f.htm**. This copy may be more up-to-date.

The cabarc.exe program presents a simpler interface than the diamond.exe program. Cabarc.exe is an easy way to create a simple CAB file. Cabarc uses command line options for specifying its options. Cabarc will be used later in this chapter where appropriate. Listing 25.5 shows the parameter usage for the cabarc.exe program. From the commands you see that cabarc.exe can: 1) List a CAB file, 2) create a New CAB file, or 3) extract files from a CAB file.

Listing 25.5   CABinet Archive Program Usage Information

```
Microsoft (R) Cabinet Tool - Version 1.00
Copyright (c) Microsoft Corp 1996. All rights reserved.

Usage: CABARC [<options>] <command> <cabfile> [<filelist...>] [dest_dir]

Commands:
   L   List contents of cabinet (e.g. cabarc l test.cab)
   N   Create new cabinet (e.g. cabarc n test.cab *.c app.mak *.h)
   X   Extract file(s) from cabinet (e.g. cabarc x test.cab foo*.c)

Options:
  -c   Confirm files to be operated on
  -o   When extracting, overwrite without asking for confirmation
  -m   Set compression type [MSZIP | NONE], (default is MSZIP)
  -p   Preserve path names (absolute paths not allowed)
  -P   Strip specified prefix from files when added
  -r   Recurse into subdirectories when adding files (see -p also)
  -s   Reserve space in cabinet for signing (e.g. -s 6144 reserves 6K bytes)
  -i   Set cabinet set ID when creating cabinets (default is 0)
  --   Stop option parsing

Notes
-----
When creating a cabinet, the plus sign (+) may be used as a filename
to force a folder boundary; e.g. cabarc n test.cab *.c test.h + *.bmp

When extracting files to disk, the <dest_dir>, if provided, must end in
a backslash; e.g. cabarc x test.cab bar*.cpp *.h d:\test\

The -P (strip prefix) option can be used to strip out path information
e.g. cabarc -r -p -P myproj\ a test.cab myproj\balloon\*.*
The -P option can be used multiple times to strip out multiple paths
```

The Diamond Cabinet Builder program, diamond.exe (see Listing 25.6), is also used to create CAB files. The .CAB file format is based on Lempel-Ziv compression. Diamond accepts its commands in a Diamond Directive File (*.ddf). The syntax of these directives is defined in "Diamond: A Compression and Disk Layout Tool" (\CabSDK\diamond.doc). There are two sample "template" *.ddf files provided in the CAB SDK: \CabSDK\ClassPck.ddf and \CabSDK\master.ddf. The use of these files is covered later in this chapter when a Java library is built.

The Diamond.exe program is a replacement for the DIANTZ.EXE program.

Listing 25.6   Diamond.exe Cabinet Builder Usage Information

```
Microsoft (R) Diamond Cabinet Builder - Version (32) 1.00.0540 (02/01/96)
Copyright (c) Microsoft Corp 1993-1996. All rights reserved.

DIAMOND [/V[n]] [/D var=value ...] [/L dir] source [destination]
DIAMOND [/V[n]] [/D var=value ...] /F directive_file [...]

   source        File to compress.
   destination   File name to give compressed file.  If omitted, the
                 last character of the source file name is replaced
                 with an underscore (_) and used as the destination.
   /F directives A file with Diamond directives (may be repeated).
   /D var=value  Defines variable with specified value.
   /L dir        Location to place destination (default is current directory).
   /V[n]         Verbosity level (1..3).
```

Archiving Files in a Cabinet File

Internet Explorer 3.0 will run a Java applet and its classes as separately downloaded class files or as a single CAB file that contains the same class files. Besides security implications, CAB files can provide some performance improvements.

Usually opening a file uses many more resources than the actual reading of the file's contents. So if a larger single file can be transferred in the place of many small individual files, a performance gain is very likely. CAB files are also compressed.

Listing 25.7 shows the standard way an applet is placed on an HTML page so that its *.class files are downloaded. Listing 25.8 shows how to specify that the same applet class files are to be downloaded in the single States.cab file. The <APPLET> CODEBASE attribute can also be used for browsers that do not yet support the CABBASE parameter convention.

Listing 25.7   HTML Code to Download Applet's *.class Files
(\msdev\projects\chap25\Cabinet1\order1.html)

```
...
<applet code=States.class id=States>
</applet>
...
```

Listing 25.8   HTML Code to Download Applet's *.class Files in a CAB File
(\msdev\projects\chap25\Cabinet1\order2.html)

```
...
<applet code=States.class id=States>
<param name=cabbase value="States.cab">
</applet>
...
```

Part
IV

Ch
25

To create a CAB file containing the two *.class files in the Cabinet1 project, run the new_cab.bat file (see Listing 25.9). The cabarc program is used to create a simple CAB file named States.cab. If the cabarc command is rerun, it will overwrite the existing States.cab file without warning.

Listing 25.9   Command Used to Create States.cab File (\msdev\projects\chap25\Cabinet1\new_cab.bat)

```
c:\CabSDK\cabarc N States.cab *.class
```

Listing 25.10 shows the output from cabarc when the States.cab file was created.

Listing 25.10   Output from cabarc N(ew) command

```
C:\MSDEV\Projects\Chap25\Cabinet1>c:\CabSDK\cabarc N States.cab *.class

Microsoft (R) Cabinet Tool - Version 1.00
Copyright (c) Microsoft Corp 1996. All rights reserved.

Creating new cabinet 'States.cab':
  -- adding States.class
  -- adding USStates.class

Completed successfully
```

After creating the CAB file, you should list its contents to verify the operation. A batch command file (see Listing 25.11) is provided to list the contents of the States.cab file. The output of the command is shown in Listing 25.12.

Listing 25.11   Command Used to List Contents of a CAB File (\msdev\projects\chap25\Cabinet1\list_cab.bat)

```
c:\CabSDK\cabarc L States.cab
```

Listing 25.12 shows that the size of the CAB file itself is 1,105 bytes. The total size of the two *.class files is 1,982 (956 + 1,026); that represents a 55 percent compression.

Listing 25.12   Output from cabarc L(ist) Command

```
C:\MSDEV\Projects\Chap25\Cabinet1>c:\CabSDK\cabarc L States.cab

Microsoft (R) Cabinet Tool - Version 1.00
Copyright (c) Microsoft Corp 1996. All rights reserved.

Listing of cabinet file 'States.cab' (size 1105):
   2 file(s), 1 folder(s), set ID 0, cabinet #0
```

```
File name                       File size    Date      Time   Attrs
------------------------------  ---------   ----------  --------  ----
States.class                         956  1996/09/11  22:56:14   --
USStates.class                      1026  1996/09/11  22:56:14   --
```

Figure 25.4 shows the order2.html file being opened in Internet Explorer. The order2.html file (see Listing 25.8) invokes the States applet class by downloading the States.cab file. Notice that the status bar in the Internet Explorer window is displaying the message Opening Java Class cabinet: file:/C:/MSDEV/Projects/Chap 25/Cabinet1/States.cab.

Remember to run order2.html from the Visual J++ debugger or the applet will fail with the security violation because the CAB file has not been signed yet. Your Project Settings are probably still set to run order1.html. From the main menu select Build, Settings to display the Project Settings dialog box. In the Debug dialog box, select Browser from the Category combo box. In the Parameters group box make sure the Use Parameters From HTML Page check box is checked, and the HTML Page option is set to order2.html.

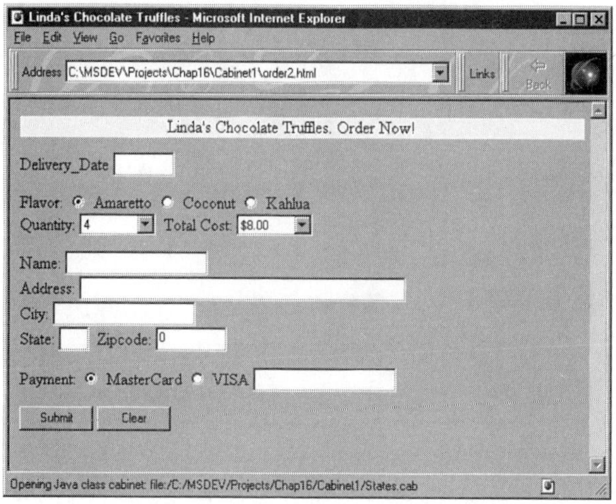

FIG. 25.4
Internet Explorer shows the status of loading the States.cab class file during applet loading.

Digitally Signing a Java Applet

In the previous section, you learned how to package your applet classes in a CAB file for Internet Explorer. Of course, the applet still must be run under the debugger because of security violations. In this section, you will learn how to digitally sign your Java code packaged in a CAB file.

Code signing CAB files is done using the Authenticode tools in Microsoft's ActiveX SDK. Real code signing requires a real digital ID. Real digital IDs must be issued by real certificate authorities like VeriSign, Inc.

Part
IV

Ch
25

Installing Microsoft's Authenticode Technology

The ActiveX Software Development Kit from Microsoft contains the Authenticode utilities used for signing files. The ActiveX SDK is available from Microsoft on the Internet at **http://www.microsoft.com/intdev/sdk/**. For the purposes of this book, the ActiveX SDK was installed in the default directory c:\INetSDK.

The ActiveX SDK files that are used in this chapter are described in Table 25.4. The rest of this section provides an overview of the use of the relevant files listed in Table 25.4.

Table 25.4   List of Authenticode Installed Files from the ActiveX SDK \InetSDK\Bin Directory

File Name	Description
Cert2spc.exe	Makes a test SPC from certificates
Chktrust.exe	Checks the code signing of a file
Dumpcert.exe	Dumps the contents of a certificate
Makecert.exe	Makes a test X.509 certificate
Pesigmgr.exe	Checks to see if file is signed
Readme.txt	Must Read! Signing code for download
Reg.txt	Explains how WinVerifyTrust uses root certificates
Root.cer	Tests "root" certificate
Signcode.exe	Signs files using SPC
Wvtstoff.reg	Regedit file to turn off WinVerifyTrust test mode
Wvtston.reg	Regedit file to turn on WinVerifyTrust test mode

TIP   The downloaded ActiveX SDK self-extracting activex.exe file contains the \INetSDK\bin\Cabdevkt.exe file. This is the CABinet SDK self-extracting file. It is not executed as part of the ActiveX installation. You can download the CABinet SDK separately from the Internet from **http://www.microsoft.com/workshop/java/cab-f.htm**. This copy may be more up-to-date.

The code signing done in the following sections will require a Software Publishing Certificate (SPC). An SPC requires an X.509 certificate. The MakeCert.exe program (see Listing 25.13) can make an X.509 certificate for testing purposes. Normally, a Class 2 or Class 3 digital ID is required, but a test digital ID can also be used. The output from MakeCert.exe is a *.cer file.

Listing 25.13   MakeCert.exe Usage Display Produced by Running MakeCert with no Options

```
Usage: MAKECERT [options] outputCertificateFile
    -u:subjectKey      subject's CryptoAPI keyset name
    -U:subjectCertFile certificate with existing subject public key to use
    -k:subjectKeyFile  subject's .pvk file
    -n:name            certificate subject X500 name (eg: "CN=Fred Dews")
    -d:displayname     certificate subject display name
    -s:issuerKey(File) loc'n of issuer's key; default to test root key
    -i:issuerCertFile     ... issuer's certificate
    -#:serialNumber    2^31 max; default is good: is guaranteed unique
    -l:policyLink      link to SPC Agency policy info (a URL, etc)
    -I                 cert explicitly allowed for individual software pub use
    -C                 cert explicitly allowed for commercial software pub use
    -C:f               ... and the publisher met the minimal financial criteria
    -S:session         use enrollment session
    -P:purpose         enrollment purpose (default CodeSigning)
    -x:providerName    CryptoAPI provider to use
    -y:nProviderType   CryptoAPI provider type to use
    -K:keyspec         'S' signature key (default), 'E' key-exchange key
    -B:dateStart       start of validity period; defaults to 'now'
    -D:nMonths         duration of valdity period
    -E:dateEnd         end of validity period; defaults to 2039
    -h:numChildren     max height of the tree below this cert
    -t:types           cert type: either/both of 'E'nd-entity; 'C'ert auth'ty
    -g                 create a glue certificate
    -r                 create a self-signed certificate
    -m                 use MD5 hash algorithm (default)
    -a                 use SHA1 hash algorithm
    -N                 include netscape client auth extension

  * For the -u and -k options, if the indicated subject's key (key pair)
    cannot, be found then it is created. For -u, it is created in the Crypto
    API keyset; for -k, it is created in a file.

    Alternatively, the subject public key can be obtained from an already
    existing certificate using the -U option. -U changes the default subject
    name to be the same as that of the indicated cert. Use -g in addition to
    make a glue certificate.

  * A self signed certificate can be created using the -r option
```

The Cert2Spc.exe program (see Listing 25.14) inputs a series of *.cer files and produces a single *.spc file. Cert2Spc.exe encapsulates multiple X.509 certificates into a signed PKCS#7 object which is the SPC.

Listing 25.14   Cert2Spc.exe Usage Display

```
Usage: CERT2SPC [-k] cert1.cer ... certN.cer certBundle.spc
  or   CERT2SPC     cert1.cer ... certN.cer -S:session
```

The dumpcert.exe program (Listing 25.15) is used to list the contents of certificates. A certFile can be a *.cer or a *.spc file.

Listing 25.15   DumpCert.exe Usage Display

```
usage: DumpCert certFile(s)
```

The SignCode.exe program (see Listing 25.16) is used to sign files with an SPC and a private key.

Listing 25.16   SignCode.exe Usage Display

```
Syntax: SignCode
        -prog programFile
        -spc credentialsFile
        -pvk privateKeyFile/keysetName
        -name opusName
        -info opusInfo
        -gui
        -nocerts
        -provider crytoProviderName
        -providerType n
        -commercial ¦ -individual (default)
        -sha ¦ -md5 (default)
```

The ChkTrust.exe program (see Listing 25.17) is used to check the validity of the signing of a file. You should always specify the option for the subject type. The options -J should be used when file-name is *.class, and -C should be used when file-name is *.cab.

Listing 25.17   ChkTrust.exe Usage Display Produced by Running ChkTrust with no Options

```
Usage:   CHKTRUST [-options] file-name
Options:
 -I   subject type is PE executable image file (default)
 -J   subject type is Java class
 -C   subject type is Cabinet file
 -N   no UI in 'bad trust' case
```

WinVerifyTrust is the Win32 API used to verify the trust of certificates. By default, Internet Explorer considers the "test" certificates made by MakeCert.exe to be invalid. But for testing, a mechanism is provided to allow these "test" certificates to be recognized as certificates. So as to not totally bypass security, the word "VOID" is displayed on the certificate bitmap used in any user interface having to do with certificates.

Listing 25.18 shows Wvtston.reg. When Wvtston.reg is installed, the WinVerifyTrust test mode is turned *on* for validating "test" certificates. When Wvtstoff.reg (see Listing 25.19) is installed, WinVerifyTrust test mode is turned *off*.

Listing 25.18   Wvtston.reg Contents

```
REGEDIT4

[HKEY_CURRENT_USER\Software\Microsoft\Windows\CurrentVersion\WinTrust\Trust
Providers\Software Publishing]
"State"=dword:000000a0
```

Listing 25.19   Wvtstoff.reg Contents

```
REGEDIT4

[HKEY_CURRENT_USER\Software\Microsoft\Windows\CurrentVersion\WinTrust\Trust
Providers\Software Publishing]
"State"=dword:00000000
```

The Pesigmgr.exe program (see Listing 25.20) is used to manage certificates in a signed file.

Listing 25.20   Pesigmgr.exe Usage Display Produced by Running Pesigmgr with no Options

```
Usage: PESIGMGR [switches] image-name
           [-?] display this message
           [-l] list the certificates in an image
           [-a:<Filename>] add a certificate file to an image
           [-r:<index>]    remove certificate <index> from an image
           [-s:<Filename>] used with -r to save the removed certificate
           [-t:<CertType>] used with -a to specify the type of the certificate
           where CertType may be X509 or PKCS7 [default is X509]
```

Part

IV

Ch

25

Making a Software Publishing Certificate (SPC)

In this section, you will make a Software Publishing Certificate (SPC) that will be used to sign all code in the rest of this chapter. Listing 25.21 shows the contents of the Cabinet2\new_cert.bat file. The MakeCert.exe program is used to create cabinet0\LoneRock.cer, a X.509 certificate.

When you have your own digital ID, it will be in a *.pvk file. MakeCert.exe will create a test private key and save it in a *.pvk file if you use the -k option instead of the -u option. Then this file would be pointed to when using the SignCode.exe program.

Listing 25.21 Make Certificate Command for Applet CAB File (\msdev\projects\chap25\Cabinet2\new_cert.bat)

```
c:\INetSDK\bin\makecert -u:LoneRockKey -n:CN=LoneRock ..\Cabinet0\LoneRock.cer
```

After the Cabinet0\LoneRock.cer file is created, the Cabinet2\list_cer.bat file can be used to display its contents. The output from running this command can be seen in Listing 25.22.

Listing 25.22 Output from the DumpCert Utility for the LoneRock.cer Certificate

```
C:\MSDEV\Projects\Chap25\Cabinet2>c:\INetSDK\bin\dumpcert
➥..\Cabinet0\LoneRock.cer

Issuer:            "CN=Root Agency;"
Serial number:     62 A5 D8 7A A5 0C D0 11 88 5F 44 45 53 54
Subject:           "CN=LoneRock;"
Not before:        1996/09/12 13:56:49 (local time)
Not after:         2039/12/31 18:59:59 (local time)
Public key:        30 5C 30 0D 06 09 2A 86 48 86 F7 0D 01 01 01 05
                   00 03 4B 00 30 48 02 41 00 DA ED 28 11 33 0F D7
                   4D 8E 20 45 49 B5 27 BE 29 63 CA A8 24 4A 03 2D
                   DF 62 B9 7B E4 BD DA F9 94 EE 93 25 26 6A F7 85
                   D7 8A E8 FC 81 0F 43 AD 25 BE C0 3D 59 A1 3B A5
                   C8 82 52 B9 A2 F2 03 38 4D 02 03 01 00 01
Public key hash: F7 0D 8A 66 C1 CD 56 0A 6E 39 1C 70 66 DC 75 81
  auth key id:   digest:  12 E4 09 2D 06 1D 1D 4F 00 8D 61 21 DC 16 64 63
                 iss/ser: "CN=Root Agency;"
                          F4 35 5C AA D4 B8 CF 11 8A 64 00 AA 00 6C 37 06
  comm'l use:    yes (implicit)
  ind'l use:     yes (implicit)
  extensions:    2.5.29.1
Parent:          iss/ser: "CN=Root Agency;"
                          F4 35 5C AA D4 B8 CF 11 8A 64 00 AA 00 6C 37 06
                 - signature ok
```

Listing 25.23 shows the results of running Cabinet2\list_root.bat. It lists the contents of the Root.cer file provided with the ActiveX SDK and Authenticode.

Listing 25.23 Output from the DumpCert Utility for the Test Root.cer Certificate

```
C:\MSDEV\Projects\Chap25\Cabinet2>c:\INetSDK\bin\dumpcert
c:\INetSDK\bin\Root.cer

Issuer:            "CN=Root Agency;"
Serial number:     F4 35 5C AA D4 B8 CF 11 8A 64 00 AA 00 6C 37 06
Subject:           "CN=Root Agency;"
Not before:        1996/05/28 17:02:59 (local time)
```

```
Not after:        2039/12/31 18:59:59 (local time)
Public key:       30 5B 30 0D 06 09 2A 86 48 86 F7 0D 01 01 01 05
                  00 03 4A 00 30 47 02 40 81 55 22 B9 8A A4 6F ED
                  D6 E7 D9 66 0F 55 BC D7 CD D5 BC 4E 40 02 21 A2
                  B1 F7 87 30 85 5E D2 F2 44 B9 DC 9B 75 B6 FB 46
                  5F 42 B6 9D 23 36 0B DE 54 0F CD BD 1F 99 2A 10
                  58 11 CB 40 CB B5 A7 41 02 03 01 00 01
Public key hash: 12 E4 09 2D 06 1D 1D 4F 00 8D 61 21 DC 16 64 63
   common name:   For Testing Purposes Only Sample Software Publishing
                  ➥Credentials Agency
   auth key id:   digest:  12 E4 09 2D 06 1D 1D 4F 00 8D 61 21 DC 16 64 63
                  iss/ser: "CN=Root Agency;"
                           F4 35 5C AA D4 B8 CF 11 8A 64 00 AA 00 6C 37 06
   comm'l use:    yes (implicit)
   ind'l use:     yes (implicit)
   extensions:    2.5.4.3
                  2.5.29.1
Parent:           self - signature ok
```

The Root.cer and the LoneRock.cer files are input to Cert2SPC.exe which creates the SPC file Cabinet\0\LoneRock.spc. Listing 25.24 shows the contents of the Cabinet2\new_spc.bat file which is used to create the new SPC.

Listing 25.24   Make SPC Command for Applet CAB File (\msdev\projects\chap25\Cabinet2\new_spc.bat)

```
c:\INetSDK\bin\cert2spc c:\INetSDK\bin\Root.cer ..\Cabinet0\LoneRock.cer
..\Cabinet0\LoneRock.spc
```

Listing 25.25 shows the output from running the Cabinet2\list_spc.bat file which lists the contents of LoneRock.spc.

Listing 25.25   Listing of Contents of LoneRock.spc

```
C:\MSDEV\Projects\Chap25\Cabinet2>c:\INetSDK\bin\dumpcert
➥..\Cabinet0\LoneRock.spc

Issuer:           "CN=Root Agency;"
Serial number:    62 A5 D8 7A A5 0C D0 11 88 5F 44 45 53 54
Subject:          "CN=LoneRock;"
Not before:       1996/09/12 13:56:49 (local time)
Not after:        2039/12/31 18:59:59 (local time)
Public key:       30 5C 30 0D 06 09 2A 86 48 86 F7 0D 01 01 01 05
                  00 03 4B 00 30 48 02 41 00 DA ED 28 11 33 0F D7
                  4D 8E 20 45 49 B5 27 BE 29 63 CA A8 24 4A 03 2D
                  DF 62 B9 7B E4 BD DA F9 94 EE 93 25 26 6A F7 85
                  D7 8A E8 FC 81 0F 43 AD 25 BE C0 3D 59 A1 3B A5
                  C8 82 52 B9 A2 F2 03 38 4D 02 03 01 00 01
```

continues

Listing 25.25 Continued

```
Public key hash: F7 0D 8A 66 C1 CD 56 0A 6E 39 1C 70 66 DC 75 81
    auth key id:  digest:  12 E4 09 2D 06 1D 1D 4F 00 8D 61 21 DC 16 64 63
                  iss/ser: "CN=Root Agency;"
                           F4 35 5C AA D4 B8 CF 11 8A 64 00 AA 00 6C 37 06
    comm'l use:   yes (implicit)
    ind'l use:    yes (implicit)
    extensions:   2.5.29.1
    Parent:       iss/ser: "CN=Root Agency;"
                           F4 35 5C AA D4 B8 CF 11 8A 64 00 AA 00 6C 37 06
                  - signature ok

 - - - - - - - - - -
Issuer:           "CN=Root Agency;"
Serial number:    F4 35 5C AA D4 B8 CF 11 8A 64 00 AA 00 6C 37 06
Subject:          "CN=Root Agency;"
Not before:       1996/05/28 17:02:59 (local time)
Not after:        2039/12/31 18:59:59 (local time)
Public key:       30 5B 30 0D 06 09 2A 86 48 86 F7 0D 01 01 01 05
                  00 03 4A 00 30 47 02 40 81 55 22 B9 8A A4 6F ED
                  D6 E7 D9 66 0F 55 BC D7 CD D5 BC 4E 40 02 21 A2
                  B1 F7 87 30 85 5E D2 F2 44 B9 DC 9B 75 B6 FB 46
                  5F 42 B6 9D 23 36 0B DE 54 0F CD BD 1F 99 2A 10
                  58 11 CB 40 CB B5 A7 41 02 03 01 00 01
Public key hash: 12 E4 09 2D 06 1D 1D 4F 00 8D 61 21 DC 16 64 63
    common name:  For Testing Purposes Only Sample Software Publishing
                  ➥Credentials Agency
    auth key id:  digest:  12 E4 09 2D 06 1D 1D 4F 00 8D 61 21 DC 16 64 63
                  iss/ser: "CN=Root Agency;"
                           F4 35 5C AA D4 B8 CF 11 8A 64 00 AA 00 6C 37 06
    comm'l use:   yes (implicit)
    ind'l use:    yes (implicit)
    extensions:   2.5.4.3
                  2.5.29.1
    Parent:       self - signature ok
```

Signing a Java Class with an SPC

The States.cab file that will be signed in this section will be created in the Cabinet2 directory using the *.class files previously built in the Cabinet1 directory. Listing 25.26 shows the command that is used to create the new CAB file. The difference between this use of cabarc.exe and the previous use (see Listing 25.9) is the -s 6144 parameter. This parameter allows 6,144 bytes to be reserved for the signing information (6,144 = 6K).

Listing 25.26 Creating a New CAB File from Cabinet1*.class Files (\msdev\projects\chap25\Cabinet2\new_cab.bat)

```
c:\CabSDK\cabarc -s 6144 N States.cab ..\cabinet1\*.class
```

The new Cabinet2\States.cab file is now ready to be signed. Listing 25.27 shows the command used to sign the States.cab file. Notice the -name parameter. Its value will be seen displayed in certificate dialogs. The Web URL will be used to create an HTML link for the -name value.

**Listing 25.27 Signing the States.cab File
(\msdev\projects\chap25\Cabinet2\sign_cab.bat)**

```
c:\INetSDK\bin\signcode -prog States.cab -spc ..\Cabinet0\LoneRock.spc -pvk
➥LoneRockKey -name "States Class File-1" -info http://www.execpc.com/~lonerock/
```

The States.cab file is now signed, but it should be verified that the signing has been performed properly. Listing 25.28 shows the command used to test the signed CAB file. Figure 25.5 shows the results of running ChkTrust.exe with States.cab.

**Listing 25.28 Checking the Signing of the States.cab File
(\msdev\projects\chap25\Cabinet2\chk_sign.bat)**

```
c:\INetSDK\bin\chktrust -c States.cab
```

Part

IV

Ch

25

Figure 25.5 shows the ChkTrust.exe program running. The Authenticode Security Technology dialog shows that the States.cab file has been signed but it does verify properly. The reason is that real certificates were not used to sign States.cab; instead only a test certificate was used. The Wvtston.reg file has not been installed yet to tell WinVerifyTrust to use test mode.

FIG. 25.5

The ChkTrust.exe program checks signed Java CAB files (run with Wvtstoff.reg in effect).

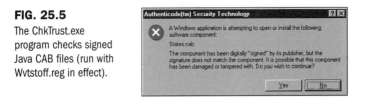

Listing 25.29 shows the command to turn on test mode certificate verification. Figure 25.6 shows the message box from the regedit.exe program after installing Wvtston.reg.

**Listing 25.29 Installing the Wvtston.reg File to Turn on WinVerifyTrust
"Test" Mode (\msdev\projects\chap25\Cabinet2\wvtston.bat)**

```
regedit \inetsdk\bin\Wvtston.reg
```

FIG. 25.6

Internet Explorer shows the Authenticode Security Technology dialog box during signed-applet loading.

Registry Editor

Information in \inetsdk\bin\Wvtston.reg has been successfully entered into the registry.

OK

After installing Wvtston.reg, you can try the ChkTrust utility again. Figure 25.7 shows the result of running the Cabinet2\chk_sign.bat file (see Listing 25.28). The SPC certificate shows information from the X.509 certificate. The underlined text of the certificate's name is a link to the publisher's Web site. If the cursor is held over the link name for a few seconds, a floating window displays the URL. The same dialog is displayed when a signed file needs to be opened for execution.

Notice the check boxes at the bottom of the dialog box. If the LoneRock check box is checked when the Yes button is clicked, then LoneRock's SPC will be installed as a trusted software publisher whose packages would be installed without prompting. If the Any Publisher With Credentials From check box is checked when Yes is clicked, then the authority that certified that software publisher will be installed. That means no prompting will occur for any software by any publisher certified by that authority.

TIP

If you do check the Any Publisher With Credentials From check box and press Yes, then any "test" signed code files will not cause prompting for installation anymore. You can remove this certificate by using the security options dialog in Internet Explorer. However, you may encounter a bug that does not allow the test certificate to be deleted by the Internet Explorer security options dialog. If you encounter this bug, then you can always use Regedit.exe to delete the Registry entry for the Root Agency. The Windows Registry entry created when the Root.cer credentials agency certificate was installed is:

[HKEY_CURRENT_USER\Software\Microsoft\Windows\CurrentVersion\WinTrust\Trust Providers\Software Publishing\Trust Database\1]

"ipippnjeaipiegabfinbdkckeacoemhd pedffmkknelimpbbikgeaakkaagmdhag"="For Testing Purposes Only Sample Software Publishing Credentials Agency"

The "garbage" characters you see above may be related to the bug described above.

Because the testing with ChkTrust.exe above showed that the file is properly signed, the next step is to open the Cabinet2\order.html file (see Listing 25.30) using Internet Explorer (*not* under the Visual J++ debugger) to check that security is working properly and that the applet can load and execute properly. You can use the Windows Explorer to double-click the Cabinet2\order.html file to open it. Figure 25.8 shows the page as it starts. When the States.cab file is opened by the browser, it detects that the file is signed. Because neither LoneRock nor the Root Agency is registered with WinTrust, the Authenticode dialog is displayed to allow the user to decide to run this signed code. Every time the browser opens this page with its signed applet, the same Authenticode dialog will be displayed. This will occur until the software publisher certificate or the issuer of credentials certificate is installed and matches the certificate of the States.cab file.

The handling of signed Java class libraries is different than the handling of signed Java applets. Java class libraries are discussed next.

FIG. 25.7

This is the result of running the Cabinet2/chk_sign.bat file.

Listing 25.30   Applet Tag and Parameters from Cabinet2\order.html (\msdev\projects\chap25\Cabinet2\order.html)

```
...
<applet code=States.class id=States>
<PARAM NAME="cabbase" value="States.cab">
</applet>
...
```

FIG. 25.8

The Cabinet2\order.html running under Internet Explorer (run with Wvtston.reg in effect).

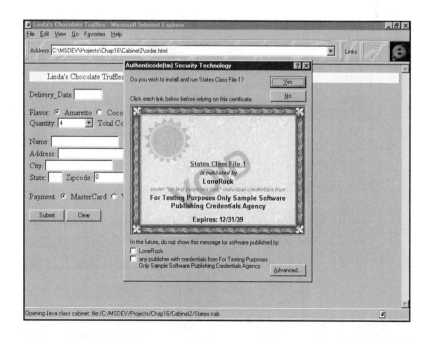

Digitally Signing a Java Class Library

In the previous section, you learned to build and digitally sign a CAB file containing an applet's classes. This applet can then run outside the normal applet security sandbox, thus being able to deliver more functionality to the clients of your Web site. Remember that each time the signed applet is run, the applet and its code must be downloaded, the user must accept the signed applet file, and the CAB file must be installed.

In this section, you will learn how to package Java classes as an installable library. A single library can be downloaded and installed once on the client's machine. When it's installed, any number of different HTML pages can use the library classes without having to download and install them each time they are used.

A Java class library is represented by a CLSDID (GUID) and a CAB file specified with an HTML <OBJECT> tag (see Listing 25.31). When the <OBJECT> tag is processed by a browser, a check of the Registry is made for the CLSID. If it is not found, then an associated CAB file specified in the CODEBASE attribute is downloaded and installed. Using a class library is a two-step process. The library must be installed before it is first referenced by an HTML page. It cannot be initially installed and used for the first time on the same page.

There are two ways a Java class library can be installed on the client's machine, as a Lib or as a Trustlib. This section will demonstrate the Lib method. The class files from a signed Java class library packaged with the Lib option are installed to \windows\java\lib. Any necessary subdirectories are created under \windows\java\lib to match the Java package structure of the library code. Because \windows\java\lib is in the ClassPath, and because the library's class files are visible in their proper subdirectories under \windows\java\lib, classes installed are available for loading by other classes.

There are different ways to reference classes within a signed class library. The simplest way is to reference an applet class from an <APPLET> tag as shown in Listing 25.32. The <APPLET> tag simply references the qualified class name.

The <OBJECT> tag above the <APPLET> tag is not actually necessary because the <OBJECT> must have been downloaded and installed previously. The <OBJECT> tag does at least associate the class library with the class specified in the <APPLET> tag. Also, if the user tried the page again, it would work because the library was installed when the page was first opened. However, a Web site should be designed to install libraries before they are used.

The Cabinet3\order0.html file (see Listing 25.31) consists solely of an <OBJECT> tag, which causes the LoneRock Utility Class Library to be downloaded and installed. Note the CLSID specified with the CLASSID attribute. A version number can be appended to the CODEBASE file name. The LRUtil.cab file is signed, so when it is first downloaded and opened, the Authenticode dialog will be presented to the user to ask acceptance to install the class library.

Listing 25.31 The HTML Page to Load and Install the LRUtil Java Class Library (\msdev\projects\chap25\Cabinet3\order0.html)

```
<HTML>

<OBJECT CLASSID="clsid:869A2AA4-07E5-11d0-885F-444553540000"
CODEBASE="LRUtil.cab#Version=1,0,0,0">
</OBJECT>

</HTML>
```

After order0.html above has been successfully run, the next page Cabinet3\order1.html (see Listing 25.32) can be run. Cabinet3\order1.html is the same chocolate truffle order form used throughout this chapter except for a change to the <APPLET> tag and the addition of the <OBJECT> tag.

Listing 25.32 The <Object> and <Applet> Tags to Use the LRUtil Java Class Library (\msdev\projects\chap25\Cabinet3\order1.html)

```
...
<OBJECT CLASSID="clsid:869A2AA4-07E5-11d0-885F-444553540000"
CODEBASE="LRUtil.cab">
</OBJECT>

<applet code=lonerock.util.States.class id=States>
</applet>
...
```

Part
IV

Ch

25

The CLASSID value used in Listing 25.32 was generated by a program called GUIDGEN.exe, which comes with Visual J++. It can be invoked from the Visual J++ Tools menu by selecting the Create GUID item. A universally unique value will be created and copied to the Clipboard in different formats. Each time the program is run, a different value will be generated; any number can be made. Figure 25.9 shows the Create GUID dialog box displayed by GUIDGEN.exe. The fourth format is the proper format for use as a class ID for your Java libraries. A value was obtained by the author and used in the examples in this chapter.

FIG. 25.9
The Create GUID dialog box copies generated globally unique identifier values to the Clipboard in various formats.

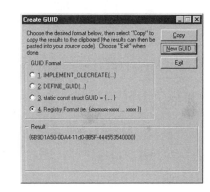

As mentioned, the sample class library used in this section is the LoneRock utility package. It consists of the two Java classes, `States` and `USStates`. The class library is packaged in a single signed file named LRUtil.cab. The contents of the LRUtil.cab file is not simply the two *.class files as was the case with a signed applet.

A downloadable Java class library using the `Lib` method requires that the CAB file specified on an <OBJECT> CODECASE attribute contain two files, one CAB file containing the *.class files and a second file named master.inf. The master.inf file contains information on how the library is installed. In this example, LRUtil.cab contains the two files: States.cab and master.inf.

Updating the States Applet to a Package

Before describing how to build the LRUtil.cab file and its contents, the master.inf and States.cab files, a small change needs to be made to the Java source code. The source code used to create the LRUtil Java class library will be the same States.java file from the Cabinet1 project. In fact, the only change to the source code is to add a `package` statement. Listing 25.33 shows the new Cabinet3\States.java file. A single line was inserted at the top: `package lonerock.util;`. This allows the proper class to be found by the class loader. It also causes a lonerock\util subdirectory to be created when the project is built from Visual J++. (However, the *.class files are not copied there by Visual J++. The files are copied later by the Cabinet3\new_lib.bat file.) The project should be rebuilt after adding the `package` statement to States.Java.

Listing 25.33 lonerock.util Package for *States* and *USStates* Classes (\msdev\projects\chap25\Cabinet3\States.java)

```
package lonerock.util;
import java.applet.*;
import java.io.*;

final public class States extends Applet
{
    static String states;
    static{
        USStates usStates;
        usStates =
            new USStates
            ➡("C:\\msdev\\projects\\chap25\\cabinet0\\statesy.txt");

        states = usStates.getStates();
        if(states == null)
            states = new String("AL,AK,AR,CA,HA,IO,NJ,NY,WI,WY");
    }

    public States()
    {
    }

    final public boolean isState(String state)
    {
```

```
            if(state.length() != 2)
                return false;
            String st = new String(state);
            st = st.toUpperCase();
            if(-1 != states.indexOf(st))
                return true;
            return false;
        }
    }

final class USStates
{
    String states;

    public  USStates(String fileName)
    {
        FileInputStream stream;
        try{
            stream = new FileInputStream(fileName);
        }
        catch(FileNotFoundException e){
            return;
        }
        DataInputStream data;
          if(null == (data = new DataInputStream(stream)))
            return;

        try{
            states = data.readLine();
        }
        catch(IOException e){
            states = null;
        }
        try{
            data.close();
        }
        catch(IOException e){
        }
    }
    final public String getStates()
    {
        return states;
    }
}
```

Building a Class Library with Class Files

After rebuilding the Cabinet3 project, the States.class and USStates.class files in the Cabinet3 project directory are the correct lonerock.util.States and lonerock.util.USStates classes to be used in the LRUtil library. These two files need to be added to a new CAB file named States.cab; States.cab will later be added to the LRUtil.cab file. Listing 25.34 shows the new_lib.bat file which is used to build the LRUtil.cab file. The build process consists of the following steps:

■ Before running the new_lib.bat file, the *.class files must exist as a result of building the Visual J++ project; and the master.inf, master.ddf, and ClassPck.ddf files must be edited.

■ The first line of new_lib.bat copies the *.class files to the lonerock\util subdirectory in preparation for the next command.

■ The second command calls the diamond.exe program to use the Diamond directives in the ClassPck.ddf file. This causes diamond to create the States.cab file containing the *.class files. The ClassPck.ddf file is an edited version of the "template" \CabSDK\ClassPck.ddf file shipped with the CABinet SDK.

■ The third command calls the diamond.exe program to use the Diamond directives in the master.ddf file. This causes diamond to create the LRUtil.cab file containing the States.cab and master.inf files. The master.ddf file is an edited version of the "template" \CabSDK\master.ddf file shipped with the CABinet SDK.

■ The last step is to call SignCode.exe to sign the LRUtil.cab file.

Listing 25.34 The Commands to Build and Sign the LRUtil.cab Java Class Library File (\msdev\projects\chap25\Cabinet3\new_lib.bat)

```
rem move class files to their directories
copy *.class lonerock\util
del *.class

c:\CabSDK\diamond /f classpck.ddf

c:\CabSDK\diamond /f master.ddf

c:\INetSDK\bin\signcode -prog LRUtil.cab -spc ..\Cabinet0\LoneRock.spc -pvk
➥LoneRockKey -name "LoneRock Utility Package 1,0,0,0" -info http://
➥www.execpc.com/~lonerock/
```

The ClassPck.ddf file is used by Diamond.exe to build the States.cab file. You will remember that the CABArc.exe program was used to build the CAB file for the States applet classes. The ClassPck.ddf file is an edited version of \CabSDK\ClassPck.ddf that comes with the CABinet SDK. The entire edited file is shown in Listing 25.35. Because the file creates States.cab, it might have been better named States.ddf.

The changes made to ClassPck.ddf to build the States.cab include:

■ The first change is the .Set CabinetNameTemplate= States.cab statement. This specifies the name of the Cabinet file to be created by the directives.

■ The next change is the .Set DestinationDir=lonerock\util statement. This specifies the directory structure for the library when it is installed. The next two statements list the name of the Java class files including their directory structure.

You may have noticed the references to using a .ZIP file to package your library; this topic is covered in detail in the next section.

Listing 25.35 The Diamond Directives File to Build States.cab
(\msdev\projects\chap25\Cabinet3\ClassPck.ddf)

```
; Template for ClassPack.ddf
; Copyright 1996, Microsoft Corporation
; Version 1.1, 30 July 1996

; This file lists all of the files that you want to place on
; a user's machine. It should contain all of your classes organized
; in the correct directory hierarchy, specified by your package
; names.

; Leave this.

.OPTION EXPLICIT

;*********************************
; Insert the name for your cab file here. You will need to
; use this name in both master.ddf and your inf, so remember your
; choice.
;
;(1).Set CabinetNameTemplate=CabFileName.cab
.Set CabinetNameTemplate=States.cab
;*********************************

; Leave these settings.

.Set DiskDirectoryTemplate=
.Set Cabinet=on
.Set Compress=on
.Set MaxCabinetSize=0
.Set MaxDiskSize=CDROM

; ***********************
; This is the main section. You will list the names of all
; of your classes here, with their full virtual pathnames.
; You also need to specify each destination directory before you
; list the files in that directory. We highly recommend that you
; make all of your packages start with a name that should be unique
; to you, so that you have your own subdirectory on the user's machine
; and don't have to worry about having your files written over.
;
; For example, say that your classes are
; Vendor.Applet.class
; Vendor.Content.ContentContainer.class
; Vendor.Content.ContentHelper.class
; Vendor.Util.Loader.class
;
; Then this file should read (don't forget to change this!)

;(2).Set DestinationDir=Vendor
;(2)Vendor\Applet.class
```

continues

Listing 25.35   Continued

```
;(2).Set DestinationDir=Vendor\Content
;(2)Vendor\Content\ContentContainer.class
;(2)Vendor\Content\ContentHelper.class

;(2).Set DestinationDir=Vendor\Util
;(2)Vendor\Util\Loader.class

.Set DestinationDir=lonerock\util
lonerock\util\States.class
lonerock\util\USStates.class

; Alternatively, if you decide to use a .ZIP file (as explained in the
; README), you just need to list one file here, without subdirectories.
; Something like

;(2)vendor.zip

; will be fine. Be sure to make your name unique, so that other vendors
; won't overwrite it.

; That's all—you're finished!

; ***********************
```

The master.ddf file is used by Diamond.exe to build the LRUtil.cab file. The master.ddf file is an edited version of \CabSDK\master.ddf that comes with the CABinet SDK. The entire edited file is shown in Listing 25.36. Because the file creates LRUtil.cab, it might have been better named LRUtil.ddf, but the original name was used to point out that the CabSDK template files are the starting point for learning about this complicated process.

The changes made to master.ddf to build the LRUtil.cab include:

- The first change is the .Set CabinetNameTemplate=LRUtil.cab statement. This specifies the name of the Cabinet file to be created by the directives. LRUtil.cab is the file that will eventually be downloaded.

- The next change is the insertion of the name of the States.cab file to be included in the LRUtil.cab file.

- Notice the .Set ReservePerCabinetSize=6144 statement. This causes 6K of space to be reserved in the LRUtil.cab file for digital signing information. Note that the LRUtil.cab file gets signed, but the States.cab file created above does *not* get signed.

- Note the name of the master.inf file to be included in the LRUtil.cab file.

Listing 25.36   The Diamond Directives File to Build LRUtil.cab
(\msdev\projects\chap25\Cabinet3\master.ddf)

```
; Template for master.ddf
; Copyright 1996, Microsoft Corporation
```

```
; Version 1.00, 16 July 1996

; Leave this setting.

.OPTION EXPLICIT

;********************************
; Insert the name for the file that you will have users download
; (i.e. the one you will call via the <OBJECT> tag). This can
; be anything you would like. Make sure to leave the .cab extension.
;
;(1).Set CabinetNameTemplate=DownloadFile.cab
.Set CabinetNameTemplate=LRUtil.cab
;********************************

; Leave these settings

.Set DiskDirectoryTemplate=
.Set Cabinet=on
.Set Compress=on
.Set MaxCabinetSize=0
.Set MaxDiskSize=CDROM

; Since you will want to consider code-signing your cab files,
; to make downloading safer and to provide you with the advantages
; coming with code signing, you will want to include the line below.
; You can comment it out if you choose not to use code-signing; however,
; if you don't, many people will not download your package.
; Depending on your certification company, the size of this may get smaller.

.Set ReservePerCabinetSize=6144

; **********************
; In this section, you will list your files.

; If these files are not located in the local directory, you must
; provide a full or relative pathname.

; The first file is the name of the first CAB you created with the
; ClassPack.ddf template.
; Its name was set in line 19 of the template, which began
; .Set CabinetNameTemplate=
; If you chose to use an uncompressed .ZIP instead, list that here.

;(2)CabFileName.cab
States.cab

; The second file is the name of the .inf you created with the
; master.inf template.
; This is the name you saved the file as and the name you included
; on the InfFile= line.

master.inf
```

continues

Listing 25.36 Continued

```
; Any DLL's or other native code you've decided to install should
; be listed here, one per line.


; That's all—you're finished!

; ************************
;
```

The previous step created the LRUtil.cab file which contains States.cab and master.inf. Listing 25.37 shows the contents of master.inf. This file is used after the LRUtil.cab file is downloaded. Master.inf contains information on how to install the files that make up the library.

Master.inf is an edited version of \CabSRC\master.inf which comes with the CABinet SDK. The changes made to master.inf to define the installation of LRUtil.cab include:

- Each change is a modification of an existing line from \CabSDK\master.inf. Each of the five changes has ; (n) inserted in front of the original line where n is the change number. The modified line is below the commented original.

- The first change (1) is the run= statement. This is the statement that is used to install the States.cab file on the client's machine.

- Change (2) is the ClassId= statement which identifies the unique CLSID that is used as the class ID for the LRUtil class library. Don't forget the braces.

- Change (3) is the PackageName= statement. This value should probably match the value specified for the -info parameter of the SignCode command shown in Listing 25.34.

- Change (4) sets the InstalledVersion number of the CLSID. The downloading of Internet components supports object versioning.

- Change (5) sets the InstalledVersion Path value. This value is used to test for the existence of the CLSID installation. If this file exists, it is assumed that the entire package is installed. If this file is missing, the object will be downloaded and reinstalled.

- There are no more changes. Notice that the default master.inf values assume a Lib installation as opposed to TrustLib.

Listing 25.37 The Installation File to Install LRUtil.cab (\msdev\projects\chap25\Cabinet3\master.inf)

```
; Template for master.inf
; Copyright 1996, Microsoft Corporation
; Version 1.1, 26 July 1996

; This inf file controls the user's installation of your Java
; classes. It is important to get all of this correct.
; This is separated into sections; be sure to make the
; necessary changes in each one.
```

```
[hook1]

; In this line, replace CabFileName.cab with the CAB file name
; you chose when filling in the template for ClassPck.ddf,
; at .Set CabinetNameTemplate=

;(1)run=extrac32.exe /e /a /y /l %49000% CabFileName.cab
run=extrac32.exe /e /a /y /l %49000% States.cab

[hook2]

; Change the name of master.inf to the name you are assigning this
; file. Leave the second line alone.

InfFile=master.inf
InfSection=RegistryData


[Strings]
; Running uuidgen in the SDK generates the ClassId you need to fill
; in here. This classId also goes in the OBJECT tag.
; Don't forget the set braces!

;(2)ClassId="{99999999-9999-9999-9999-999999999999}"
ClassId="{869A2AA4-07E5-11d0-885F-444553540000}"

; Put the name by which your packages should be referred to
; (i.e. "Bob's Text Viewer") here.

;(3)PackageName="name"
PackageName="LoneRock Utility Package 1,0,0,0"
[AddRegSection]

; Leave this line.
HKLM,"SOFTWARE\Classes\CLSID\%ClassId%",,,"%PackageName%"

; Replace <aa...> with the version number (like 1,0,0,1) of this
; version of your library. This is so that when you want to update
; your libraries, you can change the version rather then the classId
; and the problems that go with that. If the version number here
; and in the OBJECT tag match the version already stored on the
; user's machine, it will not download the classes again, which
; also saves time and energy.

;(4)HKLM,"SOFTWARE\Classes\CLSID\%ClassId%\InstalledVersion",,,"aa,bb,cc,dd"
HKLM,"SOFTWARE\Classes\CLSID\%ClassId%\InstalledVersion",,,"1,0,0,0"

; Here, replace <filename> with the name of one of the class files in
; your package, including the virtual path (specified in classpck.ddf)
; to that file. This will make sure that the classes exist on the
; user's system; if they don't, they will be downloaded, regardless
; of version numbers.
```

Part
IV

Ch
25

continues

Listing 25.37 Continued

```
;(5)HKLM,"Software\Classes\CLSID\%ClassId%\InstalledVersion","Path",,"%49000%\
➥<filename>"
HKLM,"Software\Classes\CLSID\%ClassId%\InstalledVersion","Path",,"%49000%\lonerock\
➥util\States.class"

; Leave these keys alone.

HKLM,"SOFTWARE\Classes\CLSID\%ClassId%\InProcServer32",,,"%11%\MSJAVA.DLL"
HKLM,"SOFTWARE\Classes\CLSID\%ClassId%\InProcServer32","NoJavaClass",,""
HKLM,"SOFTWARE\Classes\CLSID\%ClassId%\InProcServer32","ThreadingModel",,"Both"


; Under most circumstances, you should leave the next two keys alone.
; Only change them if
; 1) You have not expanded the classes into their subdirectories on
; the user's machine, but have instead stored them in an uncompressed
; .ZIP file; in that case, change the appropriate value
; to "%49000%\<ZipFileName>".
;
; 2) You have decided to install the files onto another, hard-coded
; directory of your choice. This is not recommended, for you will
; clutter up the user's directories and have to make other changes.
; If you do so, though, change the appropriate value to the absolute
; pathname to that directory, and change it in the run= line above.
; Also note that the "visible in scope" problem explained in the README
; for .ZIP files also applies here.
;
; If you use one of these, you will use exactly one.
; The difference between Lib and TrustLib is described in the README.

HKLM,"SOFTWARE\Classes\CLSID\%ClassId%\InProcServer32","Lib",,"%49000%"
;HKLM,"SOFTWARE\Classes\CLSID\%ClassId%\InProcServer32","TrustLib",,"%49000%"


; ************************************************************
; THE NEXT SECTION IS TO BE CHANGED IF YOU WANT TO INSTALL
; NATIVE CODE (DLLS, ETC.) ON THE USER'S MACHINE. PLEASE BE
; RESPONSIBLE ABOUT THIS USE.
; ************************************************************
;

; This template assumes you are installing all items into the
; <windir>\system directory, and that they are all in 8.3 form.
; If you need something more complex, update the INF appropriately.

; Leave these three lines.
[RegistryData]
AddReg=AddRegSection
CustomDestination=MyCustomDestination

;; If you are installing native code, you will want to uncomment all
;; the lines in the remainder of this section, except for the ones
;; that are descriptive (and have two semicolons).

; CopyFiles=OtherFiles
```

```
;[DestinationDirs]
;OtherFiles=11

;[OtherFiles]
;; List the name of each file (delimited by returns) here.
;; Just list the local name—no need for paths, etc. Example:
;; foo1.dll,,,32
;; foo2.dll,,,32

;[SourceDisksFiles]
;; For each name listed in the above section, you will want to put
;; <filename>=1 on this list. So it would look like
;; foo1.dll=1
;; foo2.dll=1

;[SourceDisksNames]
;1=%PackageName%,"",0


; ****************************************************************
; END OF NATIVE CODE SECTION
; ****************************************************************

[PackageDestination49000]

; This value should only change if you have decided to place your
; classes in the TrustedClasspath. In that case, you
; will change "LibsDirectory" to "TrustedLibsDirectory".
; The reasons to do this are explained in the README.

"HKLM","Software\Microsoft\Java VM","LibsDirectory","",""

; ************************************************
; THE REMAINDER OF THIS FILE SHOULD NOT BE CHANGED.
; ************************************************

[Setup Hooks]
hook1=hook1
hook2=hook2

[Version]
signature="$CHICAGO$"
AdvancedINF=2.0


[DefaultInstall]
CustomDestination=MyCustomDestination
AddReg=AddRegSection

[MyCustomDestination]
49000=PackageDestination49000,23
```

Part

IV

Ch

25

The files ClassPck.ddf, master.ddf, and master.inf have been prepared and reviewed. It is time to run new_lib.bat (see Listing 25.34) to create the LRUtil.cab file. After creating LRUtil.cab, it should be reviewed. Listing 25.38 shows the results of running Cabinet3\list_cabs.bat. This bat file lists the contents of States.cab and LRUtil.cab, which were created by new_lib.bat. The States.cab file along with the master.inf file are within LRUtil.cab. Notice the lonerock\util\ prefix of the file names in the States.cab file. These are necessary.

Listing 25.38   The Contents of the Two CAB Files Are Listed Using
\msdev\projects\chap25\Cabinet3\list_cabs.bat

```
C:\MSDEV\Projects\Chap25\Cabinet3>c:\CabSDK\cabarc L LRUtil.cab

Microsoft (R) Cabinet Tool - Version 1.00
Copyright (c) Microsoft Corp 1996. All rights reserved.

Listing of cabinet file 'LRUtil.cab' (size 9969):
   2 file(s), 1 folder(s), set ID 1983, cabinet #0

File name                     File size    Date      Time    Attrs
--------------------------    ---------- ---------- -------- -----
States.cab                          1151 1996/09/14 13:13:16  ---
master.inf                          5860 1996/09/13 20:34:08  ---


C:\MSDEV\Projects\Chap25\Cabinet3>c:\CabSDK\cabarc L States.cab

Microsoft (R) Cabinet Tool - Version 1.00
Copyright (c) Microsoft Corp 1996. All rights reserved.

Listing of cabinet file 'States.cab' (size 1151):
   2 file(s), 1 folder(s), set ID 5566, cabinet #0

File name                     File size    Date      Time    Attrs
--------------------------    ---------- ---------- -------- -----
lonerock\util\States.class          1012 1996/09/13 15:02:32  ---
lonerock\util\USStates.class        1054 1996/09/13 15:02:32  ---
```

The contents look correct. The Cabinet3\chk_sign.bat file can be used to check the signing of LRUtil.cab. The new library can be installed using the chk_sign.bat by clicking Yes, or the Cabinet3\order0.html file can be opened using Internet Explorer. The same Authenticode dialog will be displayed the first time the <OBJECT> tag for the LRUtil.cab file is referenced.

After the LRUtil.cab file has been installed, the States.class and USStates.class files (from the States.cab file within the LRUtil.cab file) are copied to the \windows\java\lib\lonerock\util\ directory. In addition, some Registry entries were created. Listing 25.39 shows the file created using regedit.exe to export the LRUtil entries.

Listing 25.39 The Exported Registry Entries Created When LRUtil.cab Was Installed

```
REGEDIT4

[HKEY_LOCAL_MACHINE\SOFTWARE\Classes\CLSID\{869A2AA4-07E5-11d0-885F-
➥444553540000}]
@="LoneRock Utility Package 1,0,0,0"

[HKEY_LOCAL_MACHINE\SOFTWARE\Classes\CLSID\{869A2AA4-07E5-11d0-885F-
444553540000}\InstalledVersion]
@="1,0,0,0"
"Path"="c:\\windows\\java\\lib\\lonerock\\util\\States.class"

[HKEY_LOCAL_MACHINE\SOFTWARE\Classes\CLSID\{869A2AA4-07E5-11d0-885F-
444553540000}\InProcServer32]
@="c:\\windows\\SYSTEM\\MSJAVA.DLL"
"NoJavaClass"=""
"ThreadingModel"="Both"
"Lib"="c:\\windows\\java\\lib"
```

Now that the LoneRock utility package has been installed, the Cabinet3\order1.html file can be opened and run from Internet Explorer.

Building a Class Library with Zipped Class Files

In the previous section, you learned how to build a Java class library that installed its *.class files as separate files in subdirectories created as necessary for the package structure. This configuration can result in a large number of individual files and directories on a client's machine.

An alternative configuration is supported that uses a single *.zip file of uncompressed *.class files. In the last section, LRUtil.cab contained master.inf and States.cab; States.cab contained all of the individual *.class files. Using the *.zip file option, the LRUtil.cab file still contains a master.inf and a States.cab file. However, the States.cab file contains only a single *.zip file. In this section, the *.zip file is named States.zip. States.zip contains the uncompressed *.class files. The Cabinet3 project *.class files will be used unchanged. The files for this section's examples are in the Cabinet4 directory. Listing 25.40 shows the Cabinet4\new_lib.bat file that will be used to create the "zip" Java class library. The "zip" build process consists of the following steps:

■ Before running the new_lib.bat file, the Cabinet3\lonerock\util*.class files must exist from previously building the Visual J++ project, the new States.zip file must exist, and the master.inf, master.ddf and ClassPck.ddf files must be edited.

■ The first line of new_lib.bat is a reminder to make sure the States.zip file is prepared properly.

Part
IV

Ch
25

- The second command calls the Diamond.exe program to use the Diamond directives in the ClassPck.ddf file. This causes Diamond to create the States.cab file containing the States.zip file. The ClassPck.ddf file is an edited version of the "template" \CabSDK\ClassPck.ddf file shipped with the CABinet SDK.

- The third command calls the Diamond.exe program to use the Diamond directives in the master.ddf file. This causes Diamond to create the LRUtil.cab file containing the States.cab and master.inf files. The master.ddf file is an edited version of the "template" \CabSDK\master.ddf file shipped with the CABinet SDK.

- The last step is to call SignCode.exe to sign the LRUtil.cab file.

Listing 25.40 The Commands to Build and Sign the LRUtil.cab Java Class Library File with States.zip (\msdev\projects\chap25\Cabinet4\new_lib.bat)

```
pause zip Cabinet3 *.classes into LRUtil.zip uncompressed zip file first!

c:\CabSDK\diamond /f classpck.ddf

c:\CabSDK\diamond /f master.ddf

c:\INetSDK\bin\signcode -prog LRUtil.cab -spc ..\Cabinet0\LoneRock.spc -pvk
➥LoneRockKey -name "LoneRock Utility Package 1,0,0,0" -info http://
➥www.execpc.com/~lonerock/
```

The ClassPck.ddf (see Listing 25.41) is used to create the States.cab file. Instead of setting the DestinationDir and listing the *.class file names with their directories as done in Listing 25.35 in the previous section, only the States.zip file needs to be specified.

Listing 25.41 The Bottom of the Diamond Directives File to Build the "zip" States.cab (\msdev\projects\chap25\Cabinet4\ClassPck.ddf)

```
...
; Then this file should read (don't forget to change this!)

;(2).Set DestinationDir=Vendor
;(2)Vendor\Applet.class

;(2).Set DestinationDir=Vendor\Content
;(2)Vendor\Content\ContentContainer.class
;(2)Vendor\Content\ContentHelper.class

;(2).Set DestinationDir=Vendor\Util
;(2)Vendor\Util\Loader.class

; Alternatively, if you decide to use a .ZIP file (as explained in the
; README), you just need to list one file here, without subdirectories.
; Something like
```

```
;(2)vendor.zip
States.zip

; will be fine. Be sure to make your name unique, so that other vendors
; won't overwrite it.

; That's all—you're finished!

; ************************
```

The master.ddf file is used to create the LRUtil.cab file. There are no changes from Cabinet3 to Cabinet4 to support the "zip" version of the library. LRUtil.cab still contains master.inf and States.cab.

The master.inf file specifies how to install the class library on the client's machine. Listing 25.42 shows the changes made to the previous version of master.inf (refer to Listing 25.37). The "Path" entry is used to test if the library object is already installed. The previous example listed the lonerock\util\States.class file. With the zipped version of a library, the only file that will exist on the client's machine to test for is the States.zip file. The Lib entry specifies that the *.class files are in the States.zip file. The path names for the *.class files saved in the States.zip file are significant. They determine the directory structure for the Java package classes.

Listing 25.42   Differences from Cabinet3\master (\msdev\projects\chap25\Cabinet4\master.inf)

```
...
HKLM,"Software\Classes\CLSID\%ClassId%\InstalledVersion","Path",,"%49000%\States.zip"
...
;(6)HKLM,"SOFTWARE\Classes\CLSID\%ClassId%\InProcServer32","Lib",,"%49000%"
HKLM,"SOFTWARE\Classes\CLSID\%ClassId%\InProcServer32","Lib",,"%49000%\States.zip"
...
```

The States.zip file must exist before running Cabinet4\new_lib.bat. The zip program used for this section is WinZip32.exe, version 6.1. WinZip is a shareware program available on the Internet at **http://www.winzip.com**. The important points about the States.zip file is that it is created by a program that supports *long names*, that the files are *not* compressed, and that the file also contains *the correct path names* for the Java package class files. Figure 25.10 shows the WinZip Add dialog box used to create the States.zip file in the Cabinet4 directory. The Cabinet3\lonerock\util*.class files were used unchanged to create States.zip. Notice that the File name control contains *.class for the files to be added from the Cabinet3 project directory. The States.class and USStates.class files are in the lonerock\util directory to match the Java package statement in the Java source file States.java. Note that the Compression list box has None selected, and the Recurse Folders check box is checked. The Add With Wildcards button should be clicked to add the *.class files to the Cabinet\4\States.zip file.

FIG. 25.10

The WinZip compression tool's Add files dialog box is used to create States.zip.

Before running Cabinet4\new_lib.bat, verify that your States.zip file is correctly built. Figure 25.11 shows the WinZip32 program displaying the contents of the States.zip file created previously. Make sure all the classes are in the zip file. Make sure that the path names are included, and that they match the Java package naming conventions!

FIG. 25.11

The WinZip compression tool's main window shows the files in States.zip.

Cabinet4\new_lib.bat (refer to Listing 25.40) can now be run to create the States.cab and LRUtil.cab files and to sign the LRUtil.cab file. The output from running new_lib.bat is seen in Listing 25.43.

Listing 25.43   The Output from Running Cabinet4\new_lib.bat

```
C:\MSDEV\Projects\Chap25\Cabinet4>pause zip Cabinet3 *.classes into LRUtil.zip
uncompressed zip file first!
Press any key to continue . . .

C:\MSDEV\Projects\Chap25\Cabinet4>c:\CabSDK\diamond /f classpck.ddf
Microsoft (R) Diamond Cabinet Builder - Version (32) 1.00.0540 (02/01/96)
Copyright (c) Microsoft Corp 1993-1996. All rights reserved.
2,348 bytes in 1 files
Total files:            1
Bytes before:       2,348
Bytes after:        1,107
After/Before:          47.15% compression
```

```
Time:                    0.16 seconds ( 0 hr  0 min  0.16 sec)
Throughput:              14.33 Kb/second

C:\MSDEV\Projects\Chap25\Cabinet4>
C:\MSDEV\Projects\Chap25\Cabinet4>c:\CabSDK\diamond /f master.ddf
Microsoft (R) Diamond Cabinet Builder - Version (32) 1.00.0540 (02/01/96)
Copyright (c) Microsoft Corp 1993-1996. All rights reserved.
7,118 bytes in 2 files
Total files:             2
Bytes before:            7,118
Bytes after:             3,809
After/Before:            53.51% compression
Time:                    0.16 seconds ( 0 hr  0 min  0.16 sec)
Throughput:              43.44 Kb/second

C:\MSDEV\Projects\Chap25\Cabinet4>c:\INetSDK\bin\signcode -prog LRUtil.cab -spc
➥..\Cabinet0\LoneRock.spc -pvk LoneRockKey -name "LoneRock Utility Package
➥1,0,0,0" -info http://www.execpc.com/~lonerock/

C:\MSDEV\Projects\Chap25\Cabinet4>
```

After LRUtil.cab has been created and signed, its contents can be verified by running the Cabinet4\list_cabs.bat file (see Listing 25.44 for the output).

Listing 25.44   The Listing of Contents of LRUtil.cab and States.cab from Running Cabinet4\list_cabs.bat

```
C:\MSDEV\Projects\Chap25\Cabinet4>c:\CabSDK\cabarc L LRUtil.cab

Microsoft (R) Cabinet Tool - Version 1.00
Copyright (c) Microsoft Corp 1996. All rights reserved.

Listing of cabinet file 'LRUtil.cab' (size 10063):
   2 file(s), 1 folder(s), set ID 1983, cabinet #0

File name                        File size   Date       Time     Attrs
-----------------------------    ---------   --------   -------  -----
States.cab                            1186   1996/09/14 14:55:38  ---
master.inf                            5932   1996/09/14 12:57:20  ---


C:\MSDEV\Projects\Chap25\Cabinet4>c:\CabSDK\cabarc L States.cab

Microsoft (R) Cabinet Tool - Version 1.00
Copyright (c) Microsoft Corp 1996. All rights reserved.

Listing of cabinet file 'States.cab' (size 1186):
   1 file(s), 1 folder(s), set ID 1013, cabinet #0

File name                        File size   Date       Time     Attrs
-----------------------------    ---------   --------   -------  -----
States.zip                            2348   1996/09/14 14:55:22  ---
```

Part
IV

Ch
25

Before testing the new "zip" version of the LRUtil.cab class library, you should remove the previous version if it is still installed. All the examples in this chapter use the same CLSID for the different versions of the LRUtil.cab class libraries. To completely remove the <OBJECT> from the client machine, the Registry entry found by searching for 869A2AA4-07E5-11d0-885F-444553540000 should be deleted. In addition, the \windows\java\lib\lonerock\util*.class files or the \windows\java\lib\States.zip file should be deleted.

Run Cabinet4\order0.html to initially install the new library. You should see the Authenticode dialog appear. Click Yes to install the new library. If you did not see the Authenticode dialog, then the old version may not have been removed. Or the new_lib.bat file was not run or failed.

After opening order0.html to install the library, open Cabinet4\order1.html to run the applet that uses the lonerock.util.States.class. You will not see the Authenticode dialog when you run order1.html because the LRUtil.cab library was already installed.

Calling a Signed Java Class Library

In the last section, Cabinet4\order1.html uses the installed LRUtil.cab signed library. The <OBJECT> and <APPLET> tags are shown here:

```
...
<OBJECT CLASSID="clsid:869A2AA4-07E5-11d0-885F-444553540000"
CODEBASE="LRUtil.cab#Version=1,0,0,0">
</OBJECT>

<applet code=lonerock.util.States.class id=States>
</applet>
...
```

The lonerock.util.States class extends the java.applet.Applet class. An HTML page can reference the lonerock.util.States class from an <APPLET> tag without requiring any further security authorization checks. This is because it is assumed that the software publisher did not allow anything destructive to occur by running the applet.

However, what if some other applet code is written that calls methods directly in the LRUtil.cab class library? This applet could use a different combination of calls and do some damage. Is this a security hole? Not really, because if a new applet was written that called methods in the LRUtil.cab library, then that applet would have to be signed and accepted by the client as well before it could run outside the security sandbox with the LRUtil.cab library classes.

To demonstrate this, the Cabinet5 project consists of MyStates.java, which is an applet class that "embeds" or "wraps" a lonerock.util.States object. Listing 25.45 shows MyStates.java.

Notice that a static initializer is used to create a lonerock.util.States object and save it. When the MyStates.isState method is called, it simply calls the lonerock.util.States.isState method.

The fourth statement is an import lonerock.* statement. This brings in the class definitions in the *installed* LRUtil.cab library. If the LRUtil.cab library was not installed at the time of the project build, then `MyStates.java` could not be compiled because the `lonerock.util.States` class would not be defined.

Listing 25.45 The Source of the *MyStates* Applet Class (\msdev\projects\chap25\cabinet5\MyStates.java)

```java
import java.applet.*;
import java.awt.*;
import java.io.*;
import lonerock.*;

final public class MyStates extends Applet
{
    static lonerock.util.States states;
    static{
        states = new lonerock.util.States();
    }
    public MyStates()
    {
    }

    final public boolean isState(String state)
    {
        return states.isState(state);
    }
}
```

After the project is built, the MyStates.class file is created. Before signing the `MyStates` class in a CAB file, open the Cabinet5\order3.html page. Listing 25.46 shows the <OBJECT> and <APPLET> tags from order3.html. The <OBJECT> tag's CODEBASE attribute is an absolute reference to the Cabinet4\LRUtil.cab file, i.e., the "zip" version. The <APPLET> tag references the MyStates.class file directly. You should expect that this applet would fail when opened by Internet Explorer.

Listing 25.46 The <OBJECT> and <APPLET> Tags from Cabinet5\order3.html

```
...
<OBJECT CLASSID="clsid:869A2AA4-07E5-11d0-885F-444553540000"
CODEBASE="c:\msdev\projects\chap25\cabinet3\LRUtil.cab#Version=1,0,0,0">
</OBJECT>

<applet code=MyStates.class id=States>
</applet>
...
```

Listing 25.47 shows the Javalog.txt file after opening order3.html. As explained, one applet cannot call another signed class unless that applet is also signed. The library code actually ran, but within the security sandbox. So a file-read violation occurred to stop the applet.

Listing 25.47   The \windows\java\javalog.txt Contents After the MyStates Security Violation

```
*** Security Exception: file.read:C:\msdev\projects\chap25\cabinet0\statesy.txt
***
com.ms.applet.AppletSecurityException: security.file.read:
C:\msdev\projects\chap25\cabinet0\statesy.txt
        at com/ms/applet/AppletSecurity.checkRead
        at com/ms/applet/AppletSecurity.checkRead
        at java/io/FileInputStream.<init>
        at lonerock/util/USStates.<init>
        at lonerock/util/States.<clinit>
        at java/lang/ClassLoader.findSystemClass
        at com/ms/applet/AppletClassLoader.loadClass
        at java/lang/ClassLoader.loadClassInternal
        at MyStates.<clinit>
        at java/lang/Class.newInstance
        at com/ms/applet/BrowserAppletFrame.run
        at java/lang/Thread.run
java.io.FileNotFoundException:
\C:\MSDEV\Projects\Chap25\Cabinet5\lonerock\util\States.class
        at java/io/FileInputStream.<init>
        at sun/net/www/protocol/file/FileURLConnection.connect
        at sun/net/www/protocol/file/FileURLConnection.getInputStream
        at com/ms/applet/AppletClassLoader.loadClass
        at com/ms/applet/AppletClassLoader.findClass
        at com/ms/applet/AppletClassLoader.loadClass
        at java/lang/ClassLoader.loadClassInternal
        at MyStates.<clinit>
        at java/lang/Class.newInstance
        at com/ms/applet/BrowserAppletFrame.run
        at java/lang/Thread.run
java.io.FileNotFoundException:
\C:\MSDEV\Projects\Chap25\Cabinet5\lonerock\util\States.class
        at java/io/FileInputStream.<init>
        at sun/net/www/protocol/file/FileURLConnection.connect
        at sun/net/www/protocol/file/FileURLConnection.getInputStream
        at com/ms/applet/AppletClassLoader.loadClass
        at com/ms/applet/AppletClassLoader.findClass
        at com/ms/applet/AppletClassLoader.loadClass
        at java/lang/ClassLoader.loadClassInternal
        at MyStates.<clinit>
        at java/lang/Class.newInstance
        at com/ms/applet/BrowserAppletFrame.run
        at java/lang/Thread.run
java.lang.ExceptionInInitializerError: java/lang/ClassNotFoundException
        at java/lang/Class.newInstance
        at com/ms/applet/BrowserAppletFrame.run
        at java/lang/Thread.run
```

Next, the MyStates.cab file is created, signed, and tested to verify that a signed applet can call a signed library. Listing 25.48 shows Cabinet5\new_app.bat. The first command calls cabarc.exe to create a CAB file containing the MyStates.class file. The next command calls signcode.exe to sign the MyStates.cab file.

Listing 25.48 The Commands to Build the MyStates Signed CAB File (\msdev\projects\chap25\cabinet5\new_app.bat)

```
c:\CabSDK\cabarc -s 6144 -p n MyStates.cab *.class

c:\INetSDK\bin\signcode -pvk LoneRockKey -spc ..\Cabinet0\LoneRock.spc -prog
MyStates.cab -name "My States Class File" -info http://www.execpc.com/~lonerock/
```

After running new_app.bat you can test the MyStates.cab file by opening Cabinet5\order4.html. Listing 25.49 shows the <OBJECT> and <APPLET> tags from the order4.html file. Now the <APPLET> tag has the CABBASE parameter which points to the MyStates.cab signed file. Now when order4.html is opened, it will display an Authenticode dialog for the MyStates applet (see Figure 25.12). If Yes is clicked to run MyStates, then the applet will run successfully.

Listing 25.49   The <OBJECT> and <APPLET> Tags from Cabinet5\order4.html

```
...
<OBJECT CLASSID="clsid:869A2AA4-07E5-11d0-885F-444553540000"
CODEBASE="c:\msdev\projects\chap25\cabinet4\LRUtil.cab#Version=1,0,0,0">
</OBJECT>

<applet code=MyStates.class id=States>
<PARAM NAME="cabbase" value="MyStates.cab">
</applet>
...
```

FIG. 25.12

The MyStates applet opening in Internet Explorer causes the Authenticode dialog box to be displayed.

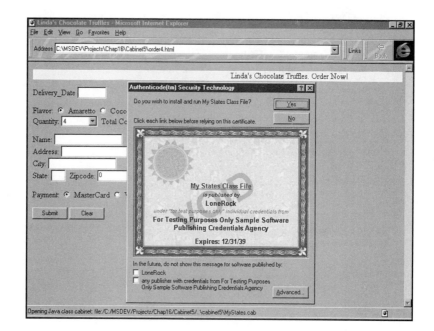

One last word about using "zip" libraries. Because the directory structure and even the class files for a "zip" library are all stored in a zip file on the client's machine, these Java classes are not in "scope" (not visible to Java). Therefore, even though the "zip" library is installed, its classes are not visible until the browser has been told to load an <OBJECT> tag that references that library. The "zip" library classes are only visible in that same browser session after the <OBJECT> tag for the library has been processed. If you exit the browser, start it again, and try to load order4.html above without the <OBJECT> tag specified, the page will fail initialization because the class would not be found (see Listing 25.50).

Listing 25.50   The Contents of JavaLog.txt After Trying to Run Applet Without Loading "zip" Library in Same Browser Session

```
java.lang.ExceptionInInitializerError: java/lang/ClassNotFoundException
        at java/lang/Class.newInstance
        at com/ms/applet/BrowserAppletFrame.run
        at java/lang/Thread.run
```

From Here...

In this chapter, you have been introduced to the CABinet SDK and the Authenticode technology for code signing. Several different detailed examples have been presented which show how to apply CABinet and Authenticode technology to Java classes. Running secure Java applets from a browser page outside the security sandbox represents a significant step forward for deploying a new generation of enhanced Java components. There are still more important related topics ahead such as:

■ See Chapter 26, "Creating an ActiveX Object with Java," to find out how Java classes can also be used to create ActiveX COM objects.

Creating an ActiveX Object with Java

by Mark Culverhouse

ActiveX components can be implemented using Java. ActiveX components can be used by programs written in other languages such as Visual Basic and C++. Java offers advantages over C++ as a language for developing ActiveX components, including portability of compiled code. In this chapter, you will learn how to use an existing ActiveX component from a Visual Basic and a Visual C++ program. Also, you will learn to create your own ActiveX component using Java. A Visual C++ program is created to test the new Java ActiveX component. ■

Creating an ActiveX component with Java

See the benefits of Java for ActiveX developers.

Using ODL to define a COM interface for the ActiveX component

Discover how the Object Definition Language can be used to initially define the ActiveX component.

Writing a Java class that implements an ActiveX component

Learn how to use various utility programs to define a Java class to implement a COM component.

Registering a Java ActiveX component

ActiveX components written in Java are accessible by clients' applications through the JavaReg utility.

Calling an ActiveX component from a C++ program

Explore the step-by-step process of building a C++ program that calls ActiveX components.

Using the *COMCallingJava* Sample

Visual J++ comes with a sample Java project called `COMCallingJava`. The `COMCallingJava` project illustrates how a simple ActiveX (COM) Automation server component can be implemented using the Java language. The new ActiveX component can then be used by any Automation controller application, such as Visual Basic.

This section will lead you through the installation, building, and testing of the `COMCallingJava` sample. Then, you will create a Visual C++ program that uses the installed ActiveX component.

This project consists of a single Java file named euclid.java. The euclid.java file contains one Java class named `CEuclid`, which implements a Java `interface` named `IGCD`. The IGCD interface implements one Java method named `GCD`.

Another file in the project is euclid.odl, which contains ODL statements defining a type library for the MkTypLib.exe or MIDL.exe utilities. The type library created from euclid.odl is used to define and register the `CEuclid` ActiveX component for use by clients. The type library defines how the Java classes, interfaces, and methods are mapped to the ActiveX classes, interfaces, and methods.

A compiled Visual Basic program, VBDriver.exe is provided to test the use of the `CEuclid` component. The source of the VBDriver.exe program is also provided.

Installing the *COMCallingJava* Sample

Installing the `COMCallingJava` sample consists of the following steps:

- Install the sample project files from the Visual J++ CD-ROM.
- Run mk_tlb.bat to make a type library.
- Use Visual J++ to build the project Java source code.
- Run reg_tlb.bat to register the COM class.
- Run VBDriver.exe to test the installation.

The first step is to install and build the COMCallingJava sample project. Insert your Visual J++ CD-ROM and start Visual J++. Select the "Visual J++ Books Online" title from the InfoViewer toolbar. Use the InfoView dialog of the Project Workspace window to expand the Samples/ Microsoft Samples topics. Double-click the COMUsingJava: Implementing a COM Object in Java item to display the InfoViewer Topic window. Click the radio button to display the Sample Application dialog box. Click the Copy All radio button to display the Copy dialog box. Navigate to the directory where you want the sample project files installed or accept the default, \msdev\samples\microsoft\comcallingjava\, and click OK. You will be prompted to create the new directories if they do not exist. After the files are copied, close the Copy All dialog box by clicking the Close button.

Use the File, Open Workspace command to open the project file, \msdev\samples\microsoft\ comcallingjava\comcallingjava.mdp. Use the Explorer to open the readme.html file. This file explains the project and how to build it. Building the project requires running two sets of batch commands—one before building the project and one after. The COMCallingJava sample project contains a single batch file, registereuclid.bat. The readme.html page describes what commands to use, but only provides registereuclid.bat to run as the last step.

This section describes the commands you can use. Two batch files are provided on the CD-ROM that comes with this book. First copy these two files, mk_tlb.bat and reg_tlb.bat, from the \msdev\projects\chap26\parts1\ directory on the companion CD-ROM to the COMCallingJava directory.

The next step is to run mk_tlb.bat (see Listing 26.1). This file has commands to create a type library and to convert the type library to create Java descriptions of the ActiveX(COM) component. Before running mk_tlb.bat, you may need to make some updates. The first line puts the Visual J++ /msdev/bin directory in front of the current path. If your path does not already include this directory, make sure the directory and drive match those on your system. If your path is already set up properly, just delete or comment out the first line. Use Explorer to double-click the mk_tlb.bat file in the project directory to run it.

Listing 26.1 The ODL File Is Used to Create a Type Library Using the Commands in mk_tlb.bat (\msdev\projects\chap26\parts1\mk_tlb.bat)

```
set path=d:\msdev\bin\;%path%
mktyplib euclid.odl /nocpp /h euclid.h
javatlb euclid.tlb
```

Listing 26.2 shows the output from running mk_tlb.bat. The MkTypLib.exe program creates the type library file, euclid.tlb, in the project directory. MkTypLib.exe also creates a header file named euclid.h. This header file will be used later in this section to call the CEuclid component from the C++ language. The JavaTLB.exe program creates a directory named euclid under c:\windows\java\trustlib. In the euclid directory are two files, CEuclid.class and IGCD.class. These class files describe the Java class and interface that implement the ActiveX (COM) component. Also, notice in the output the statement `import euclid.*;`. This statement is in the Java source file that implements the ActiveX component, euclid.java. By including this import statement, the implementation of the Java class is verified against the definition of the COM component interface. Note that the actual Java bytecodes are *not* in these files.

Part
IV
Ch
26

Listing 26.2   The Output from Running mk_tlb.bat

```
D:\MSDEV\samples\microsoft\comcallingjava>mktyplib euclid.odl /nocpp /h euclid.h

Microsoft (R) Type Library Generator  Version 2.03.3027
Copyright (C) Microsoft Corp. 1993-1995.  All rights reserved.

Successfully generated type library 'euclid.tlb'.

D:\MSDEV\samples\microsoft\comcallingjava>javatlb euclid.tlb
Microsoft (R) Visual J++ Java Typelib Conversion Utility Version 1.00.6235
Copyright (C) Microsoft Corp 1996. All rights reserved.

import euclid.*;
```

If you want to browse the contents of these trustlib class files, you can use the JavaTLB.exe utility with the /U option which unassembles a Java class file. The command is run with the trustlib\CEuclid.class and \trustlib\IGCD.class files (shown in Listing 26.3).

Listing 26.3   The Contents of the JavaTLB Generated *.class Files in \trustlib are Displayed Using the /U option of JavaTLB

```
C:\WINDOWS\JAVA\TRUSTLIB\euclid>d:\msdev\bin\javatlb /U CEuclid.class
Microsoft (R) Visual J++ Java Typelib Conversion Utility Version 1.00.6235
Copyright (C) Microsoft Corp 1996. All rights reserved.

public class euclid/CEuclid extends java.lang.Object
{
}

C:\WINDOWS\JAVA\TRUSTLIB\euclid>d:\msdev\bin\javatlb /U IGCD.class
Microsoft (R) Visual J++ Java Typelib Conversion Utility Version 1.00.6235
Copyright (C) Microsoft Corp 1996. All rights reserved.

public interface euclid/IGCD extends com.ms.com.IUnknown
{
    public abstract int GCD(int, int);
}
```

The next step, now that the euclid type library and class description files have been created, is to build the source project. With the project open, use the Visual J++ Build, Rebuild All menu command to rebuild the project. Building the project compiles the euclid.java class, which produces a single new file, CEuclid.class, in the project directory.

The next step is to copy the new CEuclid.class file to the Java VM ClassPath. You can check the ClassPath by searching the Registry for "Java VM" or "ClassPath." The c:\windows\java\classes directory is used to contain the CEuclid.class file in this example. This class file needs to be in the ClassPath in order to be found when the class is loaded for a client application.

The reg_tlb.bat file (see Listing 26.4) can be run to accomplish this step. The first line sets the path, which you may need to update as described earlier. The second line copies the CEuclid.class file to the Java VM ClassPath. The reg_tlb.bat file can be run instead of the registereuclid.bat file that comes with the COMCallingJava sample (which does not contain a copy statement). It is better to have this done automatically to keep the executables in sync, and to make sure the CEuclid.class file is placed where it belongs.

The third line calls JavaReg.exe to register the Java class as a COM component in the system Registry.

Listing 26.4   The Class File Must Be Copied to the Classpath and the Class Registered (\msdev\projects\chap26\ parts1\ reg_tlb.bat)

```
set path=d:\msdev\bin;%path%
copy CEuclid.class c:\windows\java\classes
javareg /register /class:CEuclid /clsid:{33B0ECE2-E706-11cf-A0C2-00AA00A71DD8}
```

The final step is to run the VBDriver.exe program to test the installed ActiveX component. Use Explorer to run VBDriver.exe, which is in the project directory. Figure 26.1 shows the VBDriver.exe test driver running. Enter **24** for "U" and **12** for "V." Click the Call Java! button to produce the correct results for the greatest common devisor, 12.

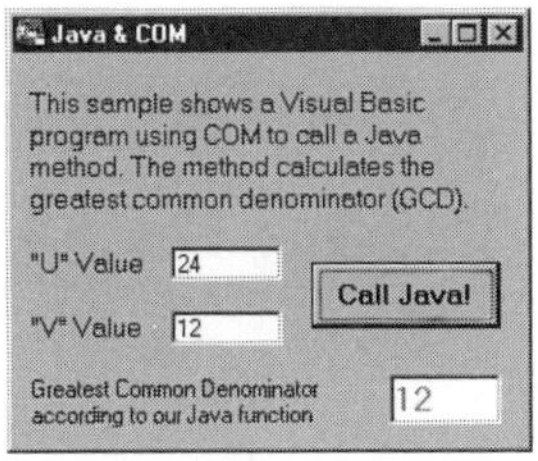

FIG. 26.1

The Java & COM dialog box is a Visual Basic program that calls the CEuclid COM component implemented in Java.

Part
IV

Ch
26

Listing 26.5 shows the euclid.java source file. Notice the import statement that brings in the CEuclid and IGCD interface descriptions. If the euclid.java file does not implement the entire IGCD interface, a compile error results.

The name of the single method in the IGCD interface, GCD, stands for *greatest common divisor*. The method has two integers as input parameters and returns the greatest common divisor, or factor, of the two input values. For example, the GCD of 24 (2*2*2*3) and 12 (2*2*3) is 12 (2*2*3).

Listing 26.5 There Is One Java Source File in the COMCallingJava Project (\msdev\samples\comcallingjava\euclid.java)

```
/*
 *
 * CEuclid
 *
 */

// import the COM interface
import euclid.*;

// Java class implements the COM interface
class CEuclid implements IGCD
{
    // public method to compute
    // greatest common denominator (GCD)
    public int GCD(int u, int v)
    {
        int t;
        while (u > 0)
        {
            if (u < v)
            {
                t=u;
                u=v;
                v=t;
            }
            u=u-v;
        }
        return v;
    }
}
```

Listing 26.6 shows the relevant sections of the source for the VBDriver.exe test program. When the form is loaded, the Form_Load subroutine is called. It creates a new CEuclid object and saves its IGCD interface in MyEuclid. When the Command1 button is clicked, Command1_Click is called. It checks U and V for numeric value and then returns MyEuclid.GCD(U, V).

TIP

Notice the version 4.0 statement in VBDriver.frm. If you do not have version 4.0 of Visual Basic installed when you run VBDriver.exe, you will get an error message saying that VB40032.dll cannot be found. You can get the VB 4.0 runtime by going to the Web page: **http://www.microsoft.com/ workshop/usage/devnav/default.htm.** This page, DevNav: The Site Navigation Bar, allows you to download a free Developer tool. It also provides a version that includes the VB 4.0 runtime. Download the version containing the VB 4.0 runtime and install it. Restart Windows and then run VBDriver.exe.

TIP

If you run VBDriver.exe and you see a message box with the message:

"Run-time error '7': Out of memory"

it may be because the c:\windows\java\trustlib\euclid\CEuclid.class and IGCD.class, or c:\windows\java\classes\CEuclid.class files are missing.

While doing development be advised that if the c:\windows\java\classes\CEuclid.class does not exist, the copy in your project directory where your driver is run from will be used.

Listing 26.6   A Portion of the VBDriver.frm Test Driver Source (\msdev\samples\comcallingjava\vbdriver\vbdriver.frm)

```
VERSION 4.00
Begin VB.Form FrmMain
...
    Begin VB.CommandButton Command1
        Caption         =   "Call Java!"
...
    End
End
...
Dim MyEuclid As IGCD

Private Sub Command1_Click()

    If Not IsNumeric(U) Then
        MsgBox "U must be numeric"
        U.SetFocus
        Exit Sub
    End If

    If Not IsNumeric(V) Then
        MsgBox "V must be numeric"
        V.SetFocus
        Exit Sub
    End If

    Final = MyEuclid.GCD(U, V)

End Sub

Private Sub Form_Load()

    Set MyEuclid = New CEuclid

End Sub
```

Part

IV

Ch

26

Listing 26.7 shows the contents of the euclid.odl file. Java interfaces can be exposed as COM interfaces, dispatch interfaces, or dual interfaces. Dual interfaces are recommended for reasons discussed later in this chapter. The euclid.odl file defines a `dispinterface`, which allows access to `CEuclid` through the `IDispatch` interface. In the next section you will learn how to call the `CEuclid` component from a C++ program.

TIP For a good discussion of the tradeoffs of the different interfaces, read "OLE Q&A" by Don Box in *Microsoft Systems Journal* (December 1995; Vol. 10, No. 12; p. 83).

Listing 26.7 A Type Library Is Created from the ODL Statements (\msdev\samples\comcallingjava\euclid.odl)

```
// This describes the library GCDLib
[
     uuid (33B0ECE0-E706-11cf-A0C2-00AA00A71DD8),
     version (1.0),
     helpstring("GCDLib 1.0 Type Library")
]
library GCDLib
{
     // GCDLib imports the interfaces, classes, structures,
     // types, and so forth from STDOLE32.TLB.
     importlib("stdole32.tlb");

     // This describes the interface IGCD, a dispinterface.
     // A dispinterface is an IDispatch-type interface.
     [
          uuid (33B0ECE1-E706-11cf-A0C2-00AA00A71DD8),
          helpstring("IGCD Interface")
     ]
     dispinterface IGCD
     {
     properties:
     methods:
          // The single method exported by the interface
          [id(1)]long GCD([in] long v, [in] long u);
     }

     // The coclass that implements the interface
     [
          uuid (33B0ECE2-E706-11cf-A0C2-00AA00A71DD8),
          helpstring("Euclid Class")
     ]
     coclass CEuclid
     {
          dispinterface IGCD;
     };
};
```

Using *CEuclid* from C++

In the last section, you learned how to install the CEuclid component built from the Microsoft COMCallingJava sample project. The component was tested using the VBDriver program. In this section, you will learn how to access the same component from a Visual C++ program. Alternative ways to access a COM component are discussed in the next section.

As described in this section, creating a Visual C++ program involves:

- Creating a new Visual C++ project.
- Copying the euclid.h file to the new project.
- Creating a wrapper C++ class for the component.
- Adding code to create and call the component.
- Testing the component.

The first step is to create a new Visual C++ project to implement a client application that uses the CEuclid component. The project will be very simple so that the focus remains on what is required to create and call the CEuclid COM component.

Start Visual C++ and choose File, New. Select Project Workspace in the New dialog box and click OK. Enter the directory name and location for the new Visual C++ project. This example uses c:\msdev\projects\chap26\EuclidClient. Click the Create button.

In the MFC AppWizard—Step 1 dialog box select the Dialog Based radio button. This will generate a simple project. Click the Next button.

In the MFC AppWizard—Step 2 of 4 dialog box, check OLE automation support. You can now click Finish or Next if you want to browse the other default options before clicking Finish. Click OK in the New Project Information dialog box to finally create the project files.

The next step is to copy the euclid.h file from the \msdev\samples\comcallingjava\ directory. The euclid.h file was created by the /h euclid.h option of the MkTypLib program (refer to Listing 26.1). The header defines the GUIDs associated with the CEuclid class and the IGCD interface. These values are needed to access the component from C++.

The next step is to create a C++ wrapper class that can be used to access the GCD method in the IGCD interface of the CEuclid class. Use the View ClassWizard menu command to display the MFC ClassWizard dialog box. Select the OLE Automation dialog tab. Click the Add Class button and select the From an OLE Typelib item (see Figure 26.2). From the Import from OLE Typelib dialog box, navigate to, and select, the euclid.tlb file from the \msdev\samples\microsoft\comcallingjava\ directory.

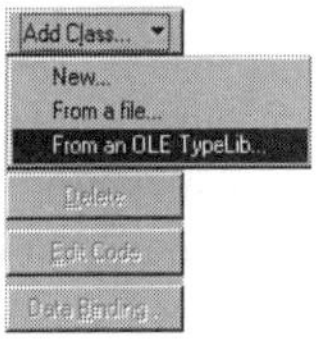

FIG. 26.2

Use the Add Class menu button in the MFC ClassWizard dialog box to add a new class to the project based on an OLE Type Library definition.

The Confirm Classes dialog box shows the IGCD interface in the list box. The name of the class should be changed from IGCD to C_IGCD, the header file name changed from euclid.h to c_euclid.h, and the implementation file name from euclid.cpp to c_euclid.cpp. The name changes avoid a conflict with the IGCD interface defined in the euclid.h file copied into the previous project. Because this is a wrapper class, it doesn't hurt to make the names reflect the additional relationship. Click OK after changing the names. Click OK to close the MFC AppWizard dialog box. The c_euclid.cpp file will be generated and automatically inserted into the EuclidClient project.

The next step is to add code to create and call the CEuclid component. For convenience, all of the lines of code to be added are on the companion CD-ROM in the \msdev\projects\chap26\parts1\ directory. The two files are i_stdafx.cpp and callGCD.cpp.

By default Visual C++ projects use compiled headers. This example does not change that. Two lines need to be appended to the contents of stdafx.cpp (see Listing 26.8). The #include of initguid.h causes the GUIDs in euclid.h to be defined and initialized properly. (For more information on this topic search the Microsoft Developers Network for "INITGUID.")

TIP   If you forget to insert the two #includes into StdAfx.cpp, you will see the following errors during the linking of the project:

EuclidClientDlg.obj : error LNK2001: unresolved external symbol _DIID_IGCD

EuclidClientDlg.obj : error LNK2001: unresolved external symbol _CLSID_CEuclid

You will see the same errors if you insert #include euclid.h, but not initguid.h.

Listing 26.8   Two Lines Are Appended to the stdafx.cpp File (\msdev\projects\chap26\EuclidClient\stdafx.cpp)

```
// stdafx.cpp : source file that includes just the standard includes
//      EuclidClient.pch will be the pre-compiled header
//      stdafx.obj will contain the pre-compiled type information

#include "stdafx.h"
#include "initguid.h" // 1 of 2 - add these 2 lines after #include "stdafx.h"
#include "euclid.h"   // 2 of 2 - add these 2 lines after #include "stdafx.h"
```

The next step is to add the code to the CEuclidClientDlg.cpp file that creates and calls the CEuclid component. Listing 26.9 shows the two changes made: 1) the two `#include` statements for euclid.h and c_euclid.h at the top of the file, and 2) the block of code that follows the `// TODO: Add extra initialization here` statement in the `CEuclidClientDlg::OnInitDialog` method.

You can enter this code manually, or you can insert the statements from a file on the companion CD-ROM. The file on the CD-ROM that contains these statements is \msdev\projects\chap26\parts1\callGCD.cpp. To copy the contents of callGCD.cpp into the EuclidClientDlg.cpp file, place the cursor in the EuclidClientDlg.cpp file and use the Insert, File command to insert the \msdev\projects\chap26\parts1\callGCD.cpp file. Be sure to 1) move the two `#include` statements to the top of the file, and 2) move the block of code beginning with the `long nGCD = 0;` to the `CDialog::OnInitDialog` method as shown in Listing 26.9.

An instance of a `CEuclid` component will be created and the `GCD` method called to set the value of the variable nGCD to GCD(24, 12).The euclid.h file is included to use the CLSIDs of the registered COM component: CLSID_CEuclid and DIID_IGCD. The c_euclid.h file is included to use the C_IGCD component wrapper class.

In the `OnInitDialog` method, a block of code is inserted whose first line defines the `long` variable named nGCD. The `CoCreateInstance` method is called to return a pointer to the `IUknown` interface of a new component of class `CLSID_CEuclid`. If this succeeds, an instance of a pointer to the `IGCD` interface (see euclid.h) is defined: igcd. The `IUknown` interface is used to call `QueryInterface` to get a pointer to the `DIID_IGCD` dispatch interface. If that succeeds, the pointer to the `DIID_IGCD` interface is in igcd. The igcd variable is used in the constructor of an instance of the wrapper class, `C_IGCD`. The c_igcd variable contains a pointer to the `C_IGCD` object, which is attached to the igcd interface pointer. The `C_IGCD` variable is then used to call the `GCD` method. Finally, the `C_IGCD` object is deleted, followed by the release of the `CEuclid` component.

Part

IV

Ch

26

Listing 26.9   A Partial Listing of EuclidClientDlg.cpp Shows the Insertions of Code to Call CEuclid Component
(\msdev\projects\chap26\EuclidClient\EuclidClientDlg.cpp)

```
// EuclidClientDlg.cpp : implementation file
//

#include "stdafx.h"
#include "EuclidClient.h"
#include "EuclidClientDlg.h"
#include "euclid.h"      // 1 of 2 - add these 2 lines after #include "stdafx.h"
#include "c_euclid.h"    // 2 of 2 - add these 2 lines after #include "stdafx.h"
```

continues

Listing 26.9   Continued

```
...
BOOL CEuclidClientDlg::OnInitDialog()
{
    CDialog::OnInitDialog();

...
    // TODO: Add extra initialization here

    {
        long nGCD = 0; // call COM object to get GCD(24, 12)

        HRESULT hr;
        LPUNKNOWN lpUnknown = NULL;

        hr = CoCreateInstance(CLSID_CEuclid, NULL,
                CLSCTX_INPROC_SERVER, IID_IUnknown,
                (void **)&lpUnknown);
        if(hr == S_OK)
        {
            IGCD *igcd = NULL;

            hr = lpUnknown->QueryInterface(DIID_IGCD, (void **)&igcd);
            if (hr == S_OK)
            {
                C_IGCD *cigcd = new C_IGCD(igcd);

                nGCD = cigcd->GCD(24, 12);

                delete cigcd;
            }
            lpUnknown->Release();
        }
    }
    return TRUE;  // return TRUE  unless you set the focus to a control
}
```

The last step is to test the changes and the access to the CEuclid component. First choose the Build, Rebuild All menu command to rebuild the entire project. After the successful build, set a breakpoint on the delete statement following the call to GCD() (see Figure 26.3). Choose the Build, Debug, Go menu item or press F5 to start debugging the application. When the program stops at the breakpoint, the value of nGCD should be 12.

FIG. 26.3

The EuclidClient application is stopped at a breakpoint in the *OnInitDialog* method.

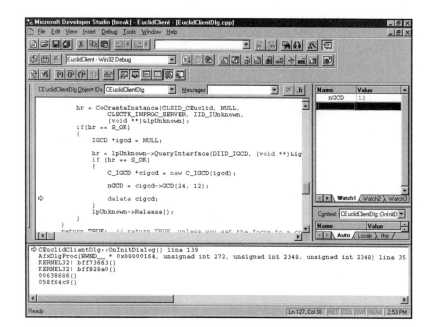

Creating a New ActiveX Object with Java

The last section illustrated how to build and test the CEuclid component from the COMCallingJava sample. CEuclid was a simple example that implemented one class with one interface. CEuclid's single interface contained one method with no parameters. In this section, you will build and test a new ActiveX component. This new component will illustrate more of the ActiveX features supported by Visual J++.

A new ActiveX component will be defined with the following features:

- ■ The class will be named JCOM.

- ■ JCOM will implement two interfaces: IJCOMAdd1 and IJCOMOther.

- ■ The IJCOMAdd1 interface will have methods to increment the value of various different data types.

- ■ The IJCOMOther interface will demonstrate throwing exceptions and other features.

- ■ The ODL will define dual interfaces.

After the new ActiveX component is built, a test program written in Visual C++ will be created.

Part
IV

Ch
26

Creating the JCOM ActiveX Visual J++ Project

First, create a new Java workspace to contain the implementation of the new ActiveX component. Start Visual J++ and choose File, New. In the New dialog box, select Project Workspace
and click OK. In the New Project Workspace dialog box, select the Java Workspace Type,
browse to the location of the new directory, and enter the Name of the new project directory.
In this section and on the companion CD-ROM, the project Name is JCOM and the Location
is \msdev\projects\chap26\JCOM\. Click Create to create the directory and project files.

The next step is to create a new file named JCOM.ODL, which will contain the definitions of
the JCOM component. This example will use dual interfaces. The COMCallingJava example has
an ODL that uses dispinterface.

Before creating JCOM.ODL, a set of GUIDs needs to be created for use in defining the JCOM
component. Four GUIDs are needed for use in the JCOM.ODL file. From Visual J++ choose
Create GUID from the Tools menu. In the Create GUID dialog box (see Figure 26.4) select
GUID Format 4. Registry Format (ie. {xxxxxx-xxxx … xxxx }). To obtain the first GUID, click
Copy and paste it into a new file. To obtain the next GUID click New GUID and Copy, now
paste the new GUID into the GUID file. Repeat this until four GUIDs have been created and
saved. Listing 26.10 shows the four GUIDs in the GUIDs.txt file. Table 26.1 shows how the four
new GUIDs are assigned to the JCOM components.

FIG. 26.4
The Create GUID dialog
box is used to create
and copy a sequence of
GUIDs.

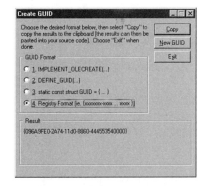

**Listing 26.10   A List of GUIDs Used to Define the ODL for JCOM
(\msdev\projects\chap26\JCOM\GUIDs.txt)**

```
{096A9FE0-2A74-11d0-8860-444553540000}
{096A9FE1-2A74-11d0-8860-444553540000}
{096A9FE2-2A74-11d0-8860-444553540000}
{096A9FE3-2A74-11d0-8860-444553540000}
```

With the four GUIDs created, the JCOM.ODL file (see Listing 26.11) can be created. The
GUIDs are assigned as follows:

Table 26.1 Assignment of GUIDs to JCOM Components

GUID	ODL Use
36908CC0-2626-11d0-8860-444553540000	library JCOMLib
36908CC1-2626-11d0-8860-444553540000	interface IJCOMAdd1 : IDispatch
36908CC2-2626-11d0-8860-444553540000	interface IJCOMOther : IDispatch
36908CC3-2626-11d0-8860-444553540000	coclass CJCOM

Listing 26.11 shows the complete ODL for JCOM. The `library` statement defines the type library. The `IJCOMAdd1` and the `IJCOMOther` interfaces are defined using the recommended `dual` attribute.

Each method in the `IJCOMAdd1` interface demonstrates how to define input parameters, in/out parameters, and function return values for the corresponding Java methods. Each function takes an input parameter value, increments it by one, and returns the value.

Listing 26.11 The ODL for JCOM Component Is in JCOM.ODL (\msdev\projects\chap26\JCOM\JCOM.ODL)

```
[
    uuid(096A9FE0-2A74-11d0-8860-444553540000),
    version(1.0),
    helpstring("JCOMLib 1.0 Type Library")
]
library JCOMLib
{
    importlib("stdole32.tlb");
  [
    uuid(096A9FE1-2A74-11d0-8860-444553540000),
    odl,
    dual,
    helpstring("IJCOMAdd1 Interface")
  ]
  interface IJCOMAdd1 : IDispatch
  {
    HRESULT Inc_boolean([in] boolean i, [out, retval]boolean *pRetVal);
    HRESULT Inc_byte([in] unsigned char i, [out, retval]unsigned char *pRetVal);
    //HRESULT Inc_char([in] wchar_t i, [out, retval] wchar_t *pRetVal);
    HRESULT Inc_double([in] double i, [out, retval]double *pRetVal);
    HRESULT Inc_float([in] float i, [out, retval]float *pRetVal);
    HRESULT Inc_int([in] int i, [out, retval]int *pRetVal);
    HRESULT Inc_intRef([in,out]int* pInt);
    HRESULT Inc_long([in] CURRENCY i, [out, retval]CURRENCY *pRetVal);
    HRESULT Inc_short([in] short i, [out, retval]short *pRetVal);
    HRESULT Inc_String([in] BSTR i, [out, retval]BSTR *pRetVal);
    HRESULT Inc_StringRef([in,out] BSTR* x);
    HRESULT Inc_void(void);
```

Part

IV

Ch

26

continues

Listing 26.11   Continued

```
}

[
  uuid(096A9FE2-2A74-11d0-8860-444553540000),
  odl,
  dual,
  helpstring("IJCOMOther Interface")
]
interface IJCOMOther : IDispatch
{
  [propget] HRESULT IntProp1([out, retval] int* IntProp1);
  [propput] HRESULT IntProp1([in] int IntProp1);
  HRESULT GetAdd1([out,retval] IJCOMAdd1** x);
  HRESULT SetAdd1([in] IJCOMAdd1* x);
  HRESULT DoAdd1([in] int i, [out, retval]int *pRetVal);
  HRESULT DoException([in] long i1);
};
    [
        uuid(096A9FE3-2A74-11d0-8860-444553540000),
        helpstring("CJCOM Class")
    ]
    coclass CJCOM
    {
        [default] interface IJCOMAdd1;
        interface IJCOMOther;
    };

};
```

Once the JCOM.ODL file is complete, it is time to make a type library from the file using the
MkTypLib.exe utility, and create the Java class files that correspond to the type library con-
tents. Listing 26.12 shows the mk_odl.bat file that contains the commands to run MkTypLib
and JavaTlb utilities. The path is set to use the MkTypLib and JavaTlb utilities from Visual J++.
The MkTypLib command will create the JCOM.tlb type library file and the jcom.h header file.
The JavaTlb command will create the three files in the c:\windows\java\trustlib\ directory:
CJCOM.class, IJCOMAdd1.class, and IJCOMOther.class. These files define the Java class and
interface definitions that correspond to the coclass and interface definitions in the jcom.tlb file.

**Listing 26.12   The JavaTlb Commands to List the JCOM Java Interfaces
(\msdev\projects\chap26\JCOM\mk_odl.bat)**

```
set path=d:\msdev\bin;%path%
mktyplib JCOM.odl /nocpp /h jcom.h
javatlb  JCOM.tlb
```

Listing 26.13 shows the output from running the mk_odl.bat file. Notice the `import jcom.*;`
statement that should be used by Java files that implement the JCOM component.

Listing 26.13   The Output from Running JavaTlb Commands to List the JCOM Java Interfaces (\msdev\projects\chap26\JCOM\listclas.bat)

```
C:\MSDEV\Projects\Chap26\JCOM>mktyplib JCOM.odl /nocpp /h jcom.h
Microsoft (R) Type Library Generator  Version 2.03.3027
Copyright (C) Microsoft Corp. 1993-1995.  All rights reserved.

Successfully generated type library 'JCOM.tlb'.

C:\MSDEV\Projects\Chap26\JCOM>javatlb  JCOM.tlb
Microsoft (R) Visual J++ Java Typelib Conversion Utility Version 1.00.6235
Copyright (C) Microsoft Corp 1996. All rights reserved.

import jcom.*;
```

Listing 26.14 shows the listclas.bat file that contains the command to list the contents of the trustlib class files created by JavaTlb in the previous step. Note that the second line in listclas.bat refers to c:\windows. This should be changed to c:\winnt if you are using Windows NT. If your windows directory is different from the defaults, then you should make the appropriate changes to listclas.bat. Listing 26.15 shows the output from running the listclas.bat file. The interfaces for IJCOMAdd1 and IJCOMOther that are described in Listing 26.15 are what must be implemented in Java.

Listing 26.14   The JavaTlb Commands to List the JCOM Java Interfaces (\msdev\projects\chap26\JCOM\listclas.bat)

```
set path=d:\msdev\bin;%path%
cd c:\windows\java\trustlib\jcom
javatlb /U CJCOM.class
javatlb /U IJCOMAdd1.class
javatlb /U IJCOMOther.class
```

Part
IV

Ch
26

Listing 26.15   The Output Listings of the listclas.bat File

```
public class jcom/CJCOM extends java.lang.Object
{
}
public interface jcom/IJCOMAdd1 extends com.ms.com.IUnknown
{
    public abstract java.lang.String Inc_String(java.lang.String);
    public abstract boolean Inc_boolean(boolean);
    public abstract double Inc_double(double);
    public abstract void Inc_intRef(int[]);
    public abstract byte Inc_byte(byte);
    public abstract float Inc_float(float);
    public abstract void Inc_void();
    public abstract short Inc_short(short);
```

continues

Listing 26.15 Continued

```
    public abstract long Inc_long(long);
    public abstract void Inc_StringRef(java.lang.String[]);
    public abstract int Inc_int(int);
}
public interface jcom/IJCOMOther extends com.ms.com.IUnknown
{
    public abstract jcom.IJCOMAdd1 GetAdd1();
    public abstract void SetAdd1(jcom.IJCOMAdd1);
    public abstract int DoAdd1(int);
    public abstract int getIntProp1();
    public abstract void putIntProp1(int);
    public abstract void DoException(int);
}
```

Before actually creating the Java source file that will implement the JCOM component, the ODL and Java definitions derived from the ODL will be examined and compared.

For example, the Inc_int method has an int input parameter and returns an int value. Below is the ODL definition of the Inc_int method and the corresponding Java method definition produced by JavaTlb. In the ODL the first parameter is input-only as specified by the [in] attribute. The last parameter is defined as [out, retval]. When defined this way, the parameter is interpreted to be the return value of the method itself. Notice the use of the * to indicate a pointer or level of indirection used to return a value. Look at the Java method definition for Inc_int. It takes a single int parameter and returns an int. The ODL shows the Inc_int method returning an HRESULT value. In Java the HRESULT value returned is set by throwing a ComException. This is discussed in the following section about the IJCOMOther interface.

```
ODL:    HRESULT Inc_int([in] int i, [out, retval]int *pRetVal);
Java:    public abstract int Inc_int(int);
```

The next example shows the Inc_intRef method. Notice the ODL definition has a single parameter with an attribute [in,out] specified. Because the retval attribute is not specified, the Java method will return void. The [in,out] attribute implies a level of indirection to be able to return a value through the parameter. In Java int parameters, as well as other primitive data types, are passed by value. There are no pointers in Java. However there are arrays that can perform the same function. Therefore, an [in,out] int parameter in ODL is mapped to a Java int *array of length one*. An array is passed as the parameter and its first element is where the int value to be read and/or written is stored.

```
ODL:    HRESULT Inc_intRef([in,out]int* pInt);
Java:    public abstract void Inc_intRef(int[]);
```

The next example shows the Inc_String method. A Java String object is represented in ODL using the BSTR data type.

```
ODL:    HRESULT Inc_String([in] BSTR i, [out, retval]BSTR *pRetVal);
Java:    public abstract java.lang.String Inc_String(java.lang.String);
```

The next example shows how to pass in and receive a new String object using only a parameter. This is similar to the int case. An array is used to pass a reference to a String object in the first array element. Notice the use of the * pointer notation for the [in,out] parameter.

```
ODL:     HRESULT Inc_StringRef([in,out] BSTR* x);
Java:     Java:     public abstract void Inc_StringRef(java.lang.String[]);
```

The IJCOMAdd1 has many similar methods for each primitive data type and the String class. (At the time of writing, the char Java data type was documented to map to the ODL char data type; however, there were problems getting it to work.)

The IJCOMOther interface illustrates some other features supported in ODL including COM properties, interface references as parameters, and returning HRESULT values. The following example shows how ODL properties are supported in Java. The IJCOMOther interface contains a COM property named IntProp1. The IntProp1 property is defined by the get and put methods. In ODL the get method is named IntProp1 and has the [propget] attribute. The corresponding Java method must be named getIntProp1. The get<property> method has no parameters and returns the property value as the method return value.

```
ODL:     [propget] HRESULT IntProp1([out, retval] int* IntProp1);
Java:     public abstract int getIntProp1();
```

The get<property> method in ODL is named IntProp1 and has the [propput] attribute. The corresponding Java method must be named putIntProp1. The put<property> method has one input parameter and returns void.

```
ODL:     propput] HRESULT IntProp1([in] int IntProp1);
Java:     public abstract void putIntProp1(int);
```

IJCOMOther has several methods that illustrate using interface references as parameters. The methods are GetAdd1, SetAdd1, and DoAdd1. SetAdd1 is used to pass a reference to an IJCOMAdd1 interface. The GetAdd1 method is used to retrieve the saved interface reference. The DoAdd1 method calls the Int_int method of the saved IJCOMAdd1 reference to increment and return the value of its parameter. These calls will be used to show that references to interfaces can be passed to and from COM and Java, and be invoked from either.

```
ODL:     HRESULT GetAdd1([out,retval] IJCOMAdd1** x);
Java:     public abstract jcom.IJCOMAdd1 GetAdd1();
```

```
ODL:     HRESULT SetAdd1([in] IJCOMAdd1* x);
Java:     public abstract void SetAdd1(jcom.IJCOMAdd1);
```

```
Java:     public abstract int DoAdd1(int);
ODL:     HRESULT DoAdd1([in] int i, [out, retval]int *pRetVal);
```

The last method in the IJCOMOther interface is DoException. This method will illustrate how various HRESULT values are returned from Java.

```
Java:     public abstract void DoException(int);
ODL:     HRESULT DoException([in] long i1);
```

The listings of the Java interfaces generated from the type library provide enough information to begin the next step—writing a Java source implementation file. The JCOM.java file (see Listings 26.16-26.18) contains the Java source code that implements the methods defined in Listing 26.16. Listing 26.18 shows the first part of the file. Two import statements identify the use of the com.ms.com library and the jcom library. The coclass name, CJCOM, in the ODL file is used to name the Java class that implements the individual methods of the IJCOMAdd1 and IJCOMOther interfaces. The IntProp1 variable is used to save the value of the IntProp1 property. The saveAdd1 variable is used to save the reference to a IJCOMAdd1 interface.

Listing 26.16   The JCOM.java Imports and Class Definition (1 of 3) (\msdev\projects\chap26\JCOM\JCOM.java)

```
// JCOM Library

// import the COM interface
import com.ms.com.*;
import jcom.*;

// Java class implements the COM interface
class CJCOM implements IJCOMAdd1, IJCOMOther
{
    int IntProp1 = 1;
    IJCOMAdd1 saveAdd1 = null;
...
```

Listing 26.17 shows the source for the methods that implement the IJCOMAdd1 interface. Every method of each implemented interface must be implemented or a compile error results. The methods of the IJCOMAdd1 interface increments its input parameter and returns the incremented value to the caller. Each method increments a different data type.

The Inc_boolean method increments the input boolean by returning the complement of the input value. The methods for byte, double, float, int, and short all use the ++ operator to increment the input value. The Inc_intRef method receives and returns the incremented value through the first element in the input array. Because int is a primitive data type, an int always exists in the array. The default value for new int array elements is 0. The Inc_String method returns s+1, which is the character 1 appended to the input string value. The Inc_StringRef method receives and returns a string value through the first element in a String array. Because Strings are objects, this method must check to see if a String reference exists in the first element before incrementing it. This method returns a String with value 1 if the first element is null. Also note that the Inc_StringRef method is written to increment each element in the array of Strings passed in. When this method is called from COM, the array will have a length of one.

Listing 26.17   The JCOM.java IJCOMAdd1 Interface Definition (2 of 3) (\msdev\projects\chap26\JCOM\JCOM.java)

```java
// interface implementation for IJCOMAdd1

// IJCOMAdd1: public methods to "increment" each data type

public boolean Inc_boolean(boolean b)
{
    return (b ? false : true);
}
public byte Inc_byte(byte y)
{
    return ++y;
}
public char Inc_char(char c)
{
    return ++c;
}
public double Inc_double(double d)
{
    return ++d + 1;
}
public float Inc_float(float f)
{
    return ++f;
}
public int Inc_int(int i)
{
    return ++i;
}
public void Inc_intRef(int[] i)
{
    ++i[0];
}
public long Inc_long(long l)
{
    return ++l;
}
public short Inc_short(short s)
{
    return ++s;
}
public String Inc_String(String s)
{
    return s+1;
}
public void Inc_StringRef(String[] s)
{
```

Part

IV

Ch

26

continues

Listing 26.17   Continued

```
    for(int n = 0; n < s.length; ++n)
    {
        if(s[n] != null)
            s[n] = new String(s[n]+1);
        else
            s[n] = new String("1");
    }
}
public void Inc_void()
{
    return;
}
```

Listing 26.18 shows the implementation of the IJCOMOther interface. The getIntProp1 and putIntProp1 methods implement the access methods for the IntProp1 property. The GetAdd1 and SetAdd1 methods provide access to a saved reference to an IJCOMAdd1 interface. The DoAdd1 method calls the Inc_int method of the saved IJCOMAdd1 reference to return the incremented value of its input parameter.

The DoException method demonstrates returning different values of HRESULT. The input parameter is used to cause a different HRESULT to be returned. An input value of 0 will cause the function to return normally without throwing any exceptions. The HRESULT returned to the caller in this case will be S_OK. (S_OK and other error codes are defined in winerror.h.) An input value of 1 causes a default ComSuccessException to be thrown. The default value of ComSuccessException is S_FALSE. ComSuccessException and ComFailException are derived from ComException. An input value of 2 causes a ComFailException initialized to a value corresponding to the E_OUTOFMEMORY error. Any other input value with default to throwing a default ComFailException exception. This results in an HRESULT of E_FAIL to be returned.

Listing 26.18   The JCOM.java IJCOMOther Interface Definition (3 of 3) (\msdev\projects\chap26\JCOM\JCOM.java)

```
// interface implementation for IJCOMOther

// IJCOMOther: properties
public int getIntProp1()
{
    return IntProp1;
}
public   void putIntProp1(int n)
{
    IntProp1 = n;
}

// interface parameters
```

```java
public IJCOMAdd1 GetAdd1()
{
    return saveAdd1;
}
public void SetAdd1(IJCOMAdd1 saveAdd1)
{
    this.saveAdd1 = saveAdd1;
}
public int DoAdd1(int i)
{
    if(saveAdd1 != null)
    {
        return saveAdd1.Inc_int(i);
    }
    return 1;
}

// IJCOMOther: exceptions and HRESULTS
public void DoException(int x)
{
    ComSuccessException successX;
    ComFailException failX;

    switch(x)
    {
    case 0:
        // HRESULT=S_OK by returning normally
        break;
    case 1:
        // HRESULT=S_FALSE
        successX = new ComSuccessException();
        throw successX;
    case 2:
        // HRESULT=E_OUTOFMEMORY
        failX = new ComFailException(0x8007000e);
        throw failX;
    default:
        // HRESULT=E_FAIL
        failX = new ComFailException();
        throw failX;
    }
}
}
```

Part
IV

Ch

26

Now that the Java source file is written, it should be inserted into the JCOM project and the project rebuilt. Building the project causes JCOM.java to be compiled, which produces the CJCOM.class file. The next step is to register and install the CJCOM class. The register.bat file (see Listing 26.19) is provided to register the CJOM component and to copy the CJCOM.class file to the Java ClassPath. Copy register.bat to the JCOM project directory and run it. After JCOM is installed, a test driver is needed to test the installation.

Listing 26.19 The Commands Used to Register and Install the JCOM Component Are in register.bat (\msdev\projects\chap26\JCOM\register.bat)

```
set path=d:\msdev\bin;%path%
javareg /register /progid:LoneRock.JCOMLib /class:CJCOM /clsid:{096A9FE3-2A74-
➥11d0-8860-444553540000}
copy CJCOM.class c:\windows\java\classes
```

Creating the *JCOMClient* Visual C++ Project

In this section, a Visual C++ application is created that tests the JCOM component installed in the previous section. The application is similar to the EuclidClient project created earlier in this chapter.

Start Visual C++ and choose File, New. Select Project Workspace in the New dialog box and click OK. Enter the directory name and location for the new Visual C++ project. This example uses c:\msdev\projects\chap26\JCOMClient. Click the Create button.

In the MFC AppWizard—Step 1 dialog box select the Dialog Based button. This generates a simple project. Click the Next button.

In the MFC AppWizard—Step 2 of 4 dialog box, check OLE Automation Support. You can now click Finish or Next if you want to browse the other default options before pressing Finish. Click OK in the New Project Information dialog box to finally create the project files. Visual C++ opens the new project.

Next copy the jcom.h file from the JCOM project to the JCOMClient project directory. Next append the following two lines to the contents of stdafx.cpp:

```
#include "initguid.h"
#include "jcom.h"
```

These lines cause CLSIDs to be defined and initialized. Next insert the statements that test the JCOM component into the JCOMClientDlg.cpp file in the OnInitDialog method after the statement:

```
// TODO: Add extra initialization here
```

The testing code is on the companion CD-ROM in the file \msdev\projects\chap26\parts2\callJCOM.cpp. To insert this file, place the cursor after the line with the TODO comment, then choose Insert, File and open the callJCOM.cpp file. After inserting the contents of callJCOM.cpp, move the #include jcom.*; statement to the top of the file as shown in Listing 26.20. The #include jcom.h; statement is all that is necessary to bring in the definitions of the JCOM interfaces.

After modifying the source, choose the menu item Build, Rebuild All to rebuild the project. The default project target is the debug version. To run the program to test JCOM choose Build, Debug, Go (or press F5). You can set a breakpoint and examine the values as they change, or run the application to completion—if any method fails, an ASSERT dialog box will notify you of the failure. No ASSERT should fail.

Listing 26.20   The #include jcom.* Statement Inserted at the Top of the JCOMClientDlg.cpp File (\msdev\projects\chap26\JCOMClient\JCOMClient.cpp)

```
// JCOMClientDlg.cpp : implementation file
//

#include "stdafx.h"
#include "JCOMClient.h"
#include "JCOMClientDlg.h"
#include "jcom.h"

#ifdef _DEBUG
#define new DEBUG_NEW
#undef THIS_FILE
static char THIS_FILE[] = __FILE__;
#endif
...
```

Listing 26.21 shows the JCOMClientDlg::OnInitDialog method, which contains the code that tests the IJCOMAdd1 interface. In the EuclidClient, the OLE Automation Wizard is used to create wrapper C++ class for the CEuclid IGCD dispinterface. In the case of the JCOM component, the ODL defines a dual interface. A dual interface supports a C++-like v-table interface and an IDispatch interface. Because of this, the MkTypLib utility command (see Listing 26.12) produces a header file that is different from the euclid.h header file. The jcom.h file contains definitions of the methods in each interface.

The first variable defined is an instance of a pointer to an IJCOMAdd1 interface, iadd1. The next is an HRESULT. In C++, each method of CJCOM explicitly returns an HRESULT. The CoCreateInstance function returns a pointer to a CJCOM object's IJCOMAdd1 interface. The first method tested is Inc_boolean. Note that the signature of the Inc_boolean method is the same as the signature in the ODL file. The result is returned in the last parameter. The test code is designed to use ASSERTs to verify the results of a call to a method.

The ASSERT macro in debug mode generates code to test its single Boolean parameter. If the value is TRUE, nothing happens; if the value is FALSE then a dialog is displayed at runtime showing the file name and the line number of the ASSERT. In non-debug mode, the ASSERT macro generates no code at all. This facility allows code to be written that is self-testing during development, but adds no overhead in the release version. The code in this example works—the ASSERT dialog is not displayed. If the call to Inc_boolean had failed, the ASSERT dialog would be displayed as shown in Figure 26.5.

Most of the test calls to IJCOMAdd1 methods are straightforward. The case for the Java data type long deserves comment. The Visual J++ documentation states that the ODL type for the Java long data type is int64. But int64 was not recognized. Some earlier documentation had mentioned using CURRENCY for the ODL mapping. This still works, so it was used.

Part
IV

Ch
26

Listing 26.21   The First Part of the Modified OnInitDialog Method in the JCOMClientDlg.cpp File Shows the Test Code that Calls the IJCOMAdd1 Interface(1 of 3) (\msdev\projects\chap26\JCOMClient\JCOMClient.cpp)

```
...

BOOL CJCOMClientDlg::OnInitDialog()
{
     CDialog::OnInitDialog();
...
     // TODO: Add extra initialization here
     IJCOMAdd1 *iadd1 = NULL;
     {
         HRESULT hr = NULL;

         hr = CoCreateInstance(CLSID_CJCOM, NULL,
                 CLSCTX_INPROC_SERVER, IID_IJCOMAdd1,
                 (void **)&iadd1);
         if(hr==S_OK)
         {
             short b = TRUE;
             hr = iadd1->Inc_boolean(b, &b);
             ASSERT (!b);

             byte y;
             y = 234;
             hr = iadd1->Inc_byte(y, &y);
             ASSERT(y==235);

             double d;
             d = 3.4567;
             hr = iadd1->Inc_double(d, &d);\
             ASSERT(d == 4.4567);

             float f;
             f = 1.23f;
             hr = iadd1->Inc_float(f, &f);
             ASSERT( f == 2.23f);

             int n;
             n = 77;
             hr = iadd1->Inc_int(n, &n);
             ASSERT( n == 78 );

             int *pn = &n;
             n = 99;
             hr = iadd1->Inc_intRef(pn);
             ASSERT( n == 100);
```

```
short s;
s = 4567;
hr = iadd1->Inc_short(s, &s);
ASSERT(s == 4568);

CY l;
l.Hi = 0;
l.Lo = 987;
hr = iadd1->Inc_long(l, &l);
ASSERT(l.Hi == 0 && l.Lo == 988);
```

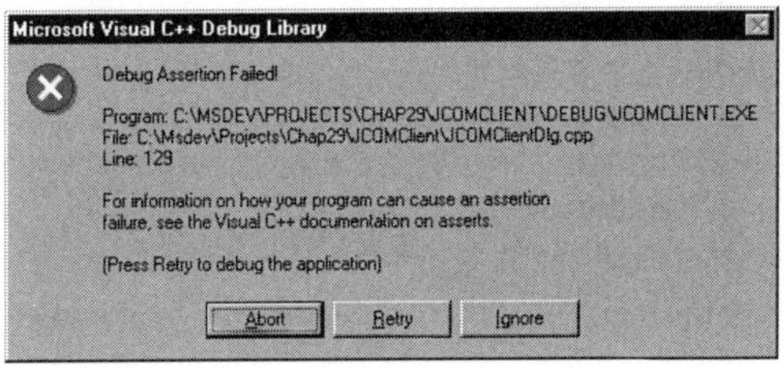

...

FIG. 26.5
The Microsoft Visual
C++ Debug Library
dialog box shows an
ASSERT failure in
line 129.

Listing 26.22 shows the next section of the OnInitDialog method. The test code for
Inc_String shows how to use a CString instance to allocate a BSTR variable. The Inc_String
method appends a 1 to the value passed in. The BSTR returned should be freed. The Inc_void
method does nothing but illustrate how to define a method that returns void.

**Listing 26.22 The Second Part of the Modified OnInitDialog Method in the
JCOMClientDlg.cpp File Shows More of the Test Code that Calls the
IJCOMAdd1 Interface(2 of 3)
(\msdev\projects\chap26\JCOMClient\JCOMClient.cpp)**

```
        ...
                  {
                          CString hello("Hello");
                          BSTR pSIn = hello.AllocSysString();
                          BSTR pSOut = NULL;
                          hr = iadd1->Inc_String(pSIn, &pSOut);

                          CString hello1(pSOut);
                          ASSERT( hello1 == "Hello1");

                          ::SysFreeString(pSOut);
                  }

                  {
                          CString hello("Hello");
                          BSTR pSInOut = hello.AllocSysString();
```

continues

Listing 26.22 Continued

```
                        hr = iadd1->Inc_StringRef(&pSInOut);

                        CString hello1(pSInOut);
                        ASSERT( hello1 == "Hello1");

                        ::SysFreeString(pSInOut);
            }
            {
                        BSTR pSInOut = NULL;

                        hr = iadd1->Inc_StringRef(&pSInOut);

                        CString hello1(pSInOut);
                        ASSERT( hello1 == "1");

                        ::SysFreeString(pSInOut);
            }
            hr = iadd1->Inc_void();

        }
...
```

Listing 26.23 shows the last section of the OnInitDialog method that tests the IJCOMOther interface. An instance of a pointer to an IJCOMOther interface is defined to store the interface pointer returned from CoCreateInstance. The test of the IntProp1 property consists of setting the property value to 23 and then getting the property value. The new value is compared with the value that was set. Notice that the Java methods are named getIntProp1 and putIntProp1, but the C++ method names generated in the jcom.h file are actually get_IntProp1 and put_IntProp1.

The iadd1 interface pointer is used to test the GetAdd1/SetAdd1/DoAdd1 methods of the IJCOMOther interface. First GetAdd1 is called to verify that the default is really set to NULL. Then, the SetAdd1 method is called to store the value of the first IJCOMAdd1 pointer obtained. Next, the GetAdd1 method is called to verify that the SetAdd1 call worked correctly. Finally, the DoAdd1 method is called with value 23. The return value is tested for 24 to verify that it was incremented by calling the Inc_int method on the IJCOMAdd1 interface set by SetAdd1.

The DoException method is tested by calling it with various input values and testing the returned HRESULT values. The Release method of the IUnknown interface is called to free the iother and iadd1 interfaces instances returned from CoCreateInstance.

Listing 26.23 The First Part of the Modified OnInitDialog Method in the JCOMClientDlg.cpp File Shows the Test Code that Calls the IJCOMOther Interface(3 of 3) (\msdev\projects\chap26\JCOMClient\JCOMClient.cpp)

```cpp
...
            IJCOMOther *iother = NULL;
            hr = CoCreateInstance(CLSID_CJCOM, NULL,
                    CLSCTX_INPROC_SERVER, IID_IJCOMOther,
                    (void **)&iother);
            if(hr==S_OK)
            {
                hr = iother->put_IntProp1(23);
                int n = 0;
                hr = iother->get_IntProp1(&n);
                ASSERT(n==23);

                ASSERT(iadd1);
                if(iadd1)
                {
                    IJCOMAdd1 *newadd1;

                    iother->GetAdd1(&newadd1);
                    ASSERT(newadd1 == NULL);

                    iother->SetAdd1(iadd1);
                    iother->GetAdd1(&newadd1);
                    ASSERT(newadd1 == iadd1);

                    int n = 0;
                    hr = iother->DoAdd1(23, &n);
                    ASSERT(n == 24);
                }
                hr = iother->DoException(0);
                ASSERT( hr == S_OK);
                hr = iother->DoException(1);
                ASSERT( hr == S_FALSE);
                hr = iother->DoException(2);
                ASSERT( hr == E_OUTOFMEMORY);
                hr = iother->DoException(-1);
                ASSERT( hr == E_FAIL);

                iother->Release();
            }
        }
        if(iadd1)
        {
            iadd1->Release();
        }
        return TRUE;  // return TRUE  unless you set the focus to a control
}
```

Part

IV

Ch

26

From Here...

In this chapter you have learned more about how to create ActiveX components using Java. Also covered was how to use Java ActiveX objects from other languages such as Visual C++. See the following chapter for more related information.

■ In Chapter 27, "Scripting Client Applets," learn how to communicate with Java applets from JavaScript and VBScript.

Scripting Client Applets

Many of your Java applets will be designed to run in a browser; and today's browsers are evolving into application platforms. Microsoft's Internet Explorer browser supports compiled Java applets, but it also supports two program scripting languages: JavaScript and VBScript. This chapter will discuss the Internet Explorer browser scripting capabilities and how to interface your Java applets with scripts.

Scripting allows embedding source code within an HTML page. The source code can communicate with objects on the HTML page like Java applets and ActiveX components. In addition, the Internet Explorer Scripting Object Model provides source code access to many of the properties of an HTML page.

This chapter will focus on the HTML features that are of interest to programmers. No attempt is made to give a complete introduction to all HTML and scripting features. ■

The following list provides some Internet Web resources that will be useful. Of particular interest to script developers will be the sites that provide detailed online documentation for the JavaScript and VBScript language syntax and functions.

ON THE WEB

http://www.microsoft.com/ie/   Microsoft Internet Explorer with ActiveX Technology page. This is the home page for Internet Explorer information and download.

http://www.microsoft.com/workshop/   Microsoft Site Builder home page for Internet technologies.

http://www.microsoft.com/vbscript/   Microsoft Visual Basic Scripting Edition home page.

http://www.microsoft.com/vbscript/us/vbslang/vbstoc.htm   Microsoft VB Scripting Language Reference. This page is an online index to VBScript keywords, functions, methods, objects, properties, and statements.

http://www.microsoft.com/jscript/   JScript comes to the Internet. This is Microsoft's JScript home page.

http://www.netscape.com/comprod/products/navigator/version_3.0/building_blocks/jscript/ Netscape Corporation's JavaScript home page.

http://www.netscape.com/eng/mozilla/3.0/handbook/javascript/   The JavaScript Guide is Netscape Corporation's page for JavaScript documentation. It has links to JavaScript syntax and language reference documents.

Scripting with VBScript and JavaScript

Internet Explorer supports scripts written in JavaScript, developed by Netscape and Sun, and VBScript developed by Microsoft. JavaScript and VBScript scripts can be in the same HTML page. Scripts written in JavaScript can call scripts written in VBScript, and vice versa.

JavaScript syntax is similar to C++ and Java. One of the main differences is that the required semicolon ending each C++ and Java statement is optional in JavaScript. JavaScript, while not object-oriented, is object-based. Objects with associated data variables and methods can be defined, but there are no classes or inheritance. JavaScript data variables are loosely typed so variables do not have to be declared before use.

Table 27.1 contains a list of JavaScript reserved words. The `function` keyword is used to declare routines in JavaScript.

Table 27.1   JavaScript Reserved Keywords

abstract	do	if	null	synchronized
boolean	double	implements	package	this
break	else	import	private	throw
byte	extends	in	protected	throws
case	false	instanceof	public	transient
catch	final	int	return	true
char	finally	interface	short	try
class	float	long	static	var
const	for	native	super	void
continue	function	new	switch	while
default	goto			with

VBScript is a subset of Visual Basic for Applications. Microsoft's Web site contains comprehensive information about the VBScript implementation.

The rest of this section will use some simple examples to introduce the basics of scripting. Figure 27.1 shows the output of the HTML page listed in Listing 27.1. The contents of an HTML file are processed from top to bottom. Any directives that cause text to be output are invoked during this initial processing when the page is loaded. After a page is loaded, other events may cause additional output to occur. The script1.html file shown in Listing 27.1 is loaded and processed from top to bottom. The <HTML> tag along with its ending tag </HTML> defines the file as an HTML document. The <TITLE> tag is used to define the title text to be displayed by the browser. In Figure 27.1, the title is displayed in the main windows caption. The <TITLE> text is not output as part of the page's output.

The <BODY> and </BODY> tags define a group of statements. Attributes specified on the <BODY> tag can define default settings that will apply to the contents of the body. There can be more than one body in a document.

The first output directive is the <H2> tag which causes the heading 2 style to be applied to the text between <H2> and </H2>, and the text to be written to the browser's main window as part of the document's output. The next two lines are written as separate paragraphs using the <P> tag.

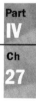

Part

IV

Ch

27

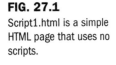

FIG. 27.1

Script1.html is a simple HTML page that uses no scripts.

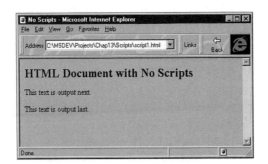

**Listing 27.1 A Simple HTML Page with No
Scripts (\msdev\projects\Chap27\Scripts\script1.html.)**

```
<HTML>
<TITLE>No Scripts</TITLE>

<BODY>

<H2>HTML Document with No Scripts </H2>
This text is output next.<P>
This text is output last.<P>

</BODY>

</HTML>
```

The HTML document script2.html is shown opened in Internet Explorer in Figure 27.2. The contents of script2.html is shown in Listing 27.2. This HTML document contains some simple scripts. Again, the document is processed from top to bottom when loaded. The <H2> text is output first. This is followed by the first script. The <SCRIPT> tag allows the specification of the scripting language to be used to process the contents of the script. Internet Explorer supports "VBScript" and "JavaScript" (case is not important) as the values that can be specified in the LANGUAGE= attribute of the <SCRIPT> tag. The contents of the first script is a call to the write method of the window.document object. Where did the window.document object come from?

The browser implements a hierarchy of objects that represents the objects that are parsed by the browser from the HTML document. This hierarchy of objects is known as the "Object Model for Scripting." The Object Model is discussed in more detail later in this chapter. At the root of the Object Model hierarchy is the window object. The window object represents the browser window that displays the HTML document. Each script runs in the context of the document's window. The document object that represents the HTML document is a property of the window object in the Object Model hierarchy.

The contents of the first script is not inside the body of a function; therefore, the statements are executed immediately as it is encountered when the page is first loaded. The window.document.write method writes a text string to the browser window. This accounts for the second line of output in Figure 27.2. Notice that the text string that is written contains an HTML <P> tag. The data that is written is interpreted as a text stream containing HTML tags as if the text came from an HTML document outside a script definition. Within a script, only statements of the respective scripting language are accepted. Any plain text or HTML tags would cause syntax errors.

The third line of output is the first line of open text after the <BODY> statement. A new paragraph tag, <P>, causes the equivalent of two line breaks (

)in the output. The <P> tag causes a first break at the end of the current line to position output to the start of the next line. In addition, another line break positions output to the next line, thus leaving a blank line between paragraphs.

All of the scripts in script2.html are inline scripts; in other works, they are invoked during the initial parsing of the document in the order they are encountered in the document. These inline scripts allow output to be formatted using expressions and environmental information. This is illustrated by the next script which writes a sentence formatted in an expression that references the document's title value. Also notice that the "window." prefix is not used to reference the document.write method. Because the script is running in the context of the window object, the explicit dereferencing of the current script's window is not required.

The last line of output is written from another script. This script uses the document.write method, but it is written in the VBScript language.

FIG. 27.2

Script2.html is a simple HTML page with text output by various scripts.

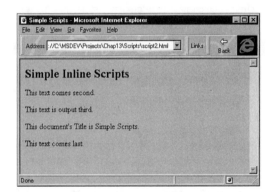

Listing 27.2   A Simple Web Page with Scripts (\msdev\projects\Chap27\Scripts\script2.html.)

```
<HTML>
<TITLE>Simple Scripts</TITLE>
<H2>Simple Inline Scripts</H2>

<SCRIPT LANGUAGE="JavaScript">
window.document.write ("This text comes second.<P>")
</SCRIPT>
```

continues

Listing 27.2 Continued

```
<BODY>
This text is output third.<P>

<SCRIPT LANGUAGE="JavaScript">
document.write("This document's Title is " + document.title + ".<P>")
</SCRIPT>

</BODY>

<SCRIPT LANGUAGE="VBScript">
document.write ("<P>This text comes last.")
</SCRIPT>
  </HTML>
```

Script3.html shows the use of scripting subroutines/functions. Figure 27.3 shows the browser display of script3.html. A function such as a JavaScript function, or a VBScript Sub or Function, can be defined in scripts. When the document is initially parsed, function definitions are saved but not invoked. A function must be explicitly or implicitly invoked. A function is explicitly invoked by being called from a statement that is executing in a script. Or, a function can be invoked implicitly as a result of being attached to an event. Listing 27.3 shows the first half of the contents of script3.html.

Here is an overview of the processing that occurs when script3.html is loaded. First the <TITLE> tag is processed. The first output is produced by the <H2> heading. The VBScript script is encountered next. Because the contents of the script are the definition of a single subroutine named myOnLoad, there are no statements actually invoked. The next script contains a single inline statement that calls the alert method of the window object. The alert method displays a string in a simple message box with an OK button. Because the statement is inline, it is invoked. Therefore, a message box will appear as the page is loaded. Click OK on the This Is Called First alert box.

Next the <BODY> tag is encountered. The <BODY> tag has two attributes specified, LANGUAGE and ONLOAD. The LANGUAGE attribute is used to specify the default scripting language within this body. The default is JavaScript. The ONLOAD attribute is used to specify some script text to be invoked. In this case, the script text is myOnLoad. Note that this "script" is actually a valid single VBScript statement that calls the myOnLoad subroutine. Multiple scripting language statements could have been entered as the value of the ONLOAD attribute. The ONLOAD script is invoked when the <BODY> tag is encountered. The myOnLoad subroutine is called, which calls the window.alert method to display a second alert box as the page is loaded. Click OK on the myOnLoad called alert box to continue.

Next are four <INPUT TYPE=Button > tags and two <A HREF= > tags which are used to demonstrate how scripts can be attached to events. The <INPUT> tags define four push buttons. The <A> tags define two dynamic links. These six objects are used to illustrate the different ways to attach scripts to object events.

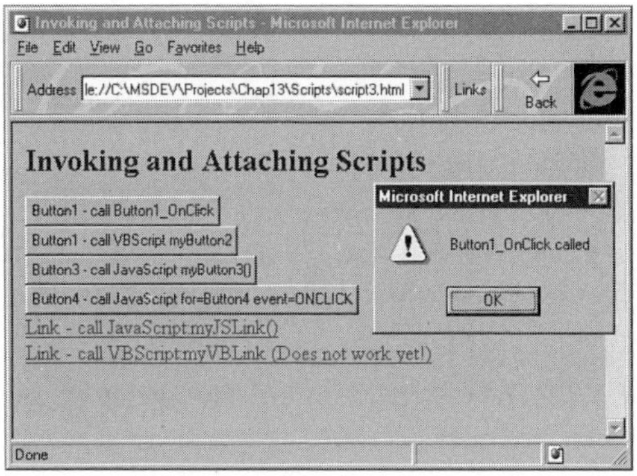

FIG. 27.3

Script3.html shows how scripts can be invoked and attached to events.

Listing 27.3   Invoking Scripts: The Form Definition—Part 1 of 2 (\msdev\projects\Chap27\Scripts\script3.html.)

```html
<HTML>
<TITLE>Invoking and Attaching Scripts</TITLE>
<H2>Invoking and Attaching Scripts</H1>

<SCRIPT LANGUAGE="VBSCRIPT">
Sub myOnLoad
    alert "myOnLoad is called second from <BODY ONLOAD="
End Sub
</SCRIPT>

<SCRIPT LANGUAGE="VBSCRIPT">
    alert "This is called first"
</SCRIPT>

<BODY LANGUAGE="VBSCRIPT" ONLOAD="myOnLoad">

<INPUT type=Button name=Button1
    value="Button1 - call Button1_OnClick"><BR>
<INPUT type=Button name=Button2
    value="Button1 - call VBScript myButton2"
    ONCLICK=myButton2><BR>
<INPUT type=Button name=Button3
    value="Button3 - call JavaScript myButton3()"
    ONCLICK="myButton3()" LANGUAGE=JavaScript><BR>
<INPUT type=Button name=Button4
    value="Button4 - call JavaScript for=Button4 event=ONCLICK"><BR>
<A HREF="JavaScript:myJSLink()">Link - call JavaScript:myJSLink()<A><BR>
<A HREF="VBScript:myVBLink">Link - call VBScript:myVBLink (Does not work
yet!)<A><BR>
...
```

Part
IV

Ch
27

Listing 27.3 shows the second half of the contents of script3.html which consists of the functions that are called for each of the six objects on the HTML document. First, look at the Button1 definition in Listing 27.3. When the button is clicked, the browser looks for a function on the page named `Button1_OnClick`. If one is found, it is called in response to clicking the button. Because `Button1_OnClick` is defined in script3.html (see Listing 27.4) it is called. Notice that Figure 27.3 shows the Button1_OnClick alert box displayed after clicking Button1. This is one way to attach a script to an object event.

Next look at the definition of `Button2` in Listing 27.3. The <INPUT> tag contains the `ONCLICK` attribute whose value is a call to the function `myButton2`. The default language is VBScript as specified in the <BODY> tag. When Button2 is clicked, `myButton2` is called.

The Button3 example is similar to Button2 except that the language used is JavaScript. The `LANGUAGE` attribute is specified on the <INPUT> tag. The syntax of the `ONCLICK` text is JavaScript, which requires parentheses () after a function name even if there are no parameters.

Button4 is similar to Button1 in that it has no `ONCLICK` attribute. The last script in script3.html (see Listing 27.4) is called when Button4 is clicked. This script uses a special `for= event=` syntax to specify that the script is associated with an object event.

The two links defined at the bottom of Listing 27.3 show a way to invoke a script by clicking a link in an HTML page. Notice that the `HREF` value is interpreted as a script when prefixed with "JavaScript:" followed by valid statements in the JavaScript language separated by semicolons. This feature works only for the JavaScript language within Internet Explorer.

In addition to `onClick`, other HTML element events include: `onFocus`, `onBlur`, `onChange`, and `onSelect`.

Listing 27.4 Invoking Scripts: The Scripts—Part 2 of 2 (\msdev\projects\Chap27\Scripts\script3.html.)

```
<SCRIPT LANGUAGE="VBSCRIPT">
     sub Button1_OnClick
     alert "Button1_OnClick called"
     end sub
     sub myButton2
     alert "myButton2 called"
     end sub
     sub myVBLink
     alert "myVBLink called"
     end sub
</SCRIPT>
<SCRIPT LANGUAGE="JavaScript">
     function myButton3()
     {
     alert("myButton3 called")
     }
     function myJSLink()
     {
     alert("myJSLink called")
```

```
    }
</SCRIPT>
<SCRIPT for=Button4 event=ONCLICK LANGUAGE="VBScript">
    alert "for Button4 event OnClick called"
</SCRIPT>

</BODY>
</HTML>
```

In the next example, script4.html (see Listings 27.5-27.7) is used to compare the use of JavaScript and VBScript. A series of push buttons, each call a method of the window object. There are two sets of the buttons, one set for VBScript and one set for JavaScript. Figure 27.4 shows script4.html in Internet Explorer.

The window object methods called in script4.html include: alert, confirm, prompt, setTimeout, open, close, and navigate. The methods alert, confirm, and prompt each display a different dialog box. The setTimeout method sets an interval timer. The methods open, close, and navigate direct the browser to open other HTML documents.

Listing 27.5 contains the button definitions for alert, confirm, and prompt. The three dialog boxes are shown in Figure 27.5. The default scripting language is the browser default JavaScript. The VBScript language context is specified using the LANGUAGE attribute of the <INPUT> and <SCRIPT> tags.

In the cases of alert and confirm, the JavaScript and VBScript text is the same. JavaScript requires parentheses around function parameters, VBScript does not. The examples use parentheses in most cases for consistency. The prompt method returns a string as opposed to void for alert and Boolean for confirm. VBScript required that an assignment be made of the string returned by prompt. JavaScript did not.

FIG. 27.4

Script4.html has buttons to demonstrate useful window object methods.

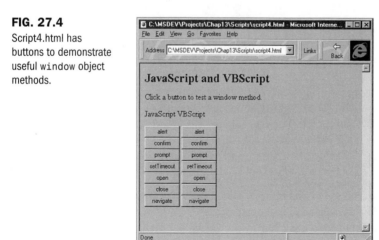

Part

IV

Ch

27

Listing 27.5 The *window* Methods: *alert, confirm,* and *prompt* (\msdev\projects\Chap27\Scripts\script4.html.)

```
<HTML>
<TITLE>JavaScript and VBScript</TITLE>
<H2>JavaScript and VBScript</H2>
<BODY>
Click a button to test a window method.
<P>
JavaScript     VBScript<P>
<INPUT TYPE=Button VALUE="alert"
       ONCLICK="window.alert('JavaScript alert')">
<INPUT TYPE=Button VALUE="alert" LANGUAGE=VBScript
       ONCLICK="window.alert('VBScript alert')"><BR>
<INPUT TYPE=Button VALUE="confirm"
       ONCLICK="window.confirm('JavaScript confirm')">
<INPUT TYPE=Button VALUE="confirm" LANGUAGE=VBScript
       ONCLICK="window.confirm('VBScript confirm')"><BR>
<INPUT TYPE=Button VALUE="prompt"
       ONCLICK="window.prompt('JavaScript', 'prompt')">
<INPUT TYPE=Button VALUE="prompt" LANGUAGE=VBScript
       ONCLICK="sPrompt = window.prompt('VBScript', 'prompt')"><BR>
...
```

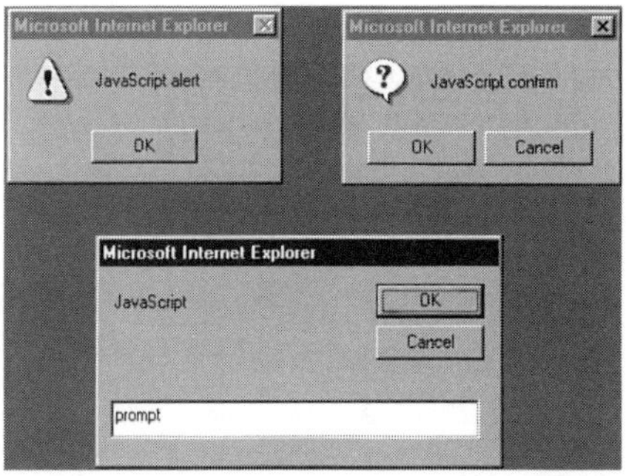

FIG. 27.5

Here are examples of the dialog boxes of the window methods `alert`, `confirm`, and `prompt`.

Listing 27.6 contains the section of script4.html that defines the buttons that invoke the open, close, and navigate methods. The open method opens a URL in a new instance of the browser. A reference to the window is returned. This can be passed to the close method to destroy the window created by open. It appears that there may be a bug in IE3.0 which closes the creating window instead of the new one. Note that the VBScript call to window.open uses a set keyword. If this is removed, an error is generated by IE3.0.

The <INPUT> tags for the close buttons show how multiple script statements can be used in the ONCLICK attribute. The navigate method causes a new URL to be loaded into the browser window to replace the current document. The JavaScript version loads script1.html. The VBScript version loads script2.html. These examples illustrate how the evolution toward object-oriented languages can contribute to the normalization of language syntax.

Listing 27.6   open, close and navigate Methods—Part 2 of 3 (\msdev\projects\Chap27\Scripts\script4.html.)

```
...
<INPUT TYPE=Button VALUE="open"
        ONCLICK="newWindowJavaScript = window.open('script1.html', '_blank',
'toolbar=yes, location=yes, directories=yes')">
<INPUT TYPE=Button VALUE="open" LANGUAGE=VBScript
        ONCLICK="set newWindowVBScript = window.open('script2.html', '_blank',
'')"><BR>
<INPUT TYPE=Button VALUE="close"
        ONCLICK="
        if(newWindowJavaScript != null)
        {
        // Bug?: this closes original window instead of new one
        window.close(newWindowJavaScript);
        newWindowJavaScript = null;
        }">
<INPUT TYPE=Button VALUE="close" LANGUAGE=VBScript
        ONCLICK="
        if not IsNull(newWindowVBScript) then
        rem Bug?: this closes original window instead of new one
        window.close(newWindowVBScript)
        newWindowVBScript = null
        end if"><BR>
<INPUT TYPE=Button VALUE="navigate"
        ONCLICK="window.navigate('script1.html')">
<INPUT TYPE=Button VALUE="navigate" LANGUAGE=VBScript
        ONCLICK="window.navigate('script2.html')"><BR>

...
```

In Listing 27.7, the `window.setTimeout` method is used. The first parameter is a script, the second parameter is a number of milliseconds. The `setTimeout` waits the number of milliseconds before invoking the script. The `clearTimeout` method is used to delete an outstanding timeout. In the script4.html example, the script is a call to the functions, `myJavaScriptTimer()` and `myVBScriptTimer()`. Each function calls the `alert` method.

Listing 27.7   window Methods: setTimeout Routines—Part 3 of 3 (\msdev\projects\Chap27\Scripts\script4.html.)

```
<INPUT TYPE=Button VALUE="setTimeout"
        ONCLICK="timeoutIDJavaScript = window.setTimeout('myJavaScriptTimer()',
1000)">
<INPUT TYPE=Button VALUE="setTimeout" LANGUAGE=VBScript
        ONCLICK="timeoutIDVBScript = window.setTimeout('myVBScriptTimer()',
1000)"><BR>
<SCRIPT LANGUAGE="JavaScript">
        var timeoutIDJavaScript
        var newWindowJavaScript = null
```

Part
IV

Ch
27

continues

Listing 27.7   Continued

```
     function myJavaScriptTimer()
     {
     alert("JavaScript timer expired")
     window.clearTimeout(timeoutIDJavaScript)
     }
 </SCRIPT>
 <SCRIPT LANGUAGE="VBScript">
     Dim timeoutIDVBScript
     Dim newWindowVBScript

     newWindowVBScript = Null

     function myVBScriptTimer()
     alert("VBScript timer expired")
     window.clearTimeout(timeoutIDVBScript)
     end function
 </SCRIPT>

 </BODY>
 </HTML>
```

The next example HTML document is script5.html. Figure 27.6 shows this document in Internet Explorer. Listing 27.6 shows the contents of script5.html. This example shows some of the object-based features of the JavaScript scripting language. JavaScript support for objects is similar to the C language support for `structs`. Despite the lack of classes, and therefore inheritance, structured objects can be created that consist of variables and functions.

This HTML document consists of a script that defines an object called `person` and creates an array of four `person` objects. Finally, the array entries are output using the `person` method sentence, and again using the `tableRow` method.

The `person` function declares instance variables by referring to the variable using the `this` notation. Object methods such as `sentence` and `tableRow` can be saved, as well as the data variables `name` and `age`. The object methods should reference the object properties defined in the "constructor" function `person`.

After the `person` "class" has been declared, an `Array` variable is declared called `persons`. The new operator is used to create a new `Array` object and save it in the `persons` variable. JavaScript, like Java, allows variables to be declared anywhere within a function.

Four `person` objects are created using the new operator with the `person` function. JavaScript does not support function overloading; in other words, only one `person` function can be declared.

After the `persons` array has been created, more inline code iterates the contents of the array. For each person, the string returned by the `person.sentence` method is written to the document using `document.write`. The `person.sentence` method returns a string in the form of a sentence including a trailing <BR> tag. The string contains information about the person.

Next, the contents of the `persons` array is formatted and output as an HTML table. First, the <TABLE> tag is written. Then, a table heading for the table which spans the two rows is output. A table header for the name and age columns is output. Next, the array is iterated using a for loop. For each person, the string returned by the `tableRow` method is output to the document. Finally, the </TABLE> tag is written.

Storing tabular data in arrays of objects can be just as effective in an HTML document as in an application. The scripts presented in this section have been very simple, yet they demonstrated that scripting offers a lot of power to HTML developers.

FIG. 27.6

Script5.html defines an array of objects and displays them twice.

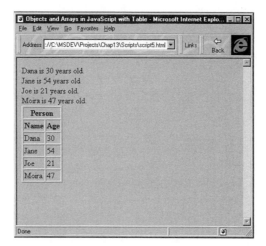

Listing 27.8   JavaScript Objects
Example (\msdev\projects\Chap27\Scripts\script5.html.)

```
<HTML>
<TITLE>Objects and Arrays in JavaScript with Table</TITLE>
<BODY>
<SCRIPT LANGUAGE=JavaScript>
    function person(name, age){
    this.name = name
    this.age = age
    this.sentence = sentence
    this.tableRow = tableRow
    }

    function sentence(){
    return this.name + " is "
    + this.age + " years old." + "<BR>"
    }
    function tableRow(){
    return "<TD>" + persons[i].name
    + "<TD>" + persons[i].age + "<TR>"
    }
```

Part
IV

Ch
27

continues

Listing 27.8   Continued

```
      // define a person array
      var persons = new Array()

      persons[0] = new person("Dana", 30)
      persons[1] = new person("Jane", 54)
      persons[2] = new person("Joe", 21)
      persons[3] = new person("Moira", 47)

      // display as sentences
      for(i=0; i < persons.length ; ++i){
      document.write(persons[i].sentence())
      }

      // display as a table
      document.write("<TABLE BORDER=1>")
      document.write("<TH COLSPAN=2>Person<TR>")
      document.write("<TH>Name<TH>Age<TR>")
      for(i=0; i < persons.length ; ++i){
      document.write(persons[i].tableRow())
      }
      document.write("</TABLE>")
</SCRIPT>
</BODY>
</HTML>
```

Using Forms

In this section HTML forms will be examined more closely. There are many opportunities to enhance HTML forms using Java applets. The example HTML document used in this section is order.html (see Listings 27.9-27.15). This HTML document contains a simple form to order chocolate truffles using a credit card. Figure 27.7 shows the form document running in Internet Explorer. An error alert box is displayed announcing that an invalid state code was entered when the Submit button was pressed.

Listing 27.9 below shows the beginning of order.html. It shows a <MARQUEE> tag. The Marquee feature allows the specification of a text string that will be scrolled automatically within the marquee object.

**Listing 27.9   The Order Form: The Marquee Source—Part 1 of 7
(\msdev\projects\Chap27\Forms\order.html.)**

```
<HTML>
<HEAD><TITLE>Linda's Chocolate Truffles</TITLE></HEAD>
<BODY Language =JavaScript onLoad="Clear()">
<MARQUEE BGCOLOR=#FFFFBB
     DIRECTION=LEFT BEHAVIOR=ALTERNATE
     SCROLLAMOUNT=10 SCROLLDELAY=200>
<FONT COLOR="WHITE">
```

```
Linda's Chocolate Truffles. Order Now!
</FONT>
</MARQUEE>
```

FIG. 27.7

Order.html is a form to order chocolates by credit card.

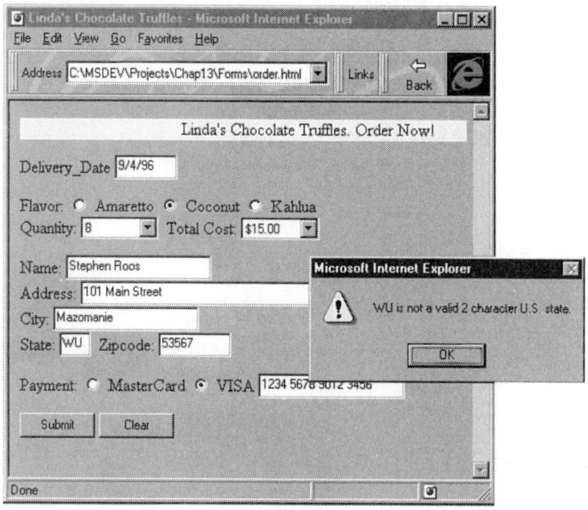

Listing 27.10 shows the second part of order.html in which the form and its elements are defined. The Object model uses the term "element" to describe document or form controls like radio buttons, check boxes, text controls, combo boxes, and push buttons. The <FORM> tag has a NAME attribute. The form name can be used to reference elements within it from scripts.

The <INPUT> tag is used to define a set of elements. The TYPE attribute value determines the type of element created. Values of the TYPE attribute include CHECKBOX, HIDDEN, IMAGE, PASSWORD, RADIO, RESET, SUBMIT, TEXT, and TEXTAREA. The first element created in the form is the Delivery_Date TEXT element. A TEXT element is an input text control.

OptFlavor is a set of three RADIO elements. Note that each RADIO element in the same group has the same NAME. The CHECKED attribute is used to specify the initial radio button in the group to be checked.

The <SELECT> tag is used to define a drop-down list box element named selQuantity. The ONCHANGE attribute is used to call the quantityChange function when the selection changes. Similarly, the selCost SELECT element uses the ONCHANGE attribute to call the costChange function when the selection changes. These two elements need to be set to the same relative entry. When one changes, the other must be set to the same selection.

Name, Address, City, State, and Zip are all INPUT TEXT elements. The OptCredit RADIO group has two elements. The last two INPUT elements are push buttons. The Submit and Clear buttons call the SubmitOrder and Clear functions, respectively, when clicked.

Finally, there is a Java applet defined whose name is States and class name is States.class. This applet and the functions called by the form elements are discussed later.

Part
IV

Ch
27

Listing 27.10   The Order Form: The Form Source—Part 2 of 7 (\msdev\ projects\Chap27\Forms\order.html.)

```
<FORM Name="form1">
Delivery_Date  <INPUT NAME="Delivery_Date" TYPE="Text" SIZE=8 >
<P>
Flavor:
<INPUT TYPE=RADIO NAME=OptFlavor CHECKED> Amaretto
<INPUT TYPE=RADIO NAME=OptFlavor> Coconut
<INPUT TYPE=RADIO NAME=OptFlavor> Kahlua
<BR>
Quantity:
<SELECT NAME="selQuantity" SIZE=1 ONCHANGE="quantityChange()">
<OPTION VALUE=4 SELECTED> 4
<OPTION VALUE=8> 8
<OPTION VALUE=16> 16
</SELECT>
Total Cost:
<SELECT NAME="selCost" SIZE=1 ONCHANGE="costChange()" >
<OPTION VALUE=8 SELECTED> $8.00
<OPTION VALUE=15> $15.00
<OPTION VALUE=16> $28.00
</SELECT>
<P>
Name: <INPUT NAME="Name" TYPE="Text" SIZE=24 >
<BR>
Address: <INPUT NAME="Address" TYPE="Text" SIZE=60 >
<BR>
City: <INPUT NAME="City" TYPE="Text" SIZE=24 >
<BR>
State: <INPUT NAME="State" TYPE="Text" SIZE=2 >
Zipcode: <INPUT NAME="Zip" TYPE="Text" SIZE=10 VALUE="0">
<P>
Payment:
<INPUT TYPE=RADIO NAME=OptCredit CHECKED> MasterCard
<INPUT TYPE=RADIO NAME=OptCredit> VISA
<INPUT NAME="Credit_Card" TYPE="Text" SIZE=24 >
<P>
<INPUT TYPE=BUTTON VALUE="Submit" NAME="BtnSubmitOrder" onClick="SubmitOrder()">
<INPUT TYPE=BUTTON VALUE="Clear" NAME="BtnClear" onClick="Clear()">
<BR>
</FORM>
<P>
<applet code=States.class id=States></applet>
</BODY>
...
```

Listing 27.11 shows the beginning of the script. A global variable, f, is set to document.form1. This is the syntax that uses the <FORM> NAME attribute to reference a document's forms and a form's elements directly. The costChange function is called when the selection changes in the selCost SELECT element. When called, costChange selects the corresponding entry in the selQuantity SELECT element. The converse is true for the quantityChange function. When the selQuantity SELECT element selection changes, quantityChange is called. The quantityChange function selects the corresponding entry in the selCost SELECT element. The element object and its options property are more examples of using the Object Model.

Listing 27.11   The Order Form: The *costChange* and *quantityChange* EventHandlers—Part 3 of 7 (\msdev\projects\Chap27\Forms\order.html.)

```
<SCRIPT LANGUAGE="JavaScript">
    var f = document.form1
    var daysToDeliver = 10

    function costChange()
    {
    f.selQuantity.options[f.selCost.selectedIndex].selected = true
    }
    function quantityChange()
    {
    f.selCost.options[f.selQuantity.selectedIndex].selected = true
    }
```

...

Listing 27.12 shows the Clear function. Its purpose is to reset the values of each element on the order form. The value property is used to set data values for appropriate input elements. A SELECT element's selection can be set using its options.selected property.

Listing 27.12   The Order Form: The *Clear* EventHandler—Part 4 of 7 (\msdev\ projects\Chap27\Forms\order.html.)

```
    function Clear()
    {
    f.Delivery_Date.value = ""
    d = new Date()
    d.setDate(d.getDate() + daysToDeliver)
    f.Delivery_Date.value =
    (d.getMonth() + 1) + "/" + (d.getDate()+1) + "/" + d.getYear()

    f.Name.value = ""
    f.Address.value = ""
    f.City.value = ""
    f.State.value = ""
    f.Zip.value = ""
    f.selCost.options[0].selected = true
    costChange()
    f.Credit_card.value = ""
    }
```

...

Part
IV

Ch
27

Listing 27.13 shows the SubmitOrder function. It is called when the Submit button is clicked. Each text element is validated by calling the ValidateRequired function. The State element is validated by calling the ValidateState script function.

Listing 27.13   The Order Form: EventHandlers: _SubmitOrder_—Part 5 of 7 (\msdev\projects\Chap27\Forms\order.html.)

```
function SubmitOrder()
{

if( ValidateRequired(f.Delivery_Date)
&& ValidateRequired(f.Name)
&& ValidateRequired(f.Address)
&& ValidateRequired(f.City)
&& ValidateState(f.State)
&& ValidateRequired(f.Zip)
&& ValidateRequired(f.Credit_Card))
{
alert("Thank you for your order!")
// TODO:  process real order here.
}
}
...
```

Listing 27.14 shows the ValidateRequired function. Its purpose is to validate that the element passed in has a non-null value. If the element's value is null, then an alert box is displayed with the element's name in the message. Then, the focus is put in that element and false is returned.

By passing a single parameter to ValidateRequired which represents the element object, properties like the element's name and value can be accessed. Also, the element's methods like focus can be called.

Listing 27.14   The Order Form: _ValidateRequired_ Routine—Part 6 of 7 (\msdev\projects\Chap27\Forms\order.html.)

```
function ValidateRequired(Field)
{
if (Field.value == "")
{
alert("Please enter " + Field.name)
Field.focus()
return false
}
return true
}
...
```

Listing 27.15 shows the last part of order.html. The ValidateState function is passed the State element as the Field parameter. The element's value is checked for null first. If not null, the isState method of the State Java applet is called to validate the name of the state. If the Java method returns false, an alert box is displayed and the focus is set to the element.

Listing 27.15   The Order Form: *ValidateState* Routine—Part 7 of 7 (\msdev\ projects\Chap27\Forms\order.html.)

```
    function ValidateState(Field)
    {
    if( ! ValidateRequired(Field) )
    return false
    if( window.document.States.isState(Field.value) )
    return true

    alert(Field.value + " is not a valid 2 character U.S. state.")
    Field.focus()
    return false
    }
</SCRIPT>
</HTML>
```

Listing 27.16 shows the Script.java source used to create the States.class file used in order.html. The states string only contains several states. The compiled States.class file has a size of 731 bytes. Java applets can be reused across HTML documents.

Listing 27.16   The States.java Source Code Called from Script (\msdev\ projects\Chap27\Forms\States.java.)

```
import java.applet.*;
import java.awt.*;

final public class States extends Applet
{
    final static String states = "AL,AK,AR,CA,HA,IO,NJ,NY,WI,WY";
    public States()
    {
    }

    final public boolean isState(String state)
    {
    String st = new String(state.toUpperCase());
    if(-1 != states.indexOf(st))
    return true;
    return false;
    }
}
```

Part

IV

Ch

27

Using Frames

This section will examine the use of the HTML <FRAME> and <FRAMESET> tags. Frames partition an HTML document's window into one or more panes or frames, each of which displays an URL. The <FRAMESET> tag is used to specify a set of <FRAME> tags. The frames within a frame set can be configured as columns or rows. The amount of space used by each frame can be specified. The <FRAME> tag has a NAME attribute to name the frame. The SRC attribute defines the initial HTML document to load into the frame. The SCROLLING attribute controls the frame's scroll bars.

Figure 27.8 shows the frame1.html document in Internet Explorer. The window has three frames configured as columns. Listing 27.17 shows the frame1.html document contents. The frame set contains three frame columns. The first column gets 35 percent of the width of the window, the next two columns share what's left. Only the third frame has scroll bars turned on. The <NOFRAME> tag is used to define output to be displayed by browsers that do not support frames.

FIG. 27.8

Frame1.html initially shows its three columns of window frames.

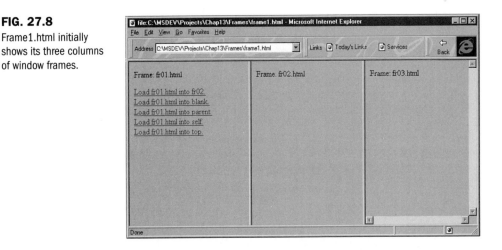

Listing 27.17 The Frame1.HTML Main Frame (\msdev\projects\Chap27\ Frames\frame1.html.)

```
<html>
<title Frame1.html>

<frameset cols="35%,*,*" marginheight=4 marginwidth=4>
<frame name="fr01" src="fr01.html" scrolling=no>
<frame name="fr02" src="fr02.html" scrolling=no>
<frame name="fr03" src="fr03.html" scrolling="yes">

</frameset>

<noframe>
<body>
```

```
Browser does not support frames!
</body>
</noframe>

</HTML>
```

Listing 27.18 shows the contents of fr01.html which are the initial contents of the first frame in frame1.html. Fr01.html contains a set of <A> tags which define links. These links illustrate some of the features available to support management of frame content. The <A> tag supports a TARGET attribute. The target is the name of the frame to use when loading the linked document. In the first <A> or anchor tag, the TARGET value is fr02. This is the name of a frame in the document's window. If clicked, fr01.html will be loaded into the fr02 frame.

The second link uses blank as a target which causes the new document to be displayed in a new browser window. The parent value is used to specify the immediate parent of the current frame (which might be another frame) as the target for the document. The self target value specifies the current frame as the target. The top target value specifies the topmost window of all frames to be the target.

Listing 27.18   The FR01.HTML Frame (\msdev\projects\Chap27\Frames\fr01.html.)

```
<HTML>
<TITLE>Frame Sample</TITLE>
<BODY>
Frame: fr01.html
<P>
<A TARGET="fr02" HREF="fr01.html">
Load fr01.html into fr02.</A><BR>
<A TARGET="_blank" HREF="fr01.html">
Load fr01.html into blank.</A><BR>
<A TARGET="_parent" HREF="fr01.html">
Load fr01.html into parent.</A><BR>
<A TARGET="_self" HREF="fr01.html">
Load fr01.html into self.</A><BR>
<A TARGET="_top" HREF="fr01.html">
Load fr01.html into top.</A>

</BODY>
</HTML>
```

Part
IV

Ch

27

Figure 27.9 shows the frame1.html document after the first two links were clicked. Clicking the first link caused the fr01.html document to be loaded into frame fr02. Clicking the second link caused the new window to be created to contain fr01.html.

FIG. 27.9

Frame1.html is shown
after the first two links
were clicked.

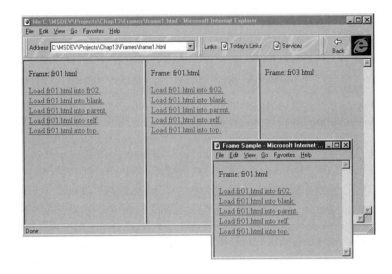

Listings 27.19 and 27.20 show the contents of fr02.html and fr03.html. Each file is a very simple document.

Listing 27.19   The FR02.HTML Frame (\msdev\projects\Chap27\Frames\fr02.html.)

```
<HTML>
<TITLE>Frame: fr02.html</TITLE>
<BODY>
Frame: fr02.html
</BODY>
</HTML>
Listing 13.20  The FR03.HTML Frame(\msdev\projects\Chap27\Frames\fr03.html.)
<HTML>
<TITLE>Frame: fr03.html</TITLE>
<BODY>
Frame: fr03.html
</BODY>
</HTML>
```

The next example shows how a frame set can be nested within another frame set. By nesting frame sets, a window can be configured similar to the Java java.awt.BorderLayout layout manager class. Frame2.html replaces the fr02 frame in frame1.html with a frame set that contains two frames configured as rows. Figure 27.10 shows the frame2.html document running in Internet Explorer. Listing 27.21 shows the contents of frame2.html.

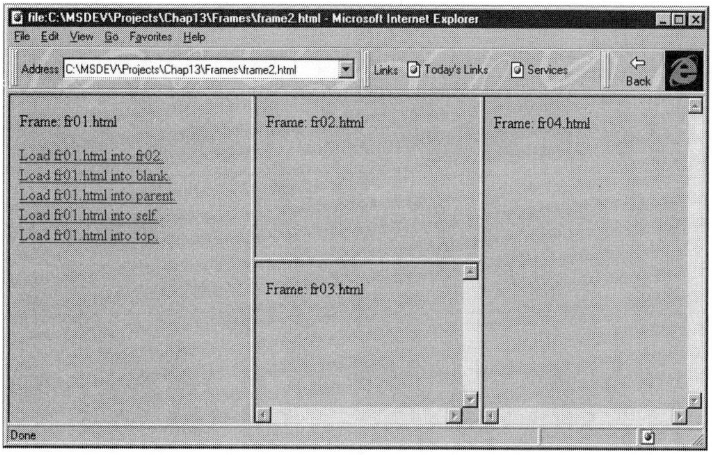

FIG. 27.10

Frame2.html initially shows three columns of frames with the middle column containing two rows of frames.

Listing 27.21   The Frame2.HTML Main Frame (\msdev\projects\Chap27\ Frames\frame2.html.)

```
<html>
<title Frame2.html>

<frameset cols="35%,*,*" marginheight=4 marginwidth=4>
<frame name="fr01" src="fr01.html" scrolling=no>

<frameset rows="*,*">
<frame name="fr02" src="fr02.html" scrolling=no>
<frame name="fr03" src="fr03.html" scrolling="yes">
</frameset>

<frame name="fr04" src="fr04.html" scrolling="yes">
</frameset>

<noframe>
<body>
Browser does not support frames!
</body>
</noframe>

</HTML>
```

Part
IV

Ch
27

Listing 27.22 shows the contents of fr04.html which is used to initialize the frame fr04.

**Listing 27.22 The FR04.HTML Frame
(\msdev\projects\Chap27\Frames\fr04.html.)**

```
<HTML>
<TITLE>Frame: fr04.html</TITLE>
<BODY>
Frame: fr04.html
</BODY>
</HTML>
```

Browsing with the Object Model

Internet Explorer supports the Object Model for Scripting. This hierarchy of objects represents the parsed contents of an HTML document including frames and forms. The Internet Explorer Object Model is compatible with the Netscape Navigator JavaScript Object Model. The Internet Explorer supports access to the Object model from JavaScript and VBScript.

The previous sections of this chapter have made references to the Object Model such as the `window` object methods `alert`, `prompt`, and `confirm`. In this section, the Object Model will be looked at in more detail. The Object Model is a hierarchy of related objects, and the hierarchy is illustrated in Table 27.1. The object names in monospace type are possible multiple objects; the others are single objects. You have seen that the `document` object was a property of the `window` object.

Table 27.1 Hierarchy of Objects in the Object Model for Scripting

WINDOW

              FRAME
              HISTORY
              NAVIGATOR
              LOCATION
              SCRIPT

                                    DOCUMENT
                                    LINK
                                    ANCHOR
                                    FORM
                                    ELEMENT

To demonstrate the capabilities of the Object Model, a sample HTML document is used. Browser.html (see Figure 27.11) has three frames, a top frame containing instructions, a lower-left frame containing a sample HTML document with a form, and a lower-right frame that will contain formatted report output. Any URL can be specified in the top frame and then loaded into the lower-left frame. Clicking the Report button causes a report of the contents of the loaded URL to be displayed in the lower-right frame.

The Object Model is used to enumerate each object and each object's properties in the report. The report has three different views or styles: Table, List, and Definition. These correspond to the HTML features used to format the output report contents.

Listing 27.23 shows the contents of browser.html which is the main frame for the browser. In Figure 27.12, the Report button has been clicked to produce a report on the default contents of the browser1 frame.

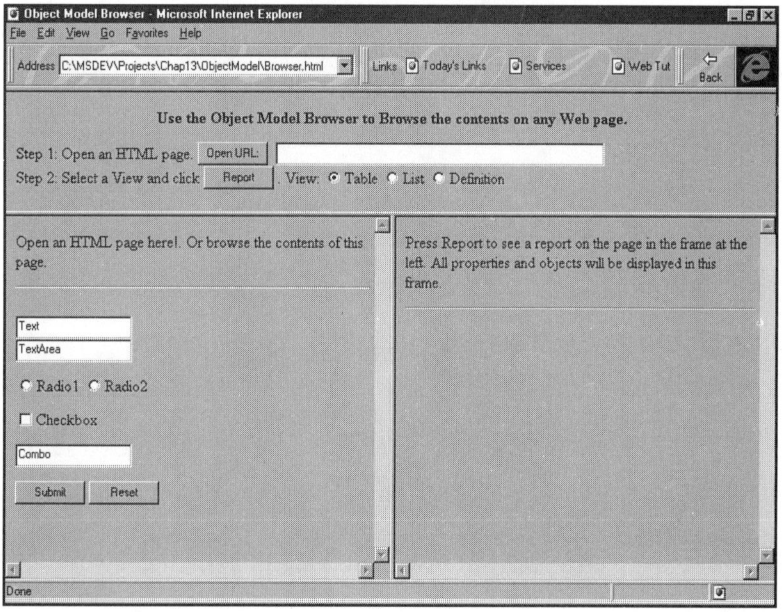

FIG. 27.11

Browser.html reports the contents of the HTML page in the lower-left frame window.

Listing 27.23 The Main Browser Page
(\msdev\projects\Chap27\ObjectModel\Browser.html.)

```html
<html>
<head>
<TITLE>Object Model Browser</TITLE>
</head>

<frameset ROWS="25%,*" MARGINHEIGHT=4 MARGINWIDTH=4>

<frame NAME="browser1" src="browser1.html" SCROLLING=no>

<frameset COLS="50%,50%">
<frame NAME="browser2" src="browser2.html" scrolling="yes">
<frame NAME="browser3" src="browser3.html" scrolling="yes">
</frameset>
```

Part
IV

Ch

27

continues

Listing 27.23   Continued

```
</frameset>

<noframe>
<body>Browser does not support frames!</body>
</noframe>

</HTML>
```

FIG. 27.12

Browser.html reports the contents of the HTML page in the lower-left frame window.

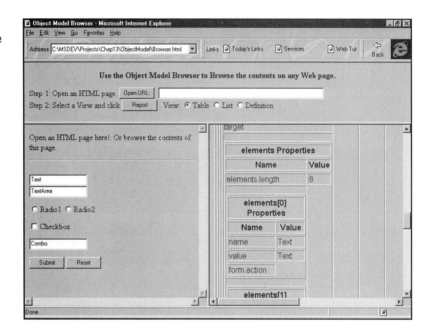

Listings 27.24-27.31 show the contents of browser1.html. This document is loaded into the browser1 frame of the browser.html document. Browser1.html consists of the form to open a specific URL, and generate a report on the contents of the URL. All of the routines to generate the report are contained in browser1.html. Listing 27.24 shows the first part of browser1.html containing the user interface elements. The Init function is called when the <BODY> is loaded. The LoadPage function is called when the Open URL button is clicked. The setView function is called with a parameter indicating which view is being set by clicking a radio button. The report is generated by clicking the WindowInfo button.

Listing 27.24   The Browser Code: The Form Definition—Part 1 of 8 (\msdev\ projects\Chap27\ObjectModel\Browser1.html.)

```
<HTML>
<TITLE>Object Model Browser</TITLE>
<BODY LANGUAGE="VBSCRIPT" ONLOAD="Init">
```

```
<CENTER><H4>Use the Object Model Browser to Browse the contents on any Web page.
</H4></CENTER>
Step 1: Open an HTML page.
<INPUT TYPE=Button NAME="LoadPage" VALUE="Open URL:">
<INPUT TYPE=TEXT NAME="AddressText" SIZE=64>
<BR>
Step 2: Select a View and click
<INPUT TYPE=Button Value="Report" NAME="WindowInfo">.
View:
<INPUT TYPE=Radio NAME="RadioView" ONCLICK="setView(1)" CHECKED>Table
<INPUT TYPE=Radio NAME="RadioView" ONCLICK="setView(2)">List
<INPUT TYPE=Radio NAME="RadioView" ONCLICK="setView(3)">Definition
...
```

Listing 27.25 shows the event-handling functions in browser1.html. The Init function sets a global variable, OutFrame to the browser3 frame, Window.parent.Frames(2). OutFrame will be used as the target for any report output. The setView function sets the global OutputView variable to match the view radio buttons. The LoadPage_Click function is called when the LoadPage push button is clicked. The window.navigate method is used to load the URL specified in the text element, AddressText, into the browser2 frame. The WindowInfo_Click function is called when the "Report" button, WindowInfo, is clicked. This function causes the report on the document in browser1 frame to be output to browser3 frame, OutFrame.

The document.open method opens the document window for rewriting. The putln function, described as follows, is called to output a string to the target frame. The <BODY> and <FONT> tags are written out first. The putWindow function is called with the browser1 frame window as the parameter. Finally, the document.close method is called.

**Listing 27.25   The Browser Code: The Form EventHandlers—Part 2 of 8
(\msdev\projects\Chap27\ObjectModel\Browser1.html.)**

```
<SCRIPT LANGUAGE="VBSCRIPT">
Dim OutFrame
Dim OutputView

Sub Init
    Set OutFrame = Window.parent.Frames(2)
    OutputView = 1
End Sub

Function setView(view)
    OutputView = view
End Function

Sub LoadPage_OnClick()
    Window.parent.Frames(1).navigate AddressText.value
End Sub
```

continues

Listing 27.26   Continued

```
Sub WindowInfo_OnClick()
    OutFrame.document.open
    putln "<BODY TOPMARGIN=0>"
    putln "<FONT FACE=""Arial"" SIZE=1>"
    putWindow Window.parent.Frames(1)
    OutFrame.document.close
End Sub
...
```

Listing 27.26 shows the putWindow function which is the high-level function that outputs each property of the window object. A helper function, putProperty, is used to write a property value. There are separate functions to write each window property that is an object or array of objects, such as putLocation to write the location object, putFrames to write the frames array, putNavigator to write the navigator object, and so on.

Listing 27.26   The Browser Code: The *putWindow* Routine—Part 3 of 8 (\msdev\projects\Chap27\ObjectModel\Browser1.html.)

```
Rem Object Model "put" object and property routines

Sub putWindow(win)
    startPropertyGroup "Window Properties"
    putProperty "name", win.name
    putProperty "parent.name", win.parent.name
    putProperty "self.name", win.self.name
    putProperty "top.name", win.top.name
    putProperty "history.length", win.history.length
    putLocation "Window", win.location
    rem putProperty "defaultStatus", win.defaultStatus
    rem putProperty "status", win.status
    putFrames win
    putNavigator win.Navigator
    putDocument win.document
    stopPropertyGroup
End Sub
...
```

Listing 27.27 shows the putDocument function. Its purpose is to write each property value and object of the document object. A set of helper functions, startPropertyGroup and stopPropertyGroup, write start and stop HTML code for the selected view. There is a function in browser1.html to put each object type found in the Object Model. The putAnchors, putLinks, and putForms functions write the set of anchors, links, and forms that belong to the document object.

Listing 27.27 The Browser Code: The *putDocument* Routine—Part 4 of 8 (\msdev\projects\Chap27\ObjectModel\Browser1.html.)

```
Sub putDocument(doc)
    startPropertyGroup "Window.document Properties"
    putProperty "linkColor", doc.linkColor
    putProperty "alinkColor", doc.alinkColor
    putProperty "vlinkColor", doc.vlinkColor
    putProperty "bgColor", doc.bgColor
    putProperty "fgColor", doc.fgColor
    putProperty "lastModified", doc.lastModified
    putProperty "title", doc.title
    putProperty "cookie", doc.cookie
    putProperty "referrer", doc.referrer
    putAnchors doc
    putLinks doc
    putForms doc
    stopPropertyGroup
End Sub
...
```

Listing 27.28 shows the putLinks function. This function is an example of a function that enumerates each entry in an array of link objects. The for loop uses the links.length array attribute to enumerate each link object. The same helper functions discussed above are used again to write each output value in a link object.

Listing 27.28 The Browser Code: The *putLinks* Routine—Part 5 of 8 (\msdev\projects\Chap27\ObjectModel\Browser1.html.)

```
Sub putLinks(doc)
    if IsNull(doc.links) then exit sub
    startPropertyGroup "Window.document.links Properties"
    putProperty "links.length", doc.links.length
    for i = 0 to doc.links.length - 1
    startPropertyGroup "Link["&i&"] Properties"
    putProperty "href", doc.links(i).protocol
    putProperty "protocol", doc.links(i).protocol
    putProperty "host", doc.links(i).host
    putProperty "hostname", doc.Links(i).hostname
    putProperty "port", doc.Links(i).port
    putProperty "pathname", doc.links(i).pathname
    putProperty "search", doc.links(i).search
    putProperty "hash", doc.links(i).hash
    putProperty "target", doc.links(i).target
    stopPropertyGroup
    next
    stopPropertyGroup
End Sub
...
```

Part
IV

Ch
27

Figure 27.13 shows the browser.html document running after loading and reporting on Microsoft's home page on the Web.

FIG. 27.13

Here, Browser.html reports the contents of www.microsoft.com using the Table view.

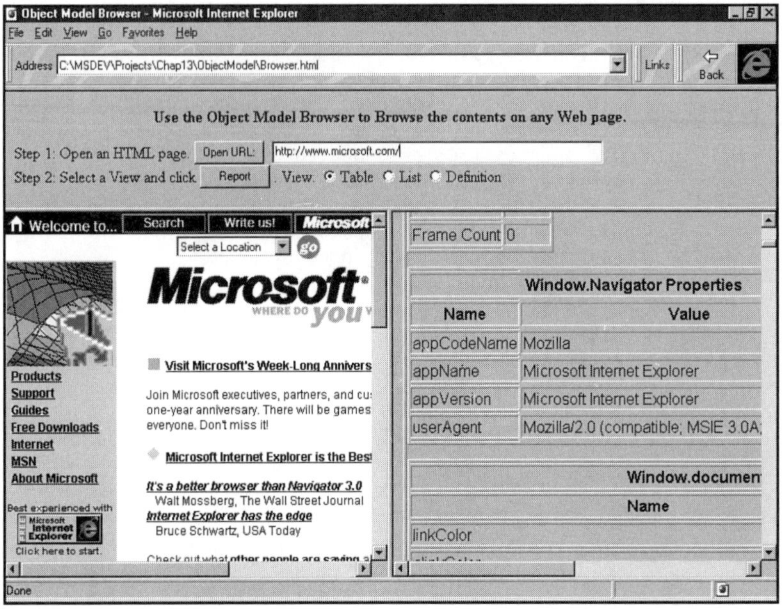

Listing 27.29 shows the two formatting helper functions, `startPropertyGroup` and `stopPropertyGroup`. These functions use the `OutputView` value set by the View radio buttons to output the appropriate HTML code. The views use the HTML <TABLE> tag for the Table view, the <UL> tag is used for the List view, and the <DL> tag is used for the Definition view.

Listing 27.29   The Browser Code: The *start/stopPropertyGroup* Routines— Part 6 of 8 (\msdev\projects\Chap27\ObjectModel\Browser1.html.)

```
Rem Text formatting and output routines...
Sub startPropertyGroup(title)
     Select Case OutputView
     Case 1
     putln "<table border=1>"
     putln "<tr><th colspan=2>" & title & "</th></tr>"
     Case 2
     putln "<strong>" & title & "</strong>"
     putln "<ul>"
     Case 3
     putln "<strong>" & title & "</strong>"
     putln "<dl>"
     End Select
     putPropertyHeader "Name", "Value"
End Sub
```

```
Sub stopPropertyGroup()
     Select Case OutputView
     Case 1
     putln "</table>"
     Case 2
     putln "</ul>"
     Case 3
     putln "</dl>"
     End Select
End Sub
```

. . .

Listing 27.30 shows the putPropertyHeader and putProperty functions. These functions and the other formatting functions encapsulate the related HTML features used for formatting. All output is passed to the putln function.

Listing 27.30   The Browser Code: The *putPropertyHeader* and *putProperty* Routines—Part 7 of 8 (\msdev\projects\Chap27\ObjectModel\ Browser1.html.)

```
Sub putPropertyHeader(propKey, propValue)
     Select Case OutputView
     Case 1
     putln "<tr><th>" & propKey & "</th><th>" & propValue & "</th></tr>"
     Case 2
     rem putln "<li><Bold>" & propKey & ": " & propValue & "</Bold></li>"
     Case 3
     rem putln "<dt><Bold>" & propKey & "<dd>" & propValue & "</Bold>"
     End Select
End Sub

Sub putProperty(propKey, propValue)
     Select Case OutputView
     Case 1
     putln "<tr><td>" & propKey & "</td><td>" & propValue & "</td></tr>"
     Case 2
     putln "<li>" & putBold(propKey) & ": " & propValue & "</li>"
     Case 3
     putln "<dt>" & propKey & "<dd>" & propValue
     End Select
End Sub
```

. . .

Part
IV

Ch
27

Listing 27.31 shows the low-level functions putBold and putln. Not all functions in browser1.html are shown in this section. The companion CD-ROM that comes with this book contains the complete HTML files for the browser presented. It shows how to access most of the supported properties in the Object Model.

Listing 27.31   The Browser Code: The *putBold* and *putln* Routines—Part 8 of 8 (\msdev\projects\Chap27\ObjectModel\Browser1.html.)

```
Function putBold(text)
     putBold = "<b>" & text & "</b>"
End Function

Sub putln(text)
     OutFrame.document.write text & "<BR>"
End Sub

</SCRIPT>

</BODY>
</HTML>
```

Listing 27.32 shows the contents of browser2.html. This is the sample form that is initially loaded into the browser2 frame when browser.html is loaded. Refer to Figure 27.12 which shows the report of the contents of the document.

Listing 27.32   The Lower-Left Frame Definition (\msdev\projects\Chap27\ObjectModel\Browser2.html.)

```
<html>
<body>
Open an HTML page here!. Or browse the contents of this page.
<HR>
<FORM NAME=FORM1>
<INPUT TYPE=Text Value="Text" NAME=Text><BR>
<INPUT TYPE=TextArea Value="TextArea" NAME=TextArea><P>
<INPUT TYPE=Radio NAME=Radio VALUE=1>Radio1
<INPUT TYPE=Radio NAME=Radio VALUE=2>Radio2<P>
<INPUT TYPE=Checkbox Value=true NAME=Checkbox>Checkbox<P>
<INPUT TYPE=Combo Value="Combo" NAME=Combo><P>
<INPUT TYPE=Submit Value="Submit" NAME=Submit>
<INPUT TYPE=Reset Value="Reset" NAME=Reset>
</FORM>
</body>
</html>
```

Listing 27.33 shows the contents of browser3.html. This document is initially loaded into the browser3 frame. It is replaced when the first report is generated.

Listing 27.33   The Lower-Right Frame Definition (\msdev\projects\Chap27\ ObjectModel\Browser3.html.)

```
<html>
<body>
Press Report to see a report on the page in the frame at the left.
All properties and objects will be displayed in this frame.
<HR>
</body>
</html>
```

From Here...

This chapter introduced you to many of the scripting features supported by Internet Explorer. The JavaScript and VBScript languages can be used together to activate HTML documents. The Object Model can be accessed to query and modify information parsed from the HTML document file. Java applets can be added to an HTML document, and its public methods can be called from scripts to enhance the intelligence of your documents. These capabilities will be used in the following chapter.

■ In Chapter 25, "Code Signing Java with Authenticode," learn how to digitally code sign Java classes for secure downloading over the Internet. The States applet code in this chapter is enhanced for use with code signing.

Part
IV

Ch
27

Appendixes

Visual J++ Program Utilities and Options

by Mark Culverhouse

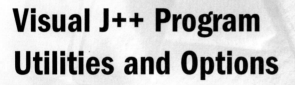This appendix lists the usage of utility programs used with Visual J++. The programs listed below were run from the DOS command line either with no parameters or with the /? or /help parameter to produce the output listing describing their usage. ■

The programs include:

- CabArc.exe—CABinet Archive
- Cert2Spc.exe—Certificate to Software Publishing Certificate
- ChkTrust.exe—Check Code Signed File
- Diamond.exe—Diamond Cabinet Builder
- DumpCert.exe—Dump Certificate Utility
- JavaReg.exe—Microsoft Visual J++ Compiler
- JavaTlb.exe—Java Type Library Conversion Utility
- JVC.exe—Microsoft Visual J++ Compiler
- JView.exe—Microsoft Visual J++ Command-line Interpreter
- MIDL.exe—Microsoft IDL Compiler
- MakeCert.exe—Make X.509 Certificate Utility
- MkTypLib.exe—Type Library Generator
- PESigMgr.exe—Check Signed PE File
- RegSvr32.exe—Control Registration Utility
- SignCode.exe—Sign Code Utility

CabArc.exe—CABinet Archive

```
Microsoft (R) Cabinet Tool - Version 1.00
Copyright (c) Microsoft Corp 1996. All rights reserved.

Usage: CABARC [<options>] <command> <cabfile> [<filelist...>] [dest_dir]

Commands:
    L   List contents of cabinet (e.g. cabarc l test.cab)
    N   Create new cabinet (e.g. cabarc n test.cab *.c app.mak *.h)
    X   Extract file(s) from cabinet (e.g. cabarc x test.cab foo*.c)

Options:
    -c   Confirm files to be operated on
    -o   When extracting, overwrite without asking for confirmation
    -m   Set compression type [MSZIP | NONE], (default is MSZIP)
    -p   Preserve path names (absolute paths not allowed)
    -P   Strip specified prefix from files when added
    -r   Recurse into subdirectories when adding files (see -p also)
    -s   Reserve space in cabinet for signing (e.g. -s 6144 reserves 6K bytes)
    -i   Set cabinet set ID when creating cabinets (default is 0)
    --   Stop option parsing

Notes
——
When creating a cabinet, the plus sign (+) may be used as a filename
to force a folder boundary; e.g. cabarc n test.cab *.c test.h + *.bmp
```

When extracting files to disk, the <dest_dir>, if provided, must end in
a backslash; e.g. cabarc x test.cab bar*.cpp *.h d:\test\

The -P (strip prefix) option can be used to strip out path information
e.g. cabarc -r -p -P myproj\ a test.cab myproj\balloon*.*
The -P option can be used multiple times to strip out multiple paths

Cert2Spc.exe—Certificate to Software Publishing Certificate

```
Usage: CERT2SPC [-k] cert1.cer ... certN.cer certBundle.spc
  or   CERT2SPC    cert1.cer ... certN.cer -S:session
```

ChkTrust.exe—Check Code Signed File

```
Usage:   CHKTRUST [-options] file-name
Options:
   -I   subject type is PE executable image file (default)
   -J   subject type is Java class
   -C   subject type is Cabinet file
   -N   no UI in 'bad trust' case
```

Diamond.exe—Diamond Cabinet Builder

```
Microsoft (R) Diamond Cabinet Builder - Version (32) 1.00.0540 (02/01/96)
Copyright (c) Microsoft Corp 1993-1996. All rights reserved.

DIAMOND [/V[n]] [/D var=value ...] [/L dir] source [destination]
DIAMOND [/V[n]] [/D var=value ...] /F directive_file [...]

   source        File to compress.
   destination   File name to give compressed file.  If omitted, the
                 last character of the source file name is replaced
                 with an underscore (_) and used as the destination.
   /F directives A file with Diamond directives (may be repeated).
   /D var=value  Defines variable with specified value.
   /L dir        Location to place destination (default is current directory).
   /V[n]         Verbosity level (1..3).
```

DumpCert.exe—Dump Certificate Utility

```
usage: DumpCert certFile(s)
```

JavaReg.exe—Microsoft Visual J++ Compiler

```
JavaReg [/?][/register][/unregister][/class:<JavaClass>
[/clsid:<clsid>][/progid:<ProgID>][options]]
/?     Help.
```

```
/register      Registers the specified Java class.
/unregister    Unregisters the specified Java class.
/surrogate     Runs or registers as LocalServer wrapper for Java class.
/class         Specifies the JavaClass to register/unregister.
/clsid         Specifies the CLSID to use for Java class (optional).
/progid           Specifies the ProgID to use for the Java class (optional).
/defappid      Indicates that the CLSID should be used as the ApplID (optional).
/single        Forces the same object instance to be returned (optional).
/console       Creates a console window to capture stdout (and System.out) (for
               ➥debugging).
```

JavaTlb.exe—Java Type Library Conversion Utility

Usage: JAVATLB [options] <filename>

```
/d <directory>   root directory for class file output
/p <package>     set package for types
/p:b[-]          include basename as package <default=include>
/X:m[-]          auto-marshal COM parameters <default=on>
/U               unassemble class file
/U:T             generate type library summary information
```

JVC.exe—Microsoft Visual J++ Compiler

Usage: JVC [options] <filename>

```
/?     list all options
/cp <classpath>    set class path for compilation
/cp:p <path>       prepend path to class path
/cp:o[-]    print classpath
/d <directory>     root directory for class file output
/g[-] full debug information (g:l, g:d)
/g:l[-]     generate line numbers <default=none>
/g:t[-]     generate debug tables <default=none>
/nowarn     turns off warnings <default=warn>
/nowrite    compile only - do not generate class files
/O[-] full optimization (O:I,O:J)
/O:I[-]     optimize by inlining <default=no opt>
/O:J[-]     optimize bytecode jumps <default=no opt>
/verbose    print messages about compilation progress
/w{0-4}     set warning level <default=2>
/x[-] disable extensions <default=enabled>

'-' turns flag off
```

JView.exe—Microsoft Visual J++ Command-line Interpreter

Usage: JView [options] <classname> [arguments]

Options:

```
/?      displays usage text
/cp <classpath>   set class path
/cp:p <path>      prepend path to class path
/cp:a <path>      append path to class path
```

Classname:
    .CLASS file to be executed.

Arguments:
    command-line arguments to be passed on to the class file

MakeCert.exe—Make X.509 Certificate Utility

```
Usage: MAKECERT [options] outputCertificateFile
    -u:subjectKey       subject's CryptoAPI keyset name
    -U:subjectCertFile  certificate with existing subject public key to use
    -k:subjectKeyFile   subject's .pvk file
    -n:name             certificate subject X500 name (eg: "CN=Fred Dews")
    -d:displayname      certificate subject display name
    -s:issuerKey(File)  loc'n of issuer's key; default to test root key
    -i:issuerCertFile      ... issuer's certificate
    -#:serialNumber     2^31 max; default is good: is guaranteed unique
    -l:policyLink       link to SPC Agency policy info (a URL, etc)
    -I                  cert explicitly allowed for individual software pub use
    -C                  cert explicitly allowed for commercial software pub use
    -C:f                ... and the publisher met the minimal financial criteria
    -S:session          use enrollment session
    -P:purpose          enrollment purpose (default CodeSigning)
    -x:providerName     CryptoAPI provider to use
    -y:nProviderType    CryptoAPI provider type to use
    -K:keyspec          'S' signature key (default), 'E' key-exchange key
    -B:dateStart        start of validity period; defaults to 'now'
    -D:nMonths          duration of valdity period
    -E:dateEnd          end of validity period; defaults to 2039
    -h:numChildren      max height of the tree below this cert
    -t:types            cert type: either/both of 'E'nd-entity; 'C'ert auth'ty
    -g                  create a glue certificate
    -r                  create a self-signed certificate
    -m                  use MD5 hash algorithm (default)
    -a                  use SHA1 hash algorithm
    -N                  include netscape client auth extension
```

* For the -u and -k options, if the indicated subject's key (key pair)
  cannot, be found then it is created. For -u, it is created in the Crypto
  API keyset; for -k, it is created in a file.

  Alternatively, the subject public key can be obtained from an already
  existing certificate using the -U option. -U changes the default subject
  name to be the same as that of the indicated cert. Use -g in addition to
  make a glue certificate.

* A self signed certificate can be created using the -r option

MIDL.exe—Microsoft IDL Compiler

```
                        -MIDL COMPILER OPTIONS-
                               -MODE-
     /ms_ext            Microsoft extensions to the IDL language (default)
     /c_ext             Allow Microsoft C extensions in the IDL file (default)
     /osf               OSF mode - disables /ms_ext and /c_ext options
     /app_config        Allow selected ACF attributes in the IDL file
     /mktyplib203       MKTYPLIB Version 2.03 compatiblity mode


                               -INPUT-
     /acf filename      Specify the attribute configuration file
     /I directory-list  Specify one or more directories for include path
     /no_def_idir       Ignore the current and the INCLUDE directories


                        -OUTPUT FILE GENERATION-
     /client none       Do not generate client files
     /client stub       Generate client stub file only
     /out directory     Specify destination directory for output files
     /server none       Generate no server files
     /server stub       Generate server stub file only
     /syntax_check      Check syntax only; do not generate output files
     /Zs                Check syntax only; do not generate output files
     /old               Generate old format type libraries
     /new               Generate new format type libraries


                          -OUTPUT FILE NAMES-
     /cstub filename    Specify client stub file name
     /dlldata filename  Specify dlldata file name
     /h filename        Specify header file name
     /header filename   Specify header file name
     /iid filename      Specify interface UUID file name
     /proxy filename    Specify proxy file name
     /sstub filename    Specify server stub file name
     /tlb filename      Specify type library file name


                  -C COMPILER AND PREPROCESSOR OPTIONS-
     /cpp_cmd cmd_line  Specify name of C preprocessor
     /cpp_opt options   Specify additional C preprocessor options
     /D name[=def]      Pass #define name, optional value to C preprocessor
     /no_cpp            Turn off the C preprocessing option
     /nocpp             Turn off the C preprocessing option
     /U name            Remove any previous definition (undefine)


                            -ENVIRONMENT-
     /char signed       C compiler default char type is signed
     /char unsigned     C compiler default char type is unsigned
     /char ascii7       Char values limited to 0-127
     /dos               Target environment is MS-DOS client
     /env dos           Target environment is MS-DOS client
     /env mac           Target environment is Apple Macintosh
     /env powermac      Target environment is Apple PowerMac
     /env win16         Target environment is Microsoft Windows 16-bit (Win 3.x)
     /env win32         Target environment is Microsoft Windows 32-bit (NT)
     /mac               Target environment is Apple Macintosh
```

```
/ms_union            Use Midl 1.0 non-DCE wire layout for non-encapsulated unions
/oldnames            Do not mangle version number into names
/powermac            Target environment is Apple PowerMac
/rpcss               Automatically activate rpc_sm_enable_allocate
/use_epv             Generate server side application calls via entry-pt vector
/no_default_epv      Do not generate a default entry-point vector
/prefix client str   Add "str" prefix to client-side entry points
/prefix server str   Add "str" prefix to server-side manager routines
/prefix switch str   Add "str" prefix to switch routine prototypes
/prefix all str      Add "str" prefix to all routines
/win16               Target environment is Microsoft Windows 16-bit (Win 3.x)
/win32               Target environment is Microsoft Windows 32-bit (NT)

                    -ERROR AND WARNING MESSAGES-
/error none          Turn off all error checking options
/error allocation    Check for out of memory errors
/error bounds_check  Check size vs transmission length specification
/error enum          Check enum values to be in allowable range
/error ref           Check ref pointers to be non-null
/error stub_data     Emit additional check for server side stub data validity
/no_warn             Suppress compiler warning messages

                        -OPTIMIZATION-
/align {1|2|4|8}     Designate packing level of structures
/pack {1|2|4|8}      Designate packing level of structures
/Zp{1|2|4|8}         Designate packing level of structures
/Oi                  Generate full interpreted stubs
/Oi2                 Generate full interpreted stubs with extensions
/Os                  Generate semi-interpreted stubs

                        -MISCELLANEOUS-
@response_file       Accept input from a response file
/?                   Display a list of MIDL compiler switches
/confirm             Display options without compiling MIDL source
/help                Display a list of MIDL compiler switches
/o filename          Redirects output from screen to a file
/W{0|1|2|3|4}        Specify warning level 0-4 (default = 1)
/WX                  Report warnings at specified /W level as errors
```

MkTypLib.exe—Type Library Generator

```
Usage: MKTYPLIB <options> [inputfile]
Valid options are:
/help or /?     Displays usage.
/tlb <filename> Specifies type library output filename.  Defaults to input name

                with extension replaced by ".tlb".
/h [filename]   Specifies .H file output filename.
/<system>       Specifies kind of type library to make (win16, win32, mac, mips
, alpha, ppc or ppc32).
                Defaults to win32.
/align <#>      Override default alignment setting.
/o filename     Redirects output from screen to specified file.
/nologo         Don't display the copyright banner.
```

```
/w0             Disable warnings.
/nocpp          Don't spawn the C pre-processor.
/cpp_cmd <path> Specifies path for C pre-processor.
                Defaults to CL.EXE.
/cpp_opt "<opt>" Specifies options for C pre-processor.  Defaults to:
                "/C /E /D__MKTYPLIB__".
/Ddefine[=value] Defines value for C pre-processor.
/I includepath  Specifies path for include files.
```

PESigMgr.exe—Check Signed PE File

```
Usage: PESIGMGR [switches] image-name
              [-?] display this message
              [-l] list the certificates in an image
              [-a:<Filename>] add a certificate file to an image
              [-r:<index>]    remove certificate <index> from an image
              [-s:<Filename>] used with -r to save the removed certificate
              [-t:<CertType>] used with -a to specify the type of the certificate
              where CertType may be X509 or PKCS7 [default is X509]
```

RegSvr32.exe—Control Registration Utility

```
RegSvr32 [/u][/s] dllname
/u      Unregister server
/s      Silent; display no message boxes
/c      Console output
```

SignCode.exe—Sign Code Utility

```
Syntax: SignCode
    -prog programFile
    -spc credentialsFile
    -pvk privateKeyFile/keysetName
    -name opusName
    -info opusInfo
    -gui
    -nocerts
    -provider crytoProviderName
    -providerType n
    -commercial ¦ -individual (default)
    -sha ¦ -md5 (default)
```

Java Resources on the Web

by Mark Culverhouse

This appendix contains a list of Java resources available on the Internet. Resources include Web sites and newsgroups. ■

NewsGroups

comp.lang.java.advocacy

comp.lang.java.announce

comp.lang.java.api

comp.lang.java.misc

comp.lang.java.programmer

comp.lang.java.security

comp.lang.java.setup

comp.lang.java.tech

comp.lang.javascript

microsoft.public.internetexplorer.java

microsoft.public.internetexplorer.java.cabdevkit

microsoft.public.visualj.com-support

microsoft.public.visualj.compiler

microsoft.public.visualj.debugger

microsoft.public.visualj.dev-environment

microsoft.public.visualj.discussion

microsoft.public.visualj.installation

microsoft.public.visualj.misc-tools

Web Sites

The format of each entry is:

TITLE

URL

DESCRIPTION

CAB Technology

http://www.microsoft.com/workshop/java/cab-f.htm

Microsoft provides information about using the Cabinet technology.

Cup O' Joe Java Shop

http://www.cupojoe.com/

Cup O' Joe Java Shop provides Java resources for the professional developer. Resources include: Applets, Applications, Classes, JDK, References, and Utilities.

Digital Espresso

http://www.io.org/~mentor/jnIndex.html

Digital Espresso is a weekly summary of information from mailing lists and newsgroups about the Java language and the HotJava browser. The search facility is very popular.

Gamelan

http://www.gamelan.com

EarthWeb's Gamelan Project organizes Java resources and provides a medium for exchanging ideas about Java.

Java Applet Rating Service (JARS)

http://www.jars.com

JARS provides ratings for Java applets. Applets are reviewed by a panel of judges, and worthy applets are awarded a JARS rating.

Java Around the World

http://www.mcp.com/que/javarc/worldwide.html

Java Around the World provides a listing of Java sites in languages other than English including: French, Dutch, German, Chinese, Italian, Danish, and Hungarian.

Java Centre

http://www.java.co.uk/

Java Centre provides information on Java news, contacts, seminars, and exhibitions in the United Kingdom.

Java Developer

http://www.digitalfocus.com/faq/

This site's Java developer resources include Java Resources, How Do I..., The Java Store, and Jobs and Services.

Java Developer's Organization

http://www.jade.org/

Java Developer's Organization bills itself as the trade association for Java developers worldwide, aiming to promote the interests of Java and its developers.

Java Performance Report

http://www.webfayre.com/pendragon/jpr

The Java Performance Report provides information and performance ratings of Java Virtual Machines.

Java Repository

http://java.wiwi.uni-frankfurt.de/

The Java Repository is a collection of resources for Java programmers, including: Ecash support to sell software, downloads, registration of applets, and links to other sites. The site uses English.

Java Resources

http://www.infospheres.caltech.edu/resources/java.html

This site is Adam Rifkin's list of links to Java developer resources which include: Documentation, Java Developers, JavaOne, Journals and Magazines, Packages and Templates, Search Engines, Specific Platforms, Tools, Distributed Systems, Internet and Networking, Java-Specific Efforts, Object-Oriented Technology, Patterns, Commercial Products, and Tutorials.

Java User Resource Network, or Java URN

http://www.nebulex.com/URN

Resources include Applets, Consultants, Java Sites, News, and Submit URL.

JavaScript Resource Center

http://jrc.livesoftware.com/

JavaScript Resource Center has resources for JavaScript developers including code samples and links to JavaScript documentation.

JavaSoft

http://java.sun.com

The JavaSoft site is Sun Microsystems's site for Java information. The site's resources include: Documentation, The Java Platform, JavaSoft News, Newly Published, Products and Services, and Developer's Info.

List archives at LISTSERV.MSN.CO

http://microsoft.ease.lsoft.com/archives/index.html

This page provides Web links to online archives of various Microsoft mailing lists including: Authenticode, Distributed COM-Based Code, Internet Explorer Automation, Internet Explorer—HTML , ISAPI, Microsoft Internet Component Download, Java and COM, VBScript, and so on.

Microsoft ActiveX SDK

http://www.microsoft.com/intdev/sdk/

The Microsoft ActiveX SDK is available for download here.

Microsoft Authenticode—Technology

http://microsoft.com/intdev/security/misf8-f.htm

This site contains information about Authenticode technology.

Microsoft: How Software Publishers Can Use Authenticode Technology

http://www.microsoft.com/intdev/signcode/

This site contains information about Authenticode technology.

Microsoft Internet Development Mailing Lists

http://www.microsoft.com/workshop/resource/mail-f.htm

This page allows you to subscribe to various mailing lists and newsgroups related to Internet development.

Microsoft on Java

http://www.microsoft.com/java/

Microsoft's Java home page is a starting point for information about FAQ, Resources, Java in the news, Java support in Internet Explorer, Visual J++, CAB, Java VM, Java, and ActiveX.

Microsoft Power Toys

http://www.microsoft.com/windows/software/powertoy.htm

Power Toys are free extensions for Internet Explorer that treat CAB files like folders. With Power Toys installed you can conveniently drag files in and out of CAB files.

Microsoft SDK for Java

http://www.microsoft.com/java/sdk/

This is the Microsoft Java SDK home page. Resources include: Release Notes, Bug Report, Packages & Classes, Tools, Java & COM, Raw Native Interface, DBCS, Unicode & Java, Working with MS VM, Standard Java References: Java Language, Java Packages.

Online eZine of Java News and Opinion

http://www.javology.com/javology/

Javology is a Java magazine by Magnastar.

Que's Java and JavaScript Resource Center

http://www.mcp.com/346101391083736/que/javarc/

At this site Que's Java and JavaScript books and a list of Java resources are available.

App

B

Sun's Worldwide Java Developer Conference

http://java.sun.com/javaone

JavaOne is Sun's Worldwide Java Developer Conference. This site has keynote addresses, as well as presentation slides from sessions, exhibitors, and other news.

Team Java

http://www.teamjava.com

Team Java promotes Java and assists Java consultants in finding contract positions. Resources include: Software, Net Search, Universities, Cult of Mac, qtvr, vrml, Stocks, and TechNews.

VeriSign Digital ID Center

http://digitalid.verisign.com/

VeriSign issues Class 1, 2, and 3 digital IDs for code signing with Authenticode.

WebWare

http://www.webwareonline.com

WebWare is an online store that sells and distributes platform-independent software products for the Internet. Developers can submit software in the following categories: Developer Tools, Web Authoring, Communications, Commerce, Entertainment, and Utilities.

WinZip by Nico Mak Computing, Inc.

http://www.winzip.com

WinZip offers a zip utility with long-name support necessary for use with Java class files.

Yahoo Index of Java Language

http://www.yahoo.com/Computers_and_Internet/Languages/Java

This is Yahoo's index for the Java language. Indices include: Applets, Companies, Contests, Events, Games, Guides, Tutorials, Documentation, JavaScript, Mailing Lists, People, Porting Projects, Security, User Groups, and Utilities.

What's on the CD?

by Mark Culverhouse

The CD included with this book contains the source pages and reference materials that have been referred to throughout the book. The goal of this approach is to enable you to cut and paste any applicable code examples so you can quickly reuse them.

The other, perhaps most exciting goal of the CD is to provide new, unique, and helpful materials, including software, shareware, and evaluation software that you can use in conjunction with Visual J++. To that end, you'll find an array of software, including the add-ins, viewers, utilities, and other software packages that we've been able to arrange for you. ■

Here's an overview of what you can expect:

- All of the sample code and applications from the book.
- A collection of demonstration applications, scaled-down software, and shareware.
- An electronic version of this book in HTML format, which can be read using any World Wide Web browser on any platform.
- A version of this book as a Windows Help File document, that you can browse, bookmark, and annotate with your own observations and notes.
- *Java by Example* electronic book in HTML format, a great way to introduce yourself to the Java language.
- *Special Edition Using Java* online book—this book, also included in HTML format, is the definitive guide to working with the Java language. It's provided here as a testament to the invaluable tool this book will be in your library.
- *Special Edition Using Visual C++* online book—this book is included in HTML format. This book will help you grasp the fundamentals of the Visual C++ language and development environment.

The CD contains several subdirectories located off of the root directory. The directories you'll find on the CD will be as follows, with application, code, or chapter-specific subdirectories under each of these (see Table C.1).

Table C.1   Directory Structure on the CD

\EBOOKS	HTML and HELP subdirectories direct you to the various versions of Que's electronic books.
\CODE	The source code and samples from the book. Each chapter that contains sample files, source code, and so on will be contained in a subdirectory named for the chapter it references.
\SOFTWARE	The software provided for your use and evaluation.

N O T E   The products on the CD are demos and shareware. You may have some difficulty running them on your particular machine. If you do, feel free to contact the vendor. (They'd rather have you evaluate their product than ignore it.) ▪

Using the Electronic Book

Special Edition Using Visual J++ is available to you as an HTML document that can be read from any World Wide Web browser that you may have currently installed on your machine (such as Internet Explorer or Netscape Navigator). If you don't have a Web browser, we have included the Microsoft Internet Explorer for you. The book can also be read on-screen as a Windows Help File.

Reading the Electronic Book as an HTML Document

To read the electronic book, you will need to start your Web browser and open the document file TOC.HTML located on the \HTMLVER subdirectory of the CD. Alternatively, you can browse the CD directory using File Manager and double-click TOC.HTML.

Once you have opened the TOC.HTML page, you can access all of the book's contents by clicking the highlighted chapter number or topic name. The electronic book works like any other Web page; when you click a hot link, a new page is opened or the browser will take you to the new location in the document. As you read through the electronic book, you will notice other highlighted words or phrases. Clicking these cross-references will also take you to a new location within the electronic book. You can always use your browser's forward or backward buttons to return to your original location.

Installing the Internet Explorer

If you don't have a Web browser installed on your machine, you can use Microsoft's Internet Explorer 3.0 on this CD-ROM.

The Microsoft Internet Explorer can be installed from the self-extracting file in the \EXPLORER directory. Double-click the MSIE20.exe or use the Control Panel's Add/Remove Programs option and follow the instructions in the install routine. Please be aware you must have Windows 95 installed on your machine to use this version of Internet Explorer. Other versions of this software can be downloaded from Microsoft's Web site at **http://www.microsoft.com/ie**.

Finding Sample Code

This book contains code examples that include listing headers, for example, "see Listing 10.1," and sample documents presented for planning purposes. For example, consider the following listing reference:

Listing 10.1 (10_01.HTM) — Creating the New Snarfle Page

This listing indicates that this particular code snippet (or example) is included electronically on the CD. To find it, browse to the \CODE subdirectory on the CD and select the file name that matches the one referenced in the listing header from the chapter indicated. In this example, you'd look in the Chapter 10 subdirectory and open the 10_01.HTM file. Table C.2 lists the file directories that contain sample Visual J++ and Visual C++ projects, HTML, and other files referenced throughout the book.

Table C.2   File Directories Located Throughout This Book

File Name	Description
\msdev\samples\que\QueChap3.java	Chapter 3 Java sample code.
\msdev\project\AppWizard0\	Chapter 15 "Building a Sample Applet" sample project.
\msdev\project\AppWizard1\	Chapter 15 "Building a Sample Applet" sample project.
\msdev\project\AppWizard2\	Chapter 15 "Building a Sample Applet" sample project.
\msdev\project\AppWizard3\	Chapter 15 "Building a Sample Applet" sample project.
\msdev\project\AppWizard4\	Chapter 15 "Building a Sample Applet" sample project.
\msdev\project\AppWizard5\	Chapter 15 "Building a Sample Applet" sample project.
\msdev\project\chap17\MyJavaApp\	Chapter 17 "Using AppStudio" sample project.
\msdev\project\chap25\Cabinet0\	Chapter 25 "Code Signing Java with Authenticode" sample project.
\msdev\project\chap25\Cabinet1\	Chapter 25 "Code Signing Java with Authenticode" sample project.
\msdev\project\chap25\Cabinet2\	Chapter 25 "Code Signing Java with Authenticode" sample project.
\msdev\project\chap25\Cabinet3\	Chapter 25 "Code Signing Java with Authenticode" sample project.
\msdev\project\chap25\Cabinet4\	Chapter 25 "Code Signing Java with Authenticode" sample project.
\msdev\project\chap25\Cabinet5\	Chapter 25 "Code Signing Java with Authenticode" sample project.
\msdev\project\chap27\Scripts\	Chapter 27 "Scripting Client Applets" sample project.
\msdev\project\chap27\Forms\	Chapter 27 "Scripting Client Applets" sample project.
\msdev\project\chap27\Frames\	Chapter 27 "Scripting Client Applets" sample project.
\msdev\project\chap27\ObjectBrowser\	Chapter 27 "Scripting Client Applets" sample project.

Index

G

J

Licensing Agreement

By opening this package, you are agreeing to be bound by the following:

The software contained on this CD is, in many cases, copyrighted and all rights are reserved by the individual software developer and/or publisher. You are bound by the individual licensing agreements associated with each piece of software contained on the CD. THIS SOFTWARE IS PROVIDED FREE OF CHARGE, AS IS, AND WITHOUT WARRANTY OF ANY KIND, EITHER EXPRESSED OR IMPLIED, INCLUDING, BUT NOT LIMITED TO, THE IMPLIED WARRANTIES OF MERCHANTABILITY AND FITNESS FOR A PARTICULAR PURPOSE. Neither the book publisher nor its dealers and distributors assumes any liability for any alleged or actual damages arising from the use of this software. (Some states do not allow exclusion of implied warranties, so the exclusion may not apply to you.)